CELEBRATING 30 YEARS

ZAGAT SURVEY

Back in 1979, we never imagined that an idea born during a wine-fueled dinner with friends would take us on an adventure that's lasted three decades – and counting.

The idea – that the collective opinions of avid consumers can be more accurate than the judgments of an individual critic – led to a hobby involving friends rating NYC restaurants. And that hobby grew into Zagat Survey, which today has over 350,000 participants worldwide weighing in on everything from airlines, bars, dining and golf to hotels, movies, shopping, tourist attractions and more.

By giving consumers a voice, we – and our surveyors – had unwittingly joined a revolution whose concepts (user-generated content, social networking) were largely unknown 30 years ago. However, those concepts caught fire with the rise of the Internet and have since transformed not only restaurant criticism but also virtually every aspect of the media, and we feel lucky to have been at the start of it all.

As we celebrate Zagat's 30th year, we'd like to thank everyone who has participated in our surveys. We've enjoyed hearing and sharing your frank opinions and look forward to doing so for many years to come. As we always say, our guides and online content are really "yours."

We'd also like to express our gratitude by supporting **Action Against Hunger,** an organization that works to meet the needs of the hungry in over 40 countries. To find out more, visit www.zagat.com/action.

Nina and Tim

Nina and Tim Zagat

ZAGAT ®
CELEBRATING 30 YEARS

Top U.S. Hotels, Resorts & Spas
2009

EDITOR
Donna Marino Wilkins

Published and distributed by
Zagat Survey, LLC
4 Columbus Circle
New York, NY 10019
T: 212.977.6000
E: travel@zagat.com
www.zagat.com

ACKNOWLEDGMENTS

We thank Olga Boikess, Carolyn Heller, Pualana Lemelle, Napua Leong, Lori Midson, Sandra Ramani, John Rambow, Shelley Sawyer, Robert Seixas and Amy Serafin, as well as the following members of our staff: Josh Rogers (associate editor), Stacey Slate (editorial assistant), Brian Albert, Sean Beachell, Maryanne Bertollo, Jane Chang, Sandy Cheng, Reni Chin, Larry Cohn, John Deiner, Alison Flick, Jeff Freier, Sharon Gintzler, Roy Jacob, Ashunta Joseph, Cynthia Kilian, Natalie Lebert, Mike Liao, Dave Makulec, Andre Pilette, Kimberly Rosado, Becky Ruthenburg, Aleksandra Shander, Sharon Yates, Anna Zappia and Kyle Zolner.

Contents

* This book is organized alphabetically by state, with cities and towns listed alphabetically within each state. We've listed some major cities here for quick reference.

Ratings & Symbols

Zagat Top Spot	Name	Symbols								Zagat Ratings				

Location, Contact, Room info

Z Tim & Nina's 👪 | ROOMS 18 | SERVICE 5 | DINING 14 | FACIL. 22 | COST $110 ▽

4 Columbus Circle | 212-977-6000 | fax 212-977-9760 | 800-977-9000 | www.zagat.com | 20 rooms, 2 suites

Review, surveyor comments in quotes

Despite "dazzling views" of Central Park and a "lovely rooftop public space", surveyors split over this "minuscule" "mini-priced" Midtown boutique hotel; fans tout its "handy location", but critics knock "rooms too small to change your mind", dining at Chez Z that's "outshone by the corner hot dog stand" and staffers who "never notice you unless they're angry."

Ratings

Rooms, Service, Dining and public **Facilities** are rated on the Zagat 0 to 30 scale. Properties listed without ratings are **newcomers** or survey **write-ins.**

0	–	9	poor to fair
10	–	15	fair to good
16	–	19	good to very good
20	–	25	very good to excellent
26	–	30	extraordinary to perfection
	▽		low response	less reliable

Cost

Reflects the hotel's high-season rack rate, i.e. its asking price for a standard double room. It does not reflect seasonal price changes and special rates.

Symbols

Z Zagat Top Spot (highest ratings, popularity and importance)

👪	children's programs	👓	views
✗	exceptional restaurant	⌐	18-hole golf course
Ⓗ	historic interest	Ⓢ	notable spa facilities
🍳	kitchens	🎿	downhill skiing
🐾	allows pets	🎾	tennis

Hotel Chains

In the Hotel Chains section, cost is indicated as follows:

I	$149 and below	E	$250–$349
M	$150–$249	VE	$350 or more

Top Lists

Except where noted, the score listed is the average of the hotel's scores for Rooms, Service, Dining and Facilities.

About This Survey

Here are the results of our **2009 Top U.S. Hotels, Resorts & Spas Survey,** covering 1,001 properties and chains in the U.S., Puerto Rico and the U.S. Virgin Islands. Like all our guides, this one is based on the collective opinions of avid consumers like you. Although ratings have been updated throughout, we've retained last year's review for some places that have had no significant factual or ratings changes.

WHO PARTICIPATED: Input from 14,049 frequent travelers and travel professionals forms the basis for the ratings and reviews in this guide (their comments are shown in quotation marks within the reviews). These surveyors are a diverse group: 49% are women, 51% men; 7% are in their 20s; 24%, 30s; 25%, 40s; 24%, 50s; and 20%, 60s or above. Collectively they bring roughly 493,000 nights worth of annual experience to this Survey. We sincerely thank each of these participants – this book is really "theirs."

HELPFUL LISTS: Our top lists and indexes can help you find exactly the right place for any occasion. See Websites & Toll-Free Numbers (pages 8–9), Key Newcomers (page 10), Top Ratings (pages 11–17), Best Buys (page 18) and the 38 handy indexes starting on page 237.

ABOUT ZAGAT: This marks our 30th year reporting on the shared experiences of consumers like you. What started in 1979 as a hobby has come a long way. Today we have over 350,000 surveyors and now cover airlines, bars, dining, entertaining, fast food, golf, hotels, movies, music, resorts, shopping, spas, theater and tourist attractions in over 100 countries.

VOTE AND COMMENT: We invite you to join any of our surveys at **ZAGAT.com.** There you can rate and review establishments year-round. In exchange for doing so, you'll receive a free copy of the resulting guide when published.

AVAILABILITY: Zagat guides are available in all major bookstores as well as on **ZAGAT.com.** You can also access our content when on the go via **ZAGAT.mobi** and **ZAGAT TO GO** (for smartphones). All three enable reserving at thousands of places with just one click.

FEEDBACK: There is always room for improvement, thus we invite your comments about any aspect of our performance. Did we miss something? Just contact us at **travel@zagat.com.**

New York, NY
November 3, 2008

Nina and Tim Zagat

What's New

THE DOWNTURN'S UPSIDE: While the nation's economic crisis has cast a widespread pall, there may be an upside for travelers. For several years, hotels have enjoyed a seller's market, commanding ever-higher prices in the face of healthy occupancy rates. But that picture is about to change. As businesses restrict travel and spending, hotels are likely to respond by dropping rates and ramping up promotions, which is good news for leisure travelers who might otherwise have opted for "stay-cations." Already, resorts from Florida to Hawaii (including our No. 1–rated resort, the Big Island's **Four Seasons**) are offering free-night deals, along with meal, spa or golf credits. Given that 35% of our surveyors say price is a top consideration in choosing vacation lodging, these discounts can be a deciding factor.

BRAND BOOSTERS: Sixty-six percent of our surveyors prefer to stay at national and international chains – borne out by our Survey, in which they account for 7 of the top 10 resorts and nine of the top 10 hotels. And 22% of the leisure travelers in our Survey ranked brand as important – not surprisingly, the **Ritz-Carlton** and **Four Seasons** head our lists, claiming between them 13 of the top 20 hotels and resorts. The latter was also voted the country's Top Chain.

GOING GREEN: The race to be green is in full swing and our surveyors have taken note, with 26% listing it among the top three best hotel trends. Some 48% say they're more likely to stay in an eco-friendly property, and 31% will pay more to do so. **Starwood** launched an eco-friendly brand, **Element,** and others, including the new **Proximity Hotel** in Greensboro, N.C., focus on energy saving.

 COMEBACK KIDS: A number of major renovations have come to fruition: Maui's **Ritz-Carlton Kapalua,** DC's **St. Regis** (home to a new Alain Ducasse restaurant), Dallas' venerable **Stoneleigh,** Chicago's historic **Blackstone Hotel** (now branded a Renaissance), the **Marriott New Orleans,** the **Vail Cascade Resort** and the **Millennium Bostonian** have all emerged from mega-million revamps. Also slated for imminent reopening are Santa Monica's **Hotel Shangri-La** and DC's **Jefferson Hotel.** These upgrades count, say our surveyors who list WiFi, high-end bath products and flat-screen TVs among key in-room features.

MANHATTAN MANIA: Ranked by our surveyors as the top U.S. destination for business and leisure, NYC is seeing a slate of openings. New Downtown boutiques include NoHo's **Bowery Hotel,** TriBeCa's **Duane Street** and the West Village's **Jane,** while in Midtown both the **Empire** and **The Plaza** reopened after extensive renovations.

SERVICE STARS: Poor service tops the list of what irritates our readers most (48%), followed by bad rooms (25%). Properties that get both right, win. Our Survey's No. 1 Small Hotel, Vermont's **Twin Farms,** was also cited as having the country's Top Service and Top Rooms.

New York, NY
November 3, 2008

Donna Marino Wilkins

Travel Tips

ASK AND YOU SHALL RECEIVE: With the demand for travel slowing down, consumers should be more able to negotiate for special rates and deals, particularly if dates are flexible and at off-peak times. Remember that a hotel's 'rack rates' are just a jumping-off point – always ask if there's a better rate or a special promotion (such as free fourth- or fifth-night stays). To get the best results, call the on-site hotel reservationist directly rather than the toll-free operator. And when you check in, don't forget to ask if it's possible to get an upgrade.

NET WORTH: The best bargains often reside on the web, particularly for last-minute lodging. You can get marked-down excess inventory by booking online through individual hotels or via sites such as Expedia, Priceline and Travelocity. If you sign up for automatic e-mail updates, you can get late-breaking specials sent directly to you. With 82% of our surveyors buying their airline tickets and 74% reserving hotel rooms online, it's clear that the Net has become most people's travel agent. As for the best online booking services, Expedia ranks first (28%), followed by Kayak and Orbitz (13% each). We have listed key Websites and Toll-Free Numbers on pages 8–9, and throughout this guide.

 BEYOND A ROOM WITH A VIEW: Make sure you know what you're getting when you book. There's a tremendous difference in room type, so find out where yours is located, what floor it's on, when it was last updated and what kind of view it has. Also inquire whether the hotel is undergoing renovation or hosting a convention that might disrupt your stay. Once you get to your room, it you're not satisfied, ask for another. We have added icons in this guide to help you find the features you seek.

HIDE-AND-SEEK COSTS: Sometimes a deal isn't a deal once you scratch the surface so be leery of taxes and extra charges, particularly for WiFi, health clubs, parking and in-room phones (it's possible to nearly double your room charge by using the hotel phone, so you're better off using your own cell phone). Daily resort fees and taxes can add up as well. To avoid nasty surprises at check-out, ask in advance about these fees.

WIRED WEARY: Wireless Internet access varies with each hotel. While some offer it for free, others can charge hefty per-hour fees. And connections may not always be stellar. High-end properties that do charge for in-room WiFi often have a support staff and better service than lower-end properties. Check the availability, cost and types of connections if this is important to you.

YOU'VE GOT A FRIEND: Even sophisticated travelers rely on the expertise of others. Despite the trend toward using the Net, a good travel agent is worth knowing because he or she can offer years of experience and on-property contacts, saving you both time and money.

Websites & Toll-Free Numbers

HOTEL CHAIN	WEBSITE	PHONE
Adam's Mark	adamsmark.com	800-444-2326
Aman Resorts	amanresorts.com	800-477-9180
AmeriSuites	amerisuites.com	800-833-1516
Best Western	bestwestern.com	800-780-7234
Caesars	caesars.com	800-223-7277
Clarion	clarionhotel.com	877-424-6423
Comfort Inn	comfortinn.com	877-424-6423
Courtyard by Marriott	courtyard.com	888-236-2427
Crowne Plaza	crowneplaza.com	877-227-6963
Days Inn	daysinn.com	800-329-7466
DoubleTree	doubletree.com	800-222-8733
Embassy Suites	embassysuites.com	800-362-2779
Fairfield Inn	fairfieldinn.com	888-236-2427
Fairmont	fairmont.com	800-257-7544
Four Points	fourpoints.com	800-368-7764
Four Seasons	fourseasons.com	800-819-5053
Grand Hyatt	hyatt.com	800-233-1234
Hampton Inn	hamptoninn.com	800-426-7866
Harrah's	harrahs.com	800-427-7247
Hilton	hilton.com	800-445-8667
Holiday Inn	holiday-inn.com	888-465-4329
Homewood Suites	homewood-suites.com	800-225-5466
Howard Johnson	hojo.com	800-446-4656
Hyatt	hyatt.com	800-233-1234
Hyatt Regency	hyatt.com	800-233-1234
Indigo	hotelindigo.com	866-246-3446
InterContinental	interconti.com	800-327-0200
Joie de Vivre	jdvhospitality.com	800-738-7477
Kimpton Group	kimptonhotels.com	800-546-7866
La Quinta	laquinta.com	800-753-3757
Leading Hotels	lhw.com	800-223-6800
Le Méridien	lemeridien.com	800-543-4300
Loews	loewshotels.com	866-563-9792
Luxury Collection	luxurycollection.com	800-325-3589
MainStay Suites	mainstaysuites.com	877-424-6423
Mandarin Oriental	mandarinoriental.com	866-526-6567
Marriott	marriott.com	888-236-2477
Millennium Hotels	millenniumhotels.com	866-866-8086
Morgans Hotel Group	morganshotelgroup.com	800-697-1791
Nikko	jalhotels.com	800-645-5687
NYLO	nylohotels.com	866-391-6956
Omni	omnihotels.com	888-444-6664
Pan Pacific	panpacific.com	877-324-4856
Park Hyatt	hyatt.com	800-233-1234
Peninsula	peninsula.com	866-382-8388
Preferred Hotels	preferredhotels.com	800-323-7500
Radisson	radisson.com	888-201-1718
Ramada	ramada.com	800-272-6232
Regent	regenthotels.com	800-545-4000
Relais & Châteaux	relaischateaux.com	800-735-2478
Renaissance	renaissancehotels.com	888-236-2427
Residence Inn	residenceinn.com	888-236-2427
Ritz-Carlton	ritzcarlton.com	800-542-8680
Rosewood	rosewoodhotels.com	888-767-3966
Sheraton	sheraton.com	800-325-3535

Shoney's Inn	shoneysinn.com	800-552-4667
Small Luxury Hotels	slh.com	800-525-4800
Sonesta	sonesta.com	800-766-3782
St. Regis	stregis.com	800-598-1863
Swissôtel	swissotel.com	888-737-9477
Travelodge	travelodge.com	800-578-7878
Westin	westin.com	800-937-8461
W Hotels	whotels.com	877-946-8357
Wingate Inns	wingateinns.com	800-228-1000
Wyndham	wyndham.com	877-999-3223

AIRLINE

AirTran	airtran.com	800-247-8726
Alaska Airlines	alaskaair.com	800-252-7522
American	americanair.com	800-433-7300
Continental	continental.com	800-523-3273
Delta	delta.com	800-221-1212
Frontier	frontierairlines.com	800-432-1359
Hawaiian Airlines	hawaiianair.com	800-367-5320
JetBlue	jetblue.com	800-538-2583
Midwest Airlines	midwestairlines.com	800-452-2022
Northwest	nwa.com	800-225-2525
Southwest	southwest.com	800-435-9792
Spirit Airlines	spiritair.com	800-772-7117
Sun Country	suncountry.com	800-359-6786
United	united.com	800-864-8331
US Airways	usairways.com	800-428-4322
Virgin America	virginamerica.com	877-359-8474

CAR RENTAL

Alamo	alamo.com	800-462-5266
Avis	avis.com	800-331-1212
Budget	budget.com	800-527-0700
Dollar	dollar.com	800-800-3665
Enterprise	enterprise.com	800-261-7331
Hertz	hertz.com	800-654-3131
National	nationalcar.com	800-227-7368
Payless	paylesscar.com	800-729-5377
Thrifty	thrifty.com	800-847-4389

RAILROAD/BUS

Amtrak	amtrak.com	800-872-7245
Greyhound	greyhound.com	800-231-2222

WEBSITE/TRAVEL AGENCY

AAA	aaa.com	800-272-2155
American Express	americanexpress.com/travel	800-528-4800
Carlson Wagonlit	carlsonwagonlit.com	800-783-9200
CheapTickets	cheaptickets.com	888-922-8849
11th Hour Vacations	11thhourvacations.com	800-291-8968
Expedia	expedia.com	800-397-3342
Hotels.com	hotels.com	800-346-8357
Hotwire	hotwire.com	866-468-9473
Kayak	kayak.com	203-899-3100
Liberty Travel	libertytravel.com	888-271-1584
OneTravel	onetravel.com	866-883-0908
Orbitz	orbitz.com	888-656-4546
Priceline	priceline.com	866-925-5373
Quikbook	quikbook.com	800-789-9887
Travelocity	travelocity.com	888-872-8356
Uniglobe	uniglobetravel.com	604-718-2600
Virtuoso	virtuoso.com	866-401-7974

Key Newcomers

Here are some of the most notable hotels and resorts that opened in the past year. For a full list, see the index on page 267.

Blackstone	*Chicago*	Liberty	*Boston*
Bowery Hotel	*New York City*	London West Hollywood	*LA*
Chelsea	*Atlantic City, NJ*	Mansion on Peachtree	*Atlanta*
Donovan House	*Washington, DC*	Murano	*Tacoma, WA*
Four Seasons	*Seattle*	NYLO Plano	*Dallas/Ft. Worth*
Four Seasons	*St. Louis, MO*	Omaha Magnolia	*Omaha, NE*
Gansevoort South	*Miami*	Palazzo Resort & Casino	*Las Vegas*
Hard Rock	*San Diego*	Regent Bal Harbour	*Miami*
Ivy	*San Diego*	Ritz-Carlton	*Westchester County, NY*
Liaison Capitol Hill	*Washington, DC*	Solage Calistoga	*Wine Country, CA*

Also this past year, well-known brand names opened multiple spots. **W** came to Atlanta (its second in that city, with a third planned for 2009), and Minneapolis; **Trump International** debuted in Chicago and Las Vegas; **MGM** moved into Connecticut's Foxwoods Resort and Detroit; Kimpton opened two **Palomar** hotels in Arlington, VA, and LA; and the new Intercontinental offshoot, **Hotel Indigo,** set up shop in Atlanta, Boston and Nashville.

Trendy new boutiques and small hotels continue apace. Chicago's **Dana Hotel & Spa,** NYC's **Six Columbus,** Dallas' **Joule Hotel** and the lush **Hidden Pond** in Kennebunkport, Maine, were all welcomed on the scene.

Just over the horizon are a slew of NYC openings including Downtown's **Cooper Square Hotel,** Thompson Hotels' **Thompson LES** and **Smyth** (in TriBeCa), Kimpton Hotels' **VU** (in Times Square) and Andre Balazs' long-awaited **Standard NYC.** Elsewhere, the **Setai** enters San Diego; Steve Wynn bets big on the **Encore** in Vegas; the **21C** arty brand branches out to Austin; **W** arrives in Miami Beach; and **Ritz-Carlton** sets up shop in Charlotte, N.C., Lake Tahoe and Rancho Mirage, California, and outside Tucson.

Top Ratings

Excludes places with low votes.

HOTEL CHAINS & MARKETING GROUPS RANKINGS

CHAIN		MARKETING GROUP	
28	Four Seasons (35)	27	Relais & Châteaux (45)
27	Ritz-Carlton (39)	26	Leading Hotels (58)
24	Fairmont (17)		Luxury Collection (16)
23	Grand Hyatt (12)	25	Small Luxury Hotels (47)
22	Westin (75)	24	Preferred Hotels (110)
	Loews (16)		
	Renaissance (70)		
	Kimpton Group (45)		
	InterContinental (24)		
21	W Hotels (21)		
	Hyatt Regency (99)		
	Omni (36)		
	Marriott (350)		
19	Hilton (269)		
	Homewood Suites (220)		
	Embassy Suites (190)		
	Wyndham (84)		
18	Millennium (14)		
	DoubleTree (160)		
	Sheraton (198)		
	Crowne Plaza (130)		
17	Harrah's (17)		
16	Radisson (172)		

The above list includes chains with at least 10 hotels in the U.S. (in parentheses is the number of locations). We've also listed marketing groups such as Relais & Châteaux and Leading Hotels of the World. Most of the top-rated chains are expensive. The following chains offer the best bang for the buck.

BEST CHAIN VALUE

1. Homewood Suites (220)

2. Embassy Suites (190)

3. DoubleTree (160)

4. Sheraton (198)

5. Crowne Plaza (130)

6. Harrah's (17)

7. Radisson (180)

With 100 or more rooms.

<u>28</u> Ritz-Carlton | *Dallas/Ft. Worth*
Peninsula | *Chicago*
<u>27</u> Four Seasons | *New York City*
Four Seasons | *Chicago*
Wynn | *Las Vegas*
Ritz-Carlton | *San Francisco*
Four Seasons | *Boston*
Mandarin Oriental | *New York City*
Peninsula | *Los Angeles*
Four Seasons | *Las Vegas*
<u>26</u> Four Seasons | *San Francisco*
Rosewood Mansion | *Dallas/Ft. Worth*
Four Seasons | *Philadelphia*
Mandarin Oriental | *Miami*
Four Seasons | *Washington, DC*
Mandarin Oriental | *Washington, DC*
Beverly Hills Hotel | *Los Angeles*
Park Hyatt | *Chicago*
Bellagio | *Las Vegas*
Ritz-Carlton Central Park | *New York City*
Ritz-Carlton | *Chicago*
Ritz-Carlton Coconut Grove | *Miami*
St. Regis | *New York City*
St. Regis | *San Francisco*
<u>25</u> Four Seasons Beverly Hills | *Los Angeles*
Rosewood Crescent | *Dallas/Ft. Worth*
Borgata | *Atlantic City, NJ*
St. Regis | *Ft. Lauderdale*
Mandarin Oriental | *San Francisco*
Four Seasons | *Austin, TX*
Ritz-Carlton | *Washington, DC*
Peninsula | *New York City*
Setai | *Miami*
Charleston Place | *Charleston, SC*
Jefferson | *Richmond, VA*
Venetian | *Las Vegas*
Four Seasons | *Miami*
Ritz-Carlton | *Boston*
Ritz-Carlton Battery Park | *New York City*
Four Seasons | *Houston*
Raffles L'Ermitage | *Los Angeles*
InterContinental Buckhead | *Atlanta*
Ritz-Carlton | *Atlanta*
Beverly Wilshire | *Los Angeles*
Washington Duke Inn | *Durham, NC**
Windsor Court | *New Orleans*
<u>24</u> Ritz-Carlton Buckhead | *Atlanta*
Grand America | *Salt Lake City*
Townsend | *Detroit*
Four Seasons Silicon Valley | *San Francisco*

LARGE RESORTS

With 100 or more rooms.

28 Four Seasons Resort | *Big Island, HI*
Four Seasons Resort | *Maui, HI*

27 Cloister | *Georgia Coast*
Sanctuary | *Kiawah Island, SC*
Montage Resort | *Orange Co. Beaches, CA*
Ritz-Carlton | *Naples, FL*
Four Seasons Resort | *Jackson Hole, WY*
Four Seasons Aviara | *San Diego*
Ritz-Carlton Bachelor Gulch | *Beaver Creek, CO*
Four Seasons/Koele | *Lanai, HI*
Ritz-Carlton Laguna Niguel | *Orange Co. Beaches, CA*
Ritz-Carlton Amelia Island | *Northeast Florida*

26 Greenbrier | *White Sulphur Springs, WV*
Meadowood | *Wine Country, CA*
Canyon Ranch | *Tucson, AZ*
Ritz-Carlton | *Half Moon Bay, CA*
St. Regis | *Orange Co. Beaches, CA*
Inn at Spanish Bay | *Carmel Area, CA*
St. Regis | *Aspen, CO*
Ritz-Carlton Grande Lakes | *Orlando Area*
Four Seasons Troon North | *Phoenix/Scottsdale, AZ*
Disney's BoardWalk Villas | *Orlando Area*
Ritz-Carlton Reynolds | *Lake Oconee, GA*
Broadmoor | *Colorado Springs, CO*
Halekulani | *Oahu, HI*
Four Seasons Biltmore | *Santa Barbara, CA*
Lodge at Pebble Beach | *Carmel Area, CA*
Four Seasons Resort/Manele | *Lanai, HI*
Boulders | *Phoenix/Scottsdale, AZ*
Ritz-Carlton | *Las Vegas*
Four Seasons | *Dallas/Ft. Worth*
Enchantment Resort | *Sedona, AZ*
Ritz-Carlton Kapalua | *Maui, HI*
Disney's Beach Club Villas | *Orlando Area*
Breakers | *Palm Beach, FL*
Lodge at Torrey Pines | *San Diego*
Ritz-Carlton Golf Resort | *Naples, FL*
Canyon Ranch/Berkshires | *Lenox, MA*
Phoenician | *Phoenix/Scottsdale, AZ*
Sonnenalp | *Vail, CO*

25 Ritz-Carlton | *Sarasota, FL*
Sanctuary/Camelback Mtn. | *Phoenix/Scottsdale, AZ*
American Club | *Kohler, WI*
Four Seasons Resort | *Palm Beach, FL*
Stein Eriksen Lodge | *Park City, UT*
Nemacolin Woodlands | *Farmington, PA*
Palazzo Resort & Casino | *Las Vegas*
Disney's Grand Floridian | *Orlando Area*
Fairmont Scottsdale | *Phoenix/Scottsdale, AZ*
Disney's Animal Kingdom | *Orlando Area*

SMALL HOTELS, INNS, LODGES & RESORTS

With less than 100 rooms.

29 Twin Farms | *Woodstock Area, VT*
28 Blackberry Farm | *Walland, TN*
Casa Palmero | *Carmel Area, CA*
27 Amangani | *Jackson Hole, WY*
Auberge du Soleil | *Wine Country, CA*
Château du Sureau | *Yosemite, CA*
Little Palm Island | *Keys, FL*
Inn at Little Washington | *Washington, VA*
Post Ranch Inn | *Carmel Area*
Tu Tu' Tun Lodge | *Gold Beach, OR*
Bel-Air | *Los Angeles*
Lodge at Sea Island | *Georgia Coast*
Canoe Bay | *Chetek, WI*
Lake Austin Spa | *Austin, TX*
Rancho Valencia | *San Diego*
Point | *Adirondacks, NY*
26 Little Nell | *Aspen, CO*
Mirbeau Inn | *Catskills, NY*
Bernardus Lodge | *Carmel Area, CA*
Rittenhouse | *Philadelphia*
Wheatleigh | *Lenox, MA*
San Ysidro Ranch | *Santa Barbara, CA*
Willows Lodge | *Seattle*
Blantyre | *Lenox, MA*
Keswick Hall | *Charlottesville, VA*
Calistoga Ranch | *Wine Country, CA*
Wauwinet | *Cape Cod & The Islands*
25 Acqualina Resort | *Miami*
Gaige House Inn | *Wine Country, CA*
L'Auberge Carmel | *Carmel Area, CA*
Watermark | *San Antonio, TX*
Woodlands Resort | *Charleston, SC*
White Barn Inn | *Southern Coast, ME*
Horned Dorset | *Rincon, PR*
Mayflower Inn | *Washington, CT*
Hana-Maui | *Maui, HI*
Ritz-Carlton Georgetown | *Washington, DC*
Lodge at Woodloch | *Hawley, PA*
Salish Lodge | *Seattle*
Ventana Inn | *Carmel Area, CA*
24 Inn at Perry Cabin | *Eastern Shore, MD*
Fearrington House | *Pittsboro, NC*
Tides | *Miami*
Grove Isle | *Miami*
Lodge & Spa/Cordillera | *Beaver Creek, CO*
Arizona Inn | *Tucson, AZ*
Virginia | *Cape May, NJ*
Chambers | *Minneapolis/St. Paul, MN*
Oheka Castle | *Long Island, NY*
Inn of the Anasazi | *Santa Fe, NM*

ROOMS

29 Twin Farms | *Woodstock Area, VT*
   Amangani | *Jackson Hole, WY*
   Casa Palmero | *Carmel Area, CA*
   Four Seasons Resort | *Big Island, HI*
   Peninsula | *Chicago*
28 Post Ranch Inn | *Carmel Area, CA*
   Acqualina Resort | *Miami*
   Blackberry Farm | *Walland, TN*
   Rancho Valencia | *San Diego*
   Four Seasons | *New York City*
   Four Seasons Resort | *Maui, HI*
   Palazzo Resort & Casino | *Las Vegas*
   Wynn | *Las Vegas*
   Lodge at Sea Island | *Georgia Coast*
   Ritz-Carlton Bachelor Gulch | *Beaver Creek, CO*
   Ritz-Carlton | *Dallas/Ft. Worth*
   Gaige House Inn | *Wine Country, CA*
   Auberge du Soleil | *Wine Country, CA*
   Sanctuary | *Kiawah Island, SC*
   Carneros Inn | *Wine Country, CA*
   Inn at Little Washington | *Washington, VA*
   Canoe Bay | *Chetek, WI*
   Mandarin Oriental | *New York City**
27 Four Seasons Resort | *Jackson Hole, WY*
   Peninsula | *Los Angeles*

SERVICE

29 Twin Farms | *Woodstock Area, VT*
   Château du Sureau | *Yosemite, CA*
   Four Seasons Resort | *Big Island, HI*
28 Casa Palmero | *Carmel Area, CA*
   Four Seasons Resort | *Maui, HI*
   Inn at Little Washington | *Washington, VA*
   Ritz-Carlton | *Dallas/Ft. Worth*
   Peninsula | *Chicago*
   Lowell | *New York City*
   Ritz-Carlton | *San Francisco*
   Tu Tu' Tun Lodge | *Gold Beach, OR*
   Ritz-Carlton | *Naples, FL*
   Four Seasons | *Chicago*
   Blackberry Farm | *Walland, TN*
   Four Seasons | *New York City*
   Four Seasons | *San Francisco*
   Point | *Adirondacks, NY*
   Little Palm Island | *Keys, FL*
   Four Seasons Aviara | *San Diego*
   Four Seasons | *Philadelphia*
   Amangani | *Jackson Hole, WY*
   Bel-Air | *Los Angeles*
   Four Seasons/Koele | *Lanai, HI*
   Lake Austin Spa | *Austin, TX*
   St. Regis | *Aspen, CO**

DINING

29 | Ritz-Carlton | *Dallas/Ft. Worth*
28 | Inn at Little Washington | *Washington, VA*
Blackberry Farm | *Walland, TN*
Château du Sureau | *Yosemite, CA*
Twin Farms | *Woodstock Area, VT*
White Barn Inn | *Southern Coast, ME*
Auberge du Soleil | *Wine Country, CA*
Rosewood Mansion | *Dallas/Ft. Worth*
27 | Woodlands Resort | *Charleston, SC*
Little Palm Island | *Keys, FL*
Inn at Langley | *Seattle*
Four Seasons Resort | *Big Island, HI*
Wheatleigh | *Lenox, MA*
Tu Tu' Tun Lodge | *Gold Beach, OR*
L'Auberge Carmel | *Carmel Area, CA*
Bellagio | *Las Vegas*
Virginia | *Cape May, NJ*
Wynn | *Las Vegas*
Ritz-Carlton | *San Francisco*
Homestead Inn | *Greenwich, CT*
Willows Lodge | *Seattle*
Wauwinet | *Cape Cod & The Islands*
Post Ranch Inn | *Carmel Area, CA*
Four Seasons Resort | *Maui, HI*
Four Seasons | *Boston*

FACILITIES

29 | Four Seasons Resort | *Big Island, HI*
Cloister | *Georgia Coast*
Disney's Beach Club Villas | *Orlando Area*
Twin Farms | *Woodstock Area, VT**
Canyon Ranch/Berkshires | *Lenox, MA*
Lake Austin Spa | *Austin, TX*
Greenbrier | *White Sulphur Springs, WV*
28 | Casa Palmero | *Carmel Area, CA*
Ritz-Carlton Reynolds | *Lake Oconee, GA*
Canyon Ranch | *Tucson, AZ*
Four Seasons Resort | *Jackson Hole, WY*
Lodge at Pebble Beach | *Carmel Area, CA*
Lodge at Woodloch | *Hawley, PA*
Montage Resort | *Orange Co. Beaches, CA**
Sanctuary | *Kiawah Island, SC*
Disney's BoardWalk Villas | *Orlando Area*
Broadmoor | *Colorado Springs, CO*
Grand Hyatt | *Kauai, HI*
Blackberry Farm | *Walland, TN*
Canoe Bay | *Chetek, WI*
Lodge at Sea Island | *Georgia Coast**
Peninsula | *Chicago*
Four Seasons Aviara | *San Diego*
Ritz-Carlton | *Naples, FL*
Inn at Spanish Bay | *Carmel Area, CA*

DESTINATION & RESORT SPAS

28 Four Seasons Resort | *Big Island, HI*
Blackberry Farm | *Walland, TN*
Four Seasons Resort | *Maui, HI*
27 Sanctuary | *Kiawah Island, SC*
Montage Resort | *Orange Co. Beaches, CA*
Lake Austin Spa | *Austin, TX*
Mandarin Oriental | *New York City*
26 Greenbrier | *White Sulphur Springs, WV*
Canyon Ranch | *Tucson, AZ*
St. Regis | *Orange Co. Beaches, CA*
Mirbeau Inn | *Catskills, NY*
Golden Door▽ | *San Diego*
Boulders | *Phoenix/Scottsdale, AZ*
Enchantment Resort | *Sedona, CA*
Canyon Ranch/Berkshires | *Lenox, MA*
Phoenician | *Phoenix/Scottsdale, AZ*
25 Miraval Spa | *Tucson, AZ*
Sanctuary/Camelback Mtn. | *Phoenix/Scottsdale, AZ*
Nemacolin Woodlands | *Farmington, PA*
Mayflower Inn | *Washington, CT*
Bacara Resort | *Santa Barbara, CA*
24 Lodge & Spa/Cordillera | *Beaver Creek, CO*
23 El Monte Sagrado | *Taos, NM*
Grand Wailea Resort | *Maui, HI*
22 La Costa Resort | *San Diego*
Two Bunch Palms | *Palm Springs Area, CA*

RESORT GOLF COURSES

Based on Course score in Zagat's *America's Top Golf Courses*.

30 Straits, Whistling Straits, American Club | *Kohler, WI*
Ocean, Kiawah Island, Sanctuary | *Kiawah Island, SC*
Casades, Homestead | *Hot Springs, VA*
Gold, Golden Horseshoe, Williamsburg Inn | *Williamsburg, VA*
29 Pebble Beach, Lodge at Pebble Beach | *Carmel Area, CA*
Plantation, Kapalua, Kapalua Villas/Ritz-Carlton Kapalua | *Maui, HI*
North, Lake of Isles, Foxwoods Resort | *Ledyard, CT*
28 Challenge at Manele, Four Seasons Resort/Manele | *Lanai, HI*
Ocean, Ginn Hammock Beach Resort | *Palm Coast, FL*
River, Blackwolf Run, American Club | *Kohler, WI*
Fazio Canyons, Barton Creek | *Austin, TX*
Greenbrier Course, Greenbrier | *White Sulphur Springs, WV*
The General, Eagle Ridge Resort | *Galena, IL**
Great Waters, Ritz-Carlton Reynolds | *Lake Oconee, GA*
No. 2, Pinehurst Resort | *Pinehurst, NC*
Seaside, Sea Island, Lodge at Sea Island | *Georgia Coast*
No. 8, Pinehurst Resort | *Pinehurst, NC*
Oconee, Ritz-Carlton Reynolds | *Lake Oconee, GA*
27 Coeur d'Alene Resort | *Coeur d'Alene, ID*
Bluff/Cove/Ridge, Ritz-Carlton Reynolds | *Lake Oconee, GA*

Best Buys

LARGE HOTELS

With 100 or more rooms.

1. Disney's Fort Wilderness | *Orlando Area*
2. Paris | *Las Vegas*
3. MGM Grand | *Las Vegas*
4. Desert Springs | *Palm Springs Area, CA*
5. Stratton Mtn. Resort | *Southern Vermont*
6. Rio All-Suite | *Las Vegas*
7. Westward Look Resort | *Tucson, AZ*
8. Bellagio | *Las Vegas*
9. Old Faithful Inn | *Yellowstone Nat'l Park, WY*
10. Signature at MGM Grand | *Las Vegas*
11. Tropicana | *Atlantic City, NJ*
12. Hyatt Regency | *San Antonio, TX*
13. Fairmont | *Dallas/Ft. Worth*
14. Palazzo Resort & Casino | *Las Vegas*
15. Hilton Short Hills | *Short Hills, NJ*
16. Mirage | *Las Vegas*
17. Sun Valley Resort | *Sun Valley, ID*
18. Argonaut | *San Francisco*
19. Red Rock | *Las Vegas*
20. Wentworth by the Sea | *Newcastle, NH*

SMALL HOTELS

With less than 100 rooms.

1. Timberline Lodge | *Mount Hood, OR*
2. Deetjen's Big Sur Inn | *Carmel Area, CA*
3. Mission Ranch | *Carmel Area, CA*
4. Beekman Arms | *Hudson Valley, NY*
5. Half Moon Bay Lodge | *Half Moon Bay, CA*
6. Inn at Montchanin | *Wilmington, DE*
7. Hacienda del Sol | *Tucson, AZ*
8. Albion River | *Northern California Coast*
9. Mirbeau Inn | *Catskills, NY*
10. Tabard Inn | *Washington, DC*
11. Tu Tu' Tun Lodge | *Gold Beach, OR*
12. Harraseeket Inn | *Freeport, ME*
13. Taos Inn | *Taos, NM*
14. Marco Beach Resort | *Naples, FL*
15. El Tovar | *Grand Canyon, AZ*
16. White Swan Inn | *San Francisco*
17. Casa Madrona | *San Francisco*
18. Napa River Inn | *Wine Country, CA*
19. Two Bunch Palms | *Palm Springs Area, CA*
20. Fearrington House | *Pittsboro, NC*

40,000 places to eat, drink, stay & play – free at ZAGAT.com

HOTEL & RESORT CHAIN DIRECTORY

	ROOMS	SERVICE	FACIL.	COST

Caesars
23 | 21 | 24 | E

800-223-7277 | www.caesars.com

"From the shores of Atlantic City to the indulgent mire of Vegas" to the Indiana heartland, this trio is "always a good choice for a casino property" say its fans; sure, the "glitzy" "Roman stuff gets silly" sometimes and they can be "chaotic", but most find "reliable" service and "well-furnished" rooms, adding that the City of Sin location, with its "excellent Forum Shops", "sets the bar high" for sister spots that may not rise to those standards.

Crowne Plaza
18 | 17 | 18 | M

877-227-6963 | www.crowneplaza.com

The 130 U.S. hotels in this "middle-of-the-road" chain, part of the InterContinental Hotels group, offer "adequate" lodging say fans of the "newly renovated spots" with "nice" in-room features like "calming CDs", "lavender spray, sleeping masks" and WiFi access; even if some find "nothing special" with "no real amenities", the "smiling staff" "knows how to treat people" and deliver a "dependable" stay.

DoubleTree
19 | 18 | 17 | M

800-222-8733 | www.doubletree.com

They're "not elegant by any stretch", but the 160 U.S. hotels in this "moderately priced" chain (part of the Hilton family) are usually a "safe bet" for a "one- or two-night quickie stay" with "spacious", "family-friendly" suites that are "often priced the same as a regular room elsewhere"; most guests "love getting a freshly baked cookie at check-in", but otherwise this budget-friendly chain is "not too exciting."

Embassy Suites
20 | 18 | 19 | M

800-362-2779 | www.embassysuites.com

"Whether for vacation, business or a bit of both", this chain's 190 hotels offer "efficient service", "expansive" suites with "separate living areas that afford privacy" ("an added plus when traveling with kids") and "free breakfasts and happy hours" for added "bang for the buck"; just "don't look for anything more than "tacky", "bland interiors", since, no matter how "hard they try", these "don't make it to the A list."

☑ Fairmont
24 | 25 | 24 | VE

800-257-7544 | www.fairmont.com

Encompassing "absolutely wonderful" resorts, "top-quality" city center hotels and "restored, grand, historic" properties, all imbued with "high-end service", the 17 "well-situated" U.S. outposts in this group come "highly recommended" and, not surprisingly, highly priced; "nothing beats the Gold floors for amenities" or the "perks for frequent guests", and with NYC's Plaza Hotel now in the fold, they've upped their quota of spots "exemplifying old-world luxury."

☑ Four Seasons
28 | 29 | 28 | VE

800-819-5053 | www.fourseasons.com

Voted our Survey's No. 1 Chain once again, this "fine choice if cost is no object" "rarely disappoints" at any of its 35 U.S. hotels; the "extraordinary" service "can't be beat", and it's matched by "fabulous" restaurants, "gorgeous rooms" with "beautiful baths", "the best spas and fitness facilities" and "surprisingly kid-friendly" facilities; you'll get

ROOMS | SERVICE | FACIL. | COST

"consistently excellent" everything at this "cream of the crop" choice; N.B. see our Top lists where this chain dominates.

Grand Hyatt
23 | 22 | 23 | E

800-223-1234 | www.grand.hyatt.com

"There's a wide range" among the 12 U.S. outposts of this "business" chain – some (Seattle, Kauai) are "super" with "up-to-date" rooms and "well-maintained facilities", others are "convention-over-run" and "not exactly grand"; still, you can expect "glossy mall-like" public spaces, "central locations" and modern fitness centers, plus a Gold Passport frequent guest program that can yield free nights and special offers.

Harrah's
17 | 16 | 19 | M

800-427-7247 | www.harrahs.com

Critics contend that at any of the 17 locations in this casino-centric chain, "you stay for the gambling", not for the "below-average" rooms or the "boring food"; though the staff "tries its best", and some fans say the refurbished Atlantic City outpost has "charm", most report "spotty experiences" overall; P.S. the "reward program offers free nights as you earn points" on the gaming floor.

Hilton
20 | 19 | 19 | E

800-774-1500 | www.hilton.com

Being an "HHonors [frequent guest] member", with "terrific" perks like upgrades and room amenities, "makes a difference" at the "commuter train" of hotels, a "solid", if sometimes "less-than-stellar", choice for a "home away from home"; the chain of 270-plus outposts may "not be what it once was" ("I bet Paris wouldn't stay in one!"), but you can still expect "reasonable prices" and decent service.

Historic Hotels of America
∇ 21 | 22 | 20 | E

800-678-8946 | www.historichotels.org

It's "almost always unique and interesting" when you stay in one of the 211 properties in this alliance since all are at least 50 years old or listed on the National Register of Historic Places; "you never know exactly what you're going to get" ("pick your spots" wisely because "comfort varies"), but more often than not they're "quaint, enjoyable" and filled with "history" – such as New York City's Algonquin, The Ahwahnee in Yosemite and Dallas' Stoneleigh.

Homewood Suites by Hilton
21 | 18 | 19 | M

800-225-5466 | www.homewood-suites.com

"Get Hilton points" while staying at one of the 220 members of this group, where all-suite accommodations with cost-saving microwaves and fridges are "more like a home than a hotel room"; tot-toters tout the "terrific value" for families, especially when given the "complimentary breakfast", while the briefcase brigade finds a "safe bet" for "long business stays"; so even if there's "no personality" and the "thin walls" make privacy impossible, it's a "functional" choice.

Hyatt Regency
22 | 21 | 22 | E

800-223-1234 | www.hyatt.com

You "get what you pay for" at the 105 U.S. locations in this group that boasts "comfortable", "well-equipped" rooms, especially at its "beautiful" resorts, along with "helpful service"; sure, some outposts are "more excellent than others" and leisure travelers tsk they're "better for conventions", but amenities like the Stay Fit Gym program and an "excellent reward system" make it the "favorite chain" of many.

InterContinental

23 | 22 | 22 | E

800-424-6835 | www.interconti.com

This 24-member business chain is "always a good value" even if it's not quite up to the best out there; the "properties vary" from "elegant" to a bit "dated", but most are "decent places to spend the night", with "proper facilities", "strong service" and "great locations"; indeed, "you know what to expect and you won't be disappointed"; N.B. the group is expanding its moderate-priced, hip boutique brand, Hotel Indigo, with three new openings in the past year.

Kimpton Group

23 | 23 | 21 | E

800-546-7866 | www.kimptongroup.com

Each of the 45 locations of this "never drab" pet-friendly boutique chain offers a "unique" spin - from the dramatic striped upholstery of Boston's Nine Zero to the playfully nautical Argonaut in San Francisco - and all offer "an experience unlike what you'd expect" (including at its "reliable" Monaco brand); fans flock for the "hospitable" service, "impressive use of space" (in mostly "small rooms"), "hopping" bars that are "places to be seen", "complimentary happy hours" and "gay-friendly" attitude.

☑ Leading Hotels of the World

27 | 26 | 25 | VE

800-745-8883 | www.lhw.com

"A wonderful collection, each with its own special personality" (e.g. Napa Valley's Calistoga Ranch, San Francisco's Campton Place), this "well-vetted" 58 U.S.-member marketing alliance provides an "extra sense of security" that you'll get "facilities worth the cost"; its "individual properties" are "expensive, yes", but most are "number one in terms of ambiance, service" and "location", so shell out the bucks because this group's "name says it all."

Le Méridien

23 | 21 | 22 | VE

800-543-4300 | www.lemeridien.com

The verdict is mixed on the eight "quasi-French" North American outposts of this Starwood-affiliated, mostly international chain; proponents praise "elegant" decor, "breathtaking rooms" and a staff full of "smiles and local knowledge", but critics cry they're "not as good as they cost", with some locations "outdated" and "behind the times technologically."

Loews

23 | 22 | 22 | E

866-563-9792 | www.loewshotels.com

Fans of these 16 U.S. "gems" find "individual" hotels that "strive for uniqueness" with "pet-friendly" rooms that "don't feel cookie-cutter", along with an "agreeable" staff and solid conference facilities; called out for special mention are the "fantastic" Florida properties and NYC's "perfectly located" Regency, plus the frequent guest program which offers extra amenities such as free fitness club access, airline miles and room upgrades.

	ROOMS	SERVICE	FACIL.	COST

☑ Luxury Collection, The   26 | 25 | 25 | VE
800-325-3589 | www.luxurycollection.com

The "best of the Starwood hotels", this upscale collection of 16 (another 67 are outside the U.S.) includes "top-notch" resorts like Phoenix's Wigwam and Kauai's Princeville as well as "high-end" city spots such as San Diego's U.S. Grant; though the "experience ranges depending on the place", most offer "quite luxurious" accommodations, "outstanding service" and "appealing" architecture.

☑ Mandarin Oriental   28 | 27 | 27 | VE
800-526-6566 | www.mandarinoriental.com

"What a way to go" laud loyalists of the "classy" hotels in this expanding Asia-based chain with four U.S. outposts that are "bastions of fine service"; from "unmatched" Zen-like decor with "excellent feng shui" to "luxurious rooms with high-end finishes" and "swanky" bath amenities " to spas that "transport you to nirvana", you "couldn't ask for a better experience" – or a more "expensive" tab.

Marriott Hotels & Resorts   21 | 21 | 21 | E
800-228-9290 | www.marriott.com

"Dependable, if not spectacular", the 350-plus U.S. members of this chain, where "corporate America lives and meets", are "always consistent", with service that's "happy to help", "comfortable rooms", "decent fitness facilities" and "all-around good value considering locations" (especially "on weekends"); even critics who find them "unexciting" ("seen one, seen 'em all") admit the Rewards Member program, in which points can be used for rooms, miles, cruises, car rentals and more, is "great."

Millennium Hotels   18 | 19 | 18 | E
866-866-8086 | www.millenniumhotels.com

For a "reasonably priced" stay with "efficient" service and contemporary decor, business types head to one of the 15 U.S. properties of this otherwise "nothing special" chain; its hotels "vary significantly", so it's a "hit-or-miss" option that can leave you either "pleasantly surprised" or convinced that a "major renovation" is necessary.

Morgans Hotels   ▽ 21 | 18 | 20 | VE
800-697-1791 | www.morganshotelgroup.com

These nine "self-consciously hip" spots from the company originally founded by boutique-master Ian Schrager come complete with the "best bars" in which to "people-watch", a staff with appropriate amounts of "attitude" and "interesting", "stylish" public spaces; value-seekers, however "expected more" than "closet-size rooms" given the "expensive" price tag.

Omni   21 | 21 | 20 | E
888-444-6664 | www.omnihotels.com

Loyalists of this chain of 36 U.S. hotels wish there "were one in every city" saying each "gives the competition a run for its money" with a staff that "goes out of its way to make sure you're happy" (they "really appreciate members" of the frequent stay club), "inviting lobbies" and "consistently above-average facilities", especially at the "newer", "trendier" properties; even if the rooms at some of "the older spots could use a face-lift", extras like in-room excercise equipment and WiFi access make them a "safe business bet."

Orient-Express
▽ 26 | 26 | 25 | VE

800-237-1236 | www.orient-express.com

Possessing a "select" U.S. collection of five "high-end" hotels including Chesapeake Bay's Inn at Perry Cabin and Charleston Place in South Carolina (plus 33 international hotels and five luxury trains), these "unique" spots are "some of the best" in their areas with a "great mixture of regional decor and modern conveniences" along with "spectacular service" and food; they each make for "expensive vacations", but you'll "smile" "when your business meeting is held" at one.

Pan Pacific
▽ 25 | 23 | 23 | E

877-324-4856 | www.panpacific.com

Since it has just two U.S. locations (there are 15 additional international outposts), the "contemporary", "Asian-inspired" luxury of this Tokyo-based chain is spread too thin for many to experience; those who do alight at the Seattle or Big Island of Hawaii hotels say there "should be more like these" given the "fabulous" facilities, "personalized service", high-quality restaurants and "exceptional rooms" with luxurious baths (the Pacific Floor offers complimentary breakfasts, evening cocktails, butler service and express check-in/check-out).

Park Hyatt
26 | 25 | 25 | VE

800-233-1234 | www.park.hyatt.com

Hyatt's "luxury brand" is "often undervalued by those who think it's just a Hyatt" rather than a lodging where "you'll likely run into stars" at the bar; the "modern", "designer-feel" rooms have flat-screen TVs and beds you want to "dive into and never leave", while the "excellent" service is "often memorable"; sure, they're "pricey", but they're also "often the swankiest place in town."

☑ Peninsula Hotels
28 | 28 | 28 | VE

866-382-8388 | www.peninsula.com

With just three U.S. hotels and five others worldwide, this "unparalleled" chain that's "right up there with the Four Seasons" may have "limited locations", but it "takes hosting very seriously" and "nothing gets in the way of the perfect service"; any of the outposts "can rank among the top hotels" in the world given their "top-notch" restaurants, "incredible rooms" with the "absolute finest" high-tech amenities and "extra-special attention to detail" all around; it's too bad this "outstanding" group is "not in more cities."

Preferred Hotels & Resorts Worldwide
25 | 23 | 24 | VE

800-323-7500 | www.preferredhotels.com

Everything is "top-of-the-line" say fans of the 110 U.S. locations in this 40-plus-year-old "eclectic" marketing "collection of individual hotels" that make for "special vacation experiences"; the lodgings are "not of equal quality", but they're "typically remarkable", "usually expensive" and "frequently worth it" – e.g. The Broadmoor in Colorado Springs, Stein Eriksen Lodge in Park City, Utah – and they can make you "feel like royalty" with "super rooms" and close "attention to detail."

	ROOMS	SERVICE	FACIL.	COST

Radisson Hotels & Resorts
`17` `16` `15` `M`

800-333-3333 | www.radisson.com

It'll "do in a pinch" say patrons who've stayed at this middle-of-the-road, "no-frills" chain of 180 U.S. hotels that some find "more inconsistent than some comparable" brands; while fans find "welcoming" staffers, "comfortable" rooms and a "decent" price, critics cite "dowdy" locations that "need much improvement."

⊠ Relais & Châteaux
`28` `27` `25` `VE`

800-735-2478 | www.relaischateaux.com

Who wouldn't want to "stay in them all" ask admirers of this "absolutely reliable" collection of 45 small, privately owned properties (there's a total of 475 members worldwide) that "fire on all cylinders" – from "superb" settings (e.g. Canoe Bay in Chetek, Wisconsin, Auberge du Soleil in Napa) to "grand" rooms and "pampering service"; they're "always a surprise from one place to the next" and "you pay for the luxe", but it's "difficult to be disappointed" at any of these "unique" hotels, especially since they all offer outstanding dining.

Renaissance Hotels & Resorts
`23` `22` `22` `E`

888-236-2427 | www.renaissancehotels.com

With 70 "standard", "business"-friendly, Marriott-affiliated properties, this "safe bet" usually offers a "helpful staff", "freebies for returning guests", "lovely facilities" that can "feel luxurious" and "decent-size rooms"; you "get a lot for your money" here, but regulars recommend staying at the "newer", "trendier" properties to avoid "disappointment."

⊠ Ritz-Carlton
`27` `27` `27` `VE`

800-542-8680 | www.ritzcarlton.com

An "incredible" experience awaits guest of this "top luxury chain" with 39 U.S. hotels that "never disappoint", with "first-class service" ("they want you back and they show it"), "always pleasant" dining, extra-amenity-laden club floors that "spoil you" and "surprisingly good" "children's programs that make vacations more enjoyable"; it's "super all-around", though some sticklers say the English club decor looks "too much the same" "from city to city."

Rosewood Hotels & Resorts
`27` `27` `26` `VE`

888-767-3966 | www.rosewoodhotels.com

The nine U.S. properties in this collection of "gems" – from NYC's venerable Carlyle to St. John's Caneel Bay – pay "attention to detail" with "superior rooms" that "make sleeping a pleasure" and staffers who "remember your name"; it's "one of the best" chains "in the business" report regulars, and "all the properties share the same special taste" – it's just "too bad they don't manage more" locations.

Sheraton
`18` `18` `18` `M`

888-625-5144 | www.sheraton.com

"Widely available" with 198 U.S. properties, this "reasonably priced" and "trusted" Starwood brand draws patrons looking for "convenient locations" and keeps them with "ample amenities and facilities", "cordial service" and "tremendous package" deals at various times; the locations that some reviewers say "need help" may soon receive it given the many upgrades planned (i.e. Waikiki's venerable Royal Hawaiian).

	ROOMS	SERVICE	FACIL.	COST

ⓩ Small Luxury Hotels of the World · 26 | 26 | 23 | VE

800-525-4800 | www.slh.com

Any of the "remarkable" 47 U.S. members of this marketing alliance of "boutique" properties is a "sure bet" if you want to "live like a royal" for a time; "beautiful facilities" with loads of "character" (e.g. Big Sur's Post Ranch Inn, Seattle's Hotel Andra); along with "flawless service" and some of the "best restaurants imaginable" make for an "indulgent getaway" that's "definitely worth the cost."

Sofitel · 22 | 22 | 21 | E

800-763-4835 | www.sofitel.com

Fans of this "reliable" chain with nine stateside hotels – "ideally located in cities" – "like the French touch", the "consistent" service and the "stylish rooms" with "European flair" boasting signature down feather beds; too bad there are "too few of them" in the U.S. say those who consider it an "economical" choice.

ⓩ St. Regis · 28 | 27 | 27 | VE

800-598-1863 | www.stregis.com

"Old-fashioned elegance" awaits "for those who can afford" to stay at one of the seven U.S. hotels in this Starwood brand that "makes you feel special" with "fantastic private butlers", "tech"-filled rooms", "fabulous" settings with lots of "stargazing" potential and "incredible" fine-dining; so "enjoy the moment and pray your credit card bill gets lost in the mail."

Westin · 24 | 22 | 22 | E

800-937-8461 | www.westin.com

The 76 U.S. locations of this "reliable" Starwood brand "blur the line between business and pleasure" with Heavenly beds topped with "soft sheets" and "fabulous pillows", "efficient" service and "better-than-average" food; other pluses that make it a "solid choice for a business trip" include in-room Starbucks coffee, frequent-guest perks and a no-smoking policy.

W Hotels · 22 | 21 | 22 | E

877-946-8357 | www.whotels.com

Sure, it's "a bit like being in a nightclub 24/7" when you stay at one of the hotels in this 21-member Starwood chain but all the "beautiful" people "dressed in black" creating a "sexy" vibe, as well as the "stylish rooms and amenities", are worth the "loud atmosphere"; fans "love the creative decor" and on-site Bliss spas, but those "not hip enough to stay here anymore" take swings at the "snobby" service and snap "if you look under the dark lighting", the "small quarters" are "nothing special."

Wyndham Hotels & Resorts · 19 | 18 | 19 | E

877-999-3223 | www.wyndham.com

They may be "inconsistent" in service and facilities, but the 84 U.S. members of this chain are "never below par", with "well-maintained rooms", "appropriate amenities and services" and a "reward program that remembers your preferences" (e.g. they "prepare the room before arrival exactly the way you want it"); families laud the kids' programs and all-inclusive packages, while history buffs like the historic collection.

HOTEL, RESORT & SPA DIRECTORY

| | ROOMS | SERVICE | DINING | FACIL. | COST |

Alabama

Birmingham

Renaissance Ross Bridge Golf Resort & Spa 🏌⛷⚲Ⓢ🔍

| ∇ 25 | 25 | 23 | 28 | $209 |

4000 Grand Ave. | 205-916-7677 | fax 205-945-8218 | 866-480-7677 | www.rossbridgeresort.com | 248 rooms, 11 suites
Combine an "unbelievable" Robert Trent Jones golf course with a "bagpiper playing at sunset" and you get a "mystical" experience boast boosters of this "ultimate getaway"; the "castle"-like "retreat" sates with "well-appointed rooms", "spacious baths", "superior" service and a "huge pool"; the "only downside" may be its "limited" dining.

Point Clear

Marriott Grand Hotel 🏌♨⚲Ⓢ🔍

| 21 | 23 | 20 | 24 | $249 |

1 Grand Blvd. | 251-928-9201 | fax 251-928-1149 | 888-236-2427 | www.marriottgrand.com | 371 rooms, 34 suites
Offering "afternoon tea" and "holiday buffets", this Point Clear "grande dame" offers a "wonderful combination" of "relaxed elegance" and "Southern charm"; its "sprawling" grounds impress with "moss-covered trees", "waterside strolls", "fabulous golf courses" and a "fantastic" pool – and "nearby Fairhope" offers "great shopping."

Alaska

Anchorage

Alyeska Resort ♨Ⓢ⚹🎿

| 21 | 21 | 21 | 23 | $309 |

1000 Arlberg Ave. | Girdwood | 907-754-1111 | fax 907-754-2200 | 800-880-3880 | www.alyeskaresort.com | 249 rooms, 53 suites, 2 townhouses
Although it's 45 minutes from Anchorage, "spend at least one night" at this "romantic" "haven" in the "rough-and-tumble" "wilderness" where "every inch" of the "newly remodeled rooms" is as "breathtaking" as the "fabulous views" of the Seven Glaciers; travel "up the mountain for dinner", but be forewarned, some find service "lacking."

Arizona

TOPS IN STATE

26 Canyon Ranch | *Tucson*
Four Seasons Troon North | *Scottsdale*
Boulders | *Carefree*
Enchantment Resort | *Sedona*
Phoenician | *Scottsdale*
25 Miraval Spa | *Catalina*
Sanctuary/Camelback Mtn. | *Paradise Valley*
Fairmont Scottsdale | *Scottsdale*
24 Royal Palms | *Phoenix*
Arizona Inn | *Tucson*

Grand Canyon

El Tovar ⊕ 🏚   16 | 19 | 19 | 20 | $166

1 Main St. | 303-297-2757 | fax 928-638-9810 | 888-297-2757 |
www.grandcanyonlodges.com | 66 rooms, 12 suites

It's "all about the view and location" at this "historic hotel" with "rustic", "vintage charm" "on the South Rim" of the Grand Canyon where the vistas are "breathtaking", "especially at sunset", and there are "deer outside the windows"; despite its "cramped", "spartan" rooms, "nothing-special" food and "minimal" services, most would "go back in a heartbeat" – if they could land another "hard-to-get" reservation.

Phoenix/Scottsdale

Arizona Biltmore 🏌️✕⊕🏚🍴🛁⚲☉❀   23 | 24 | 23 | 26 | $495

2400 E. Missouri Ave. | Phoenix | 602-955-6600 | fax 602-381-7600 |
800-950-0086 | www.arizonabiltmore.com | 638 rooms, 100 suites

"Book a casita" at this "magnificent" Frank Lloyd Wright–inspired "masterpiece", a "classy and grand" "world unto itself" that "shines" with "wonderful service", "lush grounds" ("love, love, love the life-size chessboard in the garden!"), "beautiful golf course views", a "fabulous spa", "fire pits at night", "delicious dining" and "awesome" pools with cabanas "that are a godsend in the Phoenix heat"; while some naysayers nitpick over the "steep prices" and "tiny", "aging" rooms, most agree that the "peaceful setting" "does wonders for your frame of mind."

Arizona Grand Resort 🏌️🍴🛁⚲☉❀   ▽ 19 | 18 | 16 | 20 | $399
(fka Pointe South Mountain)

8000 S. Arizona Grand Pkwy. | Phoenix | 602-438-9000 | fax 602-431-6535 |
877-800-4888 | www.arizonagrandresort.com | 640 suites

"Go for the elegance . . . stay for the pool" recommend jet-setters who say it's the highlight of this resort, given a "lazy river" that's a "blast" and lots of space for "playing water basketball, volleyball and riding the slides"; the rest doesn't rate as high, say surveyors, citing "dissapointing" rooms, "dull decor" and food that's "not outstanding"; N.B. renovations should be completed in 2009.

🇿 Boulders, The 🍴🛁⚲☉❀   26 | 26 | 23 | 28 | $599

34631 N. Tom Darlington Dr. | Carefree | 480-488-9009 | fax 480-488-4118 |
866-397-6520 | www.theboulders.com | 160 casitas, 55 villas

"A fabulous place to unwind" that "melts into the mountains" of the Sonoran Desert outside Scottsdale, this "unique venue" is "a treat for the senses"; "outstanding" for golfers and a "magnificent" spot even for non-duffers (try the "couples massage in a VIP suite" at the "A++" Golden Door Spa), it boasts "secluded" grounds, "breathtaking views", "luxurious" casitas in which you "could live forever", a "can-do" staff that "goes above and beyond" and "excellent" dining.

Fairmont Scottsdale 🏌️🍴🛁⚲☉❀   25 | 25 | 24 | 27 | $479

7575 E. Princess Dr. | Scottsdale | 480-585-4848 | fax 480-585-0091 |
800-344-4758 | www.fairmont.com | 506 rooms, 119 casitas,
23 suites, 1 house

"Don't waste your time on castles in Europe" when you can slumber at this "huge", "elegant" and "kid-friendly" Scottsdale "princess" that's a "perfect place to wind down" amid the "beautiful grounds", "challenging golf course" and "breathtaking sunsets"; the "fantastic" spa comes complete with a "waterfall treatment room, saunas, Jacuzzi and innovative treatments", and devotees suggest "springing" for one of the "wonderfully appointed casita rooms" for the "true experience."

⚡ Four Seasons Resort Troon North 🎿🍴♨️🅂🔍

| 27 | 27 | 24 | 27 | $565 |

10600 E. Crescent Moon Dr. | Scottsdale | 480-515-5700 |
fax 480-515-5599 | 888-207-9696 | www.fourseasons.com |
188 rooms, 22 suites

"Always book a casita" prod proponents who are "drawn like a magnet" to this "tucked-away", "to-die-for" Scottsdale "desert paradise" near Pinnacle Peak; with "incredible landscapes", an "incomparable spa", "impeccable service", a "wonderful pool" and "absolutely lovely rooms" bedecked with "plasma TVs, fireplaces and your own private balcony", it's a "fantastic overall experience" that "never disappoints."

Hermosa Inn 🖐🍴♨️

| 22 | 24 | 26 | 19 | $389 |

5532 N. Palo Cristi Rd. | Paradise Valley | 602-955-8614 |
fax 602-955-8299 | 800-241-1210 | www.hermosainn.com |
17 rooms, 11 casitas, 3 haciendas, 4 villas

For a "step back in time" to "old Phoenix", book a "cozy room" at this "jewel" in a 1930s-era building that's "hidden in a residential neighborhood" and prime for a "relaxing" "romantic getaway"; "extremely accommodating" service adds to the allure, as does the "outstanding" LON's restaurant offering "intimate dining in the wine room" and "views of Camelback Mountain" from its outdoor patio.

Hyatt Regency at Gainey Ranch 🎿🖐♨️Ⓛ🅂🔍

| 21 | 21 | 19 | 25 | $259 |

7500 E. Doubletree Ranch Rd. | Scottsdale | 480-444-1234 |
fax 480-483-5550 | 800-554-9288 | www.hyatt.com | 460 rooms, 30 suites

This "upscale family-vacation" "mega-resort" provides relaxation with its "secluded, grassy" grounds and "lush landscaping", yet is also "close to shopping, restaurants and all the action" of Scottsdale; there's a water park and "fabulous swimming pools" for the kids, and an "unbelievable spa" and a "bar with live entertainment" for adults, though some sniff at the "generic" rooms and public areas that "need updating."

JW Marriott Camelback Inn 🎿🖐🍴♨️Ⓛ🅂🔍

| 23 | 24 | 20 | 25 | $499 |

5402 E. Lincoln Dr. | Scottsdale | 480-948-1700 |
fax 480-951-8469 | 800-582-2169 | www.camelbackinn.com |
431 casitas, 22 suites

Combining the "original charm of the Old West with updated comforts for business and pleasure travelers", this "sprawling" "Valley of the Sun" "luxury resort" soothes sybarites with its "gorgeously landscaped" Scottsdale desert setting and "world-class spa" that's "as close to heaven as you'll find on earth"; the "Sunday brunch is to die for" and you "can lose yourself for hours" relaxing inside the "well-decorated" casitas or by the two pools, so few complain about food that "could be improved."

	ROOMS	SERVICE	DINING	FACIL.	COST

JW Marriott Desert Ridge Resort & Spa 슈ㅤ⚎⚑⚐⚒

| 24 | 23 | 22 | 26 | $549 |

5350 E. Marriott Dr. | Phoenix | 480-293-5000 | fax 480-293-3600 |
800-835-6206 | www.jwdesertridgeresort.com | 869 rooms, 81 suites
A "top-of-the-line" mega-resort with a "magnificent setting" just 20
minutes north of Sky Harbor Airport, this "huge facility" "serves up
convention-style hospitality with flair and panache" while still "managing to be personal"; the rooms are "large and gorgeous", the spa is
"excellent" and the "beautifully landscaped" grounds include "fire pits
scattered throughout the property", "amazing golf courses" and "awesome pools" (don't miss the "kid-friendly" lazy river); but a few tired
trekkers complain it's "just too big."

Phoenician, The 슈⚔⚎⚑⚐⚒

| 26 | 25 | 24 | 27 | $730 |

6000 E. Camelback Rd. | Scottsdale | 480-941-8200 | fax 480-947-4311 |
800-888-8234 | www.thephoenician.com | 621 rooms, 14 suites, 12 casitas
For "all the luxury money can buy", "move in" to this "crème de la crème"
Scottsdale "diamond in the desert" that's "heaven on earth" with an
"amazing location at the foot of Camelback Mountain" with "beautifully
landscaped cactus gardens"; features like "fabulous casitas" with "opulent decor", "exceptional service" from a "staff that treats guests like royalty", "superb spa treatments" and an "incredible array of swimming
pools" make "taking out a loan" to pay for a stay seem reasonable.

Pointe Hilton Squaw Peak 슈⚎⚑⚐⚒

| 19 | 19 | 16 | 21 | $249 |

7677 N. 16th St. | Phoenix | 602-997-2626 | fax 602-997-2391 |
800-685-0550 | www.pointehilton.com | 485 suites, 78 casitas
"A big hit with the kids", this "sprawling, family-oriented" resort is
"what you'd expect to find in Arizona", what with a "spectacular water
park and lazy river", "great recreational facilities" and "warm, welcoming attitudes" from a "helpful and informative staff"; "huge casitas with large private rooftop decks" are a "highlight", even if several
squawk about "ordinary food" and the need for "renovations."

Pointe Hilton Tapatio Cliffs 슈⚎⚑⚐⚒

| 19 | 20 | 18 | 21 | $309 |

11111 N. Seventh St. | Phoenix | 602-866-7500 | fax 602-993-0276 |
800-876-4683 | www.hilton.com | 585 suites
"Spectacular views at night", "a beautiful setting" and "no shortage of
steep hills" are the first signs that you're "spread out among the cliffs"
in an "off-the-beaten-track location" at this "exceptionally comfortable" resort "overlooking the city"; the "newly redone" quarters near
"romantic, small pools" (the "sound of water is everywhere") are
"spacious", but "bring walking shoes" as you may have a "20-minute
stroll to your room" or to the so-so restaurant.

Renaissance Scottsdale Resort ⚎⚐

| 21 | 19 | 17 | 20 | $415 |

6160 N. Scottsdale Rd. | Scottsdale | 480-991-1414 | fax 480-951-3350 |
800-468-3571 | www.renaissancehotels.com | 65 rooms, 106 suites
A "beautiful location" and "relaxing casitas" with "private outdoor hot
tubs" elevate this otherwise "just ok" resort with "warm service" near
one of Scottsdale's toniest malls; though "pleasantly surprised"

guests would stay there again, others who mark it "dated" "thought it'd be a lot nicer that it was."

Ritz-Carlton, The 🐕 🏋 — 22 | 24 | 22 | 21 | $459

2401 E. Camelback Rd. | Phoenix | 602-468-0700 | fax 602-468-0793 | 800-241-3333 | www.ritzcarlton.com | 267 rooms, 14 suites

"It's exactly what you'd expect from a Ritz-Carlton" opine patrons of this "fabulous" hotel "close to Downtown", where the "super pool", "flawless" service and location "just across the street from a high-end mall" win applause; still, some sigh "if only" this "citified" "coporate" lodging "were more of a resort", because it isn't the best "for a weekend stay."

Royal Palms Resort & Spa 🍴 🐕 🏋 [S] — 24 | 25 | 25 | 24 | $450

5200 E. Camelback Rd. | Phoenix | 602-840-3610 | fax 602-840-6927 | 800-672-6011 | www.royalpalmsresortandspa.com | 63 rooms, 44 casitas, 5 villas, 7 suites

"What Phoenix living is all about" declare devotees who frequent this "absolutely beautiful" "old hacienda" "hideout" in a "central location" on "stunning", "serene" grounds; a "helpful, informative" staff, an "amazing" spa with "great special touches" and "outstanding" fare at T. Cook's Mediterranean restaurant help create a "luxurious experience"; but watch out for "some undesirable rooms" – "if you have a casita, you're in business."

[Z] Sanctuary on Camelback Mountain 🛏 🐕 🏋 [S] 🎾 — 26 | 25 | 25 | 26 | $520

5700 E. McDonald Dr. | Paradise Valley | 480-948-2100 | fax 480-483-7314 | 800-245-2051 | www.sanctuaryaz.com | 98 rooms, 7 houses

"A bit of heaven on earth", this "classy" member of Small Luxury Hotels of the World "nestled at the foot of Camelback Mountain" is "perfect" for "hiding from the rest of the world" given its "incredible" casitas ("almost as big as a small house"), a "beyond serene spa" and "delicious" fare; other highlights include "personal service", "great tennis" courts, "exquisite" overall facilities and "views to die for"; N.B. a new outdoor bar opened in 2008.

Sheraton Wild Horse Pass Resort & Spa 👪 🐕 🏋 ⛳ [S] 🎾 — 23 | 24 | 23 | 26 | $429

5594 W. Wild Horse Pass Blvd. | Phoenix | 602-225-0100 | fax 602-225-0300 | 888-218-8989 | www.wildhorsepassresort.com | 474 rooms, 26 suites

A "pleasant" "surprise in the middle of nowhere" (actually, an Indian reservation 11 miles south of the airport), this resort "isn't just a hotel, it's an experience", "infusing Native American culture" throughout the decor, activities and even the "wonderful" food in Kai restaurant (voted No. 1 for Food in Phoenix in our *America's Top Restaurants* Survey); rooms are "spacious", and with "so much to see and do", including gambling, golf, a spa, swimming and horseback riding, "one never has to leave."

Valley Ho, Hotel [H] 🐕 🏋 [S] — ∇ 24 | 22 | 21 | 22 | $359

6850 E. Main St. | Scottsdale | 480-248-2000 | fax 480-248-2002 | 866-882-4484 | www.hotelvalleyho.com | 187 rooms, 6 suites, 36 condos

"It's definitely a scene" at this "fun, retro throwback to a 1950s motel" "with all the amenities of the 21st century"; "beautiful bathrooms", "modern, funky decor", "great cabanas" with "your own private patio facing the pool", a "top-notch spa" and a "uniformly friendly staff" make it "one of the coolest places to stay" and a "popular hangout for locals", even if some insist it "can't shake its motel roots."

Westin Kierland Resort & Spa 彡≪ﭮﻌﺴﺴﻌ

| 24 | 23 | 21 | 26 | $349 |

6902 E. Greenway Pkwy. | Scottsdale | 480-624-1000 |
fax 480-624-1001 | 800-354-5892 | www.kierlandresort.com |
672 rooms, 60 suites

"If you've never been" to this "absolutely wonderful" Scottsdale resort, "go now" for "an amazing escape" catapulted by "excellent rooms", "luxuriant landscaping" offset by an "awesome golf course", "service beyond compare", "wonderful massages" and a "gorgeous" swimming pool with a "large kids' area, waterslide" and "wonderful lazy river"; still, it's "too large and noisy" for sedate types who "can't decide if it's a business hotel or a resort"; P.S. there's "shopping and nightlife" at nearby Kierland Commons mall.

Wigwam Golf Resort & Spa 彡≪ﭮﻌﺴﺴﻌ

| 24 | 23 | 20 | 24 | $629 |

300 E. Wigwam Blvd. | Litchfield Park | 623-935-3811 |
fax 623-935-3737 | 800-327-0396 | www.wigwamresort.com |
259 casitas, 72 suites

"Everything, down to the shampoo, is top quality" at this "remotely located", but "wonderfully renovated" "favorite" where "gorgeous landscaping" and the "desert serenity" set the stage for "lovely", "bungalow-style suites" bedecked with "unbelievably comfortable beds"; the "excellent golf" (via Robert Trent Jones Sr. and Red Lawrence), "great pool", "lovely" Elizabeth Arden Red Door spa, "bar with live entertainment" and "impeccable staff" make the 30-mile drive from Phoenix worth it.

Sedona

Z Enchantment Resort 彡×≪ﻌﺴﻌ

| 26 | 26 | 23 | 28 | $450 |

525 Boynton Canyon Rd. | 928-282-2900 | fax 928-282-9249 |
800-826-4180 | www.enchantmentresort.com | 116 rooms, 120 suites

"Can I move in?" beg guests of this "magical", "hedonistic" "oasis in Sedona" that "literally takes your breath away" with its "vortex of luxury" set amid the "natural beauty" of "idyllic Boynton Canyon" and its famous Red Rocks; there's "hiking right outside the front door", a "fabulous spa" with "heavenly treatments", "outstanding" service that "makes you feel right at home", "delicious" food and "romantic, relaxing rooms", all of which makes the "sky-high" prices "worth every penny."

Hilton ≪ﻌﺴﻌ

| ▽ 23 | 22 | 18 | 22 | $169 |

90 Ridge Trail Dr. | 928-284-4040 | fax 928-284-6940 | 877-273-3762 |
www.hilton.com | 48 rooms, 171 suites

"You can't go wrong" at this "well-maintained", "kid-friendly resort" in a "gorgeous" Oak Creek location "just a stone's thrown from the heart of Sedona"; it offers "spectacular views" "at every turn" plus "excellent service", "great pools", a "nice spa and golf course" and "comfortable" accommodations, but the "restaurant choices" are merely "adequate."

L'Auberge de Sedona ✕ ⬝ ♨ Ⓢ
| 23 | 23 | 25 | 22 | $325 |

301 L'Auberge Ln. | 928-282-1661 | fax 928-282-1064 | 800-905-5745 | www.lauberge.com | 31 cottages, 21 rooms, 1 house

"Tucked away in the woods" by "a creek in the heart of Sedona's red rock country", this *très français* "romantic" "destination resort" is a "fabulous splurge" that's "worth the money if you want to feel pampered"; "well-appointed" rooms, cottages or houses ("it feels like Provence in the lovely waterside cabins") beckon with the "most comfortable beds on the planet", and L'Auberge restaurant, "with a tremendous wine list" and "great creekside seating", is "phenomenal"; N.B. notable additions include a spa and an alfresco wine bar.

Los Abrigados ♨ ⬝ ♨ Ⓢ ✎
| ▽ 22 | 21 | 18 | 23 | $139 |

160 Portal Ln. | 928-282-1777 | fax 928-282-2614 | 800-258-2899 | www.losabrigados.com | 150 suites, 9 cottages, 2 houses

With 22 acres of "beautiful grounds" and "spacious rooms" (renovations in 2008 upgraded the suites), this creekside destination is popular with families "especially during the holiday season"; there's a range of spa services, tennis courts, a golf course and a summer camp for kids, but because it's an ownership resort "beware the time-share sales" pitches or escape to the "adjacent art galleries."

Tucson

Arizona Inn ♨ ⊕ ♨ ✎
| 23 | 26 | 23 | 25 | $329 |

2200 E. Elm St. | 520-325-1541 | fax 520-881-5830 | 800-933-1093 | www.arizonainn.com | 75 rooms, 20 suites, 2 houses

Family-owned and -operated for 78 years, this "lovely oasis in the desert" is "elegant and rich in history"; the "idyllic setting", "fabulous staff" that "gets everything right", "old-fashioned" (some say "dreary") rooms and "little touches" (DVDs, afternoon tea, "a pool area like your rich aunt's backyard") prompt some to assert "I'd live here if I could."

⦿ Canyon Ranch ✕ ⬝ ♨ Ⓢ ✎
| 24 | 27 | 25 | 28 | $880 |

8600 E. Rockcliff Rd. | 520-749-9000 | fax 520-749-1646 | 800-742-9000 | www.canyonranch.com | 135 rooms, 19 casitas

"Even a coach potato is motivated to move" at this "seriously life-changing", "health-oriented" "Zen experience" in a "spectacular desert setting" that "never disappoints", thanks to a "decadent spa" with "exotic treatments", "excellent yoga classes", "divine dining" (no, you can't "bring the chef home"), "wonderful kitchen demonstrations" and a "super staff"; indeed, you'll "arrive beleaguered and leave feeling like a million bucks" both in "body and soul"; N.B. no alcohol.

Hacienda del Sol ✕ ⊕ ♨ ♨ Ⓢ
| 19 | 23 | 25 | 21 | $175 |

5601 N. Hacienda del Sol Rd. | 520-299-1501 | fax 520-299-5554 | 800-728-6514 | www.haciendadelsol.com | 22 rooms, 5 suites, 3 casitas

"One of the Sonoran Desert's most precious flowers", this "lovely boutique hotel" boasts a "mixture of Victorian and Old West decor" with an overall "relaxing atmosphere" and "spectacular" setting that includes a "great courtyard for parties"; its "charming", if "small", rooms are outfitted with "wonderful toiletries", and the "gem" of a restaurant peddles "simply stunning" food that's complimented by a "great wine list" and "beautiful" sunsets.

	ROOMS	SERVICE	DINING	FACIL.	COST

ARIZONA – TUCSON

Hilton El Conquistador 🐂🏊♨⚓☉🔍

	19	20	19	21	$229

10000 N. Oracle Rd. | 520-544-5000 | fax 520-544-1222 | 800-325-8131 | www.hilton.com | 346 rooms, 39 suites, 43 casitas

It's "fun in the sun for the whole family" at this "fabulously located" "desert hideaway" featuring a "pool area with waterslides", "gorgeous views" and "nice little casitas" "overlooking the golf course"; critics, however, lament the "predictable" eats, "screaming kids" and "older" rooms that "could use a renovation", deeming it all "a bit ordinary compared to local competition."

JW Marriott Starr Pass Resort & Spa 🐂♨⚓☉🔍

	25	23	21	26	$349

3800 W. Starr Pass Blvd. | 520-792-3500 | fax 520-670-0427 | 800-503-2898 | www.starrpassmarriott.com | 540 rooms, 35 suites

"What a view!" sigh smitten surveyors of this "blissfully peaceful", "modern" "oasis" in the "heart of the Tucson desert" that "exceeds all expectations" with "luxurious rooms" and hiking right "out the door"; though the atmosphere is "wonderfully Southwestern and laid-back", the staff remains "dedicated and attentive" and includes a "fantastic concierge service", plus there's an "inviting" golf course, spa and variety of dining choices (try the "excellent" Primo).

Lodge at Ventana Canyon 🐕🏊♨⚓☉🔍

	22	23	20	25	$259

6200 N. Clubhouse Ln. | 520-577-1400 | fax 520-577-4065 | 800-828-5701 | www.thelodgeatventanacanyon.com | 50 suites

"Don't tell anyone how beautiful it is" plead patrons of this "overwhelmingly huge", "great golf getaway" in a "gorgeous", 600-acre nature preserve in the "northern foothills of Tucson"; guests can "hike to the waterfall", indulge in "fabulous dining at Ventura" where "each course is a touch of delight" and relax in "spacious", newly renovated rooms.

Loews Ventana Canyon 🐂✕🏊♨⚓☉🔍

	24	24	23	25	$339

7000 N. Resort Dr. | 520-299-2020 | fax 520-299-6832 | 800-234-5117 | www.loewshotels.com | 371 rooms, 27 suites

Many say this is simply "*the* place to stay in Tucson", a "majestic resort at the base of the foothills with breathtaking views" and "all the prerequisites for fun": "fabulous food", "magnificent golf course", "professional staffers" that "take great care of you" and "beautiful desert trails"; the only dilemma for some is "when you're on the grounds, you don't want to return to your room" and when you're in your "amazingly comfortable" quarters, you "don't want to go out."

Miraval, Life in Balance ✕♨☉🔍

	24	26	25	27	$800

5000 E. Via Estancia Miraval | Catalina | 520-825-4000 | fax 520-825-5163 | 800-232-3969 | www.miravalresort.com | 104 rooms, 14 suites

Expect "ultraluxury" at this "deluxe adult camp" north of Tucson where the "excellent" treatments, "healthy and interesting" fare, "great classes and activities" (mountain-biking, hiking and rock climbing) make it one of "the best destination spas in the country"; though non New-Agey types tsk "too much Oprah has gone to their heads", most simply "love" the focus on "mind-body awareness" that allows you to "leave all your worries behind."

	ROOMS	SERVICE	DINING	FACIL.	COST
Tanque Verde Ranch 👫🔭🎾	▽ 20	24	22	23	$420

14301 E. Speedway Blvd. | 520-296-6275 | fax 520-721-9426 | 800-234-3833 | www.tanqueverderanch.com | 74 rooms, 23 suites, 4 houses

It's easy to "play the cowboy" at this "real" dude ranch relish wranglers who "saddle up" and experience an "all-around", "down-home" experience; there are solid sunrise breakfasts and evening dinners, and non-horse-focused diversions like spa services, hiking and nature walks, but a few "wish they'd remodel" some of the rooms.

	ROOMS	SERVICE	DINING	FACIL.	COST
Westin La Paloma 👫🐕🔭⛳Ⓢ🎾	22	21	22	24	$479

3800 E. Sunrise Dr. | 520-742-6000 | fax 520-577-5878 | 800-228-3000 | www.westinlapalomaresort.com | 462 rooms, 25 suites

"Spectacular" "golf and sunshine equals paradise" for duffers at this "sprawling" spot with "full-service convention facilities" and "a fantastic pool area" "for both families and adults without kids"; "indulgent spa treatments", "breathtaking views" and a "great restaurant" make it "a relaxing getaway", even if some snip that "rooms need a makeover."

	ROOMS	SERVICE	DINING	FACIL.	COST
Westward Look Resort 👫🐕🔭Ⓢ🎾	20	21	19	21	$129

245 E. Ina Rd. | 520-297-1151 | fax 520-297-9023 | 800-722-2500 | www.westwardlook.com | 238 rooms, 6 suites

A "lovely" resort with "plant-filled" grounds in the Catalina foothills, this destination may "not be as luxurious as others" in the area, but the "manageable scale" and "memorable" dining that incorporates produce from the chef's garden is enough to win fans; an ongoing redo may address concerns that it "feels like a stripped-down" hotel.

Arkansas

Little Rock

	ROOMS	SERVICE	DINING	FACIL.	COST
Peabody, The	▽ 20	25	21	20	$199

3 Statehouse Plaza | 501-906-4000 | fax 501-375-4721 | 800-732-2639 | www.peabodylittlerock.com | 395 rooms, 23 suites

"Business and leisure travelers" find "comfortable" rooms, an "eager-to-please" staff and an Eclectic steakhouse at this Downtown staple famous for the "ducks that walk out of the elevator" accompanied by John Philip Sousa marches; it may be somewhat "average" in general, but it's "one of the best in the Little Rock area."

California

TOPS IN STATE

28 Casa Palmero | *Pebble Beach*
27 Auberge du Soleil | *Rutherford*
Château du Sureau | *Oakhurst*
Post Ranch Inn | *Big Sur*
Montage Resort | *Laguna Beach*
Four Seasons Aviara | *Carlsbad*
Bel-Air | *Bel-Air*
Ritz-Carlton | *San Francisco*
Ritz-Carlton Laguna Niguel | *Dana Point*
Rancho Valencia | *Rancho Santa Fe*

Carmel Area

Bernardus Lodge 🍴🐾[S]🎾

ROOMS	SERVICE	DINING	FACIL.	COST
26	26	26	26	$535

415 Carmel Valley Rd. | Carmel Valley | 831-658-3400 | fax 831-659-3529 | 888-648-9463 | www.bernardus.com | 56 rooms, 1 suite

"You're welcomed with a glass of wine" ("poured like water") by an "attentive staff" "as you enter the lobby" of this "amazing sanctuary" "tucked into the Carmel Valley"; "superb rooms with terraces, fireplaces and Jacuzzis" "situated in the middle of a vineyard" along with an "outstanding spa" and "unreal" fare at "culinary genius" Cal Stamenov's restaurant make it the "ultimate" spot for "pampering, indulgence and relaxation."

Carmel Valley Ranch 🐾⛳🎾

ROOMS	SERVICE	DINING	FACIL.	COST
23	21	20	23	$550

1 Old Ranch Rd. | Carmel | 831-625-9500 | fax 831-624-2858 | 800-422-7635 | www.carmelvalleyranch.com | 144 suites

"Huge suites" on "peaceful, tranquil grounds" "await the weary traveler" at this "gem in the Carmel Valley" that's "perfect for a romantic getaway" what with the "comfortable rooms" "right on the golf course" trumpeting "wonderful, wood-burning fireplaces"; there are "fabulous views of the mountains" and "wild deer and turkeys wander the grounds", but some sigh that it's "not as luxurious as expected" since the decor "still looks like it's out of the '80s."

[Z] Casa Palmero at Pebble Beach 👪⛳[S]🎾

ROOMS	SERVICE	DINING	FACIL.	COST
29	28	25	28	$815

1518 Cypress Dr. | Pebble Beach | 831-622-6650 | fax 831-622-6655 | 800-654-9300 | www.pebblebeach.com | 19 rooms, 3 suites, 2 studios

"The pinnacle of Pebble Beach" assert aficionados of this "delightfully cloistered environment" in an "intimate and elegant setting" where the "beautifully furnished", almost perfect rooms include a "pillow menu"; under the same management as the Inn at Spanish Bay and the Lodge at Pebble Beach, it's the "height of pampered luxury" where you can "relax in a hot tub alongside the second fairway" and soak up "wonderful, personalized attention" before hitting the famous links; it's no wonder that most guests "don't ever want to leave."

Deetjen's Big Sur Inn 🐾

ROOMS	SERVICE	DINING	FACIL.	COST
15	20	22	16	$95

48865 Hwy. 1 | Big Sur | 831-667-2377 | fax 831-667-0466 | www.deetjens.com | 20 rooms

"Rough it" by "sleeping next to a redwood at this rustic" "hideaway" "in Big Sur's dramatic landscape" that attracts "Hollywood actors trying to get away from the LA bustle", "tree-huggers with expense accounts" and "former hippies"; it's a "perfect place to read a book and relax" since there are "no TVs or radios" in the "pleasant cabins" serviced by a "wonderful" staff, and the "first-rate" restaurant features "fresh, organic" fare; still, some take a look at the "makeshift" quarters and carp this one "needs to be brought into the modern world."

Green Gables Inn [H]🐾

ROOMS	SERVICE	DINING	FACIL.	COST
▽ 24	22	22	23	$135

301 Oceanview Blvd. | Pacific Grove | 831-375-2095 | fax 831-375-5437 | 800-722-1774 | www.greengablesinnpg.com | 11 rooms

The "panorama of Monterey Bay" "can't be beat" at this "lovely" 1888 Queen Anne Victorian B&B in Pacific Grove, boasting a "peaceful" waterside setting, a staff that "couldn't be more accommodating", "comfortable" individually decorated rooms (though "small") and a full breakfast buffet; no question, it's quaint ("twee?"), but it's hard not to be charmed by a place that puts cookies on the table and wine and hors d'oeuvres in the parlor.

Highlands Inn, Hyatt 🍴🐾👪

23	23	24	23	$595

120 Highlands Dr. | Carmel | 831-620-1234 | fax 831-626-8105 | 800-682-4811 | www.highlandsinn.hyatt.com | 37 rooms, 11 suites

A "magical atmosphere" that's "perfect for an affair" or a "weekend of romance", this "simply stunning" Carmel property "tucked away on top of an ocean cliff surrounded by forests" overlooks the "rugged coastline of Big Sur", yielding "incomparable" "views of the Pacific"; the "unparalleled" setting is matched by a "reliable" staff, a "wonderful restaurant" and bar, and rooms with "wood-burning fireplaces, Jacuzzi tubs for two" and "binoculars to watch the whales" - so "take a deep breath, swallow hard and pay up."

Inn at Spanish Bay 🍴👪⛳Ⓢ🎾

26	26	25	28	$580

2700 17-Mile Dr. | Pebble Beach | 831-647-7500 | fax 831-644-7960 | 800-654-9300 | www.pebblebeach.com | 252 rooms, 17 suites

"Not just a resort for golfers" (though the course is "legendary"), this "romantic" Pebble Beach "paradise" is "exceptional" even "if you stay off the links" entirely; "get ready to shell out the bucks" for "breathtaking grounds", "top-notch" service, "gorgeous" public areas, "country-estate-like", "luxurious" rooms with fireplaces and free WiFi ("splurge for an ocean view") and "dynamite restaurants", plus "fire pits and a bagpiper" who plays at dusk - "what more can you ask for?"

La Playa Hotel Ⓗ🐾👪Ⓢ

18	21	19	21	$210

Camino Real & 8th Ave. | Carmel | 831-624-6476 | fax 831-624-7966 | 800-582-8900 | www.laplayahotel.com | 73 rooms, 2 suites, 5 cottages

It's all about the "location", "within walking distance of Carmel's shops" and two blocks from the ocean that sells this "grande dame" on the National Register of Historic Places; despite a soft goods renovation over the past few years, it's still a bit "long in the tooth" say those who find "old and cold rooms" with baths that "can use updating" - so head out to the "enchanting" grounds and soak up the "peaceful ambiance" instead.

[Z] **L'Auberge Carmel** 🍴Ⓗ👪

25	26	27	23	$310

Monte Verde St. | Carmel | 831-624-8578 | fax 831-626-1018 | www.laubergecarmel.com | 20 rooms

It's all about "understated luxury" at this adults-only Relais & Châteaux hotel in Carmel that's "outstanding in every respect", especially when it comes to the "superb" 10-course contemporary Californian meals at Aubergine and the "fantastic" breakfasts; the rest of the "world-class" experience includes a staff that makes "every effort", "beautiful rooms" with French doors and deep-soaking tubs, and "luxurious" grounds.

[Z] **Lodge at Pebble Beach, The** 🍴🏇👪⛳Ⓢ🎾

26	25	24	28	$675

1700 17-Mile Dr. | Pebble Beach | 831-647-7500 | fax 831-625-8598 | 800-654-9300 | www.pebblebeach.com | 150 rooms, 11 suites

"A golfer's dream", this legendary lodge two hours from San Francisco is "absolutely out of this world" and "sets the standard for others";

	ROOMS	SERVICE	DINING	FACIL.	COST

from the "fantastic, flawless" rooms and "stunning setting" to the "luxurious" service, "exceptional dining" and "lovely spa", it's not just for duffers – but if you do play and have "buckets of money", "why would you stay anywhere else?"

Mission Ranch 🏨🔍

	21	21	20	21	$120

26270 Dolores St. | Carmel | 831-624-6436 | fax 831-626-4163 | 800-538-8221 | www.missionranchcarmel.com | 29 rooms, 2 cottages

"Kick back" at Clint Eastwood's "little hideaway", a "charming, comfortable" former ranch with "gorgeous" views of sheep-filled meadows and Point Lobos across the bay; though it's "sparse on luxury", fans cheer the "wide variety" of accommodations, including those in "well-maintained" cottages and barns, its location in Carmel ("everything is within reach") and the "fantastic" Sunday jazz brunch; P.S. you may catch Clint "making a cameo" at the "great evening piano bar."

Monterey Plaza Hotel & Spa 🏨Ⓢ

	22	21	19	22	$550

400 Cannery Row | Monterey | 831-646-1700 | fax 831-646-0285 | 800-334-3999 | www.montereyplazahotel.com | 286 rooms, 4 studios

"Jutting out over Monterey Bay" and within "walking distance to the shops of Cannery Row and to the aquarium", this "luscious" location becomes even better when you "pay a little extra" and "get a corner room" with "views of the ocean"; you'll have "the area's best sea otter" sightings (and maybe "a hawk sitting on your window ledge"), go to "sleep with the sound of seals barking" and enjoy a spa with two rooftop hot tubs; but a few find "motellike" quarters and "limited" facilities.

☒ Post Ranch Inn ✕🏨Ⓢ

	28	27	27	26	$550

Hwy. 1 | Big Sur | 831-667-2200 | fax 831-667-2512 | 800-527-2200 | www.postranchinn.com | 39 cottages

For "peace and tranquility" in an "edge-of-the-world" location, few come close to this "secluded", "absolutely stunning" coastline marvel earning accolades for its "spectacular" ocean views, "luxurious rusticity" (the treehouses are "fantastic"), "super" spa and "sensational" fare at Sierra Mar restaurant; high prices can be expected at this "blissful" member of Small Luxury Hotels of America, but so can "every amenity possible."

Quail Lodge 🏨LⓈ🔍

	23	21	20	22	$380

8205 Valley Greens Dr. | Carmel | 831-624-2888 | fax 831-624-3726 | 888-828-8787 | www.quaillodge.com | 79 rooms, 14 suites, 4 villas

Duffers "disappear for the weekend" at this "unsung", "peaceful" Carmel Valley resort catering to an "older" crowd that adores the "beautiful" golf course, "large, lodgelike" rooms with heated bathroom floors and a staff that makes your stay "special"; still, there are "better places in the area" for dining, and modernists maintain the "unrenovated rooms are trapped in the '60s."

Seven Gables Inn ⓌⒽ🏨

	▽ 24	25	20	22	$200

555 Ocean View Blvd. | Pacific Grove | 831-372-4341 | www.pginns.com | 23 rooms, 2 suites

No matter which of the "cozy" rooms you choose at this family-run Victorian B&B in Pacific Grove, it's "hard to beat" the views of Monterey Bay or the "peace and quiet" you'll experience; its other "charms" include "wonderful" hospitality and "late-night cookies and milk"; N.B. it's part of a five-building complex that includes an adjacent inn, cottages and a 1940s-era guesthouse.

Spindrift Inn 🏨

▽ 23 | 22 | 18 | 19 | $279

652 Cannery Row | Monterey | 831-646-8900 | fax 831-646-5342 | 800-841-1879 | www.spindriftinn.com | 42 rooms

"The Cannery Row action is at your doorstep", but the bayside location is an even bigger draw at this "lovely" inn on Monterey Bay, where some rooms offer panoramic water views and all feature "exquisitely comfortable" canopy beds (and for added "romance", fireplaces); P.S. the continental breakfast "delivered to your room" is a treat, but it's the only meal served here.

Tickle Pink Inn 🏨

24 | 22 | 17 | 19 | $249

155 Highland Dr. | Carmel | 831-624-1244 | fax 831-626-9516 | 800-635-4774 | www.ticklepinkinn.com | 23 rooms, 11 suites, 1 cottage

The "view is the draw" of this "romantic", "intimate" inn "perched on a cliff" four miles south of Carmel, where some of the "sumptuous" rooms feature fireplaces or whirlpool tubs, and all have "incomparable" "multi-angled views" and 32-inch, flat-screen TVs; guests are tickled pink over the champagne on arrival and the "continental breakfast on the oceanside terrace" served by "gracious hosts", so even if this "charmer" "is not chic, sophisticated or worldly, it's just damned adorable."

Ventana Inn ✕🏨Ⓢ

25 | 24 | 23 | 25 | $500

Hwy. 1 | Big Sur | 831-667-2331 | fax 831-667-0573 | 800-628-6500 | www.ventanainn.com | 20 rooms, 27 suites, 13 villas

"Luxury meets log cabin" at this "dreamy" Big Sur resort providing a near "mystical" experience for those seeking to "nip stress in the bud"; the "extraordinary", "natural" setting is complemented by a staff that "meets every need", food that easily "satisfies", "exceptional" rooms and a "super spa"; P.S. "bring the checkbook" and leave the clothes, as there's a "clothing optional" policy at some pools and hot tubs.

Half Moon Bay

Half Moon Bay Lodge 🏨

23 | 23 | 20 | 23 | $169

2400 S. Cabrillo Hwy. | 650-726-9000 | fax 650-726-7951 | 800-710-0778 | www.halfmoonbaylodge.com | 75 rooms, 5 suites

"Lovely, lovely, lovely" is how devotees describe this "relaxing" "weekend getaway" where you "can walk amid the fog and driftwood", sleep in "big rooms overlooking the ocean" ("it's hard to see anything else" because of the "beautiful views!") and be coddled by "wonderful service"; even if some say the facilities are "nothing special", the "outstanding location" saves the day.

Ritz-Carlton
Half Moon Bay 🎿🏨Ⓢ🔍

27 | 26 | 25 | 28 | $499

1 Miramontes Point Rd. | 650-712-7000 | fax 650-712-7070 | 800-293-0524 | www.ritzcarlton.com | 239 rooms, 22 suites

You "leave the real world behind" when you come to this "fantastic" lodging "at the top of its game" with a "magnificent view of the grand Pacific" (30 minutes from San Francisco); some experience the "best massage they've ever had", "killer" nearby golf, "elegant", "scrupu-

	ROOMS	SERVICE	DINING	FACIL.	COST

lously clean" rooms, an "attentive staff" and "fine dining" at Navio; still, a few fret over the often "foggy" weather.

Lake Tahoe Area

Resort at Squaw Creek 紫🏊⛷️👥⬆️🕐⛷️🔍

	22	21	19	25	$249

400 Squaw Creek Rd. | Olympic Valley | 530-583-6300 | fax 530-581-5407 | 800-327-3353 | www.squawcreek.com | 205 condos, 200 suites

"Ski with ease" right out of the hotel and onto the lift at this "wonderful" year-round Squaw Valley resort with "plenty to do" (including "hiking and biking in summer"); the "limited" dining "passes muster" (though more restaurants are a "short shuttle ride away") and the newly renovated rooms have "fabulous views", but it's "more about the outside than the inside" insist those who'll "be back next year."

Los Angeles

TOPS IN CITY

- 27 Bel-Air, Hotel
   Peninsula
- 26 Beverly Hills Hotel
- 25 Four Seasons Beverly Hills
   Raffles L'Ermitage
   Beverly Wilshire
- 24 Langham Huntington
   Four Seasons Westlake
   Ritz-Carlton Marina del Rey
   Shutters on the Beach

Avalon 🏊🍴👥

	18	20	20	17	$259

9400 W. Olympic Blvd. | Beverly Hills | 310-277-5221 | fax 310-277-4928 | 800-670-6183 | www.avalonbeverlyhills.com | 82 rooms, 2 suites

"Excellent for hip businessmen", this "retro-chic" Beverly Hills boutique can be an "adorable alternative to bigger" places, with a "nightly party around the pool" (it gets "noisy") equipped with a "great bar", restaurant and cabanas; fans find the "postmodern-meets-midcentury" rooms "quite functional despite their small size", but critics cavil that they "could use a refresh" – and so can the front desk staff that sometimes acts "like aliens who know nothing about LA."

🅭 Bel-Air, Hotel ✕⊕🍴

	27	28	27	26	$395

701 Stone Canyon Rd. | Bel-Air | 310-472-1211 | fax 310-476-5890 | 800-648-4097 | www.hotelbelair.com | 52 rooms, 39 suites

"Everyone should stay" at this "fairy-tale hideaway" "tucked away" "from the craziness of LA" at "least once" say romantics who revel in this "lover's paradise" where "everyone is treated like a star" by a "telepathic staff"; "spectacular" renovated rooms, "stellar dining" in the "legendary restaurant", a bar voted No. 1 in both Appeal and Service in our *Los Angeles Nightlife* Survey, a "fabulous oval pool" and "glorious gardens" are all part of the "world-class" experience, so "take out a mortgage" and wallow in the "elegance"; N.B. they plan to open a spa in 2009.

[Z] Beverly Hills Hotel & Bungalows 👪 Ⓗ 🛎 🐕 🔭 Ⓢ 🎾

ROOMS	SERVICE	DINING	FACIL.	COST
26	26	25	26	$485

9641 Sunset Blvd. | Beverly Hills | 310-276-2251 | fax 310-887-2887 | 800-283-8885 | www.beverlyhillshotel.com | 166 rooms, 38 suites

A "classic gem loved by both locals and tourists", this "historic landmark on Sunset" with "an exclusive 1950s country club feel" embodies "what a luxury hotel should be"; the "bungalows are a touch of heaven", the pool area is "divine", the location is "really close to Rodeo Drive" and there are "celebs everywhere" (especially at the "infamous" Polo Lounge, still "the place to see and be seen"), but "even if you're not a star", the "personalized service" "sure makes you feel like one."

Beverly Hilton 🐕 🔭 Ⓢ

ROOMS	SERVICE	DINING	FACIL.	COST
21	21	18	20	$295

9876 Wilshire Blvd. | Beverly Hills | 310-274-7777 | fax 310-285-1313 | 800-774-1500 | www.thebeverlyhilton.com | 469 rooms, 101 suites

"Stylish new rooms converge" with "Hollywood glitz and glamour" at this "reborn" "modernist masterpiece" "with the soul of a boutique property" that's "perfect for vacationing city dwellers" who want to sleep in "beds as soft as clouds", lounge near the "clubby-feeling" "crown jewel pool" and "spot a star" or take advantage of the "convenient" Beverly Hills location "close to attractions" and Rodeo Drive; to those who snap it's "still a tarted-up, airport-type hotel", others reply she may be "showing her age, but she's doing it gracefully."

Beverly Wilshire Four Seasons 🐕 🔭 Ⓢ

ROOMS	SERVICE	DINING	FACIL.	COST
25	26	24	23	$545

9500 Wilshire Blvd. | Beverly Hills | 310-275-5200 | fax 310-274-2851 | 800-545-4000 | www.fourseasons.com | 280 rooms, 115 suites

"Be your own *Pretty Woman*" at this "elegant" Hollywood "classic" where you can "step out the front door" into "all the Rodeo Drive glam" in the "heart of Beverly Hills"; overseen by an "exceptional", "professionally managed" staff, it's a "great place to star-watch", enjoy a "simply superb" dinner at Wolfgang Puck's Cut steakhouse and luxuriate in the spa before retiring to "wonderful rooms" with luxe amenities, but just "make sure to ask for a view."

Casa Del Mar, Hotel 🍴 🔭 Ⓢ

ROOMS	SERVICE	DINING	FACIL.	COST
25	24	24	23	$520

1910 Ocean Way | Santa Monica | 310-581-5533 | fax 310-581-5503 | 800-898-6999 | www.hotelcasadelmar.com | 125 rooms, 4 suites

"Elegance and beauty never go out of style" at this "beautifully restored" "beachfront" "boutique hotel", "a grand old dame" with a "superb staff", "top-notch spa services" and "panoramic views of the pier and ocean" from the "fantastic restaurant" and "happening lounge" (with "frequent live music" and a "lively weekend bar scene"); rooms boast "jetted tubs that melt away your cares", or you can get an outdoor massage that'll do the same.

Chateau Marmont 🍴 Ⓗ 🛎 🐕

ROOMS	SERVICE	DINING	FACIL.	COST
21	23	22	22	$370

8221 Sunset Blvd. | Hollywood | 323-656-1010 | fax 323-655-5311 | 800-242-8328 | www.chateaumarmont.com | 11 rooms, 36 suites, 9 cottages, 4 bungalows

"Oozing with history, legends and '30s charm", this perpetually "hot hipster spot" in the Hollywood Hills allows you to "rub elbows with the rich and famous" amid "funky" Gothic decor; "some rooms are amazing" while others are "sparse", and service can act "too cool for school", but there's an "old Hollywood mystique", "stargazing at its finest" and an "outdoor bar that's the best in town", so only the cynical snap "what a bunch of hype."

Disneyland Hotel, The 👪

ROOMS	SERVICE	DINING	FACIL.	COST
16	21	17	21	$275

1150 W. Magic Way | Anaheim | 714-778-6600 | fax 714-956-6597 | 800-227-1500 | www.disneyland.com | 935 rooms, 55 suites

"Still magical after 50 years", this Disneyland original is a "fairy tale come true" for die-hard Mouse fans thanks to "totally unique" and "beautiful landscaping", "adorable" "1950s nostalgic rooms" pasted with "glowing Tinker Bell wallpaper", the "best character dining at Goofy's Kitchen" and a "convenient" location "close to the monorail" "that takes you directly" to Anaheim's "happiest place on earth"; still, some wish upon a star that the "long" check-in lines were faster.

Disney's Grand Californian Hotel & Spa 👪🔭Ⓢ

ROOMS	SERVICE	DINING	FACIL.	COST
22	24	23	25	$519

1600 S. Disneyland Dr. | Anaheim | 714-635-2300 | fax 714-300-7300 | 800-227-1500 | www.disneyland.com | 701 rooms, 44 suites

"California Adventure theme park is your backyard" at this "huge" Anaheim resort, architecturally a "redwood paradise" with a "drop-dead stunning lobby" and "rustic" "Craftsman theme"; this being the work of the "Disney Imagineers", it's no wonder there are "wonderful activities" for children and it's staffed by a highly "friendly crew" – though there's "surprisingly amazing dining at the Napa Rose" for adults, but skeptics snap it's "overpriced", even if the "kids love the bunk beds."

Disney's Paradise Pier Hotel 👪🔭

ROOMS	SERVICE	DINING	FACIL.	COST
16	21	16	18	$265

1717 S. Disneyland Dr. | Anaheim | 714-999-0990 | fax 714-776-5658 | 800-227-1500 | www.disneyland.com | 469 rooms, 20 suites

Go "surfin' safari, Disney-style" at this "budget-minded" Anaheim resort that's a "true paradise" for "young children" who "love" the "Goofy waterslides in the rooftop pool area" and the "stunning views of the California Adventure" park next door; while some sniff that the "outdated" "rooms need a major face-lift", most agree it's "good for families"; N.B. the pool's new wooden roller coaster-inspired waterslide is the latest attraction.

Fairmont Miramar Ⓗ🐕🔭Ⓢ

ROOMS	SERVICE	DINING	FACIL.	COST
21	21	19	20	$429

101 Wilshire Blvd. | Santa Monica | 310-576-7777 | fax 310-458-7912 | 866-540-4470 | www.fairmont.com | 207 rooms, 61 suites, 32 bungalows

"The view of the sun setting over the ocean is fantastic" at this "lovely property" "tucked away" "in a wonderfully secluded area in Santa Monica" "right near the beach"; a "romantic" and "amazing place" with "old-world elegance" and an "exceptional" staff that "meets requests with a smile", it offers a "beautiful pool", an "excellent spa" and "pleasantly sized" cabanas and villas, but some find the food "disappointing."

Four Seasons Beverly Hills ✕ 🍴 🏋 Ⓢ | 25 | 27 | 24 | 25 | $455

300 S. Doheny Dr. | Beverly Hills | 310-273-2222 | fax 310-859-3824 |
800-332-3442 | www.fourseasons.com | 185 rooms, 100 suites
You'll "feel like a star (plus, you're guaranteed to see several of them)"
at this "gracious" "see-and-be-seen" "cocoon" with "impeccable service", an "amazing spa", a "spectacular rooftop pool" and "exquisite
furnishings"; while a few complain that the rooms are "not on par with
other Four Seasons", the overall facilities (including "one of the best
bars for people-watching") "more than make up" for them.

Four Seasons Hotel | 25 | 24 | 22 | 25 | $475
Westlake Village 👫 🏋 Ⓢ

2 Dole Dr. | Westlake Village | 818-575-3000 | fax 818-575-3100 |
800-332-3442 | www.fourseasons.com | 242 rooms, 27 suites
Loyalists of this "top-drawer" property "wish it were closer to LA", given
the "brilliant" spa "with a wellness and longevity clinic" that "knows
what it's doing", the "cosseting service" and the "spacious" rooms; set
in the "sleepy suburb" of Westlake Village, it's more of a "resortlike
business hotel" than a leisure one, and several Seasoned travelers say
"it just isn't where it needs to be yet."

Grafton on Sunset 🍴 🏋 | ▽ 19 | 20 | 22 | 19 | $349

8462 W. Sunset Blvd. | West Hollywood | 323-654-4600 | fax 323-654-5918 |
800-821-3660 | www.graftononsunset.com | 104 rooms, 4 suites
This "wonderfully located" West Hollywood boutique hotel "on the
Sunset Strip" is a "fun" place to stay with a "hip", modern vibe, "cool
pool area" ("the heated saltwater is a plus"), garden with a cascading
fountain and "affordable" rates (for the area); "small and discreet",
it's "the place to be without getting overwhelmed", and even if the
rooms are "average", "most have a nice view of Downtown";
P.S. check out Boa, "one of the best steakhouses" in the city.

Hilton Checkers ✕ 🏋 Ⓢ | 19 | 19 | 18 | 16 | $499

535 S. Grand Ave. | 213-624-0000 | fax 213-626-9906 | 800-445-8667 |
www.hilton.com | 183 rooms, 3 suites, 2 penthouses
An "undiscovered gem" in an "excellent Downtown location", this
"classy" "business boutique hotel" with a Spanish Moor design offers "large rooms" with "comfy beds", "gorgeous rooftop views"
from the "nice pool", a "friendly staff" and a "beautiful restaurant"
touting "power lunches" and "outstanding Sunday brunches"; if
some naysayers note it's "already seen its day", most agree it
has some "charm."

Hollywood Roosevelt Hotel | 17 | 18 | 19 | 19 | $399

7000 Hollywood Blvd. | Hollywood | 323-466-7000 | fax 323-462-8056 |
800-950-7667 | www.thompsonhotels.com | 176 rooms, 69 suites,
55 cabanas
"Updated old Hollywood glamour" abounds at this "super-cool" and
"spooky" hotel "haunted by" "Marilyn Monroe's ghost"; the "extravagant ambiance and architecture" (the "breathtaking red curtains are
very Moulin Rouge"), "above-average service", "world-famous ham-
burgers" at the "diner downstairs" and "great bar" in the "cute pool area"
are pluses, but "you have to be ready for a see-and-be-seen" "poseur
paradise" that's "fine if you're under 25 and easily impressed."

	ROOMS	SERVICE	DINING	FACIL.	COST

InterContinental
Los Angeles Century City ♯ ⅍♨Ⓢ

21 | 19 | 18 | 20 | $345

2151 Ave. of the Stars | Century City | 310-284-6500 |
fax 310-284-6501 | 888-424-6835 | www.intercontinental.com |
212 rooms, 151 suites

A former Park Hyatt, this "solid" Century City choice reels in "business travelers" and those "meeting friends for drinks" with its walkable location to 20th Century Fox Studios and Rodeo Drive, and its popular Cal-French restaurant and bar; "surprisingly spacious" rooms have large work areas, private balconies and marble baths with oversized tubs, but many say the "convenient" location is "the best thing" this "typical" chainster "has to offer."

Langham Huntington
Hotel & Spa ✕⅍♨Ⓢ🔍

24 | 25 | 23 | 25 | $299

(fka Ritz-Carlton Huntington Hotel & Spa)

1401 S. Oak Knoll Ave. | Pasadena | 626-568-3900 | fax 626-568-3700 |
800-591-7481 | www.langhamhotels.com | 342 rooms, 38 suites

Situated at the foot of the San Gabriel Mountains on "exquisite grounds", this "stately", "gracious" and "spacious" former Ritz-Carlton screams "old money, through and through"; "outstanding service", a "marvelous" 11,000-sq.-ft. spa, three lighted tennis courts, dining fit for "gods" and "relaxing" rooms (though some say they're "tiny" and "need a redo") add up to a "peaceful retreat"; N.B. a $25-million upgrade is in the works for 2009.

Le Merigot, a JW Marriott
Beach Hotel & Spa ♯⅍♨Ⓢ

23 | 24 | 20 | 22 | $410

1740 Ocean Ave. | Santa Monica | 310-395-9700 | fax 310-395-9200 |
800-228-9290 | www.lemerigothotel.com | 160 rooms, 15 suites

Regulars relish this "fabulous" resort that "costs less" than the "other big Santa Monica beachfront hotels", but still pulls off a "pleasurable" experience given the "pleasant", "conscientious" staff, "spacious" accommodations and "relaxing" spa; the bonus is the location that's just a "short walk to the sights" and Third Street Promenade.

Le Parc Suites 🐾⅍♨🔍

▽ 21 | 19 | 13 | 20 | $379

733 NW Knoll Dr. | West Hollywood | 310-855-8888 | fax 310-659-7812 |
800-578-4837 | www.leparcsuites.com | 154 suites

More "low-key" than glamorous, this West Hollywood "secret" on a tree-lined residential street continues to please guests with its "spacious" suites that stock "every amenity", along with a "beautiful" pool deck and lounge; sticklers "avoid dining or making too many service requests", however, claiming "it's not up to par" in those areas.

Loews Santa Monica Beach ♯⅍♨Ⓢ

20 | 20 | 19 | 22 | $399

1700 Ocean Ave. | Santa Monica | 310-458-6700 | fax 310-458-6761 |
800-235-6397 | www.loewshotels.com | 325 rooms, 17 suites

The "perfect" beachside location provides guests with a "beautiful" panorama of the Pacific at this Santa Monica "value" within striking distance of Venice Beach; the "staff is friendly" and the "nicely appointed" rooms have 300-thread-count linens, Bloom toiletries and flat-screen TVs, but some say they "lack charm" so book oceanfront – "location makes a huge difference."

	ROOMS	SERVICE	DINING	FACIL.	COST

NEW London
West Hollywood ✕ 🛱 🏛

| - | - | - | - | $349 |

1020 N. San Vicente Blvd. | West Hollywood | 310-854-1111 |
fax 310-854-0926 | 877-597-9696 | www.thelondonla.com | 200 suites
The few surveyors who've visited this long-awaited newcomer just off
Sunset Strip say it's "the best hotel they've stayed at in a long time",
with interiors by David Collins Studio (London's Claridge's Bar, the
Langham Hotel's Artesian Bar) and "terrific" rooms sporting huge
baths they "could live in"; with an on-site restaurant via celeb chef/TV
star Gordon Ramsay, and an exclusive rooftop pool and lounge, it's
expected to become a "see and be seen place soon."

Malibu Beach Inn 🏛

| ▽ 20 | 18 | 19 | 19 | $500 |

22878 Pacific Coast Hwy. | Malibu | 866-265-5360 | fax 310-456-1499 |
888-875-9723 | www.malibubeachinn.com | 40 rooms, 7 suites
Thank David Geffen for the "brilliant" refurb of this Malibu building,
once a ramshackle property that has a new life as a "tastefully" designed inn; the "modern" interior is marked by natural color palettes
along with works by California painter Glenn Ness, and the location,
on so-called "billionaire's beach", is a treat for those who adore soaking up the "amazing" views of the Pacific.

Millennium Biltmore ✕ ⊕ 🏛

| 17 | 20 | 20 | 20 | $375 |

506 S. Grand Ave. | 213-624-1011 | fax 213-612-1545 | 800-245-8673 |
www.millenniumhotels.com | 627 rooms, 56 suites
Squarely in the "grand-hotel tradition", this 1923 Downtown landmark
still emits an "Old Hollywood" ambiance, right down to the bar area
that "takes you back in time"; while the lobby (with its marble floors
and coffered ceiling) is "unforgettable" in its "grandeur", critics prefer
to cede this "decent but not awesome" "aging dowager" to "history
buffs", given the "merely serviceable rooms" that need an "update."

Mondrian ✕ 🏛 Ⓢ

| 19 | 18 | 23 | 21 | $495 |

8440 Sunset Blvd. | West Hollywood | 323-650-8999 |
fax 323-650-5215 | 800-697-1791 | www.morganshotelgroup.com |
54 rooms, 183 suites
The "ultra" in cool and design, this Philippe Starck–conceived Sunset
Strip "whitewashed" "scene" is a "classic LA experience" considering
the "fabulous" pool with its "truly spectacular" view of the Hollywood
Hills, the "who's who" crew that shows up at the "hip" outdoor Skybar
and Asia de Cuba restaurant, and the staff's "Hollywood-style attitude"; the "tired rooms" received a renovation post-Survey, but there's
usually "more partying than relaxing" going on at this "hot spot."

Mosaic Hotel 🛱 🏛

| ▽ 23 | 23 | 21 | 19 | $450 |

125 S. Spalding Dr. | Beverly Hills | 310-278-0303 | fax 310-278-1728 |
800-463-4466 | www.mosaichotel.com | 44 rooms, 5 suites
A "wonderfully intimate" Beverly Hills boutique, this "fabulous" "little
jewel" offers "personal attention" from a "relaxed" staff, "well-
equipped" rooms done in neutral tones (though a bit "small" for some
tastes), a restaurant set near a courtyard pool that serves regional
European cuisine and access (for a fee) to the nearby Sports Club/LA
fitness center; a "location "within walking distance" of shopping is
a further benefit.

Omni California Plaza 👪 🐕 👣 Ⓢ | 20 | 20 | 19 | 20 | $179

251 S. Olive St. | 213-617-3300 | fax 213-617-3399 | 800-843-6664 | www.omnilosangeles.com | 439 rooms, 14 suites

"Perfect for business travelers", this "towering, Asian-themed" hotel features "luxurious" rooms with "soft and exquisite" beds, "great meeting and banquet spaces" and a "convenient" address with views overlooking California Plaza and the Disney Concert Hall; if some conclude it's "nothing special", the majority agrees that "whether you're Downtown for work or play, it's a good place to stay."

[NEW] **Palomar, Hotel** 🐕 👣 | - | - | - | - | $409

10740 Wilshire Blvd. | 310-475-8711 | fax 310-475-5220 | 800-472-8556 | www.hotelpalomar-lawestwood.com | 238 rooms, 26 suites

Eco-friendly touches (i.e. energy efficient lighting) go hand-in-hand with the Cheryl Rowley-designed modern decor and upscale amenities (flat-screen TVs, iPod docks, free WiFi) at this Westwood newcomer courtesy of Kimpton Hotels; additional perks include in-room spa services, complimentary morning coffee and wine receptions, and the on-site BLVD 16, serving New American fare.

[Z] **Peninsula Beverly Hills** ✗ 🏊 🐕 👣 Ⓢ | 27 | 27 | 25 | 26 | $525

9882 S. Santa Monica Blvd. | Beverly Hills | 310-551-2888 | fax 310-788-2319 | 800-462-7899 | www.peninsula.com | 153 rooms, 27 suites, 16 villas

"Perfection is in the details" at the "brightest jewel in Beverly Hills" where the "best" staff "ever" "treats you like a star" (you'll see some actual ones at the "fantastic" "power-breakfast" scene); there's a "superb" spa, a "cool bar" and "extravagant" chambers with "plush bedding and multiple pillows" (you'll be "tempted to cancel meetings and just curl up in the room"), so it's a good thing the prices are so "high" 'cause you'd "never check out" otherwise.

Raffles L'Ermitage ✗ 🐕 👣 Ⓢ | 27 | 26 | 21 | 24 | $655

9291 Burton Way | Beverly Hills | 310-278-3344 | fax 310-278-8247 | 800-768-9009 | www.raffles.com | 102 rooms, 17 suites

A "private hideaway in the midst of the typical LA scene", this "quiet" Beverly Hills outpost is close to Rodeo Drive, and boasts "elegant, sophisticated" rooms with "everything you could want", as well as "world-class service"; "curbside check-in" "makes you feel like a celebrity" (you'll see more of the real ones "hanging around than you'll find in a wax museum"), while the "stunning outdoor patio" brings it all "close to perfection"; too bad a few frown over the "slightly disappointing" food; N.B. there are new poolside cabanas.

Renaissance Hollywood 🏊 👣 Ⓢ | 22 | 20 | 18 | 21 | $299

1755 N. Highland Ave. | Hollywood | 323-856-1200 | fax 323-856-1205 | 800-468-3571 | www.renaissancehotels.com | 604 rooms, 33 suites

The "fantastic", though "touristy", location in the "heart of" town bumps this "hip" and kitschy" chainster up a notch, since it's accessible to "old Hollywood sites like Grauman's Chinese Theater"; fans like the '50s-style decor, the "fabulous", "large" rooms and the "professional staff", but nitpickers note it's "ok if you want to trip over swarms of conference-goers"; N.B. a spa opened in 2008.

	ROOMS	SERVICE	DINING	FACIL.	COST

Ritz-Carlton
Marina del Rey ⚅♨Ⓢ⌖

24	25	23	24	$489

4375 Admiralty Way | Marina del Rey | 310-823-1700 | fax 310-823-2403 | 800-241-3333 | www.ritzcarlton.com | 292 rooms, 12 suites

A "first-rate staff" that "knows what you want before you ask" coupled with "easy access to LAX" make "tired travelers" "fans forever" of this "out-of-the-way" harborside property; if "small", slightly "dated" rooms detract from the experience, "marina views", "chic dining" (at Jer-Ne), a "luxurious spa" and a "wonderful" pool and work-out facilities make a big impression.

Shutters on the Beach ✕♨Ⓢ

25	23	23	24	$520

1 Pico Blvd. | Santa Monica | 310-458-0030 | fax 310-458-4589 | 800-334-9000 | www.shuttersonthebeach.com | 186 rooms, 12 suites

A "getaway for the well-heeled" in Santa Monica, this veteran with "snob appeal" may be "the most charming hotel on the whole West Coast" say its fans; the "idyllic" beachfront location is "almost everything", though the "fabulous rooms", "not-to-be-missed" Sunday brunch and "laid-back" vibe are strong selling points as well; still, those who complain of "boisterous revelers" heard through "flimsy walls" advise "stay somewhere else and party at Shutters"; N.B. there are new poolside cabanas.

Sofitel ⚅♨Ⓢ

22	21	20	21	$349

8555 Beverly Blvd. | West Hollywood | 310-278-5444 | fax 310-657-2816 | 800-521-7772 | www.sofitel.com | 267 rooms, 28 suites

The "prime location" near nightclubs, sightseeing and shopping, "well-designed rooms", a "warm" staff and a spa all help put this "modern, elegant" West Hollywood address "on the map"; expect "wonderful food" (and "better-than-average room service") from Simon LA, and a "sexy vibe" overall, thanks in part to the Stone Rose Lounge, where you might spot some "starlets at the bar."

Standard, The ⚅♨

16	17	19	18	$215

8300 Sunset Blvd. | West Hollywood | 323-650-9090 | fax 323-650-2820 | www.standardhotel.com | 137 rooms, 2 suites

Serving up "fun" with "no frills", this "motel-chic" West Hollywood pad "right on the Strip" via hotelier André Balazs is a "reliable bet" for "young" nightcrawlers lured by the "legendary" pool parties, rooftop bar scene and "late-night eats"; partyer-patrons can expect "simple"-yet-"comfortable" accommodations and an overall "good", "noisy" value.

Standard Downtown ⚅♨

19	18	18	21	$225

550 S. Flower St. | 213-892-8080 | fax 213-892-8686 | www.standardhotel.com | 205 rooms, 2 penthouses

The city's "stylishly fearless" set meets those looking for a "change of pace" at hotelier Andre Balazs' "funky" art deco Downtown boutique, a showcase of "eclectic" rooms featuring "see-through showers", a "fabulous rooftop bar" with "spectacular views" and a "lively" scene of "twentysomethings to 30-desperates"; but the "cool vibe" translates for some to service with a "slight 'tude" and "minimalist" quarters that "aren't for everyone."

	ROOMS	SERVICE	DINING	FACIL.	COST

Sunset Tower Hotel ⊕⅍♨Ⓢ

▽ 21	21	20	18	$345

(fka Argyle, The)

8358 Sunset Blvd. | West Hollywood | 323-654-7100 |
fax 323-654-9287 | 800-225-2637 | www.sunsettowerhotel.com |
40 suites, 34 rooms

Once the favored destination of the famous and infamous (e.g. Howard
Hughes and Bugsy Siegel), this 1929 "art deco classic" Hollywood
landmark on Sunset Boulevard has what it takes to make you "feel like
a star", since you'll always be "warmly welcomed, even without an en-
tourage"; the rooms may seem "tiny", but this "aging queen" has a
"new sheen with recent renovations."

Viceroy ⅍♨

21	21	22	23	$499

1819 Ocean Ave. | Santa Monica | 310-260-7500 | fax 310-260-7515 |
800-670-6185 | www.viceroysantamonica.com | 144 rooms, 18 suites

"Terminally hip" is how some voters describe this "see-and-be-
seen" British Regency-style boutique hotel near "all good things in
Santa Monica"; featuring "cool, all-white-themed" accommodations and "wonderful" baths with "oodles of mirrors", it also offers a
"bar scene" on weekends, but some are "put off" by its "ultrahip
crowd" of "painful wannabes."

Westin Pasadena ⅋⊕⅍♨

22	21	17	20	$345

191 N. Los Robles Ave. | Pasadena | 626-792-2727 | fax 626-792-3755 |
866-716-8132 | www.westin.com | 345 rooms, 5 suites

"Good for business travel or a quick stopover", this chainster near Old
Town Pasadena "looks more like a W than a Westin" say those who
maintain it "manages to make standard rooms seem quite fabulous"
("comfy pillows", "luxurious bedding"); one of the "best picks in the
area", it has "solid" service, the "best morning buffet" and a good location "within walking distance to shopping and dining."

W Westwood ✗⅍♨Ⓢ

22	20	19	21	$659

930 Hilgard Ave. | Westwood | 310-208-8765 | fax 310-824-0355 |
877-946-8357 | www.whotels.com | 258 suites

It has that "Hollywood" vibe "in spades" say supporters of this
Westwood hangout that stays true to the W formula, namely with
its "sexy" lounge and "mod" (and in this case, "spacious") suites;
mutterings of "more hype than substance" are easily muffled by
those happy to indulge in the "way-cool" scene that includes WiFi-
enabled poolside cabanas and a "delightful" Bliss Spa all serviced
by "beautiful people."

Mammoth Lakes

Tamarack Lodge & Resort ⅋☕⅍♨

▽ 15	21	21	18	$129

85 Twin Lake Loop Rd. | 760-934-2442 | fax 760-934-2281 | 800-616-6684 |
www.tamaracklodge.com | 11 lodges, 35 cabins

Set on the banks of Twin Lakes, this "quaint" 1924 mountain retreat is
a throwback to simpler times with its "huge stone fireplace in the
lobby", "small pine rooms" and "exemplary service" and food; there
are no TVs in the lodge quarters or in cabins that range from rustic to
deluxe, but the focus is on outdoor activities (e.g. boating, hiking,
cross-country skiing), so "get lost in nature" to have the best time.

Northern California Coast

Albion River Inn ✕ ♨

| 24 | 24 | 25 | 20 | $195 |

3790 Hwy. 1 N. | Albion | 707-937-1919 | fax 707-937-2604 |
800-479-7944 | www.albionriverinn.com | 22 rooms

"The view is the star" at this "relaxing property" perched in a "nearly
perfect location" "on top of a bluff overlooking the Pacific Ocean" on
the Mendocino Coast (with its "crashing waves and high cliffs"); highlights include "gourmet dining", a bar with an "incredible collection of
scotches" and an "extremely helpful staff", but some warn of the "in-
cessant fog horn" that either puts you "right to sleep" or "keeps you
awake" (try the "earplugs in the bathroom").

Bodega Bay Lodge & Spa ♨ⓢ

| 23 | 20 | 19 | 21 | $260 |

103 Coast Hwy. | Bodega Bay | 707-875-3525 | fax 707-875-2428 |
888-875-3525 | www.bodegabaylodge.com | 76 rooms, 8 suites

For a "laid-back" "couples destination" with a "wonderful" wine country location, look no further than this "unexpected" hillside "gem"
"near the water" in Bodega Bay; "don't expect opulence" since the
"rooms are pretty ordinary", but you can "lounge" in the sun by the
"lovely pool" "listening to the barking sea lions and fog horns", indulge
in a "bowl of to-die-for crab bisque" or a "fantastic breakfast" in
the Duck Club Restaurant, and enjoy a massage at the "outdoor spa
by the sea."

Heritage House ✕ ♨

| 25 | 24 | 21 | 22 | $399 |

5200 Hwy. 1 N. | Little River | 707-937-5888 | fax 707-937-0318 |
800-235-5885 | www.heritagehouseinn.com | 20 rooms, 20 suites

You'll have "one of the most breathtaking views of the Pacific" from
the "private deck" attached to your "incredible suite" ("go for one of
the wonderfully private bungalows on the cove") at this "totally isolated", "romantic getaway" that "creates dreams" "just outside
charming Mendocino"; there are "no cell phones" allowed, so it's the
"perfect place for a quiet hike", watching the "fog roll in" across a
"spectacular coastline" or serenely sipping wines from a "superb list";
N.B. a spa and fitness center are set to open in early 2009.

NEW Nick's Cove & Cottages ♨ ♨

∇ | 25 | 23 | 24 | 22 | $350 |

23240 Hwy. 1 | 415-663-1033 | fax 415-663-9751 | 866-636-4257 |
www.nickscove.com | 12 cottages

For solitude just one hour north of San Francisco, sea lovers head
to the shores of Tomales Bay for this 1930s restored complex of
"fabulous" nautically themed cottages (some on pilings set over
the beach, one fashioned from an old boathouse) with wood-burning
fireplaces, plasma televisions, WiFi and bathrooms with deep-
soaking tubs and heated marble floors; breakfast is delivered to
your door each day, and the "great" on-site restaurant focuses on
local, sustainable seafood.

St. Orres ✕ ♨ ♨

| - | - | - | - | $95 |

36601 Coast Hwy. 1 | Gualala | 707-884-3303 | fax 707-884-1840 |
www.saintorres.com | 8 rooms, 13 cottages

Over 50 acres of creek, meadows and redwoods give a sense of "pro-
found calm" to this Mendocino County "treasure" resting above a cove

three hours north of San Francisco; the "private" setting is complemented by "marvelous", Russian-inspired rustic architecture and "charming" accommodations - including main rooms with shared baths and "spacious" cabins; overall, it's a "must visit", especially when you factor in the "excellent" food.

Whale Watch Inn 💑🔭 ▽ 24 | 23 | 21 | 19 | $198

35100 Hwy. 1 | Gualala | 707-884-3667 | fax 707-884-3100 | 800-942-5342 | www.whalewatchinn.com | 18 rooms

"Romantics" couldn't ask for more than this "lovely little", oceanside Mendocino County complex, where the quarters feature private decks, fireplaces and "huge" bathtubs, along with "amazing" views of the Pacific and its wildlife (from sea lions to whales); indeed, the only interruption in the "quiet" of this "secluded" spot is the "pounding of the surf" below; N.B. rooms have no TVs or phones.

Orange County Beaches

Balboa Bay Club & Resort Ⓢ 24 | 23 | 22 | 23 | $315

1221 W. Coast Hwy. | Newport Beach | 949-645-5000 | fax 949-630-4215 | 888-445-7153 | www.balboabayclub.com | 150 rooms, 10 suites

Newport Beach's "best-kept secret" is also its only full-service waterfront hotel, "right on the coast and boardwalk", with a storied history of visits from the likes of Garbo and Bogart; "excellent" accommodations (the "bay-view rooms are the best") and "luxurious spa treatments" leave fans "feeling like part of *The O.C.*"; but dissenters deem it "a shame" guests are barred from the club-"members-only section", including the "tiny beach."

Hyatt Regency Resort & Spa 👪🔭Ⓢ🎾 24 | 22 | 21 | 25 | $290

21500 Pacific Coast Hwy. | Huntington Beach | 714-698-1234 | fax 714-845-4990 | 800-554-9288 | www.huntingtonbeach.hyatt.com | 460 rooms, 57 suites

"Surf City USA's most elegant resort" has a "drop-dead beautiful" setting "across the PCH" from the beach yet close to "anything you'd want to see in O.C."; "lovely" accommodations with "great views of the Pacific" are spread over a "gigantic" Mediterranean-style complex with "family-friendly" amenities - "and plenty of kids to go with them"; still, grown-ups find it "delightful and serene" with "superb service", an "impressive spa" and "numerous outdoor nooks" with fireplaces and grotto whirlpools.

Island Hotel 💑🔭Ⓢ🎾 25 | 25 | 23 | 24 | $405

690 Newport Center Dr. | Newport Beach | 949-734-4414 | fax 949-759-0568 | 866-545-0751 | www.theislandhotel.com | 212 rooms, 83 suites

"Carrying on the tradition of excellence" with a more "down-to-earth vibe", this former Four Seasons in Newport Beach is "first-class, from top to bottom", with "beautiful" rooms featuring large baths with "lovely" products, "professional" service, a "heavenly spa" and "exceptional" dining at the Palm Terrace restaurant; even if it doesn't have quite the "same panache" as before, it's just as close to the "fabulous" Fashion Island open-air shopping mall.

	ROOMS	SERVICE	DINING	FACIL.	COST
Marriott Laguna Cliffs Resort 🔭Ⓢ🎾	20	20	17	21	$279

25135 Park Lantern St. | Dana Point | 949-661-5000 | fax 949-661-5358 | 800-533-9748 | www.lagunacliffs.com | 362 rooms, 15 suites

From its "glorious location" in Dana Point overlooking the Pacific and "close to the harbor and restaurants", this "pleasant" if "sprawling" resort has "stunning" views from some of its "hit-or-miss" rooms; though a "friendly" staff and "big inviting" spa help to create a "comfortable stay", the "pretty average dining" and the "continuous weddings and parties on the front lawn" "don't make for a truly relaxing weekend."

	ROOMS	SERVICE	DINING	FACIL.	COST
[Z] Montage Resort & Spa 👪✕🔭Ⓢ	27	26	26	28	$795

30801 S. Coast Hwy. | Laguna Beach | 949-715-6000 | fax 949-715-6100 | 866-271-6953 | www.montagelagunabeach.com | 190 rooms, 60 suites

Find a "slice of paradise" at this cliffside "hidden jewel on the Southern California coast", where the food is "divine", the spa "consistently excellent" and the setting "unbelievable" with "everlasting" views; there are "fabulous" rooms with goosedown pillows, flat-screen TVs and oversized tubs, and the "amazing" staff "knows what you want before you do" - so "come to be pampered and live the high life", just "bring your trust fund" for the "splurge."

	ROOMS	SERVICE	DINING	FACIL.	COST
[Z] Ritz-Carlton Laguna Niguel 👪✕🔭Ⓢ🎾	27	27	26	27	$700

1 Ritz-Carlton Dr. | Dana Point | 949-240-2000 | fax 949-240-0829 | 800-241-3333 | www.ritzcarlton.com | 363 rooms, 30 suites

Sea-centric surveyors extol the "glorious" Pacific Ocean views at this "grand" bluff-top resort with a "lovely restaurant" and "heavenly spa"; "supremely comfortable rooms" with 42-inch plasma TVs, "superior" facilities (including an oceanfront fitness center) and "extraordinary" service add up to "true luxury"; P.S. be sure to "walk down to the fantastic beach."

	ROOMS	SERVICE	DINING	FACIL.	COST
[Z] St. Regis Monarch Beach 👪🐕🔭⛳Ⓢ🎾	27	25	25	28	$645

1 Monarch Beach Resort | Dana Point | 949-234-3200 | fax 949-234-3201 | 800-722-1543 | www.stregis.com | 326 rooms, 74 suites

"Pure paradise" is on hand at this "outstanding resort" where the "attention to detail is unmatched" ("ice pops at the pool", "freshly squeezed exotic juice each morning") and the "lush surroundings" are "glorious"; from the "beautifully appointed suites ("larger than some apartments" and boasting "butler service" and "decadent" baths) to the "breathtaking views" to the Robert Trent Jones, Jr. golf course to Michael Mina's "showstopper" Stonehill Tavern, "you can't go wrong here"; P.S. "the only drawback is having to shuttle to the beach."

	ROOMS	SERVICE	DINING	FACIL.	COST
Surf & Sand Resort 👪🐕🔭Ⓢ	21	21	21	22	$695

1555 S. Coast Hwy. | Laguna Beach | 949-497-4477 | fax 949-494-2897 | 800-837-9202 | www.surfandsandresort.com | 152 rooms, 13 suites

"Waking up" and "falling asleep" to the "sounds of waves rolling in" convinces surf-centrics that this Laguna Beach resort is in the "perfect" oceanside location; the food is "good", the staff "couldn't be nicer" and the rooms "cozy", but it's the "spectacular setting" and "unbelievable views" that provide the "wow" factor.

ROOMS | SERVICE | DINING | FACIL. | COST

Palm Springs Area

TOPS IN AREA

Desert Springs, A JW Marriott Resort & Spa 🛏🏊🛗⬆️ⓈⲀ

| 21 | 21 | 21 | 25 | $129 |

74855 Country Club Dr. | Palm Desert | 760-341-2211 | fax 760-341-1872 | 800-228-9290 | www.marriott.com | 833 rooms, 51 suites

"Big-time glitz" abounds at this "Palm desert gem" where the public spaces "sparkle" with "waterfalls everywhere", "multiple pools", "electric boats that ferry patrons" to the "phenomenal sushi bar and Tuscany restaurant" and 36 holes of championship golf, "great tennis" and a "magnificent spa"; it's "fun" for a family getaway, but a few complain about "getting lost" at this "spread-out" spot that often "feels like Spring Break."

Hyatt Grand Champions 🛏🐕🍴🏊🛗⬆️ⓈⲀ

| 22 | 22 | 19 | 24 | $350 |

44-600 Indian Wells Ln. | Indian Wells | 760-341-1000 | fax 760-568-2236 | 800-233-1234 | www.grandchampions.hyatt.com | 454 rooms, 35 suites, 43 villas

A "grand location" for a family "getaway from Los Angeles", this recently renovated "wonderful vacation experience" in "a beautiful setting" is "still a desert favorite" thanks to "state-of-the-art work-out facilities", "unbelievable views", a "top-notch spa", an "awesome pool area" and an "outdoor bar that makes for a relaxing afternoon with an umbrella'd drink"; "rooms are spacious", but "spring for" a villa "with its own butler, barbecue grills" and "privacy."

La Quinta Resort & Club 🛏✕🕐🐕🍴🏊🛗⬆️ⓈⲀ

| 22 | 22 | 20 | 25 | $329 |

49-499 Eisenhower Dr. | La Quinta | 760-564-4111 | fax 760-564-5718 | 800-598-3828 | www.laquintaresort.com | 700 rooms, 27 suites, 69 chalets

Exuding an "Old Hollywood glamour", this former "playground of the stars" from the '20s and '30s (19 miles from Palm Springs) draws raves for its "magnificent grounds" full of "beautiful flowers", more than 40 swimming pools sprinkled among the "delightful" casitas and suites, and "exceptional" golf and tennis facilities; but foes find an "unremarkable" spa, "dining that needs improvement" and an overall "tiredness" – and not just because the "too-spread-out" design is exhausting.

Le Parker Méridien Palm Springs 🍴ⓈⲀ

| 22 | 22 | 22 | 24 | $395 |

4200 E. Palm Canyon Dr. | Palm Springs | 760-770-5000 | fax 760-324-2188 | 800-543-4300 | www.theparkerpalmsprings.com | 131 rooms, 12 villas, 1 village house

Designer Jonathan Adler's "fingerprints" are all over the "fabulous" "retro-chic" decor at this "offbeat" boutique prized for the "great" spa and fitness facility, "fantastic" brunch at Norma's, and lots of "sexy and funky" lounging areas; accommodations include specialty residences (try the two-bedroom Gene Autry unit), free-standing villas and patio rooms, but you'll spot a lot of "Hollywood types" along with assorted trendsetters, so "bring your ego to survive."

Miramonte 鈴齒Ⓢ | ▽ 23 | 21 | 20 | 23 | $339

45000 Indian Wells Ln. | Indian Wells | 760-341-2200 | fax 760-568-0541 | 800-237-2926 | www.miramonteresort.com | 192 rooms, 23 suites

The Santa Rosa Mountains provide the frame for this "hidden" Indian Wells desert "oasis" about 30 minutes from Palm Springs whose "stunning" grounds – complete with olive trees and citrus groves – make it an ideal choice for "intimate" getaways; minor annoyances such as the "limited" facilities are counterbalanced by the "divine spa" and "lovely", "well-appointed" rooms with marble baths and private terraces.

Renaissance Esmeralda
Resort & Spa 齒∟ⓈQ | 21 | 22 | 20 | 23 | $459

44-400 Indian Wells Ln. | Indian Wells | 760-773-4444 | fax 760-346-9308 | 800-468-3571 | www.renaissanceesmeralda.com | 538 rooms, 22 suites

It "has everything you could want" aver visitors to this "huge", family-friendly hotel at the base of the Santa Rosa Mountains that sports "excellent" facilities and entertainment options, namely a "great" spa, two "fantastic" golf courses and "spectacular" pools; "long walks from the elevator lobbies to some rooms" as well as "large meetings" that make it "crowded" are small concessions given the "good" value here.

Two Bunch Palms ⮳ⓈQ | 19 | 23 | 21 | 25 | $225

67-425 Two Bunch Palms Trail | Desert Hot Springs | 760-329-8791 | fax 760-329-1317 | 800-472-4334 | www.twobunchpalms.com | 22 rooms, 19 suites, 11 villas

Your "stress level drops the moment you drive through the gates" sigh devotees of this "secret", "mellow" adults-only sanctuary in Desert Hot Springs that bans loud talking and public use of cell phones; it's not "five-star luxury", but for the Hollywood types who come here, it adds up to a "great getaway from the glitz" with "unique spa treatments" and "amazing" mineral pools.

Viceroy Palm Springs ⮳鈴齒Ⓢ | 21 | 22 | 20 | 21 | $399

415 S. Belardo Rd. | Palm Springs | 760-320-4117 | fax 760-323-3303 | 860-891-0948 | www.viceroypalmsprings.com | 45 rooms, 6 suites, 13 villas

Kelly Wearstler's "sexy", "cheeky" Hollywood Regency design baits the "hot" and the "young" to this "groovy" Downtown Palm Springs boutique featuring "fabulous" pools, a "trendy" lounge and a staff that "goes out of its way"; opinion is divided on the rooms ("comfortable" vs. "not great"), so "book a villa" for a real "escape."

Westin Mission Hills 齒鈴齒∟ⓈQ | 21 | 20 | 18 | 23 | $399

71333 Dinah Shore Dr. | Rancho Mirage | 760-328-5955 | fax 760-770-2199 | 800-236-2427 | www.starwoodhotels.com | 472 rooms, 40 suites

"Bring your roller blades" or use the "free shuttle" to navigate this "sprawling" family "oasis" where the facilities include "two great golf courses", tennis courts and a 60-ft. waterslide at the main pool; accommodations are available in "large but dated" rooms and "lovely" villas, and "consistent" service helps make up for the "minimal" dining options; but regulars warn "beware" of the "time-share pitch" and "convention" "crowds"; N.B. both the rooms and spa are being remodeled.

	ROOMS	SERVICE	DINING	FACIL.	COST

Riverside

Mission Inn Hotel & Spa Ⓗ Ⓢ   ▽ | 19 | 21 | 19 | 20 | $215 |

3649 Mission Inn Ave. | 951-784-0300 | fax 951-341-6730 | 800-843-7755 | www.missioninn.com | 211 rooms, 28 suites

It's "worth the trip just to see" this "quirky" Spanish Mission–style inn, a National Historic Landmark that takes up an entire Downtown city block and boasts "unique" architecture (e.g. "real Tiffany windows in the on-site chapel") and an ambiance fit for a "romantic" rendezvous; though the majority focuses on the "grandeur" of this "classic" property that's "like staying on the *Frankenstein* movie set – and enjoying it", some say the room quality "varies greatly" and the "area is only fair."

San Diego

TOPS IN AREA

27 Four Seasons Aviara
    Rancho Valencia
26 Lodge at Torrey Pines
23 La Valencia
22 La Costa Resort

Barona Valley Ranch   ▽ | 19 | 19 | 17 | 21 | $249 |
Resort & Casino ♨ Ⓛ Ⓢ

1932 Wildcat Canyon Rd. | Lakeside | 619-443-2300 | fax 619-443-8186 | 888-722-7662 | www.barona.com | 368 rooms, 32 suites

"Tucked away in the mountains of San Diego County", this "beautiful", "off-the-beaten-path" property touts "glorious suites" with private balconies and Jacuzzis, an "excellent buffet", a "nice casino" and solid service; but a few thirsty high rollers sigh "no booze is served on the premises", which "ruins any chance that you'll think you're in Vegas."

Cal-a-Vie Ⓛ Ⓢ ✎ | - | - | - | - | $942 |

29402 Spa Havens Way | Vista | 760-945-2055 | fax 760-630-0074 | 866-772-4283 | www.cal-a-vie.com | 24 villas

This "consistently exceptional" destination spa perched on 200 private acres 40 miles north of San Diego draws devotees for its "luxurious" villas (that accommodate up to 30 guests at a time), a five-to-one staff-to-guest ratio that ensures personalized service and "so many" activities – European spa treatments, yoga, Pilates, tennis, an Olympic-size swimming pool, a newly acquired adjacent private country club and golf course – that "you might be the only participant"; too bad it's so "outrageously expensive" (the above nightly rate is based on a three-night minimum stay).

del Coronado, Hotel ♔ Ⓗ ☂ ♨ Ⓢ | 20 | 22 | 22 | 24 | $325 |

1500 Orange Ave. | Coronado | 619-435-6611 | fax 619-522-8262 | 800-582-2595 | www.hoteldel.com | 687 rooms, 70 suites

"Home to kings, presidents and their lovers", this "iconic" "grande dame" in a "staggeringly beautiful beach local" on "charming" Coronado Island offers an "incredibly dreamy experience" due to its "timeless setting", "gorgeous sunsets" and "spectacular holiday decorations"; though most are satisfied with the "classic elegance" of the 18th-century decor and further laud the "wonderful spa" and "fabulous brunch", others are vexed by "uneven room quality" and swarms of "looky-loos" passing by.

Z Four Seasons Aviara 🏨✕🍴🏊♨️⬆️Ⓢ🔍 | 27 | 28 | 25 | 28 | $395

7100 Four Seasons Point | Carlsbad | 760-603-6800 | fax 760-603-6801 | 800-332-3442 | www.fourseasons.com | 285 rooms, 44 suites

"Always a pleasure", this "knockout" resort about a half-hour from town is truly "impeccable in every way"; "a perfect getaway for couples or families", it manages to "go the extra mile for kids" while "keeping it sane" for adults, via a "tropical garden–like golf course", in-room WiFi, "fabulous food", "frozen treats by the pool" and "terrific" spa treatments; although it has "everything you'd expect from a first-class Four Seasons – including an "outstanding" staff - a few find the location "secluded."

Golden Door 🏨Ⓢ🔍 | ▽ 24 | 28 | 28 | 25 | $1142

777 Deer Springs Rd. | San Marcos | 760-744-5777 | fax 760-471-2393 | 800-424-0777 | www.goldendoor.com | 40 rooms

A "heaven on earth" awaits at this "serious" destination spa 40 miles northeast of San Diego that has spawned five more locations across the U.S; "who knew healthy living could be such fun?" ask admirers of its custom programs, world-class treatments and new 4,000-sq.-ft. Fitness Pavilion; it's "expensive" for sure, but "worth every hard-earned penny."

Z NEW Grand Del Mar, The 🏨✕🍴🏊♨️⬆️Ⓢ🔍 | ▽ 26 | 25 | 25 | 27 | $450

5300 Grand Del Mar Ct. | 858-314-2000 | fax 858-314-2001 | 888-314-2030 | www.thegranddelmar.com | 218 rooms, 31 suites

A "luxury hotel" that "puts San Diego on the map", this "over-the-top" newcomer is graced with "incredible architecture", "exceptional rooms with all the bells and whistles" ("love tea and snacks in the morning and afternoon"), "tasty Mediterranean cuisine" in the "fabulous" Addison restaurant, an "outstanding" staff, "nice golf course" and "glorious views"; sure, it's "expensive", but "it's an A+ experience" that's "totally worth it."

NEW Hard Rock Hotel Ⓢ | ▽ 20 | 21 | 19 | 20 | $225

207 Fifth Ave. | 619-702-3000 | fax 619-702-3007 | 866-751-7625 | www.hardrockhotelsd.com | 284 rooms, 136 suites

It's "almost as if San Diego is turning into Vegas or New York" what with this "new hotel" "with lots of eye candy" in the Gaslamp Quarter "where the young and hip come to stay and play"; the "turndown service makes you feel like a VIP", there are "special perks" in the "rock-star themed" rooms like complimentary VOSS water, fresh flowers and *Rolling Stone* magazine, and there's an on-site branch of the sushi restaurant Nobu.

Hilton La Jolla Torrey Pines 🍴🏨⬆️🔍 | 20 | 20 | 17 | 22 | $329

10950 N. Torrey Pines Rd. | La Jolla | 858-558-1500 | fax 858-450-4584 | 800-762-6160 | www.hilton.com | 377 rooms, 17 suites

It's all about "location" at this "relaxing" resort "beautifully situated" "high on a bluff" "overlooking the ocean" in La Jolla; "wonderful service", "comfortably furnished rooms", "great conference facilities", "in-

	ROOMS	SERVICE	DINING	FACIL.	COST

credible views" and the added perk of Torrey Pines golf course "right outside your door" "make this an excellent choice" that "can't be beat."

Hyatt Regency
La Jolla at Aventine ⓈⓆ

| | 20 | 19 | 17 | 19 | $294 |

3777 La Jolla Village Dr. | 858-552-1234 | fax 858-552-6066 | 800-233-1234 | www.hyatt.com | 394 rooms, 25 suites

The "chic" Michael Graves "design wears well" at this "solid business traveler's choice" in an "easy" "location right off the freeway" that's a "fast connection" to the "heart of La Jolla"; the "rooms are bright, modern" and "spacious" ("avoid the lower floors, as they can be very noisy"), and there's a "wonderful pool", a "beautiful gym" and "attentive" service, but finicky foodniks suggest "saving your bucks to eat" off-site.

Inn at Rancho Santa Fe ⓗⓑⓈⓆ

| | 21 | 23 | 21 | 22 | $285 |

5951 Linea de Cielo | Rancho Santa Fe | 858-756-1131 | fax 858-759-1604 | 800-843-4661 | www.theinnatrsf.com | 74 rooms, 13 suites

Delivering "old Southern California charm", this "secluded" North San Diego County "retreat" has all the trappings of "understated elegance" on its "beautiful" 23-acre property, where both "hipsters" and the "old guard" enjoy a "leisurely" lunch on the patio or take up a game of croquet on the regulation lawn, abetted by a "staff who knows what you want"; although the area around this 1924 Spanish Colonial inn provides a "great" opportunity for strolling, a few feel it "needs a redo."

NEW Ivy Hotel

| | ▽ 24 | 22 | 23 | 25 | $499 |

600 F St. | 619-814-1000 | fax 619-531-7955 | 877-489-4489 | www.ivyhotel.com | 141 rooms, 18 suites

They "do hip better than anyone else" marvel those who've stepped into this Gaslamp Quarter newbie, San Diego's latest "it" spot that seduces with a "gorgeous" rooftop lounge and pool, "chic" suites with "funky decor" (one suite features an "outrageous stripper pole", fully stocked wet bar and shower walls that turn opaque – or not), VIP access to the on-site, multilevel nightclub, Envy, and "delicious" fare from Damon Gordon's Quarter Kitchen; no surprise, "people-watching" is a favored sport here.

La Costa Resort & Spa ⌖⌖⌖ⓈⓆ

| | 22 | 22 | 21 | 25 | $350 |

2100 Costa Del Mar Rd. | Carlsbad | 760-438-9111 | fax 760-438-3758 | 800-854-5000 | www.lacosta.com | 452 rooms, 77 suites, 81 villas

The "gorgeous facilities" at this Carlsbad "paradise", including the "peaceful Spanish Colonial–style spa" and Chopra Center, "make you feel like you're a million miles away from everything"; there are "fun" options for kids (e.g. game rooms and "many pools" with "amazing waterslides"), lots of "different" accommodation types and a solid golf course, but the food is "fairly standard."

L'Auberge Del Mar ⌖ⓈⓆ

| | 23 | 23 | 20 | 21 | $410 |

1540 Camino Del Mar | Del Mar | 858-259-1515 | fax 858-755-4940 | 800-245-9757 | www.laubergedelmar.com | 112 rooms, 8 suites

A "perfect" location within "easy walking distance to the village, beach and dining", this boutique also pleases patrons with a spa, pool and tennis; though surveyors describe rooms as alternately "bright and airy" or "small and cramped", they argue that "parts of this jewel" "overshadow the smudges"; N.B. a new spa will open in 2009.

	ROOMS	SERVICE	DINING	FACIL.	COST

La Valencia Hotel ⑪❄️🔭

| 22 | 24 | 23 | 22 | $300 |

1132 Prospect St. | La Jolla | 858-454-0771 | fax 858-456-3921 |
800-451-0772 | www.lavalencia.com | 75 rooms, 25 suites, 15 villas

The "wonderful" La Jolla location is "near everything", but the "spectacular" ocean views may mean you'll never want to leave this "classic" veteran where the "attentive" staff "genuinely cares" and the "beautifully decorated" quarters "overlook the ocean"; with "loads of charm" and history, most choose to overlook the "enormous variation in room quality", with some "not as fancy as you'd think for the price."

Lodge at Torrey Pines 🏃❄️🔭⇅Ⓢ

| 25 | 26 | 25 | 27 | $675 |

11480 N. Torrey Pines Rd. | La Jolla | 858-453-4420 |
fax 858-453-0691 | 800-656-0087 | www.lodgetorreypines.com |
168 rooms, 7 suites

The "divine" coastal setting is alone "worth the price" of staying at this "spectacular" Craftsman-style luxury resort set on "magnificent", "immaculately" manicured grounds; it has the "best pool area", a "tranquil" spa, "beautifully furnished" yet rustic rooms, "top-notch" fare at A.R. Valentien, an appropriately "efficient" staff and "exhilarating" golf at the legendary Torrey Pines course; in sum, most "can't wait to go back."

Loews
Coronado Bay Resort 🏃❄️🔭Ⓢ🔍

| 21 | 20 | 20 | 22 | $369 |

4000 Coronado Bay Rd. | Coronado | 619-424-4000 | fax 619-424-4400 |
800-235-6397 | www.loewshotels.com | 403 rooms, 37 suites

A "big", "welcoming" "kid-friendly" "monster resort" "off the beaten path", this "pleasant surprise" on Coronado Island feels like it's "far from civilization"; with a "friendly staff" and lots of activities, including a "fantastic spa", three lighted tennis courts, three pools, gondola rides, a surfing academy and direct access to Silver Strand beach, some can overlook "average" rooms.

Manchester
Grand Hyatt 🏃🖼️❄️🔭Ⓢ🔍

| 22 | 20 | 18 | 22 | $380 |

1 Market Pl. | 619-232-1234 | fax 619-233-6464 | 800-233-1234 |
www.hyatt.com | 1530 rooms, 95 suites

"Strategically located" "within walking distance of the convention center", this "huge" two-tower Downtown complex "right on the marina" features "grand views of the harbor", "beautiful rooms" and "helpful", "friendly" service; while the hotel can seem "even wilder than the San Diego Animal Park" during a convention, some guests escape by "walking to the famous Gaslamp Quarter", blowing off steam on the tennis courts or relaxing in the top-floor bar while "catching the sunset."

Marriott
Coronado Island Resort 🏃❄️🔭Ⓢ🔍

| 23 | 20 | 19 | 22 | $335 |

2000 Second St. | Coronado | 619-435-3000 | fax 619-435-4183 |
800-228-9290 | www.marriott.com | 273 rooms, 27 suites

You "couldn't ask for a better location" than this island "oasis" just a short ride via harbor taxi from the city; expect "incredible views" of San Diego Bay, "big" rooms with WiFi, down comforters and coffeemakers, and "nice facilities" including tennis, a spa and a beach; naysayers, however, note it's "not as fine as they thought it'd be for the price."

	ROOMS	SERVICE	DINING	FACIL.	COST

Marriott Gaslamp Quarter ♨

| 23 | 23 | 20 | 22 | $250 |

660 K St. | 619-696-0234 | fax 619-231-8199 | 800-228-9290 |
www.marriott.com | 291 rooms, 15 suites

Right in the center of San Diego's most "happening" district – two
blocks from the convention center, adjacent to PETCO Park and within
walking distance to shopping – this Gaslamp Quarter favorite "feels
more like a boutique hotel than part of a nationwide chain", thanks to
"incredibly comfortable rooms" (down comforters, designer duvets,
butter-soft 300-count linens), a "retro lobby" ("loved the 'baby
boomer' candy at the front desk"), an "ultracool" rooftop bar (where
you can glimpse a Padres game) and a "helpful" staff.

Marriott Hotel & Marina ♨

| 19 | 19 | 16 | 21 | $335 |

333 W. Harbor Dr. | 619-234-1500 | fax 619-234-8678 | 800-228-9290 |
www.marriott.com | 1306 rooms, 56 suites

They "treat you well" at this harborside hotel selling itself on its "gorgeous" views of the marina and "unbeatable" location, the latter perfect
for those attending meetings at the adjacent convention center or others who want to enjoy the "sights and dining" of the Gaslamp Quarter
and Seaport Village; sure, it's "standard", but you'll have a "nice stay"
in one of the "roomy" accommodations, plus the price is "good."

Omni ♨

| 22 | 21 | 18 | 21 | $379 |

675 L St. | 619-231-6664 | fax 619-231-8060 | 888-444-6664 |
www.omnihotels.com | 478 rooms, 33 suites

"Fantastic perks" come with the territory at this Gaslamp Quarter
high-rise prized for its "fabulous" location, particularly by baseball
fans who can "take the sky bridge that connects directly to Petco
Park and watch a Padres game"; all in all, it's a "perfect" pad for a
"guys' weekend", especially when you throw in the "gorgeous", "modern" rooms, "eye-bulging views of the bay" and on-site seafooder
McCormick & Schmick's.

Rancho Bernardo Inn ♨

| 21 | 22 | 23 | 23 | $259 |

17550 Bernardo Oaks Dr. | Rancho Bernardo | 858-675-8500 |
fax 858-675-8501 | 877-517-9342 | www.ranchobernardoinn.com |
275 rooms, 12 suites

This "sprawling" "landmark" 30 miles north of San Diego is hailed for
its "player-friendly" golf course, "excellent" tennis facilities, "enjoyable" spa and "gourmet" restaurant, El Bizcocho; sure, you'll see your
share of "corporate outings" and it feels like it's "in the middle of nowhere", but it's "comfortable" enough for most.

Ⓩ Rancho Valencia Resort ♨

| 28 | 27 | 25 | 27 | $550 |

5921 Valencia Circle | Rancho Santa Fe | 858-756-1123 |
fax 858-756-0165 | 800-548-3664 | www.ranchovalencia.com |
48 suites, 1 hacienda

"Worth every penny", this "serene", "romantic" Relais & Châteaux
hacienda-inspired standout showcases "first-class" facilities including "gorgeous" grounds dotted with orange trees, a "great spa" and
"huge, luxurious" rooms (fitted with "enormous" bathtubs), along
with "outstanding" housekeeping; a haven for "tennis buffs"
(18 courts) and for gourmands who appreciate the "incredible" food,
it's a "perfect getaway" that no one "ever wants to leave."

	ROOMS	SERVICE	DINING	FACIL.	COST

Solamar, Hotel ✕ 🍴 ♨

| ▽ 26 | 21 | 18 | 22 | $299 |

435 Sixth Ave. | 619-531-8740 | fax 619-531-8742 | 877-230-0300 | www.hotelsolamar.com | 221 rooms, 14 suites

Polka dots and stripes in the "modern" rooms match the "hip" pattern of thinking at this "fun" Kimpton boutiquer perfectly postioned for "Padres games and Gaslamp dining"; the "fabulous" nightlife (at the "happening rooftop bar") is fueled 'round the clock by a "young crowd" and a "gracious staff."

Westgate Hotel, The ♨Ⓢ

| 23 | 23 | 21 | 20 | $350 |

1055 Second Ave. | 619-238-1818 | fax 619-557-3737 | 800-221-3802 | www.westgatehotel.com | 215 rooms, 8 suites

"All the modern comforts in an old-world hotel" is the lure of this "well-run" Downtown "classic" featuring a "lovely" setting replete with antiques, French tapestries, Persian rugs and "beautiful" chambers that are all "decorated differently"; although "pleasant" service and a rooftop that's "nice for sunsets" are pluses, a few advise "stay elsewhere" "for fun."

W San Diego 🍴 ♨Ⓢ

| 21 | 20 | 18 | 19 | $399 |

421 W. B St. | 619-398-3100 | fax 619-231-5779 | 866-837-4147 | www.whotels.com | 259 rooms, 19 suites, 1 penthouse

The "fantastic" rooftop beach bar complete with fire pits gives it away: this "terminally hip" property near the Gaslamp Quarter caters to the "under-30" crowd; the "good-looking", "attentive" staff that sometimes "takes itself too seriously" matches the look and attitude of the "beautiful" clientele, and everyone seems to be having a "wild" time after dark, so who cares if the rooms are so "teensy" "only a lilliputian could love them."

San Francisco Bay Area

TOPS IN AREA

27	Ritz-Carlton
26	Four Seasons
	St. Regis
25	Mandarin Oriental
24	Four Seasons Silicon Valley
	Campton Place
23	Vitale
	Huntington
22	Fairmont
	Palace

Argonaut Hotel 🍴 ♨

| 23 | 22 | 17 | 20 | $169 |

495 Jefferson St. | San Francisco | 415-563-0800 | fax 415-563-2800 | 866-415-0704 | www.argonauthotel.com | 239 rooms, 13 suites

When you "cruise into" this "appropriately nautical" "boutique hotel" "in the heart of Fisherman's Wharf", expect "Kimpton classic" "whimsical decor" and a "funky vibe" complemented by a "personable and extremely polite staff"; the "eclectic" rooms are "smallish" but offer "L'Occitane bath products", while the daily "wine happy hours", "free parking for hybrid cars", "fantastic bay views" and "wonderful" location "a block from Ghirardelli Square" add to the allure.

	ROOMS	SERVICE	DINING	FACIL.	COST

Campton Place Hotel ✕ ☆ 🏃

| 24 | 25 | 25 | 20 | $575 |

340 Stockton St. | San Francisco | 415-781-5555 | fax 415-955-5536 |
866-332-1673 | www.tajhotels.com | 101 rooms, 9 suites

"Understated" "luxurious comfort" abounds at this "outstanding
treat" boasting an "excellent location" "right in Union Square" that's a
"real find"; among its standout features are "top-notch service" that's
"personalized" "on every level", "beautifully decorated rooms" with
"enormous baths", "soft linens" and "appropriate amenities", plus
"great food" in a "relaxing restaurant"; while a few argue that it should
be called "Crampton Place" for the "closet-size" quarters, most agree
it's simply "delightful."

Casa Madrona ✕ ⓘ 🗂 ☆ 🏃 Ⓢ

| 23 | 21 | 20 | 20 | $199 |

801 Bridgeway | Sausalito | 415-332-0502 | fax 415-332-2537 |
800-288-0502 | www.casamadrona.com | 56 rooms, 2 suites, 5 cottages

Get set for a "romantic weekend getaway" proclaim proponents of this
"undiscovered gem" with "spectacular views" "overlooking the harbor"
in a "fabulous location in the heart of Sausalito"; it feels "like a quick trip
to Italy" complete with Poggio, the "divine" "on-site Italian ristorante",
while the "newly renovated addition" contains "elegant rooms" with
"gorgeous marble baths and spa tubs" (the "historic" quarters are "full
of charm", but they "lack space and other modern comforts").

Claremont Resort 🏃 ☆ 🏃 Ⓢ 🔍

| 18 | 21 | 20 | 24 | $309 |

41 Tunnel Rd. | Berkeley | 510-843-3000 | fax 510-843-3229 | 800-551-7266 |
www.claremontresort.com | 247 rooms, 32 suites

Some describe this hotel as a little "slice of heaven" "tucked away" "in
the Berkeley Hills", with "breathtaking views of San Francisco Bay", a
"pampering spa" and an "out-of-this-world Sunday brunch at Jordan's";
but others note the "need for some nip and tuck" to its "faded" face,
and warn that the "musty" rooms "vary from huge to closet-size."

Clift ⓘ 🏃

| 20 | 21 | 21 | 20 | $345 |

495 Geary St. | San Francisco | 415-775-4700 | fax 415-441-4621 |
800-606-6090 | www.clifthotel.com | 310 rooms, 52 suites

Guests say this "stunningly chic" Ian Schrager "über-modern" boutique in Union Square boasts a "beautiful and striking lobby", "fabulous dining" at Asia de Cuba and a "vibrant night scene" whose
"biggest draw is people-watching" at the Redwood Room, "one of the
greatest hotel bars anywhere"; but it's "not the place to catch some
zzzs" snap light-sleepers who feel trapped in the "microscopic-sized"
quarters of a "loud" "hip hell."

Fairmont, The ⓘ ☆ 🏃 Ⓢ

| 22 | 24 | 21 | 23 | $359 |

950 Mason St. | San Francisco | 415-772-5000 | fax 415-772-5013 |
800-441-1414 | www.fairmont.com | 529 rooms, 62 suites

A "historic" "bastion of refinement" in a "pristine location" "atop Nob
Hill", this "lovely grande dame" "provides everything from an incredible
night's sleep" to a staff that "stops at nothing to exceed expectations";
"it's a little slice of heaven" offering "views of the bay", "classic
European decor" and a "spectacular lobby", so even if critics cry foul
over the "widely varying" quarters ("go for the newer wing"), most
agree it's "still majestic after all these years"; P.S. "have a cocktail" in
the "legendary Tonga Room" tiki bar.

	ROOMS	SERVICE	DINING	FACIL.	COST

Fairmont San Jose ⚬⚬⚬

| 22 | 22 | 19 | 21 | $239 |

170 S. Market St. | San Jose | 408-998-1900 | fax 408-287-1648 |
800-866-5577 | www.fairmont.com | 731 rooms, 74 suites

A "luxury business hotel" "right in Downtown San Jose", this "highly recommended" "pleasant surprise" "for the older crowd" boasts a "wondrous lobby", "modern" and "spacious rooms and suites" and a staff that provides "little extras that help busy travelers" (i.e. "a machine that prints boarding passes"); but while there's "an abundance of restaurants" and "no better place to people-watch than in the piano lounge", finicky foes find "facilities could use an upgrade."

☑ Four Seasons ⚬⚬⚬⚬

| 27 | 28 | 25 | 26 | $480 |

757 Market St. | San Francisco | 415-633-3000 | fax 415-633-3001 |
800-332-3442 | www.fourseasons.com | 231 rooms, 46 suites

"I left my heart" here gush guests of this "spectacular" SoMa/Union Square property with "marvelous views", service that "can't be beat" and "acres of marble" in the "stunning lobby"; "modern rooms" have an "understated elegance" and "special touches" (like fresh fruit and truffles), while the "wonderful dining" and "impeccable" staff "keeps up with the Four Seasons tradition"; N.B. its bar was voted No. 1 for Service in our *San Francisco Nightlife* Survey.

Four Seasons Silicon Valley ⚬⚬⚬

| 26 | 25 | 23 | 24 | $345 |

2050 University Ave. | East Palo Alto | 650-566-1200 | fax 650-566-1221 |
800-819-5053 | www.fourseasons.com | 173 rooms, 27 suites

Despite its "concrete jungle" "location right on the highway" with "views of Ikea", this East Palo Alto "suburban gem" "convenient to Silicon Valley" is a "terrific business hotel" with "ultramodern" and "spacious" "high-tech rooms" bedecked with "floor-to-ceiling, wall-to-wall windows"; all in all, it's a "wonderful property" with "great dining", a "state-of-the-art gym" and an "impeccable and well-trained staff" "who never uses the word 'no.'"

Garden Court Hotel ⚬⚬

| ▽ 24 | 23 | 19 | 19 | $369 |

520 Cowper St. | Palo Alto | 650-322-9000 | fax 650-324-3609 |
800-824-9028 | www.gardencourt.com | 48 rooms, 14 suites

"Still the place to stay" in the "heart of Palo Alto", this "beautiful boutique hotel" in a "fabulous location" near Stanford offers "first-class", "personalized service", "home-baked cookies, fresh squeezed OJ and muffins" in the morning, "pretty gardens" and "restful" rooms outfitted with fireplaces, whirlpools, private balconies, marble bathrooms and Aveda bath products.

Grand Hyatt ⚬⚬

| 20 | 19 | 16 | 19 | $189 |

345 Stockton St. | San Francisco | 415-398-1234 | fax 415-848-6091 |
800-233-1234 | www.grandhyattsanfrancisco.com | 649 rooms, 36 suites

"Good and solid for business travel" and anchored in an "excellent location" "overlooking Union Square" that's "within walking distance of many" San Francisco "sites and attractions", this "surprisingly elegant and serene" hotel sports "comfortable" and "beautifully decorated rooms" and a "fantastic" "rooftop bar" with "spectacular city views"; but while an "excellent brunch buffet" "in the sky is a delight", the building seems to "sway" "when the wind blows" and the "cramped quarters" "could be better."

	ROOMS	SERVICE	DINING	FACIL.	COST

Huntington Hotel & Nob Hill Spa ⓗ☕♨ⓢ

| 21 | 25 | 21 | 23 | $350 |

1075 California St. | San Francisco | 415-474-5400 | fax 415-474-6227 | 800-227-4683 | www.huntingtonhotel.com | 96 rooms, 40 suites

"Takes me back to a time of quiet elegance" sigh devotees of this "refined" member of Small Luxury Hotels of the World that boasts white-gloved doormen and a "top-of-the-world" Nob Hill perch over-looking "beautiful" Huntington Park; the"attentive" staff is "exem-plary in kindness", and though fans say the recently renovated rooms are "beautifully appointed", some feel they're "not great"; still, a "to-die-for" spa with a "stunning" indoor pool and a "grand" outdoor deck are bonuses.

Inn Above Tide ♨

| 26 | 22 | 13 | 20 | $325 |

30 El Portal | Sausalito | 415-332-9535 | fax 415-332-6714 | 800-893-8433 | www.innabovetide.com | 26 rooms, 3 suites

"The view is the thing" at this "beautiful" bayside boutique hotel where "charming" rooms - most with private balconies "so close to the water you almost get seasick"- treat guests to "unbelievable" vis-tas and the sounds of seagulls and "whispering fishermen"; with a staff that "bends over backwards" to please, an "amazing selection" of breakfast items and complimentary afternoon wine, it's "definitely one of the best finds around"; P.S. "opt for a grand deluxe room for a splurge you'll long remember."

Inn Marin

| - | - | - | - | $184 |

250 Entrada Dr. | Novato | 415-883-5952 | fax 415-883-5058 | www.innmarin.com | 66 rooms, 4 suites

This simple, family-owned Novato inn recently completed an eco-friendly renovation, incorporating sustainable materials (bamboo flooring, shams and coverlets), water-conserving bath fixtures and or-ganic toiletries in rooms that also offer refrigerators, iPod docks, com-plimentary WiFi, flat-screen TVs and large work desks with ergonomic chairs; housekeeping now uses non-toxic cleaners, while a solar cover warms the on-site pool.

NEW InterContinental ♨ⓢ

| ∇ 25 | 24 | 20 | 24 | $589 |

888 Howard St. | San Francisco | 888-811-4273 | fax 415-520-6662 | 800-496-7621 | www.intercontinental.com | 546 rooms, 15 suites

"Ask for a room with a view" say fans of this new glass-encased SoMa outpost since you "can't beat" the "spectacular" views from the "floor-to-ceiling" windows; "comfortable" rooms have "every-thing you need", including 42-inch plasma TVs, iPod docks, minibars and large work areas, and there are 24-hour fitness and business cen-ters, a spa and a Californian restaurant, Luce, that serves Italian fare in the evenings.

JW Marriott ♨
(fka Pan Pacific San Francisco, The)

| 22 | 21 | 17 | 19 | $299 |

500 Post St. | San Francisco | 415-771-8600 | fax 415-398-0267 | 800-228-9290 | www.jwmarriottunionsquare.com | 329 rooms, 8 suites

It feels "brand-new" thanks to the "nicely" remodeled interior that's now finally complete at this centrally located property near Union

	ROOMS	SERVICE	DINING	FACIL.	COST

Square; the "large", "fresh" rooms please, the "prices are excellent" and the staff is "helpful" and "friendly", making this spot a real "sleeper."

Kabuki, Hotel 👥

▽ 20 | 18 | 16 | 19 | $249

1625 Post St. | San Francisco | 415-922-3200 | fax 415-614-5498 | 800-533-4567 | www.jvdhotels.com | 195 rooms, 18 suites

A recent "face-lift" has sparked renewed interest in this "lovely" '60s Japantown hotel featuring both Eastern and Western aesthetic touches throughout, along with "fantastic" saunas, "friendly" staffers and access to "traditional" communal baths (a few blocks away); in all, it's a "nice" alternative if you want somewhere "away from the city's touristy areas."

Lafayette Park Hotel & Spa 👥Ⓢ

▽ 21 | 20 | 20 | 21 | $269

3287 Mt. Diablo Blvd. | Lafayette | 925-283-3700 | fax 925-284-1621 | 800-368-2468 | www.lafayetteparkhotel.com | 126 rooms, 12 suites

Arguably the "only civilized place to stay" in the area, this East Bay hotel with French-château architecture, a three-story domed lobby and a "friendly staff" lures loyalists who also like the heated indoor pool and fitness facilities; but nitpickers nix the "dated rooms" and "way too small spa", saying it's time to "remodel" this "suburban" spot.

Le Méridien San Francisco 👥

23 | 22 | 17 | 20 | $579

333 Battery St. | San Francisco | 415-296-2900 | fax 415-296-2901 | 866-837-4184 | www.lemeridien.com | 324 rooms, 40 suites

You get a "spectacular" view of the Golden Gate Bridge and San Francisco Bay from the top floor of this "professionally" run property situated between the Embarcadero and the Financial District; "best for corporate travelers", it has "quality" in spades, as evidenced by the "excellent" service and "large", "modern" rooms, but a few say the restaurant is "mediocre."

Mandarin Oriental ✕👒👥

27 | 27 | 23 | 24 | $700

222 Sansome St. | San Francisco | 415-276-9888 | fax 415-276-9304 | 800-622-0404 | www.mandarinoriental.com | 154 rooms, 4 suites

Experience pure "bliss" and "utter luxury" at this "sublime" Financial District hotel, thanks to "sumptuous" rooms with "spectacular" baths (you'll "feel like an emperor in the tubs"), an "impeccable" staff that "genuinely cares", "excellent" food at Silks and "postcard"-perfect, panoramic views of the city and bay; it's all so "calm" and "soothing" that even the top-dollar pricing doesn't rattle.

Mark Hopkins InterContinental ⓘ👥

22 | 23 | 21 | 21 | $329

1 Nob Hill | San Francisco | 415-392-3434 | fax 415-421-3302 | 800-662-4455 | www.markhopkins.net | 340 rooms, 40 suites

"Gracious service" is one of this Nob Hill "landmark's" best virtues, along with "huge", "nicely appointed" rooms that "resemble luxury suites"; the upper floors and the aptly named Top of the Mark lounge ("Sunday brunch is a must") offer "spectacular" city views that make you feel "as if you are a bird or a star", and though detractors call it a "shabby" "grande dame" that "needs some serious nip and tuck", loyalists say this "stylish" spot "keeps earning its reputation."

	ROOMS	SERVICE	DINING	FACIL.	COST

Marriott Downtown ⓢ
19 | 19 | 15 | 19 | $199

55 Fourth St. | San Francisco | 415-896-1600 | fax 415-486-8101 |
800-228-9290 | www.marriott.com | 1362 rooms, 137 suites
The "fantastic" location (near MoMA and the Moscone Center) of this
"bustling" jumbo-size Downtowner is a magnet for "tourists", "business
travelers" and "convention"-goers; "friendly" service, "adequate"
rooms and a "well-equipped" fitness center make it a solid bet, while
a post-Survey renovation may liven up what a few call "boring" decor.

Monaco, Hotel ⍋
20 | 22 | 19 | 18 | $279

501 Geary St. | San Francisco | 415-292-0100 | fax 415-292-0111 |
866-622-5284 | www.monaco-sf.com | 169 rooms, 32 suites
The "cozy", "cool" rooms may be a little "tight", but their "playful" design
charms devotees of this "whimsical" Downtown Kimpton boutique
whose "wonderful" staff is more than happy to loan you an in-room goldfish; there's "color" and "character" in abundance, and the "super"
Theater District location, "reasonable" rates and "fun" (and free)
"wine/cheese hour" help distinguish this hotel from its "big-box rivals."

Nikko, Hotel ✕⍋♨
22 | 22 | 20 | 21 | $520

222 Mason St. | San Francisco | 415-394-1111 | fax 415-394-1106 |
800-248-3308 | www.hotelnikkosf.com | 510 rooms, 22 suites
"Well-located near Union Square", this hotel is "often overlooked" but
imparts "a cool Japanese elegance", with "understated" (and "small")
rooms sporting pillowtop beds and Frette linens, an "accommodating"
staff and an indoor solarium with a pool and hot tub; corporate folks
consider it a "solid choice" given the on-site business center, 24-hour
fitness facility, "great steak and sushi" at the Euro-Japanese restaurant, Anzu, and chic Rrazz Room featuring headline entertainers.

Omni ♔⍋
22 | 22 | 20 | 22 | $599

500 California St. | San Francisco | 415-677-9494 | fax 415-273-3038 |
800-843-6664 | www.omnisanfrancisco.com | 347 rooms, 15 suites
A "charming" preserved 1926 bank building with a marble-clad lobby
and arched windows is the setting for this "beautiful" Downtowner
with a "great location" for business and "wonderful" flavor for vacationers as well; "pleasant" rooms feature "updated amenities", including minibars with "spa products and candles", while "fantabulous"
service and a solid restaurant complete the picture.

Orchard Hotel, The ⓘ♨
▽ 22 | 23 | 17 | 17 | $329

665 Bush St. | San Francisco | 415-362-8878 | fax 415-362-8088 |
888-717-2881 | www.theorchardhotel.com | 104 rooms, 9 suites
The "extremely helpful" staff pulls off a "great experience" for clients of
this "charming", "ecologically correct" address on Nob Hill boasting
"exceptionally comfortable" rooms and "spacious" suites; the "nice
touches" (e.g. an "excellent" free breakfast and DVDs) further cement
this "true find"; P.S. the location "close to Union Square, subway and
buses" provides a "launching pad for sightseeing excursions."

Palace Hotel, The ⓘⓢ
21 | 23 | 22 | 22 | $569

2 New Montgomery St. | San Francisco | 415-512-1111 | fax 415-543-0671 |
888-625-5144 | www.sfpalace.com | 499 rooms, 53 suites
Luxuristas longing for a taste of "old San Francisco" flock to this "decadent" Financial District "classic" offering "first-class service", a

"stunning lobby", "Victorian-esque decor" and "tastefully appointed" rooms with "high ceilings"; the "amazing" Garden Court serves an "awesome brunch" and "wonderful tea service", and if some say "getting a nice room is hit-and-miss" at this "rather tired old lady", others reply "they don't call it the Palace for nothing."

Palomar, Hotel ✕ ⍣ 🛌   22 | 23 | 23 | 18 | $479

12 Fourth St. | San Francisco | 415-348-1111 | fax 415-348-0302 | 866-373-4941 | www.hotelpalomar-sf.com | 180 rooms, 16 suites

They "go out of their way to take care of you" at this "sorta hip but not too hip" Kimpton boutique in SoMa that's equally adored for its "serene", "modern" rooms (each with distinctive headboards) as it is for its location (near the "shopping bonanza" of Union Square); while foodies focus on the "to-die-for" fare at the Fifth Floor restaurant, others praise the "fun, funky decor" and service so "amazing" you'll think "you have a pal at the Palomar."

Petite Auberge   ▽ 20 | 22 | 16 | 15 | $189

863 Bush St. | San Francisco | 415-928-6000 | fax 415-673-7214 | 800-365-3004 | www.jdvhotels.com | 25 rooms, 1 suite

"Small, but wonderful" sums up this "comforting" Nob Hill auberge noted for a "welcoming" French countryside ambiance and "lovely" breakfasts (along with *gratis* wine and cheese at nights); "cute", "cozy" rooms and reasonable rates make it sound a bet for travelers on a "budget" and seeking a "true B&B" experience.

Prescott Hotel, The ✕ ⍣   18 | 22 | 22 | 17 | $220

545 Post St. | San Francisco | 415-563-0303 | fax 415-563-6831 | 866-271-3632 | www.prescotthotel.com | 132 rooms, 32 suites

A "genuinely interested" staff (including an "attentive" front desk) and "top-notch" food at Wolfgang Puck's adjoining Postrio restaurant are the bright lights of this "cozy" hotel in a "fabulous" Union Square location; true, it "may not have the fancy amenities" of others, and the quarters could use a "real makeover", but few quibble with the prices, which add up to a "bargain" for the area.

🅱 Ritz-Carlton, The ✕ ⍣ ⓢ   26 | 28 | 27 | 26 | $545

600 Stockton St. | San Francisco | 415-296-7465 | fax 415-291-0288 | 800-241-3333 | www.ritzcarlton.com | 276 rooms, 60 suites

"A+ all the way" is the word on this "quintessentially classy" Nob Hill hotel that's "still the favorite" of acolytes who adore the "beautiful", "spacious" accommodations, "wonderful food" (including an "amazing jazz brunch"), "immaculate service" and overall ambiance of "comfortable elegance"; although the high prices make it "unmistakably a Ritz", so do "outstanding" virtues such as a "heavenly club floor" and "blissful spa."

Serrano Hotel ⍣ 🛌   ▽ 18 | 20 | 17 | 15 | $299

405 Taylor St. | San Francisco | 415-885-2500 | fax 415-474-4879 | 866-289-6561 | www.serranohotel.com | 217 rooms, 19 suites

The rooms are "cozy" (i.e. "really small") and "not super luxe", but they have "nice amenities" pledge patrons of this Kimpton Spanish revival boutique with a fun-and-games theme near the Theater District and Union Square; "charm" to spare, an "attentive staff" and a "lively wine hour" make up for "dissapointing" food and "older" facilities; P.S. "for space and views, a suite is the way to go."

Sofitel 🎐🏨

21	21	18	20	$309

223 Twin Dolphin Dr. | Redwood City | 650-598-9000 |
fax 650-598-9383 | 800-763-4835 | www.sofitel.com | 379 rooms,
42 suites

Business travelers looking for "nice" accommodations and "value" bet on this "corporate" hotel "in an office park" in "quiet" Redwood City; though it's a "little far" from San Francisco and offers "nothing spectacular", the beds are "puffy" and "plush", the staff is "attentive" and the location offers proximity to the airport and Silicon Valley.

Stanford Court, A Renaissance Hotel 🎐🏨

21	22	21	20	$329

905 California St. | San Francisco | 415-989-3500 | fax 415-391-0513 |
800-468-3571 | www.stanfordcourt.com | 360 rooms, 4 suites,
28 studios

Hop on one of the cable cars that stop right in front of this "ideally located" Nob Hill standby where stained-glass domes adorn the lobby, rooms are "well appointed" and the "knowlegeable" staff "takes great care" of you; those who call it a "golden oldie" will be happy a post-Survey top-to-bottom renovation could liven things up (and outdate the above scores).

Stanford Park Hotel ✕🏨

23	21	19	20	$299

100 El Camino Real | Menlo Park | 650-322-1234 |
fax 650-322-0975 | 800-368-2468 | www.stanfordparkhotel.com |
154 rooms, 9 suites

At this "delightful" address near Stanford University - an English Colonial–style "change of pace from the typical business" property – they offer "warm homemade cookies" in the lobby and serve up "one of the best brunches" in the area; but ambivalent types are torn over this "not bad, not great" spot, saying it "could be much better."

St. Regis ✕ⓗ🎐🏨ⓢ

27	26	25	25	$409

125 Third St. | San Francisco | 415-284-4000 | fax 415-284-4100 |
877-787-3447 | www.stregis.com | 214 rooms, 46 suites,
102 condos

Experience "luxe quality" at this "phenomenal hotel in a great location", next to the SF MoMA, that earns superlatives all around for its "sleek", "high-tech" rooms (think "remote-controlled shades") with "plush bathrooms", a "flawless" staff, chef Hiro Sone's "terrific" Ame restaurant and a "wonderful" Remède spa; in short, "every amenity" and service imaginable makes staying at this "gorgeous" property worth the price.

Vitale, Hotel 🎐🏨ⓢ

25	24	22	22	$429

8 Mission St. | San Francisco | 415-278-3700 | fax 415-278-3750 |
888-890-8688 | www.hotelvitale.com | 178 rooms, 21 suites

The "clean", "serene" design and service that "sets a high standard" are part of the "winning" profile of this "chic" hotel in a "fantastic" Embarcadero location with "amazing" bay views and proximity to the nearby Ferry Building (a paradise for foodies); aside from the "fantastic" spa and all those luxe amenities in the "fabulous" rooms (Fresh brand toiletries, 440-thread-count linens), there are complimentary rooftop yoga and stretching classes every morning.

Westin San Francisco Market Street ♨🔭

ROOMS	SERVICE	DINING	FACIL.	COST
21	18	17	20	$319

(fka Argent Hotel)
50 Third St. | San Francisco | 415-974-6400 | fax 415-974-8742 | 888-627-8561 | www.westin.com | 652 rooms, 24 suites
The "chic" "boutique-hotel feel" is a "wonderful surprise" at this "ideally located" SoMa outpost where the "outstanding views" from its "floor-to-ceiling windows" come at a "bargain price" for the city; "Heavenly beds" are the highlight of the "modern" rooms, the staff is "helpful" and if some find the restaurant disappointing, there are "plenty of other options nearby."

Westin St. Francis, The 👪🍴[H]♨🔭[S]

ROOMS	SERVICE	DINING	FACIL.	COST
20	20	21	20	$389

335 Powell St. | San Francisco | 415-397-7000 | fax 415-774-0124 | 888-625-5144 | www.westinstfrancis.com | 1156 rooms, 39 suites
Revisit the "luxury" of the "gold rush days" at this San Francisco "landmark" that "oozes" "history" in a "phenomenal" "heart-of-Union-Square" location; though the "rooms vary in size and grandeur" (the newer tower has "more modern touches" vs. the older section's "small", "quaint" lodgings), the main "charm" resides in the "elegant" building's "amazing public spaces" and its "over-the-top" dining courtesy of the "über-luxe Michael Mina" restaurant.

White Swan Inn

ROOMS	SERVICE	DINING	FACIL.	COST
22	24	19	19	$189

845 Bush St. | San Francisco | 415-775-1755 | fax 415-775-5717 | 800-999-9570 | www.whiteswaninnsf.com | 25 rooms, 1 suite
This "funky but charming" B&B amid Nob Hill's "hubbub" has a "big heart" according to smitten surveyors who salute its "friendly, helpful staff", "intimate" rooms with "remote-control fireplaces" and "wonderful value"; its "limited" eats include a "lovely breakfast", homemade cookies in the lobby and "nice" complimentary wine and hors d'oeuvres in the evening.

W San Francisco ♨🔭[S]

ROOMS	SERVICE	DINING	FACIL.	COST
23	21	20	22	$529

181 Third St. | San Francisco | 415-777-5300 | fax 415-817-7823 | 877-946-8357 | www.whotels.com | 395 rooms, 9 suites
It's probably "not the best place to take grandma", but this "trendy", "clublike" South of Market hotel provides plenty of joy for those into "hot" bar scenes, "modern" amenities, "dark" hallways and "minimalist" design; even if the food is only "pretty good" and the service a bit "snide", most applaud the "plush" beds in the "beautifully equipped" rooms.

Santa Barbara

Alisal Guest Ranch & Resort 👪🔭⛳🎾

ROOMS	SERVICE	DINING	FACIL.	COST
17	21	18	23	$475

1054 Alisal Rd. | Solvang | 805-688-6411 | fax 805-688-2510 | 888-425-4725 | www.alisal.com | 36 rooms, 37 suites
Take a lot of time off because "you'll want to stay longer" at this "truly unique", "upscale dude ranch" a short jaunt from Solvang that's "high-end fun" for the "entire family"; with "no phones or TVs", it allows you to "get away from it all" – enjoying "amazing breakfasts" before "fish-

ing on the lake", taking "nature walks", "playing tennis or golf" or horseback riding "through the beautiful countryside"; even if the "dated" "rooms have a motel-ish quality", most "love it."

Bacara Resort & Spa, The

| 26 | 24 | 24 | 27 | $550 |

8301 Hollister Ave. | 805-968-0100 | fax 805-968-1800 | 877-422-4245 | www.bacararesort.com | 311 rooms, 49 suites

"Pretend you're a celeb" at this multi-tiered "oasis", a "Spanish-style", "gorgeous, romantic getaway" north of Santa Barbara where the "facilities are fabulous": "sublimely comfortable" rooms, eateries with Basque, Med and "healthy" cuisine, "entertainment for even the most high-maintenance kids", an "outstanding" spa ("with prices to match"), "gorgeous infinity pools" with "sweeping ocean views" and even a movie theater; while service can range from "haughty and uncaring to incredible", most leave "longing for another night."

Fess Parker's Wine Country Inn & Spa

| 21 | 20 | 20 | 20 | $295 |

2860 Grand Ave. | Los Olivos | 805-688-7788 | fax 805-688-1942 | 800-466-2455 | www.fessparker.com | 16 rooms, 5 suites

A "classic country inn" in a "great location for wine tasting", this "little hideaway" about five miles from Solvang is "worth the trip" for its "spacious accommodations", proximity to the "vineyards of the Santa Rita hills", a "friendly staff" – and the opportunity to meet owner Fess, who occasionally entertains in the piano bar ("we sang the theme to Davy Crockett all the way home"); but while loyalists laud its "above-average" charms, others opine it's in "desperate need of a remodeling."

Four Seasons, The Biltmore

| 26 | 27 | 25 | 27 | $600 |

1260 Channel Dr. | 805-969-2261 | fax 805-565-8323 | 800-332-3442 | www.fourseasons.com | 181 rooms, 26 suites

"A king's ransom buys royal treatment" at this "splendid resort" with a "lovely oceanside setting" (there are "frequent dolphin sightings from the beach") and "elegant" "old-time Santa Barbara class"; you'll "feel like a pampered celeb", what with the "luxurious" cottages sporting "beautiful bathrooms" and "private terraces", "impeccable service", "fantastic spa services", "unbelievable health club", "excellent" "sunset dining" and "out-of-this-world Sunday brunch"; P.S. "dogs are welcome" too.

Inn of the Spanish Garden

| 26 | 24 | 19 | 23 | $359 |

915 Garden St. | 805-564-4700 | fax 805-564-4701 | 866-564-4700 | www.spanishgardeninn.com | 17 rooms, 6 suites

"Immaculate" rooms with "private gardens", "balconies", "fireplaces" – plus oversized tubs, French press coffee makers and Frette linens – distinguish this "impeccably" run Spanish Colonial boutique in a "great" location in the historic Presidio District, just a "short walk" from shops and cultural attractions; a "unanimously friendly" staff rounds out the "charm"; P.S. while there is no on-site restaurant, there's a "nice" complimentary continental breakfast and plenty of dining options in town.

	ROOMS	SERVICE	DINING	FACIL.	COST
Ojai Valley Inn & Spa 👪 🐕 🔭 ⛳ [S] 🎾	25	24	22	27	$300

905 Country Club Rd. | Ojai | 805-646-5511 | fax 805-646-7969 | 800-422-6524 | www.ojairesort.com | 233 rooms, 75 suites

Even those who say they "never return to the same place" "can't wait to go back" to this "classic" Mediterranean-style resort 35 miles south of Santa Barabara where the "stunning natural beauty", "expert spa treatments", "unsurpassed golf", tennis and kids' programs, and staffers who "love their jobs" create a "heaven on earth"; to those who tsk "the grounds are littered with children", others reply "though it's bustling, it's easy to find a place to relax"; N.B. a fourth pool is slated to open shortly.

	ROOMS	SERVICE	DINING	FACIL.	COST
San Ysidro Ranch 🐕 🔭	26	26	25	25	$650

900 San Ysidro Ln. | 805-565-1700 | fax 805-565-1995 | 800-368-6788 | www.sanysidroranch.com | 41 cottages

"What's not to love?" about this "incredibly romantic" Relais & Châteaux lodging that was "good enough for a Kennedy honeymoon" (JFK and Jackie's) and for "droves of Hollywood royalty"; the "gorgeous facility" is set on "incredible grounds" ("rural yet sophisticated") in the Montecito foothills near Santa Barbara, and the staff "treats you like royalty", the "lovely"cottages are "secluded" (outdoor rain showers and hot tubs delight) and the dining is "fabulous"; it's "pricey", but the recent $150-million renovation has made this one "worth every penny."

	ROOMS	SERVICE	DINING	FACIL.	COST
Simpson House Inn [H] 🔭	25	26	23	21	$255

121 E. Arrellaga St. | 805-963-7067 | fax 805-564-4811 | 800-676-1280 | www.simpsonhouseinn.com | 7 rooms, 4 suites, 4 cottages

Within walking distance of Downtown Santa Barbara, this "outstanding", "charming and quaint" 1874 Victorian B&B - set behind tall hedges on a "lovely" estate featuring an English country garden - entices with "beautifully decorated" quarters and a staff displaying "amazing attention to detail"; though penny-pinchers find the "smaller rooms overpriced", most love "celebrating a special weekend" at this "romantic" spot.

		ROOMS	SERVICE	DINING	FACIL.	COST
Upham Hotel & Country House [H] 🔭	▽	20	24	21	18	$245

1404 De La Vina St. | 805-962-0058 | fax 805-963-2825 | 800-727-0876 | www.uphamhotel.com | 41 rooms, 9 cottages

A "quintessentially California B&B" awaits guests of this 1871 "romantic" Santa Barbara retreat where the "airy" rooms have "cushiony" four-poster beds, the continental breakfast is "delicious" and the surrounding "pretty gardens" "add to the delight"; its "wonderful location" is "only a short walk to State Street", but be warned that only some of the quarters are air-conditioned.

Wine Country

		ROOMS	SERVICE	DINING	FACIL.	COST
Applewood Inn [H]	▽	19	21	24	19	$185

13555 Hwy. 116 | Guerneville | 707-869-9093 | fax 707-869-9170 | 800-555-8509 | www.applewoodinn.com | 19 rooms

This "charming" 1922 B&B set amid towering redwoods in an "off-the-beaten-path" location is a welcome retreat for journeying through the Russian River Valley wine country; it may not be a luxury destination per se (there's no room service), and you may have to "ask to stay in the newer building for a more updated room", but visitors have no is-

	ROOMS	SERVICE	DINING	FACIL.	COST

sue with the inn's highly regarded restaurant, serving "tasty" meals along with "fabulous" wines.

☑ Auberge du Soleil ✕♨☺☌

| 28 | 27 | 28 | 27 | $700 |

180 Rutherford Hill Rd. | Rutherford | 707-963-1211 | fax 707-963-8764 | 800-348-5406 | www.aubergedusoleil.com | 34 rooms, 16 suites, 2 maisons

"Oh, let me stay here forever" plead patrons of this Relais & Châteaux inn, a "dramatically gorgeous" "Mediterranean dream" where "memories of a lifetime" are etched in abundance thanks to "outstanding" rooms and "suites with wood-burning fireplaces", service that personifies "country elegance and charm at its best", "lovely views" of "magical sunsets", and "amazing starry skies and zephyr breezes"; an "incredible sculpture garden", "transporting spa" and "fabulous food" are also at hand, along with "astronomical prices."

Calistoga Ranch ♔✕☆♨☺

| 26 | 27 | 25 | 25 | $845 |

580 Lommel Rd. | Calistoga | 707-254-2800 | fax 707-254-2888 | 800-942-4220 | www.calistogaranch.com | 46 cottages

A "luxurious" "secluded retreat" for a "quiet weekend", this Napa valley "hideaway" is "like your own private" "pristine valley" "in the heart of Calistoga", complete with "grazing horses and cattle and lots of fruit trees and flowers" spread across "beautiful gardens"; "extraordinary suites" with "opulent baths, extensive decks and outdoor showers", a "rejuvenating spa" with "a hot tub worthy of a photo shoot", a "bar with a great wine selection" and a "fantastic restaurant" with "incredible food" are part of the "dreamy" experience.

Carneros Inn ♔✕☆☺

| 28 | 25 | 24 | 27 | $580 |

4048 Sonoma Hwy. | Napa | 707-299-4900 | fax 707-299-4950 | 888-400-9000 | www.thecarnerosinn.com | 86 cottages, 15 villas

"Set on a low, rolling hill overlooking the wine country", this "idyllic" Napa inn "perfect for honeymooners" is a "budding star", thanks to "off-the-chart cottages" bedecked with "outdoor showers", "heated bathroom floors" and "secluded patios", plus "impeccable service" and "out-of-this-world cuisine" "offering innovative twists on local produce"; "drink fabulous wines" in the "hip, open-air bar", "enjoy the best massage of your life followed by a dip" in the "beautiful pool" and say "aaahhh!" to an "absolutely wonderful" "weekend retreat" that's "worth every Ben Franklin"

Fairmont Sonoma Mission Inn & Spa ☆♨ℒ☺

| 21 | 23 | 21 | 24 | $329 |

100 Boyes Blvd. | Sonoma | 707-938-9000 | fax 707-938-4250 | 800-441-1414 | www.fairmont.com | 166 rooms, 60 suites

The "magnificent spa" and "beautiful", natural mineral springs take center stage at this Sonoma spot ("you must try the bathing ritual" that "takes you out of this world"); while the "grounds are calm and pretty", the staff "attentive" and the "suites fabulous", a few find the "regular rooms small", the layout "convoluted" and the lobby "marginal."

Gaige House Inn ✕

| 28 | 27 | 24 | 24 | $395 |

13540 Arnold Dr. | Glen Ellen | 707-935-0237 | fax 707-935-6411 | 800-935-0237 | www.gaige.com | 14 suites, 9 rooms

"Don't skip the breakfast, no matter what" advise patrons who laud chef Diane Peck's "unbelievable" meals at this "serene, romantic" inn on the banks of Calabasas Creek in the "homey" wine country town of Glen Ellen; "not your typical antiques-filled B&B", this "funky", "modern inn" with an "invisible housekeeping staff" and a "Zen-like atmosphere" (decor has Asian and Indonesian influences) boasts rooms with silky-soft linens and wonderful artwork; P.S. it was recently purchased by Thompson Hotels.

Harvest Inn ⚘♨Ⓢ | 23 | 20 | 14 | 19 | $399 |

1 Main St. | St. Helena | 707-963-9463 | fax 707-963-4402 | 800-950-8466 | www.harvestinn.com | 71 rooms, 3 suites

The "wonderful location" of this "beautiful" and "hospitable" inn on eight "lush acres" in the Napa Valley, boasting views of the Mayacama Mountains, means oenophiles can "taste wine and wobble back" to their "cavernous" rooms (boasting "top-shelf" L'Occitane bath products); two outdoor heated pools and a "top-notch" spa offering treatments under a tented cabana draw raves, but the "ho-hum" breakfast means you'll want to explore off-site eateries.

Healdsburg, Hotel ⚘♨Ⓢ | 24 | 23 | 24 | 21 | $340 |

25 Matheson St. | Healdsburg | 707-431-2800 | fax 707-431-0414 | 800-889-7188 | www.hotelhealdsburg.com | 49 rooms, 6 suites

"Fabulously trendy", "ultrachic" and pulsating with "lots of energy", this "totally killer" "boutique hotel" "in the heart of Healdsburg" is a "perfect" location "for sampling Sonoma County's best wineries", but it also offers "soothing rooms" bedecked with "big, cloud comforters", "beautifully tiled baths" and "a lavender scent that carries you home"; the "pleasant service" and "welcoming lobby bar" are added extras, but the "superb" Dry Creek Kitchen (courtesy of chef Charlie Palmer) may be "reason enough" to "make a return visit."

Inn at Southbridge ♨ | ▽ 20 | 22 | 18 | 21 | $400 |

1020 Main St. | St. Helena | 707-967-9400 | fax 707-967-9486 | 800-520-6800 | www.innatsouthbridge.com | 20 rooms, 1 suite

Within "walking distance to restaurants and shopping in St. Helena", this member of Small Luxury Hotels of the World is "by no means opulent, but it's a nice option" in wine country; a "caring" staff, "modern" rooms with French doors that open onto private balconies and free access to a "terrific fitness center" win points, but a few complain that, overall, this one "needs a refreshening."

Kenwood Inn ♨Ⓢ | ▽ 26 | 23 | 20 | 25 | $600 |

10400 Sonoma Hwy. | Kenwood | 707-833-1293 | fax 707-833-1247 | 800-353-6966 | www.kenwoodinn.com | 27 rooms, 3 suites

"Your cares seem a million miles away" at this "quiet" Sonoma retreat with "amazing rooms" offering "the most comfortable beds anywhere"; the "grounds are incredible", the ambiance "romantic" (no kids under 18 allowed) and the spa "outstanding" ("where else can you put on your bathrobe or swimsuit and never take it off for the duration of your stay?"), but regulars report that dining is "limited during the week."

Les Mars Hôtel | ▽ 28 | 22 | 27 | 17 | $575 |

27 North St. | Healdsburg | 707-433-4211 | fax 707-433-4611 | 877-431-1700 | www.lesmarshotel.com | 16 rooms

A "chic" experience awaits guest of this adult-only Relais & Châteaux boutique, where the Swiss-trained staff, 18th- and 19th-century antiques and "incredible" Cyrus restaurant present a "formal" option in "sleepy Sonoma"; expect "service that other hoteliers only dream about", and the "ultimate" rooms with draped, four-poster beds, marble baths, fireplaces and Louis XV armoires that hide 21st-century amenities; it's too "pretentious" for down-to-earth sorts, but the rest wallow in the "luxury."

MacArthur Place 卌Ⓢ
25 | 22 | 19 | 24 | $349

29 E. MacArthur St. | Sonoma | 707-938-2929 | fax 707-933-9833 | 800-722-1866 | www.macarthurplace.com | 33 rooms, 29 suites, 2 cottages
The "stunning" Victorian-style accommodations at this wine-country inn, including rooms, cottages and specialty suites (the cabana suite features a private tented outdoor space with a fountain and rain shower), are truly impressive say fans; and while the "charming garden setting", "eager-to-please" staff and "fine, small spa" also please, the dining doesn't quite measure up to the rest.

Madrona Manor ✕
23 | 23 | 26 | 20 | $375

1001 Westside Rd. | Healdsburg | 707-433-4231 | fax 707-433-0703 | 800-258-4003 | www.madronamanor.com | 19 rooms, 3 suites
Seems "like Scarlett O'Hara is going to come around the corner any moment" at this 1881 hilltop mansion overlooking Sonoma's Dry Creek Valley, with its "stunning surroundings" that are the "perfect accompaniment to a wine-country weekend"; chef Jesse Mallgren's "divine" restaurant "emphasizes local and on-site produce" and "romantic" rooms feature Frette linens, hypoallergenic beds and fireplaces, but a few say they're a "little tired", veering "more toward old than antique."

Maison Fleurie 卌
▽ 18 | 20 | 17 | 16 | $130

6529 Yount St. | Yountville | 707-944-2056 | fax 707-944-9342 | 800-788-0369 | www.maisonfleurienapa.com | 13 rooms
"Sleep off all the excesses" you've indulged in (i.e. from vineyard hopping) at this "adorable" French-country B&B in Napa, a "preferred stop" for wine-country connoisseurs; "cozy" rooms, a "cordial" staff that pays "careful attention to detail" and "delicious" baked goods at breakfast create a "sweet and romantic" stay.

ⓩ Meadowood Napa Valley 卌✕卌Ⓢ🔍
27 | 26 | 25 | 27 | $650

900 Meadowood Ln. | St. Helena | 707-963-3646 | fax 707-963-3532 | 800-458-8080 | www.meadowood.com | 56 rooms, 44 suites
"Simply spectacular" sums up this "premier" Relais & Châteaux resort treasured for so many virtues, namely the "idyllic", "secluded" Napa Valley setting, "wonderful" cottages and cabins that dot the "beautiful" property, servers that "make you feel like a dignitary" and dining at "one of the finest restaurants in California"; "thank God for expense accounts", but even if you don't have one, it's worth splurging on this "magical" experience.

Milliken Creek Inn & Spa 卌Ⓢ
▽ 26 | 23 | 18 | 20 | $575

1815 Silverado Trail | Napa | 707-255-1197 | fax 707-255-3112 | 800-810-7814 | www.millikencreekinn.com | 12 rooms
"Exceeding the expectations" of the most discerning travelers, this Napa "oasis of calm and beauty" is truly "splendid", with "every detail

	ROOMS	SERVICE	DINING	FACIL.	COST

and every guest attended" to by a "fantastic" staff; quarters contain "sumptuous" linens, oversized hydrotherapy tubs and the "finest" in-room amenities, and the idyllic, "romantic" setting overlooking the Napa River (there are waterside spa treatments) creates a "blissful" "heaven on earth"; P.S. though there's "no real dining here", breakfasts and evening wine receptions offer a "collection of local delights."

Napa River Inn ⊕✦♨

22	20	21	16	$199

500 Main St. | Napa | 707-251-8500 | fax 707-251-8504 | 877-251-8500 | www.napariverinn.com | 59 rooms, 7 suites

"In a great location to walk to fab food and shops", this "funky" former grain mill in Downtown Napa (located in three separate buildings) "can't be beat, for the price"; service makes your stay "happy and memorable", rooms are "cozy" and "non-kitschy" and the breakfast that "arrives in the morning for you to enjoy on your balcony" is "amazing"; ongoing "construction", including a spa renovation, bothers some, but others "completely forget about it" once inside.

Napa Valley Marriott Hotel & Spa ♨

19	21	14	19	$289

3425 Solano Ave. | Napa | 707-253-8600 | fax 707-258-1320 | 800-228-9290 | www.marriott.com | 270 rooms, 4 suites

In "a field of tough competitors" this Napa Valley chainster holds its own, mostly due to a spa that's "a real surprise", especially "after a long flight from the East Coast"; most maintain the rest is "about what you'd expect" – "ok for a chain" with "comfortable" rooms, "adequate service" and "reasonably affordable" rates, but "lacking in charm."

Silverado Resort ✕🐾♨⚘☉🔍

18	20	19	23	$205

1600 Atlas Peak Rd. | Napa | 707-257-0200 | fax 707-257-2867 | 800-532-0500 | www.silveradoresort.com | 140 rooms, 280 suites

The "price is right" and the golf is "excellent" for duffers who've stayed and played at this "sprawling", "country club"-like complex whose "excellent" location is ideal for "exploring lower Napa Valley" and "the beautiful wine country"; two Robert Trent Jones, Jr. courses, 17 tennis courts and 10 swimming pools make it "family-friendly", but those who come away "unimpressed" say the "so-so" rooms need "sprucing up."

NEW Solage Calistoga ✦✿♨☉

▽ 23	21	21	24	$425

755 Silverado Trail | Calistoga | 707-226-0800 | fax 707-226-0809 | 866-942-7442 | www.solagecalistoga.com | 83 studios, 6 suites

Evoking the essence of the wine country, this Calistoga newcomer has a quintessential "Napa feel" thanks to the rustic-contemporary studio-style accommodations (named for stars in the sky) with fireplaces, outdoor patios, flat-screen TVs and iPod hookups; the service is "still a bit spotty" but there are "nice touches" ("everyone gets a bicycle" to tour the area), so some say this "property should get better with age"; P.S. the "fantastic" spa has a mud bar and 14 treatment rooms.

Villagio Inn & Spa ♨☉🔍

24	23	19	23	$375

6481 Washington St. | Yountville | 707-944-8877 | fax 707-944-8855 | 800-351-1133 | www.villagio.com | 86 rooms, 26 suites

"If you can't relax and enjoy yourself here, you need professional help" tease sensualists enthralled by the "peaceful Tuscan atmosphere" at this "charming" Napa inn that's near "some of Northern Cal's best restaurants"; "expansive rooms" with fireplaces and balconies "surround a beautiful pool and well-manicured grounds" ("make sure you aren't facing the highway"), the "helpful staff" serves a "fabulous" daily champagne breakfast buffet and there's a new "high-quality" spa.

Vintage Inn ⚑⚐⚘

ROOMS	SERVICE	DINING	FACIL.	COST
23	21	18	20	$480

6541 Washington St. | Yountville | 707-944-1112 | fax 707-944-1617 | 800-351-1133 | www.vintageinn.com | 68 rooms, 12 suites

"Upscale amenities" and a "peaceful" setting are among the "delightful" attributes of this "friendly" Country French B&B-like Napa lodge boasting "romantic" brick fireplaces in all of its "spacious" rooms and an "outstanding breakfast buffet"; the staff is "amazing, and the "perfect" location serves as a "convenient" launching pad for taking in the wineries and "great restaurants within walking distance"; N.B. guests have access to the spa at sister property Villagio.

Vintners Inn ✕⚘

ROOMS	SERVICE	DINING	FACIL.	COST
25	22	22	22	$275

4350 Barnes Rd. | Santa Rosa | 707-575-7350 | fax 707-575-1426 | 800-421-2584 | www.vintnersinn.com | 38 rooms, 6 suites

For a "relaxing respite in Sonoma County", enthusiasts endorse this "lovely" inn (residing in the midst of the Russian River Valley's wineries) for its "nicely decorated" rooms, "many with vineyard views", "delicious" food at the on-site John Ash & Co. restaurant and "intimate" setting; even more "memorable" are the relatively "affordable" tabs.

Yosemite

Ahwahnee, The ⚑⊕⚘⚐

ROOMS	SERVICE	DINING	FACIL.	COST
20	22	23	24	$449

Yosemite National Park | 209-372-1407 | fax 209-372-1463 | www.yosemitepark.com | 93 rooms, 6 suites, 24 cottages

For fans of "luxurious, rustic living" and "bygone days", this National Park lodging is the right " idea of camping", where the "incomparable" Yosemite setting means you can "enjoy the outdoors", then "come inside and feel pampered"; the "stunning" building, blending elements of the Arts & Crafts Movement with art deco and Native American, boasts "cathedral ceilings", hand-stenciled beams and tapestries, while the "gorgeous" restaurant serves up "the best buffet you'll have anywhere"; still, some are disappointed in the "tired" rooms.

⛝ Château du Sureau ✕⚘⚐

ROOMS	SERVICE	DINING	FACIL.	COST
27	29	28	25	$385

48688 Victoria Ln. | Oakhurst | 559-683-6860 | fax 559-683-0800 | 800-735-2478 | www.chateaudusureau.com | 10 rooms, 1 villa

"This must be what it was like at the country" estates of "nobility in the Gatsby age" muse admirers of this "spectacular" Relais & Châteaux-affiliated "little hideaway" just 20 minutes from Yosemite that's "exquisite in every way" – from the "sumptuous cuisine at Erna's Elderberry House" and "healing magic of the art deco-inspired spa" to the "impeccable service" ("nothing is too much trouble") and "extravagant accommodations"; sure, the prices give pause, but with standards "this high", it's "worth every penny."

Tenaya Lodge at Yosemite ⚑⚐⚘

ROOMS	SERVICE	DINING	FACIL.	COST
19	21	17	20	$285

1122 Hwy. 41 | Fish Camp | 559-683-6555 | fax 559-683-6147 | 800-635-5807 | www.tenayalodge.com | 224 rooms, 20 suites

The word is mixed on this "rustic", but "comfortable" lodging, "convenient" to the park's southern entrance and nearby Sierra National

Forest; though some find a "kid-friendly" "respite" that's a "good base for exploring", others frown over the "fairly long drive from Yosemite Valley", the "noisy", "nothing special" rooms and the "subpar food."

Colorado

TOPS IN STATE

27 | Ritz-Carlton Bachelor Gulch | *Avon*
26 | Little Nell | *Aspen*
St. Regis | *Aspen*
Broadmoor | *Colorado Springs*
Sonnenalp | *Vail*
24 | Lodge & Spa/Cordillera | *Edwards*
Teatro | *Denver*
St Julien | *Boulder*

Aspen

Jerome, Hotel ⊕⌘⌂⌘

22	22	21	19	$570

330 E. Main St. | 970-920-1000 | fax 970-920-2050 | 800-331-7213 | www.hoteljerome.com | 77 rooms, 15 suites

This 1889 Victorian "landmark" "oozing with history" "in the heart of" "chic Aspen" was a "scene"-stealer even "before Versace and Gucci arrived", and after several renovations it's still a "cool place", with "gorgeous" "turn-of-the-century decor" "preserved" in "warm and comfortable" rooms, and "one of the best bars in town"; but while this "grand old" prop in "a skiing mecca" offers such amenities as a fitness center, outdoor pool and access to a nearby spa, some say it's not "the same" since new management took over.

☑ Little Nell, The ✕⌘⌂⌘⌂

27	27	26	25	$810

675 E. Durant Ave. | 970-920-4600 | fax 970-920-4670 | 888-843-6355 | www.thelittlenell.com | 77 rooms, 15 suites

"As long as money is no object" this "ski-in/ski-out" Relais & Châteaux "icon" "on the slopes" of Aspen is "everything a luxury resort should be" – a "perfect mix of style, comfort and service"; with "to-die-for rooms" offering "many thoughtful details" ("like chimneys"), an "outstanding staff", "fabulous dining" (at Montagna, featuring chef Ryan Hardy's locally sourced 'American Alpine' cuisine) and a "pool area with whirlpools and waterfalls" – it's no wonder the smitten say "every place else comes in second."

St. Regis ✕⌘⌂⌘Ⓢ⌂

26	28	24	27	$1000

315 E. Dean St. | 970-920-3300 | fax 970-925-8998 | 888-454-9005 | www.stregisaspen.com | 155 rooms, 24 suites

Get the "royal Aspen treatment" at this "terrific" ski resort with an "amazing location" at the base of the mountain and "within walking distance to everything in town"; expect "excellence in every respect", from the "faultless service" and "luxurious" rooms to the "amazing amenities" that include a "sexy coed spa and grotto" and "live music in the bar" ("lots of jet-setter sightings"); although a small flock of foodniks find Olives restaurant a little "disappointing" and penny-pinchers pout over "absurd" rates, most say this one "has it all."

Beaver Creek

Beaver Creek Lodge 🐾🛶🛷

| 24 | 23 | 21 | 24 | $499 |

26 Avondale Ln. | 970-845-9800 | fax 970-845-8242 | 800-525-7280 |
www.beavercreeklodge.net | 72 suites

"A fairy-tale setting" greets guests at this "something-for-everyone",
all-suite boutique resort in "beautiful" Beaver Creek village that offers
"every comfort imaginable": a "terrific ski-in/ski-out location", "relaxing", "carefully decorated" rooms "with new furniture and fixtures"
(flat-screen TVs, private balconies), "family-oriented" amenities
(babysitting – for a fee, a playground) and nearby spa, golf and upscale "shopping and dining" options.

Lodge & Spa
at Cordillera, The ✕🛶⬆️☺️🛷🔍

| 25 | 23 | 22 | 26 | $549 |

2205 Cordillera Way | Edwards | 970-926-2200 | fax 970-926-2714 |
800-877-3529 | www.cordilleralodge.com | 46 rooms, 10 suites

You'll feel like you're "on top of the planet" when you gaze upon the
"spectacular" sweeping views of the Vail Valley at this "mountain
heaven" 15 minutes from Beaver Creek, 25 minutes west of Vail and
"close to the charming village of Edwards" (there's complimentary shuttle service to both ski resorts); the "secluded" setting and "great food
that can be enjoyed in your cushy room" by a "wood-burning fireplace"
lit by a butler ensure lots of "quiet nights" and a "romantic-as-heck" vibe,
while "tremendous golf" gives you something to do in warmer weather.

Park Hyatt 🚶✕🐾🛶⬆️☺️🛷🔍

| 23 | 23 | 20 | 27 | $650 |

50 W. Thomas Pl. | 970-949-1234 | fax 970-949-4164 | 800-233-1234 |
www.parkhyatt.com | 184 rooms, 6 suites

"Wow" exclaim escapees to this "excellent hotel" providing a "fabulous" "ski-in/ski-out" "slopeside location" in "posh Beaver Creek" and
"spacious rooms" sporting "beautiful views"; "top-notch" service that
includes "valets for your skies", an "amazing flight of water experiences" in the "terrific spa", "nightly s'mores" "at the fire pit" ("a silver
fox is a regular visitor") and an "incredible atmosphere" make up for a
kitchen that "could use an overhaul."

Pines Lodge ✕🛶🛷

▽ | 24 | 28 | 27 | 21 | $629 |

141 Scott Hill Rd. | 970-754-7200 | fax 970-754-7295 | 866-605-7625 |
www.rockresorts.com | 60 rooms, 21 townhouses, 12 condos

They "really know service" at this slopeside "favorite" right among aspen
and pine groves, whose ski-in/ski-out feature attracts winter-sports
fanatics; it's also "highly recommended" for other reasons: "well-
appointed" accommodations (including condos and townhouses), in-
room massages and the acclaimed Grouse Mountain Grill, whose food
gourmets guarantee "should not be missed"; N.B. there are complimentary shuttles to Beaver Creek Village, a regional shopping mecca.

⚡ Ritz-Carlton
Bachelor Gulch 🚶🍴🛶☺️🛷🔍

| 28 | 27 | 24 | 28 | $795 |

0130 Daybreak Ridge | Avon | 970-748-6200 | fax 970-343-1070 |
800-576-5582 | www.ritzcarlton.com | 139 rooms, 41 suites

"A true ski-in/ski-out getaway", this "luxurious log cabin" "oh-so-
convenient to the ski lift" "doesn't get any more perfect" thanks to its

ROOMS | SERVICE | DINING | FACIL. | COST

"spectacular" surroundings; with "everything you'd expect" from a "magnificent resort", including "casually elegant rooms", most with balconies, "world-class service", a "sublime spa" with "outdoor-inspired treatments" ("the grotto is fantastic") and "great" dining at the "recently added Spago outpost", it's the "best" choice in Beaver Creek.

Clark

Home Ranch 👯

ROOMS	SERVICE	DINING	FACIL.	COST
-	-	-	-	$400

54880 RCR 129 | 970-879-1780 | fax 970-879-1795 | www.homeranch.com | 8 cabins, 6 rooms

For an upscale "cowboy" experience, this "fantastic" Relais & Châteaux guest ranch 18 miles north of Steamboat Springs is a "wonderful" choice; you can feast on "amazing" dinners, "learn to horseback ride" and enjoy activities like hiking and cross-country skiing in rustic surroundings; accommodations include rooms in a main lodge, and one- to three-bedroom cabins with wood-burning stoves, Indian rugs and down comforters.

Colorado Springs

☑ Broadmoor, The 👯✗🍴🛁⚓☝☺🔍

ROOMS	SERVICE	DINING	FACIL.	COST
26	26	24	28	$420

1 Lake Ave. | 719-634-7711 | fax 719-577-5700 | 866-837-9520 | www.broadmoor.com | 593 rooms, 107 suites

"A true American treasure" laud loyalists of this "wonderful institution" that's "been around for years and years" and rightly so; from the "world-class" golf (via Donald Ross, Robert Trent Jones and Jack Nicklaus) to the "fantastic service" to the "loads of dining options" to the "incredible" mountain views from "luxurious rooms", it prompts a few to consider spending "their life savings to stay" for good.

Cliff House at Pikes Peak ✗🌐🛁

ROOMS	SERVICE	DINING	FACIL.	COST
-	-	-	-	$199

306 Canon Ave. | Manitou Springs | 719-685-3000 | fax 719-685-3913 | 888-212-7000 | www.thecliffhouse.com | 38 suites, 17 studios

At the foot of Pikes Peak rests this Manitou Springs "find" (45 minutes south of Denver and 10 minutes from Colorado Springs) offering "quaint" rooms with WiFi, Aveda bath products, jetted tubs, fireplaces and other amenities that "don't interfere with the historic" Victorian ambiance; the "sweeping" wraparound porch is an ideal location for dining on "awesome" fare and wines, while the "great staff" brings it all together; N.B. high-tech, state-of-the-art meeting and event spaces draw the corporate crowd.

Denver

Boulderado, Hotel 🌐🛁

ROOMS	SERVICE	DINING	FACIL.	COST
▽ 19	20	20	17	$214

2115 13th St. | Boulder | 303-442-4344 | fax 303-442-4378 | 800-433-4344 | www.boulderado.com | 139 rooms, 21 suites

"They don't build them like this anymore" sigh nostalgics of this "grand" "Old West" National Landmark in Boulder (45 minutes from Denver) and "just a short walk" from the Downtown pedestrian Pearl Street mall; globe-trotting guests gawk over the "grand lobby" overseen by a "warm and inviting staff" that points foodies to chef John Platt's Q's restaurant "on the mez", then to "vintage-style" rooms with "quirky antiques"; but "stay in the old part if you can" because the chambers in the "new, modern" section are "sterile."

Brown Palace Hotel ⓗ✻♨ⓢ | 20 | 22 | 21 | 21 | $289

321 17th St. | 303-297-3111 | fax 303-312-5900 | 800-321-2599 | www.brownpalace.com | 190 rooms, 52 suites

Admirers of this "venerable" 1892 Downtown "classic" take a "lovely look at the past with a modern twist" at this "majestic" "beauty"; highlights include a soaring atrium lobby, "exceptional" suites (with LCD flat-screen TVs), "fine dining" (an "amazing" Sunday brunch, "superb" afternoon tea), a unique spa (with soaks that draw from a natural well located 750 feet beneath the hotel) and an "excellent" staff; calls for a "needed upgrade" are being addressed by ongoing remodeling.

C Lazy U Ranch ✻♨✎ | ▽ 22 | 24 | 23 | 26 | $350

3640 Colorado Hwy. 125 | Granby | 970-887-3344 | fax 970-887-3917 | www.clazyu.com | 35 rooms, 5 suites

Those who've "never been to a guest ranch" "won't go anywhere else" after they visit this 1946 family-friendly outpost west of Denver; "impeccable service" keeps all activities – a children's program, a 12,000-sq.-ft. indoor riding arena and trap shooting – running smoothly, while the "outstanding", Western-influenced accommodations include private cabins; in sum, it's the "most fun you'll have with your clothes on"; N.B. there's a minimum weeklong stay.

Curtis, The ✻♨ | - | - | - | - | $339

1405 Curtis St. | 303-571-0300 | fax 303-825-4301 | 800-525-6651 | www.thecurtis.com | 334 rooms, 2 suites

"Welcome to the hippest hotel in Denver" proclaim proponents of this Downtown "retro modern" new kid on the block that provides "as much fun as you can have" amid a "cool" pop-culture setting; given the comic books and a five-and-dime candy kiosk in the lobby, wake-up calls from a crooning Elvis (in rooms outfitted with modern furnishings, flat-screen TVs and iPod docks), campy-themed floors with names like "One-Hit Wonders" and "Chick Flick", and a "great" Eclectic restaurant, it's no wonder that some locals choose it for their "out-of-town guests."

Denver Marriott City Center | ▽ 19 | 20 | 16 | 19 | $184

1701 California St. | 303-297-1300 | fax 303-298-7474 | 800-228-9290 | www.marriott.com | 601 rooms, 14 suites

If you want to stay in the "middle of all the Downtown Denver action" *and* "make it to the convention on time, look no further" than this "decent" "conference hotel" overseen by an "attentive staff" that's the "standout" feature here; though the "rooms are cavernous" and "well designed", boasting "huge showers that could fit a dozen people", discriminating guests declare that it's just a "typical Marriott" with a "boring bar" and a "work-out room that needs to be updated."

Grand Hyatt ♨✎ | ▽ 22 | 23 | 19 | 21 | $259

1750 Welton St. | 303-295-1234 | fax 303-292-2472 | 800-233-1234 | www.hyatt.com | 486 rooms, 26 suites

"Fabulous service" is one of the draws at this "beautiful hotel" in a "convenient" Downtown location that "lives up to its name", exhibiting "excellent decor" ("especially in the lobby bar area"), nightly live piano music in the lounge, "wonderful mountain views" from "lovely rooms" outfitted with "comfy beds" and a "must-see rooftop bar"; it's a "great value", even if some foodies find the "expensive" food "mediocre, at best"; N.B. room renovations were recently completed.

Hyatt Regency Convention Center ⓢ   21 | 20 | 17 | 22 | $175

650 15th St. | 303-436-1234 | fax 303-486-4450 | 800-233-1234 | www.denverregency.hyatt.com | 1028 rooms, 72 suites

This "impressive" Downtown chainster pleases patrons with rooms sporting "fancy flat-panel TVs" and "beautiful views of the Rockies and Pikes Peak"; other pluses are the "friendly" staff, a mile-high bar with "spectacular panoramic" city vistas, a "terrific gym" and a pool that's "just about the best ever."

JW Marriott at Cherry Creek ⅍♨ⓢ   25 | 25 | 20 | 23 | $309

150 Clayton Ln. | 303-316-2700 | fax 303-316-4697 | 800-228-9290 | www.jwmarriottdenver.com | 191 rooms, 5 suites

A "wonderful visit" awaits guests at this "gorgeous" chainster that feels like "an independent boutique hotel" just "minutes from Downtown" in the Cherry Creek shopping district; "modern" and "dog-friendly" ("watch out for poochies in the lobby"), it satisfies sojourners with a "superb" staff that "bends over backwards to make sure your needs are met" and "nice rooms" (some with panoramic mountain views) that are "perfect for business or a personal getaway."

Loews ♛⅍♨   ▽ 21 | 23 | 19 | 17 | $159

4150 E. Mississippi Ave. | 303-782-9300 | fax 303-758-6542 | 800-345-9172 | www.loewshotels.com | 166 rooms, 17 suites

"Service, service and more service" distinguishes this "charming hotel" whose staff "pampers you" and "remembers your name"; while in an "unlikely location" – near the Cherry Creek Mall, but "a bit away" from Downtown ("forget about walking if it's winter", though there's a shuttle service) – it's "perfect for business"-types and animal lovers ("they allow pets"); even if a few grouse it's "nothing special", advocates assert "it's not your typical hotel – so points for that."

Monaco, Hotel ⅍♨ⓢ   22 | 23 | 21 | 20 | $349

1717 Champa St. | 303-296-1717 | fax 303-296-1818 | 800-990-1303 | www.monaco-denver.com | 157 rooms, 32 suites

This "quirky but fun" Downtown Kimpton boutique hotel in a "historic building" acquires accolades for its "warm service", "eclectic" rooms bedecked with "big beds, high ceilings", "lots of color" and pet-friendly policy ("don't forget to ask for your complimentary" "loaner goldfish" if you arrive sans-pooch); a "fantastic restaurant", "enjoyable wine hour" and "nice massages" in the "vibrant lobby buzzing with activity" make it a "good choice" for both business and pleasure.

St Julien Hotel & Spa ✕♨ⓢ   26 | 25 | 19 | 25 | $285

900 Walnut St. | Boulder | 720-406-9696 | fax 720-406-9697 | 877-303-0900 | www.stjulien.com | 189 rooms, 12 suites

An "über-cool hotel" "right smack in Downtown" near "shopping, restaurants and nightlife", this "upscale" "favorite" that's "perfect for a romantic stay" showcases "fantastic Flatiron views", "terrific rooms" bedecked with "amazingly comfortable beds and glorious baths", a "beautiful pool and spa" ("loved the pedicure cocktail combo"), "live music in the lobby", "five-star service" and "complimentary bikes" for "cruising" around town; while some warn the food "is nothing to write home about", others counter "dining and drinks are tops."

Teatro, Hotel ✕⊕✿♨ — 24 | 26 | 25 | 20 | $269

1100 14th St. | 303-228-1100 | fax 303-228-1101 | 888-727-1200 | www.hotelteatro.com | 102 rooms, 7 suites, 1 apartment

"A sublime experience" awaits guests at this "historic boutique hotel in an "excellent" Downtown location in the theater district across from the Denver Center for the Performing Arts; "from the elegant lobby" and "impeccable service" to the "trendy", "immaculate" and "modern rooms" ("liked the chaise lounge, work desk and extra amenities") to the "best food" at Restaurant Kevin Taylor, it's a "beautiful" "oasis."

Westin Tabor Center ♔✿♨Ⓢ — 21 | 19 | 18 | 19 | $349

1672 Lawrence St. | 303-572-9100 | fax 303-572-7288 | 800-937-8461 | www.westin.com | 421 rooms, 9 suites

The "fantastic" location "right in the heart of the action" and within walking distance of Downtown's 16th Street Mall is the highlight of this "solid" chainster with "mountain views", a "cool pool", "competent service" and "quality" dining at the Palm; still, some say it's a "typical", "uninspiring" convention hotel.

Keystone

Keystone Resort ♔⌚✿♨⬆Ⓢ⛷⚲ — 20 | 20 | 20 | 23 | $189

22010 Hwy. 6 | 970-496-4000 | fax 970-496-4215 | 888-222-9298 | www.keystone.snow.com | 1173 condos, 255 rooms

"Endless activities" welcome visitors to this "awesome family vacation spot" in a "gorgeous" "storybook setting" 90 miles from the Denver Airport that's "wonderful for skiers", but "even better in the summer" when biking, hiking, fishing and boating are available; the "large complex" includes "rooms, apartments and lodges", but a few feel there's "nothing spectacularly exceptional" about this resort.

Pagosa Springs

Keyah Grande ✕♨Ⓢ — - | - | - | - | $895

13211 W. Hwy. 160 | 970-731-1160 | fax 970-731-1162 | 800-577-9769 | www.keyahgrande.com | 8 suites

Luxury and intimacy await guests at this gated 4,000-acre all-inclusive resort in the San Juan Mountains southwest of Denver that boasts suites outfitted with whirlpools, wet bars, sophisticated artwork – and a one-to-one staff-to-guest-ratio; activities include horseback riding, skiing, an on-site spa and nearby whitewater rafting, and the on-site restaurant features a bar, lounge and 5,000-bottle wine collection; N.B. the per diem rate includes breakfast, dinner and one activity.

Telluride

Peaks Resort & Golden Door Spa, The ♔⌚✿♨⬆Ⓢ⛷⚲ — ▽ 20 | 18 | 15 | 25 | $189

136 Country Club Dr. | 970-728-6800 | fax 970-728-6175 | 800-789-2220 | www.thepeaksresort.com | 136 rooms, 38 suites, 33 penthouses, 15 cabins

The highlights of this "true ski-in/ski-out" Telluride resort are the "location" with "spectacular views" of the Colorado Rockies and the "great facilities" that include a well-regarded, full-service, renovated Golden Door spa with wellness classes, and a supervised children's program for tots as young as 12 weeks; however, some find it a "pity" that "multiple ownership changes" have meant "little continuity in service."

Vail

Lodge at Vail, The 🏃✕🏊🏋🛷 | 23 | 24 | 22 | 25 | $519 |

174 E. Gore Creek Dr. | 970-476-5011 | fax 970-476-7425 | 877-528-7625 | www.rockresorts.com | 107 rooms, 38 suites

Guests at this "unbeatable" "ski-in/ski-out" RockResorts property in a "fantastic location" "in the heart of Vail village" are gaga not only for its "glamour, pampering and great service" but for its "old-world charm", "luxurious rooms", the "best brunch in Vail" and "awesome pool and hot tub" ("it's worth the cost"); better yet, "it's outstanding even in the summer, when hiking and biking await"; N.B. a 7,500-sq.-ft. state-of-the-art spa recently debuted.

Sonnenalp 🏃✕🏊🏋⬆️☺️🔍 | 27 | 25 | 23 | 27 | $525 |

20 Vail Rd. | 970-476-5656 | fax 970-476-1639 | 800-654-8312 | www.sonnenalp.com | 115 suites, 12 rooms

"Sinking into the down bed is like skiing in fresh, deep powder" sigh smitten surveyors of this "real touch of Europe" "deep in the heart of Vail Village"; you'll "yodel in delight over the bountiful breakfasts", "spacious rooms with heated bathroom floors", "wonderful spa", "beautiful indoor/outdoor pool" and "superb" staff, plus the wing added a few years ago means it might not be as hard to get into during high season.

Vail Cascade   ▽ | 22 | 21 | 19 | 25 | $699 |
Resort & Spa 🏃🏋☺️🛷🔍

1300 Westhaven Dr. | 970-476-7111 | fax 970-479-7050 | 800-282-4183 | www.vailcascade.com | 165 rooms, 27 suites, 80 condos, 18 resort homes

"It's big, but it works" declare disciples of this "dark-wooded, leather and antler-motifed" Vail resort; the "beautiful slope-side" setting has "true ski-in/ski-out" access, while the "peaceful" spa (a "bit of a hike" away) is nevertheless "terrific"; regulars also rave about staffers who "remember you year after year" and are pleased by the $30-million renovation, completed in spring 2008, that updated the restaurant, bar, pool, deck, rooms and conference facilities.

Connecticut

Greenwich

Homestead Inn ✕⊕ | 21 | 25 | 27 | 17 | $495 |

420 Field Point Rd. | 203-869-7500 | fax 203-869-7502 | www.homesteadinn.com | 11 rooms, 7 suites

Chef-inkeeper Thomas Henkelmann's "gracious", "delicious" self-titled Relais Gourmand New French eatery (voted the No. 1 Restaurant in our *Connecticut Restaurants* Survey) is the "real thing" at this "exquisite" "old-money B&B" "in the heart of Greenwich" that dates from 1799; satisfied suppers "go for the food and stay over to relax" in the "antiques-filled" rooms, complete with Frette linens and bold colors and serviced by a "superb" staff; N.B. kids under 14 not permitted.

	ROOMS	SERVICE	DINING	FACIL.	COST

Hyatt Regency Ⓢ

| 18 | 20 | 17 | 20 | $289 |

1800 E. Putnam Ave. | Old Greenwich | 203-637-1234 | fax 203-637-2940 |
800-233-1234 | www.greenwich.hyatt.com | 361 rooms, 12 suites

"Live trees, a waterfall and bridges" make the four-story lobby of this
"solid" Old Greenwich hotel "feel like a botanical garden", while the
"friendly" staff, "fabulous weekend brunch" and full-service spa are
further pluses; but even though it's one of the "best places to stay in
the area", it "needs an overhaul" say critics who complain it's "not
what you'd expect in this affluent" neighborhood.

Ledyard

Foxwoods Resort ♨ ⌐ Ⓢ

| 20 | 19 | 19 | 21 | $225 |

39 Norwich Westerly Rd. | Mashantucket | 860-312-3000 |
fax 860-312-5044 | 800-369-9663 | www.foxwoods.com | 1416 rooms

With three hotels (not counting the separately run MGM Grand),
340,000 sq. ft. of casino space, 30 restaurants, spas, theaters and two
18-hole golf courses, even those who loathe gambling find something to
do at this "mini-metropolis in the middle of nowhere" (it lies 50 minutes
from Hartford, two-and-a-half hours from NYC); although critics report
the "rooms and public areas need a face-lift" and it can be "impossible
to get a dinner reservation" at prime times, most find it a "pleasant
surprise" and advise staying in the "elegant" Grand Pequot Tower.

NEW MGM Grand at Foxwoods ☕ ♔ ♨ ⌐ Ⓢ

| - | - | - | - | $347 |

39 Norwich-Westerly Rd. | Mashantucket | 866-646-0050 |
fax 860-312-8384 | 800-488-7777 | www.mgmatfoxwoods.com |
688 rooms, 137 suites

The latest lodging at the Foxwoods resort, this newly opened tower
features luxe rooms designed by Dallas' Wilson & Associates (Arizona
Biltmore, Four Seasons Hong Kong) featuring 300-thread-count linens,
WiFi, 32-inch high-def, flat-screen TVs and iPod docks; two Rees Jones–
designed courses, a golf academy, an Italian restarant with outdoor
seating and a spa join the 50,000-sq.-ft. casino to offer plenty of action.

Mystic

Mystic Marriott Ⓢ

| 20 | 20 | 19 | 21 | $239 |

625 North Rd. | Groton | 860-446-2600 | fax 860-446-2601 |
800-228-9290 | www.mysticmarriott.com | 281 rooms, 4 suites

With a handy location for visiting "Mystic, Groton and the other beautiful towns" nearby, this otherwise "standard Marriott" set in a yellow
mid-rise off of I-95 boasts "updated" rooms with down comforters,
"attentive" service and a "nice" indoor pool, steakhouse and Elizabeth
Arden Red Door spa; N.B. there's shuttle service to the Mohegan Sun.

New Preston

Boulders, The ♨

| 20 | 21 | 21 | 19 | $365 |

E. Shore Rd. | 860-868-0541 | fax 860-868-1925 | 800-455-1565 |
www.bouldersinn.com | 18 rooms, 2 suites

"Warm and cozy in the cold months and beautiful in the fall", this "upscale" but "unpretentious" B&B 45 minutes from Hartford on New

	ROOMS	SERVICE	DINING	FACIL.	COST

Preston's Lake Waramaug is "what a New England inn should be" – the water view from the dining room alone is "worth the trip"; the accommodations, divided among two buildings and some "lovely" hillside cottages, may seem a "little precious" to some, but most feel that the "fabulous setting" makes up for it; N.B. no kids under 12 permitted.

Winvian ♨

	-	-	-	-	$1450

155 Alain White Rd. | Morris | 860-567-9600 | fax 860-567-9660 | www.winvian.com | 18 cottages, 1 suite

Melding "luxury with creativity" in the Litchfield Hills, this "fascinating", "romantic" sister property to Vermont's Pitcher Inn (and a member of Relais & Châteaux) attracts monied guests in search of a "special different world" – its individually designed cabins include a Medieval cottage, a restored helicopter and an actual tree house; on a more traditional note, there's an Eclectic restaurant, a spa, a fly-fishing pond and cross-country skiing on-site; N.B. all meals and liquor (but not wine) are included in rates.

Norwich

Mohegan Sun Casino Hotel ♨♨Ⓢ

23	20	22	23	$299

1 Mohegan Sun Blvd. | Uncasville | 860-862-8000 | fax 860-862-7419 | 888-226-7711 | www.mohegansun.com | 1015 rooms, 185 suites

A "piece of Vegas" "in the middle of Connecticut", this "flashy", totally "surreal" 34-story tower nestled near Norwich comes with "more dining options than you can shake a stick at" (the "awesome" choices include Todd English's Tuscany), a two-story mall with over 30 stores, a sports arena, performance spaces and, for the kids, a "fantastic game room"; its "sleek" accommodations are enhanced by "stunning baths" and "quick, polite" service; N.B. the massive new Casino of the Wind includes a Jimmy Buffet Margaritaville.

Spa at Norwich Inn, The ☕♨Ⓢ⚲

20	23	20	23	$225

607 W. Thames St. | 860-886-2401 | fax 860-886-9483 | 800-275-4772 | www.thespaatnorwichinn.com | 45 rooms, 4 suites, 51 villas

"You'll relax here even if you don't want to" thanks to this "beautiful" retreat's "country charm", "friendly" staff and "peaceful grounds" with rooms in both a 1930 Colonial main house and "much-nicer" condolike villas; though some feel its accommodations "need a face-lift", the "exquisite" spa treatments receive raves – plus you can have your "gourmet lunch while wearing a big, white, fluffy bathrobe"; P.S. "for a break from the healthiness", the "nearby gambling adds some excitement."

Old Saybrook

Saybrook Point Inn & Spa ♨♨Ⓢ

21	21	21	20	$329

2 Bridge St. | 860-395-2000 | fax 860-388-1504 | 800-243-0212 | www.saybrook.com | 65 rooms, 16 suites

A "charming" New England inn right on the Connecticut River and Long Island Sound, this "comfortable" spot two hours from New York City boasts "roomy" accommodations with "inviting fireplaces" (about half have water views) and a "restaurant with a varied menu"; but those who find "nothing spectacular" complain there's "no beach, just a concrete marina" and conclude that the spa may be "high-end for Old Saybrook", but it's "unfortunately middle-of-the-road" for most other places.

Washington

Mayflower Inn & Spa 🔭 [S] 🎾 | 27 | 25 | 23 | 25 | $550

118 Woodbury Rd. | 860-868-9466 | fax 860-868-1497 | www.mayflowerinn.com | 19 rooms, 11 suites

Expect "amenities galore" - marble baths, fireplaces, 18th-century antiques, plus WiFi and flat-panel TVs - inside the "stunning" rooms at this "bucolic" Relais & Châteaux Dutch Colonial "hideaway" set in four separate buildings on 58 "serene" acres; its restaurant gets mixed reviews, but the "world-class" spa wows fans who label this "expensive" Litchfield County getaway "fit for a Goldman Sachs partner"; N.B. no children under 12.

Westport

Inn at National Hall, The [H] 🔭 | 27 | 23 | 17 | 19 | $325

2 Post Rd. W. | 203-221-1351 | fax 203-221-0276 | 800-628-4255 | www.innatnationalhall.com | 8 rooms, 8 suites

"It doesn't get better than staying right on the river in Downtown Westport" say fans of this Relais & Châteaux "European boutique" inn that's "worth the splurge" (it "costs an arm and a leg") and features an on-site spa; each of the "truly unique" rooms in its 1873 Italianate building is a "jewel" bedecked with fanciful, hand-painted walls, and although there's nowhere to eat in-house, it's just a "short walk to the restaurants and shops on Main Street."

Delaware

Rehoboth Beach

Bellmoor, The 🛏 🔭 [S] | 25 | 22 | 19 | 22 | $325

6 Christian St. | 302-227-5800 | fax 302-227-0323 | 800-425-2355 | www.thebellmoor.com | 56 rooms, 21 suites, 1 cottage

You'll "feel like you aren't anywhere near the sand" at this "surprisingly elegant" Rehoboth Beach B&B with "immaculate rooms", including "top-shelf" suites on a child-free "private floor"; sybarites savor the "divine" massages while relaxing at its "upstairs pool" and "wonderful" spa, and surveyors unanimously swoon over the "delightful" complimentary breakfasts "overlooking the garden"; alas, there's no full-service eatery, so for other meals, ask the "helpful" staff for nearby dining recommendations.

Wilmington

du Pont, Hotel 🍴 [H] 🐕 | 24 | 25 | 25 | 22 | $409

11th & Market Sts. | 302-594-3100 | fax 302-594-3108 | 800-441-9019 | www.hoteldupont.com | 206 rooms, 11 suites

"Intimate class" abounds at this "stately" "old-world" haunt, the "grande dame of Wilmington", that's "still genteel" if a bit "tired" after 95 years; its "gorgeous" rooms ("can they come decorate my house?")

include modern amenities like "large soaking tubs", the staff has a "can-do attitude" and the Green Room's Sunday brunch (reservations suggested) is "phenomenal."

Inn at Montchanin Village, The ✕ ⊕ ⋒ ₳

ROOMS	SERVICE	DINING	FACIL.	COST
26	24	25	21	$185

Kirk Rd. & Rte. 100 | Montchanin | 302-888-2133 | fax 302-888-0389 | 800-269-2473 | www.montchanin.com | 12 houses, 16 suites

Three miles from Wilmington, this former mining village turned "lovely country inn" (a member of Small Luxury Hotels of the World) is "too charming and unique for words", made up of restored "workers' houses" in a garden setting that's well-situated for "weekend escapes", since it's "close to Brandywine Valley sites"; the "at-home feel" extends to the "well-appointed" rooms and suites, and epicures label the "outstanding", "whimsically purr-fect" Krazy-Kat "highly recommended"; N.B. a spa was in the works at Survey time.

District of Columbia

TOPS IN DISTRICT

26	Four Seasons
	Mandarin Oriental
25	Ritz-Carlton
	Ritz-Carlton Georgetown
24	Willard InterCont.
	Hay-Adams
23	Sofitel
	St. Regis

Washington, DC

NEW Donovan House ₳

ROOMS	SERVICE	DINING	FACIL.	COST
-	-	-	-	$699

1155 14th St. NW | Washington | 202-737-1200 | fax 202-521-1410 | 800-383-6900 | www.thompsonhotels.com | 158 rooms, 17 suites, 18 studios

Sleek, sexy and relatively cheap, this Holiday Inn remake on burgeoning Thomas Circle, by the hotel group that owns NYC's 60 Thompson, offers chic rooms with leather wraparound beds and baths boasting Kiehl's toiletries and ceiling-mounted spiral showers; other highlights are the guest-only roof deck, pool and lounge, state-of-the-art fitness center and restaurant courtesy of Equinox's Todd Gray.

Fairmont, The ⚶ ₳ Ⓢ

ROOMS	SERVICE	DINING	FACIL.	COST
23	23	21	23	$499

2401 M St. NW | Washington | 202-429-2400 | fax 202-457-5010 | 800-257-7544 | www.fairmont.com | 392 rooms, 23 suites

One of DC's "most amenable" staffs keeps things running smoothly at this "beautiful" West End venue where the "airy" rooms give travelers a "feeling of luxury and spaciousness", making it "great for a conference" or event; "welcoming" touches like a "fabulous" flower-filled courtyard, "innovative" brunch and complimentary "cucumber water and fresh fruit" served in the "well-appointed" lobby distinguish it from a host of other "business"-oriented choices that share its "close-to-everything" (by Metro or cab) location.

	ROOMS	SERVICE	DINING	FACIL.	COST
DIST. OF COLUMBIA – WASH.					

ⓩ Four Seasons ⚹✕⌗♨ⓢ
26 | 27 | 25 | 25 | $595

2800 Pennsylvania Ave. NW | Washington | 202-342-0444 |
fax 202-944-2076 | 800-332-3442 | www.fourseasons.com |
160 rooms, 51 suites

"Terrific" even before its makeover, this "amazing" hotel on the edge of Georgetown offers rooms, dining and service "you just can't get anywhere else"; "every stay tops the last" say regulars who relish its feeling of "understated luxury", from the "discreet" staff to the "lovely, classical" accommodations to the sightings of "George Clooney eating at the next table"; in sum, you've "got everything you need" at this "fabulous" "power" property.

George, Hotel ✕⌗
21 | 23 | 23 | 18 | $409

15 E St. NW | Washington | 202-347-4200 | fax 202-347-4213 |
800-576-8331 | www.hotelgeorge.com | 138 rooms, 1 suite

Well-situated for "people with business on the Hill", this "chic" Kimpton boutique boasts "big, luscious beds and amazing room service" that ready them for "work" the next day; "celeb-spotting" at the bar and in the "hot" French-accented restaurant, Bistro Bis ("especially pleasant at breakfast"), counterbalances the "small" (but "artfully" designed) rooms and limited public facilities.

Hay-Adams, The ✕⊕⌗♨
24 | 26 | 23 | 22 | $515

800 16th St. NW | Washington | 202-638-6600 | fax 202-638-2716 |
800-424-5054 | www.hayadams.com | 125 rooms, 20 suites

Guests immerse themselves in the "mix of politics and intrigue" at this "sophisticated" "classic" that's across from the White House and known for the "power-breakfast" scene in its Lafayette Room, as well as for its rooftop bar and service that treats every visitor "like royalty" ("I doubt Hay or Adams would be treated better!"); the "comfortable" rooms that face Lafayette Park Square have "picture-postcard views", leading loyalists to aver "it doesn't get better than this in DC – unless you're counting the Lincoln Bedroom!"

Helix, Hotel ⚹☕⌗
▽ 23 | 21 | 16 | 19 | $329

1430 Rhode Island Ave. NW | Washington | 202-462-9001 |
fax 202-332-3519 | 800-706-1202 | www.hotelhelix.com |
160 rooms, 18 suites

A "boutique hipster" that's maybe "a little over the top with the '60s theme", this "funkalicious" Logan Circle lodging via Kimpton is all "retro" "Pop Art", with "leopard-print robes" in the "interesting" rooms and a "lively", "bass-thumping" bar; "you'll either love it or hate it", but those in the former group soak up all the "silly" "fun."

JW Marriott ♨
21 | 21 | 17 | 21 | $339

1331 Pennsylvania Ave. NW | Washington | 202-393-2000 |
fax 202-626-6991 | 800-228-9290 | www.marriott.com | 738 rooms,
34 suites

An "unbeatable" location just two blocks from the White House makes this "quality" "mega-Marriott" "wonderful" for sightseeing families as well as suits seeking a "solid business and convention facility"; pampered guests report the "services on the concierge level far exceed" average, and most find even the "small" rooms "comfortable", though a few shrug "run-of-the-mill."

[NEW] Liaison Capitol Hill

ROOMS	SERVICE	DINING	FACIL.	COST
-	-	-	-	$209

415 New Jersey Ave. NW | Washington | 202-638-1616 | fax 202-638-0707 | 866-246-2203 | www.affinia.com | 343 rooms

An urbane recent arrival on Capitol Hill, this Affinia-branded retreat (a $12-million redo of a former Holiday Inn) offers guests customized comforts like a pillow menu and in-room spa services, along with a sophisticated lobby and spectacular views from its rooftop bar; celebrity chef Art Smith's restaurant, Art & Soul, opened post-Survey and features his take on Mid-Atlantic cuisine.

Madera, Hotel 👪🍴🐾

ROOMS	SERVICE	DINING	FACIL.	COST
▽ 20	19	17	15	$359

1310 New Hampshire Ave. NW | Washington | 202-296-7600 | fax 202-293-2476 | 800-430-1202 | www.hotelmadera.com | 82 rooms

"A real find in an easy-to-reach" area "convenient" to Dupont Circle, this "cool" Kimpton boutique in a converted 1940s apartment building has "spacious", "well-appointed" rooms, some of them themed - e.g. the 'cardio room' comes complete with its own work-out equipment; a "helpful" staff, fun "bar scene" and the popular New American restaurant Firefly round out the picture, which has gotten more eco-friendly with a recent renovation.

Madison, A Loews Hotel, The 🐾Ⓢ

ROOMS	SERVICE	DINING	FACIL.	COST
19	21	18	18	$319

1177 15th St. NW | Washington | 202-862-1600 | fax 202-785-1255 | 800-424-8577 | www.loewshotels.com | 337 rooms, 16 suites

Many fabled guests have stayed at this "fairly luxurious" "business person's hotel" in the heart of Downtown with a "European" "boutique" feel and "efficient" staff; the "solid" rooms feature "comfortable bedding", American Empire and Georgian furnishings, and "lovely bath products", while the Palette restaurant offers a "creative menu"; still, some find the experience "stuffy" and wonder whether this "classic" "has been eclipsed by newcomers."

Mandarin Oriental 🍴🐾🔭Ⓢ

ROOMS	SERVICE	DINING	FACIL.	COST
27	25	26	26	$590

1330 Maryland Ave. SW | Washington | 202-554-8588 | fax 202-554-8999 | 888-888-1778 | www.mandarinoriental.com | 347 rooms, 53 suites

"East meets West" in "luxurious", "feng shui-inspired" rooms and suites with "beautiful views" of the Tidal Basin and Jefferson Memorial at this "stunning" property; a "first-class" spa, "Zen-like" vibe and "exceptional dining options" (including the "not-to-be-missed" New American CityZen and Asian-accented Café MoZU) mean some sybarites "have to be dragged from the hotel to go sightseeing" - which is just as well, since the "only real problem (other than cost) is an isolated location" that's a "cab ride from everywhere."

Monaco, Hotel 👪Ⓗ🐾🔭

ROOMS	SERVICE	DINING	FACIL.	COST
20	21	19	18	$459

700 F St. NW | Washington | 202-628-7177 | fax 202-628-7277 | 800-649-1202 | www.monaco-dc.com | 166 rooms, 17 suites

"Close to everything" ("restaurants, Verizon Center, clubs" and museums), this former "neo-classical marble-and-granite government building" is now a "funky, fun" Kimpton boutique featuring a "delightful lobby and outdoor dining courtyard" that's favored by DC's "young and chic"; "keen design" marks the "adorable" (if "a little tight") accommodations where "huge tapestries" lend a "sultanlike" feel and "nice" staffers are the crowning touch.

	ROOMS	SERVICE	DINING	FACIL.	COST
Palomar, Hotel 👪 🐕 🏋	23	20	18	19	$359

2121 P St. NW | Washington | 202-448-1800 | fax 202-448-1801 | 877-866-3070 | www.hotelpalomar-dc.com | 317 rooms, 18 suites

With "comfortable rooms, a decent gym, free Internet" and a "quaint" setting close to Dupont Circle and Georgetown, this Kimpton apartment-house conversion is "definitely worth a try, especially if you're traveling with Fido", since it's "super dog-friendly"; it's also "quirky, in a pleasant way" ("tiger-stripe robes and leopard-print bedspreads"), with "great evening wine-and-cheese gatherings" where visitors pick up tips from locals, staffers and other guests, so few mind that the restaurant doesn't live up to the rest of the package.

	ROOMS	SERVICE	DINING	FACIL.	COST
Park Hyatt 👪 🍴 🛏 🐕 🏋	24	23	22	21	$575

1201 24th St. NW | Washington | 202-789-1234 | fax 202-419-6795 | 800-633-7313 | www.parkhyatt.com | 205 rooms, 20 suites

For a "business trip or leisurely getaway", "park yourself" at this "oasis of calm and sophistication" in the "fashionable West End", opt for a "beautifully appointed" deluxe room and don't miss the "fantastic spalike bathroom"; all appreciate the "terrific" regional American restaurant and "top-notch" service that's "less stuffy than competing high-end hotels", but old-schoolers are put off by the "minimalist" decor and recent renovations they say place "form over function."

	ROOMS	SERVICE	DINING	FACIL.	COST
Renaissance Mayflower [H] 🐕	21	21	18	20	$369

1127 Connecticut Ave. NW | Washington | 202-347-3000 | fax 202-776-9182 | 800-228-7697 | www.renaissancehotels.com | 583 rooms, 74 suites

A "legend" among Downtown hotels, this "centrally located", recently "refurbished" "grande dame" "reeks of political movers and shakers" - not to mention "brides, blue bloods, blowhards" and quite a few curious tourists checking out the place New York's disgraced former governor Eliot Spitzer met his call girl; the "lovely common areas" and "suites with all the comforts of home" make "you feel rich", but dissenters, citing the "cranky staff" and "too many meetings and events", smell a "faded flower."

	ROOMS	SERVICE	DINING	FACIL.	COST
Ritz-Carlton, The 👪 🐕 🏋	26	26	23	26	$700

1150 22nd St. NW | Washington | 202-835-0500 | fax 202-835-1588 | 800-241-3333 | www.ritzcarlton.com | 268 rooms, 32 suites

Expect "over-the-top" "Ritz-Carlton treatment from the minute you enter" this West End "class act" where they "greet you by name" and the "bathrooms are bigger than the bedrooms (which is a good thing)!"; adding to the allure, the "club floor is fantastic", there's an "incredible" Sports Club/LA on-site (albeit for an extra charge) and a new "Eric Ripert-backed" American bistro - so it's no surprise there's "great people-watching" too.

	ROOMS	SERVICE	DINING	FACIL.	COST
[Z] **Ritz-Carlton Georgetown** 👪 🏋 [S]	27	27	22	24	$650

3100 South St. NW | Washington | 202-912-4100 | fax 202-912-4199 | 800-241-3333 | www.ritzcarlton.com | 52 rooms, 34 suites

"Another incredible Ritz" say regulars of this "hip" outpost in a "terrific" Georgetown location close to "shopping and restaurants" and an "easy walk to the waterfront"; the "interesting architecture" (it was "uniquely" fashioned from "an old incinerator") wins points, while "wonderful rooms", a "swank bar", the "lovely" Fahrenheit eatery – not to mention "welcoming" service – round out the picture.

Sofitel Lafayette Square ⊕✦

| 24 | 25 | 22 | 22 | $350 |

806 15th St. NW | Washington | 202-730-8800 | fax 202-730-8500 | 800-763-4835 | www.sofitel.com | 220 rooms, 17 suites

A "stone's throw from the White House", this "upscale Euro" favorite satisfies with "French flair" and "boutique ambiance" overseen by an "impeccable" staff; its "sumptuous" rooms sport a "retro, art deco design" with "trendy" accents and baths beautifed by "fresh orchids" and Roger & Gallet toiletries, and the on-site fitness center is "top-notch"; P.S. the "large, welcoming bar" is a local "after-work" "hot spot."

St. Regis ✦♨

| 23 | 25 | 21 | 22 | $695 |

923 16th St. NW | Washington | 202-638-2626 | fax 202-638-4231 | 877-787-3447 | www.stregis.com | 150 rooms, 25 suites

A "fabulous" $52-million renovation, completed in early 2008, "preserved the opulence and beauty of this classic property", from the Italian Renaissance chandeliers in the "stunning lobby" to the rooms you can "just sink into"; guests also benefit from a "perfect location" near the White House and "first-rate" service that leaves most "feeling a bit spoiled"; N.B. the new Adour restaurant by Alain Ducasse opened post-Survey.

Tabard Inn, Hotel ✦♨

| 16 | 19 | 24 | 14 | $158 |

1739 N St. NW | Washington | 202-785-1277 | fax 202-785-6173 | www.tabardinn.com | 40 rooms

"Full of Colonial character", with a "welcoming fire roaring in the winter" and "attractive alfresco dining in warmer months", this "quaint" "best DC secret" is a "funky, cozy" lodging "for the alternative crowd"; the "great" restaurant is a "favorite lunchtime venue" and the service is "welcoming", but what seems "eclectic" and "homey" to some is more of a "dumpy" "philanderer's oasis" to others.

Topaz Hotel ♥♥✦

| ▽ 21 | 22 | – | 15 | $369 |

1733 N St. NW | Washington | 202-393-3000 | fax 202-785-9581 | 800-775-1202 | www.topazhotel.com | 99 rooms

"Kimpton has done it again" rave impressed guests of this "flavorful", "converted residential" boutique hotel on a "quiet street" where the "stylish" rooms that feature an in-room yoga channel and complimentary yoga gear are a standout feature; the "wonderful" staff contributes to its "friendly atmosphere", and though there's no full-service restaurant (just a "rockin'" Asian-influenced bar), the "proximity to Dupont Circle more than compensates."

Willard InterContinental ⊕✦♨Ⓢ

| 24 | 25 | 23 | 23 | $649 |

1401 Pennsylvania Ave. NW | Washington | 202-628-9100 | fax 202-637-7326 | 800-827-1747 | www.interconti.com | 292 rooms, 40 suites

This "stately" "residence of presidents" ("Lincoln's bill is on display") with "beautifully appointed" accommodations and a "prime location" near the National Mall oozes "old-school class", especially in its "lovely public rooms" where longtimers insist "lobbying was invented"; the "elegant" dining areas are "fantastic" for a "power coffee" or formal tea, and though it "may seem stuffy" to modernists, most love being made to "feel like an ambassador or dignitary" amid the "historic" splendor.

Florida

TOPS IN STATE

<u>27</u> Little Palm Island | *Little Torch Key*
  Ritz-Carlton | *Naples*
  Ritz-Carlton | *Amelia Island*
<u>26</u> Ritz-Carlton Grande Lakes | *Orlando*
  Disney's BoardWalk Villas | *Lake Buena Vista*
  Mandarin Oriental | *Miami*
  Disney's Beach Club Villas | *Lake Buena Vista*
  Breakers | *Palm Beach*
  Ritz-Carlton Golf Resort | *Naples*
  Ritz-Carlton Coconut Grove | *Coconut Grove*

Ft. Lauderdale

Atlantic Resort & Spa, The

	ROOMS	SERVICE	DINING	FACIL.	COST
	26	22	19	21	$429

601 N. Ft. Lauderdale Beach Blvd. | 954-567-8020 | fax 954-567-8040 | 866-837-4274 | www.luxurycollection.com | 66 rooms, 53 suites, 5 penthouses

This "jewel of a boutique resort", "terrifically located" across the street from the ocean and a mile from the massive Galleria mall, offers "big rooms" done in minimalist whites and outfitted with "extremely comfortable beds", flat-screen TVs and balconies that afford "excellent views"; surveyors are split on the service ("sublime" vs. "forgetful"), however, and aren't impressed with the Med restaurant, Trina, or the "too-small" pool that's "in shade by mid-afternoon."

Boca Raton Resort & Club

	ROOMS	SERVICE	DINING	FACIL.	COST
	21	22	22	25	$350

501 E. Camino Real | Boca Raton | 561-447-3000 | fax 561-447-3183 | 800-327-0101 | www.bocaresort.com | 789 rooms, 134 suites, 120 bungalows

"Golf, water and views: they have it all" at this "sprawling" Addison Mizner–designed "pseudo-Italian" "oasis" from 1926, just choose your accommodations wisely, since experiences "vary depending on where you stay"; the "breathtakingly beautiful" grounds, "first-class" beach, "terrific" spa and Angela Hartnett's Cielo restaurant win praise (a branch of Morimoto is on the way); N.B. the Beach Club is closed until 2009 as it completes a total renovation.

Hilton

	ROOMS	SERVICE	DINING	FACIL.	COST
	21	19	16	19	$259

505 N. Ft. Lauderdale Beach Blvd. | 954-760-7177 | fax 954-414-2223 | 800-445-8667 | www.hilton.com | 224 rooms, 150 suites

"Surf's up, baby!" say admirers of this "newer", recently refurbed 25-story white tower on North Beach with "stunning" suites featuring kitchens or kitchenettes, the chain's signature Serenity beds, flat-screen HDTVs and "grand views" from "large, well-appointed balconies"; though sand crabbies contend this one's "nothing special" overall, a "beautiful" pool with private cabanas, an on-site spa and access to golf at the Parkland Country Club brighten their mood.

	ROOMS	SERVICE	DINING	FACIL.	COST

Lago Mar Resort & Club ♂️ 🏖️ 🛁 Ⓢ 🔍 | 20 | 23 | 20 | 24 | $315 |

1700 S. Ocean Ln. | 954-523-6511 | fax 954-524-6627 | 800-524-6627 | www.lagomar.com | 40 rooms, 164 suites

"One of the best hidden treasures on the Atlantic", this "family-friendly" Harbor Beach resort lies "directly on" a "huge", "sandy" private beach, an enviable location "unusual for Ft. Lauderdale"; this "older" lodging may be starting to show its age, particularly in rooms, but its many fans still deem it "outstanding" for the "professional yet personal" staff, a pool surrounded by palms and a playground that helps make it "perfect" for "younger kids."

Marriott Harbor Beach Resort & Spa ♂️ 🛁 Ⓢ 🔍 | 21 | 20 | 20 | 24 | $359 |

3030 Holiday Dr. | 954-525-4000 | fax 954-766-6152 | 800-222-6543 | www.marriottharborbeach.com | 615 rooms, 35 suites

Sitting on 16 acres of private oceanfront property, this seaside resort boasts a "gorgeous pool and tiki bar", "superb spa", "gracious staff" and freshly renovated rooms with "wonderful water views"; there are "lots of facilities" to make it family-friendly, including "one of the best South Florida seafood restaurants" (3030 Ocean), and the location makes it perfect for "pre-cruise" stays.

Seminole Hard Rock Hotel & Casino Hollywood 🏖️ 🛁 Ⓢ | 20 | 18 | 17 | 22 | $189 |

1 Seminole Way | Hollywood | 954-327-7625 | fax 954-327-7655 | 800-937-0010 | www.seminolehardrockhollywood.com | 418 rooms, 63 suites

"Live like a rock star" at this Mediterranean-style, "mad-crazy resort" that "packs lots of fun into one place", including new nonsmoking gaming areas, "displays of rock 'n' roll costumes" and "spacious, modern" rooms that "make you feel like a high roller"; the spa is "luxurious", the staff "caring" and while the hotel is "nowhere near the beach", its "landscaped" 4.5-acre lagoon-style pool is "a must-do"; dining, however, runs from "adequate to good."

St. Regis ✕ 🏖️ 🛁 Ⓢ | 27 | 25 | 24 | 25 | $689 |

1 N. Ft. Lauderdale Beach Blvd. | 954-465-2300 | fax 954-465-2340 | 877-787-3447 | www.stregis.com | 166 rooms, 25 condos

Deemed "a far cry from the Ft. Lauderdale of yore", this "über-luxurious" hotel "lives up to the name" with "large", "extremely well-appointed" rooms and a "lovely pool" that "takes full advantage of the ocean view"; the "excellent staff" ("personal butlers", "gorgeous pool boys") provides the "best service" that many surveyors have experienced, but given the "off-the-charts food and drink prices", your wallet may "be empty when you leave."

Westin Diplomat Resort & Spa ♂️ 🛁 ⤒ Ⓢ 🔍 | 24 | 22 | 19 | 25 | $400 |

3555 S. Ocean Dr. | Hollywood | 954-602-6000 | fax 954-602-7000 | 888-627-9057 | www.westin.com | 898 rooms, 100 suites

"Without the pretentiousness of the South Beach scene", this "luxurious", modern "soaring high-rise" in Hollywood, between Ft. Lauderdale and Miami, is not only "a great conference location", but also "a first-class establishment" for vacationers, who come to enjoy the "breath-

	ROOMS	SERVICE	DINING	FACIL.	COST

taking views", "tastefully decorated rooms" and "fabulous", "oceanside" glass-bottomed infinity pool (though it can "get very crowded"); while the golf course, tennis courts and spa are "a short shuttle ride away" at the Diplomat Golf Resort & Spa, they're worth the "special trip."

Ft. Myers Area

Casa Ybel Resort ⚷☺♨☜

▽ 20	18	19	22	$550

2255 W. Gulf Dr. | Sanibel | 239-472-3145 | fax 239-472-2109 | 800-276-4753 | www.casaybelresort.com | 114 suites
The first resort built on Sanibel Island, this "charming" lodge is next to 14 miles of "shell-studded beaches" with views of the Gulf of Mexico (it makes a "gorgeous spot for a wedding"); one- and two-bedroom bungalow-style suites are equipped with kitchens, sleeper sofas and a terrace or balcony, while child-friendly amenities include a kids' club and pool.

Sanibel Harbour Resort & Spa ⚷☺♨☺☜

21	21	20	23	$249

17260 Harbour Pointe Dr. | Ft. Myers | 239-466-4000 | fax 239-466-6050 | 800-767-7777 | www.sanibel-resort.com | 240 rooms, 107 suites, 54 condos
It may be a bit of a "throwback to the days when Debbie Gibson was popular", but "sunsets out of the movies" and an air of "casual elegance" make this "one of the best places" in the area for regulars who appreciate the "reasonable rates", "lovely accommodations" and "wonderful" staff; you'll also find "great golf", free boat rides, a tennis club and nightly dinner cruises on a 100-ft. yacht, so despite there being " a hundred better places" to stay, it's still a "favorite" of many.

South Seas Island Resort ⚷☺☺☜

21	20	18	25	$349

5400 Plantation Rd. | Captiva Island | 239-472-5111 | fax 239-472-7541 | 800-965-7772 | www.southseas.com | 346 villas, 105 rooms, 14 houses
"Wouldn't trade it for the world" assert fans of this "wonderful" "family resort" "nestled" "in a sleepy setting" on "beautiful Captiva Island" that's "still getting back on track from hurricane" damage; there's a "beautiful beach" with "tons of seashells", an "adequate nine-hole golf course", swimming pools, tennis and "daily kids activities" ("trams" navigate the "huge setting"); although dining options are "limited", there's a wide "variety" of room types and the staff "tries hard to please."

Keys

Casa Marina Resort & Beach Club ⊕♨☺
(fka Wyndham Casa Marina Resort)

21	20	18	22	$300

1500 Reynolds St. | Key West | 305-296-3535 | fax 305-296-4633 | 800-626-0777 | www.casamarinaresort.com | 240 rooms, 71 suites
Built in 1920 by railway tycoon Henry Flagler, this lodging (on the National Register of Historic Places) has the "best location" in the area, and it's also just about the only one with "its own beachfront" and two oceanfront pools; the "redone rooms are lovely", the staff pleasant and the atmosphere very "old Key West", but you'll have to "go down to Duval Street" for decent dining say those who judge the food "mediocre."

	ROOMS	SERVICE	DINING	FACIL.	COST

Cheeca Lodge & Spa 🏃🏻🏊🐕⛱🌊⛳ | 21 | 21 | 20 | 22 | $369 |

81801 Overseas Hwy. | Islamorada | 305-664-4651 | fax 305-664-2893 |
800-327-2888 | www.cheeca.com | 49 rooms, 25 suites, 33 bungalows,
92 villas

Located two hours north of Key West in Islamorada, this "luxurious waterfront" member of Small Luxury Hotels of the World offers "posh rooms and pretty grounds" that combine with "well-designed and impeccably maintained" facilities; even if "thin walls make whispering a must in most rooms", the "enviable" sports-fisherman-friendly location, the on-site Camp Cheeca for kids and the "unexpectedly large selection of activities" for young and old mean you won't spend much time inside.

Hawk's Cay Resort 🏃🏻🏊🐕⛱🌊⛳ | 21 | 20 | 20 | 23 | $595 |

61 Hawk's Cay Blvd. | Duck Key | 305-743-7000 | fax 305-743-5215 |
888-814-9104 | www.hawkscay.com | 225 villas, 162 rooms, 15 suites

There's "a lot for everyone to do" at this "highly recommended" 40-acre Duck Key "resort for families", where a "wonderful" $30-million renovation to the rooms, suites and one- to four-bedroom villas (beds make you feel like "you're sleeping on a cloud"), the addition of Nueva Latina restaurant, Alma, and a "relaxing" new lobby rum bar brings everything up a notch; from "feeding and swimming with the resident dolphins" ("a big hit") to diving, fishing and partaking in a "great children's program", it's a "dream vacation" for most.

Hyatt Key West
Resort & Marina 🐕⛱ | 23 | 21 | 18 | 22 | $325 |

601 Front St. | Key West | 305-809-1234 | fax 305-809-4050 |
800-233-1234 | www.hyatt.com | 118 rooms

Beaming sun-seekers say this "fine little resort's" location near Mallory Square – "ideally positioned for sunsets and views of the ships" – "helps a great deal" in making it a "perfect place to enjoy the Keys", as well as a "pleasant relief from big beach resorts"; "excellent" spa services, good water sports and access to the Gulf of Mexico add to the charms, as do the "newly decorated" rooms.

🄴 Little Palm Island ✕🐕⛱ | 27 | 28 | 27 | 27 | $1300 |

28500 Overseas Hwy. | Little Torch Key | 305-515-4004 | fax 305-872-4843 |
800-343-8567 | www.littlepalmisland.com | 30 bungalows

It may be hard "for a place this expensive" to be "worth every penny . . . but it is" purr patrons of this "intimate getaway" on a private island (reachable by boat or seaplane), where the "spacious" bungalow suites have their own private decks and no TVs; the "most romantic" spot in the Keys includes "impeccable service", "exceptional" dining and no children under 16 – plus the use of cell phones in public areas is highly discouraged.

Marquesa Hotel, The ✕🌐🐕 | 25 | 25 | 25 | 20 | $350 |

600 Fleming St. | Key West | 305-292-1919 | fax 305-294-2121 |
800-869-4631 | www.marquesa.com | 14 rooms, 13 suites

Enjoy "total seclusion" or a "romantic getaway" at this "terrific" boutique, where a "quiet" "garden oasis" sits surrounded by "spacious and well-appointed" accommodations in restored 1884 conch houses; meals at the "innovative" Cafe Marquesa are "excellent" and the "amazing spaces" - "lush with tropical vegetation and wonderful pools" - are "impeccably" maintained by an "amazing staff" that makes a stay feel "like going home to visit special friends."

Pier House Resort & Caribbean Spa 🔭Ⓢ 20 | 19 | 20 | 21 | $329

1 Duval St. | Key West | 305-296-4600 | fax 305-296-7569 | 800-723-2791 | www.pierhouse.com | 116 rooms, 26 suites

Located within "walking distance to everything" and set in a former Hemingway haunt, this hotel is "the civilized, elegant" place in town, especially considering its "continual" upgrades that have resulted in "stylish" rooms with "hardwood floors, rustic fans" and "flat-screen TVs"; though some say the service "could improve", most folks "love their small beach", the "colorful and happy" digs and the "cool", "historic" Chart Room bar where Jimmy Buffet got his start.

Sunset Key Guest Cottages, A Westin Resort 🫖🔭🎾 26 | 24 | 21 | 25 | $495

245 Front St. | Key West | 305-292-5300 | fax 305-292-5395 | 888-477-7786 | www.sunsetkeyisland.com | 37 cottages

"For sunsets and pampering", this "dreamy" "private paradise" just a "short boat ride to Key West" offers a "unique experience" with "well-appointed rooms", an "amazing staff" and a vibe that gives guests an "instant attitude adjustment into vacation-minded bliss"; the "fabulous Sunday brunch" at the "open-air restaurant" is "better than dinner", and fans of the whole experience consider it "worth the price", since "you feel like you are 10,000 miles away from civilization."

Miami & Miami Beach

TOPS IN AREA

26 Mandarin Oriental
Ritz-Carlton Coconut Grove
25 Acqualina Resort
Setai
Four Seasons
Fairmont Turnberry Isle
24 Ritz-Carlton Key Biscayne
Ritz-Carlton South Beach
Tides
Grove Isle

[Z] Acqualina Resort & Spa 👫🫖🐕🔭Ⓢ 28 | 23 | 24 | 27 | $850

(fka Acqualina, A Rosewood Resort)

17875 Collins Ave. | Sunny Isles Beach | 305-918-8000 | fax 305-918-8100 | 888-804-4338 | www.acqualina.com | 54 rooms, 43 suites

In an "odd" but "rapidly developing" location that "so far" "lacks the Miami Beach crowds" farther south, this "beautiful" three-year-old hotel/condo on 4.5 oceanfront acres is "fabulous all the way 'round"; the large rooms boast serious "wow factor", with "flat-screen TVs that rise up out of the furniture" and "spectacular" water views from the balconies; boosters tout the "terrific" ESPA spa, "wonderful beach and pools" and the "best Italian food south of NYC" at Il Mulino, but sticklers say they "expected the service to be" better.

Biltmore, The 🍴[H]🐕🔭⛳[S]🎾

ROOMS	SERVICE	DINING	FACIL.	COST
23	24	23	26	$425

1200 Anastasia Ave. | Coral Gables | 305-445-1926 | fax 305-913-3159 | 800-915-1926 | www.biltmorehotel.com | 238 rooms, 37 suites

"They just don't make them like this anymore" sigh fans of this "opulent" Jazz Age "landmark" that's "worth a visit just for the pool" (the largest hotel swimmery in the continental U.S.) and "knockout" of a lobby; its 18-hole Donald Ross golf course, "spectacular" updated spa and "Sunday brunch in the courtyard" at the Palme d'Or restaurant win acclaim, though the "antiques-filled" rooms, while "charming" to some, come off as "cramped" to others; P.S. Coral Gables can be "quiet at night, but it's a quick drive to anywhere in Miami."

Conrad ☕🔭[S]🎾

ROOMS	SERVICE	DINING	FACIL.	COST
23	19	16	17	$499

1395 Brickell Ave. | Miami | 305-503-6500 | fax 305-503-6599 | 800-560-7966 | www.conradmiami.com | 189 rooms, 14 suites, 103 apartments

"Stunning and cutting-edge modern", this Downtown steel-and-glass tower "five minutes from Key Biscayne" has some calling it "the most beautiful building in Miami", with renovated rooms sporting a "devastating expanse of windows", especially in the baths, and a 25th-floor bar and restaurant with "spectacular views"; still, some say "too many elevator" banks make it all a bit "confusing."

Delano 🍴🔭[S]

ROOMS	SERVICE	DINING	FACIL.	COST
21	21	24	25	$895

1685 Collins Ave. | Miami Beach | 305-672-2000 | fax 305-532-0099 | 877-679-1791 | www.delano-hotel.com | 208 rooms, 8 bungalows, 1 apartment, 1 penthouse

"Is this a movie set?" wonder guests upon entering this "slinky" hotel that "pioneered the modern-cool Miami era", with its "MTV atmosphere" and "surreal" "white-on-white" decor; "pack lightly" because you'll have a "ridiculously cramped" room ("I just paid how much for this?") – though why linger there when "the party's in the lobby and around the pool", the "spa's sublime" and the Blue Door restaurant leaves you "awestruck"; even if "the bloom is off the rose" for some, the majority believes it's still "trendy after all these years."

Doral Golf Resort & Spa 👪🔭⛳[S]

ROOMS	SERVICE	DINING	FACIL.	COST
19	19	17	24	$379

4400 NW 87th Ave. | Miami | 305-592-2000 | fax 305-591-6653 | 800-713-6725 | www.doralresort.com | 494 rooms, 199 suites

"If it's good enough for Tiger Woods, it's good enough for me" say duffers delighted by the fabled Blue Monster and four other "amazing" courses at this "beautiful" "golfers' paradise" that's "close to the airport" but a "little far from the beach"; "high marks" go to the spa rooms and the "simply stunning" spa itself, but still detractors claim it's a "tired, old Marriott" that misses the cut with "dated" quarters and food that "could be better."

Fairmont Turnberry Isle Resort & Club 👪🐕🔭⛳[S]🎾

ROOMS	SERVICE	DINING	FACIL.	COST
26	24	22	27	$539

19999 W. Country Club Dr. | Aventura | 305-932-6200 | fax 305-933-6554 | 800-327-7028 | www.fairmont.com | 351 rooms, 41 suites

"If I die and heaven isn't like this, I want to be reincarnated" claim luxury lovers lured to this "newly renovated" Mediterranean-style "oasis" declared "worth every dime spent"; kudos go to rooms with all the amenities "you could ask for" (it recently underwent a $150-million redo), "exemplary" service, a "huge" Willow Stream Spa, "incredible" pool, two "outstanding" golf courses and chef Michael Mina's "fantastic" Bourbon Steak; even if you have to take a "shuttle to the beach", at least the "upscale" Aventura mall is within "walking distance" - though really "you don't ever need to leave this resort."

Fisher Island Hotel & Resort 👫 Ⓗ ☕ 🔭 Ⓢ 🎾

ROOMS	SERVICE	DINING	FACIL.	COST
23	23	20	25	$900

1 Fisher Island Dr. | Miami Beach | 305-535-6000 | fax 305-535-6003 | 800-537-3708 | www.fisherisland.com | 2 rooms, 49 suites, 7 villas, 3 cottages

"As private and relaxing as it gets", this "spectacular" "hidden oasis" set in a 1928 Vanderbilt mansion on its own island (a seven-minute ferry ride from SoBe) allows you to "live the lifestyle of the rich and famous"; though there's the renowned Spa Internazionale, a nine-hole P.B. Dye-designed golf course, 18 tennis courts (most of them clay), five pools and a private beach, been-there, done-that types say they love it "not because it's fancy", but because it's a "refreshing change of pace from the Miami scene."

Fontainebleau 👫 🍴 Ⓗ ☕ 🐕 🔭 Ⓢ

ROOMS	SERVICE	DINING	FACIL.	COST
18	17	16	21	$329

(fka Fontainebleau Hilton Resort)

4441 Collins Ave. | Miami Beach | 305-538-2000 | fax 305-532-8145 | 800-548-8886 | www.fontainebleau.com | 658 suites

A "classic, old Miami Beach" hotel built by Morris Lapidus and featured in *Goldfinger,* this resort is "reinventing itself once again" after a billion dollars of renovations to the original building and the addition of two all-suite towers; among the improvements are an update of the iconic freeform pool, a new 40,000-sq.-ft. spa, four nightclubs and a steakhouse by Alfred Portale of NYC's Gotham Bar & Grill.

Four Seasons ☕ 🐕 🔭 Ⓢ

ROOMS	SERVICE	DINING	FACIL.	COST
26	26	23	25	$475

1435 Brickell Ave. | Miami | 305-358-3535 | fax 305-358-7758 | 800-819-5053 | www.fourseasons.com | 182 rooms, 39 suites

Though this "monumental" Financial District tower is "strictly business", "tourists can do well here" too proclaim partisans of this "luxurious" "oasis" a block from Biscayne Bay; the "well-appointed rooms" boasting "great views", "unparalleled" service "without the SoBe attitude", "state-of-the-art" gym, "flat-out cool" rooftop pool and "top-rate" dishes at Acqua make up for the lack of a beach.

[NEW] **Gansevoort South** ☕ 🐕 🔭 Ⓢ

ROOMS	SERVICE	DINING	FACIL.	COST
∇ 26	23	19	26	$695

2377 Collins Ave. | Miami Beach | 305-604-1000 | fax 305-604-6886 | www.gansevoortsouth.com | 248 rooms, 86 suites, 259 condos

The new South Beach branch of NYC's trendy boutique Hotel Gansevoort boasts rooms with '80s-style hot pink and green walls, high-thread-count sheets, 40-inch flat-screen TVs and balconies with ocean, bay or city views; the private beach complete with cabanas, fire pits and water features turns into a VIP lounge after sunset, while the monster palm-tree-lined rooftop pool features an oversized Jacuzzi and cafe/bar; upping the scenester factor are an eponymous Philippe Chow eatery, a 42,000-sq.-ft. David Barton gym and swank nightclubs.

	ROOMS	SERVICE	DINING	FACIL.	COST

Grove Isle Hotel & Spa ✕♨ⓈⓆ

| 26 | 22 | 25 | 25 | $689 |

4 Grove Isle Dr. | Coconut Grove | 305-858-8300 | fax 305-858-5908 |
800-884-7683 | www.groveisle.com | 41 rooms, 8 suites

You'll "sleep like a baby" amid the "Biscayne Bay breezes" at this "amazing", "romantic" hotel on a 20-acre "private isle" that's "far away from reality" but still "close to the action of Coconut Grove"; "beautifully appointed" rooms, "oh-so-comfortable" beds, the "excellent" SpaTerre and the "off-the-charts" Baleen, serving New World cuisine on the oceanfront, have fans saying it's "worth the splurge."

Hilton Bentley Beach ⓘⒹ♨♨

| ▽ 21 | 20 | 16 | 18 | $500 |

101 Ocean Dr. | Miami Beach | 305-938-4600 | fax 305-938-4601 |
866-236-8539 | www.thebentleyhotels.com | 109 suites

It's hard to beat this boutique hotel's "excellent" SoBe location "south of Fifth and out of the fray" but still within walking distance of good restaurants – and it's also "perfect" "if you love to swim in the ocean" since it's a "stone's throw" from the beach; now owned by Hilton, it boasts condo-style suites with "large" terraces and kitchens that most call "comfortable", though others cry "needs attention."

Hotel, The ✕♨

| 19 | 22 | 24 | 21 | $275 |

801 Collins Ave. | Miami Beach | 305-531-2222 | fax 305-531-3222 |
877-843-4683 | www.thehotelofsouthbeach.com | 49 rooms, 4 suites

With interiors by Todd Oldham, this art deco boutique hotel offers stylishly "beautiful surroundings" and a "hip" vibe in a "trendy SoBe location" that nevertheless remains "nice and quiet" (it's "one block back from the madness" of the Strip); the "comfortable" rooms, done in bright colors, "aren't as small as many make them out to be", but they aren't the main reason for staying – that honor goes to the rooftop pool and to Wish restaurant, which serves "amazingly" "delicious" food in a "garden setting."

JW Marriott ♨Ⓢ

| 22 | 22 | 17 | 21 | $249 |

1109 Brickell Ave. | Miami | 305-329-3500 | fax 305-371-8820 |
800-228-9290 | www.marriott.com | 274 rooms, 22 suites

"It's all business (and conventions)" at this "surprisingly upscale" 22-story Financial District tower with a "magnificent" lobby, fitness center, spa, stainless-steel rooftop pool and "particularly attentive" service; true, the "contemporary rooms" lean toward "cramped" ("almost NYC-size"), but they've been nicely "renovated" with work areas, marble tubs and 42-inch flat-screen TVs; one drawback is the on-site dining, which "needs improvement."

Loews Miami Beach ♔✕♨♨Ⓢ

| 21 | 21 | 20 | 24 | $499 |

1601 Collins Ave. | Miami Beach | 305-604-1601 |
fax 305-604-3999 | 800-235-6397 | www.loewshotels.com |
740 rooms, 50 suites

"Gorgeous grounds, fabulous restaurants and a hip lobby lounge" more than make up for this "lovely waterfront" hotel's sometimes "unknowing" service and "tiny rooms with paper-thin walls" (just renovated in spring 2008); still, you probably won't be inside very long anyway, given the "huge", "seashell-shaped" pool, "wonderful" Emeril's restaurant and "great beach location" near Lincoln Road and "most of SoBe's restaurants and bars."

	ROOMS	SERVICE	DINING	FACIL.	COST

🇿 Mandarin Oriental ✕ ⚄ ♨ Ⓢ | 27 | 26 | 26 | 26 | $655

500 Brickell Key Dr. | Miami | 305-913-8288 | fax 305-913-8300 |
866-888-6780 | www.mandarinoriental.com | 295 rooms, 31 suites
"You get what you pay for" at this "beautiful", "comfortably Zen" "alternative to South Beach", where "minimalism is done right", the "impeccable staff" "spoils you" and the "stunning rooms" sport "marvelous views"; fans also rave about the "fantastic restaurants" – "Azul is one of the best" in town and "Cafe Sambal is right behind it" – not to mention what some call the "top spa in the world."

Mayfair Hotel & Spa ⚄ ♨ Ⓢ | ▽ 23 | 20 | 19 | 20 | $269

3000 Florida Ave. | Coconut Grove | 305-441-0000 | fax 305-447-9173 |
800-433-4555 | www.mayfairhotelandspa.com | 179 suites
Surveyors "leaving on a cruise from Miami" and those in search of a "true bohemian experience" deem this "charming" Coconut Grove boutique hotel "a treat" thanks to its "cute rooms" with a Japanese hot tub "on the balcony" and the "fun" atmosphere complemented by a spunky staff (including "some of the best spa personnel" around); the "wedding"-worthy atrium as well as the rooftop deck complete with infinity pool and 13,000-sq.-ft. sunning area boost the appeal.

National Hotel South Beach ⑪ ♨ | 18 | 19 | 18 | 21 | $399

1677 Collins Ave. | Miami Beach | 305-532-2311 | fax 305-534-1426 |
800-327-8310 | www.nationalhotel.com | 142 rooms, 8 suites
The longest pool in Florida, "great beach access" and a "prime" location within "walking distance to all the clubs and restaurants" ensure this "chic, but not over-the-top" "value" is perfect for "families wanting someplace cool or couples trying to avoid the disco scene"; fans appreciate the "classic art deco feel" and find the "cabana rooms outstanding" (others are just "average"), but critics bemoan the "mediocre" service, and say this hotel "isn't looking after itself very well."

Raleigh, The ⚄ ♨ | 19 | 22 | 20 | 24 | $375

1775 Collins Ave. | Miami Beach | 305-534-6300 | fax 305-538-8140 |
800-848-1775 | www.raleighhotel.com | 104 rooms
Boasting a "chill vibe" conducive to "fun and frolic", hotelier André Balazs' "chic and trendy" art deco-style boutique spoils guests with its "beach location" within "walking distance to shops and restaurants", and "fantastic", "alfresco dining" "under the trees" "overlooking an incredible pool" (the "outdoor lounge/cabana area is what makes" the place); rooms are "nicely decorated" but "small", but the "super staff" helps keep this a "favorite place for relaxing, pampered getaways."

NEW Regent Bal Harbour ⚄ ♨ Ⓢ | – | – | – | – | $790

10295 Collins Ave. | Bal Harbour | 305-455-5400 | fax 305-455-5399 |
800-545-4000 | www.regenthotels.com | 63 suites, 61 studios
Cutting-edge types compliment the "wonderful location" of this brand-new luxury resort located "on the ocean at Haulover Inlet" with "exquisite shopping at your door" and South Beach only 15 minutes away; suites and studios sport "stunning baths" with showers overlooking the "white-sand" beach, and a swimming pool, spa (with foot therapy lounge), beautiful lobby and nearby clothing-optional beach are also part of the package.

	ROOMS	SERVICE	DINING	FACIL.	COST

Ritz-Carlton Coconut Grove ✕ 🏨 ⓢ   26 | 27 | 25 | 24 | $429

3300 SW 27th Ave. | Coconut Grove | 305-644-4680 | fax 305-644-4681 | 800-241-3333 | www.ritzcarlton.com | 98 rooms, 17 suites

Both vacationers and "upscale business travelers on an expense account" go nuts over the "quiet luxury" of this "off-the-beaten-path", "top-notch classic", where the "incredible", "caring" staff "bends over backward for your every whim" and the "excellent" dining options include a "fantastic Sunday brunch" and a "fun terrace bar"; some consider the location "weird", but most agree this "small, laid-back and beautiful" spot is a "bargain for a Ritz-Carlton."

Ritz-Carlton Key Biscayne 👪 ✕ 🏨 ⓢ 🔍   24 | 25 | 22 | 26 | $559

455 Grand Bay Dr. | Key Biscayne | 305-365-4500 | fax 305-365-4505 | 800-241-3333 | www.ritzcarlton.com | 365 rooms, 37 suites

From "wake-up to sleepy time", this "smashing", "family-friendly resort" is "heaven on earth" with "gorgeous pools and gardens", "excellent tennis facilities", a "phenomenal spa" and a "pleasant stretch of beach" "on a private island" that are as good as the "peerless" staff that delivers "before you even have a chance to ask"; although a few say the "limited restaurant choices" offer only "adequate" fare, others say don't miss the "insane football stadium–size brunch" or "trendy", "new burger bar, Dune", where you can dine with your "toes in the sand."

Ritz-Carlton South Beach 👪 ✕ 🏨 ⓢ   25 | 25 | 22 | 25 | $550

1 Lincoln Rd. | Miami Beach | 786-276-4000 | fax 786-276-4001 | 800-241-3333 | www.ritzcarlton.com | 334 rooms, 41 suites

This "high-end" outpost is "hipper than other Ritz's", with a "picture-perfect" pool (sporting VIP cabanas and "boys serving cocktails") and "many features" intact from the "original 1953 Morris Lapidus-designed Dilido hotel"; it "doesn't disappoint", from a staff that's "delightful" to the "well-equipped" rooms to the multimillion-dollar art collection, plus there's a new Modern American eatery, Bistro One LR.

Setai, The 🖾 & 🏨 ⓢ   26 | 24 | 23 | 27 | $1070

2001 Collins Ave. | Miami Beach | 305-520-6000 | fax 305-520-6600 | 888-625-7500 | www.setai.com | 165 suites

"An oasis from the fast-paced Miami Beach scene", this "Asian-inspired", earth-toned hotel and adjoining residential tower is "insanely great", boasting "rooms decorated to perfection", a "beautiful bar under the stars" and "three overflowing waterholes you can pool-hop between"; "courteous, efficient" staffers "cater to your every whim", but just "bring buckets of money" to pay the bill.

Shore Club, The ✕ & 🏨 ⓢ   16 | 18 | 22 | 21 | $545

1901 Collins Ave. | Miami Beach | 305-695-3100 | fax 305-695-3299 | 877-640-9500 | www.shoreclub.com | 307 rooms, 70 suites, 7 bungalows, 1 penthouse

Those who "like to party" "happily pay through the nose" to partake in the "see-and-be-seen" scene of this "Morrocan-Miami oasis of chic", where Sobe's "most beautiful", "rich and famous" play by the "posh pool" manned by "hunky beach boys" and "nosh" at the "fabulous Nobu restaurant" ("the saving grace of this hip-hop mecca according to some); however, the unimpressed liken the "stark" rooms to "high-end jails", and grimly endure the "hipper than thou service."

	ROOMS	SERVICE	DINING	FACIL.	COST

Standard, The ♶Ⓢ

▽ 20 | 19 | 20 | 26 | $300

40 Island Ave. | Miami Beach | 305-673-1717 | fax 305-673-8181 | www.standardhotel.com | 104 rooms, 1 suite

With "one of the finest spas in town", complete with "large Turkish soaking tubs", a "killer pool" and "hot slabs of marble for lounging and drifting off to sleep on", this "fantastic option" courtesy of hotelier André Balazs, overlooking Biscayne Bay, is "close enough to, but away from, the SoBe tumult"; "dining options are flexible but not incredibly creative", while "trendy", "pure-white" rooms are "small, but soothing" with flat-panel TVs and DVD libraries; too bad there "never seems to be enough staff", and when it's there, it's "nonchalant."

Tides, The ♶♶

26 | 25 | 24 | 23 | $595

1220 Ocean Dr. | Miami Beach | 305-604-5070 | fax 305-503-3275 | 866-891-0950 | www.tidessouthbeach.com | 44 suites, 1 penthouse

Those who "like being in the heart of the action" check into this "timeless" 1936 art deco hotel that's set in a "perfect location" and "defines South Beach cool", with a $14-million redesign courtesy of Kelly Wearstler; "sensual", "roomy suites", "all facing the beach", sport "awesome views" and "telescopes to keep track of the activities", while "breakfast on the terrace" offers "good people-watching" as well as "impeccable service"; indeed, this "sophisticated" scene feels straight "out of an old movie."

Townhouse ♶

▽ 22 | 22 | 22 | 19 | $195

150 20th St. | Miami Beach | 305-534-3800 | fax 305-534-3811 | 877-534-3800 | www.townhousehotel.com | 67 rooms, 2 penthouses

For a "hip vibe without all the attitude" – and a "great bargain" to boot – reviewers "highly recommend" this "all-white", "super-trendy" "European-style boutique hotel" "one block from the beach"; "comfortable rooms" are complemented by a "wonderful" free breakfast and a "courteous staff", while the rooftop terrace and the "casual" "underground" Bond St. Lounge are both "don't-miss" venues.

Victor, Hotel ♶♶Ⓢ

22 | 21 | 24 | 20 | $799

1144 Ocean Dr. | Miami Beach | 305-428-1234 | fax 305-421-6281 | 800-233-1234 | www.hotelvictorsouthbeach.com | 72 rooms, 8 suites, 6 bungalows, 2 penthouses

Check out the "jellyfish tank" at this "happening", "dripping-in-chic" South Beach hotel that's known for its "bright, modern decor" and the "innovative" VIX eatery, which consensus calls "one of the best restaurants" in the area; while the "beautiful" rooms are "tiny", and service varies ("could not have been more helpful" vs. "lackadaisical, even by Miami standards"), the beach is just "several steps out the front door."

Naples

Hyatt Regency Coconut Point Resort & Spa ♶♶▲Ⓢ♘

25 | 24 | 21 | 26 | $499

5001 Coconut Rd. | Bonita Springs | 239-444-1234 | fax 239-390-4344 | 888-591-1234 | www.hyatt.com | 427 rooms, 27 suites

The "private beach" accessible by a free catamaran is an "amazing feature" at this "wonderful resort" in Bonita Springs (20 minutes north of Naples) since there's an added benefit of possibly "seeing manatees and dolphins" in the waters; "well-run" facilities include the Raptor Bay Golf Course, Camp Coconut for kids, "fabulous pools" (including a 140-ft. corkscrew slide) and an all-around "beautiful setup", but foodies find the restaurants "inadequate for dinner."

La Playa Beach & Golf Resort ♨ ⅃ ☺   22 | 22 | 20 | 25 | $579

9891 Gulf Shore Dr. | 239-597-3123 | fax 239-597-6278 | 800-237-6883 | www.laplayaresort.com | 180 rooms, 9 suites

A "wonderful quiet beach" and a "million-dollar view" are highlights at this "lovely, boutiquey resort" next to Vanderbilt Bay; every room has a balcony and twice-daily maid service, but for some that's not enough to make up for their not-so-large size; still, most love the "first-class" staff and "lovely grounds", which include a tiki bar, waterfall pools and an 18-hole Bob Cupp–designed golf course.

Marco Beach Ocean Resort ☕♨☺   24 | 23 | 21 | 23 | $200

480 S. Collier Blvd. | Marco Island | 239-393-1400 | fax 239-393-1401 | 800-260-5089 | www.marcoresort.com | 98 suites

"Elegant" and "quiet", this "first-class" venue on Marco Island's Crescent Beach boasts "large rooms", "top-notch" "spa and sports facilities", a "pristine beach" and a "helpful" staff willing to "cater to your every need"; despite having one of the "most beautiful dining rooms on the Gulf Coast", it serves just "average" food, and critics say "inconsistency on all levels" detracts from an otherwise "great getaway."

Marco Island Marriott Beach Resort ♔♨⅃☺⚲   22 | 22 | 19 | 24 | $499

400 S. Collier Blvd. | Marco Island | 239-394-2511 | fax 239-642-2672 | 800-438-4373 | www.marcoislandmarriott.com | 664 rooms, 63 suites

"You'll easily slip into a relaxing pace" at this "tropical paradise", thanks to the "fantastic beach", "beautiful" "updated rooms" with "wraparound balconies" and an "infinity pool to die for" (and there's another with a "waterslide" that's "more geared toward kids"); service is "prompt" and "Quinn's casual dining is a treat", so there's really "no need to leave the property" – though you may get transported to another planet at the "out-of-this-world spa."

Naples Grande Beach Resort ♔♨☺⚲   24 | 23 | 21 | 24 | $439

(fka Naples Grande Resort & Club)

475 Seagate Dr. | 239-597-3232 | fax 239-594-6777 | 888-422-6177 | www.naplesgranderesort.com | 395 rooms, 29 suites, 50 bungalows

"Bird-watching" tourists and business travelers alike enjoy this "beautiful high-rise" where "amazing new renovations" have resulted in "spacious" rooms, "splurge-worthy" "Zen bungalows", an "über-cool bar" and a "to-die-for" Golden Door Spa, along with a "more Miami feel to the lobby"; though "dinner choices are limited" and the "golf course is miles away", most guests are content to take a "delightful walk through mangroves to the great beach" aided by a "friendly staff."

🅉 Ritz-Carlton, The ♔✕♨☺⚲   27 | 28 | 25 | 28 | $679

280 Vanderbilt Beach Rd. | 239-598-3300 | fax 239-598-6690 | 800-241-3333 | www.ritzcarlton.com | 415 rooms, 35 suites

"Hope the staff" is "in charge of running heaven" pray patrons of this "gorgeous confection" "perfectly located on the Gulf Coast of

Naples" where "stellar" service is "unparalleled", as are the "impeccable grounds" with an "exquisite beachfront" offering "sublime sunsets"; "elegant interiors" include a "huge", "world-class spa", "spacious", "beautifully decorated" rooms (the "club level is a must") and "incredible" dining (Artisans was voted No. 1 for Food in Naples in our *America's Top Restaurants* Survey); it "can get crowded during peak seasons", but it's a "beautiful escape" that's deemed "well worth the price tag."

[Z] Ritz-Carlton Golf Resort 👫🐕🔭⛳Ⓢ🎾

26	27	24	26	$399

2600 Tiburon Dr. | 239-593-2000 | fax 239-254-3300 | 800-241-3333 | www.ritzcarlton.com | 257 rooms, 38 suites

The "wonderful golf" facility with an "excellent practice range" is the highlight of this "less-expensive alternative to the Ritz" down the street, and you have "full use of both" via free shuttle; but even those who can't swing a club find much to love given the "best staff", "impeccably maintained grounds" ("there isn't a blade of grass out of place") and "fresh" rooms that are "a bargain in the off-season"; too bad visits to both the beach and spa "require a trip."

Northeast Florida

Amelia Island Plantation 👫🚲🐕🔭⛳Ⓢ🎾

22	22	20	26	$298

6800 First Coast Hwy. | Amelia Island | 904-261-6161 | fax 904-277-5945 | 800-874-6878 | www.aipfl.com | 361 villas, 249 rooms

"Bike trails snake through" the 18 square miles of this "paradise on earth", blessed with four "wonderful" golf courses, a "world-class spa", "beautiful sand beaches and intercoastal marshes" and "lots of woods"; non-cyclers take advangage of "trams that take you everywhere" and other "top-notch" services, and though dissatisfied sorts declare the dining options and some condos "need updating", "on the whole, it's a lovely experience."

Casa Monica Hotel Ⓗ🔭

▽ 23	25	24	23	$209

95 Cordova St. | St. Augustine | 904-827-1888 | fax 904-819-6065 | 800-648-1888 | www.casamonica.com | 124 rooms, 14 suites

Listed on the National Register of Historic Places, this "classy" 1888 hotel overlooking Matanzas Bay in the nation's oldest city leaves "no detail left undone" (they "even give the kids teddy bears"); "wonderful" Moroccan-Spanish-influenced rooms, "fantastic" fare and a "fabulous" location "right in the heart" of the old district add up to St. Augustine's "best-kept secret."

Ponte Vedra Inn & Club 👫🚲🔭⛳Ⓢ🎾

▽ 25	26	22	27	$385

200 Ponte Vedra Blvd. | Ponte Vedra Beach | 904-285-1111 | fax 904-285-2111 | 800-234-7842 | www.pvresorts.com | 217 rooms, 33 suites

For "unsurpassed views of the Atlantic" and "Florida elegance" "steeped in tradition", guests - many who have been coming here for "generations" - rely on this 300-acre "old-style resort", where a "departure from everyday reality" comes courtesy of an "over-the-top" staff that "remembers your name, likes and dislikes"; the "beautiful facilities" include seven "convenient" dining options, four oceanfront pools, a "memorable health club" and "schizophrenic" rooms that range from "brand-new" to "upgrade" ready.

[Z] Ritz-Carlton Amelia Island 👪✕🔭⛳Ⓢ🎾

ROOMS	SERVICE	DINING	FACIL.	COST
26	27	25	27	$349

4750 Amelia Island Pkwy. | Amelia Island | 904-277-1100 | fax 904-261-9064 | 800-241-3333 | www.ritzcarlton.com | 400 rooms, 44 suites

Those who "prefer the 'resorty' casual Ritz to the stuffy Victorian ones" find "heaven by the sea" along with "miles and miles of beach" and "bend-over-backwards service" at this "relaxing" resort; couples come for "romance" in the "heavenly" rooms (try the club floors for an "exquisite experience"), but it's also "a great place to bring the kids", who "love the campfire on the beach with s'mores"; other pluses include a "fantastic" spa and the "outstanding" New American restaurant, Salt.

Orlando Area

TOPS IN AREA

26 Ritz-Carlton Grande Lakes
Disney's BoardWalk Villas
Disney's Beach Club Villas
25 Disney's Grand Floridian
Disney's Animal Kingdom
Disney's Wilderness
24 JW Marriott
Disney's BoardWalk Inn
Disney's Saratoga Springs
23 Disney's Yacht Club

Buena Vista Palace, Walt Disney World Resort 🔭Ⓢ🎾

ROOMS	SERVICE	DINING	FACIL.	COST
20	19	16	21	$279

1900 N. Buena Vista Dr. | Lake Buena Vista | 407-827-2727 | fax 407-827-6034 | 866-397-6516 | www.buenavistapalace.com | 888 rooms, 124 suites

This modern tower block has an "excellent" Downtown Disney location across from Pleasure Island but costs just a "fraction" of what some of this brand's other hotels charge; "spacious rooms" have 32-inch LCD TVs, and facilities include six restaurants, three pools, a 24/7 fitness center and a 10,000-sq.-ft. spa; although some guests conclude that "it's better as a convention hotel than a fantasy family getaway", if you're visiting the theme parks it's a fine "staging point."

Celebration Hotel 🔭

	ROOMS	SERVICE	DINING	FACIL.	COST
▽	21	20	18	18	$309

700 Bloom St. | Celebration | 407-566-6000 | fax 407-566-1844 | 888-499-3800 | www.celebrationhotel.com | 92 rooms, 23 suites

A "fantastic find in this tourist area", this "cozy and comfortable" quasi-Victorian, owned by the Kessler group and "right on the lake", exchanges "Orlando's hustle and bustle" for the nostalgia of Celebration, the "quaint and lovely" (if a little too "Stepford Wives"-ish) planned community five minutes away from Disneyworld; rooms are outfitted with four-poster beds and other classic furnishings, while an 18-hole golf course designed by Robert Trent Jones, Sr. and Jr. is nearby.

	ROOMS	SERVICE	DINING	FACIL.	COST

Disney's Animal Kingdom Lodge 유 ᵬᵬⓈ

| 24 | 25 | 24 | 27 | $335 |

2901 Osceola Pkwy. | Lake Buena Vista | 407-938-3000 | fax 407-938-4799 |
800-227-1500 | www.disneyworld.com | 1274 rooms, 19 suites

"A more amazing view cannot be found" say fans who "go wild" over the "spectacular" vistas ("the animals are right there") from the Savannah rooms at this safari-themed spot; the "unique" experience includes two "amazing" restaurants, "perfectly conceived" decor with "superlative attention to detail, down to animal footprints imbedded in the walkways" and a lobby that pays "homage to African culture and folklore"; better yet, there's "wonderful kids' entertainment" from a staff that "couldn't be more gracious", so even if a few find it "a bit far away from the Disney parks", others contend there's "nothing like it anywhere in America."

Disney's Beach Club Resort 유 ᵬᵬ🔍

| 22 | 24 | 21 | 27 | $475 |

1800 Epcot Resorts Blvd. | Lake Buena Vista | 407-934-8000 |
fax 407-934-3850 | 800-227-1500 | www.disneyworld.com |
527 rooms, 56 suites

It's "like the Jersey Shore in Orlando" at the sister property to Disney's Yacht Club next door with an "incredible" seaside theme and a location "steps away from Epcot and MGM"; the "fantastic", three-acre "mini-waterpark" with a sandy bottom is "worth the price alone", although regulars also find "just the right mix of charm, fantasy and efficiency" to offset the "pedestrian" rooms.

☑ Disney's Beach Club Villas 유 🏕ᵬᵬ🔍

| 27 | 24 | 23 | 29 | $429 |

1800 Epcot Resorts Blvd. | Lake Buena Vista | 407-934-8000 |
fax 407-934-3850 | 800-227-1500 | www.disneyworld.com |
171 villas, 109 studios

It's often "hard to get a rez" at this Disney Vacation Club "favorite" with "excellent service", "lovely, serene" Victorian-style villas with full kitchens that are "ideal for families" and a location an "easy walk" to Epcot; access to the "best of the Disney pools", including the "incredible" sand-bottomed Stormalong Bay, also contributes to a "magical stay."

Disney's BoardWalk Inn 유 🔍

| 24 | 24 | 23 | 25 | $475 |

2101 N. Epcot Resorts Blvd. | Lake Buena Vista | 407-939-5100 |
fax 407-939-5150 | 800-227-1500 | www.disneyworld.com |
357 rooms, 14 suites

What could be a better combination than "an old-fashioned wooden boardwalk with a luxurious resort to match"? ask fans of this "festive" "beauty" with the "bustling" atmosphere of "turn-of-the-century" Atlantic City; outside is the Flying Fish Café, serving "some of the best seafood in central Florida", while inside are "wonderfully maintained public areas" and "plush" rooms serviced by an "excellent" staff; P.S. if you "want quiet", ask for one facing the "serene pools and gardens."

☑ Disney's BoardWalk Villas 🏕ᵬᵬ🔍

| 27 | 26 | 23 | 28 | $560 |

2101 N. Epcot Resorts Blvd. | Lake Buena Vista | 407-939-6200 |
fax 407-939-5150 | 800-227-1500 | www.disneyworld.com |
533 villas, 372 rooms

This "awesome" Disney Vacation Club option with the "relaxation" of a "seaside resort" earns praise for a staff that "pampers guests" and a "can't-beat" location "between Hollywood Studios and Epcot"; the "super", "home-away-from-home" conveniences in the "spacious", "comfortable" villas include kitchens and washer/dryers, while the "bustling" BoardWalk, with its multitude of eateries, further sweetens the deal; for "serenity", head to the on-site "pools and gardens."

Disney's Caribbean Beach Resort 🏃

| 19 | 21 | 15 | 23 | $185 |

900 Cayman Way | Lake Buena Vista | 407-934-3400 | fax 407-934-3288 | 800-227-1500 | www.disneyworld.com | 2112 rooms

"Festive and bright", this "no-frills" hotel consists of villages of "basic", motel-style rooms ("pay a little more to be near" the bus stop and food court) that sport "fun" "island" decor; though fans appreciate the "tropical feeling" and "affordable prices", others warn "be prepared to walk a lot" and don't expect gourmet food 'cause "it's not here"

Disney's Contemporary Resort 🏃Ⓢ🔍

| 20 | 20 | 20 | 22 | $339 |

4600 N. World Dr. | Lake Buena Vista | 407-824-1000 | fax 407-824-3539 | 800-227-1500 | www.disneyworld.com | 997 rooms, 11 suites

The first hotel at Disney World, this "comfortable" *Jetsons*-ish A-frame has an "unbeatable location" (the "monorail goes right through the lobby", so the Magic Kingdom is "just a skip away"); while fans say the refurbed rooms, "giant" by Mouse standards, have helped the "Contemporary earn its name yet again", others gripe that it's all "still a bit tired"; P.S. the rooftop California Grill "continues to wow" with excellent" Californian fare and fireworks views.

Disney's Coronado Springs Resort 🏃Ⓢ

| 19 | 22 | 18 | 22 | $185 |

1000 W. Buena Vista Dr. | Lake Buena Vista | 407-939-1000 | fax 407-939-1001 | 800-227-1500 | www.disneyworld.com | 1875 rooms, 46 suites

Disneyphiles gush over the "manicured grounds" at this moderately priced "expansive" Southwestern-themed resort and convention center that's "centered on a gorgeous lake" and feels "like a tropical paradise"; the "excellent facilities" include four "awesome" pools (one designed like a Mayan temple), a spa, a fitness center and the "unique" Pepper Market food court, but spoilsports snap the "long walk" to your "difficult-to-find", "motellike" room can feel "like miles."

🅩 Disney's Fort Wilderness Resort & Campground 🐾🏃🔍

| 24 | 23 | 21 | 25 | $67 |

4510 N. Ft. Wilderness Trail | Lake Buena Vista | 407-824-2900 | fax 407-824-3508 | 800-227-1500 | www.disneyworld.com | 784 campsites, 409 cabins

"One of the best-kept secrets" at Disney, this "campground" (rated the Best Buy among large resorts in this Survey) offers tents, RV campsites and "well-appointed" cabins with a/c, kitchens and patio decks; the "many outdoor activities" include canoeing, hiking, horseback riding and "watching an outdoor movie while roasting marshmallows and making s'mores", but getting to the parks is a hassle if you don't have a car.

Disney's Grand Floridian Resort & Spa 🧖🏃Ⓢ🔍

| 25 | 25 | 25 | 26 | $555 |

4401 Floridian Way | Lake Buena Vista | 407-824-3000 | fax 407-824-3186 | 800-227-1500 | www.disneyworld.com | 837 rooms, 25 suites

The "jewel in Disney's crown", this "amazing" Victorian-style spot with "breathtaking" views of Cinderella's Castle across the lagoon is

ROOMS SERVICE DINING FACIL. COST

"so close to the Magic Kingdom via monorail" that it makes up for the "long walk to it from your room"; an "excellent all-around venue" – "from the character meals to the food" (Victoria & Albert's was voted No. 1 for Food in our *Orlando Restaurants* Survey) to the "fabulous" spa and "amazing views of the fireworks" – this "flagship" is "perfect" for "adults with or without kids."

Disney's Old Key West Resort 🖎🖐☺🔍

| 25 | 22 | 16 | 25 | $485 |

1510 N. Cove Rd. | Lake Buena Vista | 407-827-7700 | fax 407-827-7710 | 800-227-1500 | www.disneyworld.com | 761 villas

Goofy and Co. feel "a hundred miles away" from this "quaint retreat" near Downtown Disney, a "relaxing and private", pastel-heavy "home away from home" with "well-appointed" studios and villas that are "extremely large in comparison to other resorts"; get-up-and-goers praise the Lake Buena Vista golf course, which "wraps around the resort", and the "many pools and other recreational activities", but a few foodies fret over "limited" dining options.

Disney's Polynesian Resort 🏃🖐

| 22 | 24 | 22 | 25 | $499 |

1600 Seven Seas Dr. | Lake Buena Vista | 407-824-2000 | fax 407-824-3174 | 800-227-1500 | www.disneyworld.com | 815 rooms, 32 suites

One of the original Disney resorts, this "taste of the Pacific" boasts "tropical" grounds with "swaying palms and flaming tikis" that "make you feel far removed from a theme park"; with "convenient" monorail service, "great views of the evening light parade on the lake", a "luau that's a must", a lush "volcano" pool area with waterfalls and a staff that "bends over backwards", it's the "favorite" of traditionalists; but a few mention a "badly needed renovation" and a "cheesy" theme.

Disney's Port Orleans Resort - French Quarter 🖐

| 21 | 22 | 18 | 25 | $185 |

2201 Orleans Dr. | Lake Buena Vista | 407-934-5000 | fax 407-934-5353 | 800-227-1500 | www.disneyworld.com | 1008 rooms

Melding the "flavor of New Orleans" with "Disney charm", this "moderately priced", "lush and tranquil" resort has "beautiful landscaping" and an "old-time French Quarter" feel that earns raves; while it's "easy to get around" (there's a "wonderful river cruise to Downtown Disney"), and the "cool pool" comes with a grand waterslide, "don't expect elegant dining", just "decent quick options", from the on-site food court.

Disney's Port Orleans Resort - Riverside 🖐

| 22 | 24 | 18 | 24 | $185 |

1251 Riverside Dr. | Lake Buena Vista | 407-934-6000 | fax 407-934-5777 | www.disneyworld.com | 2048 rooms

With "phenomenal grounds" that allow for "quiet walks through magnolia trees", this "midpriced" "gem" with an old-time Mississippi River town theme is a "peaceful and relaxing" "escape from the Mouse"; a fishing hole and "pools scattered all around" make it "fantastic for families", and though some say the "spacious" rooms are "nothing fancy", most river rats just go with the flow; P.S. guests can take a "boat ride direct from the resort" to nearby Downtown Disney.

	ROOMS	SERVICE	DINING	FACIL.	COST

Disney's Saratoga Springs Resort & Spa 🏨🌊☺🔍

27	24	18	26	$485

1960 Broadway | Lake Buena Vista | 407-827-1100 | fax 407-827-4444 | www.disneyworld.com | 552 villas, 288 studios

Styled after upstate New York's horse-y resort, this "humongous" complex "across the water from Downtown Disney" is "great for, you guessed it, families", who gallop from the "nicely equipped" rooms to the "fantastic" pools; "top-notch" service and a spa with "unique treatments" have a stable of admirers, but neigh-sayers snort that it's "way too spread out" and "could use more food options."

Disney's Wilderness Lodge 👪🏨

24	25	24	27	$335

901 Timberline Dr. | Lake Buena Vista | 407-824-3200 | fax 407-824-3232 | www.disneyworld.com | 700 rooms, 27 suites

Guests arriving at this "gorgeous" "family resort" wonder if they've taken a "wrong turn somewhere and ended up in the Pacific Northwest" when they see the "cavernous" split-log lobby replete with totem poles, a "river-stone fireplace" and "inviting chairs scattered all over the place"; sure, the "comfortable" rooms are "somewhat smaller than most hotels", but all have balconies or patios, and the "wonderful activities" (including a "picturesque" pool with an "awesome" geyser), the "outstanding" Artist Point restaurant and "phenomenal grounds" offer more than enough distraction.

Disney's Yacht Club Resort 👪🏨🔍

23	24	22	26	$415

1700 Epcot Resorts Blvd. | Lake Buena Vista | 407-934-7000 | fax 407-934-3450 | 800-227-1500 | www.disneyworld.com | 610 rooms, 11 suites

"Outstanding service" and an "awesome" waterfront location "within walking distance to Epcot" make this New England–themed resort "great for families"; "well-appointed" rooms with nautical motifs and "beautiful views" are "a bit classier" than those at its sister Beach Club, but the highlight here is the same: the "fantastic" sand-bottomed pool and three-acre "mini water park"; penny-pinchers pout that "for the price" they "expected larger" quarters and more dining options.

Gaylord Palms 👪🐾🏨☺

22	21	20	25	$379

6000 W. Osceola Pkwy. | Kissimmee | 407-586-0000 | fax 407-586-1999 | 866-972-6779 | www.gaylordpalms.com | 1300 rooms, 106 suites

"If you don't have to stay inside" Disney, it's "the place to be" say devotees of this "humongous" Kissimmee mega-property with "everything for business and pleasure", including "wonderfully appointed" rooms, a recreation park with putting greens and a "relaxing" Canyon Ranch spa; a "cool" 4.5-acre, "greenhouse"-like atrium with "incredible flowers, plants" and even "live alligators" re-creates Florida habitats, but cold-blooded critics cringe over this "simulated reality" that's "chock-full of crying children and boozed-up conventioneers."

Grand Bohemian Hotel 🍴🏨 (fka Westin Grand Bohemian)

24	23	22	23	$499

325 S. Orange Ave. | Orlando | 407-313-9000 | fax 407-313-9001 | 888-663-0024 | www.grandbohemianhotel.com | 214 rooms, 36 suites

"Right in the center of Downtown" is this "true gem" shining with a staff that's "hip without being obnoxious", "original artwork throughout the hotel and in-house gallery" and a "vibrant bar" built around a "gorgeous", rare Bösendorfer grand piano whose "music permeates the lobby every evening"; "bordellolike" rooms are "draped in rich reds and dark woods", with "plush bedding", while dining ranges from a "Starbucks in the lobby" to the surf 'n' turf at Bohème, but since it's a 20-minute ride to Disney, it's "not recommended for families" with kids.

Hilton Walt Disney World ♨

| 19 | 20 | 17 | 20 | $159 |

1751 Hotel Plaza Blvd. | Lake Buena Vista | 407-827-4000 |
fax 407-827-3890 | 800-782-4414 | www.hilton.com | 708 rooms,
106 suites
"Steps away from Downtown Disney, where you can jump on a bus to any" of the parks, this enormous "conference hotel" is the "place to be" "if you don't want to stay in" (or pay extra for) an "actual WDW hotel"; "with the perks, but without the price tag" of some of the Mouse-owned houses, it offers a "conscientious staff" and "pool facilities with distinct areas for splashing toddlers, boisterous kids and margarita-sipping floaters."

Hyatt Regency Grand Cypress ♟ ⌂ ☜

| 21 | 22 | 20 | 26 | $279 |

1 Grand Cypress Blvd. | Orlando | 407-239-1234 | fax 407-239-3800 |
800-233-1234 | www.hyattgrandcypress.com | 750 rooms, 67 suites
Just "outside the House of the Mouse", this "gargantuan" 1,500-acre resort is a "wonderful oasis" with "magnificent grounds", four "outstanding" Jack Nicklaus–designed golf courses and a "fabulous", "cavernlike" pool with waterslides and "hidden hot tubs"; even if some find the "cramped" rooms in "need of an upgrade", most vow that it's "still one of the best", with a "staff that can't do enough for you"; N.B. teetotalers might prefer the affiliated Villas of Grand Cypress, which are closer to the links.

International Plaza Resort & Spa ♨ ♨ Ⓢ

| - | - | - | - | $299 |

10100 International Dr. | Orlando | 407-352-1100 | fax 407-354-5007 |
800-327-0363 | www.intlplazaresortandspa.com | 1046 rooms, 56 suites
Expect a fresh look at this palm-tree-lined former Sheraton adjacent to SeaWorld and 10 minutes from Disney, which underwent renovations throughout 2008; the rooms, divided between a motellike building and a main tower, will sport a Balinese look, along with dark woods, granite countertops and flat-screen TVs, and the spa, three swimming pools and four restaurants are also being updated.

JW Marriott Grande Lakes ♟ ♨ ⌂ Ⓢ ☜

| 24 | 23 | 22 | 26 | $469 |

4040 Central Florida Pkwy. | Orlando | 407-206-2300 |
fax 407-206-2301 | 800-228-9290 | www.grandelakes.com |
934 rooms, 64 suites
This "excellent resort" and "massive" convention center is an "always consistent" "oasis" that's "away from the 'Mouse crowd'" (the "only characters" at dinner are "competent waiters"); notable features include a "wonderful", "lazy river pool" that "kids love", "fantastic landscaping" and "superbly appointed rooms"; there's also a 40,000-sq.-ft. "world-class fitness center and spa" and a "beautiful" 18-hole Greg Norman–designed golf course, both of which are shared with the Ritz-Carlton next door.

	ROOMS	SERVICE	DINING	FACIL.	COST

Loews Portofino Bay �

| 24 | 22 | 22 | 25 | $344 |

5601 Universal Blvd. | Orlando | 407-503-1000 | fax 407-503-1010 |
800-232-7827 | www.loewshotels.com | 705 rooms, 45 suites

Get "transported to Italy" at this "wonderful escape" "in the middle of
town", where the "stunning re-creation" of a "seaside village" comes
complete with "singing waiters" at Mama Della's, a "phenomenal
beach pool", a "great spa" and "pretty" (but "tiny") rooms with "super-
comfortable" beds; a "convenient" location a "10-minute ferry ride
from Universal Studios" and "front-of-the-line privileges" for guests
have some fans asking "who needs Disney?"

Loews Royal Pacific Resort ♚♘

| 20 | 20 | 22 | 24 | $284 |

6300 Hollywood Way | Orlando | 407-503-3000 | fax 407-503-3010 |
800-232-7827 | www.loewshotels.com | 949 rooms, 51 suites

With its "fast-pass tickets", "complimentary boat rides" "to the parks"
and an "awesome", "expansive pool" complete with interactive water
features (water cannon, anyone?), this "gorgeous" resort "in the middle of Universal" is the "hands-down favorite" for "families with kids"
(or pets); rooms are "solid", the "number and variety of resturants is
good" and things are "well run" "for such a large property."

Marriott Orlando World Center
Resort & Convention Center ♚♘⊥☺🔍

| 20 | 19 | 18 | 23 | $369 |

8701 World Center Dr. | Orlando | 407-239-4200 |
fax 407-238-8777 | 800-228-9290 | www.marriottworldcenter.com |
1890 rooms, 110 suites

It feels like "the whole world" is staying at this "enormous" "Marriott on
steroids" (the largest in the world), where it's "easy to get lost" on the
200-plus acres of "stunning grounds" that include "two golf courses"
and "wonderful pools" complete with "waterslides"; guests can watch
"Disney fireworks from the balconies" of some rooms (they all have
"spectacular views"), but while there are "lots of meal choices" on-
site, quality ranges from "excellent" to "terrible"; luckily the "prompt
and friendly" staffers "know how to handle large groups with ease."

Peabody, The ♚♘☺🔍

| 21 | 22 | 21 | 22 | $395 |

9801 International Dr. | Orlando | 407-352-4000 | fax 407-351-0073 |
800-732-2639 | www.peabodyorlando.com | 834 rooms, 57 suites

"All it's quacked up to be" crack converts of this "close-to-the-
Convention-Center" hotel famed for its "don't-miss morning and
evening march of the Peabody ducks" through the lobby; given its locale
that attracts "too many conventioneers" and the "tired" rooms, this "big"
property is "more about business than a vacation or resort experience."

Renaissance Resort
at SeaWorld ♚♘☺🔍

| 21 | 21 | 18 | 21 | $300 |

6677 Sea Harbor Dr. | Orlando | 407-351-5555 | fax 407-351-9991 |
800-468-3571 | www.renaissancehotels.com | 716 rooms, 65 suites

With "rooms large enough for Shamu to swim in", this "newly renovated" resort offers "convenience" (you can "walk to SeaWorld"), as
well as a "lovely atrium", "several dining choices" and solid service;
though it "caters more to business travelers", if you get a room with a
"view of the fireworks" and take advantage of the "excellent pools",
it's a fun family respite too.

[Z] Ritz-Carlton Grande Lakes 👪 🍴 ⛳ 🏊 Ⓢ 🎾

ROOMS	SERVICE	DINING	FACIL.	COST
27	26	25	28	$390

4012 Central Florida Pkwy. | Orlando | 407-206-2400 | fax 407-206-2401 | 800-241-3333 | www.ritzcarlton.com | 520 rooms, 64 suites

Its South Orlando location is "in the middle of nowhere, but who cares?" when you've got "the best of the Ritz-Carltons in Florida" say surveyors who swoon over this "super-sized, yet surprisingly intimate" "Italian palace-like" resort filled with "everything you never knew you needed, [like] a chilled towel and lemonade upon check-in", "amazing rooms", "outstanding" cuisine at Norman's, "top-notch activities" and an "Epcot of spas combining services from around the world"; P.S. the "wonderful" staff "takes care of kids as if they're the ones paying the bill."

Rosen Shingle Creek 💼 ⛳ 🏊 Ⓢ 🎾

ROOMS	SERVICE	DINING	FACIL.	COST
23	21	19	22	$375

9939 Universal Blvd. | Orlando | 407-996-9939 | fax 407-996-9938 | 866-996-6338 | www.rosenshinglecreek.com | 1362 rooms, 139 suites

Despite the "zillions of conventioneers and their spouses", "you won't feel crowded" at this "surprisingly nice" "mega-resort" deemed "a sanctuary in the middle of town", thanks in part to the "good-for-lounging" pool area, golf courses and enjoyable "wildlife trail"; the rooms are "serene", service is "impeccable" and there's "something to do and eat for every age group", but tired trekkers tsk it takes "time to get from one end" of this "cavernous" hotel "to the other."

Villas of Grand Cypress 👪 💼 ⛳ 🏊 🎾

ROOMS	SERVICE	DINING	FACIL.	COST
∇ 26	24	20	25	$450

1 N. Jacaranda St. | Orlando | 407-239-4700 | fax 407-239-7219 | 877-330-7377 | www.grandcypress.com | 73 suites, 73 villas

Duffers and tot-toters "can't wait to return" to this "fabulous" "secluded" Lake Buena Vista "hideaway" with "stellar grounds" and "terrific" "individual suites" "conveniently" situated on the Jack Nicklaus-designed "Scottish-style golf courses" (45 holes worth); the "above-par" staff "takes care of every little detail", and with a spa and pools with slides and waterfalls available at sister property Hyatt Regency Grand Cypress, there's "so much to do" for families.

Walt Disney World Dolphin 👪 Ⓢ 🎾

ROOMS	SERVICE	DINING	FACIL.	COST
19	19	20	22	$439

1500 Epcot Resorts Blvd. | Lake Buena Vista | 407-934-4000 | fax 407-934-4099 | 800-227-1500 | www.swandolphin.com | 1509 rooms, 129 suites

Deemed "Disney without the saccharine", this resort (connected by a causeway to its sister, Swan) is a "respite from all the kiddie stuff" yet still a "family-friendly" spot within an easy "boat ride or walk" to "all the parks"; the "superb location" is matched by "dining choices for everyone" (Todd English's "bluezoo is fantastic"), while "rooms are modern" with "amazing beds"; even if dissers dub it either "depressing" or "tacky" ("you're fine as long as you can't see the decor"), the crowds of "conventioneers" don't seem to mind.

Walt Disney World Swan 👪 Ⓢ 🎾

ROOMS	SERVICE	DINING	FACIL.	COST
21	21	21	22	$439

1200 Epcot Resorts Blvd. | Lake Buena Vista | 407-934-3000 | fax 407-934-4499 | 800-227-1500 | www.swandolphin.com | 756 rooms, 55 suites

The "smaller", "quieter" sister to the Dolphin, this "happy" place boasts "easy access to Epcot and MGM" without being too close to the "frenzy"; even "grumpy conventioneers" don't dissuade those who find "luxurious beds", a "choice" of restaurants ("Il Mulino New York and Kimonos are a big plus") and an overall "super atmosphere"; but fusspots find "nothing spectacular" in this "standard" spot.

Palm Beach

Brazilian Court ✕ [H] 🐕 🔭 [S] — 23 | 23 | 25 | 20 | $599

301 Australian Ave. | 561-655-7740 | fax 561-655-0801 | 800-552-0335 | www.thebraziliancourt.com | 40 rooms, 40 suites

Fresh from a recent renovation, this "intimate", "elegant" eight-decade-old "hot spot" is a "true Palm Beach experience", with "spacious, immaculate and incredibly well-appointed" rooms (complete with wine coolers and Jacuzzi tubs) located "walking distance to Downtown" and "just two blocks from the beach"; as for the eats, the French-American Café Boulud is "as good as it gets", with a "buzzing evening cocktail scene" that "must be seen to be believed."

Breakers Palm Beach, The 👪 ✕ [H] 🔭 ⛷ [S] 🎾 — 24 | 27 | 25 | 28 | $550

1 S. County Rd. | 561-655-6611 | fax 561-659-8403 | 800-833-3141 | www.thebreakers.com | 492 rooms, 58 suites

"From the moment you arrive until you leave, you feel like a valued guest" at this "premier" "grande dame" that "still maintains her charm" after all these years; despite being a "little too fancy" for some (the "magnificent lobby" has "ceilings worthy of the Sistine chapel"), it's "surprisingly family-friendly" with "terrific pools" and a beachfront that was redone a few years ago, along with "amazing" food; just beware, the "size of rooms varies enormously."

Chesterfield, The 🐕 🔭 — 20 | 24 | 21 | 19 | $495

363 Cocoanut Row | 561-659-5800 | fax 561-659-6707 | 800-243-7871 | www.chesterfieldpb.com | 41 rooms, 11 suites

It "feels like you're visiting your great aunt" by way of "Tarzan" and "Laura Ashley" at this Small Luxury Hotels of the World member with "traditional English touches" incorporated into the "funky" decor; an "outstanding staff" and a location "walkable to Worth Avenue" help you get a "great sample of life on the island", especially if you don't require ocean views or large rooms.

Four Seasons Resort 👪 ✕ 🐕 🔭 [S] 🎾 — 24 | 26 | 25 | 26 | $674

2800 S. Ocean Blvd. | 561-582-2800 | fax 561-547-1557 | 800-432-2335 | www.fourseasons.com | 197 rooms, 13 suites

"Supreme service" ("black napkins in the restaurant so we wouldn't get white fuzz on our clothes"), a "sophisticated setting" just "steps from the ocean" and some of "the best food in Palm Beach" combine to "make this hotel a winner" you'll "return to every year"; while a few fret about "average" rooms (for a Four Seasons) and facilities "loaded with small kids during high season", others just head to the "relaxing" spa for relief.

Jupiter Beach Resort & Spa 🔭 [S] 🎾 — ▽ 20 | 21 | 21 | 21 | $359

5 North A1A | Jupiter | 561-746-2511 | fax 561-744-1741 | 800-228-8810 | www.jupiterbeachresort.com | 133 rooms, 35 suites

"What's not to like?" ask fans of this "beautiful", white midsize complex on the Atlantic; although it's a little "off the beaten path" (25 miles from

	ROOMS	SERVICE	DINING	FACIL.	COST

the Palm Beach airport), that's part of what makes it a "quiet family place" that lets you get "away from it all"; an "accommodating staff" and a 7,500-sq.-ft. spa are other pluses, but "food is the weak link."

PGA National Resort & Spa ⚐ 🛁 ⊾ ⓢ ⚲

17	18	17	23	$495

400 Ave. of the Champions | Palm Beach Gardens | 561-627-2000 | fax 561-622-0299 | 800-633-9150 | www.pga-resort.com | 241 rooms, 56 suites, 42 cottages

"Even if you think a wedge is lettuce and a mulligan is soup", this "recently renovated" "quintessential golf resort" with five "pristine" courses offers "something for everyone": "pampering" at the "expansive spa", relaxing at the "refurbished pool" and working out at the extensive gym facilities; "rooms are well kept", service is "pretty good" and while dining can be "variable", the new Ironwood Grille is a notable option.

Ritz-Carlton, The 🏨 ✕ ⚐ 🛁 ⓢ ⚲

26	26	23	25	$649

100 S. Ocean Blvd. | Manalapan | 561-533-6000 | fax 561-588-4202 | 800-241-3333 | www.ritzcarlton.com | 268 rooms, 32 suites

After spending "zillions in renovations" (and they're "still spending"), this "absolutely beautiful hotel" is deemed a solid "benchmark for high-end lodging" with "spacious" rooms matching the "overstuffed, old-fashioned luxury" of the "inviting lobby"; "magnificent grounds" include a "top-notch" pool area, the staff is "totally committed to quality at every level" and the "dining is excellent", so it's only the "small", "rocky" beach that some wish were better.

Palm Coast

Ginn Hammock Beach Resort 🏨 🏖 🛁 ⊾ ⓢ ⚲
(fka Club at Hammock Beach)

-	-	-	-	$349

200 Ocean Crest Dr. | 386-246-5500 | fax 386-246-5600 | 866-502-6228 | www.ginnhammockbeachresort.com | 280 condos, 19 rooms

Duffers drive to the edge of the Altantic to golf at this "super-size" oceanfront resort where the courses come courtesy of Jack Nicklaus and Tom Watson and there's lots of "fabulous" kid-friendly features ("pool with sand beach, waterslide, lazy river"); given the "wonderful" staff and accommodations from upscale lodge rooms to multi-bedroom condos scattered along the sea, it's "surprising" that this four-year-old is "not that well known"; N.B. sushi and cigar bars were recently added.

Panhandle

WaterColor Inn & Resort 🏨 ✕ 🏖 ⓢ ⚲

▽ 27	25	26	28	$520

34 Goldenrod Circle | Santa Rosa Beach | 850-534-5000 | fax 850-534-5001 | 888-376-0424 | www.watercolorresort.com | 150 cottages, 60 rooms

Hooked surveyors paint a pretty picture of this Santa Rosa Beach inn, a member of Small Luxury Hotels of the World, where "Southern comfort" meets "great views" in a "casually elegant" atmosphere on one of the "most beautiful white sand" stretches of the Emerald Coast; adding to the "perfect" experience are "cool" rooms, a staff that delivers "expert attention to every detail" and the "amazing" Fish Out of Water restaurant; N.B. guests get free use of kayaks, canoes, fishing gear and bicycles.

Sarasota

Colony Beach & Tennis Resort, The ♯🏖♨⚲🔍 | 18 | 21 | 22 | 24 | $395

1620 Gulf of Mexico Dr. | Longboat Key | 941-383-6464 |
fax 941-383-7549 | 800-426-5669 | www.colonybeachresort.com |
234 suites

"If you're a tennis player, this may be your ideal" lodging praise proponents of this "low-key" "family-oriented" resort on Longboat Key that has 21 courts, 10 pros and lots of clinics to improve your swing; tottoters tout the "wonderful" kids' program, "gorgeous beach", pool and lots of water sports for little ones, but a few warn it's "aging less than gracefully" when it comes to "tired" rooms and a restaurant menu that needs an "update."

Longboat Key Club & Resort ♯🏖♨⚲🔍 | 22 | 21 | 18 | 23 | $375

301 Gulf of Mexico Dr. | Longboat Key | 941-383-8821 |
fax 941-383-0359 | 800-237-8821 | www.longboatkeyclub.com |
195 suites, 23 rooms

Deemed "one of Florida's great treasures", this "old-fashioned" "Gulffront" resort is most appreciated for its "glorious, long beach", "plentiful amenities" (including a "new state-of-the-art tennis facility") and "terrific" rooms, most of which have kitchens and "great sea views"; the "pleasant staff" "hits all the high notes", food is "good but nothing special" and while recent "renovations" helped refine the "elegant" atmosphere, yet another "major upgrade" has been announced for the near future.

Ritz-Carlton, The ♯🏖♨⚲🔍 | 26 | 27 | 24 | 26 | $519

1111 Ritz-Carlton Dr. | 941-309-2000 | fax 941-309-2100 | 800-241-3333 |
www.ritzcarlton.com | 235 rooms, 31 suites

"Absolutely superb throughout", this sizable property boasts a "wonderful beach club" (a "short" shuttle ride away), "exceptional service", "plush rooms", a "full spa" and "outstanding, player-friendly golf"; while sun-worshipers who wish the beach weren't off-site find something "to be desired" here, most are ready to "let Ritz-Carlton be in charge of heaven."

Tampa Bay Area

Chalet Suzanne Country Inn ✕♨⚲ | ▽ 16 | 21 | 22 | 15 | $169

3800 Chalet Suzanne Dr. | Lake Wales | 863-676-6011 | fax 863-676-1814 |
800-433-6011 | www.chaletsuzanne.com | 26 rooms

Built in 1931 and "so unique it's hard to rate", this "laid-back" B&B "in a time warp" serves "hearty" Traditional American dishes that "aren't for weight watchers" and offers "old-fashioned" chambers styled with "kitschy, off-the-wall decorations" perfect for those wanting "old-time Florida" (with "facilities from the same era"); guests who think it "badly needs an overhaul", however, suggest you "eat and run" rather than "putting up with aged rooms."

	ROOMS	SERVICE	DINING	FACIL.	COST
Clearwater Beach Marriott Suites on Sand Key 👪 🔭 Ⓢ	▽ 18	21	19	20	$269

1201 Gulf Blvd. | Clearwater Beach | 727-596-1100 | fax 727-595-4292 | 800-228-9290 | www.marriott.com | 220 suites

An "excellent location" overlooking Clearwater Harbor and a half-mile from a "wonderful" beach, this all-suite spot on Sand Key is a good choice "for families with children"; it offers all the "classic amenities" of a Marriott, as well as a pool with its own cabanas and a 35-ft. cascading waterfall.

	ROOMS	SERVICE	DINING	FACIL.	COST
Don CeSar Beach Resort, A Loews Hotel 👪 Ⓗ 🐕 🔭 Ⓢ	21	24	21	24	$360

3400 Gulf Blvd. | St. Pete Beach | 727-360-1881 | fax 727-367-6952 | 800-282-1116 | www.doncesar.com | 237 rooms, 40 suites, 2 penthouses

Stalwarts liken sojourns at this "elegant" 1928 Spanish-Mediterranean "pink palace" to "staying inside a birthday cake" - an "old-world" confection modeled on Waikiki's Royal Hawaiian that has "direct access" to an "outstanding stretch" of St. Pete Beach, a "great pool" and multiple restaurants (the "oceanfront casual dining is a winner at sunset"); if some carp that rooms vary from "suite to broom closet"-size, others are "tickled pinker than the paint job" by the "fantastic" new 11,000-sq.-ft. spa.

	ROOMS	SERVICE	DINING	FACIL.	COST
Grand Hyatt 🐕 🔭 🎾	22	22	20	21	$359

2900 Bayport Dr. | Tampa | 813-874-1234 | fax 813-207-6790 | 800-233-1234 | www.grandtampabay.hyatt.com | 377 rooms, 23 suites, 45 casitas

"So close to the airport you think you're on the runway", this huge high-rise is a "good venue for business travelers", and depending on whom you ask, it's either in a "nice location on the bay" or "in the middle of nowhere"; regardless, surveyors applaud the "terrific" service, the free-form pool and the "fabulous sunsets" from Armani's and Oystercatchers (which has "wonderful seafood"); P.S. rooms seem "a bit dated" to some, but renovations are planned for '09.

	ROOMS	SERVICE	DINING	FACIL.	COST
Renaissance Vinoy Resort & Golf Club 👪 Ⓗ 🔭 Ⓢ 🎾	24	24	24	24	$349

501 Fifth Ave. NE | St. Petersburg | 727-894-1000 | fax 727-822-2785 | 888-303-4430 | www.vinoyrenaissanceresort.com | 346 rooms, 14 suites

This "grande dame of the Gulf Coast" is "still reigning" praise "pampered" patrons who are "made to feel special" "from the moment" they arrive at this peachy-pink Downtown Mediterranean Revival resort; "top-rate" facilities include tennis, golf, a spa and some of "the best" dining "in the area, particularly at Sunday brunch, and "guests are treated like stars" in the "relaxed atmosphere"; it's all an "unexpected oasis" many hope to "return to."

	ROOMS	SERVICE	DINING	FACIL.	COST
Saddlebrook Resort 👪 🍳 🔭 ⛳ Ⓢ 🎾	▽ 22	20	19	25	$280

5700 Saddlebrook Way | Wesley Chapel | 813-973-1111 | fax 813-973-1312 | 800-729-8383 | www.saddlebrookresort.com | 200 rooms, 600 suites

"If you love tennis and golf" you'll "have a great time" at this 480-acre resort 30 miles north of Tampa where the "amazing tennis program" (on grass, clay and hard courts) is run by "talented and passionate instructors", and "two great" Arnold Palmer-designed golf courses are favorites with beginners and pros alike (and alligators too); the "superb service focuses on the guest at all times", while the "awesome pools" and "beautiful spa" offer relaxation, but some say you'll have to overlook "decor reminiscent of the '70s and '80s."

Vero Beach

Disney's Vero Beach Resort 👪 🍳 🔭 🎾 ▽ 23 | 25 | 18 | 25 | $309

9250 Island Grove Terr. | 772-234-2000 | fax 772-234-2030 | 800-227-1500 | www.disneyvacationclub.com | 211 apartments

"Don't tell anyone about this amazing place!" say selfish fans of this oceanfront "away from it all" resort two hours southeast of Disney World; there's "just a hint of the Mouse here", but it shines through in the "impeccable" service and the "huge", "amazing" pool (there's also the "beach at your door"); the apartmentlike rooms are "not luxurious, but are designed for families", with kitchens and (in most cases) porches or balconies.

Georgia

TOPS IN STATE

27 Cloister | *Sea Island*
Lodge at Sea Island | *St. Simons Island*
26 Ritz-Carlton Reynolds | *Greensboro*
25 InterContinental Buckhead | *Atlanta*
Ritz-Carlton | *Atlanta*
24 Ritz-Carlton Buckhead | *Atlanta*

Atlanta

Atlanta Marriott Downtown 18 | 20 | 17 | 19 | $219

160 Spring St. NW | 404-688-8600 | fax 404-524-5543 | 866-316-5959 | www.marriott.com | 286 rooms, 26 suites

Downtown denizens "love" this "moderately priced", "atrium-centered hotel" with a "convenient location" near the Aquarium and Coca-Cola museum, where the staff is "wonderful" and the traditional digs "comfortable"; but some call it "noisy" ("bring earplugs if you want your beauty sleep") and somewhat "dated."

Four Seasons 👪 🍴 🐕 🔭 Ⓢ 25 | 26 | 24 | 23 | $410

75 14th St. | 404-881-9898 | fax 404-873-4692 | 800-819-0642 | www.fourseasons.com | 226 rooms, 18 suites

"Who cares if it doesn't have a Buckhead address?" ponder patrons of this "top-notch" Midtown hotel where the "standout" staff "wishes to please" and the "impressive common areas" include a huge marble lobby with a "busy bar" that's "packed with celebrities on weekends" and a health club with indoor saltwater pool; a "good location" for business or arts district activities and "delicious" fare are other pluses, but well-seasoned sojourners say, given the caliber of this luxury brand's other outposts, their "expectations for the rooms were much higher."

	ROOMS	SERVICE	DINING	FACIL.	COST

Grand Hyatt 🦢

| 22 | 23 | 19 | 23 | $389 |

3300 Peachtree Rd. NE | 404-237-1234 | fax 404-233-5686 | 800-233-1234 | www.hyatt.com | 416 rooms, 22 suites

"Worthy of the 'grand'" moniker praise patrons of this "upscale" "model hotel" whose "Japanese-Zen theme is relaxing after a day of shopping" or hitting the "many popular bars and restaurants" nearby; guests report a "high level of service" and "dependable rooms", as well as a "surprisingly chic" and "well-maintained" facility with a "beautiful main lobby"; "you won't go wrong" at this "good value for the money."

Hilton 🦢🏃🔍

| ▽ 19 | 18 | 17 | 19 | $299 |

255 Courtland St. NE | 404-659-2000 | fax 404-221-6368 | 800-445-8667 | www.hilton.com | 1201 rooms, 25 suites

Boosters of this "big convention hotel" set "off the beaten path" on the edge of Downtown claim "it caters to everyone's needs" with an "extremely helpful and friendly" staff, "nice rooms" (especially the "remodeled" ones) and "lots of choices" from the "very good" "breakfast buffet"; but travelers disillusioned with the generaly "old" digs and lack of a spa pine "Hilton, thou have forsaken us."

Hyatt Regency

| 20 | 18 | 18 | 20 | $169 |

265 Peachtree St. NE | 404-577-1234 | fax 404-588-4137 | 800-233-1234 | www.hyattregencyatlanta.com | 1208 rooms, 52 suites

It's "what you'd expect in a Downtown business hotel" report reviewers of this "well-maintained", "convenient" chainster with the expected "atrium lobby"; "old rooms are spacious and shabby, new ones are tiny but chic", say some, but all are "moderately priced", so you can overlook service that sometimes "just does not exist."

Indigo, Hotel 🦢

| ▽ 18 | 22 | 16 | 17 | $179 |

683 Peachtree St. NE | 404-874-9200 | fax 404-873-4245 | 800-972-2404 | www.hotelindigo.com | 140 rooms

Deemed "a wonderful alternative to the big hotels in town" and boasting an "unbeatable location" (especially "if you're seeing a show at the Fox" across the street), this "cute", pet-friendly offering (a newish brand from InterContinental) earns points for its "coffee/wine bar" with a "nice indoor/outdoor seating area", and rooms "decorated with flair"; but "tight" baths and no full restaurant on-site are drawbacks.

InterContinental Buckhead ✕🦢🏃Ⓢ

| 26 | 25 | 22 | 25 | $399 |

3315 Peachtree Rd. NE | 404-946-9000 | fax 404-946-9001 | 877-422-8254 | www.intercontinental.com/buckhead | 401 rooms, 21 suites

Hotel hounds "highly recommend" this "solid property" in an "amazing location" near upscale malls, citing the "exquisite rooms", "top service" (they're "wonderful with children") and "surprisingly good" food from the "24-hour " Au Pied de Cochon as major pluses; regulars who "catch a glimpse of celebrities" in the lobby bar and deem the "rooftop pool and hot tub" "a must" say that while the prices can be "high", it's "well worth the money" for business or a "romantic getaway."

JW Marriott Buckhead 🏃

| 21 | 20 | 19 | 21 | $299 |

3300 Lenox Rd. NE | 404-262-3344 | fax 404-262-8689 | 800-228-9290 | www.jwmarriottbuckhead.com | 367 rooms, 4 suites

"Shoppers" and those with business in Buckhead report a "pleasant stay" at this "convenient" midsized hotel adjacent to Lenox Square

Mall and the Marta, thanks in part to the "nice steakhouse", "quality rooms", "wonderful club level" and "consistently good service"; the not-so-happy harrumph this "faded lady" "needs some renovation."

🆕 Mansion on Peachtree, The ✕ 🍴🛁Ⓢ
-	-	-	-	$495

3376 Peachtree Rd. | 404-995-7500 | fax 404-995-7501 | 888-767-3966 | www.mansiononpeachtree.com | 96 rooms, 31 suites

Rosewood lifts Buckhead's level of luxury to a new high with this ultra-chic hotel where art deco marble interiors in soothing neutral tones impart a serene vibe that continues to the understated rooms and suites, boasting personal butlers, 37-inch flat-screen TVs, Bose music systems, fresh daily flowers, WiFi and deluxe bath amenities; views of a beautifully landscaped courtyard complement the modern Italian-inspired fare at NEO, while Tom Colicchio's Craft will soon take center stage; N.B. the on-site 29 Spa, the first developed by Lydia Mondavi, uses exclusive grape seed antioxidant products.

Omni Hotel at CNN Center 🏃 🍴🛁Ⓢ
20	18	15	21	$199

100 CNN Ctr. | 404-659-0000 | fax 404-525-5050 | 888-444-6664 | www.omnihotels.com | 1036 rooms, 31 suites

Guests needing a "fine business hotel" in "the heart of Downtown" like this rather "ordinary" spot's "modern, spacious, cushy" quarters, "excellent fitness" room and location "attached to CNN" and mere "blocks from the aquarium", park, Marta stop, convention center and Atlanta Dome; while the dining isn't impressive and the facilities may need "some freshening", it's otherwise considered a "well-managed" choice.

Ritz-Carlton, The ✕🛁
26	26	24	23	$395

181 Peachtree St. NE | 404-659-0400 | fax 404-688-0400 | 800-241-3333 | www.ritzcarlton.com | 422 rooms, 22 suites

"Party in Buckhead, but sleep here" counsel carousing critics who enjoy "nothing but the best" from this recently renovated "grand" Downtown hotel deemed "far superior to big convention" properties in the area thanks to the "beautifully appointed, quiet rooms" and a "superb staff" that "accommodates" "requests without blinking"; "wonderful cuisine" from the Atlanta Grill can be taken on a charming balcony overlooking Peachtree Street.

Ritz-Carlton Buckhead ✕🍴🛁
24	25	25	24	$479

3434 Peachtree Rd. NE | 404-237-2700 | fax 404-239-0078 | 800-241-3333 | www.ritzcarlton.com | 524 rooms, 29 suites

Enjoy a "cocoon of civility" at this business hotel where the "wonderful facilities" include "the best restaurant in the city", a "fantastic" week-end brunch and a "hip" lobby bar perfect for "celeb-stalking"; fans say "service is superb" and plush rooms make them "feel like royalty", but others claim that the "peach has lost a bit of its fuzz" and hope the on-going renovations – to double the number of suites – will help.

🆕 W Atlanta - Midtown 🍴🛁Ⓢ
-	-	-	-	$509

(fka Sheraton Midtown at Colony Square)

188 14th St. NE | 404-892-6000 | fax 404-733-6990 | 877-822-0000 | www.whotels.com | 433 rooms, 33 suites

Moxie with a dash of mojo is the name of the game at this new and typically modern Starwood sandwiched between Piedmont Park and the

	ROOMS	SERVICE	DINING	FACIL.	COST

magnificent Midtown Mile; highlights include the waterfall-bedecked Living Room lounge, the Southeast Asian Spice Market restaurant, a Bliss Spa and a suitably chic crowd.

W Atlanta - Perimeter 🏊🛜🏋️

	21	20	19	20	$349

111 Perimeter Ctr. W. | 770-396-6800 | fax 770-399-5514 | 800-683-6100 | www.whotels.com | 154 suites, 121 rooms

Deemed "convenient" if you need to be in the "suburbs" or are "visiting the malls" "directly across the street", this "older" hotel – "one of the first W's in existence" – is considered a "nice place to stay" by those who find the "minimalist" digs "beautiful"; but many who complain it's a "mediocre" property with "average rooms" "in need of a remodel" say it "doesn't feel up to par with others" in this brand.

Westin Buckhead 🛜🏋️

	23	21	19	22	$365

3391 Peachtree Rd. NE | 404-365-0065 | fax 404-365-8787 | 800-937-8461 | www.westin.com | 365 rooms, 11 suites

Given the "Heavenly beds" (and heavenly cribs, too) plus what some call the "best club floor in the country" guests "can't wait to come back" to this "upscale business hotel" in a "superb location" just a Prada pump's throw from Buckhead's tony Lenox Mall and Phipps Plaza; the service is "hospitable", and dining comes courtesy of the Palm restaurant.

Braselton

Château Élan 🍴🏋️⛰️Ⓢ🔍

	23	23	20	24	$259

100 Rue Charlemagne | 678-425-0900 | fax 678-425-6000 | 800-233-9463 | www.chateauelan.com | 275 rooms, 14 suites, 10 villas

"For a perfect weekend getaway" or "meeting location" surveyors head for the "hills north of Atlanta", to this "beautiful winery"-centered resort deemed "simply exquisite" by those who toast the "efficiency-meets-old-South" service; although "underwhelmed" whiners who find a "tacky" "concrete castle" just "a stone's throw off I-85" "don't get it", the rest relax at the "full-service" "spa" or happily play golf away "from the chaos" of city life.

Georgia Coast

Ⓩ Cloister Hotel, The 🍴🛜🏋️⛰️Ⓢ🔍

	27	27	26	29	$750

100 First St. | Sea Island | 912-638-3611 | fax 912-638-5159 | 800-732-4752 | www.seaisland.com | 124 rooms, 32 suites

The "downside of visiting" this "magical" Sea Island resort is that "everything else will seem second rate" sigh smitten surveyors "captivated" by the "awesomely remodeled", "beyond heavenly" facilities of this "golfer's paradise" where "no detail goes unnoticed" ("is there nothing these people don't think of?"); further "exceptional" aspects include the "superb new beach club", the "divine" dining and the "amazing" beach – no wonder it's so "outrageously expensive."

Jekyll Island Club Hotel 🍴Ⓗ🏋️

	∇ 21	23	23	23	$199

371 Riverview Dr. | Jekyll Island | 912-635-2600 | fax 912-635-2818 | 800-535-9547 | www.jekyllclub.com | 122 rooms, 35 suites

"Take a walk back in time" at this fanciful, turreted Victorian-style hotel whose "historic elegance" makes you "feel like one of the billionaires who established" this "laid-back" late-19th-century island resort an hour south of Savannah; guests enjoy "incredible Georgia sunsets" from "wide porches", the "stunning" dining room's "well-prepared regional dishes", "charming", refurbished chambers and "excellent" service; there's nearby golf and fishing, but "don't go expecting late-night entertainment."

[Z] Lodge at Sea Island, The 🍴🔭⛳Ⓢ 28 | 27 | 24 | 28 | $650

100 Retreat Ave. | St. Simons Island | 912-638-3611 | fax 912-634-3909 | 800-732-4752 | www.seaisland.com | 38 rooms, 2 suites

"As nice as Pebble Beach but without the tourists", this "posh, comfortable" resort - consistently "one of the best in the U.S." - is beloved for its "top-notch food", "Southern elegance", "divine views" of the ocean and fairway and "private butlers" who proffer "warm cookies" and "rose petal baths"; fans find the "bagpiper at sundown a nice touch" after a day spent "horseback riding on the private beach", teeing off on a golf course that "doesn't get much better" or taking target practice in the "fine shooting facility."

Lodge on Little St. Simons Island 🍴🔭 ▽ 23 | 28 | 24 | 25 | $650

1000 Hampton Point Dr. | Little St. Simons Island | 912-638-7472 | fax 912-634-1811 | 888-733-5774 | www.littlessi.com | 15 rooms

It feels like "your own private island" when you're at this "peaceful", remote retreat (accessible only by boat off the Georgia coast), a 10,000-acre resort you "can't wait to go back to"; there's a "wonderful" staff, "family-style dining on Low Country meals (included in the rate) and activities including bird-watching (nearly 300 species), horseback riding and "sublime" day trips that skirt along the seven miles of beaches.

Lake Oconee

[Z] Ritz-Carlton Reynolds Plantation 👪🐕🔭⛳Ⓢ🎾 26 | 26 | 24 | 28 | $375

1 Lake Oconee Trail | Greensboro | 706-467-0600 | fax 706-467-7124 | 800-241-3333 | www.ritzcarlton.com | 246 rooms, 5 suites, 6 cottages, 1 house

Likened to a "sophisticated summer camp", this "oasis in the 'sticks'" "feels much further than 90 minutes" from Atlanta thanks to its "relaxed vibe" and "elegantly rustic", "picturesque" "setting on Lake Oconee"; along with a "golfers' paradise" of five "excellent" courses, facilities include an "infinity pool" "that's relaxing just to look at", a "top-notch spa" and "huge rooms" with "wonderful showers", all accented by "awesome service" and "high-quality" dining, plus kids love "the huge fire pit and s'mores" on the shore.

Savannah

Ballastone Inn Ⓗ ▽ 26 | 26 | 21 | 26 | $235

14 E. Oglethorpe Ave. | 912-236-1484 | fax 912-236-4626 | 800-822-4553 | www.ballastone.com | 13 rooms, 3 suites

Savannah's historic district is blessed by this Southern "charmer", a "stately" antebellum inn housed in a restored four-story 1838 Victorian mansion; it emits a truly "gracious" air, from the "delightful" staff to the "fantastic" hardwood furnishings and canopy beds in all

	ROOMS	SERVICE	DINING	FACIL.	COST

the individually decorated Victorian rooms to the "lovely" courtyard that's a "perfect spot for breakfast"; guests also appreciate "fabulous" nearby shopping; N.B. no children under 16.

Mansion on Forsyth Park, The ♨ⓢ

	26	22	21	23	$299

700 Drayton St. | 912-238-5158 | fax 912-238-5146 | 888-711-5114 | www.mansiononforsythpark.com | 120 rooms, 6 suites

"See Savannah in style" from this "eclectic" boutique hotel described as both a "mixture of classy meets Las Vegas" and a "breath of fresh air"; "fantastic rooms" are "unique", food is "excellent", "surroundings are delightfully posh" (think "big white columns and statues"), the service includes "free limos" and the "incredible spa and cooking school" please most; foes, however, find the staff merely "adequate."

Westin Savannah Golf Resort & Spa ♯♒♨⚓☺♨

	24	22	21	25	$309

1 Resort Dr. | 912-201-2000 | fax 912-201-2001 | 800-937-8461 | www.westinsavannah.com | 390 rooms, 13 suites

For a "fine day's golf" in "luxurious surroundings", surveyors suggest checking into this "genteel" "favorite" on the banks of the Savannah River with "quick" ferry service to Downtown (though the trip can become a "hassle" "after the first day or two"); the "sumptuous accommodations include "excellent rooms" with "river views", though mixed reviews go to the staff and dining, which range from "superb" to "mediocre."

Hawaii

TOPS IN STATE

- 28) Four Seasons Resort | *Kaupulehu-Kona, Big Island*
  Four Seasons Resort | *Wailea, Maui*
- 27) Four Seasons/Koele | *Lanai City, Lanai*
- 26) Halekulani | *Honolulu, Oahu*
  Four Seasons Resort/Manele | *Lanai City, Lanai*
  Ritz-Carlton Kapalua | *Kapalua, Maui*
- 25) Hana-Maui | *Hana, Maui*
  Fairmont Kea Lani | *Wailea, Maui*
  Kahala | *Honolulu, Oahu*
  Grand Hyatt | *Koloa, Kauai*
- 24) Mauna Lani Resort | *Kamuela, Big Island*
  Fairmont Orchid | *Kamuela, Big Island*

Big Island

Fairmont Orchid ♯✕♒♨⚓☺♨

	25	24	23	26	$579

1 N. Kaniku Dr. | Kamuela | 808-885-2000 | fax 808-885-5778 | 800-257-7544 | www.fairmont.com | 486 rooms, 54 suites

"Gorgeous rooms and perfectly manicured grounds", a "private beach with sea turtles" and the "not-to-be-missed spa without walls" are enough to sell this Kohala Coast resort as a "favorite"; even if a few say "the food could be better" and the "beach is a little shrimpy", the "super-friendly staff" that "meets every need" and the overall "welcoming" environment make up for that.

	ROOMS	SERVICE	DINING	FACIL.	COST
[Z] **Four Seasons Resort Hualalai** 👪✕🐕🏖⛳Ⓢ🎾	29	29	27	29	$775

72-100 Ka'upulehu Dr. | Kaupulehu-Kona | 808-325-8000 | fax 808-325-8200 | 888-340-5662 | www.fourseasons.com | 212 rooms, 30 suites, 1 villa

You may "cry when you check out" of this "indescribably beautiful" "paradise in paradise", and not just because of the "jaw-dropping cost" - rated the No. 1 U.S. Resort, it boasts "fantastic", "almost perfect", rooms (some with "sexy outdoor lava rock showers"), service that's "unrivaled yet unobtrusive" and an atmosphere that's "never overly crowded"; it's also rated our Survey's No. 1 for Facilities given the "over-the-top spa", "magnificent Jack Nicklaus golf course", a "lagoon where you can feed the rays" and a "great variety of dining", including Alan Wong's Hualalai Grille.

	ROOMS	SERVICE	DINING	FACIL.	COST
Hapuna Beach Prince Hotel 👪🏖⛳Ⓢ🎾	23	22	20	25	$415

62-100 Kauna'oa Dr. | Kamuela | 808-880-1111 | fax 808-880-3200 | 866-774-6236 | www.princeresortshawaii.com | 314 rooms, 36 suites

The "best beach on the island", combined with access to an "excellent" Arnold Palmer/Ed Seay-designed golf course, makes this "quiet" Kohala Coast lodging a sometimes "overlooked gem"; some of the otherwise "ordinary" rooms have "fantastic" ocean views, but a few faultfinders feel it "fails in the dining department"; N.B. its sister resort, the Mauan Kea, was closed for renovations at press time.

	ROOMS	SERVICE	DINING	FACIL.	COST
Hilton Waikoloa Village 👪🛁🏖⛳Ⓢ🎾	21	21	20	26	$299

69-425 Waikoloa Beach Dr. | Waikoloa | 808-886-1234 | fax 808-886-2900 | 800-445-8667 | www.hilton.com | 1155 rooms, 57 suites, 28 cabanas

"Walt Disney would approve" of this "large, large, large" "kid paradise" where you can "take a tram or boat to your room" or "hoof it" to burn calories (wags dub it the "Walk-a-lot-a"); "beautiful grounds with a Zen theme", waterslides that slosh into "a gazillion pools", a "top-notch spa" and a "cool" "dolphin encounter" program give it "lots of wow factor", so even if naysaysers deem the rooms "nothing special" and gripe there's "not much of a beach", fans still liken it to the "greatest show on earth"; N.B. suites are currently undergoing renovation.

	ROOMS	SERVICE	DINING	FACIL.	COST
Kona Village Resort 👪🏖🎾	25	25	21	26	$660

Queen Ka'ahumana Hwy. | Kailua-Kona | 808-325-5555 | fax 808-325-5124 | 800-367-5290 | www.konavillage.com | 125 bungalows

Escapists looking to "drop off the face of the planet" "love" the "luxurious" bungalows "nestled in the tropical garden or on the beach" at "one of the last authentic Hawaii hideaways", this all-inclusive Kona veteran with a "no TV, no radio, no telephone" rule ("go elsewhere for nightlife"); loyalists rhapsodize over the "excellent" food, the "wonderful" staff and the "first-class entertainment, from the luau to the cowboys", but critics cry for a "makeover"; N.B. rates include three daily meals.

	ROOMS	SERVICE	DINING	FACIL.	COST
Mauna Lani Resort 👪✕🛁🏖⛳Ⓢ🎾	24	24	23	26	$445

68-1400 Mauna Lani Dr. | Kamuela | 808-885-6622 | fax 808-885-1484 | 800-367-2323 | www.maunalani.com | 328 rooms, 10 suites, 5 bungalows

It "always feels like home" at this "fabulous" Kohala Coast resort, "an oasis in nature" sporting some of the Big Island's "best snorkeling

ROOMS SERVICE DINING FACIL. COST

spots", a "beautiful beach", "excellent golf" on reclaimed lava beds and "lots of sealife" (including turtles) cavorting in ancient fishponds; quibblers insist that this "grande dame" is "in need of a face-lift", but devotees shrug it off given the "considerate service", "gracious dining" and "unbelievable" rooms; N.B. the Mauna Lani Spa offers some treatments in open-air, thatched-roof huts.

Kauai

Grand Hyatt ♯♠☕♨☺🔍 | 24 | 24 | 23 | 28 | $550 |

1571 Poipu Rd. | Koloa | 808-742-1234 | fax 808-742-1557 | 800-233-1234 | www.grandhyattkauai.com | 565 rooms, 37 suites

"Bring your walking shoes" to this sprawling Poipu "hideaway" that's the "definition of casual elegance" with its "gorgeous" grounds (awash in "more flowers than a funeral"), "vibrant Hawaiiana-style rooms" and "accommodating" staff that's "well trained in 'aloha'"; it offers lots of "family-friendly" "free activities, from lei making to parrot talks", and is "rightly known" for its "amazing pools", but some say it may be best to "avoid in summer months if you're kid-free."

Hanalei Bay Resort ♯♠☕♨🔍 | 20 | 21 | 18 | 22 | $215 |

5380 Honoiki Rd. | Princeville | 808-826-6522 | fax 808-826-6680 | 800-827-4427 | www.hanaleibayresort.com | 30 rooms, 15 suites

"The real star is the beach" at this "affordable", "cozy" option on Kauai's North Shore, a "good all-around family hotel" that also manages to have a "romantic Bali Hai atmosphere"; though rooms (some are time-shares) are merely "fine", they're undergoing renovation, and compensations include a "great outdoor bar" and some of the "best views anywhere."

Hilton Kauai Beach Resort ♯♨☺ | ▽ 21 | 19 | 14 | 20 | $329 |

4331 Kauai Beach Dr. | Lihue | 808-245-1955 | fax 808-246-9085 | 888-243-9178 | www.hilton.com | 343 rooms, 7 suites

Fans find "bang for the buck" at this 25-acre "family fun" resort in a "nice location near Lihue" where the "pretty grounds", "beautiful" open-air spa (a "mandatory visit") and recently refurbished "contemporary" (if "small") rooms win over fans; but sourpusses snap it's "not up to standards" given the unimpressive dining, spotty service and "beach" location where "swimming is not recommended."

Kauai Marriott Resort & Beach Club ♯♨☺ | 21 | 22 | 20 | 24 | $390 |

3610 Rice St. | Lihue | 808-245-5050 | fax 808-245-5049 | 800-220-2925 | www.marriott.com | 345 rooms, 11 suites

"Make sure you ask for an ocean view, it's worth it" say fans of this chainster that's "convenient to the airport" and features "one of the biggest pools you've ever seen", a "secluded bay beach", a "Vegas-type" lobby and "friendly service"; the "dated" rooms and hallways "could use an upgrade", however, and the large size means you "shouldn't go here if you want to get away from all the other mainland tourists."

Sheraton ♯☕♨☺🔍 | 20 | 22 | 17 | 23 | $420 |

2440 Hoonani Rd., Poipu Beach | Koloa | 808-742-1661 | fax 808-742-9777 | 888-488-3535 | www.sheraton-kauai.com | 386 rooms, 8 suites

"Pay more" and "upgrade to the oceanfront rooms" with "lanais to die for" ("it's so worth it") at this "intimate" resort on Poipu Beach offering "all the amenities you would want without being overly touristy"; admirers laud a staff that's "friendly, courteous and helpful" and the "nightly entertainment with complimentary mai tais", though others gripe that the "food's not great" ("stay here and eat elsewhere").

Lanai

☑ Four Seasons Lanai, The Lodge at Koele ⑪ఘ⬆️�🌙☺🔍

| 27 | 28 | 25 | 27 | $375 |

1 Keomoku Hwy. | Lanai City | 808-565-4000 | fax 808-565-4561 | 800-321-4666 | www.fourseasons.com | 91 rooms, 11 suites

For a "totally different Hawaiian experience", consider this "sanctuary of relaxation", a "hunting lodge"-like resort perched "high on a hill-side" amid "vast gardens" in "quiet" Lanai's Central Highlands; the "rooms and service are everything you'd expect from the Four Seasons" (quarters feel like private cottages with "secluded lanais"), while the "dining room alone is worth the visit"; guests can golf on the "amazing" Greg Norman–designed course, take afternoon tea, relax in the classic library or try "skeet shooting", "lawn bowling, croquet and horseback riding"; N.B. a shuttle runs to sister property Manele Bay.

Four Seasons Resort Lanai at Manele Bay ⚤✕ఘ⛤⬆️☺🔍

| 27 | 26 | 24 | 27 | $445 |

1 Manele Bay Rd. | Lanai City | 808-565-7700 | fax 808-565-2483 | 800-321-4666 | www.fourseasons.com | 215 rooms, 21 suites

"If you want luxury in a quiet Hawaiian location" with "ocean views from almost everywhere", this "sprawling" "little piece of heaven" on Lanai's south shore – where you can snorkel, swim or watch "whales breaching right outside your windows" – is "paradise for the whole family"; the "opulent" rooms "make you feel you've arrived", ditto service that's "laid-back but still special", and given its "wonderful" restaurants, "beautiful" Jack Nicklaus–designed golf course and "excellent" kids' club, there's "no need to leave the premises"; N.B. a shuttle runs to sister property Lodge at Koele.

Maui

Fairmont Kea Lani ⚤☃ఘ⛤☺

| 27 | 25 | 23 | 26 | $525 |

4100 Wailea Alanui Dr. | Wailea | 808-875-4100 | fax 808-875-1200 | 800-441-1414 | www.fairmont.com | 413 suites, 37 villas

"Elegantly appointed all-suite" lodgings with a "vibrant Hawaiian ambiance" and "enormous bathrooms" are the highlights of this "fabulous" "Moroccan-inspired" Wailea resort where "aloha greets you at every turn", the staff provides "superb personalized service" and "the views from high floors are hypnotizing"; with "really nice pools and its own beach", it's "great for families" yet also has a "very adult feel"; P.S. fans say Nick's Fishmarket is a "big winner" for on-site dining.

☑ Four Seasons Resort Maui at Wailea ⚤✕ఘ⛤☺🔍

| 28 | 28 | 27 | 28 | $495 |

3900 Wailea Alanui Dr. | Wailea | 808-874-8000 | fax 808-874-2244 | 800-334-6284 | www.fourseasons.com | 328 rooms, 52 suites

The vibe is "LA in Hawaii" at this "beautiful" oasis where the recently upgraded rooms are "spacious and luxurious", the "outstanding food"

	ROOMS	SERVICE	DINING	FACIL.	COST

(at restaurants including Spago) is paired with "amazing sunset/ocean views" and the "seamless service" is exemplified by an "amazing concierge staff" – you'll be "addressed by name everywhere"; relaxation seekers sigh "ah, the spa", while sun-worshipers choose between a "perfect stretch of beach" or "pristine" pools where guests are pampered with "Evian face spritzes" and there may be "a celebrity in the next cabana."

Grand Wailea Resort 忭蛥⑤⚲ | 24 | 22 | 21 | 27 | $780 |

3850 Wailea Alanui Dr. | Wailea | 808-875-1234 | fax 808-879-4077 | 800-888-6100 | www.grandwailea.com | 728 rooms, 52 suites

When you enter this "gorgeous" Hawaiian "Disneyland" on Wailea, with an "awesome beach", "winding paths through lush gardens", "eye-catching sculptures", the "planet's best spa" and a "magnificent" water park, you'll find it's "perfect for the whole family" (tip: "if you don't have kids, avoid school-break periods" when it's "filled to the brim"); although a handful say this property "seems to be slipping of late" and needs "more focus on service" and food, others "come here for the best pool" on the islands, not the "overpriced dining."

Hana-Maui, Hotel 忭蛥⑤⚲ | 27 | 26 | 23 | 25 | $495 |

5031 Hana Hwy. | Hana | 808-248-8211 | fax 808-248-7202 | 800-321-4262 | www.hotelhanamaui.com | 47 cottages, 22 suites, 1 house

For a "breathtaking look into old Hawaii", this "secluded" Maui member of Small Luxury Hotels of the World is "super-luxurious yet simple at the same time"; the "adventurous" drive to get there along the winding Hana Highway is "almost as spectacular as watching the waves" from your lanai or "riding bareback on the beautiful beach", and the "friendly" staff "goes out of its way" to "pamper" you; the "romantic", "remote" setting, "excellent" spa and "serene" rooms ("stay in the plantation-style cottages") further impresses; so "the only drawback" is the "limited" dining.

Hyatt Regency 忭蛥⑤⚲ | 22 | 23 | 21 | 25 | $535 |

200 Nohea Kai Dr. | Lahaina | 808-661-1234 | fax 808-667-4498 | 800-233-1234 | www.maui.hyatt.com | 774 rooms, 32 suites

"You feel transported the minute you drive up" to this "stunning" hotel on Kaanapali Beach, starting with the "breathtaking lobby" and its "gorgeous water elements and resident penguins"; though there's "not much beachfront", the "lush gardens", "first-class spa" and "fabulous" pool (with its "waterfalls, grotto bar and waterslide") more than compensate, and while some praise the "attractive" rooms, quibblers say the "baths need updating."

Kaanapali Beach Hotel 忭蛥⑤ | 17 | 22 | 16 | 22 | $209 |

2525 Kaanapali Pkwy. | Kaanapali | 808-661-0011 | fax 808-667-5978 | 800-262-8450 | www.kbhmaui.com | 419 rooms, 13 suites

"Let the breezes carry your stress away" at this "charming", "family-friendly hotel" in the "heart of Kaanapali" that's "Hawaiian all the way" from the "extraordinary" staff to the "beautiful grounds" and "wide sandy beach"; it may not be the "most plush hotel" around – it's "on the older side" with "simple" rooms and a "somewhat small" pool – but it's a "reasonably" priced option in a "wonderful location."

	ROOMS	SERVICE	DINING	FACIL.	COST

Kapalua Villas ♔🐾🏊⚲⚲ ▽ 23 | 21 | 19 | 23 | $299

500 Office Rd. | Kapalua | 808-665-5400 | fax 808-669-5234 |
800-545-0018 | www.kapaluavillas.com | 230 villas

The "spacious" rooms at this "upscale condo" on the bay are "great for families who want seclusion and couples who need a romantic getaway", since there's "everything you'd want to do nearby" yet it's "away from the bustle of nearby tourist areas"; the upgraded villas are "beautifully decorated" and some feature "unbelievable ocean views", plus there are "wonderful restaurants within a 15-minute drive" and guests have signing privileges at the newly reopened Ritz-Carlton.

Maui Prince Hotel ♔🏊⚲⚲ 19 | 21 | 20 | 20 | $380

5400 Makena Alanui Rd. | Makena | 808-874-1111 | fax 808-879-8763 |
888-977-4623 | www.princeresortshawaii.com | 291 rooms, 19 suites

"Plenty of sea turtles" share the "awesome beach" at this "quiet", "uncrowded" Makena resort with a "warm staff" that "may work for those looking for total seclusion" (or a bargain, as veterans insist it's a "great value"); but critics find the property "a little long in the tooth", with "simple" rooms that "could use updating"; N.B. the South golf course is closed for more than a year for renovations.

☑ Ritz-Carlton Kapalua ♔✕🏊⚲🕓⚲ 25 | 27 | 25 | 26 | $719

1 Ritz-Carlton Dr. | Kapalua | 808-669-6200 | fax 808-665-0026 |
800-262-8440 | www.ritzcarlton.com | 331 rooms, 132 suites

A "spectacular" $180-million refurb has enthusiasts buzzing about this "huge, lush" "golf paradise" that "you won't want to leave"; besides its "two amazing courses", devotees cite the "beautiful" rooms (with dark-wood floors, private lanais and "fantastic views"), the "superb" food at its six restaurants (including the Asian-inspired Banyan Tree) and the "exceptional" service; yes, it's "too windy to be perfect" and the beach is "small, rough and fairly distant", but fans focus on the "well-appointed" spa and "wonderful pool" instead.

Sheraton 🏊🕓⚲ 22 | 23 | 19 | 24 | $500

2605 Kaanapali Pkwy. | Lahaina | 808-661-0031 | fax 808-661-0458 |
800-325-3535 | www.sheraton.com | 464 rooms, 46 suites

They've got "the best spot" on Kaanapali Beach say fans of this "comfortable" chainster with a "superb location" at Black Rock where you "can snorkel from the beach", enjoy "awesome sunsets" from a "quiet" stretch of sand and be "within walking distance" of many restaurants at Whalers Village; though some say the "small" rooms are strictly "standard", a staff that's "willing to help with anything" makes up for it; N.B. a new spa opened in 2008.

Westin Maui Resort & Spa ♔🍴🏊⚲🕓 22 | 22 | 19 | 25 | $545

2365 Kaanapali Pkwy. | Lahaina | 808-667-2525 | fax 808-661-5764 |
800-937-8461 | www.westinmaui.com | 731 rooms, 27 suites

A "fantastic lobby with waterfalls and pools" greets visitors to this "lush Kaanapali resort" where the "impressive scenery", "friendly service", "fabulous spa" and "awesome swimming pools" are the highlights; but it can be so "crowded with conventions that remind you of the business you left at home" that it "lacks traditional Hawaiian charm", and further disappointment is found in the "mediocre" dining; P.S. critics caution "keep your hands on your wallet" given the extra resort fees.

Oahu

Ala Moana Hotel 🔭

ROOMS	SERVICE	DINING	FACIL.	COST
18	18	16	18	$239

410 Atkinson Dr. | Honolulu | 808-955-4811 | fax 808-944-6839 | 800-367-6025 | www.alamoanahotelhonolulu.com | 1103 rooms, 51 suites

"Away from the crowds of Waikiki Beach", this renovated older tower appeals to those looking to be "close to everything but not in the middle of everything"; it's the "perfect location" for high-end shopping at the adjacent Ala Moana Center and just a "couple of blocks" from the beach, with "updated" accommodations that can be "quite nice" and a "pleasant" staff; P.S. "wonderful views" from some rooms are a bonus.

Halekulani 👫🍴🔭Ⓢ

ROOMS	SERVICE	DINING	FACIL.	COST
25	27	26	25	$445

2199 Kalia Rd. | Honolulu | 808-923-2311 | fax 808-926-8004 | 800-367-2343 | www.halekulani.com | 412 rooms, 43 suites

It's an "oasis of sanity" in the "midst of tourist action" applaud admirers who give this "amazing" hotel on the beach a "standing ovation"; the warm staffers "somehow always know your name" and offer the "best service anywhere", the oceanside New French restaurant, La Mer, is "simply outstanding", the "gorgeous" pool is a "work of art" and sipping sunset cocktails while listening to Hawaiian music at House Without a Key is a "romantic way to end the day"; it's "still the best" in Waikiki, even if you have to trip over all the brides and grooms "having their pictures taken" in the lobby.

Hawaii Prince Hotel Waikiki 🔭Ⓢ

ROOMS	SERVICE	DINING	FACIL.	COST
21	24	20	20	$390

100 Holomoana St. | Honolulu | 808-956-1111 | fax 808-946-0811 | 888-977-4623 | www.princeresortshawaii.com | 464 rooms, 57 suites

Dream big ("pretend it's your yacht" at the adjoining marina) or eat big (via the "abundant buffets") at this "well-run", "good-priced" "respite from the madness of Waikiki" near Ala Moana Center and a "short walk to some very nice beaches"; the "friendly" staff "goes out of its way to satisfy", but while some appreciate the rooms for their "water views" and "zero noise", others carp that they're "starting to show their age" and "aren't what the Prince name" suggests.

Hilton Hawaiian Village 👫🐕🔭Ⓢ

ROOMS	SERVICE	DINING	FACIL.	COST
20	20	19	24	$229

2005 Kalia Rd. | Honolulu | 808-949-4321 | fax 808-951-5458 | 800-445-8667 | www.hilton.com | 3515 rooms, 345 suites

"Everything is at your fingertips" at this "extremely kid-friendly" "mega-resort" in a "wonderful location" "away from the noise and traffic" of the rest of Waikiki; it's best if you "like being in a crowd" because this "city unto itself" with "adorable penguins", myriad shopping and dining options, an "awesome" renovated lagoon and pools, and the "best beachfront in Honolulu" attracts a lot of "families with kids"; although it may be "too big" for some, the great "variety" of rooms in six towers and the full-scale spa and medical wellness center allow for serenity.

Hyatt Regency Waikiki Resort & Spa 👫🔭Ⓢ

ROOMS	SERVICE	DINING	FACIL.	COST
20	20	19	19	$300

2424 Kalakaua Ave. | Honolulu | 808-923-1234 | fax 808-926-3415 | 800-233-1234 | www.waikiki.hyatt.com | 1212 rooms, 18 suites

The zoo, aquarium and "one of the most scenic stretches of Waikiki" are a short walk from these two "well-maintained", if "ho-hum", high-

	ROOMS	SERVICE	DINING	FACIL.	COST

rise towers with "excellent views" "in the center of the action" and "across the street from the beach"; while the "accommodating" staff (particularly on the club floor and poolside) wins points, the "scores of shops on the first three levels" make some feel as if they're bunking "on top of a shopping mall."

JW Marriott Ihilani Resort & Spa 🛎✕🏊⛱Ⓢ☜

26	23	22	26	$485

92-1001 Olani St. | Kapolei | 808-679-0079 | fax 808-679-0080 | 800-626-4446 | www.ihilani.com | 351 rooms, 36 suites

If you want "a wonderful place to forget about winter", this "beautiful resort" with "doting service" about 30 minutes "away from Waikiki" is "well worth the drive"; "play golf in the morning", hit the "relaxing spa" in the afternoon, "have a sunset dinner" at the "wonderful" Azul or neaby Roy's, then "sit under the moonlight at the lagoon" before heading back to your "spacious" room; indeed it's "pure bliss" for all except techies who tsk that the quarters could use flat-screen TVs.

Kahala Hotel & Resort, The 🛎✕🏊🅐Ⓢ

25	24	25	25	$395

5000 Kahala Ave. | Honolulu | 808-739-8888 | fax 808-739-8800 | 800-367-2525 | www.kahalaresort.com | 312 rooms, 31 suites

A 15-minute drive from Waikiki in the "luxe residential area" of Kahala, this "quiet, unrushed" beachfront resort with "apartment-sized rooms" sporting "mahogany poster beds and 450-thread-count sheets" is "by far the favorite" Oahu lodging for many; maybe it's the "mesmerizing dolphin lagoon", the "excellent restaurants", the "glorious spa" with private suites or the staff that "treats you like royalty from check-in to check-out" that keep regulars returning, but even if you can't afford to stay here, stop in for the "decadent" Sunday brunch.

Marriott Waikiki Beach 🅐Ⓢ

21	21	18	21	$425

2552 Kalakaua Ave. | Honolulu | 808-922-6611 | fax 808-921-5255 | 800-367-5370 | www.marriottwaikiki.com | 1297 rooms, 13 suites

Flip-flop your way to the "beautiful beach across the street" from this "nicely located" twin-towered giant within "walking distance" of "plenty of dining options" and the "best Waikiki can offer"; the "attractive", "refurbished" rooms (some with "spectacular views") all have balconies, the "staff is extremely friendly" and there's a spa and two freshwater pools, but detractors note the complex has a "mall-meets-paradise type feel."

Moana Surfrider, A Westin Resort 🛎Ⓗ🅐

21	23	19	22	$450

2365 Kalakaua Ave. | Honolulu | 808-922-3111 | fax 808-923-0308 | 800-325-3535 | www.moana-surfrider.com | 747 rooms, 46 suites

Order a mai tai, "sit under the banyan tree" and take in the "wonderful atmosphere" of this refurbished beachfront "resort treat" "in the heart of Waikiki" that was "rebranded a Westin" in mid-2007, but has been "the place to be seen since 1901"; expect "elegant", "old-fashioned Hawaiian ambiance", with an "attentive" staff and some of the area's top "people-watching", but be careful which of the "hit-or-miss" rooms you book (insiders insist the Ocean Tower quarters are "killer"); N.B. the ocean-front Beachouse serves up surf 'n' turf overlooking the surf.

	ROOMS	SERVICE	DINING	FACIL.	COST

Outrigger Reef on the Beach ♨Ⓢ   ∇ 16 | 20 | 15 | 15 | $289

2169 Kalia Rd. | Honolulu | 808-923-3111 | fax 808-924-4957 |
800-688-7444 | www.outrigger.com | 195 rooms, 5 suites

Undergoing a "redo in a big way", this "beautiful" twin-towered ocean-
fronter near the Waikiki Beach Walk is "great for families", with a
"premier" beach footsteps from the resort's refurbished lobby (and its
collection of Polynesian canoe art); fans report the "new rooms are
gorgeous and comfortable", while the über-connected praise the "free
Internet and telephone calls to the mainland"; N.B. ongoing construction may outdate the above scores.

Outrigger Waikiki ♨Ⓢ   ∇ 19 | 19 | 17 | 20 | $369

2335 Kalakaua Ave. | Honolulu | 808-923-0711 | fax 808-921-9798 |
800-688-7444 | www.outrigger.com | 494 rooms, 30 suites

Positioned "front and center on Waikiki Beach", Outrigger's "friendly"
flagship has an "ideal" oceanfront location that offers "incredible"
views of Diamond Head and the Pacific (even from "the cheapest city-
view rooms"); thanks to the "wonderful" service, the penthouse-level
Waikiki Plantation Spa and Duke's, its venerable beach bar, even the
fussiest may overlook the "postage stamp–size pool."

Sheraton Waikiki Hotel ♨🐾♨   19 | 17 | 18 | 20 | $365

2255 Kalakaua Ave. | Honolulu | 808-922-4422 |
fax 808-923-8785 | 800-782-9488 | www.sheraton-waikiki.com |
1636 rooms, 128 suites

Guests at this "huge" high-rise "with a Hawaii-meets–Las Vegas feel" are
divided over whether it's a "bustling, fun place" or an "overcrowded,
hectic" behemoth; devotees are inspired by the "renovated rooms",
"gorgeous views", shops that may "entice you to max out your credit
card" and "interesting" restaurants (including the new oceanfront
RumFire), but others can't overlook those "convention mobs."

Turtle Bay Resort ♨♨⊥Ⓢ🔍   21 | 20 | 18 | 22 | $470

57-091 Kamehameha Hwy. | Kahuku | 808-293-6000 |
fax 808-293-9147 | 800-203-3650 | www.turtlebayresort.com |
375 rooms, 26 suites, 42 cottages

"Watch the sea turtles and the surfers" from your balcony at this
"North Shore hideaway" where the "spacious rooms" offer "spectacular views" and "the beach cottages are romantic"; with "an award-
winning golf course", hiking, tennis, a "beautiful beach" and a variety
of "tolerable" dining options, it pleases most; but others find this
"windy" option "too far off the beaten path" with rooms that are "not
the latest and greatest"; P.S. you "need your own transportation"
since taxis to the airport or elsewhere will break the bank.

Idaho

Coeur d'Alene

Coeur d'Alene, The ♨♨♨⊥Ⓢ🔍   ∇ 25 | 25 | 25 | 27 | $229

115 S. Second St. | 208-765-4000 | fax 208-664-7276 | 800-688-5253 |
www.cdaresort.com | 304 suites, 34 rooms

You get "sublime views" and "the best of all worlds" at this "little paradise" of a resort that's "right on" "beautiful" Lake Coeur d'Alene,

| | ROOMS | SERVICE | DINING | FACIL. | COST |

"surrounded by mountains"; its 18-hole Scott Miller course (with its showy floating green) is a legend in its own right, but even non-golfers rave about this "true find" because of its "wonderful food", "attentive and friendly staff" and two-level spa with "fabulous facilities" and deep-woods–influenced treatments.

Ketchum

Knob Hill Inn ✕👥

| - | - | - | - | $275 |

960 N. Main St. | 208-726-8010 | fax 208-726-2712 | 800-526-8010 | www.knobhillinn.com | 22 rooms, 2 suites, 2 penthouses

This Relais & Châteaux chalet-style B&B in Sun Valley, within walking distance of Ketchum, is "beyond belief" say its fans; there's "luxury at every turn", from the rooms outfitted with DVD players, fireplaces, marble-tiled baths, flat-panel TVs and balconies with extensive flowerboxes to the "fabulous" (included) breakfast that's "so good locals turn out for it"; in short, it's "the best in town"; N.B. closes for seven weeks every spring, reopening in June.

Sun Valley

Sun Valley Resort 👥👥👥

| 21 | 23 | 22 | 26 | $189 |

1 Sun Valley Rd. | 208-622-4111 | fax 208-622-2030 | 800-786-8259 | www.sunvalley.com | 191 rooms, 227 suites, 227 condos, 7 houses

"Nostalgia rules" at this "comfortable" 1930s European-style lodge and spa that's "dedicated to taking care of guests" with "old-fashioned" service and condo-style rooms; a true Sun Valley escape, it's "full of activity" year-round, with ice-skating and outdoor hot tubs as well as the slopes in winter, and a Robert Trent Jones Jr. golf course, three outdoor pools, 18 tennis courts and horseback riding in summer.

Illinois

Chicago

TOPS IN CITY

28	Peninsula
27	Four Seasons
26	Park Hyatt
	Ritz-Carlton
23	James
	Burnham

NEW Blackstone, A Renaissance Hotel

| - | - | - | - | $389 |

636 S. Michigan Ave. | 312-447-0955 | fax 312-765-0545 | 800-468-3571 | www.marriott.com | 328 rooms, 4 suites

A $128-million restoration of a historic 1910 beaux arts hotel (once a favorite of movie stars, sports legends and U.S. presidents, listed on the National Register of Historic Places), this new smoke-free South Loop lodging mixes traditional architecture with modern elements, including 1,600 original works by contemporary local artists (the two-story lobby houses an avant-garde video installation); rooms feature eclectic furnishings, flat-screen TVs and Internet access, while the

23rd-floor Hubbard Place boasts a lounge, two private boardrooms and luxury suites overlooking Lake Michigan.

Burnham, Hotel ⊕❄♨ | 25 | 26 | 21 | 20 | $219 |

1 W. Washington St. | 312-782-1111 | fax 312-782-0899 | 877-294-9712 | www.burnhamhotel.com | 103 rooms, 19 suites
Part of the quirky Kimpton chain, this "stunningly" renovated landmark with lots of plate glass was one of the world's first skyscrapers when it was finished by Daniel Burnham in 1895; although the "ultra-professional" staff can't make the "charming" rooms any bigger, you can "splurge on a corner suite" to up your square footage; P.S. given its "excellent" but busy location "in the center of the Loop", be sure to "ask about nearby construction when booking."

Conrad ❄♨ | 26 | 23 | 19 | 23 | $525 |

521 N. Rush St. | 312-645-1500 | fax 312-645-1550 | 800-543-4300 | www.conradhotels.com | 278 rooms, 33 suites
The "large", "well-furnished" rooms with 42-inch plasma TVs, Pratesi linens, Bose stereos and Molton Brown products in the "spectacular baths" are the standout feature of this "classy" Magnificent Mile hotel set inside a 1920s-era landmarked building; there's a "sublime" "staff that listens" and a convenient indoor connection to the "high-end" Shops at North Bridge that allows for "shopping in the Windy City" without "mussing one's hair", but some say the on-site fitness center and the restaurant are "a bit weak."

NEW Dana Hotel & Spa ❄Ⓢ | - | - | - | - | $695 |

660 N. State St. | 312-202-6000 | fax 312-202-6033 | 888-301-3262 | www.danahotelandspa.com | 196 rooms, 20 suites
Chicago's newest boutique, this River North newcomer utilizes natural, sustainable woods and warm earth tones in luxe rooms featuring floor-to-ceiling windows and baths with Italian rain shower fixtures and handcrafted tiles; an on-site spa and a rooftop lounge with fire pit, signature cocktails and live music are fit for the see-and-be-seen crowd.

Drake, The ⊕☕❄♨ | 20 | 23 | 21 | 20 | $367 |

140 E. Walton Pl. | 312-787-2200 | fax 312-787-1431 | 800-553-7253 | www.thedrakehotel.com | 461 rooms, 74 suites
Built in 1920, this "timeless" Gold Coast "landmark" has a "knowledgeable" staff, an "overwhelmingly beautiful" lobby brimming with flowers, "fine dining" (including Drake Bros. Steaks Chicago) and a harpist-assisted afternoon tea that's "worth the visit alone"; the underwhelmed claim that this Italianate "grande dame is a little tired", with "elegant" but "stylistically dated" rooms that "vary greatly" – luckily, a renovation is underway.

Embassy Suites Downtown Lakefront | ▽ 21 | 20 | 15 | 21 | $289 |

511 N. Columbus Dr. | 312-836-5900 | fax 312-836-5901 | 800-362-2779 | www.embassysuites.com | 455 suites
A "great choice" "when toting the kids", this all-suites Streeterville outpost offers a free hot breakfast, "lots of space inside and out" and "a pool with views"; the prime location two blocks from Navy Pier and "an easy walk to Michigan Avenue", along with "suburban family-friendly prices" and "nice service" further recommend this one.

	ROOMS	SERVICE	DINING	FACIL.	COST

Fairmont, The ✵♨ⓢ
23 | 24 | 21 | 23 | $350

200 N. Columbus Dr. | 312-565-8000 | fax 312-565-1032 | 800-441-1414 | www.fairmont.com | 622 rooms, 64 suites

"A room on a high floor facing the lake is worth the high price of admission" at this convention/conference hotel that's "a little removed from the main strip" of the Mag Mile – and that's "probably a good thing"; more pluses: "stellar" service, a "gorgeous", newly expanded spa and restaurant Aria – a "wonderful place to relax"; N.B. the quarters were recently refurbished and feature marble baths and 42-inch flat-panel TVs.

🅉 Four Seasons ✿✕✵♨ⓢ
27 | 28 | 26 | 27 | $575

120 E. Delaware Pl. | 312-280-8800 | fax 312-280-1748 | 800-332-3442 | www.fourseasons.com | 175 rooms, 168 suites

Serving up "elegance by the mile, on the Mile" – and "costing a mile" – this luxe option next to the upscale 900 North Michigan Shops "always excels"; the "pampering" consists of "perfect service", "newly refurbished rooms" (a "nice mix of retro and modern") with "exquisite" Loop views, a "stunning" Roman-style pool, "awesome health club" and "amazing" flower arrangements throughout – "it doesn't get any better."

Hilton Suites Chicago/Magnificent Mile ✵♨
∇ 22 | 20 | 15 | 19 | $359

198 E. Delaware Pl. | 312-664-1100 | fax 312-664-9881 | 800-222-8733 | www.hilton.com | 345 suites

It's a "suites-style hotel with real style" exclaim enthusiasts of this former Streeterville DoubleTree, which received a "nice redo" in 2007 after it was Hiltonized; while the "upgraded" rooms, complete with flat-screen TVs, complement the "great lake views" and "excellent Downtown location" one block off the Mag Mile, the "shockingly sparse", "no-frills" dining options leave some hungry for more.

InterContinental ⑪♨
22 | 20 | 18 | 21 | $299

505 N. Michigan Ave. | 312-944-4100 | fax 312-944-1320 | 800-628-2112 | www.interconti.com | 721 rooms, 71 suites

Built as the Medinah Athletic Club in 1929, this "reliable" "business hotel", divided between old and new wings, has fans pumped up by its "prime location" on the Mag Mile and "amazing architectural features" including a "wonderful" art deco "tiled indoor pool"; the rooms, however, range from "plushly furnished with gorgeous decor" to a bit "dumpy" (opt for the "historic wing"), and meanwhile service can be "unimpressive."

NEW InterContinental Chicago O'Hare
- | - | - | - | $229

5300 N. River Rd. | Rosemont | 847-544-5300 | fax 847-349-5201 | 888-424-6835 | www.icohare.com | 556 rooms, 70 studios

With its own art gallery and full-time curator, this brand-new airport-area chainster in Rosemont (14 miles west of Downtown) surprises many; features include a 24-hour state-of-the-art fitness center, an extensive business center, rooms with plenty of workspace and eateries that include a branch of seafooder McCormick & Schmick's and the contemproray Italian Osteria di Tramonto.

James, The 🐕Ⓢ

ROOMS	SERVICE	DINING	FACIL.	COST
24	24	23	22	$539

55 E. Ontario St. | 312-337-1000 | fax 312-660-7183 | 877-526-3755 | www.jameshotels.com | 191 rooms, 52 studios, 26 loft rooms, 26 apartments

This "super-chic" "makeover of the old Lenox Suites" in River North (the "place to be for an out-of-towner") offers rooms that are "modern without seeming cold" and boast "comfortable beds", "alarm clocks that project time on the ceiling" and impressive baths ("loved the Kiehl's products"); although a few who find it "too trendy" say "if you're not a hipster" or you're "over the age of 45" "look elsewhere", carnivores say stay for the "aged steaks" at David Burke's Primehouse.

Monaco, Hotel 🐕🔭

ROOMS	SERVICE	DINING	FACIL.	COST
21	22	17	18	$239

225 N. Wabash Ave. | 312-960-8500 | fax 312-960-1883 | 866-610-0081 | www.monaco-chicago.com | 170 rooms, 22 suites

"In the heart of the Loop", this "offbeat", "worn-around-the-edges" member of the Kimpton Group (set in a 1912 former hat factory building) has that "funky in a nice way" vibe, with "small", "cute" rooms in vivid colors and wacky patterns (some have "great river views" through "big picture windows"); schmoozers smile at the complimentary wine and appetizers in the evening, but say the rest of the "food leaves a little to be desired."

Omni 👪🐕🔭

ROOMS	SERVICE	DINING	FACIL.	COST
24	22	19	20	$359

676 N. Michigan Ave. | 312-944-6664 | fax 312-266-3015 | 888-444-6664 | www.omnihotels.com | 347 suites

"I can see why Oprah has her guests stay here" say fans fond of this "excellent" all-suiter that draws more "locals and business types than tourists"; it's a "surprisingly good value" given its "superb location" - you can "jump out of bed and into the shops on the Magnificent Mile" - and rooms have "beautiful city views", plasma TVs and "granite" bathroom countertops, but the dining is "average."

Palmer House Hilton Ⓗ🫖🐕🔭

ROOMS	SERVICE	DINING	FACIL.	COST
19	21	18	20	$459

17 E. Monroe St. | 312-726-7500 | fax 312-917-1707 | 800-445-8667 | www.hilton.com | 1594 rooms, 45 suites

"Big" and "oh-so-busy", this "Queen of the Chicago scene" has an "excellent" location that puts it in "walking distance to Millennium Park, the Art Institute and late-night restaurants" and "next door" to the El; on the plus side are the "first-rate fitness center", "spectacular lobby" and "ambitious" $170-million renovation, but rooms are still a crapshoot - some are "tiny and dank" - and there's "not much personal service"; N.B. a new spa is in the works.

Park Hyatt 👪🍴🐕🔭Ⓢ

ROOMS	SERVICE	DINING	FACIL.	COST
27	26	25	26	$545

800 N. Michigan Ave. | 312-335-1234 | fax 312-239-4000 | 800-778-7477 | www.parkhyatt.com | 185 rooms, 13 suites

"Zen garden meets corporate boardroom" at this "sleek" yet "serene oasis" with an "unbeatable location" facing "the old Water Tower" from which you can "walk to everything"; you'll return to a "dreamy room" with "appointments to die for" ("instantly engulfing" beds), a "friendly staff that shows you're welcome", an "outstanding pool, fitness center" and Tiffani Kim spa, plus "one of Chicago's best restaurants", NoMI.

	ROOMS	SERVICE	DINING	FACIL.	COST

⧉ Peninsula, The 🛎✕🏊🛍Ⓢ

| | 29 | 28 | 27 | 28 | $550 |

108 E. Superior St. | 312-337-2888 | fax 312-751-2888 | 866-288-8889 |
www.peninsula.com | 257 rooms, 82 suites

"Everything a posh big-city hotel should be, but usually isn't", this "exquisite" branch of the Hong Kong chain is truly a "spectacular hotel" with the "most gorgeous rooms" and baths some have "ever seen"; the "unbelievable" staff "anticipates your every whim", a "fantastic" spa offers "bracing rooftop views of the Windy City" and the central Near North area, and the dining is "excellent"; so "if you can afford" this "sublime", "gold standard" (or your company can), "go for it."

Renaissance 🛍Ⓢ

| | 23 | 21 | 17 | 21 | $620 |

1 W. Wacker Dr. | 312-372-7200 | fax 312-372-0093 |
800-468-3571 | www.renaissancechicagodowntown.com |
513 rooms, 40 suites

This high-rise chainster's head-of-State-Street location makes it "good for business stays", as being a "bit away from shopping" means "no crowds on the sidewalk in front", and there's "easy access to the El" line direct to O'Hare; inside, the "lovely" rooms have large work desks and baths furnished with wood and "elegant" marble, and some offer pleasing views of the Chicago skyline.

Ritz-Carlton
(A Four Seasons Hotel) 🛎✕🏊🛍Ⓢ

| | 26 | 27 | 25 | 25 | $510 |

160 E. Pearson St. | 312-266-1000 | fax 312-266-1194 | 800-621-6906 |
www.fourseasons.com | 344 rooms, 91 suites

"Incredible service (the "second-to-none" concierge can even score *Oprah* tickets with a few weeks' notice – don't tell anyone)", "impeccable dining" and "classically decorated, spacious" rooms, some with "sweeping Mag Mile views, are the highlights of this "five-star retreat" inside Water Tower Place; though a few say it's "a bit in the shadow of the Peninsula", most find it "in keeping with the wonderful Ritz tradition."

Sofitel 🏊🛍

| | 25 | 23 | 21 | 22 | $575 |

20 E. Chestnut St. | 312-324-4000 | fax 312-324-4026 | 877-813-7700 |
www.sofitel.com | 388 rooms, 27 suites

"Contemporary luxury with a European feel" lurks "in the heart of the Gold Coast" at this "swanky" scene of "modern" furnishings, "fresh flowers throughout", "wonderfully bright" suites and "airy rooms" "with real character" (and "magnificent beds"); factor in French cooking at the Café des Architectes – some surveyors "go here to eat even when staying elsewhere" – and "attentive" service, and vets say it's a "great value" "for business travelers who don't need all the extra gilding."

Sutton Place 🏊🛍

| | ▽ 23 | 22 | 14 | 19 | $395 |

21 E. Bellevue Pl. | 312-266-2100 | fax 312-266-2103 | 866-378-8866 |
www.suttonplace.com | 206 rooms, 40 suites

A "fabulous location" in the heart of the Gold Coast that's perfect for "roaming on Michigan Avenue", as well as rooms with 27-inch flat-screen TVs, deep soaking tubs and European-style furnishings recommend this 20-year-old veteran; though cutting-edgers contend the "tired" decor is "straight outta the '80s" and gym rats report a "joke" of a fitness center, they're shushed by shopaholics who smile this relative "bargain" "saves money you can spend in neighboring stores."

	ROOMS	SERVICE	DINING	FACIL.	COST
Swissôtel 👪 🔭	23	22	19	21	$549

323 E. Wacker Dr. | 312-565-0565 | fax 312-565-0315 | 888-737-9477 | www.swissotel.com | 596 rooms, 36 suites

A "wonderful choice" if you're looking for "proximity to the Mile" and Millennium Park, this Euro chainster earns points for "fabulous views over the Chicago River" from some of its "modern rooms"; but those who declare it "bland" and somewhat "soulless" further knock an "impersonal" staff that's more "convention-friendly" than "people-friendly" as well as a restaurant that's best suited for a "stuffy, traditional power lunch."

	ROOMS	SERVICE	DINING	FACIL.	COST
[NEW] **Trump International Hotel & Tower** 🛁 🐕 🔭 Ⓢ	-	-	-	-	$525

401 N. Wabash Ave. | 312-588-8000 | fax 312-588-8001 | 877-458-7867 | www.trumpchicagohotel.com | 218 rooms, 121 suites

This "luxurious" hotel portion of The Donald's storied glass-and-steel skyscraper, across the river from the Loop, opened in early 2008 with suites that some say are "half the size of a house", featuring custom-designed furnishings and cabinetry, 10-ft. floor-to-ceiling windows and 42-inch flat-screen HDTVs (most also have fully equipped kitchens with Sub-Zero fridges); "Downtown high-fliers" also find "attentive" service, the "world-class" 23,000-sq.-ft. Spa at Trump, the mez-level Rebar nightclub and Sixteen, serving New American from 16 flights up.

	ROOMS	SERVICE	DINING	FACIL.	COST
Westin Chicago River North 👪 🐕 🔭	22	21	17	21	$319

320 N. Dearborn Ave. | 312-744-1900 | fax 312-527-2650 | 877-866-9216 | www.westinchicago.com | 407 rooms, 17 suites

With a "great location for shoppers focused on the Magnificent Mile", this smoke-free River North entry retains "some Asian touches" from its days as the Hotel Nikko, including a sushi bar and "beautiful Japanese gardens" in and around the lobby; rooms have a similar "low-key elegance", and those on the recently renovated top floors have "all the bells and whistles", including "large marble baths", Westin's "trademark Heavenly beds" and (at club level) Macintoshes with free Internet; but critics advise "if you don't like crowds, stay clear."

	ROOMS	SERVICE	DINING	FACIL.	COST
Whitehall Ⓗ 🐕 🔭 Ⓢ	20	22	20	18	$500

105 E. Delaware Pl. | 312-944-6300 | fax 312-944-8552 | 800-948-4255 | www.thewhitehallhotel.com | 197 rooms, 25 suites

Built in 1928, this "elegant", European-style hotel with "old-fashioned grace" has a "fantastic" Downtown location "just slightly away from the hubbub" but still "perfect" "for a Michigan Avenue shopping trip"; the rooms, which tend to be "small", come with restored mahogany antiques, baths with marble floors and granite countertops, and high-thread-count Egyptian cotton bedding, but snipsters snap "the furniture is more tired than most guests."

	ROOMS	SERVICE	DINING	FACIL.	COST
W Lakeshore 🐕 🔭 Ⓢ	20	20	19	21	$399

644 N. Lake Shore Dr. | 312-943-9200 | fax 312-255-4411 | 877-946-8357 | www.whotels.com | 490 rooms, 30 suites

"Hip"-sters hail this "ultramodern", "high-energy" Streeterville "concept hotel", "opposite Navy Pier along the lake", where there's "always

	ROOMS	SERVICE	DINING	FACIL.	COST

something happening" in the "trendy bars" (especially the rooftop night-club); but some find that "small", "oddly furnished" rooms and "pretentious service" overshadow the pluses, including a "nice indoor swimming pool" and "fabulous" Bliss Spa.

Galena

Eagle Ridge Resort & Spa 🕴🏖🏌🏊⛷☺🔍

▽ 19	20	19	24	$219

444 Eagle Ridge Dr. | 815-777-5000 | fax 815-777-4502 | 800-892-2269 | www.eagleridge.com | 72 rooms, 8 suites, 287 resort homes

In the hills near the "charming town" of Galena, 160 miles northwest of Chicago, this "gorgeous" "weekend getaway" is "like summer camp for adults", with 63 holes of golf, tennis courts, an indoor/outdoor pool, cross-country ski trails and the Stonedrift Spa – a "getaway of its own"; eagle-eyed lodgers say the homes and townhouses outfitted with "comfortable beds, well-equipped kitchens" and fireplaces offer "a better value" than the "hit-or-miss" rooms in the main inn.

Indiana

Indianapolis

Conrad 🏊☺

▽ 27	25	23	26	$399

50 W. Washington St. | 317-713-5000 | fax 317-638-3687 | 800-445-8667 | www.conradhotels.com | 218 rooms, 23 suites

This "fantastic" "addition to Downtown", a block from Monument Circle and next to the Artsgarden, boasts "huge", "plush" rooms with baths sporting "multiple showerheads, an LCD-TV and a separate" soaking tub; the staff operates "above expectations", while a "fantastic" fitness center, the solid Capital Grille and 10,000 sq. ft. of meeting space make it a "paradise for the business traveler."

NEW West Baden Springs Hotel ⊕🏊⬆

-	-	-	-	$399

8538 W. Baden Ave. | West Baden Springs | 812-936-1902 | fax 812-936-2100 | 888-694-4332 | www.frenchlick.com | 208 rooms, 38 suites

An "amazing" restoration of a 1902 landmarked hotel that was closed since the Depression has resurrected this "gorgeous" property along with its jaw-dropping, six-story gilt atrium dome and huge mosaic floor; rooms have luxuriously printed fabrics and balconies that overlook the dome, while the extensive amenities include a 14,000-sq.-ft. spa and a shuttle that runs to the affiliated French Lick Resort, with its 42,000-sq.-ft. casino and 18-hole Donald Ross golf course (another designed by Pete Dye is planned for '09).

Westin 🕴🏊🏌

▽ 20	19	17	19	$259

50 S. Capitol Ave. | 317-262-8100 | fax 317-231-3928 | 800-937-8461 | www.westin.com | 533 rooms, 40 suites

"Central, solid and reliable", this Downtown business hotel that's connected by sky bridge to the Indiana Convention Center and near the Capitol is always filled "with people wearing little name badges" (consequently it's often "hard to book"); once you're in, it man-

| | ROOMS | SERVICE | DINING | FACIL. | COST |

ages to be "plush and indulgent" at times, with those "awesome' trademark Heavenly beds and road-warrior-friendly outlets of Shula's Steakhouse and Starbucks.

Iowa

Iowa City

Vetro & Conference Center, Hotel 🕭 🍴

| | - | - | - | - | $299 |

201 S. Linn St. | 319-337-4961 | fax 319-337-7037 | 800-592-0355 | www.hotelvetro.com | 56 suites

It's "hard to believe" this "minimalist and hip" all-suites sophisticate is "in Iowa City and not New York City" say fans of this three-year-old in the Old Capitol Cultural District "surrounded by the University of Iowa campus"; expect sleekly contemporary smoke-free accommodations with polished concrete floors, pillow-top beds, full kitchens and high-speed Internet, and a location within the Plaza Towers building with easy access to meeting rooms, the Japanese restaurant, Formosa, a fitness center and the adjacent Sheraton Hotel's indoor pool and rooftop garden.

Kansas

Overland Park

Sheraton 🍴

| | ∇ 19 | 19 | 15 | 18 | $289 |

6100 College Blvd. | 913-234-2100 | fax 913-234-2111 | 800-325-3535 | www.starwoodhotels.com | 394 rooms, 18 suites

Attached to the Overland Park Convention Center and in the affluent 'burbs 25 minutes from KC, this chain outpost has rooms with "classic, warm touches" and Sheraton's "fantastic" signature beds, along with other "up-to-date amenities" such as a lounge, work-out facilities, indoor pool and business center that make it "perfect" for the corporate crowd; the on-site OP1906 Bar and Grille gets comparatively low marks, but a post-Survey overhaul may change that.

Kentucky

Louisville

21c Museum Hotel 🛏️ Ⓢ

| | ∇ 27 | 27 | 30 | 28 | $299 |

700 W. Main St. | 502-217-6300 | fax 502-217-6301 | 877-217-6400 | www.21cmuseumhotel.com | 83 rooms, 7 suites

"How often do you get the chance to stay in a 24-hour museum?" demand the fans of this "feast for the senses"; the "stunning" lobby is given over to rotating exhibits of "engaging" works by living artists, and numerous pieces adorn the halls, elevators and "phenomenal" adjoining Proof on Main restaurant; the cool-toned rooms sport exposed brick and all the latest toys (42-inch HDTVs, WiFi, 500-thread-count sheets), but also "funky" touches like rubber duckies in the bath and silver cups (for mint juleps, natch).

	ROOMS	SERVICE	DINING	FACIL.	COST

Louisiana

New Orleans

TOPS IN CITY

25 Windsor Court
24 Ritz-Carlton
22 Omni Royal Orleans
   W French Quarter
21 Monteleone
   W New Orleans

Bourbon Orleans ⊕♨

∇ 18	20	16	20	$139

717 Orleans St. | 504-523-2222 | fax 504-571-4666 |
www.bourbonorleans.com | 177 rooms, 41 suites

A "super", "accessible" location "close to Jackson Square and the action on Bourbon Street", as well as two-story suites with balconies, earn points for this former Wyndham housed in an 1817 French Quarter building by the river; but "loud street noise" (get a room "overlooking the courtyard" if you want to sleep) and "variable" quarters that "still need improvement", "despite the renovations" make it hard to "recommend."

Chateau Sonesta ♨

∇ 22	23	20	22	$279

800 Iberville St. | 504-586-0800 | fax 504-586-1987 |
www.chateausonesta.com | 226 rooms, 25 suites

Operating behind an 1849 neo-Classical facade, this French Quarter hotel sports "lovely" common areas, a courtyard and a prime location right near Bourbon and Dauphine streets; if the "rooms vary in size" and "loud" acoustics are an issue (depending on which area of the hotel you're staying in), most agree it's a "wonderful" choice.

Harrah's New Orleans ✕♨

∇ 23	24	22	24	$139

228 Poydras St. | 504-533-6000 | fax 504-593-8010 | 800-427-7247 |
www.harrahs.com | 366 rooms, 84 studios

"Centrally located" "close to the convention center and all the action" "without being in the chaos of Bourbon Street", this "Vegas South" hotel "surprises" with "lovely rooms", "good service", a "gorgeous lobby" and "great entertainment" (there's a "casino right there"); despite having "no pool" and "no spa", this "value" is "well worth the stay."

**Hilton New Orleans
Riverside** ✕♨♨⚲

19	18	16	19	$219

2 Poydras St. | 504-561-0500 | fax 504-584-3989 | 800-445-8667 |
www.hilton.com | 1540 rooms, 76 suites

"Lounge at the riverfront pool and watch the barges float by" suggest supporters of this "sprawling" "convention hotel" in a "convenient, safe location" "attached to a unique mall"; some rooms boast "tremendous views" of the Mississippi, the staff is "well trained" and there's an "amazing health club", but the dining is just "ok."

Hilton St. Charles Ave. ✕

-	-	-	-	$369

333 St. Charles Ave. | 504-524-8890 | fax 504-524-8889 | 800-445-8667 |
www.hilton.com | 225 rooms, 25 suites

Dining at Luke's is "reason enough to stay" at this "tidy" convention property, formerly Kimpton's Hotel Monaco, where you can "eat and drink extremely well" and be serviced by a "professional staff"; overall, fans find a "good value" for a "convenient" city location.

Iberville Suites 🐕 Ⓢ ▽ 20 | 21 | - | 19 | $249

910 Iberville St. | 504-523-2400 | fax 504-524-1321 | 866-229-4351 | www.ibervillesuites.com | 232 suites

Thrifty travelers "on a Courtyard budget" enjoy high-end perks "at a fraction of the cost" at this "quaint" hotel on the "upper end of the French Quarter" that's "adjoined to the Ritz-Carlton" and has "access" to its amenities; "spacious rooms" with "nice furnishings" and "friendly service" "make it easy to forget" there's "no bar or dining room", just a "genteel lobby" "graced" with "oriental carpets and antiques."

InterContinental ☕ 🔭 ▽ 23 | 21 | 17 | 21 | $499

444 St. Charles Ave. | 504-525-5566 | fax 504-523-7310 | 888-424-6835 | www.interconti.com | 458 rooms, 21 suites

"It never disappoints" say road warriors of this "tried-and-true" convention hotel "centrally located" in the CBD and on the Mardi Gras "parade route"; while some throw beads at the "nondescript" dining, they toast the "stellar service", "nice gym on the top floor" and "immaculate" but "smallish" rooms with "good amenities", deeming this "a steal" despite "insane" "parking prices."

JW Marriott 🔭 19 | 20 | 17 | 18 | $189

614 Canal St. | 504-525-6500 | fax 504-525-8068 | 800-771-9067 | www.marriott.com | 487 rooms, 7 suites

The "lobby bar with soaring ceilings" is the "best place to rebuild New Orleans one drink at a time" jest guests of this "typical conference hotel" "right in the heart of things" in the Central Business District and "convenient to the French Quarter"; "small" but "well-furnished" rooms and "competent" service have most calling it "pleasant", though "disappointed" surveyors deem it "devoid of style."

Le Pavillon Hotel 🔭 ▽ 19 | 25 | 18 | 19 | $279

833 Poydras St. | 504-581-3111 | fax 504-620-4130 | 800-535-9095 | www.lepavillon.com | 219 rooms, 7 suites

Guests of this business district "grande dame" feel like they're "staying at Tara" thanks to the "columned entrance", the "old-world luxury" of the "magnificent lobby" and, most of all, the "top-notch" (and top-hatted) staff delivering "a heavy dose of New Orleans charm" and complimentary "nighttime snacks of peanut-butter-and-jelly sandwiches"; rooms are "smallish but comfortably appointed", and while "parking leaves a lot to be desired", the location is "one block from the streetcar."

Loews 👫 🐕 🔭 Ⓢ ▽ 26 | 26 | 25 | 25 | $249

300 Poydras St. | 504-595-3300 | fax 504-595-3310 | 800-235-6397 | www.loewshotels.com | 273 rooms, 12 suites

"You can't go wrong" praise patrons of this "well-located" business hotel deemed "practically perfect in every way" from the "spacious rooms" with "huge baths" to the "accommodating" staff to the "fabulous food" (including "room service by the Brennan" restaurant group); "contemporary Southern design" defines the "absolutely beautiful" public spaces, including a "fabulous bar and lounge area" with "great people-watching" and a "lovely indoor Jacuzzi and pool" - indeed, it's all so "wonderful", you'll want to "check back in" next week.

ROOMS | SERVICE | DINING | FACIL. | COST

Maison Dupuy ⚶

▽ 22 | 24 | 23 | 19 | $109

1001 Toulouse St. | 504-586-8000 | fax 504-525-5334 | 800-535-9177 | www.maisondupuy.com | 187 rooms, 12 suites, 1 cottage

"Perfectly charming" aptly sums up this "budget" boutique whose "excellent" location in the French Quarter provides a retreat from all the ongoing activities on nearby Bourbon Street; clients adore the "inviting" atmosphere and courtyard, "quick" service, "excellent" fare at Dominique's and "cozy", if also "small", rooms; P.S. expect to see a lot of "wedding receptions."

Marriott Metairie at Lakeway ⚶

- | - | - | - | $195

3838 N. Causeway Blvd. | Metairie | 504-836-5253 | fax 504-836-5258 | 888-364-1200 | www.neworleanslakesidehotel.com | 186 rooms, 34 suites

Enjoy room service overlooking Lake Pontchartrain at this "newly redone" "beautiful property", where the visitors who like the lobby level "food and drinks", "on-site exercise facility" and "walks along the levee" say they'd prefer "never to leave"; the tastefully refurbished accommodations feature 32-inch plasma HDTVs with Internet, signature Revive bedding with allergy-tested duck down and work areas with swivel desks and ergonomic chairs.

Marriott New Orleans ⚶

▽ 18 | 19 | 15 | 19 | $375

555 Canal St. | 504-581-1000 | fax 504-523-6755 | 888-771-4429 | www.marriott.com | 1275 rooms, 55 suites

A $38-million renovation has spruced up this smoke-free French Quarter lodging "right in the middle of everything"; the chambers feature "improved bedding" (the chain's signature Revive brand) and large workstations, but "if you're spending time in your room this close to Bourbon Street, you're missing the point" say celebrating surveyors; expect "decent" food, a "lively" wine bar and a "very W" "new lobby" complete with its own Starbucks.

Monteleone, Hotel ⑪⚶⚶Ⓢ

22 | 23 | 19 | 21 | $319

214 Royal St. | 504-523-3341 | fax 504-681-4491 | 800-535-9595 | www.hotelmonteleone.com | 530 rooms, 40 suites

"As comforting as a beignet and café au lait on a cold morning", this (allegedly haunted) "Big Easy landmark" is known for its "independent ethos, amiable staff" and one-of-a-kind "revolving" Carousel Bar, which keeps "your head spinning and your beverages swirling"; admirers appreciate the "fantastic spa", "exquisite rooftop pool", "grand" public spaces "full of antiques" and "elegant" suites that bear the names of authors who once stayed here.

Omni Royal Orleans ⚶✕⚶⚶

21 | 24 | 21 | 23 | $279

621 St. Louis St. | 504-529-5333 | fax 504-529-7089 | 888-444-6664 | www.omniroyalorleans.com | 321 rooms, 25 suites

"Sipping drinks and watching paddleboats on the Mississippi" from the "marvelous rooftop terrace and pool" is a must at this "gracious" "old French Quarter hotel" say fans, who also praise the "perfect location" "in the center of everything" (yet "far enough from Bourbon"), "wonderful staff" and "excellent" eats from the Rib Room ("a favorite with the local lunch crowd"); rooms, though "comfortable and elegant", "could do with a bit of an upgrade."

	ROOMS	SERVICE	DINING	FACIL.	COST

Renaissance Arts Hotel 🛏

-	-	-	-	$179

700 Tchoupitoulas St. | 504-613-2330 | fax 504-613-2331 |
800-431-8634 | www.renaissanceartshotel.com | 210 rooms,
7 suites

Erudite excursionists say this "superb" place "lives up to its name"
since it's "like staying in an art gallery": installations (including
"Chihuly glass") adorn "the rooms, lobby and restaurant, and there's
a sculpture garden inside"; the "ideal location" in the Warehouse
District and the on-site Creole seafooder, LaCôte Brasserie, are further reasons why this chainster comes "highly recommended."

Ritz-Carlton, The 🏨✕🛏Ⓢ

25	24	22	25	$519

921 Canal St. | 504-524-1331 | fax 504-670-2884 | 800-241-3333 |
www.ritzcarlton.com | 491 rooms, 36 suites

"The little touches really add up" at this "ultra-luxe" French Quarter
hotel deemed "better than ever" after a "gorgeous renovation" that's
resulted in "flawless rooms", "de-lish food" and "amazing facilities"
like a "fantastic spa" and "lively courtyard" "complete with parrot";
though a few picky patrons cite "post-Katrina issues" (the staff is "still
learning"), most say extras, like the "amazing piano bar entertainment", are "icing on the cake."

Royal Sonesta 🛏🛏

20	21	21	21	$250

300 Bourbon St. | 504-586-0300 | fax 504-586-0335 | 800-766-3782 |
www.sonesta.com | 478 rooms, 22 suites

You can be "in the middle of the action" and "stay up all night" if you
book balcony quarters "above Bourbon Street" at this French Quarter
veteran, but "if you want to sleep" get a "beautiful room overlooking
the courtyard"; it "retains its old-world charm" say fans, and the staff
"labors tirelessly" to keep service "excellent."

Soniat House ⓗ🛏

▽ 26	26	16	22	$265

1133 Chartres St. | 504-522-0570 | fax 522-7208 | 800-544-8808 |
www.soniathouse.com | 33 rooms, 12 suites, 1 cottage

Quintessentially "refined" and utterly "genteel", this luxury boutique
comprising three 1830s townhouses in the lower, residential French
Quarter is "top-notch in every respect"; expect "lovely flowers all
around" and "charming" rooms (some with balconies overlooking
Chartres Street) decorated in "fine" period furnishings and stocked
with Frette linens; in short, this member of Small Luxury Hotels of the
World is a true "New Orleans experience" that makes you feel like "a
royal"; N.B. the proprietors also own the adjacent antique shop.

Westin New Orleans
Canal Place 🛏🛏

▽ 21	20	17	21	$200

(fka Wyndham at Canal Place)

100 Iberville St. | 504-566-7006 | fax 504-553-5120 | 800-937-8461 |
www.westin.com | 398 rooms, 40 suites

A location that's "wonderfully convenient to the Quarter or
Warehouse District" and across the street from Harrah's Casino is the
draw at this CBD convention hotel with "breathtaking views of the
Mississippi" from the lobby and from some of the "huge" rooms;
though many moan that it's "understaffed", the "friendly" crew "tries
to be helpful."

	ROOMS	SERVICE	DINING	FACIL.	COST

W French Quarter 🍴♨

| 23 | 21 | 20 | 22 | $489 |

316 Chartres St. | 504-581-1200 | fax 504-523-2910 | 877-946-8357 | www.whotels.com | 94 rooms, 2 suites, 2 carriage houses

"Everything you expect in a W and more (or less?)" is how fans describe this typically "sparse-but-cool" spot "in the heart of the French Quarter" with "large", "modern" rooms and "outstanding" food at Bacco restaurant; some find the "beautiful courtyard" with a "wonderful pool" the "main attraction" of this "oasis from the chaos", but others pout over the "'whatever, whenever' attitude of the staff."

⦿ Windsor Court Hotel ✕☕🍴♨

| 24 | 25 | 24 | 25 | $250 |

300 Gravier St. | 504-523-6000 | fax 504-596-4513 | 888-596-0955 | www.windsorcourthotel.com | 56 rooms, 266 suites

"The good times are rollin' again" assert aficionados who rank this "sophisticated" CBD spot a "first choice" thanks to its "beautiful, spacious rooms", "unrivaled" service from a "well-mannered staff" and "out-of-this-world" dining that includes an "old-world" "high tea in the lobby"; if aesthetes find it all a "tad shabby", fans who "could live here" simply see "lots of patina" and suggest "spending more for a club level room."

W New Orleans 🍴♨

| 23 | 22 | 18 | 21 | $469 |

333 Poydras St. | 504-525-9444 | fax 504-581-7179 | 877-946-8357 | www.whotels.com | 400 rooms, 23 suites

This "chic" hotel "right outside of the French Quarter" gets "two thumbs up" from the "young professional crowd" and "tourists with a need for contemporary consistency" who appreciate its "modern ambiance" and "boutique-hotel" feel despite its "large" size; the "nicely decorated", "intimate" rooms (some say "claustrophobic") with "great amenities" ("love the bath products") and "good views of the Mississippi" are enhanced by a "trendy" staff and rooftop pool.

Wyndham Riverfront New Orleans ✕♨

| ∇ 23 | 22 | 20 | 19 | $299 |

701 Convention Center Blvd. | 504-524-8200 | fax 504-524-0600 | 800-996-3426 | www.wyndham.com | 190 rooms, 12 suites

Fresh from a $9-million total renovation, this "big conference hotel" is "surprisingly nice" gush groupies who savor the "comfortable" rooms with pillow-top mattresses and ergonomic work chairs (the "corner" units are particularly "spacious"); other pluses include "quite reasonable" dining, some of "the best river views" and a Warehouse District location just a few blocks from the French Quarter that's "great for shopping."

White Castle

Nottoway Plantation ⊕♨

| ∇ 24 | 22 | 22 | 23 | $300 |

31025 Louisiana Hwy. 1 | 866-527-6884 | fax 225-545-8632 | 866-527-6884 | www.nottoway.com | 12 rooms, 3 suites

For a truly "nostagic experience", head an hour-and-a-half from New Orleans to this "authentically restored" 1859 plantation, "one of the best-maintained in Louisiana" and listed on the National Register of Historic places; "high ceilings", "fine linens", "elegant" architecture and "beautifully" landscaped grounds boasting "grand oak trees" are complemented by an "accommodating" staff, and if you "stay in the main house" you can "overlook the Mississippi River" in a "huge, antique bed."

Maine

Bar Harbor

Bar Harbor Inn [H] 🐕 🔭 [S] — 21 | 21 | 18 | 22 | $199

Newport Dr. | 207-288-3351 | fax 207-288-8454 | 800-248-3351 | www.barharborinn.com | 149 rooms, 4 suites

The "grounds are a perfect place to sit and be happy to be alive" enthuse lovers of this location near Acadia National Park that "can't be beat"; "get a room overlooking the ocean" to experience "waking up to the fog" and "watching the cruise ships come in", then enjoy all the "little shops and restaurants" within walking distance (picky palates find the on-site dining "needs an upgrade").

Freeport

Harraseeket Inn 🫖 🐕 🔭 — 20 | 25 | 24 | 20 | $195

162 Main St. | 207-865-9377 | fax 207-865-1684 | 800-342-6423 | www.harraseeketinn.com | 84 rooms, 4 suites, 9 townhouses

"If your idea of heaven is lobster and L.L. Bean, you've found it" at this "surprisingly pleasant", pet-friendly inn that's "in the heart" of "shopping crazy Freeport" (and two blocks north of the outdoorswear retailer); "rural luxury" extends to an indoor swimming pool and "wonderful" tavern meals "cooked up from local meat and produce", and "afternoon tea is a nice bonus" after a day spent raiding the outlets.

Portland

Inn by the Sea 🫖 🐕 🔭 [S] — 21 | 23 | 19 | 23 | $399

40 Bowery Beach Rd. | Cape Elizabeth | 207-799-3134 | fax 207-799-4779 | 800-888-4287 | www.innbythesea.com | 14 rooms, 43 suites

This "lovely" inn on "beautifully landscaped" grounds steps from the "perfect" Crescent Beach (and "just over the bridge" from Portland) recently completed a multimillion dollar upgrade of its rooms, added a spa and opened a restaurant with an Argentine chef; it "hits the high mark" on many counts, say fans, who find "something special" in this "romantic" spot.

Rockport

Samoset Resort 👫 🔭 ⛳ 🎾 — 19 | 21 | 19 | 23 | $279

220 Warrenton St. | 207-594-2511 | fax 207-594-0722 | 800-341-1650 | www.samosetresort.com | 156 rooms, 22 suites

With an "incredible" oceanfront location just south of Camden, this resort boasts an 18-hole championship golf course with a "beautiful view" of Penobscot Bay, a staff that "tries hard" and 230 acres featuring tennis courts, a health club, shuffleboard, badminton and a children's day camp; refurbished rooms have 32-inch, flat-screen TVs, granite vanities and marble-top mahogany furniture, but the less-enamored "go for the golf or not at all."

Southern Coast

Breakwater Inn & Spa 🏨Ⓢ

| ▽ 20 | 23 | 23 | 18 | $289 |

127 Ocean Ave. | Kennebunkport | 207-967-5333 | fax 207-967-0675 | www.thebreakwaterinn.com | 33 rooms, 2 suites

"All-around lovely" is what vacationers say about this Kennebunkport harbor retreat featuring the necessary luxury amenities, e.g. a spa facility with on-call consultants and medical treatments, accommodations within inn rooms, cottages and serviced apartments that reflect the nautical setting, and "excellent" fare complemented by views of the rugged coastline at Stripers Waterside.

Captain Lord Mansion

| 27 | 24 | 21 | 21 | $285 |

6 Pleasant St. | Kennebunkport | 207-967-3141 | fax 207-967-3172 | 800-522-3141 | www.captainlord.com | 19 rooms, 1 suite

The individually decorated rooms – many with "canopy beds" and fireplaces – are "so pretty you won't want to leave", except to dig into the "fabulous breakfasts" at this "homey" B&B "near the heart of Kennebunkport" (though "thankfully" enough of a distance from the Bush compound); "warm and friendly owners" offer "home-baked cookies" and other daily snacks, while "no TVs" in most of the rooms mean "total relaxation"; N.B. children over age 12 preferred.

Cliff House, The Ⓗ🍴🏨Ⓢ🔍

| 20 | 20 | 19 | 22 | $265 |

Shore Rd. | Ogunquit | 207-361-1000 | fax 207-361-2122 | www.cliffhousemaine.com | 192 rooms, 2 suites

"Location, location, location" is the draw at this "elegant" 19th-century resort where 70 oceanfront acres provide "spectacular views" of "the rocky coast of Maine at its glorious best" and private balconies make guests feel like they're "sitting on the veranda of an ocean liner"; the somewhat "motel-type" rooms in the three older buildings are a bit "austere" and the service "needs to be more attentive", but the spa accommodations are a "lovely" alternative.

NEW Hidden Pond 🍴🏨

| - | - | - | - | $695 |

354 Goose Rocks Rd. | Kennebunkport | 207-967-9050 | fax 207-967-9055 | 888-967-9050 | www.hiddenpondmaine.com | 14 cottages

Consisting of private cottages wiith screened-in porches, gas fireplaces set in river stone, kitchens with floor-to-ceiling windows and bedrooms with Frette linens and down duvets, this new Kennebunkport resort spread over 60 acres of lush birch and balsam fir offers a temporary home in the woods; other lovely features include a main lodge with a stone fireplace and a mezzanine overlooking the pool, a unique, tented spa, daily yoga classes and hiking trails.

Z White Barn Inn & Spa ✕🏨Ⓢ

| 25 | 26 | 28 | 22 | $420 |

37 Beach Ave. | Kennebunkport | 207-967-2321 | fax 207-967-1100 | www.whitebarninn.com | 12 rooms, 13 suites, 1 cottage

It's "worth a detour from anywhere" to this "beautiful" barn in Kennebunkport, but "leave the kids at home" because it's "the ultimate romantic getaway" with a "wonderful" full-service spa and "one of the best" restaurants (chef Jonathan Cartwright's Relais Gourmand "gem") that offers a "once-in-a-lifetime" dining experience; a renovation in 2008 elevates the already "gorgeous" accommodations, while the "top-notch" staff lives up to the rest with "pampering beyond" belief.

Maryland

Baltimore

Antrim 1844 ✕ ⊕ ♟ ♦   ▽ 24 | 24 | 23 | 22 | $180

30 Trevanion Rd. | Taneytown | 410-756-6812 | fax 410-756-2744 | 800-858-1844 | www.antrim1844.com | 132 rooms, 18 suites

Civil War buffs bivouac at this "charming base for visiting Gettysburg" (15 minutes away), a former plantation–turned-B&B; "gorgeous rooms" have antiques, wood-burning or gas fireplaces, feather beds and double Jacuzzis (but no phones), and sophisticated touches include afternoon tea in the drawing room, croquet on the lawn and "divine" gourmet dinners; the "exceptional service" and "romantic ambiance" (along with a policy that doesn't allow children under 12) inspire some guests to "propose."

NEW Gaylord National Resort &   - | - | - | - | $299
Convention Center ♟ ♦ Ⓢ

201 Waterfront St. | Oxon Hill | 301-965-2000 | fax 301-965-2030 | 866-972-6779 | www.gaylordhotels.com | 1890 rooms, 110 suites

This new "gigantotel" in the DC suburbs has Potomac travelers abuzz over its "stunning" design and amenities that please the "big convention crowd", matched by "unconventionally good service"; early reviewers complain there's "no easy transportation into the city", but the numerous dining outlets and a million square feet of shops make up for that.

NEW Hilton Baltimore ⚐ ♦   - | - | - | - | $439

401 W. Pratt St. | 443-573-8700 | fax 443-573-8799 | 800-445-8667 | www.hilton.com | 737 rooms, 20 suites

The corporate crowd convenes at this Inner Harbor smoke-free newcomer connected to the convention center via pedestrian sky bridge; a full-service, 24-hour business center, an on-site New American restaurant and rooms with WiFi, ergonomic desk chairs and voicemail (along with baths offering Crabtree and Evelyn La Source products) make doing work easier.

Hyatt Regency ♦ ♦   22 | 19 | 17 | 19 | $399

300 Light St. | 410-528-1234 | fax 410-685-3362 | 800-233-1234 | www.baltimore.hyatt.com | 461 rooms, 27 suites

"Perfectly located" for business travelers (there's a skyway connection to the convention center) and sightseers (it's "close to all attractions"), this "sophisticated" spot in the Inner Harbor offers a "fantastic view" from the rooftop restaurant and "looks fabulous" after a "much-needed" renovation; the "comfortable" rooms may "lack charm", but they're full of "nice small touches" like "bath salts" and other toiletries that are kept stocked by a "responsive" staff.

	ROOMS	SERVICE	DINING	FACIL.	COST

InterContinental Harbor Court ✕🛇🔍

| 23 | 21 | 20 | 21 | $389 |

550 Light St. | 410-234-0550 | fax 410-659-5925 | 866-484-1958 | www.harborcourt.com | 173 rooms, 22 suites

"Take advantage of high tea at Brightons" say caffeinehounds who enjoy the "great bar and lounge" at this "family-friendly" chainster's new restaurant; the views of the Inner Harbor are "lovely", there's a "nice" indoor pool and hot tub, and the staff is generally "helpful", notwithstanding a few who say the service "isn't always up to par."

Marriott Waterfront 🛇

| 23 | 21 | 19 | 22 | $339 |

700 Aliceanna St. | 410-385-3000 | fax 410-895-1900 | 800-228-9290 | www.marriott.com | 733 rooms, 20 suites

"Gorgeous views of the Inner Harbor" set the scene at this "spiffy" waterfront lodging and convention-goer's mainstay that's also "accessible" to "plentiful" shopping, restaurant and nightlife options; its "genuinely first-rate" facilities (most "love" the business center) and "ready-to-serve" staff have surveyors calling a stay here a "classy break."

Renaissance Harborplace 🛇

| 21 | 19 | 18 | 20 | $379 |

202 E. Pratt St. | 410-547-1200 | fax 410-539-5786 | 800-535-1201 | www.renaissancehotels.com | 586 rooms, 36 suites

"Baltimore is your oyster" at this "solid" chain outpost offering a "perfect view of the Inner Harbor" and attached to the "high-end" Harborplace shopping mall; families find the indoor pool "wonderful on a cold winter day", while convention-goers welcome "excellent service for events and corporate meetings", and both groups appreciate the "comfortable" rooms.

Eastern Shore

Hyatt Regency Chesapeake Bay 🛇🔍

| 21 | 20 | 18 | 26 | $319 |

100 Heron Blvd., at Rte. 50 | Cambridge | 410-901-1234 | fax 410-901-6301 | 800-233-1234 | www.hyatt.com | 380 rooms, 20 suites

A "dynamite" Eastern Shore location sets the scene at this "beautiful resort in the heart of nowhere" that's "perfect" for a "five-star", "adventurous" "family-oriented" vacation, drawing "boat and golf enthusiasts", yet is also "suited for business meetings"; the grounds evoke "a nature preserve" and include "huge indoor and outdoor pools", a 150-slip marina and an outside fireplace for making s'mores at night; the main downside seems to be the dining, which "lacks" excitement.

Inn at Perry Cabin ✕🛇

| 25 | 24 | 24 | 24 | $340 |

308 Watkins Ln. | St. Michaels | 410-745-2200 | fax 410-745-3348 | 866-278-9601 | www.perrycabin.com | 36 rooms, 42 suites

"Exquisite views" abound at this "romantic and delightful" Orient-Express "relaxation spot" in a "lovely waterside location" on the Chesapeake Bay with access to sailing lessons and yacht cruises; the "light, airy" rooms feature Molton Brown toiletries, French doors, fireplaces and lots of "charm", while the service is "awesome"; though some find the fare "excellent", others only recommend having a "scotch in the cozy bar" before "walking or biking into town" for dinner.

Massachusetts

Boston

TOPS IN CITY

- 27 Four Seasons
- 25 Ritz-Carlton
- 23 Boston Harbor
- 22 InterContinental
  - Commonwealth
  - Fifteen Beacon
  - Taj Boston
  - Nine Zero
  - Eliot
  - Fairmont Copley Plaza

Boston Harbor Hotel 👪 🍴 ♨ 🔭 [S] — 24 | 23 | 21 | 23 | $525

70 Rowes Wharf | 617-439-7000 | fax 617-951-9307 | 800-752-7077 | www.bhh.com | 204 rooms, 26 suites

The "city has never looked better" than from this "classic" waterfront hotel where there are "gorgeous views of the harbor" from "expansive" rooms; better still, service is "superb", Meritage Restaurant is "top-notch" and the "indoor pool is terrific for kids"; N.B. hop on the water ferry from Logan International to beat the Boston traffic.

Boston Marriott Cambridge 🔭 — 20 | 20 | 15 | 19 | $209

2 Cambridge Ctr. | Cambridge | 617-494-6600 | fax 617-494-0036 | 888-236-2427 | www.marriott.com | 431 rooms

Ask for a "comfortable", "high-floor" room for "great views of Boston across the river" advise habitués of this Kendall Square tower, a "no-nonsense" business hotel that "can't be more convenient to the T" (the station entrance is steps away); while the "solid" spot offers all the standard amenities like an indoor pool and fitness center, and "service is responsive", fashionistas fuss that the decor is "frozen in the '80s" and the on-site American bistro is "not gourmet."

Charles Hotel 🍴 ♨ 🔭 [S] — 23 | 22 | 23 | 22 | $399

1 Bennett St. | Cambridge | 617-864-1200 | fax 617-864-5715 | 800-882-1818 | www.charleshotel.com | 249 rooms, 45 suites

Offering "a contemporary spin on traditional New England style", this "classy" hotel with a "wonderful location" "in the heart of Harvard Square" is frequently "packed with proud parents", "reunion" groups and other university guests who settle into the "comfy rooms" with "Shaker-inspired furnishings"; the "top-tier food" options include Rialto and Henrietta's Table ("don't miss the weekend brunch"), and surveyors give "extra credit for the Regattabar jazz club" that books national and regional acts; P.S. tuition-payers tut-tut about inflated prices "during college events."

Colonnade 👪 ♨ 🔭 — 20 | 21 | 20 | 19 | $559

120 Huntington Ave. | 617-424-7000 | fax 617-425-3222 | 800-962-3030 | www.colonnadehotel.com | 276 rooms, 9 suites

"Oh, the pool" gush groupies who've graced Boston's only rooftop swimming space, long considered the best feature of this "European"-style hotel that's "convenient to the convention center and to Back Bay shopping"; Francophiles favor the on-site Brasserie Jo, and a 2008 redo has moved the formerly "adequate" rooms "up several notches", so this property opposite the Prudential Center is a "good value" in an expensive nabe.

Commonwealth, Hotel ✕⊕✵♨ | 24 | 21 | 22 | 20 | $325
500 Commonwealth Ave. | 617-933-5000 | fax 617-266-6888 | 866-784-4000 | www.hotelcommonwealth.com | 73 rooms, 75 suites
Alumni of nearby Boston University "wish their dorms" had been as "spacious" and "comfortable" as the traditionally turned-out chambers in this Kenmore Square boutique member of Small Luxury Hotels of the World, where the modern "luxuries" include flat-panel TVs and L'Occitane toiletries, and the "helpful staff" "bends over backwards to assist you"; on-site dining includes the Great Bay seafood restaurant, and as a bonus, "you can walk" to nearby Fenway Park (or have a view of it from some rooms).

Eliot Hotel ♯✕✵♨ | 23 | 22 | 24 | 17 | $365
370 Commonwealth Ave. | 617-267-1607 | fax 617-536-9114 | 800-443-5468 | www.eliothotel.com | 16 rooms, 79 suites
"We'd run the Boston Marathon every year just to stay here" declare devotees of this "sophisticated" "little treasure" "well-situated" in the Back Bay up the street from the Copley Square finish line; they race in for the "luxurious, but petite, rooms" and for "top-notch dining" at Clio Restaurant and the "cool" Uni Sashimi Bar; contenders confirm that "what it lacks in features" - there's no pool or gym - "it compensates for" with "old-world service" from a "professional" staff that "always remember you."

Fairmont Copley Plaza ♯✕⊕✵♨ | 22 | 23 | 21 | 21 | $429
138 St. James Ave. | 617-267-5300 | fax 617-375-9648 | 800-441-1414 | www.fairmont.com | 366 rooms, 17 suites
Aided by Catie, the hotel's "live-in Labrador" mascot, staffers make guests "feel like royalty" at this "true grande dame [decorated] with gilt plasterwork and crystal" on Copley Square; fussbudgets fume she's looking "tired" - in particular, the "rooms need updates", unless you go for the "wonderful Gold floor" - but there's a "terrific lobby", the Oak Bar serves the "best martinis in town" and it's in a "prime location", especially "in April, when the Boston Marathon ends near the front door."

Fifteen Beacon ✕⊕✵♨ | 24 | 23 | 22 | 18 | $495
(aka XV Beacon)
15 Beacon St. | 617-670-1500 | fax 617-670-2525 | 877-982-3226 | www.xvbeacon.com | 39 rooms, 3 suites, 18 studios
Managing to "keep up with tradition but shake off old-school ideas", this "wonderful boutique hotel" in a 1903 Beacon Hill beaux arts building boasts "sleek and stylish" "rooms with fireplaces and lots of amenities" including mini-TVs in the baths, surround-sound stereo systems with CD libraries and original artwork; add "first-class service", power dining in the Mooo steakhouse and "complementary car" service for guests, and the result is a "warm abode" in an often-cold metropolis.

Four Seasons 🛏✕🍴🐕Ⓢ

| 27 | 27 | 27 | 25 | $650 |

200 Boylston St. | 617-338-4400 | fax 617-423-0154 | 800-332-3442 |
www.fourseasons.com | 197 rooms, 76 suites

From the "sumptuous", "generously sized guestrooms" to the "magical Aujourd'hui restaurant" to the "legendary Four Seasons service", "you'll feel like a celebrity" at this "opulent" Back Bay hotel with a "perfect location" "right across from the Public Garden"; "the staff goes out of its way to get anything you need", even providing "great amenities for kids", so the smitten swoon it's "worth every penny."

NEW Indigo, Hotel

| - | - | - | - | $229 |

399 Grove St. | Newton | 617-969-5300 | fax 617-454-3493 | 800-980-6429 |
www.hotelindigo.com | 189 rooms, 2 suites

Near Route 128 in Newton, this newcomer (part of the boutique Hilton brand) may be "off the beaten path" for Downtown touring, but it's well-located for business travelers or visitors to the western suburbs; aiming for a mix of style and value, with minimalist design, duvet-topped beds and free WiFi, it also offers an in-house restaurant, BOKX 109, that's a modern take on the American steakhouse.

InterContinental Ⓢ

| 25 | 21 | 19 | 25 | $499 |

510 Atlantic Ave. | 617-747-1000 | fax 617-217-5190 | 866-493-6495 |
www.intercontinental.com | 386 rooms, 38 suites

A "chic" property in the Waterfront District, this chainster may "not be what you think of as 'Boston'", but if "hip" rooms with "all the latest gadgets", a "happening bar scene" (RumBa lounge features a collection of international rums) and a staff that "makes you feel like you matter" are important to you, then this one could "eclipse others in the area."

Jacob Hill Inn ✕⊕🐕✎

| ▽ 28 | 28 | 26 | 28 | $199 |

120 Jacob St. | Seekonk | 508-336-9165 | 888-336-9165 |
www.inn-providence-ri.com | 9 rooms, 3 suites

Ranking among "the best hosts on the planet", the "hospitable inn-keepers" "make you feel comfortable" at this "getaway", a lavishly decorated B&B where the main building dates back to 1722; "set in beautiful, rural surroundings", this "romantic" "retreat is just outside of Providence", but with on-site activities ranging from tennis to billiards to simply "relaxing", you may never want to leave; N.B. no kids under 13.

Jurys ⊕

| 22 | 23 | 18 | 20 | $505 |

350 Stuart St. | 617-266-7200 | fax 617-266-7203 |
www.jurys-boston-hotels.com | 222 rooms, 3 suites

A genuine Irish hotel in this most Gaelic of American cities, built out of "a 1920s architectural landmark, the former Boston Police Headquarters", this "trendy" boutique sports a Back Bay location that's "good for shopping on Newbury Street"; while some of the rooms "can be small" (though still "huge for Boston"), all of them are "exquisitely appointed" with "fabulous baths", and the "rocking" "bar pours generous drinks", so all told, this "sleek" spot is "kind of fun for a police station."

Langham Hotel 🍴🐕

| 21 | 22 | 20 | 20 | $505 |

250 Franklin St. | 617-451-1900 | fax 617-423-2844 | 800-791-7764 |
www.langhamhotels.com | 301 rooms, 17 suites

"In a converted Federal Reserve building" in the Financial District, this "refined" property has "more character than the usual business hotel"; sybarites swoon over the "fabulous new spa", the "chocolate buffet held every Saturday from fall to spring" and "all the amenities you might expect"; but a few who find the "quiet" ambiance rather "stodgy" quip that "European central bankers" would feel right at home here.

NEW Le Méridien Cambridge 🐕 🍴 👥 | 22 | 19 | 14 | 17 | $459 |
(fka Hotel @ MIT)
20 Sidney St. | Cambridge | 617-577-0200 | fax 617-494-8366 | 800-543-4300 | www.lemeridien.com | 196 rooms, 14 suites

"Geek chic reigns" at this "cool spot in Cambridge" (formerly known as the Hotel @ MIT) where the "quirky", "high-tech" theme – "even the blankets have mathematical formulae woven into them" – "reflects the brainiacs" who work in the neighborhood (at nearby technology and pharmaceutical companies); there's "not much in the way of facilities", though, and dining options are optimistically described as "improving", but the recent ownership transfer may bring some needed changes.

Lenox, The 👥 | 19 | 21 | 19 | 17 | $395 |
61 Exeter St. | 617-536-5300 | fax 617-267-1237 | 800-225-7676 | www.lenoxhotel.com | 198 rooms, 16 suites

"Either you love it or you don't" is the mixed verdict on this "old-style hotel" that nonetheless has surprisingly "happening" bars as well as an "ideal" Back Bay location steps from Copley Square; traditionalists have some "nostalgia" for "family-owned and -operated" properties like this one, appreciating its "historic feel", "sensible staff" and long-established environmentally friendly policies, but detractors are "disappointed" that some rooms are "small" and "more than a little tatty."

NEW Liberty Hotel 🍴 | ▽ 24 | 22 | 23 | 23 | $550 |
215 Charles St. | 617-224-4000 | fax 617-224-4001 | 866-507-5245 | www.libertyhotel.com | 288 rooms, 10 suites

Prison rehab gets a luxury take at this "hip" new Beacon Hill hotel in a "fabulously restored" 19th-century former penitentiary that's a National Historic Landmark; a "fantastic" lobby attracts lots of "late-night" "socializing", deluxe suites afford "panoramic" views of the city and the Charles River (along with flat-panel HDTVs) and Lydia Shire's Scampo restaurant is "amazing", but humorless inmates dis decor that "overdoes the jail connection in a cloying way."

Marlowe, Hotel 🍴 👥 | ▽ 23 | 23 | 18 | 20 | $309 |
25 Edwin Land Blvd. | Cambridge | 617-868-8000 | fax 617-868-8001 | 800-825-7140 | www.hotelmarlowe.com | 222 rooms, 14 suites

Take a walk on "the wild side" in your "leopard print robe" (to match the carpeting, natch) at this "chic" East Cambridge Kimpton hotel, where the "colorful" rooms are "luxurious", "fun" and a "good value" too); the "friendly" staffers are "helpful", and admirers "love the daily wine social in the lobby", the "lively bar scene" and the welcome given to "encourage canine guests", though a handful of their human companions howl that the restaurant could be better.

Marriott Copley Place 👥 | 20 | 19 | 18 | 20 | $299 |
110 Huntington Ave. | 617-236-5800 | fax 617-236-5885 | 888-236-2427 | www.copleymarriott.com | 1100 rooms, 47 suites

Those who "want to be in the center of things" check into this Copley Square chainster, a "huge hotel" with enclosed skywalks to the convention center and malls "that seems as if it should have its own ZIP code"; it's "just average", with rooms that are "a little tired", but there's a "nice sushi bar in the lobby" and a "friendly" staff.

Marriott Long Wharf 🔭 — 20 | 19 | 16 | 20 | $449

296 State St. | 617-227-0800 | fax 617-227-2867 | 888-236-2427 | www.marriott.com | 391 rooms, 11 suites

"Paul Revere would certainly ride to this" "ideal location" - a "scenic" Waterfront spot "right on the harbor", "close to Faneuil Hall, the aquarium" and the Freedom Trail; whether they come by land or by sea, loyalists insist it's a "a good bet most of the time", but revolutionaries retort the "rooms are average" unless you have "a water view", the service is just "ok" and the dining is "middle-of-the-road."

Millennium Bostonian Hotel 🔭 — ∇ 21 | 19 | 17 | 18 | $429

26 North St. | 617-523-3600 | fax 617-523-2454 | 866-866-8086 | www.millenniumhotels.com | 177 rooms, 24 suites

"Walk out of the hotel and have history at your feet" when you stay at this "sophisticated" "boutique-type property" "right across the street from the Faneuil Hall Marketplace" that recently completed a $25-million renovation; rooms have "varied quite widely" in the past, but the revamped quarters (flat-panel TVs, faux-leather finishes), upgraded public areas and new restaurant are adding an "elegance" not seen before.

Nine Zero Hotel 🍴🐕🔭 — 23 | 23 | 21 | 20 | $399

90 Tremont St. | 617-772-5800 | fax 617-772-5810 | 866-646-3937 | www.ninezero.com | 185 rooms, 4 suites, 1 penthouse

"A young, hip crowd awaits" at this "oasis of service and style", a "swank" "ultramod boutique hotel" with "location, location, location" right at Downtown Crossing; the "comfy beds" and "great beauty products" earn kudos for these Kimpton quarters, as does the "chic dining" at KO Prime, "a nontraditional steakhouse" with a menu by local celeb chef Ken Oringer (of Restaurant Clio fame); some rooms are quite "small", however, so request a "corner one" or go for a "top-floor" perch with "wonderful views" of Boston Common.

Omni Parker House 👪[H]🐕 — 16 | 20 | 19 | 17 | $499

60 School St. | 617-227-8600 | fax 617-742-5729 | 888-444-6664 | www.omniparkerhouse.com | 489 rooms, 62 suites

There's no lack of "old-world" charm at this "historic" Downtown property, built in 1855 and reported to be America's longest continuously operating hotel; the staff knows how to "make special occasions truly special" - perhaps that's why former president John F. Kennedy held his bachelor party here - and Parker's Restaurant, which still serves all "the standards" including the namesake rolls, is a nostalgic favorite; just beware that the "shoebox-size" rooms, though "newly renovated", "make steerage on a cruise ship seem spacious."

[NEW] **Renaissance Hotel Waterfront** [S] — - | - | - | - | $450

606 Congress St. | 617-338-4111 | fax 617-338-4138 | 800-468-3571 | www.renaissancehotels.com | 450 rooms, 21 suites

Taking its design cues from the sea, this newly opened hotel in the Seaport District is done up with curvaceous modern furnishings, nautical artwork and bright aqua-inspired colors; many of the WiFi-equipped rooms have ocean views, there's an indoor lap pool and, in keeping with the maritime theme, the tapas-style 606 Congress restaurant specializes in New England seafood.

Ritz-Carlton
Boston Common 🛏️✕🏊👥Ⓢ

| 25 | 26 | 23 | 25 | $745 |

10 Avery St. | 617-574-7100 | fax 617-574-7200 | 800-241-3333 | www.ritzcarlton.com | 150 rooms, 43 suites

"All it's cracked up to be" – "from the moment you enter until check-out" – this totally madeover "grande dame" is "sleek, sexy" and sports a "stellar" location within "walking distance of Newbury Street restaurants and shops"; there's "free use of the Sports Club/La gym in the same building" and a staff that can "write the book on service", so "if you like to be pampered, this is the place."

Royal Sonesta 👥Ⓢ

| 21 | 20 | 19 | 20 | $299 |

40 Edwin H. Land Blvd. | Cambridge | 617-806-4200 | fax 617-806-4232 | 800-766-3782 | www.sonesta.com | 377 rooms, 23 suites

"Enjoy the views" of the Charles River and the Downtown skyline at this "reliable" choice that's within "walking distance of the Museum of Science" in East Cambridge; from the exterior, "you may not think it's upscale", but inside, there's an "impressive" contemporary art collection, and the rooms are "spacious" and "reasonably priced"; the modern Mediterranean restaurant, Dante, can be "quite good" as well.

Taj Boston 🏊👥

| 22 | 23 | 20 | 21 | $670 |

15 Arlington St. | 617-536-5700 | fax 617-536-1335 | 877-482-5267 | www.tajhotels.com | 228 rooms, 45 suites

"Thankfully, it's really still the Ritz" insist admirers of this "lovely, old-world hotel" that's now owned by the Taj group; the "impressive service" continues to earn praise (there are specialized butlers for the bath, the fireplace and technology), "its famous bar is as excellent as ever" and, of course, it will always have the "perfect" Back Bay location opposite the Public Garden; note that the type of room you get "makes a big difference", since some are "large" and "comfy", others are "cubbyholes."

Westin
Boston Waterfront, The 🖥️🏊👥

| 22 | 18 | 15 | 22 | $429 |

425 Summer St. | 617-532-4600 | fax 617-532-4630 | 800-937-8461 | www.westin.com | 758 rooms, 35 suites

"It's a professional outfit" report road warriors who've bedded down at this "refreshing business" lodging in the Waterfront District with a "sexy lobby" and modern "high-tech rooms"; vacationers should note, however, that it's primarily a "big", "impersonal" "conference hotel" that "isn't convenient to anything but the adjoining convention center", and the on-site food can be "ho-hum."

Westin Copley Place 🛏️🏊👥Ⓢ

| 22 | 21 | 19 | 21 | $499 |

10 Huntington Ave. | 617-262-9600 | fax 617-424-7483 | 800-937-8461 | www.westin.com | 763 rooms, 142 suites

"Great location, fine hotel" sums up this bustling Back Bay lodging that's directly connected to Copley Place (offering some of "the best shopping in Boston"); regulars recommend rooms on the "upper floors" since you'll feel like you're on "top of the world overlooking the entire city", while the "numerous dining options", including seafood at Turner Fisheries and steak in The Palm, along with "pleasant" staffers", make this lodging "much better than the average convention" destination.

Cape Cod & The Islands

Charlotte Inn, The ✕ 🏨
| 23 | 23 | 25 | 20 | $395 |

27 S. Summer St. | Edgartown | 508-627-4751 | fax 508-627-4652 | www.charlotteinn.net | 23 rooms, 2 suites

"Like staying in an English aunt's home", this "romantic" Edgartown Relais & Châteaux inn that dates to 1864 is a "charming" "choice for a weekend on the Vineyard"; "wonderfully kept lawns", "cozy common areas with fireplaces" and "sophisticated dining" at the seafood-centric Catch at The Terrace restaurant are to be expected from a member of Relais & Châteaux, although a few find all the "bric-a-brac" and "antique tchotchkes" a little "fussy"; P.S. kids under 14 are not allowed.

Chatham Bars Inn 🛉 🏨 ⓢ ✎
| 22 | 23 | 23 | 25 | $580 |

297 Shore Rd. | Chatham | 508-945-0096 | fax 508-945-6785 | 800-332-1577 | www.chathambarsinn.com | 158 rooms, 59 suites

Occupying a "gorgeous spot on a bluff", this 1914 "grande dame of the Chatham cruise set" is a "place to take the family", what with the "great pool and beach", children's programs, spa, nearby "wide nine-hole golf course", championship croquet and tennis courts whose "mixture of carpet, sand and clay" means you "can play even after heavy rain"; though "small", the rooms are "much better post-renovations", and you "still get the old Cape Cod ambiance."

Jared Coffin House ⓗ 🏨
| ▽ 21 | 22 | 21 | 16 | $280 |

29 Broad St. | Nantucket | 508-228-2400 | fax 508-228-8549 | 800-248-2405 | www.jaredcoffinhouse.com | 50 rooms

You "don't have to mortgage the house" for a Nantucket getaway when you stay at this "lovely, old-style inn", set inside an 1845 stately brick mansion, since the rooms range in type and price; highlights include a "central location" "in the heart of town", a relaxing garden and a library with fireplace; N.B. the renovated Harbor Wok restaurant opened post-Survey.

Ocean Edge
Resort & Golf Club 🛉 ⛱ 🏨 ⬆ ⓢ ✎
| ▽ 21 | 19 | 18 | 23 | $430 |

2907 Main St. | Brewster | 508-896-9000 | fax 508-896-9123 | 800-343-6074 | www.oceanedge.com | 90 rooms, 246 villas

"If you like golf" or want a base for "exploring in the mid-Cape", particularly if you're traveling with children, this "family-oriented" resort in Brewster with a "pleasant setting overlooking Cape Cod Bay" is a solid choice; the "grounds are lovely" and there are tons of activities for the youngsters, but if you're not *en famille*, the "pools teaming with screaming kids" may not appeal; N.B. a significant renovation post-Survey may outdate some scores.

Wauwinet, The ✕ 🏨 ⓢ ✎
| 25 | 26 | 27 | 25 | $750 |

120 Wauwinet Rd. | Nantucket | 508-228-0145 | fax 508-228-6712 | 800-426-8718 | www.wauwinet.com | 34 rooms

This "ultimate romantic hideaway for a summer weekend" is the "best place to stay if you want quiet" say sojourners who relish the

ROOMS | SERVICE | DINING | FACIL. | COST

"small but elegant rooms", the "exquisite dining" at Topper's restaurant and the "location, location, location" nine miles from the mayhem of Downtown Nantucket; other highlights at this "gorgeous" Relais & Châteaux member include "exceptional service" and an updated spa.

Wequassett Resort & Golf Club 斧✕战⌐📵

21 | 24 | 24 | 25 | $475

Rte. 28, Pleasant Bay | Chatham | 508-432-5400 | fax 508-430-3131 | 800-225-7125 | www.wequassett.com | 114 rooms, 7 suites

It's "like staying at your own cottage with a private deck overlooking the water" say fans of this veteran with a "beautiful setting", "top-notch food", access to the nearby private Cape Cod National Golf Club and "service that compensates for minor shortcomings"; just opt for a "well worth it" room with a view of Pleasant Bay (a new luxury Signature Collection focuses on impressive vistas), rather than get stuck in one of the "dark" quarters.

White Elephant 战

23 | 23 | 22 | 22 | $600

50 Easton St. | Nantucket | 508-228-2500 | fax 508-325-1195 | 800-445-6574 | www.whiteelephanthotel.com | 23 rooms, 30 suites, 11 cottages

"If you have big bucks to spend in Nantucket", surveyors suggest a stay at this "top-of-the-line hotel", a "well-managed property" "on the edge of town" that's run by an "accommodating crew"; you can't beat the "beautiful setting", especially in the Brant Point Grill ("one of the few waterfront restaurants that overlooks the harbor"), but since the place "can be a bit noisy on weekends", regulars recommend visiting off-season – "the value goes up, when the crowds go down."

Lenox

☑ Blantyre ✕⊕战☺📵

26 | 26 | 26 | 25 | $550

16 Blantyre Rd. | 413-637-3556 | fax 413-637-4282 | www.blantyre.com | 12 rooms, 8 suites, 4 cottages

"Ever wonder what it would feel like to lead the life of a Tudor?" – head to this "formal" 1902 Berkshires country estate, a Relais & Châteaux lodging where "luxury comes in many forms"; arise from your "charming" room ("be sure to stay in the main building"), "play shuffleboard or go touring or hiking" and then finish with a "superlative" meal that's "unlike anything you've ever experienced"; indeed, it "lives up to all reports", so there's "no better place to stay in the area."

☑ Canyon Ranch in the Berkshires 战☺📵

22 | 27 | 24 | 29 | $923

165 Kemble St. | 413-637-4400 | fax 413-637-0057 | 800-326-7080 | www.canyonranch.com | 104 rooms, 22 suites

"Whether you're here to nourish your body or soul", this "grande dame of spas" is "as up-to-date as when it first opened"; "tucked away in the Berkshires'" town of Lenox, this "fabulous fitness and wellness resort" offers an "incredible variety" of "dusk-to-dawn activities", from "health and nutrition" programs to hiking and yoga, led by a crew of "outstanding instructors"; even the "food is delish", so as long as you "don't come for luxurious rooms" and can cough up the "astronomical" tariffs, it's "worth it"; N.B. no kids under 14.

	ROOMS	SERVICE	DINING	FACIL.	COST

Cranwell Resort, Spa & Golf Club ⓘ🐾♨️🛗☺🔍

21 | 22 | 21 | 26 | $405

55 Lee Rd./Rte. 20 | 413-637-1364 | fax 413-637-4364 | 800-272-6935 | www.cranwell.com | 79 rooms, 26 suites

From the "lovely" 1894 Tudor-style mansion that serves as its main building to the "gorgeous grounds", the "beautiful setting" is the draw at this "all-around family resort" in the Lenox area; there's "lots to do", whether you'd like a base for a "New England getaway", "good golf" or "excellent spa facilities", but a disappointed few declare that the rooms "need a freshening up", particularly "in comparison to some of the Berkshires' competition."

🆉 Wheatleigh ✕ⓘ♨️🔍

26 | 26 | 27 | 24 | $655

Hawthorne Rd. | 413-637-0610 | fax 413-637-4507 | www.wheatleigh.com | 10 rooms, 9 suites

Take someone special to this "romantic getaway", one of "the most luxurious" places in western Massachusetts, and "remind them why you fell in love"; the "marvelous experience" includes an "excellent" staff that "bends over backwards to insure perfection", "amazing grounds", "gourmet meals", "superb accommodations" and "proximity to the Tanglewood music festival"; even so, a minority is bothered by the "high cost" of this "elegant" nirvana.

Michigan

Detroit

Dearborn Inn, The ⓘ

▽ 18 | 20 | 19 | 20 | $149

20301 Oakwood Blvd. | Dearborn | 313-271-2700 | fax 313-271-7464 | 800-228-9290 | www.dearborninnmarriott.com | 207 rooms, 21 suites

Service is always "top-notch" at this "grand", "historic" Colonial (a Marriott-affiliated property) built in 1931 on the grounds of the Ford Motor Company a few minutes from Downtown Detroit and "close to the Henry Ford Museum and Greenfield Village"; while "the history is great", the restaurants "consistently good" and the staff "pleasant", unimpressed guests say the accommodations and public facilities "could use some spiffing up" (luckily, it recently completed a multimillion-dollar renovation of the main inn, two lodges and five Colonial guest homes).

NEW MGM Grand ✕♨️☺

▽ 26 | 22 | 24 | 24 | $399

1777 Third St. | 313-393-7777 | fax 313-463-4470 | 877-888-2121 | www.mgmgranddetroit.com | 322 rooms, 78 suites

"The only place to stay Downtown", this "hot" new property "raises the bar", with a "beautiful 'living room' lobby" and luxurious accommodations including 1,000-sq.-ft. corner suites with marble foyers and floor-to-ceiling wraparound windows; "pricey" signature restaurants from Michael Mina and Wolfgang Puck "rival those of the MGM in Vegas", and while children are permitted, they have limited access due to the location of the casino (only one restaurant allows kids); P.S. if some note "a slightly rocky start", it doesn't detract from the overall "wow" factor.

	ROOMS	SERVICE	DINING	FACIL.	COST

Ritz-Carlton, The ✗ ⚲♨

| 24 | 25 | 23 | 22 | $315 |

300 Town Center Dr. | Dearborn | 313-441-2000 | fax 313-441-2051 | 800-241-3333 | www.ritzcarlton.com | 293 rooms, 15 suites

"Beautiful rooms, delicious food" and a staff with "smiles that will warm you even during Detroit's crazy-cold winters" distinguish this "conveniently located", "classic, personal and reliable" Dearborn hotel; a recently completed $3-million renovation of the main lobby, meeting space and ballrooms should allay complaints about the need for an "upgrade."

St. Regis ♨ⓢ

| - | - | - | - | $189 |

3071 W. Grand Blvd. | 313-873-3000 | fax 313-873-2574 | 800-598-1863 | www.hotelstregisdetroit.com | 117 rooms, 8 suites

A recent $2-million renovation of the restaurant, lobby and rooms (inviting color schemes, marble vanities, iPod docks, superior bedding) of this Motor City hotel makes it a "romantic and warm" "oasis" "in the New Center City area", just minutes from all the major Downtown attractions; still, some wonder what the future holds for this property, given half the rooms are being converted into condominiums.

Townsend Hotel, The ⚲♨

| 24 | 27 | 24 | 23 | $395 |

100 Townsend St. | Birmingham | 248-642-7900 | fax 248-645-9061 | 800-548-4172 | www.townsendhotel.com | 92 rooms, 58 suites

"Stay with the stars and athletes" at this "intimate" boutique in suburban Birmingham (40 minutes from Detroit) where the "excellent" service delivers "quality without pretension"; the "chic" location is "within walking distance" of "lots of great shopping", the recently upgraded rooms are "tasteful and comfortable", and the on-site Rugby Grille restaurant has "one of the best burgers to splurge on."

Westin Detroit
Metropolitan Airport ⚻ ⚲♨

| 24 | 20 | 18 | 20 | $269 |

2501 Worldgateway Pl. | 734-942-6500 | fax 734-942-6600 | 800-Westin-1 | www.westin.com | 394 rooms, 10 suites

"If I have to spend a night at the airport, this is where I want to be" admit admirers of this "trendy", "affordable" property in the Midfield Terminal that offers "a respite from travel"; "updated rooms", "hip lobby dining", an "accommodating staff", flight monitors and a "special security entrance that puts you right on the concourse with no wait" ensure a "Zen-like ambiance" – and the "perfect antidote to the adjacent terminal"; P.S. try cocktails at the "exceptional bar."

Grand Rapids

Amway Grand Plaza ⊕♨

| ▽ 23 | 21 | 23 | 22 | $215 |

187 Monroe Ave. NW | 616-774-2000 | fax 616-458-6641 | 800-253-3590 | www.amwaygrand.com | 638 rooms, 44 suites

"One of the classiest hotels in the Midwest", this "monster"-size property provides a dizzying number of dining options, in addition to more than 40 meeting and event spaces geared toward executives; regulars appreciate the "wonderful" suites and rooms in either the old, classic section or the newer tower, while fitness fiends find on-site racquetball and tennis courts.

	ROOMS	SERVICE	DINING	FACIL.	COST

Mackinac Island

Grand Hotel ♯♯✕⊕🐾♨⌂☺🔍 | 22 | 26 | 24 | 26 | $250 |

Mackinac Island | 906-847-3331 | fax 906-847-3259 | 800-334-7263 |
www.grandhotel.com | 348 rooms, 37 suites

A truly "historic landmark", this "time warp" resort on Mackinac Island, where "you may bike, walk or take a carriage ride, but no cars!", has been "used in several films" including *Somewhere in Time* with Christopher Reeve and Jane Seymour; its horse-drawn shuttle, "long creaking halls", "world's longest porch" (660 ft.), "magnificent columns" and "outstanding" service proffer an "old-fashioned grace" that "awes" admirers, even if the "tiny rooms" are not as grand.

Iroquois on the Beach ⊕♨ | ▽ 22 | 25 | 26 | 21 | $300 |

7485 Main St. | 906-847-3321 | fax 906-847-6274 | www.iroquoishotel.com |
38 rooms, 8 suites

"Surprise elegance" at an "end-of-the-world" location distinguishes this restored 1902 Victorian mansion that overlooks the Straits of Mackinac; for views of Round Island Lighthouse, savvy travelers grab one of the deluxe rooms and suites, while others opt for the gardenside rooms, perfect for taking in one of the notable homes nearby; an "experienced" staff that can set up ferry and carriage tours of the area and "delicious" breakfasts and complimentary tea and coffee round out the picture.

Minnesota

Minneapolis/St. Paul

Chambers ✕⊕🍴 | 25 | 22 | 27 | 23 | $345 |

901 S. Hennepin Ave. | Minneapolis | 612-767-6900 | fax 617-767-6801 |
877-767-6990 | www.chambersminneapolis.com | 48 rooms, 12 suites

Find "New York style and buzz" in "the heart of Minneapolis's Downtown and Theater districts" at this "chic", "stylish" all-white David Rockwell-designed hotel (sister to the original in the Big Apple) featuring "sparsely decorated rooms" with 400-thread-count linens and "original British art throughout"; guests rave about both Jean-Georges Vongerichten's "excellent" Asian fusion Chambers Kitchen and the extensive variety of "bar options" including a "rooftop veranda overlooking the city."

Grand Hotel ♨☺ | ▽ 24 | 24 | 20 | 24 | $389 |

615 Second Ave. S. | Minneapolis | 612-288-8888 | fax 612-373-0407 |
866-843-4726 | www.grandhotelminneapolis.com | 121 rooms, 19 suites

There's "a great vibe" to this "clubby", "grand" Downtown hotel with a "better-than-average staff" that's "not too pretentious"; loyalists laud rooms combining "old-school elegance" (marble baths, nightly turn-down service) with "modern" amenities (high-speed Internet access, iPod docks), a 58,000-sq.-ft. "outstanding work-out facility" ("the best hotel gym I've ever seen!") and the "great lounge" and sushi restaurant.

Graves 601 Hotel ✕☺ | ▽ 26 | 22 | 23 | 24 | $389 |

601 First Ave. N | Minneapolis | 612-677-1100 | fax 612-677-1200 |
866-523-1100 | www.graves601hotel.com | 251 rooms, 4 suites

"Space Age meets Mary Richards" at this "cool-for-Minneapolis" "hotel" "conveniently located on Block E" near Downtown's Entertainment

District; celebrated for its "handsome, modern decor" and "fabulous", "deliciously comfortable rooms" bedecked with "two flat-screen TVs", Jacuzzis and WiFi ("stay in bed all day – they're that good"), it's a "swanky hangout even the locals love", though "service can be spotty"; N.B. a replacement for the shuttered Infinity Lounge is expected in 2009.

Marquette Hotel ⌂✦⚭

∇ 24 | 23 | 19 | 22 | $349

710 Marquette Ave. | Minneapolis | 612-333-4545 | fax 612-288-2188 | 800-328-4782 | www.marquettehotel.com | 261 rooms, 20 suites

Convenience meets comfort at this "sleek", "oversized" Hilton-affiliated business hotel in the IDS Center, easily accessible to Downtown shopping, businesses and restaurants via an enclosed skyway sytem; the "staff is helpful", and patrons praise the "redone" rooms with 42-inch, flat-panel TVs and all-new baths, but even though the 50th-floor dining room has 360-degree views, foodies find the fare "mediocre."

Saint Paul Hotel, The ⊕⚭

22 | 26 | 25 | 22 | $219

350 Market St. | St. Paul | 651-292-9292 | fax 651-228-9506 | 800-292-9292 | www.saintpaulhotel.com | 223 rooms, 31 suites

Loyalists laud this 1910 "grand old lady" in St. Paul's Downtown Rice Park district as "the cream of the crop", citing the "classic charm" and "understated elegance" of its "well-appointed" rooms and "fabulous bar and restaurant"; the superior service and location also earn praise, though a few feel this "landmark" is "showing its age."

Sofitel ✕✦⚭

∇ 22 | 21 | 22 | 20 | $239

5601 W. 78th St. | Bloomington | 952-835-1900 | fax 952-835-2696 | 800-876-6303 | www.sofitel.com | 277 rooms, 5 suites

Don't be fooled by the suburban Bloomington locale of this "gem" 15 miles southwest of Downtown and seven miles from the Mall of America; an "above-average chainster with French flair", it's "the place to stay" ("like being in Paris if you don't look outside the window"), with "spotless rooms", "attentive service" and "excellent French" fare.

NEW W Minneapolis ⚭⚭

- | - | - | - | $499

821 Marquette Ave. | Minneapolis | 612-215-3700 | fax 612-215-3705 | www.whotels.com | 111 rooms, 16 suites

The latest outpost from the hip Starwood brand is set in the historic obelisk-shaped, 1929 Foshay tower where the cool quotient comes via the sky-high Prohibition bar, the loungey Living Room and the top-shelf dining at Manny's and Key's Cafe; accommodations include modern rooms with avant-garde geometric rugs, signature beds with goosedown comforters, Bliss products, 37-inch flat-screen TVs and iPod docks, and loftlike 'Extreme Wow' suites further up the ante on luxe.

Mississippi

Natchez

Monmouth Plantation ⊕⚭

∇ 26 | 26 | 24 | 24 | $195

36 Melrose Ave. | 601-442-5852 | fax 601-446-7762 | 800-828-4531 | www.monmouthplantation.com | 16 rooms, 14 suites

Those pining "for an authentic plantation experience" appreciate this "blast from the past" – a "romantic" restored 1818 "antebellum" mansion 100 miles southwest of Jackson that brings the "old South to life"; "well-manicured grounds", "pleasant owners" and "outstanding" regional fare, along with "charming" rooms featuring period furnishings, make for a "wonderful" *"Gone With the Wind"* experience at this National Historic Landmark member of Small Luxury Hotels of the World.

Missouri

Branson

Chateau on the Lake Resort & Spa

▽ 23 | 21 | 21 | 26 | $179

415 N. State Hwy. | 417-334-1161 | fax 417-339-5566 | 888-333-5253 | www.chateauonthelake.com | 244 rooms, 57 suites

"In the middle of nowhere", this "sprawling" complex 10 miles west of Branson in the Ozarks rewards guests with its "scenic" lake and mountain location, a "Sunday brunch that leaves you busting at the belt" (work it off at the 14,000-sq.-ft. spa), activities including tennis, sailing, swimming and fishing, and a 10-story, skylit lobby complete with trees, fountains and koi ponds.

St. Louis

Chase Park Plaza

▽ 22 | 22 | 22 | 23 | $269

212-232 N. Kingshighway Blvd. | 314-633-3000 | fax 314-633-3077 | 877-587-2427 | www.chaseparkplaza.com | 50 rooms, 201 suites

A "legendary" Downtown hotel near Forest Park, with its 18-hole golf course and lots of "eclectic dining and shopping", this "historic" 1922 "grande dame" "restored to its former glory days" features "classy" rooms and suites "the size of small apartments", plus an "incredible new fitness center"; the "impressive" public rooms, "good" (if "not great") restaurants, an "extraordinary" heated outdoor pool and a "multiplex right in the lobby" are further highlights.

NEW Four Seasons

▽ 29 | 27 | 25 | 26 | $245

999 N. Second St. | 314-881-5800 | fax 314-881-5700 | 800-819-5053 | www.fourseasons.com | 186 rooms, 14 suites

The Gateway City's "outstanding, new" hotel, located minutes from the central business district, boasts "wonderful rooms" and suites with "over-the-top technology and decor", and a variety of views ("opt for one of the Gateway Arch"); an "amazing" "rooftop" pool deck with "views of St. Louis", a "well-trained", "friendly" staff, fine Italian fare at Cielo and a 12,000-sq.-ft. spa add up to an "amazing" stay for most.

Renaissance Grand Hotel

▽ 23 | 23 | 21 | 21 | $189

800 Washington Ave. | 314-621-9600 | fax 314-621-9601 | 800-397-1282 | www.marriott.com | 876 rooms, 207 suites

Incorporating the original 1917 Statler Hotel, this "truly grand" Downtown "conference" spot is distinguished by "exceptional service" and a "great location across from the convention center" near "the thriving nightlife of Washington Avenue"; "surprisingly good dining" (at An American Place and the Mediterranean-style Capri) make it ideal for a "weekend visit", "business trip" or special occasion, but a few finicky foes say it's just "average, average, average."

	ROOMS	SERVICE	DINING	FACIL.	COST

Ritz-Carlton, The ✕ 🏠 ♨ | 24 | 24 | 21 | 23 | $189 |

100 Carondelet Plaza | Clayton | 314-863-6300 | fax 314-863-3525 |
800-241-3333 | www.ritzcarlton.com | 268 rooms, 33 suites

"A big city hotel in the suburbs", this "beautiful", "business-oriented" "haven" in Clayton (eight miles west of Downtown) has a distinctly "upper-class vibe", with "comfortable", if "small", rooms sporting "marble baths", and "dependable service with a smile"; still, some say this one may not be quite "worthy of the Ritz-Carlton badge" given the "ordinary" restaurant and "stodgy" decor; P.S. jazz bands that play in the "old-money lobby" on weekends "draw a crowd that loves to dance."

Montana

Darby

Triple Creek Ranch ✕ 🏠 ♨ 🔍   ▽ 29 | 29 | 29 | 28 | $650 |

5551 W. Fork Rd. | 406-821-4600 | fax 406-821-4666 | 800-654-2943 |
www.triplecreekranch.com | 23 cabins

"Everyone should be lucky enough to go at least once" to this "romantic" Relais & Châteaux resort (78 miles south of Missoula) that delivers "way beyond expectations"; the staff "gives pampering a new name", while the "terrific" cabins, "amazing" restaurant (a "tidal wave of taste") and "spectacular" vistas of the Bitterroot Mountains make you "pinch yourself for a reality check" – and "think about it every day" after you leave; P.S. although it's an "adult playground", kids are allowed during October, December, January, February and May, or if the entire ranch has been reserved.

Missoula

Resort at Paws Up 🏇 🦮 🏠 ♨ Ⓢ | - | - | - | - | $670 |

40060 Paws Up Rd. | Greenough | 406-244-5200 | fax 406-244-5242 |
866-894-7969 | www.pawsup.com | 29 houses, 12 tents

Located 25 miles from Missoula at the foothills of the Garnet Mountains, this working ranch (member of Small Luxury Hotels) pulls double duty as a resort that "inspires relaxation", with a variety of spacious vacation homes and cabins with Internet access and flat-screen TVs, as well as tents on the property's outskirts where clients indulge in "don't miss" spa treatments; active types can go river rafting, canoeing, clay shooting, horseback riding and waterskiing in summer or snowhshoeing, sledding and snowmobiling in winter, though some just sit and "breathe the fresh mountain air."

Nebraska

Omaha

NEW Omaha Magnolia Hotel 🦮 ♨ | - | - | - | - | $149 |

1615 Howard St. | 402-341-2500 | fax 402-342-2569 | 888-915-1110 |
www.magnoliahotelomaha.com | 125 rooms, 20 suites

Set in a 1920s building, this new Downtown hotel (formerly a Sheraton) has a classic lobby with original marble floors, travertine walls, Roman columns and a vaulted ceiling, along with modern touches including leather ottomans and elliptical chandeliers; rooms feature floor-to-ceiling windows with city and courtyard views, Starbucks coffee and executive work desks, while the signature club lounge offers a daily breakfast, evening cocktails and live entertainment.

Nevada

Incline Village

Hyatt Regency
Resort & Casino ♂♀ 👥 Ⓢ

| 21 | 22 | 19 | 23 | $355 |

111 Country Club Dr. | 775-832-1234 | fax 775-831-2171 | 800-553-3288 | www.laketahoe.hyatt.com | 388 rooms, 10 suites, 24 cottages

A "rustic", "beautiful mountain setting" "on the north shore of Lake Tahoe" provides the backdrop for this "older but very well-maintained" "lodge" that "feels like a private club", offering "both relaxation and excitement" with an "elegant spa" and an "intimate casino"; look for "friendly and helpful service", a restaurant with views of the Sierra Nevadas and "spectacular facilities" – a beach, nearby golf, cross-country skiing, boating – "you name it!"; regulars recommend "a room in the new wing" or one of the "fabulous" "lakeside cottages", as some of the quarters "really need an update."

Las Vegas

TOPS IN CITY

27	Wynn
	Four Seasons
26	Bellagio
25	Palazzo Resort & Casino
	Venetian
24	Red Rock
	Mandalay Bay
23	Caesars

☑ Bellagio Hotel ✕ 👥 Ⓢ

| 26 | 23 | 27 | 27 | $169 |

3600 Las Vegas Blvd. S. | 702-693-7111 | fax 702-693-8546 | 888-987-6667 | www.bellagio.com | 3421 rooms, 512 suites

"Top-of-the-line in every respect", this landmark is "as close to taste-ful as one gets in Las Vegas", offering guests a "classic rather than plastic" experience at a true resort, "not a casino with rooms"; "plush" accommodations – the fountain views are "well worth the extra cost" – add to the "va-va-voom" factor, as do the "outstanding" public areas with "spectacular" flowers, a collection of "first-class" restaurants, "fantastic shopping" and a "phenomenal" 55,000-sq.-ft. spa.

Caesars Palace ✕ Ⓢ

| 22 | 21 | 24 | 25 | $250 |

3570 Las Vegas Blvd. S. | 702-731-7110 | fax 702-866-1700 | 866-227-5938 | www.caesarspalace.com | 3452 rooms, 245 suites

"There may be more sparkle at other spots", but the majority agrees this "immense" staple of the Strip still "exudes elegance"; "rooms vary from classic" with "round beds" and "mirrored ceilings" to "state-of-the-art refurbished" in "the newer upscale towers"; boosters report the staff is "attentive", the on-site Forum Shops are a "shopaholic's dream come true" and the restaurants are "amazing", but detractors liken this "way too big" "zoo" to a "haggard '50s cocktail waitress trapped in the '70s"; N.B. the Forum Tower is undergoing renovations, and a new Octavius Tower is set for 2009.

☑ Four Seasons ✕ ❦ ⋔ Ⓢ

| 27 | 27 | 25 | 27 | $390 |

3960 Las Vegas Blvd. S. | 702-632-5000 | fax 702-632-5195 | 877-632-5000 | www.fourseasons.com | 338 rooms, 86 suites

"In the midst of the bustling Las Vegas pulse", this "calming, luxurious" "no-casino hotel" offers the best of both worlds on the Strip with "its own entrance and all of its own facilities" as well as "easy access to the Mandalay Bay grounds and casino" located next door; fans rave about "the top-notch service" ("about as close to perfect as one can expect"), the "high-class" accommodations, the "delicious food", the "celebrity-filled private swimming pool" and –"thank goodness"– "the quiet."

Green Valley Ranch Resort & Spa ❧ ❦ ⋔ Ⓢ

| 24 | 22 | 21 | 25 | $400 |

2300 Paseo Verde Pkwy. | Henderson | 702-617-7777 | fax 702-617-7738 | 866-782-9487 | www.greenvalleyranchresort.com | 423 rooms, 73 suites

Just "a short drive" from the "cha-ching of the slots" on the Strip, this "luxurious-without-being-pretentious" resort in Henderson is an "oasis in the land of neon"; with "big fluffy beds", a "pool out of a Chanel No. 5 commercial" and plenty of "Mediterranean flair", it has "all you'll ever need", including "beautiful public spaces", plus a "fantastic" spa and "restaurants, grounds and shopping much nicer than expected"; although critics say "service tries, but misses the mark", the majority has a "relaxing" time.

Hard Rock Hotel & Casino ✕ ⋔ Ⓢ

| 20 | 18 | 20 | 23 | $299 |

4455 Paradise Rd. | 702-693-5000 | fax 702-693-5010 | 800-473-7625 | www.hardrockhotel.com | 648 rooms, 96 suites

While it's "not as trendy as it once was", this "sexy" hotel is still the place to "party like a rock star" with a "fun, young crowd" in a "festive atmosphere"; guests say "the rooms are modern" ("try to get a renovated" one), ditto the restaurants (the newest is Ago, via chef Agostino Sciandri and partner Robert De Niro), "the small gaming floor is inviting" and the pool "is the reason to stay"; but while some surveyors "like its intimacy", others warn it's "far from the Strip" and there's "nonstop music."

JW Marriott Resort & Spa ⋔ Ⓢ

| 27 | 22 | 18 | 25 | $289 |

221 N. Rampart Blvd. | 702-869-7777 | fax 702-869-7771 | 877-869-8777 | www.jwlasvegasresort.com | 471 rooms, 77 suites

Surrounded by championship golf courses and "impeccable grounds" in upscale Summerlin, this "great escape from hectic Downtown" (yet just a "shuttle to the Strip") boasts a "romantic", full-service spa, rooms with "magnificent bathrooms" (rainfall showerheads, Jacuzzi tubs) and an "excellent pool area"; the dining leaves something to be desired, however, and you'd best pack some walking shoes since it's all "a bit sprawling."

	ROOMS	SERVICE	DINING	FACIL.	COST

Loews Lake Las Vegas
Resort 🏇🏕🎿🏃⛷Ⓢ

| 22 | 23 | 20 | 24 | $369 |

101 Montelago Blvd. | Henderson | 702-567-6000 |
fax 702-567-6067 | 877-285-6397 | www.loewshotels.com |
454 rooms, 46 suites

"The ultimate man-made environment, including a huge lake in the
middle of the desert", can be found at this "lovely", "low-key"
"Mediterranean village" offering "a fun family escape" about a half-
hour from "the insanity of the Strip"; while there's "no gambling on-
site" and some balk at "cramped" accommodations and "food that's
not nearly as good as it should be", advocates assert that the recreational facilities – which include a "pool, boating" and "golf" at two
Jack Nicklaus-designed courses – and "excellent service" help make
for a "relaxing" "respite."

Mandalay Bay Resort ✕🏃Ⓢ

| 24 | 21 | 24 | 26 | $229 |

3950 Las Vegas Blvd. S. | 702-632-7777 | fax 702-632-7328 |
877-632-7000 | www.mandalaybay.com | 2662 rooms,
1553 suites

Popular with the "twenty- to thirtysomething crowd", this "classy"
spot with a "tropical" feel is "right up there with the best of them"; kudos
go to the "best pools in town" (a three-story complex), Mixx Lounge
(voted the No. 1 in overall Appeal in our *Las Vegas Nightlife* Survey),
the "spacious" rooms, the "awesome spa" and "food that does not disappoint" (from Micheal Mina's StripSteak to Rick Moonen's RM
Seafood); but if you want a "really special" experience, head to its separate "best-kept-secret rooms in the country" – THEhotel tower suites
with flat-screen TVs, wet bars and stylish lobby areas.

MGM Grand ✕🏃Ⓢ

| 19 | 18 | 22 | 22 | $109 |

3799 Las Vegas Blvd. S. | 702-891-7777 | fax 702-891-1030 |
877-880-0880 | www.mgmgrand.com | 4216 rooms, 2527 suites,
29 villas

"If size matters to you", this "sprawling", "mall-like" property with a
"freshly renovated" interior "delivers big", with "a dizzying array of
amenities" that "makes its less than central location on The Strip
worthwhile"; fans say the dining – "from coffee shop to ultra-high end"
(Joël Robuchon "is without equal" and was voted No. 1 for Food in our
Las Vegas Restaurants Survey) – impresses, "the gaming floor is out of
this world" and the remodeled rooms are "modern", but given the
"crowds", service can be "impersonal"; N.B. the all-suite Signature
(with three towers) is the newest addition.

Mirage Hotel ✕🏃Ⓢ

| 19 | 19 | 21 | 22 | $159 |

3400 Las Vegas Blvd. S. | 702-791-7111 | fax 702-891-1030 | 800-374-9000 |
www.mirage.com | 2763 rooms, 281 suites

This "quintessential grande dame of Las Vegas" "remains one of the
best mega-resorts" thanks to "a staff that's eager to serve", an interesting "restaurant lineup" and "newly remodeled rooms" boasting "all
the comforts"; with "great entertainment" for all ages (a "hot nightclub" for adults, a "kid-friendly" dolphin habitat), it's no wonder that
despite some gripes, the majority maintains this "original gem still
shines"; N.B. a $25-million upgrade is in store for its iconic erupting
faux volcano, including 120 new fireball-throwing devices.

	ROOMS	SERVICE	DINING	FACIL.	COST

Orleans Hotel & Casino ♟Ⓢ

| 18 | 18 | 17 | 18 | $175 |

4500 W. Tropicana Ave. | 702-365-7111 | fax 702-365-7500 | 800-675-3267 | www.orleanscasino.com | 1811 rooms, 75 suites

"Off the Strip" and "off the chart in value", given its "spacious rooms" and "incredibly friendly staff", this hotel "away from the bustle and congestion" has a "family-friendly" "gorgeous pool", 70-lane bowling center, video arcade and 18-screen movie theater; it may be an "average" spot overall with "nondescript" food options, but the "really good rates" save the day.

☷NEW Palazzo Resort, Hotel, & Casino ✕♨Ⓢ

| 28 | 22 | 26 | 25 | $199 |

3325 Las Vegas Blvd. S. | 702-414-1000 | fax 702-414-4884 | 877-883-6423 | www.palazzolasvegas.com | 3066 suites

"Mama mia" – there are "no bachelorette parties, buffet-seekers or fraternity bashes" at this new "gem on the Strip", a "ridiculously opulent" "all-suite property" that's "still finding its legs", but "promises to be a worthy younger sister to the Venetian" next door (the two share amenities, including "the world-famous" Canyon Ranch Spa Club); guests rave about the "pristine rooms" with "large baths", "impeccable service", "outstanding restaurant selection", "super shopping" and "beautiful casinos" that exemplify "how Vegas should be."

Palms Casino Resort ♟♨Ⓢ

| 20 | 18 | 20 | 21 | $599 |

4321 W. Flamingo Rd. | 702-942-7777 | fax 702-942-7001 | 866-942-7777 | www.palms.com | 552 rooms, 150 suites

"Though off-Strip", this "trendy hotel" that "caters to a cooler, younger crowd" is "the ultimate party scene" where "the casino is abuzz with activity at all hours, and the glitterati stay awake and dressed to the nines for most of the night"; while our respondents report the rooms "are nothing to write home about", the "service is average" and the pool is "small", enthusiasts claim there's absolutely "no substitute for the nightlife" or "the eye candy" here.

Paris Las Vegas Ⓢ

| 20 | 19 | 21 | 20 | $109 |

3655 Las Vegas Blvd. S. | 702-946-7000 | fax 702-946-4405 | 877-603-4386 | www.parislasvegas.com | 2621 rooms, 295 suites

With a "center-of-the-action" location and a casino that "isn't as hectic as most", this older property may not be "in the same league as Bellagio" but you can appreciate "French character without the attitude"; given the "average" rooms and facilities where "nothing stands out" ("other than the faux Eiffel Tower"), many are "not impressed."

Planet Hollywood Resort & Casino Ⓢ

| 18 | 16 | 18 | 18 | $199 |

3667 Las Vegas Blvd. S. | 702-785-5555 | fax 702-785-9450 | 866-517-3263 | www.planethollywood.com | 2300 rooms, 300 suites

"They certainly rubbed the lamp right when they renovated the former Aladdin" into this "flashy" hotel that "provides good value for the Strip" with "basic", "comfortable" rooms ("above-average baths") and "varied food choices" (including Koi from LA and Strip House from NYC); "they have everything you need", from a "shiny redone casino" with "dancing girls on the tables" to "a variety of stores", though the

	ROOMS	SERVICE	DINING	FACIL.	COST

required "march through the labyrinth of shops" to enter the hotel is a minus.

Platinum Hotel & Spa ✕⊟🐾M⑤

| - | - | - | - | $359 |

211 E. Flamingo Rd. | 702-365-5000 | fax 702-365-5001 | 877-211-9211 | www.theplatinumhotel.com | 255 suites

Ok, there's no gaming or smoking at this all-suite boutique hotel east of the Strip, but you will find "great rooms" that include gourmet kitchens, whirlpool tubs and private balconies with views, "good but expensive food" at chef James Sasahara's Kilawat (specializing in steaks and seafood with edgy American nuance), a "nice upper-level pool" and the rejuvenating WELL spa; just "plan for a hike" to get to the heart of Sin City action.

Red Rock Casino Resort & Spa ⛳M⑤

| 27 | 22 | 21 | 26 | $199 |

11011 W. Charleston Blvd. | 702-797-7777 | fax 702-797-7771 | 866-767-7773 | www.redrocklasvegas.com | 816 rooms

"What's not to enjoy?" at this "breathtakingly beautiful" resort from Station Casinos that's "away from the insanity of the Strip", with "comfortable rooms" boasting "gorgeous views of Red Rock Park" (just a "short drive" away) and amenities that "rival anything" near the action (and "at a lower cost"); "the pool is a high point", as is the "gaming" and the "eye-catching cocktail lounges", most notably Rande Gerber's Cherry; N.B. a recently completed tower almost doubles its capacity.

Rio All-Suite Hotel & Casino M⑤

| 20 | 18 | 19 | 20 | $120 |

3700 W. Flamingo Rd. | 702-777-7777 | fax 702-777-2360 | 866-746-7671 | www.playrio.com | 2551 suites

The views are decidedly mixed on this off-Strip, Brazilian-themed, all-suiter; fans dig the "fun", "24/7 carnival atmosphere", the lively clubs, the buffet and the "huge" accommodations, but foes frown over a "once shining star that's now a black hole", citing "marginal dining", "large rooms passed off as suites" and the "cheesy New Orleans theme" that "needs some work."

Ritz-Carlton Lake Las Vegas 👯⛳M⬆⑤

| 27 | 26 | 24 | 27 | $299 |

1610 Lake Las Vegas Pkwy. | Henderson | 702-567-4700 | fax 702-567-4777 | 800-241-3333 | www.ritzcarlton.com | 314 rooms, 35 suites

"A calming alternative to the noise and glitz of the Strip", this "practically perfect" Henderson resort offers "typically wonderful Ritz-Carlton service", "special rooms" and "nice spa facilities" in a "beautiful" desert setting; for "pure luxury", the "club-level" suites on a Tuscan-inspired bridge over the lake "are the way to go" ("awesome service"), while a "great" Jack Nicklaus–designed golf course awaits duffers; still, some say it's "way too far" from the Vegas action.

Signature at MGM Grand ⊟M⑤

| 27 | 24 | 18 | 22 | $159 |

145 E. Harmon Ave. | 702-891-7777 | fax 702-891-1275 | 877-612-2121 | www.signaturemgmgrand.com | 1728 suites

For "a quiet oasis away from the Strip", this "beautiful" three-tower "escape" with a separate entrance on the MGM Grand property offers "everything you can imagine" – "spacious", "smoke-free" suites with "top-notch facilities", "royal" treatment from an "excellent" staff and a "relaxing pool area"; if you want more action, though, "put on your walking shoes" and "trek" via "indoor walkways" to the main hotel's casino, restaurants and nightclubs.

Treasure Island 🏨Ⓢ

ROOMS	SERVICE	DINING	FACIL.	COST
-	-	-	-	$99

3300 Las Vegas Blvd. S. | 702-894-7111 | fax 702-894-7414 | 800-288-7206 | www.treasureisland.com | 2665 rooms, 218 suites, 2 penthouses

A complete refurbishment a few years back, along with renovations in 2008, have made this veteran property at the end of the Strip a "pleasant surprise" for most guests; accommodations sport modern decor, "comfortable" signature beds, iPod alarm clocks and flat-panel TVs, the swimming pool has "heavenly cabanas", the aquatic-themed Wet spa features unique water-based treatments and service is "prompt"; the "happening" atmosphere includes the "best sports betting area", Cirque du Soleil's *Mystère,* the scantily clad Sirens (performed several times daily at the hotel entrance) and a new Christian Audigier nightclub.

NEW Trump International Hotel & Tower 🏖Ⓢ

ROOMS	SERVICE	DINING	FACIL.	COST
▽ 21	22	18	19	$199

3128 Las Vegas Blvd. S. | 702-982-0000 | fax 702-476-8450 | 866-939-8786 | www.trumplv.com | 1282 suites

Fans of this new 64-floor Trump property minutes from the Strip action find it "an oasis" for the "ego-driven, jet-set crowd" with "unobtrusive service", a spa and accommodations that include 50 penthouse suites with floor-to-ceiling windows and European-style kitchens; on-site eateries include DJT, serving Modern American fare, and the poolside H2(Eau).

Venetian Hotel ✕🏨Ⓢ

ROOMS	SERVICE	DINING	FACIL.	COST
27	22	25	26	$379

3355 Las Vegas Blvd. S. | 702-414-1000 | fax 702-414-1100 | 877-883-6423 | www.venetian.com | 4027 suites

"Get swept away" at this "true Italian gem in the desert", a "huge", "all-suite" "city under one roof" in the "center of the Strip", touting "luxurious rooms", "endless quality dining options" (from top toques like David Burke and Mario Batali), a "friendly, attentive staff" (its La Scena Lounge was voted the No. 1 spot for Service in our *Las Vegas Nightlife* Survey), plus an on-site Canyon Ranch Spa and "great shopping" opportunities along the Grand Canal "mall" ("take a gondola ride"); though some bemoan the "maze"-like design, admirers ask "why would you ever leave?"; N.B. it shares amenities with its sister, Palazzo.

🅉 Wynn Las Vegas Casino Resort ✕🏨⌐Ⓢ

ROOMS	SERVICE	DINING	FACIL.	COST
28	25	27	27	$300

3131 Las Vegas Blvd. S. | 702-770-7100 | fax 702-770-1571 | 888-320-9966 | www.wynnlasvegas.com | 2108 rooms, 608 suites

There's "no need to stay anywhere else" cheer champions of this over-the-top piece of "eye candy", especially if you "get a room on the upper floors facing the Strip" for "incredible" night views; there are "dining choices for every taste", "winning nightlife", decor that's "top-notch" (the velvet-lined Tryst club was voted No. 1 for Decor in the *Las Vegas Nightlife* Survey) and a "breathtaking" golf course ("the only in-town links left"); still, sour sorts "can't figure out what all the fuss is about."

New Hampshire

Dixville Notch

Balsams, The ♞✕⊕❄♨⊾☺🔍

ROOMS	SERVICE	DINING	FACIL.	COST
▽ 19	25	25	25	$278

1000 Cold Spring Rd. | 603-255-3400 | fax 603-255-4221 | 877-225-7267 | www.thebalsams.com | 193 rooms, 11 suites

Be transported "back in time" to "the Catskills in their heyday" at this "quaint", "big-summer destination resort" built in 1866 in the Great North Woods; while it may be isolated, our voters say it "has everything", including "entertainment, golf", "incredible dining", "skiing even in April" and a "professional and friendly" staff that provides "tremendous service"; still, even admirers admit the rooms are "out of date."

Newcastle

Wentworth by the Sea by Marriott ♨☺🔍

ROOMS	SERVICE	DINING	FACIL.	COST
25	24	23	24	$199

588 Wentworth Rd. | 603-422-7322 | fax 603-422-7329 | 866-240-6313 | www.wentworth.com | 125 rooms, 18 suites, 18 condos

"Thank goodness they saved this one from the wrecking ball" exclaim enthusiasts seduced by the "beautiful restoration" of this "old grande dame" five minutes from Downtown Portsmouth and an hour north of Boston; "a throwback to the seaside resorts from the turn-of-the-century", it features accommodations "fit for kings and queens" (with water views and "gorgeous" marble bathrooms), tennis, a marina, access to a private golf club and an "exceptional" staff; P.S. the restaurants and spa "fill up quickly" when it's "busy."

White Mountains

Manor on Golden Pond ⊕♨☺🔍

ROOMS	SERVICE	DINING	FACIL.	COST
-	-	-	-	$245

31 Manor Dr. | Holderness | 603-968-3348 | fax 603-968-2116 | 800-545-2141 | www.manorongoldenpond.com | 21 rooms, 2 suites, 1 cottage

If "you want to get away" from it all, you can "switch off" at this Central New Hampshire "country inn on steroids" that fans call "the best on Squam Lake" (featured in the film *On Golden Pond*); a member of Small Luxury Hotels of the World, this "winner" offers rooms with fireplaces, Jacuzzis and luxury bath amenities (some have private decks and water views), as well as an outdoor pool, gourmet breakfasts, fine dining, afternoon high tea and a private beach with canoes and paddleboats.

Mount Washington Hotel & Resort, The ♞⊕❄♨⊾🎿🔍

ROOMS	SERVICE	DINING	FACIL.	COST
18	20	19	22	$209

Rte. 302 | Bretton Woods | 603-278-1000 | fax 603-278-8838 | 800-314-1752 | www.mountwashingtonresort.com | 283 rooms, 24 suites, 69 townhouses

"Take a step back in time" at this "picture postcard" 1902 Spanish Renaissance hotel "way up in the White Mountains" "near the exceptional family ski area of Bretton Woods" that offers guests "a little bit of old America" with a "wraparound veranda" and "views that go on for miles"; while some sniff "overrated", "lots of repeat visitors" find it "elegant"; N.B. an 18-hole Donald Ross golf course reopened in August 2008, and an ongoing $50-million renovation will include a new spa in 2009.

New Jersey

Atlantic City

Atlantic City Hilton Casino Resort 🛏️Ⓢ — 18 | 20 | 19 | 20 | $275

3400 Pacific Ave. | 609-347-7111 | fax 609-340-4858 | 800-445-8667 | www.hiltonac.com | 604 rooms, 204 suites

Gamers who "highly recommend" this Hilton outpost cite the "wonderful" lounge, "enjoyable" casino and "housekeeping that never lets you down" ("for a busy hotel", the rooms and public facilities are "spotless"); but a few find food "so-so" and accommodations that "need sprucing up."

Borgata Hotel Casino & Spa ✕Ⓢ — 26 | 22 | 27 | 26 | $279

1 Borgata Way | 609-317-1000 | fax 609-317-1100 | 866-692-6742 | www.theborgata.com | 1600 rooms, 400 suites

"Get everything you desire without ever having to leave" this "splashy" "piece of Vegas in the Northeast", where "gorgeous" rooms, "fabulous" celebrity-chef restaurants (the Adam Tihany-designed, Michael Mina–headed SeaBlue was voted No. 1 for Food in Atlantic City in our *New Jersey Restaurants* Survey), a "fantastic" spa, "superior" service, an "exciting" casino, "top" entertainment and various "outstanding" recreational facilities further propel it to "premier" status; N.B. the separate Water Club at Borgata offers an even more luxe experience.

Caesars 🛏️Ⓢ — 18 | 18 | 20 | 19 | $189

2100 Pacific Ave. | 609-348-4411 | fax 609-343-2405 | 800-443-0104 | www.caesars.com | 1127 rooms, 17 suites

"Well-maintained" public spaces, a "high-end" designer shopping mall and "eager-to-please" staffers are the pride of this large, Roman-themed casino complex in the middle of the Boardwalk; but many find the rooms "vary in quality" depending on whether you book a "comfortable" one in the "newer" Centurion wing or a "dated" one in the older tower.

NEW Chelsea, The 🛏️Ⓢ — - | - | - | - | $265

111 S. Chelsea Ave. | 609-428-4380 | 866-393-3285 | www.thechelsea-ac.com | 319 rooms, 11 suites

The first non-gaming hotel on the Boardwalk in over 40 years, this glamorous, just-opened retreat from the casino chaos is ultraluxe all the way, with a series of suites offering glorious views of the Atlantic, a cocktail lounge, a saltwater-inspired spa, poolside cabanas and attendants for the property's beach; taking care of the dining is Philly restaurateur Stephen Starr, who adds a pair of restaurants to the mix.

	ROOMS	SERVICE	DINING	FACIL.	COST

Harrah's Resort ♿Ⓢ
| 21 | 21 | 19 | 23 | $439 |

777 Harrah's Blvd. | 609-441-5000 | fax 609-348-6057 | 800-277-5990 | www.harrahs.com | 1311 rooms, 319 suites

Now that the $550-million expansion is finished, admirers say this "completely redone" Atlantic City extravaganza easily "gives other hotels a run for their money", with "spacious" rooms (including new suites in a waterfront tower boasting floor-to-ceiling windows and 24-hour butler service), a "gorgeous" tropical pool with private cabanas ("like a visit to the islands every day"), a "great" Elizabeth Arden Red Door Spa, "awesome" nightlife and dining (including a branch of McCormick & Schmick's) and 112,000 sq. ft. of "fantastic" gaming; most deem it a "luxury vacation" worth repeating.

Seaview Resort & Spa, A Marriott Resort 🎿♿⌂Ⓢ🔍
| 19 | 21 | 19 | 23 | $299 |

401 S. New York Rd. | Galloway | 609-652-1800 | fax 609-652-2307 | 800-205-6518 | www.seaviewmarriott.com | 278 rooms, 19 suites

"Redolent in Gatsby-esque splendor", this "vintage" resort with a "perky staff" offers an "affordable" "respite" just a "dice roll away from AC"; proponents call it "Marriott's jewel" with "strokes of genius" that include a "beautiful" Elizabeth Arden spa and two golf courses (one of which is a "spectacular" 1914 Donald Ross design); but it's "heaven for flies" ("native" biting greenheads) say sourpusses, who add this "grand lady" needs more "updating" or she'll lapse into a "tired old broad."

Tropicana ♿Ⓢ
| 16 | 17 | 21 | 19 | $129 |

S. Brighton Ave. | 609-340-4000 | fax 609-343-5254 | 800-345-8767 | www.tropicana.net | 2030 rooms, 100 suites

It's "nothing fancy", but this AC beachfront complex tempts "those without money to burn" on a casino hotel; while there are "no high-end amenities", the rooms are just "adequate" (but perhaps better in the "newer tower") and "service needs to come up a notch", most come for the gaming, others for the "great outdoor bar" and restaurants.

NEW Water Club, The ♿Ⓢ
| - | - | - | - | $539 |

1 Renaissance Way | www.thewaterclubatborgata.com | 800 rooms

Just steps from the casino and entertainment action at the Borgata, this newly opened 43-story tower features a two-level spa offering floor-to-ceiling water views, five indoor and outdoor pools and the lobby Sunroom lounge surrounded by gardens and drenched in light; high-end designer boutiques include Hugo Boss and La Perla, while the accommodations include three urban loft-like residences.

Bernardsville

Bernards Inn ✕Ⓗ
| ▽ 20 | 25 | 28 | 20 | $249 |

27 Mine Brook Rd. | 908-766-0002 | fax 908-766-4604 | 888-766-0002 | www.bernardsinn.com | 16 rooms, 4 suites

The staff is sure to "make your occasion special" at this "romantic" north Jersey inn where you also have the chance to dine in chef Corey Heyer's "wonderful" restaurant – "one of the best" in the state; it's "like staying in an antiques shop" in the "beautiful rooms (recent renovations may not be reflected in the above Rooms score), but it's definitely the "amazing" fare that outshines all.

	ROOMS	SERVICE	DINING	FACIL.	COST

Cape May

Congress Hall ♀♿⊕♨⑤

| 19 | 19 | 20 | 21 | $265 |

251 Beach Ave. | 609-884-8421 | fax 609-884-6094 | 888-944-1816 | www.congresshall.com | 106 rooms, 2 suites

Providing "history and comfort" year-round, this 1816 Victorian Cape May property exudes endless "charm", thanks to its "gorgeous" views of the ocean and town, its "cozy bar area" and its "superbly decorated", though "small", rooms, some sporting claw-foot tubs; foodies are relieved it's "within walking distance" of area eateries, however, since a few find the food "mediocre."

Queen Victoria, The ⊕♨

| ▽ 22 | 26 | 22 | 21 | $220 |

102 Ocean St. | 609-884-8702 | www.queenvictoria.com | 22 rooms, 10 suites

"Don't miss the afternoon tea on the porch", prepared by the "awesome staff" at this "wonderfully charming" Victorian B&B "in the heart of Cape May", "a short walk" to the beach, shopping and "excellent dining options" (lunch and dinner are not offered on the premises); "each room has individual touches" and it's open year-round, so it's "fine for a romantic autumn weekend"; N.B. no children under eight allowed.

Virginia, The ✕⊕♨

| 23 | 25 | 27 | 22 | $250 |

25 Jackson St. | 609-884-5700 | fax 609-884-1236 | 800-732-4236 | www.virginiahotel.com | 24 rooms

Continuing to make a splash, this "beautiful" 1879 Cape May landmark "perfectly situated between the beach and shopping" excels at classic "detail"-driven, "B&B hospitality"; "wonderfully inviting rooms" that combine "old-world charm" with "modern" grace notes (e.g. Bulgari bath products), plus "terrific" food at the "romantic" on-site Ebbitt Room further prompt the question "why don't more people know about this gem?"

Hamburg

Grand Cascades Lodge ♀♿✒♨⊾⑤

| – | – | – | – | $299 |

3 Wild Turkey Way | 973-827-5996 | fax 973-823-6535 | www.resortscrystalsprings.com | 73 rooms, 182 suites, 28 studios

This "outstanding" luxury endeavor in the sprawling Crystal Springs Resort in Hamburg (about 50 miles from Manhattan) pulls out all the stops with a "lovely" spa, a tropical aquarium, an indoor biosphere pool with retractable roof and a full-service salon; Adirondack-style touches throughout reflect the wooded, mountainous Northern New Jersey locale (the lobby has massive wooden beams with iron strapping and a stone fireplace flanked by torchère lighting), and guests can take advantage of six nearby golf courses and fine dining at Latour.

Short Hills

Hilton ✒♛♨⑤

| 22 | 23 | 22 | 23 | $179 |

41 John F. Kennedy Pkwy. | 973-379-0100 | fax 973-379-6870 | 800-445-8667 | www.hilton.com | 272 rooms, 32 suites

Even locals "pack their bags for a weekend" to indulge at this "luxury destination" in the suburbs north of New York City where "posh"

	ROOMS	SERVICE	DINING	FACIL.	COST

rooms, "gracious" service and "wonderful" spa treatments await; "alas, The Dining Room is no more", but The Terrace still serves a "terrific" Sunday brunch, and "world-class" shopping awaits "across the street" at the Mall at Short Hills; N.B. the spa and pool just finished a $7-million renovation.

New Mexico

Albuquerque

Hyatt Regency Albuquerque ⏸ ∇ 18 | 20 | 18 | 19 | $260

330 Tijeras Ave. NW | 505-842-1234 | fax 505-843-2710 | 800-233-1234 | www.hyatt.com | 381 rooms, 14 suites

It "beats a teepee" jest guests of this simple Downtown property that, despite providing "intermittent service" and a "curiously anonymous experience", is praised for "pleasant" accommodations, "enormous bathrooms" and a location "near many things"; even if some say it's basically "standard across the board", it's a "reliable", "comfortable" place to land.

Hyatt Regency Tamaya 🕴🐾⏣ⓢ 23 | 24 | 22 | 26 | $255

1300 Tuyuna Trail | Santa Ana Pueblo | 505-867-1234 | fax 505-771-6180 | 800-554-9288 | www.tamaya.hyatt.com | 327 rooms, 23 suites

"Your cares drift away on incense-scented breezes" at this "oasis" "in the middle of nowhere" that fans "absolutely adore" for the "gorgeous", "secluded" surroundings, "elegant rooms" and "tasty" fare ("breakfast at the cafe is fantastic"); the "wonderful" "local Pueblo tribe" staff creates a "magical setting", while the "awesome spa facilities", "beautiful pools" and "daily activities" like "fun horseback riding and ballooning" make it even more family-friendly.

Santa Fe

Bishop's Lodge Resort & Spa 🕴⏣🐾🐾ⓢ🌸 19 | 22 | 19 | 22 | $399

1297 Bishop's Lodge Rd. | 505-983-6377 | fax 505-983-0832 | 800-419-0492 | www.bishopslodge.com | 97 rooms, 15 lodges

"Warm" feelings abound for this "friendly", "adobe-and-timber getaway" spread over 15 lodges "on the outskirts of Santa Fe" that's christened "the real thing" by reviewers who "just love" its "pretty", "spacious surroundings" ("great for horseback riding") and its on-site yoga classes; still, given the varying rooms, some find the "New York expensive" rates too high.

Eldorado Hotel & Spa 🐾🐾ⓢ 22 | 22 | 23 | 21 | $359

309 W. San Francisco St. | 505-988-4455 | fax 505-995-4544 | 800-988-4455 | www.eldoradohotel.com | 199 rooms, 20 suites

Those in search of "New Mexican splendor" find it at this "well-appointed" "meeting hotel" "central to all of Santa Fe's delights"; you'll find "superb" dining at the Old House restaurant, "great guitar players" in the "outstanding lobby bar" and "excellent service" that creates a "casual yet elegant" atmosphere, but a few nitpickers deem it "a bit too big."

	ROOMS	SERVICE	DINING	FACIL.	COST

NEW Encantado Resort 🏨Ⓢ
| – | – | – | – | $450 |

198 State Rd. 592 | 505-946-5700 | fax 505-946-5888 | 877-262-4666 | www.encantadoresort.com | 9 suites, 56 casitas

Set on 57 acres in the foothills of the Sangre de Cristo Mountains and minutes from Downtown Santa Fe, this recently opened sun-dappled Auberge outpost sits on the site of the former Rancho Encantado; along with suites and casitas featuring fireplaces, soaking tubs and beds piled high with Italian linens, hedonists find a 10,000-sq.-ft. spa with 15 treatment rooms, a fitness center, nearby hiking and horseback riding and chef Charles Dale's regionally inspired Terra restaurant.

Inn of the Anasazi ✕🍴
| 24 | 25 | 25 | 22 | $349 |

113 Washington Ave. | 505-988-3030 | fax 505-988-3277 | 800-688-8100 | www.innoftheanasazi.com | 56 rooms, 1 suite

Combining "Swiss efficiency, Santa Fe charm [and] New York prices", this "simply stunning" boutique hotel in an "ideal location" "steps from the plaza" is "incomparable in every way" say its fans; it "oozes" "local flavor", with "small but charming" rooms that have their "own fireplace" (a "romantic touch"), "warm" and "sophisticated" service, and "spectacular" dining (go "for dinner" "even if you stay somewhere else"); indeed, it's "perhaps the best that Santa Fe has to offer."

Inn on the Alameda 🍴
| 22 | 23 | 20 | 19 | $215 |

303 E. Alameda St. | 505-984-2121 | fax 505-986-8325 | 888-984-2121 | www.innonthealameda.com | 59 rooms, 12 suites

"One of the least presumptuous and overbearing places in Santa Fe", this "secluded" but "close to everything" "B&B-style hotel" earns kudos for its "happy and helpful staff", "delicious breakfast", "beautiful flower-filled courtyard" and "fabulous" "afternoon wine and cheese" that's "included" in the rate; while only some of the "homey" digs have "fireplaces and Jacuzzis", "renovated old-world charm" prevails throughout – "which means things work, but in an old-fashioned way."

La Fonda 🏨Ⓢ
| 19 | 19 | 18 | 19 | $319 |

100 E. San Francisco St. | 505-982-5511 | fax 505-988-2952 | 800-523-5002 | www.lafondasantafe.com | 143 rooms, 24 suites

Dating back to 1610, this "historic beauty" is kept "quirky but fun" by "quaintly colorful public areas" and "incredible tile work and murals", while "Western swing bands" and "views from the rooftop bar" add atmosphere; "concierge-level rooms" are deemed "fantastic", but "regular" ones are clearly "built for another time, place and traveler" say modernists who maintain it's "looking ragged around the edges."

La Posada de Santa Fe
Resort & Spa ⓗ🍴🏨Ⓢ
| 21 | 20 | 20 | 22 | $379 |

330 E. Palace Ave. | 505-986-0000 | fax 505-982-6850 | 866-331-7625 | www.laposadadesantafe.com | 127 rooms, 30 suites

"Just a short walk" from the main town plaza, this "reliable" newly renovated Rock Resorts property boasts "small, but charming" "adobe-style cabins" with indigenous fabrics and "cozy", "wood-burning fireplaces", as well as "gorgeous" grounds and a staff that "could not do a better job"; the "excellent spa facilities" feature a state-of-the-art fitness center and a eucalyptus steam room, while the "wonderful" food includes the new Viga restaurant serving classic American favorites.

Taos

El Monte Sagrado ✕🛏🔭Ⓢ 25 | 21 | 23 | 24 | $299

317 Kit Carson Rd. | 505-758-3502 | fax 505-737-2985 | 800-828-8267 | www.elmontesagrado.com | 78 suites, 6 casitas

Spa-lovers seek out this "eco-friendly" resort just "steps from Taos Plaza" for an "all-day session" of herbal wraps and healing treatments at its "luxurious" facility, "followed by rattlesnake and chile pasta" at the "memorable" dining room and a "restful" overnight in "spectacular rooms" that are "like works of art"; it's just too bad a handful sigh "like an orchestra playing out of tune" the service "just isn't where it should be for such an [otherwise] deluxe" and "magical" place.

Taos Inn, The Historic Ⓗ🔭 18 | 20 | 22 | 19 | $175

125 Paseo del Pueblo Norte | 575-758-2233 | fax 575-758-5776 | 888-518-8267 | www.taosinn.com | 41 rooms, 3 suites

"History and now meet" at this "charming" "inn of a time since past" that treats guests to an "authentic New Mexico experience" (it's listed on the National Register of Historic Places); the "funky" scene includes the "marvelous" Doc Martin's restaurant and the "raucous" Adobe Bar - "ground central for visitors and locals" - while the "pretty basic" rooms, located in four buildings, have plenty of "local flavor."

New York

Adirondacks

Elk Lake Lodge 🔭 - | - | - | - | $115

1106 Elk Lake Rd. | North Hudson | 518-532-7616 | fax 518-532-9262 | www.elklakelodge.com | 8 cottages, 6 rooms

If you really want to "get away from it all", head to this seasonal "retreat" on 12,000 "fabulous" acres of mountains, woods and lakes in the Adirondacks High Peaks, where "all you do is hike, swim, row, read, nap, eat" and become "unplugged"; there's a "camplike low-keyness" to the simple rooms and food, but the setting is "so lovely" and the tab so modest that you "can't go wrong" here.

Friends Lake Inn ✕🔭 22 | 25 | 26 | 20 | $349

963 Friends Lake Rd. | Chestertown | 518-494-4751 | fax 518-494-4616 | www.friendslake.com | 16 rooms, 1 suite

Ideal for getting friendly during a "long romantic weekend", this "little gem tucked away in a quiet corner of the Adirondacks" offers up "rustic elegance" and "great atmosphere"; in the daytime, guests paddle "on a small lake with no public access" or ski at nearby Gore Mountain, while the evenings bring dining on "the best food in the region" complemented by a "terrific" 25,000-bottle wine list.

Mirror Lake Inn 👪🔭Ⓢ⛳ 23 | 25 | 24 | 23 | $290

77 Mirror Lake Dr. | Lake Placid | 518-523-2544 | fax 518-523-2871 | www.mirrorlakeinn.com | 100 rooms, 31 suites

A "true Adirondack inn", this "peaceful, relaxing" "gem in the heart of Lake Placid" offers "all the hospitality, warmth and coziness you would expect" from a member of Small Luxury Hotels; rooms are "rustic, but surprisingly plush at the same time" (particularly the "deluxe accom-

	ROOMS	SERVICE	DINING	FACIL.	COST

modations"), a "dedicated staff" provides "impeccable service" and "the spa is first-rate", leading some to list this as their "favorite."

🗹 Point, The ✕ ☆ ♨ ⚲ | 27 | 28 | 26 | 26 | $1350 |

Upper Saranac Lake | Saranac Lake | 518-891-5674 | fax 518-891-1152 | 800-255-3530 | www.thepointresort.com | 10 rooms, 1 cabin

It's "one of the musts before you die" sigh sojourners of the "once-in-a-lifetime experience" to be had at this Relais & Châteaux "escape from daily stress" on Saranac Lake in the Adirondacks; "play robber baron" and indulge in the "fabulous service", "top-notch" dining and "amazing" rooms featuring lake views, custom-made beds and eclectic antiques; it'll "cost a fortune", but it's "pure class"; N.B. no children under 18.

Sagamore, The ✿ ☜ ♨ ⌂ ⓢ ⚲ | 21 | 23 | 21 | 25 | $309 |

110 Sagamore Rd. | Bolton Landing | 518-644-9400 | fax 518-743-6036 | 800-358-3585 | www.thesagamore.com | 147 rooms, 149 suites

The "tweedy set" loves this "big, old, rambling hotel" that "brings you back to the heyday of the Adirondacks" with "rustic suites" ("stay in the main lodge") and "afternoon tea on the veranda"; the "genteel service" may be a "bit uppity" at times, and nostalgics wryly note "it's had its day in the sun . . . during the Roosevelt administration", but few can argue with the "inspiring views" of Lake George or the "spectacular" Donald Ross–designed golf course.

Whiteface Lodge ✿ ☜ ♨ ⓢ ⚲ | 23 | 23 | 22 | 23 | $350 |

7 Whiteface Inn Ln. | Lake Placid | 518-523-0500 | fax 518-523-0559 | 800-903-4045 | www.thewhitefacelodge.com | 94 suites

Built "in the style of the great camps" of the Adirondack region, this Lake Placid timber lodge boasts "magnificent" suites with "every amenity" including "heated granite tiles in the foyer and bath" and detail-oriented wood furnishings; the "enthusiastic" staff "tries its best", there's "superb food" and the on-site activities include a cigar and cognac lounge, a movie theater, an ice cream shop, a bowling alley, an indoor/outdoor pool, a spa and 'smores by an outside fire pit; "too bad it's not on the lake", but there's a free shuttle to the water.

Amenia

Troutbeck Estate & Resort ⚲ | ▽ 18 | 21 | 23 | 22 | $250 |

515 Leedsville Rd. | 845-373-9681 | fax 845-373-7080 | 800-978-7688 | www.troutbeck.com | 42 suites

The "breathtaking" scenery and secluded location make this 1920s-era Berkshires-area choice two hours north of Manhattan a no-brainer for weddings and "corporate retreats"; the "quaint" inn (actually, three separate houses) offers a taste of "country living" – tennis, fly fishing, winery tours and golf – along with solid dining, but critics contend it sometimes seems "past its prime."

Catskills

🗹 Mirbeau Inn & Spa ✕ ♨ ⓢ | 27 | 26 | 25 | 27 | $225 |

851 W. Genesee St. | Skaneateles | 315-685-5006 | fax 315-685-5150 | 877-647-2328 | www.mirbeau.com | 18 rooms, 16 cottages

Quelle surprise to find this "Monet-inspired" "bit of the French countryside in upstate NY" near the "beautiful" Skaneateles Lake; lovebirds chirp that the "charming rooms with fireplaces", "a staff that can't do enough for you" and "excellent" food at Edward Moro's Giverny restaurant are perfect for a "cozy, romantic getaway", and pamper-holics praise its on-site spa – "one of the best in the country."

Mohonk
Mountain House 👬 ⓗ ♨ ⓢ ⚲   18 | 22 | 18 | 25 | $240

1000 Mountain Rest Rd. | New Paltz | 845-255-1000 | fax 845-256-2161 | 800-772-6646 | www.mohonk.com | 258 rooms, 3 suites, 4 cottages

A "gorgeous lake setting" with "to-die-for" views is the star at this 19th-century Catskills retreat beside a lake in the Shawangunk Mountains, where city slickers soak up the "wilderness" but still enjoy lots of "creature comforts", such as a "fantastic" new spa, a "kids' camp" and an ice-skating rink; "humble yet charming rooms" remind you of "spending the weekend with your grandmother" (there's no TV or a/c), and meals are "plentiful" (though "not extraordinary"), so all in all, it's a real "trip down memory lane" for most guests.

Cooperstown

Otesaga, The 👬 ⓗ ♨ ⚓ ⚲   21 | 23 | 21 | 23 | $435

60 Lake St. | 607-547-9931 | fax 607-547-9675 | 800-348-6222 | www.otesaga.com | 110 rooms, 25 suites

It's a home run for this recently refurbished "historic" hotel owned by the same family for over a century, with "old-world charm", "phenomenal" service and a "perfect" location for visiting Cooperstown's Baseball Hall of Fame (the Leatherstocking golf course is also "worth the stay"); the "heavenly" veranda with rocking chairs "overlooking the lake" helps it maintain a "yesteryear ambiance", but the "modern amenities" bring it all into the present.

Hudson Valley

Beekman Arms & Delamater Inn ⓗ   18 | 19 | 19 | 16 | $130

6387 Mill St. | Rhinebeck | 845-876-7077 | fax 845-876-7080 | www.beekmandelamaterinn.com | 67 rooms, 6 suites

"Quaint" is the word used most often to describe "the oldest hotel in the United States", located in the heart of Rhinebeck, where visitors are "immersed in history" in "teeny", "charming" rooms with "period-style furniture" and "modern comforts"; there's "lots to do in the area" including "a walkable collection of shops and restaurants", and listening to "locals spin yarns at the bar" of this "lovely relic."

Long Island

American Hotel ✗ ⓗ   17 | 21 | 22 | 15 | $375

45 Main St. | Sag Harbor | 631-725-3535 | fax 631-725-3573 | www.theamericanhotel.com | 8 rooms

You could get "lost in time" at this 1846 hotel on Long Island's South Shore if it wasn't for the "eclectic cast" of cutting-edge "local celebrities, writers" and other "A-listers" in the bar and "fabulous restaurant" (with "the best wine list"); most say it's filled with "old-world" charm perfect for a "romantic" stay, but others who are put off by "snobby" service and "no facilities to speak of" insist it's "coasting."

	ROOMS	SERVICE	DINING	FACIL.	COST

Danfords Hotel & Marina ⊕🐾🏇 (fka Danfords Inn)

| 18 | 20 | 19 | 17 | $269 |

25 E. Broadway | Port Jefferson | 631-928-5200 | fax 631-928-9082 | 800-332-6367 | www.danfords.com | 76 rooms, 10 suites

City-ites looking for an "easy escape" head east to this "recently refurbished" Long Island "classic" near the ferry in "picturesque" Port Jeff; it's "not particularly fancy" but has "great views of the Sound" (sit on the back patio with a lemon drop martini), "lots of little shops" and eateries nearby (plus the revamped on-site Waves restaurant) and a "solid staff"; P.S. the place "comes alive at night."

Garden City Hotel ✕🐾🏇🏇

| 23 | 24 | 24 | 23 | $240 |

45 Seventh St. | Garden City | 516-747-3000 | fax 516-747-1414 | 877-547-0400 | www.gardencityhotel.com | 270 rooms, 16 suites

"Popular with brides on their wedding night", this "upscale retreat" is "an oasis" "teeming with history, class and ambiance" "in the middle of" upscale Garden City; the "elegant" lobby and various lounges are "inviting places to spend your free time", while the "amazing" Sunday brunch at Polo may cost "an arm and a leg, but who needs two arms and legs anyway?"; even if critics contend it's "time for another makeover", this is still "Long Island's finest."

Gurney's Inn Resort & Spa 🏇🐾🏇Ⓢ

| 17 | 19 | 19 | 21 | $255 |

290 Old Montauk Hwy. | Montauk | 631-668-2345 | fax 631-668-3576 | 800-848-7639 | www.gurneysinn.com | 83 rooms, 22 suites, 4 cottages

Gothamites praise this "terrific" Long Island spa getaway in Montauk with "fantastic ocean views", a "gorgeous" beach and "pools, baths and saunas that can soothe anyone after the long ride"; but while supporters say you "gotta love the location" and the "wonderful salt scrubs" among other treatments, critics claim it's all riding on "old coattails" with an "aloof" staff, "worn" quarters and food that's "nothing special."

Maidstone Arms 🏇

| 18 | 20 | 20 | 16 | $375 |

207 Main St. | East Hampton | 631-324-5006 | fax 631-324-5037 | www.maidstonearms.com | 10 rooms, 6 suites, 3 cottages

For "old-fashioned charm" in the Hamptons, this year-round Greek Revival–style inn on Main Street is a good choice for spending a "lazy weekend" out east; it offers "unique", "nicely appointed" rooms, three private cottages with fireplaces and skylights, a new restaurant and "lots of charm"; but cutting-edgers say "don't stay here if you want a hip and happening hotel", just a convenient one for in-town activities.

Mill House Inn 🏇🏇

| 24 | 23 | 22 | 20 | $550 |

31 N. Main St. | East Hampton | 631-324-9766 | fax 631-324-9793 | 800-563-8645 | www.millhouseinn.com | 5 rooms, 6 suites

With an "excellent location" in an historic area of East Hampton, this 1790 inn is the "perfect B&B", serving up "warmth and intimacy" along with "service and amenities to rival any top-notch hotel" (for example, an in-suite fridge that "they'll stock with provisions requested prior to your arrival"); "if you can't relax here", lounging on the porch in an Adirondack chair, "you can't relax anywhere" – though regulars recommend you get up for "one of the best breakfasts you've ever had."

	ROOMS	SERVICE	DINING	FACIL.	COST

NEW YORK – NEW YORK CITY

Oheka Castle
25 | 24 | 23 | 25 | $325

135 W. Gate Dr. | Huntington | 631-659-1400 | fax 631-592-5991 |
www.oheka.com | 26 rooms, 6 suites

Many a "fairy-tale" Long Island wedding takes place at this "gorgeous French-style castle" in Huntington, built in 1921 and recently "restored to its full glory" as a "charming getaway" with 23 acres of "stunning" grounds and "superb views"; the "expensive" rooms sport Frette linens and high-end toiletries, but since they're "mostly for event guests" you'll have to book this member of Small Luxury Hotels of the World "well ahead" to enjoy your "romance novel" experience.

Ram's Head Inn 🏨🔍
16 | 21 | 22 | 20 | $325

108 Ram Island Dr. | Shelter Island Heights | 631-749-0811 |
fax 631-749-0059 | www.shelterislandinns.com | 9 rooms, 4 suites

If you want a mostly "undiscovered" vacation spot, take the ferry to Shelter Island (between Long Island's North and South Forks) and head for this "charming" waterside inn that's "full of tradition", where you can "have a drink on the lawn overlooking the harbor" before enjoying a "romantic" dinner; even if the rooms and the restaurant are just "ok", "go for the view, less for the food and wine."

New York City

TOPS IN CITY

27] Four Seasons
Mandarin Oriental
26] Ritz-Carlton Central Park
St. Regis
25] Peninsula
Ritz-Carlton Battery Park
24] Plaza
Carlyle
Mark
Lowell

Alex Hotel 🛏
21 | 21 | 18 | 17 | $700

205 E. 45th St. | Manhattan | 212-867-5100 | fax 212-867-7878 |
www.thealexhotel.com | 73 rooms, 130 suites

Most are "pleasantly surprised" by this "secret" boutique whose "modern", "well-appointed" rooms with flat-screen TVs and "breathtaking views of the Chrysler building" make it "worth a look"; although surveyors split on the staff, with some finding it "responsive" and others sensing a "bad attitude", most agree you should "make sure to dine at [Marcus Samuelsson's] Riingo" restaurant.

Algonquin Hotel ⊞
16 | 21 | 19 | 16 | $599

59 W. 44th St. | Manhattan | 212-840-6800 | fax 212-944-1618 |
888-304-2047 | www.algonquinhotel.com | 150 rooms, 24 suites

New Yorker readers" listening for the "echoes of [Dorothy Parker's] Round Table" flock to this "legendary" centenarian in the Theater District for a "genuine NYC experience"; service is "friendly as all get-out", the Oak Room's cabaret "can't be beat" and the renovated rooms are nice enough, but the real reason you're here is for all that "history oozing from the cracks."

	ROOMS	SERVICE	DINING	FACIL.	COST

Benjamin, The ⚐Ⓢ

| | 21 | 22 | 16 | 18 | $450 |

125 E. 50th St. | Manhattan | 212-715-2500 | fax 212-715-2525 |
888-423-6526 | www.thebenjamin.com | 115 rooms, 94 suites

A convenient Midtown hotel for business travelers, with "high-quality
amenities", "spacious suites" and a "soothing spa", this "reliable"
lodging is "big on style"; even if the elevators can be "slow" and there
"aren't many food choices", that "pillow menu is cool" and the staff is
both "friendly and helpful."

Blue Moon Hotel ⊕⚌

| | - | - | - | - | $525 |

100 Orchard St. | Manhattan | 212-533-9080 | fax 212-533-9148 |
www.bluemoon-nyc.com | 20 rooms, 2 suites

"Love it" exclaim hipsters and history buffs who frequent this
offbeat Lower East Side boutique hotel carved out of an 1879 tenement house; its rooms, named after old-time celebrities from Benny
Goodman to Eddie Cantor, are decorated with a "crazy" mishmash of
period furnishings, while the nearby Tenement Museum offers up
more local color.

NEW Bowery Hotel ⚌

| | ▽ 21 | 22 | 20 | 18 | $525 |

335 Bowery | Manhattan | 212-505-9100 | fax 212-505-9700 |
www.theboweryhotel.com | 85 rooms, 25 suites

"If you are anyone", you already know that this "Downtown space" in
NoHo features accommodations that are "fun and different", boasting
"superb" amenities and a "sleek" design that manages to look both utterly happening and "authentically old" at the same time; big windows
offer great views (insiders "ask for the room with the private balcony"), so even if the food is just "ok", this stomping ground for the
cool crowd is "wonderful" overall.

Bryant Park Hotel, The ⚐⚌

| | 22 | 22 | 21 | 19 | $545 |

40 W. 40th St. | Manhattan | 212-869-0100 | fax 212-869-4446 |
877-640-9300 | www.bryantparkhotel.com | 111 rooms, 18 suites

"Across from charming Bryant Park" (and a quick walk to Times Square),
this "stylish" Midtown "gem" caters to a "trendy" crowd with its "clad-
in-black staff", "modern design", "hip" Koi restaurant and "rocking"
basement bar; rooms sport flat-screen HDTVs, Bose Wave radios and
park views, but less-impressed guests sigh it's all "a bit too full of itself" with a staff that "forgets who's paying."

Carlton Hotel ✕⚐⚌

| | 20 | 22 | 20 | 19 | $499 |

88 Madison Ave. | Manhattan | 212-532-4100 | fax 212-696-9758 |
800-601-8500 | www.carltonhotelny.com | 295 rooms, 21 suites

Guests gush about the "magnificent lobby" of this turn-of-the-century
building, set in a "quiet" location in Manhattan's Murray Hill neighborhood, that was "beautifully redone" and expanded by architect David
Rockwell; the "doormen and manager go out of their way" for you, and
the "classic rooms" are each "laid out differently", with some of the
"softest cotton sheets in the world."

Carlyle, The 🕭⚐⚌

| | 25 | 26 | 24 | 22 | $755 |

35 E. 76th St. | Manhattan | 212-744-1600 | fax 212-717-4682 |
800-227-5737 | www.thecarlyle.com | 122 rooms, 65 suites

"Kings, queens, presidents, celebrities" – and you – can be "spoiled"
by the "wonderful" staff at this Upper East Side "grande dame" that

epitomizes "old New York at its finest"; the vibe's "glamorous", the rooms are "elegant" and there's "nothing more sumptuous than a night at the Café Carlyle", which showcases "fantastic" performers like Elaine Stritch; admittedly, you'll "spend a fortune", but its many "repeat" guests prove it's "worth the bucks"; N.B. a two-level, 4,000-sq.-ft. spa opened in 2008.

Chambers ✕🛏🚶

▽ 21 | 18 | 21 | 17 | $575

15 W. 56th St. | Manhattan | 212-974-5656 | fax 212-974-5657 | 866-204-5656 | www.chambersnyc.com | 60 rooms, 5 suites, 12 studios
The "ultracool" chambers in this Midtown spot are so "tragically tiny" that "there are no drawers for clothing", but there are cordless phones, DVD players and contemporary art on the walls; on-site restaurant Town is "amazing" thanks to chef-owner Geoffrey Zakarian, so even if the service leans toward "snooty" (it "depends on your connections"), this "hopelessly hip" lodging is "worth it" for foodie scenesters.

NEW Duane Street Hotel 🛏🚶

- | - | - | - | $439

130 Duane St. | Manhattan | 212-964-4600 | fax 212-964-4800 | www.duanestreethotel.com | 45 rooms
This new TriBeCa luxury boutique mirrors its neighborhood's residences via rooms with oversized loft windows, 11-ft. ceilings, hardwood floors, free WiFi and furnishings designed by Paul Vega Architects; the on-site 'beca restaurant, a 24-hour business center concierge, personalized business cards for corporate clients and in-room spa services add to the charm.

Elysée, Hotel ⑪🍽🚶

▽ 22 | 25 | 20 | 20 | $465

60 E. 54th St. | Manhattan | 212-753-1066 | fax 212-980-9278 | 800-535-9733 | www.elyseehotel.com | 90 rooms, 13 suites
Built in the 1920s, "this old girl still has her devotees", plus a "wonderful" staff including the long-serving doorman, Tony; "elegant, comfortable, European" – even Elysian – this Midtowner is a "real find" "for business or a weekend getaway" with "comfortable" rooms, a "gourmet" breakfast and "weekday wine and cheese"; P.S. the "famous" Monkey Bar is closed for renovations.

Embassy Suites 🚶

22 | 18 | 14 | 19 | $569

102 North End Ave. | Manhattan | 212-945-0100 | fax 212-945-3012 | 800-362-2779 | www.embassysuites.com | 463 suites
"Off the beaten path" in the Financial District, this chainster with "generously sized" suites and a "free buffet breakfast" "caters to conventions", but is "great" for families as well (there are "two outstanding playgrounds nearby" and lots of space to spread out); while the "location is a bit of a challenge" and the decor "kind of generic", you'll get "accommodating" service and, if you're lucky, a room "overlooking the Hudson."

NEW Empire Hotel 🛏🚶Ⓢ

- | - | - | - | $499

44 W. 63rd St. | Manhattan | 212-265-7400 | fax 212-765-4201 | www.empirehotelnyc.com | 406 rooms, 14 suites
A trendy rooftop pool deck with rentable cabanas featuring minifridges, iPod docks, flat-screen TVs and daybeds is one of the rare Manhattan treats served up by this newly reopened West 60s hotel set in a 19th-century building across from Dante Park; a three-year

renovation brings sleek rooms outfitted with WiFi, Frette bed linens and 32-inch flat-screen TVs, as well as a Jeunesse spa offering VIP treatment areas.

[Z] Four Seasons 🍴🐕🔭Ⓢ 28 | 28 | 26 | 26 | $915

57 E. 57th St. | Manhattan | 212-758-5700 | fax 212-758-5711 | 800-332-3442 | www.fourseasons.com | 305 rooms, 63 suites

The "international elite" love this I.M. Pei-designed Midtown "oasis", and fortunately "it lives up to every bit of the hype"; rooms are "big enough to exercise in" and offer "spectacular" views and "fast-filling tubs", the "outstanding" staff finds "nothing impossible" and the L'Atelier de Joël Robuchon restaurant is "fabulous"; add in an "excellent" spa and "awe-inspiring" lobby, and this "super-chic" spot is nothing short of "NYC's best" - "just fill your suitcase with money" to pay the bill.

Gansevoort, Hotel 🐕🔭Ⓢ 20 | 18 | 20 | 22 | $495

18 Ninth Ave. | Manhattan | 212-206-6700 | fax 212-255-5858 | 877-426-7386 | www.hotelgansevoort.com | 166 rooms, 20 suites, 1 duplex

It's "become an expensive habit" admit addicts of this "chic, über-modern" hot spot in the Meatpacking District - especially its "sexy rooftop pool" (though locals complain that weekends, the nightclub is overrun by "the bridge-and-tunnel crowd" as well as "gawkers" "in search of celebs"); rooms might be "tiny" and service "hit-or-miss depending upon whether the aspiring actor/actress feels like working", but many "movers and shakers" claim it's the "place to crash."

[NEW] Gild Hall 🛏 - | - | - | - | $429

15 Gold St. | Manhattan | 212-232-7700 | fax 212-425-0330 | 800-268-0700 | www.thompsonhotels.com | 116 rooms, 10 suites

Just a short distance from Wall Street and the South Street Seaport, this new Financial District boutique, courtesy of Thompson Hotels, features a bi-level library and champagne bar, an English tavern courtesy of chef Todd English and rooms boasting Frette robes and Dean & DeLuca minibar snacks.

Gramercy Park Hotel 🔭Ⓢ 22 | 22 | 18 | 20 | $795

2 Lexington Ave. | Manhattan | 212-920-3300 | fax 212-673-5890 | 866-784-1300 | www.gramercyparkhotel.com | 68 rooms, 72 loft rooms, 45 suites

Another "celeb hot spot" owned by Ian Schrager, this historic boutique hotel in Gramercy is "chic beyond belief", with lounges that are "places to be seen" and a "splendid design" by artist Julian Schnabel; though old-schoolers liked it "better when it was funky and threadbare", complaining of an interior with "little or no lighting", most take one look at the "rooftop lounge" serviced by a "surprisingly friendly" staff, and say "it rocks."

Hotel on Rivington 🐕🔭 ▽ 23 | 18 | 16 | 20 | $525

107 Rivington St. | Manhattan | 212-475-2600 | fax 212-475-5959 | 800-915-1537 | www.hotelonrivington.com | 93 rooms, 16 suites, 1 penthouse

"If you're looking for super-cool - which button is the lightswitch? - this is your Manhattan abode", promise poseurs about this "beautiful" Lower East Side boutique in a "hip", "lively" neighborhood; "better for weekend fun" than business meetings (check out the on-site bar with its "pumping house music"), it sports "modern" rooms with "luxurious baths", Tempur-Pedic beds that are "sheer heaven" and floor-to-ceiling windows offering metropolitan views "to die for."

Inn at Irving Place [H] 🔭 ▽ 24 | 24 | 18 | 14 | $515

56 Irving Pl. | Manhattan | 212-533-4600 | fax 212-533-4611 | 800-685-1447 | www.innatirving.com | 4 rooms, 5 suites, 3 apartments

Like a weekend at "your rich grandmother's apartment in the city", this 1834 brownstone in the "top-notch" neighborhood of Gramercy Park is "teeth-achingly cute, with more Victorian bric-a-brac than you can shake a stick at" and "caring service" worthy of grammy; out-of-towners say they get a "feel of what it's like to live in Manhattan" at this member of Small Luxury Hotels of the World, while locals make a beeline here for the "best high tea in NYC" or an "outdoor cocktail" from the martini lounge.

InterContinental The Barclay 🔭 20 | 21 | 18 | 19 | $599

111 E. 48th St. | Manhattan | 212-755-5900 | fax 212-644-0079 | 800-972-3160 | www.intercontinental.com | 600 rooms, 86 suites

An "international clientele" gravitates to this "consistent" favorite that marries "old-world" charm with "quintessential New York elegance", from the "stunning" lobby to "comfortable", "tastefully decorated" rooms; though it's a "solid business hotel" offering an "excellent" location "near Grand Central Station" and "solicitous" service, the dining is "disappointing" and the lobby "outdated."

Iroquois 🔭 ▽ 21 | 22 | 22 | 19 | $629

49 W. 44th St. | Manhattan | 212-840-3080 | fax 212-398-1754 | 800-332-7220 | www.iroquoisny.com | 105 rooms, 9 suites

This "beautiful prewar hotel" offers "charming" (although "cramped") accommodations featuring "amazingly comfortable" beds; a Midtown boutique "classic" and member of Small Luxury Hotels of the World, it also boasts a "great location" "close to theaters and shopping" and an on-site restaurant, Triomphe, serving "tempting" French fare.

[NEW] **Jane, The** - | - | - | - | $99

113 Jane St. | Manhattan | 212-924-6700 | fax 212-924-6705 | www.thejanenyc.com | 200 rooms

Hoteliers Sean MacPherson and Eric Goode (NYC's Maritime and Bowery hotels) are the forces behind this gritty West Village boutique newcomer (a former single-room-occupancy hotel), where well-designed rooms with WiFi and flat-screen TVs can be had inexpensively - a rarity in Manhattan; the catch is the cabinlike size - 50 sq. ft. - and the shared bathrooms (though a few are larger with private baths); N.B. in 1912, the surviving crew of the *Titanic* was held here until the inquiry into the sinking was complete.

Jumeirah Essex House 🍴 🔭 [S] 22 | 22 | 20 | 20 | $919

160 Central Park S. | Manhattan | 212-247-0300 | fax 212-315-1839 | 888-645-5697 | www.jumeirahessexhouse.com | 392 rooms, 117 suites

New owners and a $90-million refurb bring this 1931 Midtown hotel into the 21st century, with "luxurious, high-tech" features that fans call "renovation bliss" (you can "change your room settings via phone pad"); old-schoolers scoff that the "baby got thrown out with the bathwater" due to "overdone" decor, a "flashy lobby" and service that could be more "responsive", but you can't deny the "prime location" with Central Park as the "fabulous front yard."

Kitano, The ♨   22 | 24 | 21 | 21 | $535

66 Park Ave. | Manhattan | 212-885-7000 | fax 212-885-7100 | 800-548-2666 | www.kitano.com | 131 rooms, 18 suites

"Why don't more people know about this hotel?" ask admirers of this "real find" "in the heart of Murray Hill", a "quiet residential neighborhood" that's "convenient to everything"; Japanese ownership is the reason for "spartan Asian-style rooms" with "understated beauty", "attentive" service, a "traditional" restaurant serving kaiseki cuisine and "cool jazz evenings" in the bar – so those in-the-know whisper "don't let the secret out – it's difficult to book already."

Le Parker Méridien ✕🏖🏊♨ⓢ   21 | 20 | 21 | 20 | $600

118 W. 57th St. | Manhattan | 212-245-5000 | fax 212-307-1776 | 800-543-4300 | www.parkermeridien.com | 510 rooms, 221 suites

"The views of Central Park are breathtaking" from the higher floors of this "fancy schmancy hotel" near Carnegie Hall, which is why the rooftop pool is "the pièce de résistance"; rooms are "stylish" (if "not stunning") and "larger than most" in the city ("spacious" suites have "a huge work desk"), and "the power-breakfast set" loves the eggs at Norma's and the lobby's "hidden" Burger Joint that's "worth the frenzied jockeying for seats" ("you can always work meals off in the on-site four-star gym").

Library Hotel   21 | 24 | 16 | 20 | $599

299 Madison Ave. | Manhattan | 212-983-4500 | fax 212-499-9099 | 877-793-7323 | www.libraryhotel.com | 60 rooms

Like a library, the rooms in this Midtown boutique hotel are "full of peace and tranquility" (though "tiny") and each one is "dedicated to a subject (love, dinosaurs, romance, etc.)"; bookworms find it "intimate and friendly" with "complimentary breakfast in the AM and wine and cheese in the evening" along with a "fancy espresso machine" in the lounge, not to mention "superb service" that extends to rainy days, when "a doorman offers umbrellas" – though you might "not want to leave" this refuge in any weather.

Loews Regency, The 🏃🐾🏊♨   23 | 23 | 21 | 19 | $669

540 Park Ave. | Manhattan | 212-759-4100 | fax 212-826-5674 | 800-233-2356 | www.loewshotels.com | 267 rooms, 86 suites

"Everyone gets the superstar treatment" at this Upper East Side "grande dame" on Park Avenue; with its "famous power breakfasts", afternoon wine in the Library, "accommodating staff" and "wish-fulfillment address", it's particularly "impressive for out-of-town business" clients; just a few nitpickers natter about "spotty" rooms.

London NYC 🏊♨   23 | 22 | 22 | 20 | $599

151 W. 54th St. | Manhattan | 212-307-5000 | fax 212-765-6530 | 866-690-2029 | www.thelondonnyc.com | 561 suites

This hotel has "notched up quite a bit" following its remodel (it was formerly the Rihga Royal), and Anglophiles adore the "hip haute" style, "spacious", "sexy" suites and "memorable meals" (both for the "divine food" and the "astronomical prices") at chef Gordon Ramsay's restaurant; the Midtown location is "good if you like to jog in Central Park", but a few say the rooms "have all the warmth of a doctor's waiting room."

☑ Lowell, The ⌂ ⌘ ⚇

| 25 | 28 | 21 | 20 | $665 |

28 E. 63rd St. | Manhattan | 212-838-1400 | fax 312-319-4230 | 800-221-4444 | www.lowellhotel.com | 25 rooms, 47 suites
Regulars of this "beautiful" Midtown "hideaway" "on a lovely, quiet street" off Madison Avenue claim it's "like being at home but better" – especially if your idea of home is "a British country house", with working "fireplaces in many rooms", "sheets so good you'll want to stay in bed" and a wonderful high tea; its "small" size means service is "phenomenally attentive", and the "low-key" vibe makes it "one of the few truly romantic hotels in New York."

☑ Mandarin Oriental ✕ ⌘ ⚇ ⊙

| 28 | 27 | 25 | 27 | $895 |

80 Columbus Circle | Manhattan | 212-805-8800 | fax 212-805-8888 | 866-801-8880 | www.mandarinoriental.com | 202 rooms, 46 suites
"New York energy meets incredible Asian serenity" at "one of the swankiest" (and "priciest") destinations in Manhattan, where "Zensational" rooms have "floor-to-ceiling windows", the staff is "trained (or born) to perfection", the "gorgeous spa" feels like a "temple" and Asiate is "one of the best hotel restuarants in town"; the only downside is the awkward entrance via public elevator, though with access to more "great restaurants and shopping in the next-door Time Warner building", you barely need to leave the hotel.

Mansfield, The ⌘

| ▽ 14 | 17 | 12 | 16 | $309 |

12 W. 44th St. | Manhattan | 212-277-8700 | fax 212-764-4477 | 800-255-5167 | www.mansfieldhotel.com | 99 rooms, 26 suites, 1 penthouse
It seems "the secret is out" about this "ultrachic" 1903 Midtown boutique where the "European-style elegance" extends to "lilliputian" rooms that are so tiny clients "can't open the door to the bathroom without moving the bed"; but these are mere details, say devotees, who "love the espresso machine" in the lovely off-lobby library, the "champagne at check-in" and the "hopping bar"; P.S. "if noise is an issue, request a room in the back."

Maritime Hotel, The ⊕ ⌘ ⚇

| ▽ 17 | 19 | 16 | 19 | $435 |

363 W. 16th St. | Manhattan | 212-242-4300 | fax 212-242-1188 | www.themaritimehotel.com | 121 rooms, 5 suites
Scenesters dock at this "shipshape" Chelsea spot known for its "hip" "young crowd" and first-class "people-watching", whether in the outdoor garden, the rooftop lounge, the lobby bars, the "fantastic" downstairs club, Hiro, or the Japanese restaurant, Matsuri; while claustrophobes cringe at rooms "the size of jail cells and almost as ugly", others salute the "cheeky" design featuring porthole windows, teak furnishings and ocean-themed fabrics.

Marriott Marquis ⌘ ⌘ ⚇

| 20 | 18 | 17 | 20 | $379 |

1535 Broadway | Manhattan | 212-398-1900 | fax 212-704-8930 | 800-843-4898 | www.marriott.com | 1892 rooms, 57 suites
A Times Square chain link that's like "a giant beehive" – this "behemoth" is one of the "best places to stay when you're seeing a Broadway show"

(it has its own theater inside and is opposite the half-price TKTS booth); "tourists abound", whether in the "rooftop revolving restaurant", the "crazy" glass elevators or the hectic lobby, but "if you're lucky", you can escape to a room with a "spectacular view" of the "chaos" below – the "fabulous" location is what it's all about.

Mercer, The ✕ 🏄🏋 — 23 | 21 | 24 | 23 | $595

147 Mercer St. | Manhattan | 212-966-6060 | fax 212-965-3838 | 888-918-6060 | www.mercerhotel.com | 68 rooms, 7 suites

"Fashionistas, actors and dot-commers flock" to "the hippest hotel in SoHo", which, as part of the André Balazs empire, "screams sexy in an understated, sophisticated way"; the "superb" Mercer Kitchen is "especially good for celeb-spotting", so while "the rooms are tiny" and the staff "haughty", everyone knows "it's about who's here" not the square footage or hospitality.

Michelangelo, The 🏋 — 24 | 23 | 18 | 19 | $495

152 W. 51st St. | Manhattan | 212-765-1900 | fax 212-541-6604 | 800-237-0990 | www.michelangelohotel.com | 124 rooms, 55 suites

"You'll feel like the view outside should be of Trevi Fountain" when you stay at this "baroque" Italian-accented "haven" in the "hectic Times Square area" where the standout features are the "larger-than-expected" rooms with "fantastic amenities" and marble baths; there's also some of "the best service in the city" that's the "essence of discreet", plus a complimentary continental breakfast; even if the lobby is "less than inspiring", Marco Canora's Italian restaurant, Insieme, is worth a try.

Millenium Hilton 🏄🏋 — 21 | 19 | 16 | 19 | $569

55 Church St. | Manhattan | 212-693-2001 | fax 212-571-2316 | 800-445-8667 | www.hilton.com | 471 rooms, 98 suites

"In the heart of the Financial District", this "sleek" hotel caters both to businesspeople and "bargain-conscious college kids and families", who say the "spotless" accommodations are "larger than is typical" and the "42-inch plasma TV is a treat"; the downside, for now, is the "noise" associated with being "in the middle of eternal construction zones", but some like having the "best view of the Ground Zero rebuild", if not the constant "sea of gawkers."

Millennium UN Plaza 🏋🔍 — 22 | 19 | 13 | 20 | $599

1 United Nations Plaza | Manhattan | 212-758-1234 | fax 212-702-5051 | 866-866-8086 | www.millenniumhotels.com | 384 rooms, 45 suites

"A favorite with diplomats" who convene at the nearby United Nations, this "unpretentious" "'60s modern" hotel is "international in flavor", yet residents of higher floors never forget where they are, thanks to "wraparound views" of "Midtown, the East River and the bridges" ("ask for the East Tower"); though it lacks "a decent place to eat", ambassadors adore a "delicious dip in the pool overlooking NYC" as well as the on-site tennis court.

Muse, The 🏄🏋 — 23 | 22 | 18 | 19 | $509

130 W. 46th St. | Manhattan | 212-485-2400 | fax 212-485-2789 | 877-692-6873 | www.themusehotel.com | 181 rooms, 19 suites

It may be "the best-kept secret in the Times Square area" say fans of this "charming" Kimpton boutique that sports "surprisingly sizable"

	ROOMS	SERVICE	DINING	FACIL.	COST

rooms with flat-screen TVs and WiFi, a "friendly" staff that "remembers your name" and "cool", "slightly quirky" decor; overall, you may find it "hard to believe you're in New York" at this "fun" alternative.

New York Marriott at the Brooklyn Bridge 🏨

| 21 | 20 | 16 | 19 | $399 |

333 Adams St. | Brooklyn | 718-246-7000 | fax 718-246-0563 | 888-436-3759 | www.marriott.com | 637 rooms, 28 suites
"No need to stay in Manhattan anymore" with this "viable alternative" "at the foot of the bridge" and "near the Federal Court" in Brooklyn that's "close enough to walk into the city" and offers "convenient access to multiple train lines"; value-seekers say it has "all the amenities of a much pricier" Big Apple address, like "spacious" rooms, convention meeting space and a health club with indoor pool.

New York Marriott Downtown 🏨

| 19 | 19 | 17 | 19 | $439 |

85 West St. | Manhattan | 212-385-4900 | fax 212-227-8136 | 800-242-8685 | www.marriott.com | 490 rooms, 7 suites
"If you have to be Downtown", it's "exciting" to stay "on a high floor overlooking the Statue of Liberty and the Harbor" at this "standard" Financial District chainster, with a location that's "handy" for business though "far from most tourist locations" (and somewhat "deserted" at night); you'll find "decent-size", "recently remodeled" rooms, a "responsive front desk" and "a great gym and spa", and though critics complain there aren't enough decent restaurants "within walking distance", "Roy's off the lobby is a huge plus."

New York Palace ⑪ 🥂 🏨 Ⓢ

| 25 | 24 | 21 | 23 | $815 |

455 Madison Ave. | Manhattan | 212-888-7000 | fax 212-303-6000 | 800-804-7035 | www.newyorkpalace.com | 806 rooms, 88 suites
"It's good to be king" say the loyal subjects of this Midtown palace with a "perfect" location "for everything" and "graciously decorated" quarters (royals "recommend the tower rooms"); an "architectural gem" that "seems to get better with age", it offers a "wonderful" fitness center, the "excellent" Gilt restaurant and a "fantastic concierge staff" – but coin-counters caution the "sticker shock might prevent a good night's sleep."

Night Hotel 🥂 🏨

| ▽ 16 | 16 | 13 | 15 | $469 |

132 W. 45th St. | Manhattan | 212-835-9600 | fax 212-835-9610 | www.nighthotelny.com | 70 rooms, 2 suites
"Fun for a night" – especially at "Halloween" – this "friendly" boutique in the West 40s "looks like a private club from the outside", but turns all black, white and "pornlike" with "tiny", "spooky", "Goth-style rooms" within; it's definitely "different" say its fans, who "wouldn't be surprised if dominatrixes were available upon request", but others scoff "painting everything dark to make it 'cool' doesn't work."

Peninsula, The 🥂 🏨

| 26 | 27 | 23 | 25 | $925 |

700 Fifth Ave. | Manhattan | 212-956-2888 | fax 212-903-3949 | 800-262-9467 | www.peninsula.com | 185 rooms, 54 suites
An "all-around outstanding" lodging that's an "oasis of calm and elegance", this "gracious" Midtowner in a 1905 landmark Fifth Avenue building "delivers" on all its promises; "super", state-of-the-art rooms have "bedside controls that adjust everything imaginable", the "im-

	ROOMS	SERVICE	DINING	FACIL.	COST

peccable" staff offers the "ultimate" service and the dramatic Salon de Ning rooftop bar draws "quite a crowd"; but some don't spend much time inside with such close proximity to "shopping, theaters, museums" and Central Park; N.B. the rooftop fitness facility and spa was scheduled to reopen after a massive renovation in October 2008.

Plaza, The ≋♨Ⓢ | 25 | 25 | 25 | 23 | $1100

768 Fifth Ave. | Manhattan | 212-759-3000 | fax 212-546-5260 | 800-759-3000 | www.fairmont.com | 180 rooms, 102 suites
Even before Eloise, this "grand old girl" was "the quintessential NYC" lodging, a "true classic" in a "perfect location" – but now that it's completely renovated ("part condo and part hotel"), veterans proclaim the "tradition is alive" and "even better than before"; yes, it's "expensive, but boy oh boy does it deliver", with "modern conveniences", "second-to-none service", "a fabulous high tea" and a bar that's "a romantic meeting spot" – no wonder it's chock-full of "beautiful people running around."

Plaza Athénée, Hôtel ♨✗≋♨ | 22 | 25 | 24 | 20 | $695

37 E. 64th St. | Manhattan | 212-734-9100 | fax 212-772-0958 | 800-447-8800 | www.plaza-athenee.com | 114 rooms, 35 suites
For un petit peu of "Paris in NYC", this "European jewel" on a "quiet" Upper East Side street has "charm" to spare, along with "old-school service" that's "discreet with a polite nod"; surveyors "could live" in the suites, but the "fabulous" restaurant, Arabelle, cool Bar Seine and "perfect" location "for shopping and strolling" draw them out of this "classy" "gem."

NEW Ravel Hotel ♨ | - | - | - | - | $399

8-08 Queens Plaza S. | Queens | 718-289-6101 | fax 718-289-7919 | 888-291-3411 | www.ravelhotel.com | 58 rooms, 5 suites
The first upscale boutique in Queens' Long Island City neighborhood, this bright newcomer offers a luxe yet lower-price-tag stay for the Manhattan-bound; there's a rooftop bar and modern quarters with 300-thread-count sheets, pillow-top mattresses, glass-enclosed showers, flat-panel TVs and (in superior rooms) private terraces, as well as a King Penthouse with 11-ft. ceilings and magnificent views of the skyscrapers just across the East River; a further plus are the shuttles to local train stations and into the Big City, for a fee.

Renaissance Times Square ≋♨ | 22 | 21 | 19 | 19 | $359

714 Seventh Ave. | Manhattan | 212-765-7676 | fax 212-765-1962 | 800-772-5897 | www.renaissancehotels.com | 305 rooms, 5 suites
"In the middle of Times Square, but away from the tumult", this just-renovated "boutiquelike" hotel offers "ultrahip" rooms with "marble baths" and "luxurious" showers, yet still feels "homey"; even those who find the cool quotient "slightly forced" admit the "spectacular bird's-eye view" from the restaurant of New York's most famous square, along with "unassuming" service, may just make this an "unsung jewel."

Ritz-Carlton Battery Park ≋♨Ⓢ | 27 | 26 | 23 | 24 | $595

2 West St. | Manhattan | 212-344-0800 | fax 212-344-3801 | 800-241-3333 | www.ritzcarlton.com | 254 rooms, 44 suites
You have to travel pretty far south for "the best view in the world", but this "exceptional" Battery Park bastion at the tip of Manhattan is so

"fabulous in every way" it's "worth it"; from the "impeccable" service to the "fantastic" 14th-floor Rise bar to the "luxurious rooms" (Liberty View ones come "with a telescope to scan NY Harbor"), this is "*the* place to stay*" "if you have business Downtown"; just be warned, it's a "$20 taxi ride to Midtown" – and "good luck getting a cab after hours"; N.B. look for weekend bargains.

Ritz-Carlton Central Park ✕ 🍴🏃Ⓢ

27 | 27 | 24 | 25 | $995

50 Central Park S. | Manhattan | 212-308-9100 | fax 212-207-8831 | 800-241-3333 | www.ritzcarlton.com | 259 rooms, 47 suites

"Gorgeous" accommodations are "the tip of the iceberg" at this "spectacular" hotel with an "outstanding location" where "suites with million-dollar Central Park views" and soundproofed windows are "well worth the hit to the wallet"; regulars relish chef Laurent Tourondel's BLT Market restaurant, the "excellent" La Prairie spa and the "flawless" staff that "calls you by name" (Norman at the bar is "an instant mood-lifter"); so whether you're "longing for that once-in-a-lifetime feeling" or you're just "accustomed to staying in the finest hotels in the world", "you won't be disappointed here."

Royalton 🍴🏃

20 | 19 | 19 | 19 | $450

44 W. 44th St. | Manhattan | 212-869-4400 | fax 212-869-8965 | 800-635-9013 | www.morganshotelgroup.com | 131 rooms, 37 suites

The recently updated lobby of this "funky" West 40s hotel, boasting steel and brass furnishings, suede upholstery, leather walls and hide-covered chairs, is still a great spot to "people-watch" over "perfect cocktails" by a "roaring fireplace"; while the reopened Brasserie 44 and Bar 44, courtesy of restaurateur John McDonald (Lever House, Lure Fishbar), are further draws, those who can see past the "cool crowd" find "minute rooms", corridors so "dark" that "after a few days you wish someone would just flick on a light" and a staff that "at best is indifferent" and "at worst, rude."

Sherry-Netherland, The ⊕🍴🏃

24 | 24 | 21 | 22 | $749

781 Fifth Ave. | Manhattan | 212-355-2800 | fax 212-319-4306 | 877-743-7710 | www.sherrynetherland.com | 30 rooms, 20 suites

From the "welcome treat" of "a box of chocolates" upon arrival to "spacious" suites (some with "great views" of Central Park), this 1927 Fifth Avenue "gem" is "the place to experience the best of classic New York" along with "top-notch", European-style service and ornate, "old-fashioned luxury"; modernists might find it "a little stodgy", but nostalgists plead, "don't touch it, please! it works just fine."

Shoreham 🍴🏃

▽ 21 | 24 | 20 | 20 | $419

33 W. 55th St. | Manhattan | 212-247-6700 | fax 212-765-9741 | 800-553-3347 | www.shorehamhotel.com | 132 rooms, 42 suites

A "relatively unknown" Midtown boutique, this "friendly" spot has a "marvelous" high-design bar, an on-site art gallery, modern rooms with plasma TVs, Bose sound systems and Frette linens, and a 24-hour complimentary espresso bar in the lobby; the "cramped" rooms are worrisome for a few, but the majority maintains that the "killer location" "convenient" to many attractions makes up for that.

	ROOMS	SERVICE	DINING	FACIL.	COST

NEW Six Columbus ✕⚎

| - | - | - | - | $495 |

6 Columbus Circle | Manhattan | 212-431-0200 | fax 212-204-3030 |
877-626-5862 | www.thompsonhotels.com | 81 rooms, 7 suites
Right off Columbus Circle across from the Time Warner Center, this boutique boasts the "wonderful" service that clients have come to expect from "all Thompson hotels" – and then some, as repeat guests gush "the doormen welcomed me back as if I were a supermodel"; "who cares" if rooms are on "the smallish side?" say modernists since they're decked out in cool, 1960s-era decor (teak, chrome and pony-skins) with flat-screen TVs and iPod docks, plus there's a Blue Ribbon Sushi Bar & Grill on-site and a rootop lounge for guests and VIPs; N.B. splurge for one of two penthouse duplex lofts with floor-to-ceiling windows and fireplaces.

60 Thompson ✕

| 20 | 20 | 20 | 19 | $619 |

60 Thompson St. | Manhattan | 212-431-0400 | fax 212-431-0200 |
877-431-0400 | www.thompsonhotels.com | 88 rooms, 8 suites, 1 duplex
The "cool vibe", "seductive rooftop bar" and "hot, hot, hot" scene pull in the "pretty" people to this SoHo "attitude hotel without the attitude"; "as long as you don't mind checking in next to the celebutante drowning in her lychee martini", you'll find "well-designed", if "small" rooms, a solid restaurant, Kittichai, and a lobby that "becomes more like a club" at night – though since you're "right in the middle of all the action" you can head out for after-dark fun.

Sofitel ⚐

| 24 | 23 | 19 | 21 | $709 |

45 W. 44th St. | Manhattan | 212-354-8844 | fax 212-354-2480 |
877-565-9240 | www.sofitel.com | 346 rooms, 52 suites
Regulars love the "feeling of reassurance" they get at this "highly competent" "French hotel chain" "in the heart of Midtown" (a "perfect location for shopping and theater"), which is "well-managed" by an "efficient" staff; "minimalist" rooms might "lack any oomph", but they're "decent"-sized for the city and "excellent" for business meetings, while sensitive sleepers appreciate the "soundproofing" – and "those feather beds!"

Soho Grand Hotel ⚐⚎

| 19 | 20 | 19 | 20 | $399 |

310 W. Broadway | Manhattan | 212-965-3000 | fax 212-965-3200 |
800-965-3000 | www.sohogrand.com | 361 rooms, 2 penthouses
The "location is sublime" at this "cool" SoHo hotel with a "great lobby scene" ("better wear your Prada") and lots of "style"; while some say this "trendsetter is staying true", others sigh I "can't wait until modern minimalism is over" 'cause squeezing into "dark" "rooms the size of closets" is getting "tired", and as for the "attitude to spare" – "leave it, you're not that good."

St. Regis ✕ⓘ☕⚎Ⓢ

| 27 | 27 | 25 | 24 | $1195 |

2 E. 55th St. | Manhattan | 212-753-4500 | fax 212-787-3447 |
877-787-3447 | www.stregis.com | 182 rooms, 74 suites
"Wish I lived here" sigh worshipers of this "posh", "European-style" "oasis amid the chaos" that "oozes history, old-world charm and luxury"; "sumptuous rooms" feature "Pratesi bed linens", "crystal chandeliers and silk wall coverings", while "unfailing service" is provided by "a real butler on call" on every floor; the King Cole Bar was voted No. 1 for

Appeal in our *NYC Nightlife* Survey, and "the opening of Alain Ducasse's Adour restaurant is the pièce de résistance" of any stay here.

Tribeca Grand Hotel 🐕🔭 20 | 19 | 18 | 20 | $695

2 Sixth Ave. | Manhattan | 212-519-6600 | fax 212-519-6700 | 877-519-6600 | www.tribecagrand.com | 196 rooms, 7 suites

A "pretty crowd" hangs at this "trendy" TriBeCa spot, sister of the Soho Grand, offering "an enticing combination of hip and comfy" with "decent-size" rooms, an "excellent lively bar" with "soaring ceilings", "pricey drinks" and "celebrity sightings" to satisfy any fan (though some find the staff have inherited "attitude to spare"); "white noise generators" do their best to cancel the hubbub from the central atrium.

Trump International Hotel & Tower 🍴🫖🔭Ⓢ 23 | 24 | 25 | 22 | $775

1 Central Park W. | Manhattan | 212-299-1000 | fax 212-299-1150 | 888-448-7867 | www.trumpintl.com | 39 rooms, 128 suites

Even if you're "unimpressed with the Donald", you can "love his hotel" say admirers of the "understated elegance" ("better taste than one might expect") at this Columbus Circle spot with "fabulous views of Central Park"; expect "personalized stationery upon arrival", "a stocked refrigerator" in the "spacious suites", an "outstanding" meal at Jean Georges, a "gorgeous" gym and "celebs everywhere" - just "be prepared to drop some dough" to breathe their same rarified air.

Waldorf=Astoria & Towers Ⓗ🫖🐕🔭 21 | 22 | 20 | 21 | $639

301 Park Ave. | Manhattan | 212-355-3000 | fax 212-872-7272 | 800-925-3673 | www.waldorf.com | 1112 rooms, 313 suites

A "place of legends" where every sitting U.S. president since Herbert Hoover has stayed, this "magical" veteran has a "glorious" art deco lobby that's an "all-time favorite" of many; the "attentive staff" makes you feel "like a prince while walking in the footsteps of kings", but "rooms vary" so much - from "woeful to wonderful" - that some guests wonder if it's "surviving on its name alone"; P.S. a $60-million renovation and the addition of a Guerlain spa may help "recapture the glory."

Wales, The ▽ 18 | 21 | 19 | 18 | $342

1295 Madison Ave. | Manhattan | 212-876-6000 | fax 212-876-7139 | 866-925-3746 | www.waleshotel.com | 46 rooms, 42 suites

Though it's "small", this "old-fashioned" hotel in the "lovely" Carnegie Hill neighborhood offers "a whale of a good time" to those who find it a "home way from home" with "outstanding" "complimentary continental breakfast" and a "relaxing" ambiance; but others say it lacks "first-class amenities" ("no turndown service, no decent newspaper"), the quarters offer little more than if you were staying on a "convertible couch in a friend's apartment" and "service ranges from excellent" to "unhelpful."

Westin 👪🐕🔭Ⓢ 23 | 19 | 17 | 21 | $399

270 W. 43rd St. | Manhattan | 212-201-2700 | fax 212-201-2701 | 866-837-4183 | www.westinny.com | 863 rooms, 27 suites

An "enormous" hotel in "crowded" Times Square, this chainster is a place for Big Apple action rather than a "relaxing getaway"; "good for families and tour groups" (part of the reason for "long check-in lines"), it's also a "solid business" choice with "contemporary" rooms offering "signature Heavenly beds" and "spectacular" views; but critics "aren't impressed" with Shula's Steakhouse.

W New York ✿Ⓢ — 14 | 17 | 17 | 18 | $659

541 Lexington Ave. | Manhattan | 212-755-1200 | fax 212-319-8344 | 877-946-8357 | www.whotels.com | 628 rooms, 60 suites

The city's "original W" in Midtown is "home of the itsy bitsy teeny weeny" rooms; those who don't mind this definition of a New York "minute" say the hotel is "slick and cool", with Bliss bathroom products from the "solid" on-site spa, "yummy food" at the Heartbeat restaurant and a "hip" bar scene where the "over-40 crowd stands out like a sore thumb" – but, at any age, it's best to come in "designer duds", since the staff "sizes you up as soon as you walk in the door."

W Times Square ✿♨Ⓢ — 20 | 20 | 19 | 19 | $669

1567 Broadway | Manhattan | 212-930-7400 | fax 212-930-7500 | 888-627-8680 | www.whotels.com | 464 rooms, 43 suites

"Walking under a suspended waterfall" in the "cool" lobby is just part of the show at this "funky" Theater District hotel where "swanky" rooms are "on the small side" yet have "fantastic views of Times Square" and "mirrored headboards" that "add spice" to the "heavenly beds"; the seafood restaurant, Blue Fin, "rocks" and there's a "great exercise room", but the staff stands accused of a "hipper-than-thou attitude" while more light would make it feel less like "a club disguised as a hotel."

W Union Square ✕ⓘ✿ — 22 | 21 | 20 | 20 | $689

201 Park Ave. S. | Manhattan | 212-253-9119 | fax 212-253-9229 | 877-782-0027 | www.whotels.com | 253 rooms, 17 suites

"It's easy to get comfortable in this" "cool" beaux arts hotel, which many find the "most functional" of New York's W constellation, with its "great Downtown location" near Union Square Park and its "quiet", "well-furnished", though often "gloomy", rooms; the "beautiful people" who call this a "fave" also praise the "accommodating, personable" staff, the on-site Todd English restaurant, Olives, and the neighborhood that features "great dining" all around.

Westchester County

Castle on the Hudson, The ✕♨Ⓢ✎ — 23 | 23 | 25 | 22 | $370

400 Benedict Ave. | Tarrytown | 914-631-1980 | fax 914-631-4612 | 800-616-4487 | www.castleonthehudson.com | 24 rooms, 7 suites

A "wonderful getaway that's close to home" (just a 30-minute drive from NYC), this "highly recommended" century-old facility with a "fairy-tale setting" features "amazing food" at the French–New American Equus, a staff that "treats you like royalty" and "picture-perfect views of the Hudson River"; the 19th-century-style rooms and suites (each "unique", some with wood-burning fireplaces) further elevate this member of Small Luxury Hotels of the World.

Renaissance Westchester ✎ — ▽ 19 | 21 | 18 | 21 | $299

80 W. Red Oak Ln. | White Plains | 914-694-5400 | fax 914-694-5616 | 888-236-2427 | www.renaissancehotels.com | 341 rooms, 6 suites

For a quick "getaway", this chain spot with "beautiful", "woodsy" grounds 35 minutes from Manhattan feels appropriately far "from route 287", though it's right "in the center of Westchester" connected to the John Carrere House; supporters say the "newly renovated rooms have a modern edge" and the "wonderful brunch spread" is impressive, but those who notice it "rents the pool out for parties" (hello, "13-and-under crowd") would "rather spend" their "money elsewhere."

NEW Ritz-Carlton, The ⚲◎ ▽ | 27 | 27 | 25 | 26 | $499 |

3 Renaissance Sq. | White Plains | 914-946-5500 | fax 914-946-5501 | 800-241-3333 | www.ritzcarlton.com | 80 rooms, 38 suites

"Westchester finally has a first-class hotel" shout boosters of this "beautiful new" building "in the heart of White Plains" where rooms feature warm wood tones, Frette linens, 42-inch flat-panel TVs, iPod docking stations and oversized dual-sink baths with Bulgari toiletries; the signature "excellent service" is on hand, as is a 10,000-sq.-ft. spa and indoor swimming pool; indeed, there's "nothing like staying at a Ritz."

North Carolina

Asheville

Greystone Inn, The ⊕♨⌐◎⚲   ▽ | 24 | 26 | 23 | 21 | $360 |

Greystone Ln. | Lake Toxaway | 828-966-4700 | fax 828-862-5689 | 800-824-5766 | www.greystoneinn.com | 30 rooms, 3 suites

A "wonderful place to relax", especially "if you like golf, hiking" and taking a "relaxing" champagne boat toar on a "beautiful lake" (Toxaway), this "charming" and "discreet" resort southwest of Asheville in the Blue Ridge Mountains| is "special" in so many ways; the 1915 Swiss-style mansion is decorated with period furnishings and boasts "personal" service, but "be sure to take whatever you want with you" say some, since the "nearest grocery store is miles back down."

Grove Park Inn
Resort & Spa, The ⚵⊕♨⌐◎⚲ | 20 | 23 | 22 | 26 | $330 |

290 Macon Ave. | 828-252-2711 | fax 828-253-7053 | 800-438-5800 | www.groveparkinn.com | 500 rooms, 12 suites

"Feel like a Vanderbilt" at this "rambling" "historic" inn that "entices you to r-e-l-a-x" with "breathtaking views of the Blue Ridge Mountains", a "terrific spa", "great golf course" and "superb lobby"; "cocktails on the terrace at sunset" are "a must", though both the rooms ("quaint" in the original buliding, "spacious" in the newer wing) and the dining rate just "ok" – and regulars warn that during weekends the "peaceful environment" can get "overcrowded" with "day-trippers" and "conventions."

Inn on Biltmore Estate ⊕♨ | 25 | 25 | 23 | 26 | $359 |

1 Antler Hill Rd. | 828-225-1660 | fax 828-225-1629 | 800-624-1575 | www.biltmore.com | 205 rooms, 8 suites

Travelers to Asheville "can't beat the beauty" of this "magnificent" "getaway" on the 8,000-acre Biltmore Estate, esteemed for its "great views" from "spacious" rooms, "top-notch service" and dining available both at the inn itself and at the winery on the grounds; though its facilities are "gorgeous, inside and out" and the vibe "welcoming", wary spenders complain that the "second-mortgage prices" can really "raid the wallet."

NORTH CAROLINA - ASHEVILLE

Richmond Hill Inn ✕ ♨Ⓢ

▽ 23 | 26 | 26 | 19 | $265

87 Richmond Hill Dr. | 828-252-7313 | fax 828-252-8726 | 888-742-4536 | www.richmondhillinn.com | 33 rooms, 4 suites

Acres of sculpture gardens and wooded trails with a Blue Ridge Mountain backdrop "charm" guests of this 1889 Asheville mansion where "nothing is left undone"; accommodations, with Victorian-era antiques and boasting "imaginative turndown amenities", include rooms in the main house, croquet cottages or a garden pavilion, and are serviced by a "friendly" staff; "outstanding" fare at Gabrielle's is another plus, but petite patrons pout "you need a stool to get into the high beds."

Charlotte

Ballantyne ♨↥Ⓢ☌

24 | 24 | 18 | 26 | $329

10000 Ballantyne Commons Pkwy. | 704-248-4000 | fax 704-248-4005 | 866-248-4824 | www.ballantyneresort.com | 200 rooms, 14 suites, 35 lodges

Despite its "strange location" "surrounded by cars and concrete" in an "upcoming area" of Charlotte, surveyors deem this "top-class" "convention hotel" "sumptuous" thanks to its "Southern-friendly" service and "beautiful rooms" with "terrific baths"; though it "caters to business travelers" and the dining is "not up to par", there are still plenty of downtime options, including a spa and golf course.

Westin ✿♨

23 | 20 | 18 | 21 | $249

601 S. College St. | 704-375-2600 | fax 704-375-2623 | 800-937-8461 | www.westin.com | 678 rooms, 22 suites

"One of the few luxury hotels in Charlotte", this "architectural work of art" boasts an "awesome" staff, "spacious rooms" and a location just "a few blocks from all the business activity" and "across the street from the convention center"; those with early-morning meetings warn of "beds so comfortable you won't want to get up", but go elsewhere for dinner, since the food doesn't find many fans.

Durham

Carolina Inn, The Ⓗ

▽ 22 | 25 | 25 | 22 | $189

211 Pittsboro St. | Chapel Hill | 919-933-2001 | fax 919-918-2795 | 800-962-8519 | www.carolinainn.com | 177 rooms, 7 suites

Expect "Southern comfort without the hangover", plus appropriately "pleasant" service, at this "delightful" plantation-style "Carolina-blue slice of heaven" "in the heart" of Chapel Hill's UNC campus; the "rooms are charming", the on-site restaurant is "one of the best" around (regulars recommend the "great brunch buffet") and the "live" Friday night bluegrass music on the "beautiful lawn" is a "don't-miss" tradition as "time-honored" as the "historic hotel" itself.

Siena Hotel ✿

▽ 24 | 27 | 26 | 21 | $209

1505 E. Franklin St. | Chapel Hill | 919-929-4000 | fax 919-968-8527 | 800-223-7379 | www.sienahotel.com | 67 rooms, 12 suites

"European ambiance with a Southern twist" is the hallmark of this "eclectic" entry just outside Downtown Chapel Hill with "elegant rooms" and "personalized service" that one overnighter rates the "best I've ever received"; Il Palio restaurant helps compensate for a "lack" of other amenities ("no swimming pool" or on-site exercise room).

Washington Duke Inn & Golf Club 🔭⛳

ROOMS	SERVICE	DINING	FACIL.	COST
23	25	24	27	$329

3001 Cameron Blvd. | 919-490-0999 | fax 919-688-0105 | 800-443-3853 | www.washingtondukeinn.com | 229 rooms, 42 suites

"Southern hospitality at its finest" is on tap at this "elegant" inn on Duke University land in Durham County that's "far and away the best in the area" and "surprisingly kid-friendly"; there's "top-notch golf", "excellent restaurants", a "gorgeous" setting and an indoor pool, but a handful finds "nothing special" about the rooms.

Greensboro

[NEW] Proximity Hotel

	ROOMS	SERVICE	DINING	FACIL.	COST
▽	23	24	19	22	$209

704 Green Valley Rd. | 336-379-8200 | fax 336-478-9123 | 800-379-8200 | www.proximityhotel.com | 137 rooms, 10 suites

"New York comes to North Carolina" with this "cool" "eco-friendly hotel" that "wows" the "green" Greensboro gang with its "great location", "21st-century" rooms (with HDTVs), "ultramodern lobby" and mandate to use 36% less energy than comparable venues; its design is deemed too "spartan" and "urban" by some comfort-seekers, but that doesn't deter the "local" "thirtysomething crowd" that fills the bar after dark.

Pinehurst

Pinehurst Resort 👫Ⓗ🐾🔭⛳Ⓢ🎾

ROOMS	SERVICE	DINING	FACIL.	COST
20	26	21	27	$206

1 Carolina Vista Dr. | 910-295-6811 | fax 910-295-8503 | 800-487-4653 | www.pinehurst.com | 345 rooms, 20 suites, 80 condos, 40 villas

The service is "magical" at this "old-school" "nirvana" for duffers, where "you'll only touch your golf bags to retrieve a club" and "nothing tops the white-jumpsuited caddy on a misty morning"; as for the "less-than-expected" rooms and the "ok" food, well, "everything is secondary" to the tees - the rest "doesn't stand on its own for these prices."

Pittsboro

Fearrington House Country Inn, The ✕🔭🎾

ROOMS	SERVICE	DINING	FACIL.	COST
24	25	26	23	$250

2000 Fearrington Village Ctr. | 919-542-2121 | fax 919-542-4202 | www.fearrington.com | 20 rooms, 15 suites

This "quaint and quirky" Relais & Châteaux "country escape", set about eight miles south of Chapel Hill, "could convince even the most hard-core urbanite to move to the farm" - a "luxurious" one, as the rooms are "commodious", the restaurant "exceptional" and the staff "eclectic and interesting"; so "plan to spend several days relaxing" on the "romantic", "beautiful" grounds that are "perfect" for "long walks."

Raleigh

Umstead Hotel & Spa Ⓢ

	ROOMS	SERVICE	DINING	FACIL.	COST
▽	28	25	26	27	$399

100 Woodland Pond | Cary | 919-447-4000 | fax 919-447-4100 | 866-877-4141 | www.theumstead.com | 123 rooms, 27 suites

"It's a winner" gush admirers of this "gorgeous" "first-class" boutique-style lodging where the "large, well-designed rooms" are matched by

	ROOMS	SERVICE	DINING	FACIL.	COST

an "amazing" (if "expensive") Southern-influenced restaurant that many rate among "Raleigh's finest"; the "lovely" lakeside property, adjacent to William B. Umstead State Park, is home to a "wonderful" 14,000-sq.-ft. spa and a "modern art" collection that's "worth the trip alone" – plus, it's "close to the airport."

Ohio

Cincinnati

Hilton Cincinnati
Netherland Plaza ⑪☕♨

▽ 16	19	17	19	$174

35 W. Fifth St. | 513-421-9100 | fax 513-421-4291 | 800-445-8667 | www.hilton.com | 490 rooms, 71 suites

Architecture addicts agree this 1931 building, "the home of art deco in Cincinnati", has an "unbelievably cool" interior with rosewood paneling and ceiling murals, and a "magnificent hall of mirrors"; even if critics cringe that "some rooms" in this National Historic Landmark "look like they haven't been updated since William Howard Taft's time", and others knock the less-than-perfect service, at least it's "right Downtown" with "nearby attractions" and an adjacent shopping mall.

Cleveland

Ritz-Carlton, The ✕♨♨Ⓢ

24	24	24	23	$279

1515 W. Third St. | 216-623-1300 | fax 216-623-1492 | 800-241-3333 | www.ritzcarlton.com | 181 rooms, 25 suites

Travelers tout this "upmarket" Public Square hotel as the "best in Downtown", where the "stately" building is a fine setting for "wonderful" rooms, a staff that "doesn't miss a beat" and "fabulous" fare; it may not be the best outpost of this luxury brand, but a post-Survey renovation may quiet some concerns.

Columbus

Blackwell Hotel, The ♨

▽ 23	23	18	23	$309

2110 Tuttle Park Pl. | 614-247-4000 | fax 614-247-4040 | 866-247-4003 | www.theblackwell.com | 135 rooms, 16 suites

"Business folks and football fans" who "need to be on campus" at Ohio State exclaim "wow" when they check into this "top-notch" hotel attached to the Fisher School of Business, saying they "love" the facilities, "fairly modern styling" and "surprisingly good service", though the restaurant doesn't draw praise.

Oregon

Cannon Beach

Stephanie Inn, The ♨

▽ 27	26	25	24	$229

2740 S. Pacific St. | 503-436-2221 | 800-633-3466 | www.stephanie-inn.com | 43 rooms, 7 suites

For a "totally relaxing escape" with "stunning" views of the Pacific and Haystack Rock, seaside sybarites choose this "gorgeous" "couples getaway" with "romantic" rooms (fireplaces, Jacuzzis, high-def LCD-TVs, DVDs) and a "pleasant" staff; "delicious" complimentary breakfasts, in-room massages and repeat-visitor promotions are further "wonderful" features; N.B. no children under 12.

Gleneden Beach

Salishan Spa & Golf Resort 🏕 ⚐ ♨ ⬆ ☯ ⚲

| 24 | 23 | 24 | 25 | $229 |

7760 Hwy. 101 N. | 541-764-2371 | fax 541-764-3510 | 800-725-4742 | www.salishan.com | 202 rooms, 3 suites

Devotees "dream about going for a break" to this "awesome", recently renovated resort "nestled in the woods overlooking the ocean" of the Oregon coast (though not directly on the water), where "golf, hiking, whale-watching or just plain hanging out in a gorgeous part of the country will keep you busy for days"; but even "a rainy day here is better than a sunny day in most other places" given the "romantic" rooms with "cozy fireplaces" serviced by a "refined" staff.

Gold Beach

🅩 Tu Tu' Tun Lodge ✕ ♨

| 26 | 28 | 27 | 27 | $233 |

96550 N. Bank Rogue | 541-247-6664 | fax 541-247-0672 | 800-864-6357 | www.tututun.com | 16 rooms, 2 suites, 2 houses

Guests gush it's too too "fabulous" at this luxury lodge on Oregon's Rogue River, where the "hospitable, friendly and personalized" staff makes them feel like "part of the family", and "wonderful" dining includes "wine tastings every night" in a dining space overlooking the water; some spy "deer in the front yard each morning" and say the evening stargazing is so "lovely" "you're likely to make loud swooning noises and wake your neighbors"; N.B. the dining room is closed November–April, and no children under 10 are allowed May–October.

Hood River

Columbia Gorge ✕ ⊕ ⚐ ♨ ☯

| ▽ 20 | 21 | 20 | 18 | $244 |

4000 Westcliff Dr. | 541-386-5566 | fax 541-386-1402 | 800-345-1921 | www.columbiagorgehotel.com | 35 rooms, 4 suites

This "lavishly redone", "historic" hotel with "spectacular gardens" and views that make it "popular for weddings" is an "elegant place to stay in casual Hood River", 60 miles from Portland; the accommodations are "fairly basic", but "management's love for the place shines through", especially during "formal" dinners and "wonderful" breakfasts in the "lovely" restaurant.

Mount Bachelor

Sunriver Resort 🏕 ⚐ ⚐ ♨ ⬆ ☯ ⚲ ⚲

| ▽ 21 | 21 | 21 | 26 | $199 |

17600 Center Dr. | Sunriver | 541-593-1000 | fax 541-593-5458 | 800-801-8765 | www.sunriver-resort.com | 128 rooms, 75 suites, 33 lodges

"Outdoorsy" types are in "paradise" at this "family-focused" Oregon resort that's like an "upscale" "summer camp" in the "high desert mountains", offering "multiple golf courses, miles of bike trails, amazing woods for hiking, pools, tennis courts", a "fantastic spa facility"

| | ROOMS | SERVICE | DINING | FACIL. | COST |

and in winter, "horse-drawn sleigh rides"; accommodations are a "mixed" bag: "the river lodge rooms are beautiful, while the lodge village rooms are ok, but a lot cheaper."

Mount Hood

☑ Timberline Lodge ⊕♨⚓ | 16 | 19 | 20 | 23 | $95 |
Hwy. 26 | Timberline Lodge | 503-272-3391 | fax 503-272-3311 | 800-547-1406 | www.timberlinelodge.com | 70 rooms
Dedicated by President Franklin D. Roosevelt in 1937, this "beautifully restored historic lodge", voted our Survey's Best Buy among small resorts, was later used as the exterior shot for *The Shining*, though you "forget about the movie" when "Mount Hood takes your breath away"; a "romantic", though "rustic", getaway, it's at its "best during the winter", with a "gorgeous" "fireplace in the lobby" and the longest ski season in North America.

Portland

Benson Hotel, The ⊕✂♨ | 20 | 21 | 19 | 19 | $224 |
309 SW Broadway | 503-228-2000 | fax 503-471-3920 | 888-523-6766 | www.bensonhotel.com | 230 rooms, 50 suites, 7 penthouses
"If you like dark wood and brocade this is your place" admit admirers of this "stylish old hotel for stylish old guests" built in 1912 and on the National Register of Historic Places (every U.S. president has stayed here since Woodrow Wilson); service is "gracious"and the Tempur-Pedic beds in the recently renovated rooms "feel better than" your perch at home (though some would just as soon "sleep in their classic bar"), but those who "skip this relic" can't see past its "faded" beauty.

Heathman Hotel, The ✕⊕✂♨ | 20 | 24 | 25 | 19 | $315 |
1001 SW Broadway | 503-241-4100 | fax 503-790-7110 | 800-551-0011 | www.heathmanhotel.com | 109 rooms, 41 suites
Enthusiasts exclaim the "public areas are drop-dead beautiful" in this historic '20s boutique hotel with "impeccable" service located next to Downtown's Center for the Performing Arts; chef Philippe Boulot's "outstanding" French-Oregonian fusion fare is "to die for" (among "the best in the Northwest"), but guests are less entranced by "disappointing" rooms that are "tiny" and "shabby" "for the price."

Lucia, Hotel ✕✂ | ▽ 19 | 21 | 21 | 19 | $159 |
400 SW Broadway | 503-225-1717 | fax 503-225-1919 | 877-225-1717 | www.hotellucia.com | 119 rooms, 8 suites
Hipsters hail the "contemporary face-lift" that's turned a "formerly awful hotel" into a "gem" with "funky" "black-and-white photographs" of politicians and celebrities throughout, a "great" restaurant and cocktail lounge, and "beautifully designed" (although "small") rooms with iPod docks and Aveda products; sure, some say it may be "a bit pretentious for Portland, but that's what makes it fun."

Monaco, Hotel ⊕✂Ⓢ | 22 | 23 | 17 | 18 | $259 |
506 SW Washington St. | 503-222-0001 | fax 503-222-0004 | 888-207-2201 | www.monaco-portland.com | 82 rooms, 139 suites
Part of the Kimpton chain, this "fun" Downtowner with a "laid-back atmosphere" "epitomizes Portland" - so feel free to "bring your dog"

and/or the kids to relax in the colorful, "electic" rooms (you can even call on a pet psychic for an extra fee); the service is "terrific" and evening wine tastings are "a nice touch", so many can overlook a restaurant they say is "holding it back."

RiverPlace Hotel ⚐🏨

| ▽ 27 | 26 | 20 | 24 | $269 |

1510 SW Harbor Way | 503-228-3233 | fax 503-295-6190 | 800-227-1333 | www.riverplacehotel.com | 40 rooms, 44 suites

The "best hotel in Portalnd" say fans of the "beautiful" rooms with "wonderful" Willamette River views at this close-to-Downtown hotel that nevertheless seems "far from everything"; though the service is "excellent" and the Craftsman-style lobby and library are "wonderful", a few foodies find the "menu needs upgrading"

Westin 🏋🍴🏨

| 21 | 22 | 16 | 17 | $339 |

750 SW Alder St. | 503-294-9000 | fax 503-241-9565 | 888-627-8401 | www.westin.com | 188 rooms, 17 suites

"In the center of a culturally vibrant Downtown area" "minutes away from Pioneer Place", this chain outpost with a "pleasant, professional" staff has "perfectly furnished" rooms "for the demanding business traveler"; though gourmets gripe there's "no really good restaurant" and "nothing notable" about the facilities, the "charming neighborhood" with dining options is a plus; N.B. it's slated for renovations in 2009.

Pennsylvania

Bradford

Glendorn 🏋☕⚐🏨🔍

| - | - | - | - | $475 |

1000 Glendorn Dr. | 814-362-6511 | fax 814-368-9923 | 800-843-8568 | www.glendorn.com | 26 cabins, 4 suites

Built as a family estate in the 1920s and open to the public since 1995, this "beautiful" Relais & Châteaux hotel is a "gem" "in the middle of nowhere" in northwestern Pennsylvania, with a "delightful old-world setting" in a redwood lodge and several cabins, a "great big pool", an "attentive staff" and "excellent food" (gentlemen: jackets required for dinner) along with outdoorsy activities such as fly fishing; N.B. a new fitness center and spa are planned.

Farmington

Nemacolin Woodlands 🏋☕🏨⚐🕒🍴🔍

| 25 | 25 | 24 | 27 | $339 |

1001 LaFayette Dr. | 724-329-8555 | fax 724-329-6947 | 800-422-2736 | www.nemacolin.com | 260 rooms, 25 suites, 45 townhouses

You "feel like you have your own personal mansion", complete with "24-hour butler service", when you stay in Falling Rock, "a Frank Lloyd Wright–inspired masterpiece" amid the many lodging choices at this "hilltop" "paradise of pleasure" in western PA; the "château rooms are worthy of royalty" too, while the facilities offer "something for everyone": "shooting to art, spa to four-wheeling", plus 18 holes of Pete Dye–designed golf and "delicious" dining at Lautrec.

	ROOMS	SERVICE	DINING	FACIL.	COST

Hawley

Ⓩ Lodge at Woodloch 🛁Ⓢ

23 | 26 | 23 | 28 | $675

109 River Birch Ln. | 570-685-8500 | fax 570-685-8612 | 866-953-8500 |
www.thelodgeatwoodloch.com | 47 rooms, 11 suites

Rebalance your chakra at this "exceptionally executed destination spa"
(and member of Small Luxury Hotels) set on 75 "tranquil", wooded acres
in Pennsylvania's Lake Region, halfway between New York and
Philadelphia; proponents praise the "ample" rooms, "wonderful" treatments, "first-class service" and gourmet spa food that's "cooked to perfection", saying this place is "just the right size" to "feel pampered."

Hershey

Hershey, The Hotel 🏃🛁⬆Ⓢ🔍

22 | 24 | 22 | 25 | $409

100 Hotel Rd. | 717-533-2171 | fax 717-534-8887 | 800-437-7439 |
www.hersheypa.com | 221 rooms, 9 suites

"As sweet as it sounds" with a "historic atmosphere" that "feels like
1950" ("dated", yet with "residual charm"), this Spanish-style family
resort predictably boasts "chocolate everywhere" – even in the "sinfully
good" spa where you can "get dipped, scrubbed and soak in it"; expect
"lots of local activities" including Hershey Park, an "excellent" golf
course and "incredible gardens" in which you can "encounter a walking
Kit Kat bar", plus "gourmet dining" that's as "decadent as it should be";
just be prepared to "kiss your money goodbye" along with your diet.

Philadelphia

Ⓩ Four Seasons ✕✽🛁Ⓢ

26 | 28 | 26 | 26 | $405

1 Logan Sq. | 215-963-1500 | fax 215-963-9562 | 866-516-1100 |
www.fourseasons.com | 288 rooms, 96 suites

"Staying here is a preview of heaven" chant those charmed by this
"phenomenal" hotel overlooking Logan Circle, where the staff "treats
you like royalty" and the "gorgeously decorated rooms" with Federal-
style furnishings impress; public spaces "filled with different fresh
flowers every day", a "superb spa" and Fountain restaurant that's
a "must-do for foodies" (it was voted No. 1 in our *Philadelphia
Restaurants* Survey) further propel this one to the "top of the heap."

Hilton Inn at Penn ☕✽🛁

▽ 19 | 19 | 15 | 18 | $219

3600 Sansom St. | 215-222-0200 | fax 215-222-4600 | 800-445-8667 |
www.hilton.com | 238 rooms

"Any college campus would be lucky to have such a fine hostelry", with a
"caring staff", "spacious and beautifully decorated public areas" and a
"grand piano in the library" say fans of this West Philadelphia chainster;
but foes, citing "small quarters" and "awful food", insist it will "succeed
as long at it can prey on parents" with "a kid at Penn", since the "convenient location" "in the center of the university" is "the best part."

Loews ⑪✽Ⓢ

23 | 21 | 18 | 21 | $239

1200 Market St. | 215-627-1200 | fax 215-231-7310 | 800-235-6397 |
www.loewshotels.com | 545 rooms, 36 suites

A converted "rare gem of an art deco building" ("formerly a bank")
houses this "gorgeous" "inner city retreat" that's "close to everything"

| | ROOMS | SERVICE | DINING | FACIL. | COST |

"in the heart of Philadelphia"; even if its lows include "inconsistent" service and an "abysmal parking situation", the highs – a "fantastic bar", "daring" seafood restaurant and "views to love" from the "modern" "pet-friendly" rooms – make up for them.

Omni Independence Park ♦♦♨Ⓢ | 23 | 22 | 18 | 19 | $379

401 Chestnut St. | 215-925-0000 | fax 215-925-1263 | 888-844-6664 |
www.omnihotels.com | 147 rooms, 3 suites

Sightseers say "historic Philadelphia" is "an easy stroll" from this "charming" hotel "facing Independence Park", with "comfortable", "old-fashioned rooms", an indoor pool and spa, and a "friendly" staff that "goes out of its way"; the food is "decent" (especially the "wonderful brunch"), but this "great location" is also steps from "dozens of fine restaurants" or a "night on the town."

Park Hyatt ✕⊕♨Ⓢ | 22 | 23 | 23 | 22 | $305

200 S. Broad St. | 215-893-1234 | fax 215-732-8518 | 800-233-1234 |
www.parkhyatt.com | 159 rooms, 13 suites

"Old-money Philadelphia" comes to life at this "classic" 1904 hotel, overlooking the river, that has maintained "its beauty and elegance through generations"; the "stylish public areas" include an "amazing" health club and the "beautiful" bar and restaurant "on the 19th floor" ("be sure to try the eggs Benedict"), and while the "traditional" rooms are "stuffy" for some tastes, those at the top offer "spectacular" views.

☑ Rittenhouse, The ✕♨♨Ⓢ | 26 | 27 | 25 | 25 | $470

210 W. Rittenhouse Sq. | 215-546-9000 | fax 215-732-3364 | 800-635-1042 |
www.rittenhousehotel.com | 87 rooms, 11 suites

The "perfect spot for a romantic getaway", this "gem on Rittenhouse Square" is the "best hotel in Philadelphia", with an "excellent, personalized" staff servicing "super-comfy" rooms sporting baths "bigger than your bedroom" back home; the food at Lacroix is "to die for", the "resort-level spa" doesn't disappoint and the "prime" Center City location puts everything at your fingertips.

Ritz-Carlton, The ✕⊕♨♨Ⓢ | 24 | 25 | 23 | 23 | $469

10 Ave. of the Arts | 215-523-8000 | fax 215-568-0942 | 800-241-3333 |
www.ritzcarlton.com | 266 rooms, 32 suites, 1 penthouse

"In true form" for RC, this "fancy" lodging in an "elegant former" beaux arts bank building has a lobby with an "awe-inspiring vaulted ceiling" and a concierge level that's "one of the best"; a new restaurant, Ten Arts, sits under the dome of the rotunda, and the "middle-of-it-all" location means you can practically "shake hands with William Penn" (his statue, anyway) from the rooms; but those who've "been to better Ritzs" are a bit "disappointed" in the chambers.

Sheraton Society Hill | 18 | 18 | 16 | 18 | $329

1 Dock St. | 215-238-6000 | fax 215-238-6652 | 888-625-5144 |
www.sheraton.com | 355 rooms, 10 suites

This "sleeper" in "quiet", residential Society Hill, "close to the river and within walking distance of the historical area", is a "perfect place to stay for a weekend"; the "welcoming personnel" treats your dog as well as you, and the heated indoor pool is "nice", but detractors dis the "old-fashioned" rooms, saying this one "tries hard", but achieves "run-of-the-mill" status.

	ROOMS	SERVICE	DINING	FACIL.	COST

Sofitel ✓ 🛏

| 24 | 22 | 19 | 21 | $525 |

120 S. 17th St. | 215-569-8300 | fax 215-569-1492 | 800-876-6303 | www.sofitel.com | 238 rooms, 68 suites

With a bit of "French flair", this "well-located" Center City chainster with "effiicent service" and "cool, modern" rooms boasting "the softest beds" provides an "all-around pleasant experience" for most; but with no pool or fancy trimmings, it's "better than average, but not the best."

Westin ✓ 🛏

| 23 | 22 | 18 | 19 | $389 |

99 S. 17th St. | 215-563-1600 | fax 215-564-9559 | 800-228-3000 | www.westin.com | 277 rooms, 17 suites

As the "former home of the Ritz-Carlton", this hotel inherited its "plush", "old-world" decor and "excellent" Downtown location "in the business section" of Philly "close to the museums", while "updated rooms have all of the Westin conveniences" including "Heavenly beds"; friends find the staff "pleasant", while foes call them "diffident" and "untrained", so though it's a "solid" choice, it offers "nothing memorable."

Pittsburgh

Omni William Penn 🛏 🅗 🛏 Ⓢ

| 22 | 23 | 20 | 21 | $200 |

530 William Penn Pl. | 412-281-7100 | fax 412-553-5252 | 888-444-6664 | www.omniwilliampenn.com | 561 rooms, 35 suites

Patrons praise "the most elegant hotel in Pittsburgh", a "grand old", "historic" institution in a "fantastic Downtown location" on Mellon Park that's "beautifully updated" with "spacious" rooms sporting "modern" details; "impeccable" service, a "dining experience par excellence" in a restaurant with "opulent decorative touches" and "reasonable prices" make this "really the only place to stay" in town.

Poconos

Skytop Lodge 🛏 🛏 ⌂ Ⓢ ✈ 🔍

| 15 | 21 | 18 | 21 | $578 |

1 Skytop | Skytop | 570-595-7401 | fax 570-595-9618 | 800-345-7759 | www.skytop.com | 165 rooms, 28 suites

Rising up "like a medieval castle" in the "lovely" Pocono Mountains and with a "*Dirty Dancing*-esque vibe", this "family-oriented hotel" that's "like a cruise on land" "attempts to provide the charm of the old" resorts - and often succeeds, say those keen for group nature activities and "attention" from the staff; but "time has not been kind" snap spoilsports staying in "subpar" rooms, who snort "1980 wants its decor back."

Puerto Rico

Fajardo

El Conquistador 🛏 ✓ 🛏 ⌂ Ⓢ 🔍

| 21 | 20 | 20 | 23 | $319 |

1000 El Conquistador Ave. | Las Croabas | 787-863-1000 | fax 787-863-6586 | 800-468-8365 | www.elconresort.com | 734 rooms, 16 suites

Built on a cliff 31 miles from San Juan, this "massive" resort with "sweeping" views, "amazing" pools and "tastefully renovated" rooms is "great for families", though "not on the water" (you catch a ferry to a "private island beach"); otherwise, there's "no need to leave", what with a spa, golf, a water park and a casino on the premises – though a few seek escape from the "crowds" and "just ok" food.

Las Casitas Village & Golden Door Spa ♔☺♨上Ⓢ✎

∇ 26 | 24 | 20 | 28 | $439

1000 El Conquistador Ave. | 787-863-1000 | 800-468-5228 | www.lascasitasvillage.com | 149 villas

"Casitas fit for a king" and other "pretty" accommodations beckon visitors to this "heavenly", villas-only enclave tucked within the El Conquistador hotel; expect a "gorgeous" ocean panorama, "exceptional" spa treatments at the renowned Golden Door, "personal butler service" and "delicious" fare at numerous restaurants (most notable, an offshoot of Manhattan's Strip House).

Rincon

◪ Horned Dorset Primavera, The ✕☺♨Ⓢ

26 | 26 | 26 | 23 | $970

Apartado 1132 | 787-823-4030 | fax 787-823-5580 | 800-633-1857 | www.horneddorset.com | 22 villas, 13 suites

"Feel like a celebrity with your own villa and private pool" at this Rincon Relais & Châteaux a "long drive from the airport" and "as far removed from the San Juan crowd as one can get"; rooms are "beautiful, the food is world-class" and "lounging" alongside your personal plunge pool is the perfect respite; this isn't the place to enjoy "lots of activities", and "for the money" some "want a beach", but it's "fantastic" if you're looking to "unwind."

San Juan

El Convento, Hotel ⊕♨

21 | 21 | 21 | 19 | $355

100 Calle Cristo | Old San Juan | 787-723-9020 | fax 787-721-2877 | 800-468-2779 | www.elconvento.com | 53 rooms, 5 suites

Get thee to this "nunnery", urge apostles of this 17th-century "repurposed convent" "in the middle of the historic city", transformed into a "wonderfully exquisite" boutique hotel with "amazing ambiance" that gives "a strong sense of old Puerto Rico" and is an easy "walk to shops and restaurants"; "cozy" rooms with high ceilings, "champagne sangria" in the courtyard and a "roof jacuzzi overlooking the city" are enough to draw lovebirds who "get married" in the original chapel, but a few wish the restaurant had better food.

El San Juan Hotel & Casino ♨Ⓢ✎ (fka Wyndham El San Juan)

20 | 19 | 21 | 23 | $349

6063 Isla Verde Ave. | Carolina | 787-791-1000 | fax 787-791-0390 | 800-468-2818 | www.elsanjuanhotel.com | 270 rooms, 47 suites, 69 lanais

This "landmark" hotel "on a perfect stretch of" Isla Verde Beach is "still buzzing", with a casino "straight out of a Bond movie", an "opulent" lobby "great for people-watching", a popular nightclub that "draws the locals for dancing" and a "beautiful" pool complex so big it's from "another era"; that said, "crowded" conditions mean you "have to get up at the crack of dawn" for a lounge chair and rooms could use "upgrading" despite a recent "trendy remodeling."

	ROOMS	SERVICE	DINING	FACIL.	COST

Rio Mar Beach
Resort & Spa 🏊🏖🛏⬆️Ⓢ🔍

	22	21	17	23	$739

6000 Rio Mar Blvd. | Rio Grande | 787-888-6000 | fax 787-888-6235 |
877-636-0636 | www.wyndhamriomar.com | 528 rooms, 72 suites
"Nestled in between the rainforest and the sea", "about an hour from
San Juan", this "relaxing" resort "recently changed hands" from
Westin to Wyndham and fans say it's "fun and family-friendly" with
"tons of activities": "two gorgeous pools just off the ocean", a "lovely"
beach, a tennis center, water sports, a "great spa" and its own conference center; "expect to pay big bucks" for "mediocre" food, but since
it's "far from everything" "the variety" of dining "is a plus."

Ritz-Carlton, The 🏊🛏Ⓢ🔍

	24	24	24	25	$799

6961 Ave. of the Governors | Carolina | 787-253-1700 | fax 787-253-1777 |
800-241-3333 | www.ritzcarlton.com | 374 rooms, 42 suites
A "luxurious" "enclave" on the beach in Isla Verde, just a few minutes
from the airport, this lodging boasts the chain's signature "attentive
staff" ("fantastic pool service" includes "spritzes of water") as well as
"amazing beds"; further praise goes to on-site eateries BLT Steak and
Il Mulino, as well as the work-out facilities, but some wish there were
"more Puerto Rican flavor" ("restaurants are direct from NYC").

Water & Beach Club 🏖🛏

	▽ 18	18	19	18	$239

2 Tartak St. | 787-728-3666 | fax 787-728-3610 | 888-265-6699 |
www.waterbeachclubhotel.com | 74 rooms, 4 suites
Donatella Versace and Pamela Anderson have both cruised the lobby
of this "stylish" San Juan boutique that's "like staying at a hip NY hotel
on the beach" with "starkly white" rooms, "cool elevators" with waterfalls, a "gorgeous rooftop bar" and pool, and a nightclub that stays
open until the last party animal leaves; and though it's "not appropriate
for families", this "trendy" spot "will appeal to the very young and rich."

Vieques

Bravo Beach Hotel 🛏Ⓢ

	-	-	-	-	$190

1 N. Shore Rd. | 787-741-1128 | www.bravobeachhotel.com | 8 rooms,
2 suites, 1 villa
A "little jewel nestled in a surprising location", this boutique on Puerto
Rico's Vieques may have the "peace and calm" associated with a "private B&B", but eschews the latter's characteristic quaintness in favor
of a "sleek", "minimalist" design; rooms have "top-quality" Frette linens and iPod docking stations, the "food is simply phenomenal" and
the service "friendly without too much pomp and circumstance."

Rhode Island

Block Island

1661 Inn & Hotel Manisses, The Ⓗ🛏

	-	-	-	-	$235

1 Spring St. | 401-466-2421 | fax 401-466-3162 | 800-626-4773 |
www.blockislandresorts.com | 69 rooms
Encompassing a small inn, a larger Victorian-inspired hotel and
various nearby cottages, this Block Island "getaway" seduces visi-

ROOMS SERVICE DINING FACIL. COST

tors with its antiques-filled rooms and views of both the ocean and the island's countryside; no matter the building you choose, you can expect a "peaceful" stay and a "bang for your buck", along with some surprises, such as the garden and farm (both behind the Manisses), the home of a fantastic array of wildlife including camels, emus, kangaroos and llamas.

Newport

Castle Hill Inn & Resort ✕ ⊕ 🏄 | 23 | 24 | 24 | 21 | $395 |

590 Ocean Ave. | 401-849-3800 | fax 401-849-3838 | 888-466-1355 | www.castlehillinn.com | 32 rooms, 3 suites
"Sit on an Adirondack chair" and "watch sailboats" "on the Narragansett Bay" at this "elegant" "historic" Relais & Châteaux member that "charms" guests with "romantic" beach houses, a "wonderful" staff that "treats" them "like family" and "fantastic dining" that includes an "exquisite brunch"; the "unique", "out-of-the-way setting" provides a "serene" atmosphere and "dramatic" views that add up to an "unforgettable vacation" for those who only "wish" they "had more money" to "stay longer."

Francis Malbone House ⊕ 🏄   ∇ | 25 | 25 | 20 | 21 | $280 |

392 Thames St. | 401-846-0392 | fax 401-848-5956 | 800-846-0392 | www.malbone.com | 17 rooms, 3 suites
The "home-cooked" "breakfast is included and never disappoints" at this 1760 "elegant" B&B "right in the center of Downtown Newport", where "charming" rooms are "well restored" to offer "modern amenities such as whirlpool tubs"; the innkeeper not only shows "attention to detail", but also has "good ideas for dining and activities", and there's "a lovely courtyard" where "they pull out all the stops for afternoon tea."

Providence

Providence, Hotel ✕ ⊕ | 21 | 19 | 17 | 19 | $339 |

311 Westminster·St. | 401-861-8000 | fax 401-861-8002 | 800-861-8990 | www.thehotelprovidence.com | 64 rooms, 16 suites
Both "business and leisure travelers" appreciate this "elegant" boutique member of Small Luxury Hotels of the World, set in a "turn-of-the-century building"; a "well-situated" location "in the center of town", a "great" staff, varied dining and "reasonable rates" make up for the "lack of some amenities that its big-chain competitors" have (though it's "a nice break" from them).

Westin ⇤ 🏄 Ⓢ | 23 | 22 | 18 | 22 | $270 |

1 W. Exchange St. | 401-598-8000 | fax 401-598-8200 | 800-368-7764 | www.westin.com | 545 rooms, 19 suites
Popular "for both business and leisure" travelers thanks to its "fantastic location" just over a "pedestrian bridge" from the convention center and an "easy walk" to many "historic" sites, this "hospitable", "good-value" lodging also earns props for its "silent" rooms and mostly "friendly service"; if the in-house dining options don't win many accolades, at least there are "great restaurants in the adjacent mall."

	ROOMS	SERVICE	DINING	FACIL.	COST

South Carolina

Charleston

Charleston Place ✕⊕❄♒Ⓢ

| 25 | 26 | 24 | 25 | $559 |

205 Meeting St. | 843-722-4900 | fax 843-722-0728 | 888-635-2350 |
www.charlestonplacehotel.com | 400 rooms, 40 suites

"There's a lot of hustle and bustle" at this "first-class" hotel with "small-town charm" in an "amazing location" "in the center of it all" within "easy walking distance" to "old homes", the Battery and the market; "pampered" patrons praise "comfortable rooms" (regulars say the "club level" is "worth the extra money"), "fantastic service" (even "dogs" are "greeted" "by name") and "grand food", while other impressive features include a "gorgeous lobby" with a "staircase right out of *Gone With the Wind*" and a "sublime" "rooftop pool."

Inn at Middleton Place ⊕♒

| - | - | - | - | $200 |

4290 Ashley River Rd. | 843-556-0500 | fax 843-556-5673 | 800-543-4774 |
www.theinnatmiddletonplace.com | 51 rooms, 1 suite

Enjoy the "best of Mother Nature's creations" along with "unique" architecture at this "serene" inn on the Ashley River that's a "perfect mix of the modern and the traditional"; four geometric buildings house "lovely", rustic rooms notable for handcrafted furniture, braided rugs and "fantastic" bathtubs, while the "lush" grounds (once part of a plantation) showcase the famed Middleton Place Gardens, a National Historic Landmark, as well as a museum exhibiting works from the 18th- and 19th-centuries.

Mills House Hotel, The ⊕♒

| ▽ 20 | 21 | 21 | 21 | $349 |

115 Meeting St. | 843-577-2400 | fax 843-722-0623 | 800-874-9600 |
www.millshouse.com | 195 rooms, 19 suites

The "elegant", "old Southern" atmosphere makes guests "feel like Rhett Butler" at this "former grande dame", set in a "historic" 1853 property within "easy walking distance" to local attractions; an "accommodating staff", "excellent" dining (including a notable Sunday brunch and a "fun bar with live music") and a "fabulous" "rooftop pool and terrace" make up for generally "small" rooms.

Planters Inn ✕⊕♒

| 22 | 24 | 26 | 20 | $375 |

112 N. Market St. | 843-722-2345 | fax 843-577-2125 | 800-845-7082 |
www.plantersinn.com | 58 rooms, 6 suites

"Ideally located in the heart of old Charleston", this "intimate" Relais & Châteaux boutique provides a "memorable experience" thanks to its "beautiful" rooms "with fireplaces and tasteful furnishings", service that "exudes Southern charm" and, most of all, "top-notch" ("but expensive") dining from "one of the best restaurants in town"; despite otherwise "limited facilities", this "quiet", "lovely" spot leaves some guests feeling like they've been "transported to another time, or planet."

Wentworth Mansion ✕⊕❄♒Ⓢ

| ▽ 27 | 27 | 27 | 23 | $370 |

149 Wentworth St. | 843-853-1886 | fax 843-720-5290 | 888-466-1886 |
www.wentworthmansion.com | 14 family rooms, 7 suites

"World-class" rooms, a "sensational" staff that "goes the extra mile to make you feel welcome" and a "marvelous" restaurant all come together in this "gorgeous", "first-rate" Victorian, formerly a private mansion and now a member of Small Luxury Hotels of the World; the "decorative" design includes hand-carved marble fireplaces, Tiffany-stained glass, a spa that retains the inn's architectural elements, and rooms with "beautiful antiques" and "bath tubs so nice you can sleep in them."

Wild Dunes Resort 👪 🏖 🏋 ⛳ [S] 🎾 ▽ 21 | 19 | 18 | 26 | $390

5757 Palm Blvd. | Isle of Palms | 843-886-6000 | fax 843-886-2916 | 888-778-1876 | www.wilddunes.com | 93 rooms, 375 villas, 82 resort homes

Fans find "something for everyone" at this "family-friendly" "mini-Hilton Head" just 20 minutes from Charleston with a "variety of accommodation choices" including hotel rooms, suites and private villas, plus an "excellent staff" and plethora of "pools, beaches, bikes" and "challenging golf"; the "community feeling" and "beautiful location" please most, though a few detractors declare it a bit "tired."

[Z] Woodlands Resort & Inn 🍴 🐕 🏋 [S] 🎾 26 | 26 | 27 | 21 | $325

125 Parsons Rd. | Summerville | 843-875-2600 | fax 843-875-2603 | 800-774-9999 | www.woodlandsinn.com | 5 rooms, 13 suites, 1 cottage

"Relaxation is paramount" at this "unbelievable" "hideaway paradise" set in a "gorgeous" Greek Revival mansion surrounded by "magnificent trees" and a "pretty pool" in the "quaint, historic town" of Summerville; with "fantastic" rooms, "wonderful hospitality" ("they think of everything") and an "exquisite" Relais Gourmand restaurant that may be the "best in the Carolinas", serving New American cuisine with a Southern accent, boosters boast it is easily "worth" the 30-minute ride from Charleston; N.B. though there's no gym, there are clay tennis courts and a croquet lawn.

Hilton Head

Hilton Head Marriott Resort & Spa 🏋 ⛳ [S] 🎾 21 | 21 | 19 | 23 | $369

1 Hotel Circle | Hilton Head Island | 843-686-8400 | fax 843-785-2419 | 800-295-5998 | www.hiltonheadmarriott.com | 477 rooms, 36 suites

The "friendly staff" with a "can-do attitude" and the "great facilities" make it "worth a repeat visit" say fans of this large chainster, part of the Palmetto Dunes resort complex that sports a "wonderful pool and beach setting", 25 tennis courts and three golf courses; finicky diners say the food is "not as stellar as it should be" and some of the rooms "need attention", but it still has "everything" some guests "need."

Inn at Palmetto Bluff 👪 🏖 🏋 ⛳ [S] 🎾 ▽ 29 | 25 | 23 | 28 | $650

1 Village Park Sq. | Bluffton | 843-706-6500 | fax 843-706-6550 | 866-706-6565 | www.palmettobluffresort.com | 42 cottages, 8 suites, 53 houses

"Sunny cottages" "scattered like Easter eggs" "among majestic oaks and rolling lawns" define this "little piece of heaven on the May River" that has groupies gushing over the "most perfect rooms you could imagine", "food to die for" and "a good dose of Southern charm"; "idyllic surroundings" next to a nature reserve, "phenomenal activities" like golf and a "sublime spa" and plenty of "relaxing" make it a "marvelous getaway" "for anyone, anytime" – it's "pricey but worth it."

Sea Pines Resort 👪🚲🏋⛳Ⓢ🎾

ROOMS	SERVICE	DINING	FACIL.	COST
22	20	17	24	$209

32 Greenwood Dr. | Hilton Head Island | 843-785-3333 | fax 843-842-1475 | 866-561-8802 | www.seapines.com | 60 rooms, 440 villas, 100 resort homes

Surveyors "never tire of coming back" to this "family-friendly" resort with "lots to do", saying it's "become a tradition" for them; the 5,200 acres of "lush surroundings" include "excellent golf", bike trails, "fabulous clay tennis courts" and a horse farm, while rooms with "the most beautiful baths", an "accommodating staff" and "all kinds of restaurants" (even if food leaves "a little to be desired"), add up to a "hassle-free vacation."

Westin 👪🐕🏋⛳Ⓢ🎾

ROOMS	SERVICE	DINING	FACIL.	COST
21	20	17	23	$479

2 Grasslawn Ave. | Hilton Head Island | 843-681-4000 | fax 843-681-1096 | 800-228-3000 | www.westin.com | 384 rooms, 28 suites

This "peaceful", "beachfront beauty" boasts "breathtaking" ocean views, a "great beach for walking", "well-kept grounds" (that are so "large" it can be a "long" trek to the rooms) and a pool area that offers "plenty of room to spread out"; added pluses are the "personal service", new 8,000-sq.-ft. spa and "lots of organized kids activities", though finicky types find fault with the "marginal" dining and "tired" furnishings.

Kiawah Island

[Z] Sanctuary at Kiawah Island Golf Resort 👪🍴🏋⛳Ⓢ🎾

ROOMS	SERVICE	DINING	FACIL.	COST
28	27	26	28	$468

1 Sanctuary Beach Dr. | 843-768-6000 | fax 843-768-5150 | 877-683-1234 | www.kiawahresort.com | 242 rooms, 13 suites

Surveyors who "keep coming back" to this "aptly named", "isolated yet reachable" resort 30 minutes from Charleston find one of the "top places to stay and eat in South Carolina" with "fabulous" rooms sporting four-poster beds, "service of the highest caliber" ("the only thing the staff can't control is the weather"), a "heavenly spa", five 18-hole "premier golf" courses and "endless white sand beaches"; sure, all this "Southern hospitality" "comes at a premium", but most say it's "worth it for the food alone."

Myrtle Beach

Myrtle Beach Marriott Resort Grande Dunes 👪🏋Ⓢ

ROOMS	SERVICE	DINING	FACIL.	COST
▽ 24	20	16	24	$129

8400 Costa Verde Dr. | 843-449-8880 | fax 843-449-8669 | 888-236-2427 | www.marriott.com | 397 rooms, 8 suites

Surveyors "highly recommend" this "sprawling convention hotel" whose facilities include a "pretty lobby", "excellent golf" and a "spacious beach"; even though surveyors snap that the food "needs improvement" and the stafffers "sometimes have no idea what they're doing", the managers are good about "fixing mistakes", while the "peaceful" vibe and "beautifully appointed" rooms with "large soaking tubs" are fully restorative.

ROOMS SERVICE DINING FACIL. COST

Tennessee

Gatlinburg

Lodge at Buckberry Creek ☎ 🏃 | - | - | - | - | $265 |

961 Campbell Lead Rd. | 865-430-8030 | fax 865-430-4659 |
866-305-6343 | www.buckberrylodge.com | 45 suites

Altogether "outstanding in every way", this Adirondack-style, all-suite mountain retreat beguiles with its "spectacular" location near the "grand and alluring" Smoky Mountains and Mount LeConte, as well as with accommodations that include private balconies, soaking tubs, kitchens and fireplaces; guests can play a round of golf at Pigeon Forge, or just indulge in the in-room massage treatments, happy they've discovered the "best-kept secret" in Tennessee; N.B. a spa is planned for 2009.

Memphis

Madison Hotel ⊕ 🏃 | ▽ 22 | 20 | 20 | 19 | $240 |

79 Madison Ave. | 901-333-1200 | fax 901-333-1299 | 866-446-3674 |
www.madisonhotelmemphis.com | 74 rooms, 36 suites

Expect "welcoming Southern hospitality with a little New York City edge" at this "intimate yet modern" 1905 Downtown "boutique" member of Small Luxury Hotels of the World within "walking distance" of many "tourist spots"; boosters love the "cozy rooms" and "personable service", and recommend "watching the sunset" from the "rooftop bar" "overlooking the Tennessee River", deeming it all a "lovely alternative" to other large hotels; detractors say the "idea is right, but the delivery is lacking."

Peabody, The ⊕ 🏃 ⑤ | 19 | 22 | 21 | 20 | $260 |

149 Union Ave. | 901-529-4000 | fax 901-529-3600 | 800-732-2639 |
www.peabodymemphis.com | 449 rooms, 15 suites

Along with the "must-see" "spectacle" of the house "ducks on parade", this "one-of-a-kind", "steeped in history" "local landmark" enjoys a "great location near Beale Street", a "beautiful lobby" and a "good choice of restaurants" yielding "yummy food"; the "attentive" staff's "quaint touches" are also "memorable", but "tourist traffic" can be "distracting" and some of the rooms are so "tired" and "small" that critics quack the famous fowl "on the roof have it better."

Nashville

Gaylord Opryland ☎ 🏃 ⫪ ⑤ | 19 | 18 | 18 | 23 | $229 |

2800 Opryland Dr. | 615-889-1000 | fax 615-871-5728 | 888-777-6779 |
www.gaylordopryland.com | 2707 rooms, 174 suites

"Bring your hiking boots" or a "GPS system" urge surveyors about this "almost too big" "mini-city" with "wonderful public facilities", "well-maintained" meeting spaces, a "plethora of activities" (like "boat rides") and "indoor atriums" that are a "marvel"; service ranges from "impeccable" to "indifferent", rooms are "no big deal", dining is "pricey" and some report feeling like they're "part of *The Truman Show*", but most insist the "domed utopia" is "fabulous" "for both work and play."

	ROOMS	SERVICE	DINING	FACIL.	COST

Hermitage ⓗ ≈ ♨ ⓢ

▽ | 27 | 27 | 25 | 24 | $339

231 Sixth Ave. N. | 615-244-3121 | fax 615-254-6909 | 888-888-9414 | www.thehermitagehotel.com | 116 rooms, 6 suites

Fresh from a "wonderful remodel", this "charming" 1910 Downtown "favorite" lures "country music stars", the business crowd and guests on a "romantic getaway" with its "beautiful rooms" with "every modern amenity", an "eager-to-please staff" and "fabulous food" at The Capitol Grille; the stained-glass ceiling in the "gorgeous lobby" transports some to Europe – and may be "reason enough" to visit Nashville.

NEW Indigo, Hotel

– | – | – | – | $184

1719 West End Ave. | 615-329-4200 | fax 615-3294205 | 800-770-5675 | www.hotelindigo.com | 131 rooms, 8 suites

This Zen-like Downtown entry from the InterContinental group is dubbed a "refreshing place to stay" by early fans of the "unique" concept that blends nature, art and architecture; rooms sport hardwood floors, CD players and coffee makers, while the on-site bistro and wine bar is a nice touch.

Loews Vanderbilt ♯♯ ≈ ♨

21 | 22 | 18 | 21 | $299

2100 West End Ave. | 615-320-1700 | fax 615-320-5019 | 800-336-3335 | www.loewshotels.com | 315 rooms, 25 suites

Even though it's "not super-exciting" and "could use some updating", "road warriors" say they'd "go back" to this "lovely hotel" "convenient to Vanderbilt and nearby businesses", thanks to the "large rooms", "five-star hospitality" and "great dining" from Ruth's Chris.

Walland

☒ Blackberry Farm ✕ ♨ ⓢ ⚲

28 | 28 | 28 | 28 | $745

1471 W. Millers Cove Rd. | 865-984-8166 | fax 865-681-7753 | 800-273-6004 | www.blackberryfarm.com | 22 rooms, 34 suites, 4 cottages

"Even" "rainy days" are "perfect" at this "cream of the crop" "getaway" in the Smoky Mountains where "beautiful" cottages with stocked pantries and a "doting but discreet" staff are "absolutely the best"; "expect to gain weight" from the "phenomenal food" at the Relais Gourmand eatery, then be distracted by "breathtaking views" and "acres of gardens" (as well as by wonderful spa services); just be warned: you may "miss your first- and second-born when you hand them over as payment."

Texas

TOPS IN STATE

ROOMS | SERVICE | DINING | FACIL. | COST

Austin

Barton Creek 👪🔭⛳[S]🎾 — 23 | 23 | 20 | 26 | $260

8212 Barton Club Dr. | 512-329-4000 | fax 512-329-4597 | 800-336-6158 | www.bartoncreek.com | 287 rooms, 16 suites

"Beautiful indoors and out", this "well-maintained" resort on the outskirts of Austin is best known as a "golf mecca" with its four "amazing" pedigreed courses; however, non-duffers also appreciate its "airy, bright" recently renovated rooms, "wonderful" full-service spa and American-Continental restaurant; still, the "prices are extreme for everything" and it's "a little overrun by conventioneers."

Driskill, The [H]🐕 — 23 | 25 | 24 | 22 | $199

604 Brazos St. | 512-474-5911 | fax 512-474-2214 | 800-252-9367 | www.driskillhotel.com | 175 rooms, 14 suites

Patrons of this "historic" "slice of old Texas" "in the heart of Downtown" have "cattle baron fantasies" given its "tradition" "serving politicos, oilmen and affluent Austinites" "for over a century"; it may be "full of legends and good times", especially given the "atmospheric bar", "some of the best food" in town at Driskill Grill and location just "steps from the nightlife" on Sixth Street, but "wildly variable rooms" "can be smaller than a coat closet or extravagant."

Four Seasons 🐕🔭[S] — 25 | 27 | 24 | 25 | $410

98 San Jacinto Blvd. | 512-478-4500 | fax 512-478-3117 | 800-332-3442 | www.fourseasons.com | 263 rooms, 28 suites

Watch the "famous Austin bats" "from the terrace" of the "best bar in town" (filled with "movers and shakers") at this "lush haven" in an "absolutely gorgeous" Downtown location on the banks of Lady Bird Lake; it's "Texas to the core" with that Four Seasons "magic", from the "courteous" staff to the "first-rate" spa to the "excellent" new restaurant, TRIO; recently renovated rooms "maintain a traditional style with a touch of local flavor", but sticklers snap that "for the rate" they're not quite as "grand" as "what you'd expect."

Hilton 🔭[S] — 20 | 18 | 16 | 20 | $299

500 E. Fourth St. | 512-482-8000 | fax 512-469-0078 | 800-774-1500 | www.hilton.com | 775 rooms, 25 suites

Deemed a "knockout" ("especially for such a large one"), this chainster earns cheers for its "incredible city views", "lobby coffee bar" with free WiFi and "small rooftop pool"; but others find spotty service, "rather ordinary" rooms and an overall "stark" "convention hotel" feel

[Z] **Lake Austin Spa Resort** 🐕🔭[S] — 25 | 28 | 25 | 29 | $485

1705 S. Quinlan Park Rd. | 512-372-7300 | fax 512-266-1572 | 800-847-5637 | www.lakeaustin.com | 36 rooms, 1 suite, 3 cabins

A "picturesque" 19-acre "retreat from the hustle and bustle of the Texas high-tech lifestyle", this lakeside Hill Country resort "lets you escape in many ways"; "beautiful" grounds and "impressive facilities" encourage water sports (sculling, kayaking, swimming, hydrobiking), hiking, yoga and a wide array of spa treatments; the staff's "hospitality" and the dining room's "healthy, delicious" meals also help make this "expensive" interlude "worth the investment"; N.B. no children under 14.

	ROOMS	SERVICE	DINING	FACIL.	COST

Renaissance 🏨
▽ 20 | 20 | 16 | 21 | $259

9721 Arboretum Blvd. | 512-343-2626 | fax 512-346-7953 | 800-468-3571 | www.renaissancehotels.com | 463 rooms, 29 suites

"Reasonable prices", "well-maintained" digs that include indoor and outdoor pools, and a "location near lots of shopping and restaurants" but "away from the hustle and bustle of Sixth Street" recommend this "pleasant" Marriott offspring; even if the "average" service, dining and amenities make it "unexceptional", it's a "good value" for most.

Dallas/Ft. Worth

Adolphus, The ✕⊕🏨
23 | 25 | 25 | 22 | $260

1321 Commerce St. | Dallas | 214-742-8200 | fax 214-651-3561 | 800-221-9083 | www.hoteladolphus.com | 416 rooms, 17 suites

Built by (and named for) a beer baron in 1912, this "beautifully appointed" Downtown hotel is anything but Busch league thanks to the "best dining in Dallas" at its French Room (voted the city's No. 1 restaurant in our *Texas Restaurants* Survey), and a staff that could be "the role model for other properties"; rooms are "old-world charming", yet boast 21st-century perks like WiFi and flat-panel TVs, while the public spaces' "exquisite" decor wraps everything in a "timeless elegance."

Ashton ⊕✍
▽ 25 | 23 | 23 | 22 | $280

610 Main St. | Ft. Worth | 817-332-0100 | fax 817-332-0110 | 866-327-4866 | www.theashtonhotel.com | 29 rooms, 10 suites

The "perfect choice" for Downtown Ft. Worth, this member of Small Luxury Hotels of the World, set in refurbished buildings listed on the National Register of Historic Places, has a "great location" "just steps to restaurants and entertainment"; many "love it" for "beds as comfortable as home" and "showstopper" baths, while others dig the solid dining at the recently revamped American bistro, 610 Grille.

Fairmont Dallas ✍🏨
22 | 23 | 20 | 21 | $159

1717 N. Akard St. | Dallas | 214-720-2020 | fax 214-720-5269 | 800-441-1414 | www.fairmont.com | 501 rooms, 50 suites

"Convenient to the Central Business District", this "elegant", if not "exceptional", stalwart in the Dallas Arts District satisfies most who cite "refined service" and "well-appointed" rooms with "some of the best views of Downtown and Uptown"; while most enjoy the "happening" bar and the Pyramid Grill for American-Continental fare, a few find it looks "kind of dated."

Four Seasons Las Colinas 🧖✍🏨⊾⊚🔍
25 | 27 | 24 | 27 | $385

4150 N. MacArthur Blvd. | Irving | 972-717-0700 | fax 972-717-2550 | 800-332-3442 | www.fourseasons.com | 377 rooms, 20 suites

An "oasis" in suburban Irving (between DFW Airport and Downtown Dallas), this outpost of the luxe group is "highly recommended" for "family vacations", "business stays" or a duffer's "getaway" given the "amazing service" and "exquisite facilities" that include an "amazing golf course", "phenomenal fitness" center, "incredible spa" and newly renovated "fantastic pool"; most maintain the rooms are "elegantly appointed", but nitpickers take issue with "uninspired" decor.

	ROOMS	SERVICE	DINING	FACIL.	COST

Grand Hyatt

| 21 | 20 | 17 | 23 | $279 |

2337 S. International Pkwy. | Dallas | 972-973-1234 | fax 972-973-1299 | 800-233-1234 | www.granddfw.hyatt.com | 263 rooms, 35 suites

"For an airport hotel", it's "a lot better than you expect" find frequent-fliers who appreciate this chainster's "excellent location" "overlooking the runway" and "amazing views from the rooftop pool", along with "a large fitness room" with "free weights and cool towels"; the staff makes "checking in for your flight easy" and "seems to understand its purpose", but "don't expect Southern hospitality here."

Hilton Anatole 🍴🏋☀🔍
(fka Wyndham)

| 20 | 19 | 19 | 21 | $219 |

2201 N. Stemmons Frwy. | Dallas | 214-748-1200 | fax 214-761-7520 | 800-822-4200 | www.hilton.com | 1479 rooms, 129 suites

"Shockingly large – even for Texas" – and with "all the charm of an air-plane hangar" ("and about the size of one too"), this business outpost in the Market Center is "a safe choice" "for large meetings" since you never "have to leave the air-conditioning" (though you'll need "com-fortable shoes" as it's "easy to get lost"); the "recently redone rooms" are "immaculate" and the spa is "wonderful", although pickier patrons say the "service is not up to the chain's usual standards."

NEW Joule Hotel 🍴🏋

| - | - | - | - | $340 |

1530 Main St. | Dallas | 214-748-1300 | fax 214-261-4575 | 866-716-8136 | www.starwoodhotels.com | 108 rooms, 20 suites, 1 penthouse

Set in a former 1920s Neo-Gothic Downtown building (and next door to the flagship Neiman Marcus), this newly opened designer boutique makes a splash with its hip rooftop lounge and glass-bottomed pool (hanging partially off the building for a view of the strolling masses be-low); the chambers boast flat-screen TVs, extra-large showerheads, energy-efficient lighting and sleek stone-and-white decor, and room service comes courtesy of the lobby-level Charlie Palmer restaurant.

Magnolia Hotel ⓗ🏃

| ▽ 24 | 22 | 16 | 22 | $179 |

1401 Commerce St. | Dallas | 214-915-6500 | fax 214-253-0053 | 888-915-1110 | www.magnoliahotels.com | 204 rooms, 125 suites

"Hip without the hype" is the pull of this "wonderful boutique hotel" "in the heart of Downtown" where the "great architectural features" include the landmark rooftop Pegasus sculpture; the "modern inte-rior" features "cozy" (read: "small"), "romantic" rooms "with an art deco flair" – plus "yummy cookies and milk at bedtime" – and the "amiable" staff is more than "competent"; there's "no restaurant", just an "excellent breakfast buffet", though you can "walk" to nearby dining.

NEW NYLO Plano 🍴

| - | - | - | - | $189 |

8201 Preston Rd. | Plano | 972-624-6990 | fax 972-624-6989 | 866-206-6956 | www.nylohotels.com | 161 rooms, 15 suites

The first outpost of this slick new midpriced, business-oriented brand features the signature urban-loft design, rooms with high ceilings, 32-inch flat-screen TVs, iPod docks, allergen-free soft goods and free WiFi, a state-of-the-art business center, an outdoor pool and a 24-hour gym; other facilities include an outdoor courtyard with barbe-cue grill, a library and a restaurant with table service as well as 24-hour, grab-and-go fare.

	ROOMS	SERVICE	DINING	FACIL.	COST
Palomar, Hotel 🐕🔭	▽ 25	23	23	23	$309

5300 E. Mockingbird Ln. | Dallas | 214-520-7969 | fax 214-520-8025 | 888-253-9030 | www.hotelpalomar-dallas.com | 189 rooms, 9 suites

"Small appreciated touches" like "fresh magazines", "flat-screen TVs" and a goldfish upon request in the "modern" rooms make for a "pleasurable stay" at this new Uptown Kimpton boutique that's a "great renovation" of an older property; an "unfailingly helpful and kind" staff, a "stylish interior" that includes a lobby with two-story windows, wood floors and a fireplace, and "wonderful food" amid a "trendy" scene at Central 214 and Trader Vic's draw "serious crowds."

	ROOMS	SERVICE	DINING	FACIL.	COST
[Z] Ritz-Carlton, The 🍴🐕Ⓢ	28	28	29	27	$369

2121 McKinney Ave. | Dallas | 214-922-0200 | fax 214-922-4707 | 800-960-7082 | www.ritzcarlton.com | 166 rooms, 52 suites

"By far the best in Dallas", this two-year-old has soared to the top of our Survey, voted the No. 1 Hotel in the U.S.; it's located "in the heart of Uptown", the "hottest area" for dining and nightlife due in part to the "extraordinary", "last-meal-worthy" "haute Texan" fare at the on-site Fearing's Restaurant (voted No. 1 for Dining in this Survey as well) and the adjacent "see-and-be-seen" Rattlesnake Bar; wallow in "fabulous luxury", with "plush" rooms, "perfect service" (the staff "calls you by name") and a "divine spa", then "rob a bank to pay" the bill.

	ROOMS	SERVICE	DINING	FACIL.	COST
Rosewood Crescent Hotel 🍴🫖🐕🔭Ⓢ	25	26	25	26	$525

(fka Crescent Court, A Rosewood Hotel)

400 Crescent Ct. | Dallas | 214-871-3200 | fax 214-871-3272 | 800-654-6541 | www.rosewoodcrescent.com | 191 rooms, 29 suites

The "public rooms are literally paved in marble" and "creature comforts abound" at this "prime Uptown hotel" that's "highly recommended" for "when you want to make an impression"; "adjacent to several tony shops" and "upscale office buildings", it seduces with a "superb spa", "amazing work-out area" and "old-world charm" that extends to the "elegant" yet "homey" rooms that are "worth the $$ in luxury bath products alone"; even better, "no request is too great or small" for the staff and there's an "amazing" on-site branch of Nobu restaurant.

	ROOMS	SERVICE	DINING	FACIL.	COST
[Z] Rosewood Mansion on Turtle Creek 🍴Ⓗ🐕🔭	26	27	28	25	$575

2821 Turtle Creek Blvd. | Dallas | 214-559-2100 | fax 214-528-4187 | 800-527-5432 | www.mansiononturtlecreek.com | 127 rooms, 16 suites

"Not a detail is left to chance" for "pampered" patrons of this "pinnacle of luxury hotels" housed in a 1925 palatial home that "knocks your socks off" with "fabulous Texas grandeur", and has "only gotten better" with a "makeover" and a "newly renovated restaurant"; "impeccable" service is "so personal it can be embarrassing" ("how everyone seemed to know my name, I'll never know") and the rooms are "charming."

	ROOMS	SERVICE	DINING	FACIL.	COST
Stoneleigh 🐕🔭Ⓢ	▽ 22	21	19	20	$455

2927 Maple Ave. | Dallas | 214-871-7111 | fax 469-375-5450 | 800-921-8498 | www.stoneleighhotel.com | 100 rooms, 70 suites

Nestled in the "lovely" Turtle Creek area, this "charming" "Dallas institution" has emerged from a "recent renovation" "that breathed luxury and opulence back into the property" ("Dorothy Draper would be proud") as well as added a "wonderful" "new restaurant" and organic-

ROOMS | SERVICE | DINING | FACIL. | COST

themed basement spa; the classic bar is still a "nice hang out", and despite being "made new" it retains its decidedly "funky character."

Warwick Melrose, The Ⓗ🐕🔭 ∇ 23 | 25 | 21 | 23 | $268

3015 Oak Lawn Ave. | Dallas | 214-521-5151 | fax 214-521-2470 | 800-521-7172 | www.melrosehotel.com | 163 rooms, 21 suites

"Spacious" rooms with marble floors and "wonderful, personal" service up the "charm" factor at this "old-world" hotel circa 1924 in Uptown's Oak Lawn area that attracts a loyal gay clientele as well as old-money types; the on-site Library Bar is "great for a cocktails", but some say the food "doesn't measure up" to the rest.

W Dallas-Victory 🍴🐕🔭Ⓢ 22 | 20 | 23 | 24 | $599

2440 Victory Park Ln. | Dallas | 214-397-4100 | fax 214-397-4105 | 877-946-8357 | www.whotels.com | 222 rooms, 30 suites

"Cool with a capital 'W'" say scenesters of this "hip" new outpost on the edge of Downtown filled with "good-looking people" ("like South Beach in Dallas"); "fabulous facilities" include a "stunning infinity pool" "with a fantastic view", a "great" Bliss spa, the "hot" Ghost Bar that's "crazy with" a "young, jet-set" crowd and Tom Colicchio's "excellent" Craft restaurant; the "edgy" rooms sport "spectacular views", but those who find it all "too loud" and "overdone" long for a sanctuary rather than a "thumping nightclub."

Westin Galleria 🐕🔭 19 | 17 | 16 | 19 | $399

13340 Dallas Pkwy. | Dallas | 972-934-9494 | fax 972-851-2869 | 888-625-5144 | www.westin.com | 435 rooms, 12 suites

There's "nothing better than shopping where you sleep" insist surveyors who find "instant gratification" from the "loads of" offerings at the Galleria "just steps away" from this chain outpost ("walk down to the mall in your slippers!"); "Texas-sized rooms" with "spacious baths" and "large tubs" sport the same "hip design" as the rest of the recently "renovated" property, but "don't look for assistance from the staff" snap some surveyors who add that the "food needs improvement" as well.

Zaza, Hotel 🐕🔭Ⓢ 26 | 23 | 24 | 23 | $315

2332 Leonard St. | Dallas | 214-468-8399 | fax 214-468-8397 | 800-597-8399 | www.hotelzaza.com | 127 rooms, 26 suites

"A breath of fresh air" sigh smitten surveyors about this "*très* fabu" "boutique hotel" that's a "lively place to stay" since "movie stars", socialites and "the beautiful people" "zwing" here ("most entertaining people-watching of all time'); "massively sized", "individually decorated" rooms with "wonderful beds and linens" "attract a diverse clientele", as does the "spot-on food at Dragonfly" and the "see-and-be-seen" "scene" of the Urban Oasis lounge, the "pool area that becomes a nightclub after dark"; a "professional staff" can be "snooty" "if you are not 'somebody'", however, and the "facilities are limited due to size."

Galveston

Galvez, Hotel Ⓗ🔭Ⓢ ∇ 18 | 22 | 21 | 22 | $269

2024 Seawall Blvd. | 409-765-7721 | fax 409-765-5780 | 800-996-3426 | www.wyhndam.com | 216 rooms, 6 suites

"The place to go" for a "weekend getaway" with a real "Galveston feel", this "old grande dame by the sea" set in a "historic" 1911 building "within walking distance of restaurants and shops" boasts "beautiful common areas", a "recently opened" "elegant spa" and "superb" service; but rooms are "tiny" and "old-school" say a few; N.B. the property was temporarily closed at press time to assess damage from Hurricane Ike.

Houston

Derek, Hotel ⍤⍤

| 22 | 21 | 21 | 22 | $350 |

2525 W. Loop S. | 713-961-3000 | fax 713-297-4393 | 866-292-7100 | www.hotelderek.com | 288 rooms, 26 suites

Just "blocks from the Galleria and Highland Village", this "edgy" boutique with a "sexy vibe" and a "good social scene" is a solid "home base for a shopping spree"; the "delightful mix" of guests that appreciate the "ultramodern", "pleasantly attractive rooms" ("love" the "window seats"), "smiling" staff and "decent dining" at bistro moderne don't seem to mind the "loud lobby bar" and "mini" quarters.

Four Seasons ⍖⍤⍤Ⓢ

| 25 | 27 | 24 | 23 | $355 |

1300 Lamar St. | 713-650-1300 | fax 713-652-6220 | 800-332-3442 | www.fourseasons.com | 292 rooms, 112 suites

Harried travelers report "a relaxing rush" when they arrive at this "longtime favorite" with a "superb staff" that makes guests "feel like" they're "on vacation despite" the Downtown location; other factors that help are "stellar" eats at Quattro restaurant, "spacious, peaceful" rooms with flat-panel TVs, a 24-hour gym, a newly renovated pool and "complimentary car service" manned by "friendly drivers."

Hilton Americas ⍤⍤Ⓢ

| ▽ 21 | 21 | 18 | 22 | $349 |

1600 Lamar St. | 713-739-8000 | fax 713-739-8007 | 800-774-1500 | www.hilton.com | 1137 rooms, 66 suites

"If a large, convention-style hotel is what you're looking for, this one delivers the goods" assert "business travelers" who like the skywalk link to the convention center and "some of the nicest public spaces"; with a "convenient" Downtown location and "comfortable" rooms, "it serves its function" even if some sigh "eh" – there's "no character" here.

Houstonian, The ⍤⍤⍤Ⓢ⍝

| 23 | 24 | 22 | 26 | $325 |

111 N. Post Oak Ln. | 713-680-2626 | fax 713-680-2992 | 800-231-2759 | www.houstonian.com | 280 rooms, 8 suites

"You'd never know it was right in the middle of Houston" assert aficionados overcome with a "peaceful feeling" at this Galleria-area hotel "gently tucked away" among "beautifully landscaped", "parklike" grounds; the "idyllic environment" includes an "unbelievable fitness facility" and swimming pool, a "magnificent Trellis Spa" and a "superb" restaurant, though a few find the "well-appointed" rooms have "walls too thin for such a fine" property.

Icon, Hotel ⍖⍤⍤Ⓢ

| ▽ 24 | 23 | 23 | 22 | $209 |

220 Main St. | 713-224-4266 | fax 713-223-3223 | www.hotelicon.com | 126 rooms, 9 suites

Dubbed "the hippest in Houston" by cutting-edgers who appreciate "unique" hotels set in "historic" buildings (a 1911 bank designed by Candra Scott and Richard Anderson), this lodging boasts "over-the-top decor", "fantastic" rooms with "excellent baths" and a staff that's "there to please"; gourmands gush over the "amazing" Voice restaurant with its "fabulous brunch", but scenesters focus mostly on a "location that's perfect for hitting the nightlife."

Inn at the Ballpark ▽ 25 | 23 | 22 | 25 | $269

1520 Texas Ave. | 713-228-1520 | fax 713-228-1555 | 866-406-1520 | www.innattheballpark.com | 148 rooms, 53 suites

This inn with an "unbeatable location" opposite the Houston Astros' Minute Maid Park hits a "home run" say fans who cheer the "pleasant" rooms, "subtle baseball-themed design" and view of "the ball park from the roof"; it covers all the bases with the "wonderful" on-site Vic & Anthony's steakhouse, a bar that's "great for grabbing a drink" pre- or post-game and state-of-the-art, WiFi-enabled meeting facilities.

InterContinental 🔭Ⓢ ▽ 21 | 22 | 20 | 22 | $279

2222 West Loop S. | 713-627-7600 | fax 713-916-3327 | 800-327-0200 | www.interconti.com | 472 rooms, 13 suites

Get some "big Texan class" along with your skyline views at this Uptown chainster "close to the financial area" and Galleria, where the "careful and informed service" makes you feel "very much at home"; "inventive and tasty offerings" at the newly renovated The Restaurant, "impeccably decorated", if "small", rooms and a club floor serving "tasty evening hors d'oeuvres" are pluses that prompt patrons to proclaim "we'll certainly stay here" again.

JW Marriott 🔭 20 | 20 | 16 | 20 | $289

5150 Westheimer Rd. | 713-961-1500 | fax 713-961-5045 | 800-228-9290 | www.jwmarriotthouston.com | 487 rooms, 28 suites

Conventioneers can "catch some rays" and then go shopping "in between business meetings" at this Uptown property, given the "wonderful rooftop pool" and the "ideal location" "right across from the Galleria"; a "frequent venue for conferences and weddings", it has "great" service and "lovely", if also "ordinary", rooms, "just don't eat here" warn foodies; P.S. a recent renovation may address concerns over "dated facilities."

Lancaster, The 🔭 18 | 22 | 20 | 16 | $269

701 Texas Ave. | 713-228-9500 | fax 713-223-4528 | 800-231-0336 | www.thelancasterhouston.com | 83 rooms, 10 suites

"Theatergoers", "lawyers" and those in need of a "romantic getaway inside a non-romantic city" check into this "small" "Downtown charmer" "situated in the heart of the theater district" and closest to the court houses; "dated but comfortable" digs have lots of "character" and the "exceptional staff" serves "superb" meals to an "eclectic crowd", but while modernists recognize the "potential" here, some insist the 1926 building is an "old dump" that "needs a makeover."

Omni 👪✕🐕🔭🎾 20 | 19 | 22 | 20 | $399

4 Riverway | 713-871-8181 | fax 713-871-0719 | 888-444-6664 | www.omnihotels.com | 344 rooms, 34 suites

The "relaxing" scene at this "secluded" Galleria-area hotel includes "well-landscaped" grounds, "a pond with swans", a "fabulous" New American restaurant and a just-opened spa; overall, it's "reliable" and "consistent", but it's "a little pricey" given what some call "tired" rooms in "need of updating."

	ROOMS	SERVICE	DINING	FACIL.	COST

St. Regis ✕⍥♨Ⓢ

| 25 | 25 | 22 | 22 | $480 |

1919 Briar Oaks Ln. | 713-840-7600 | fax 713-840-0616 | 877-787-3447 | www.stregis.com | 179 rooms, 53 suites

"You can't go wrong" at this "classy" spot that "oozes wealth" and "befits its River Oaks neighborhood", where the "regal" rooms, a "lovely" spa, "divine" New American cuisine at The Remington and "superb" staffers impress most guests; light sleepers, however, yawn if it "weren't for the trains" passing nearby this "would be the best place in town."

Marfa

Cibolo Creek Ranch ⊕⍥

| – | – | – | – | $475 |

HCR 67, Box 44 | 432-229-3737 | fax 432-229-3653 | www.cibolocreekranch.com | 30 rooms, 2 suites

"There isn't a place like this anywhere else in the world" is the refrain heard from visitors who "never want to leave" this 35,000-acre ranch close to Big Bend National Park, a true "oasis in the middle of nowhere" (200 miles southeast of El Paso and 32 miles south of the artists' colony of Marfa) that caters to horseback riders, hikers, hunters and fishers; meals are served at communal tables, and rooms are set in three restored forts with adobe walls and Mexican and Spanish antiques, but there are no in-room telephones or Internet connections.

San Antonio

Hyatt Regency
Hill Country ⍟🐾♨⌁Ⓢ⚲

| 23 | 23 | 21 | 28 | $170 |

9800 Hyatt Resort Dr. | 210-647-1234 | fax 210-681-9681 | 800-554-9288 | www.hillcountry.hyatt.com | 440 rooms, 60 suites

Even though it's "a short drive from Downtown San Antonio", this "gorgeous" "countryside" resort on a 100-year-old cattle ranch "is a destination in itself" where "great golf", a "gracious spa facility", "one of the best lazy river pools" "for kids" and hayrides make it a "favorite family getaway"; rooms are "nothing special", but "fantastic amenities", decent fare and "enthusiastic service" elicit a hearty "eye-haw" – just "don't go unless you have children" or don't mind a place "overrun" with them.

La Mansión del Rio ⍟⍥♨

| 21 | 22 | 22 | 22 | $275 |

112 College St. | 210-518-1000 | fax 210-226-0389 | 888-444-6664 | www.lamansion.com | 334 rooms, 2 suites

Nestled in a "perfect spot on the Riverwalk", this "romantic" and "unique" landmark hotel is an "absolutely charming" alternative to other "big box" chain choices here; the recently renovated Spanish Colonial–style rooms can be "tiny", but those that "overlook the pool" are "amazingly quiet", and the "Sunday brunch at Las Canarias is a don't-miss event"; N.B. guests have access to the spa of its sister property, Watermark Hotel.

Menger Hotel ⊕♨Ⓢ

| ▽ 17 | 21 | 18 | 20 | $195 |

204 Alamo Plaza | 210-223-4361 | fax 210-228-0022 | 800-345-9285 | www.mengerhotel.com | 291 rooms, 25 suites

Reviewers who "remember the Alamo" don't forget about this "grand" 1859 landmark "right across the street" that's an "integral part of Texas" lore where "history comes alive" ("literally", as "ghosts"

	ROOMS	SERVICE	DINING	FACIL.	COST

"haunt" certain rooms); the public spaces exude "classic old elegance", so even if they're "tired", they're "full of charm" as is the "great bar" once patronized by Teddy Roosevelt, but the "average" service and dining brings it down a notch.

Valencia Riverwalk, Hotel 🏨   ∇ 26 | 21 | 24 | 22 | $300

150 E. Houston St. | 210-227-9700 | fax 210-227-9701 | 866-842-0100 | www.hotelvalencia.com | 208 rooms, 5 suites
With its "plush opium den atmosphere", this boutique member of Small Luxury Hotels of the World earns accolades as the "coolest hotel on the Riverwalk" due to its "chicly dim lobby" (more like an "eerie" "bat cave entrance" to some), "trendy bar" with "leather floor" and "understated dark hallways" leading to "elegant minimalist rooms"; the "excellent restaurants", Citrus and Acenar, are "hot spots" for "beautiful locals", but service can range from "excellent" to "ragged."

Watermark Hotel & Spa 🏨🧖♨   27 | 25 | 23 | 26 | $429

212 W. Crocket St. | 210-396-5800 | fax 210-393-5813 | 866-605-1212 | www.watermarkhotel.com | 92 rooms, 6 suites
"More contemporary than its sister hotel", La Mansión del Rio (right across the footbridge), this small Riverwalk "gem" has a "pampering" staff that "calls you by name", plus "soothing, chic" rooms and an extensive array of "excellent" treatments and fitness options (including exercise classes, meditation and yoga) at the 17,000-sq.-ft. spa; add in the "prime river location" that puts plenty of dining options nearby, and most "have a great time" there.

Westin La Cantera 🏕🏨⚟♨🔍   22 | 22 | 21 | 25 | $429

16641 La Cantera Pkwy. | 210-558-6500 | fax 210-558-2400 | 888-937-8461 | www.westinlacantera.com | 444 rooms, 26 suites, 38 casitas
Though it's "on the edge of Hill Country", this "sprawling", "family-oriented" resort has "everything you could need"; duffers dig the "spectacular" links – including one course designed by Arnold Palmer – kids love the five swimming pools (there's "an adults-only area, thank God") and proximity to Six Flags, and grown-ups seeking a "quiet getaway" can partake of "wonderful spa services" or enjoy "breathtaking views" while dining at Francesca's at Sunset.

Westin Riverwalk 🏕🏨♨   22 | 22 | 16 | 21 | $539

420 W. Market St. | 210-224-6500 | fax 210-444-6000 | 800-228-3000 | www.westin.com | 406 rooms, 66 suites
The "beautiful setting" "on the tail end of the Riverwalk" ("quiet at night, but still walkable to all the hoopla") is the main "attraction" of this chain outpost that "personalizes" the "fantastic Westin name" "with Southern charm" and "generous hospitality"; the "spacious" rooms are "outstanding" (especially those "overlooking" the river) and while the food "could be better", "there are lots of restaurants within minutes" (and plans for a new on-site eatery).

Washington

Inn at Dos Brisas 🏨   - | - | - | - | $575

10000 Champion Dr. | 979-277-7750 | www.dosbrisas.com | 4 casitas
The "perfect" "romantic getaway" (about an hour from Houston), this ranch-style Relais & Châteaux inn is "one of the nicest resorts in Texas"

	ROOMS	SERVICE	DINING	FACIL.	COST

say fans of the "read-your-mind service" and the "peaceful" Spanish-style casitas with remote-controlled fireplaces, mini-kitchens, satellite HDTVs, WiFi, baths with L'Occitane toiletries and private patios overlooking meadows and ponds; each guest gets use of a golf cart to explore the 300 acres, which include a "phenomenal" restaurant with an "amazing wine list", an infinity pool, 10 miles of groomed riding trails, skeet-shooting and biking.

U.S. Virgin Islands

St. Croix

Buccaneer, The 🏋️🚶⚓🏖️⛳🔍

∇ 23	23	22	26	$360

Gallows Bay | Christiansted | 340-712-2100 | fax 340-712-2105 | 800-255-3881 | www.thebuccaneer.com | 8 cottages, 3 suites

"Gorgeous" St. Croix is home to this tropical mainstay "for couples and families" boasting "exceptional" views and surroundings, three private beaches and activities such as snorkeling, kayaking, tennis and, for young kids, a beach camp; a variety of accommodations, including villas, and a staff "interested in making your stay enjoyable", make up for some rooms that seem "dated."

St. John

Caneel Bay 🏋️🚶🔍⛵

23	25	23	26	$550

N. Shore Rd. | 340-776-6111 | fax 340-693-8280 | 888-767-3966 | www.rosewoodhotels.com | 166 cottages

"Spend a week and never visit the same beach twice" urge enthusiasts of this "über-expensive" "retreat" in an "amazing" "setting on a spectacular island" where "couples" and "families" "get away from it all" ("no TV", "no phone"); most report "lovely" service, "stunning" grounds and "wonderful" food", as well as "the best snorkeling this side of Australia", but a handful say the bungalows "could use a bit of updating."

Westin 🏋️🏊🍴🚶🔍⛵

21	21	18	25	$659

Great Cruz Bay | 340-693-8000 | fax 340-779-4985 | 888-937-8461 | www.westinresortstjohn.com | 166 rooms, 9 suites, 146 villas

"There seem to be more iguanas than people" at this "easy, breezy" resort that's prime for both a "romantic getaway" or "fun family trip" given its "beautifully landscaped" ground and "gorgeous" setting; the "endlessly kind" staff operates on "island time", but there's "free Internet in the lobby" and "easy access to town" and the island's other swim spots (good news, since the private beach is "not the best"); detractors dis the "dated" rooms and disappointing dining.

St. Thomas

Ritz-Carlton, The 🏋️🚶🔍⛵

25	23	22	25	$699

6900 Great Bay | 340-775-3333 | fax 340-775-4444 | 800-241-3333 | www.ritzcarlton.com | 161 rooms, 19 suites

"Set on the tip" of the island, this "beautiful family-friendly property" gets "no complaints" from patrons who praise the "top-notch" private beaches, "awesome spa", "cushioned lounge chairs" and "fabulous" accommodations that come complete with "terraces facing the ocean, luxurious baths" and "all the right amenities"; dining is "delectable" and "the staff completes the picture of comfort", so while sensitive types sink the "noisy" location "close to the airport", most agree this is "paradise."

Utah

Park City

Goldener Hirsch Inn ✕🔭⛷ ▽ 21 | 21 | 22 | 17 | $599

7570 Royal St. E. | 435-649-7770 | fax 435-649-7901 | 800-252-3373 | www.goldenerhirschinn.com | 8 rooms, 12 suites

"You will love it" promise pros of this "quaint" "ski-in/ski-out" spot modeled after its "Austrian namesake"; "spacious" rooms with travertine showers and wood-burning fireplaces, "high-quality food" ("don't miss the fondue") and a "helpful" staff help "balance out" the "lack of a gym", while "delighted" fans insist it's "the 'cheap' way to get slopeside at Deer Valley."

Stein Eriksen Lodge 👪✕🔭Ⓢ⛷ 24 | 26 | 25 | 26 | $835

7700 Stein Way | 435-649-3700 | fax 435-649-5825 | 800-453-1302 | www.steinlodge.com | 122 rooms, 58 suites

"Perfect in every way", this "top-notch", "mid-mountain" "ski-in/ski-out" Deer Valley resort is a "first choice" for many thanks to "well-appointed" accommodations, "superb service" including "ski valets" that "treat you like a king" and "terrific food" at the mountainside Glitretind Restaurant; an "excellent" gym and "fantastic views" are added pluses, but don't forget to "bring your platinum card" to pay for all this "finery."

Salt Lake City

Grand America Hotel 🛁🔭Ⓢ 27 | 25 | 20 | 26 | $309

555 S. Main St. | 801-258-6000 | fax 801-258-6911 | 800-621-4505 | www.grandamerica.com | 380 rooms, 395 suites

Thanks to "magnificent rooms", "luxurious" public spaces ("subtle it is not") and "superlative service", guests "feel like royalty" at this "strikingly posh", "five-star property", which seems "out of place" in otherwise "sterile surroundings"; while most agree that beyond an "extravagant Sunday brunch", the "dining needs a big push", the hotel still ranks as a "pampering" "world-class destination" "surrounded by beautiful snowcapped mountains."

Little America 🔭 ▽ 20 | 20 | 16 | 19 | $149

500 S. Main St. | 801-596-5700 | fax 801-596-5911 | 800-453-9450 | www.littleamerica.com/slc | 848 rooms, 2 suites

"Operated by the same people as the Grand America across the street", this "family favorite" has rooms that "run the gamut from top flight" in the tower to more "modest" and "charmingly run-down" in the lodge and motel sections; fans who "stay here again and again", however, overlook the "sterile surroundings" and nondescript food, and focus on the "reasonable pirces" and "dependable" service instead.

	ROOMS	SERVICE	DINING	FACIL.	COST

Monaco, Hotel 🏨👥

▽ | 21 | 23 | 22 | 19 | $269

15 W. 200 S. | 801-595-0000 | fax 801-532-8500 | 800-805-1801 | www.monaco-saltlakecity.com | 190 rooms, 35 suites

A "nice change from the standard business hotel", this "chic" Kimpton boutique, housed in a historic Downtown building, provides a "comfortable stay" to both you and your dog; "attentive but not obtrusive" service, "adorable" rooms ("whimsical" geometric patterns, Frette-linened beds and a goldfish, if you want) along with the "excellent" New American Bambara restaurant are further draws.

Snowbird Ski & Summer Resort Cliff Lodge & Spa 🏨👥

▽ | 17 | 20 | 18 | 24 | $470

Little Cottonwood Canyon Rd. | Snowbird | 801-933-2222 | fax 801-947-8227 | 800-232-9542 | www.snowbird.com | 348 rooms, 21 suites, 54 condos

"Simply unbeatable skiing" and a "terrific spa" are the highlights of this "extremely convenient" "slopeside resort" boosted for "excellent" access to both Alta and Snowbird; though some say the rooms "are somewhat dated" and the "food really needs work" ("bring some Power Bars"), it's still a good choice for "die-hard skiers with little appetite for après ski" goings-on; so "if you're here for the snow, you'll be very pleased."

Sundance 🏨✕👥

▽ | 23 | 24 | 25 | 24 | $320

8841 N. Alpine Loop Rd. | Sundance | 801-225-4100 | fax 801-226-1937 | 800-892-1600 | www.sundanceresort.com | 97 suites, 12 houses

The "environment is a star" too at Robert Redford's "charming", "secluded" resort 30 minutes outside of Provo; it's a legend for its "low-key" appeal, proximity to downhill skiing, hiking and a Sioux-inspired spa, "accessibility to Sundance Film Institute events", "fabulous" Native-American–style accommodations (from standard studios to grander mountain homes with stone fireplaces and decks) and "terrific" food at both the Foundry Grill, a brunch hot spot, and the "wonderful" upscale Tree Room (rated No. 1 in the Salt Lake area in our *America's Top Restaurants* Survey); it's easy to see why you'll "want to go back every year."

Vermont

Central Vermont

Pitcher Inn, The ✕👥

▽ | 25 | 24 | 24 | 21 | $425

275 Main St. | Warren | 802-496-6350 | fax 802-496-6354 | 888-867-4824 | www.pitcherinn.com | 9 rooms, 2 suites

"Like a B&B on steroids", this "delightful" Relais & Châteaux property "redefines what a luxurious inn can be" with its "uniquely themed and decorated" rooms – each "is a flight of architectural fancy" – "incredible", "gracious and sincere" service and "superb" on-site dining (the "chef is a goddess"), plus you can "do puzzles" "after dinner by the roaring fireplace"; even those who warn about the "hefty bill for your journey" admit this "modern Alice in Wonderland" experience "is worth it."

	ROOMS	SERVICE	DINING	FACIL.	COST

Lake Champlain Area

Basin Harbor Club ✳⊕☕✦♨⚓♦ ▽ | 19 | 21 | 19 | 22 | $250 |

4800 Basin Harbor Rd. | Vergennes | 802-475-2311 | fax 802-475-6545 |
800-622-4000 | www.basinharbor.com | 28 rooms, 14 suites, 74 cottages
Surveyors who "loved going to camp as a child" take to this "old-fashioned", fourth-generation-owned "family resort" that "feels like the set of *Dirty Dancing*; "rustic but fitting cabins" and "ordinary" food are trumped by the "fabulous" Adirondacks location and the "beautiful" views; "lose yourself on the lake" or in the Olympic-size pool, but don't forget to wear your dinner jacket to the "fussy" dining room.

Inn at Essex, The ✗☕✦♨⚓ ▽ | 21 | 23 | 25 | 20 | $189 |

70 Essex Way | Essex | 802 878-1100 | fax 802-878-0063 | 800-727-4295 |
www.vtculinaryresort.com | 92 rooms, 28 suites
"Spoil yourself with decadent food and drink" at this "quaint hotel" "not far from Burlington" (or "outlet shopping"), where a "delicious" affiliation with the New England Culinary Institute creates "incredible dining experiences" and the "cooking classes" are a "unique feature"; an "accommodating staff" and "gorgeous gardens" also "charm", but less sybaritic surveyors who report "ho-hum" rooms sniff "cooking isn't everything"; P.S. a spa in the works for 2009 "should do the place justice."

Inn at Shelburne Farms ✗♨⚓ ▽ | 22 | 24 | 24 | 20 | $155 |

1611 Harbor Rd. | Shelburne | 802-985-8498 | fax 802-985-1233 |
www.shelburnefarms.org | 24 rooms, 2 cottages
Part of a 1,400-acre working farm, this restored 19th-century "historic" inn (open May–October) in a "specatular" Lake Champlain setting charms "laid-back" types fond of "faded grandeur"; educational activities for the whole family inclue a "tour of the farm" (a National Historic Landmark), artisanal cheese-making and sheep shearing, but rooms are simple (some share baths and there's "no a/c").

Southern Vermont

Equinox, The ⊕☕✦♨⚓⊙⚓ | 20 | 22 | 21 | 23 | $399 |

3567 Main St. | Manchester | 802-362-4700 | fax 802-362-4861 |
800-362-4747 | www.equinoxresort.com | 173 rooms, 20 suites
"Outdoor types" and "inveterate shoppers" appreciate this "picture-postcard" "heavenly escape" in the Green Mountains (and near outlet stores), that dates back to 1769 and just completed a $20-million refurbishment; the "friendly service", "picturesque" location "within walking distance" of Manchester's attractions and "beautifully renovated" rooms (they're now more "urban chic" than "country charm") are top reasons to come, along with "unmatched activities" like hawking classes, off-road driving lessons and "fantastic spa treatments."

Inn at Sawmill Farm, The ✗✦♨⚓ | 22 | 22 | 23 | 19 | $450 |

7 Crosstown Rd. | West Dover | 802-464-8131 | fax 802-464-1130 |
800-493-1133 | www.theinnatsawmillfarm.com | 17 rooms, 3 cottages
Fans "enjoy all four seasons" and a dose of "old Vermont charm" at this country inn "treasure" "convenient to Mt. Snow", where the "exceedingly friendly" restaurant staff delivers "excellent, up-to-date cuisine" and wine from a "spectacular cellar"; aesthetes appreciate the

	ROOMS	SERVICE	DINING	FACIL.	COST

"great scenery", especially "during fall foliage", but report that rooms range from "lovely" to "need help", and suggest the whole place may soon require "a major overhaul."

Old Tavern at Grafton, The ♔⑪🐕🔍 ▽ | 21 | 23 | 25 | 18 | $210 |

92 Main St. | Grafton | 802-843-2231 | fax 802-843-2245 | 800-843-1801 | www.oldtavern.com | 35 rooms, 7 suites, 4 houses

Located in a town right out "of a Norman Rockwell painting", this "historic" 1801 site (one of America's oldest operating inns and a member of Small Luxury Hotels of America) is a visitor "favorite" for its "wonderfully New England" atmosphere, "charming", distinctive accommodations complete with WiFi, "excellent" food, "romantic" rooms (though there are no TVs) and proximity to the renowned Grafton Village Cheese company; N.B. kids under eight are allowed in guesthouses only.

Reluctant Panther Inn ♔🐕 ▽ | 27 | 27 | 27 | 25 | $399 |

17-39 West Rd., Manchester Vill. | Stratton Mountain | 802-362-2568 | fax 802-362-2586 | 800-822-2331 | www.reluctantpanther.com | 17 rooms, 3 suites

"Hooked" travelers are reluctant "to check out" of this "romantic", renovated boutique hotel in Manchester Village where "magnificent" rooms with fireplaces and hot tubs "make each stay special", as does the "over-the-top" staff and "great new owners" who add "their personal touches"; "delightful" Regional American fare "rivals the best in major cities", and the fun "little bar" adds to the "quirky" experience.

Stratton Mountain Resort ♔🐕🐕⬆☺🔍 | 19 | 19 | 16 | 23 | $118 |

5 Village Lodge | Stratton Mountain | 802-297-2200 | fax 802-297-4300 | 800-787-2886 | www.stratton.com | 200 rooms, 250 condos

You'll find "lots to do" at this "year-round resort" "at the base of the mountain" where snowbirds sing about "great skiing" (an "enclosed gondola" is a plus) and warm-weather warriors recommend the golf course; there's a basic "ski-lodge feel" when it comes to the "not memorable" dining, service and rooms, and on weekends, the village can get "as crowded as a NYC Uptown 4 train during rush hour."

Stowe/Smuggler's Notch

Green Mountain Inn ⑪🐕🐕 ▽ | 22 | 22 | 19 | 19 | $269 |

18 Main St. | Stowe | 802-253-7301 | fax 802-253-5096 | 800-253-7302 | www.greenmountaininn.com | 86 rooms, 19 suites, 4 townhouses, 2 apartments

This "B&B"-like mountain inn, consisting of a 19th-century National Historic Landmark building along with "comfortable" suites, apartments and townhouses, is the ideal base of operations for skiing and "catching the fall" foliage; though there's a "friendly" staff and a "fun", "quaint" tavern, head into town for decent dining.

Topnotch Resort & Spa ♔🐕🐕☺🔍 | 21 | 23 | 23 | 26 | $350 |

4000 Mountain Rd. | Stowe | 802-253-8585 | fax 802-253-9263 | 800-451-8686 | www.topnotchresort.com | 61 rooms, 7 suites, 40 townhouses

Stowe-bound surveyors get a "warm feeling after a day in the cold" from this "gorgeous", "pet-friendly" Green Mountains resort with "rustic" but "lovely rooms", a staff that "bends over backwards" with "110% professional" service and "incredible food"; but it's the "breathtaking views" and "decadent spa" that make this a "perfect place" for a "romantic getaway", despite the fact that some say it "could use a face-lift."

Trapp Family Lodge ▽ | 19 | 22 | 17 | 23 | $580

700 Trapp Hill Rd. | Stowe | 802-253-8511 | fax 802-253-5740 | 800-826-7000 | www.trappfamily.com | 86 rooms, 12 lodges, 100 houses, 8 villas

"Utterly charming in a fun European way" and "as cheesy as you'd expect", this "skiing and hiking resort" perched above Stowe is run by *The Sound of Music*'s von Trapp family and deemed a "delight for people of all ages"; "the hills are alive" with "spectacular views" ("especially during fall foliage"), and its "rustic", recently renovated, lodgings are lorded over by a staff that's "accommodating to all requests"; though some tout the "excellent happy hour", overall, the Austrian-style food is "not great"; N.B. it's a member of Small Luxury Hotels of the World.

Woodstock Area

Ⓩ Twin Farms | 29 | 29 | 28 | 29 | $1300

Royalton Tpke. | Barnard | 802-234-9999 | fax 802-234-9990 | 800-894-6327 | www.twinfarms.com | 10 rooms, 10 cottages

For "a magical stay where every wish comes true", pampered patrons head to this "across-the-board perfect" resort in "rural Vermont", voted the No. 1 Small Hotel, as well as No. 1 for both Rooms and Service, in our Survey; each of the quarters is "like a world unto itself", an "exemplary" staff is "invisible yet always there", and the food and wine "measure up by any yardstick" (the "master sommelier and chef work in divine unison"); it's all "absurdly amazing" – and "absurdly expensive" – so wags warn "have a hedge fund close by when the bill arrives."

Woodstock Inn & Resort | 22 | 22 | 22 | 23 | $269

14 The Green | Woodstock | 802-457-1100 | fax 802-457-6699 | 800-448-7900 | www.woodstockinn.com | 134 rooms, 8 suites

You'll feel as if "you've entered a Norman Rockwell painting" at this "grand inn" with "country elegance" on the green of what some call the "most beautiful town in New England"; fans "never tire of the warm welcome" and laud the "fresh" "antiques"-filled rooms, "delicious" food, sports center that's "a big plus" and proximity to the "challenging" golf course and "modest ski area"; however, a few aesthetes who report "mallard duck overkill" say some rooms are "tired."

Virginia

Charlottesville

Boar's Head Inn | 19 | 23 | 21 | 22 | $196

200 Ednam Dr. | 434-296-2181 | fax 434-972-6024 | 800-476-1988 | www.boarsheadinn.com | 148 rooms, 22 suites

This "historic" resort and convention center is set on "beautiful", "peaceful" grounds that lie just a "stone's throw" from the University of Virginia, Monticello and the Blue Ridge Mountain vineyards; its slightly

| | ROOMS | SERVICE | DINING | FACIL. | COST |

"dated" rooms rate lower than the "wonderful" service and facilities (including a "great" fitness center and spa, clay and hard tennis courts, and multiple pools) – so some surmise it "doesn't always succeed."

Clifton Inn, The ✕⊕😌🏋🕯

	ROOMS	SERVICE	DINING	FACIL.	COST
▽	21	22	26	21	$305

1296 Clifton Inn Dr. | 434-971-1800 | fax 434-971-7098 | 888-971-1800 | www.cliftoninn.net | 8 rooms, 3 suites, 7 cottages

The acres of rolling lawns and gardens with views of Monticello Mountain are part of the "pretty" setting that seduces guests of this "historic" Relais & Châteaux member 10 minutes from Charlottesville, but it's really the "magnificent" food "served with precision" that sets it apart; rooms located in several buildings are "romantic" enough, but foodies joke "I'd sleep on a cot in a broom closet" just to eat here; N.B. Thomas Jefferson's daughter and son-in-law were the architects behind the inn's original 1799 mansion.

⊠ Keswick Hall
at Monticello ✕⊕😌🏋⊾⊙🕯

ROOMS	SERVICE	DINING	FACIL.	COST
26	26	24	26	$425

701 Club Dr. | Keswick | 434-979-3440 | fax 434-977-4171 | 800-274-5391 | www.keswick.com | 45 rooms, 3 suites

A "delightful escape" that's truly "exceptional", Orient-Express' "English manor" ("more British than anything in Sussex or Essex") sits "minutes from Charlottesville" and "close to many historical sites", most notably Monticello; fans of the "stunning" "hideaway" enjoy dining in the "fabulous" Fossett's, being "pampered" at the "terrific spa" or "finding your foursome alone on the lovely [Arnold Palmer–designed] golf course."

DC Metro Area

Goodstone Inn & Estate ⊕🏋

ROOMS	SERVICE	DINING	FACIL.	COST
–	–	–	–	$385

36205 Snake Hill Rd. | Middleburg | 540-687-4645 | fax 540-687-6115 | 877-219-4663 | www.goodstone.com | 12 rooms, 5 suites

It's hard to deny the attraction of this "peaceful" Small Luxury Hotels of the World member, a "quaint", relatively unknown Middleburg inn resting on a 265-acre estate of rolling hills amid the Blue Ridge Mountains; the fare at the on-site restaurant is "always delicious", and the luxury accommodations include assorted houses and cottages, plus the "wonderful" staff is happy to arrange biking, canoeing in Goose Creek or teeing off at Stoneleigh Country Club.

Lansdowne Resort 🏌✕🏋⊙🕯

ROOMS	SERVICE	DINING	FACIL.	COST
20	21	20	23	$309

44050 Woodridge Pkwy. | Lansdowne | 703-729-8400 | fax 703-729-4096 | 877-509-8400 | www.lansdowneresort.com | 282 rooms, 14 suites

This "geared-to-groups" "conference hotel" and resort sits in a "beautiful" Lansdowne setting and keeps both business and personal visitors occupied with golf, five pools, a spa and a "fabulous Sunday brunch"; however, naysayers nag that while it's "nice for a corporate retreat", it's "too remote" for pure leisure and "expensive for what you receive."

Morrison House 🏌✕😌🏋

ROOMS	SERVICE	DINING	FACIL.	COST
23	25	22	19	$289

116 S. Alfred St. | Alexandria | 703-838-8000 | fax 703-684-6283 | 866-834-6628 | www.morrisonhouse.com | 42 rooms, 3 suites

"Tucked into" Old Town, this "absolutely elegant" Kimpton boutique may be the "nicest spot in the area" – a "graceful brick abode" that's walking distance to Alexandria's shops and restaurants and has "easy access to DC"; a "hospitable, cosmopolitan" staff services the "lovely" and "dog-friendly" rooms, while the attached restaurant offers a "fabulous wine list" and "great brunch."

NEW Palomar Arlington, Hotel 🖼🏃 | - | - | - | - | $279 |

1121 N. 19th St. | Arlington | 703-351-9170 | fax 703-894-5079 | 866-505-1001 | www.hotelpalomar-arlington.com | 79 rooms, 75 suites

Floor-to-ceiling/wall-to-wall windows showcase spectacular views of Georgetown and the local skyline at this new I.M. Pei-designed boutique Kimpton hotel across the Potomac in the Rosslyn area of Arlington; the decor, by Beverly Hills designer Cheryl Rowley, features lots of modern art, plush velvets and neutral tones, while high-tech rooms sport iPod docks, WiFi and flat-panel TVs (spa suites have elliptical machines and Fuji soak tubs); the on-site Italian restaurant, Domaso, features a separate gourmet wine and cheese shop.

Ritz-Carlton Pentagon City 🖼🏃 | 25 | 25 | 23 | 24 | $399 |

1250 S. Hayes St. | Arlington | 703-415-5000 | fax 703-415-5061 | 800-241-3333 | www.ritzcarlton.com | 345 rooms, 21 suites

Patrons proclaim the room renovations at this "lovely" outpost on the banks of the Potomac have "made a big difference", citing "excellent beds" with 400-thread-count Frette linens and "pretty baths" with Bulgari white tea products, serviced by an "amazing" staff (the "incredible" "club level is worth" the higher price); the "great" location "by the Metro" makes for "convenient sightseeing" trips, but those who find dining a bit "plain-Jane" say this "reliable" Ritz is "not too exciting."

Ritz-Carlton Tysons Corner ✕🏃ⓢ | 25 | 25 | 22 | 24 | $359 |

1700 Tysons Blvd. | McLean | 703-506-4300 | fax 703-506-2694 | 800-241-3333 | www.ritzcarlton.com | 365 rooms, 33 suites

With a "direct entrance" to the "adjoining" Tysons Galleria as well as proximity to Northern Virginia's high-tech and defense industries, this outpost 10 miles west of Downtown DC is favored by both business types and shopaholics; there's the expected "luxurious" rooms sporting new flat-screen TVs and Bulgari bath products, a concierge staff that'll "wow you" and an "impressive" Sunday brunch, but some say the rest of the food is "uninspired"; P.S. check out the "weekend specials."

NEW Westin 🏃 | - | - | - | - | $499 |

11750 Sunrise Valley Dr. | Reston | 703-391-9000 | fax 703-391-9115 | 800-937-8461 | www.westin.com | 140 rooms, 51 suites

The newest Westin in the DC Metro area, this business-friendly hotel, which launches the 35-acre Reston Heights planned community, offers modern rooms with signature Heavenly beds, ergonomic workspaces, flat-screen TVs and 24-hour room service, along with a fitness center and heated indoor pool; the stylish on-site Vinifera Wine Bar & Bistro pulls in a cool crowd for cocktails and small plates.

Hot Springs

Homestead, The 🏃✕♨⌁ⓢ🏃🔍 | 21 | 23 | 22 | 25 | $500 |

Rte. 220 Main St. | 540-839-1766 | fax 540-839-7670 | 800-838-1766 | www.thehomestead.com | 395 rooms, 88 suites

Dating back to 1766, this "old-style" Georgian estate still "echoes" its past as a "railroad spa destination" – "the hot springs are for real", as are the horseback riding, fishing and "first-rate golf" – while managing to remain "quaint" for such a "large" property just 75 minutes from the Roanoke airport; "memories are made having tea in the lobby", indulging in the "can't-be-beat" daily breakfast buffet and strolling the "sprawling campus"; as for the "quirky" quarters, some "need updating."

Irvington

Tides Inn, The 🏇 🐕 🎎 ☺ 🔍   ∇ 22 | 23 | 21 | 21 | $360
480 King Carter Dr. | 804-438-5000 | fax 804-438-5222 | 800-843-3746 |
www.tidesinn.com | 84 rooms, 22 suites
Yacht cruises, sailing school and theme parties for the kids make time fly at this "quaint", "civilized" Northern Neck resort that's been around for more than 60 years; a "friendly" staff oversees the "lovely" rooms and dining lodge, though an atmosphere that fans call a "step back in time" is interpreted as "musty" and "dilapidated" by the less-enthused.

Richmond

Jefferson Hotel, The ✕ ⊕ 🎎 🏇   24 | 26 | 25 | 25 | $345
101 W. Franklin St. | 804-788-8000 | fax 804-225-0334 | 800-424-8014 |
www.jeffersonhotel.com | 226 rooms, 36 suites
"You never know who you'll meet" at this "luxe" "crown jewel of Richmond" with "turn-of-the-century style" dating from 1895; an "awe-inspiring", marble-columned lobby, a "rock-solid" staff with "big-city focus on details along with small-town charm" and "first-class dining" that's "not to be missed" (the Sunday champagne brunch is "worthy of Mr. Jefferson himself") make it "the best in town"; N.B. Lemaire restaurant closes for renovations from January to March 2009.

Washington

🛿 Inn at Little Washington, The ✕🏇   28 | 28 | 28 | 24 | $755
309 Middle St. | 540-675-3800 | fax 540-675-3100 | 800-735-2478 |
www.theinnatlittlewashington.com | 9 rooms, 6 suites, 3 houses
"About as close to heaven as you can get while alive" gush gourmands who swear you "won't find a better meal" than at the "unbelievable" on-site Relais Gourmand restaurant at this "fabulous" inn 90 minutes from the Capitol; almost everything is "beyond perfection" – from the "over-the-top decor" to service that "consistently anticipates and fulfills your needs" to the "uniquely furnished rooms" – so "sell your first-born" if you have to and "be prepared for a shock when you get the bill."

White Post

L'Auberge Provençale ✕🏇   ∇ 23 | 24 | 26 | 19 | $155
13630 Lord Fairfax Hwy. | 540-837-1375 | fax 540-837-2004 |
800-638-1702 | www.laubergeprovencale.com | 8 rooms, 6 suites
You can have a "perfect" French multicourse dining experience – featuring herbs grown in the on-site garden – at this "old", "romantic" inn in the Virginia hunt and wine country 90 minutes from DC; though it has solid service, a "gorgeous setting" and the requisite antiques in its "charming" rooms, it's a "restaurant first and a B&B a weak second" say foodies who find a "dream come true" in the "incredible" fare.

	ROOMS	SERVICE	DINING	FACIL.	COST

Williamsburg

Kingsmill Resort & Spa ✻✻☕♨⅃☺✎ | 19 | 22 | 18 | 24 | $239

1010 Kingsmill Rd. | 757-253-1703 | fax 757-253-8237 | 800-832-5665 |
www.kingsmill.com | 246 rooms, 179 suites

"Close to Busch Gardens for the kids" and with spa treatments and
"three beautiful golf courses" for adults, this Anheuser-Busch–owned
facility – set in a 2,900-acre residential and resort community on the
James River – also offers tennis, "gorgeous landscaping" and "great
walking and biking trails"; add in six "good but not great" restaurants,
"spacious" rooms with "fine" service and "free shuttles" to area attractions, and you've got a "perfect-for-families" getaway.

Williamsburg Colonial Houses ✻✻⊞♨☺✎ | 23 | 24 | 23 | 26 | $300

136 E. Francis St. | 757-229-1000 | fax 757-565-8444 | 800-447-8679 |
www.colonialwilliamsburg.org | 26 houses

"You feel like you're in the 1700s" at this "really cool" collection of
"unique period" rooms and taverns adjacent to Colonial Williamsburg;
the accommodations range from rustic to "lovely", as "some of the
houses are nicer than others", but all have access to "excellent service" and "modern amenities" that include two Robert Trent Jones golf
courses, clay tennis courts and a spa with herbal treatments.

Williamsburg Inn ✗⊞♨☺✎ | 23 | 24 | 23 | 24 | $489

136 E. Francis St. | 757-220-7978 | fax 757-565-8444 | 800-447-8679 |
www.colonialwilliamsburg.com | 48 rooms, 14 suites

"Do Williamsburg right" at this "elegant" inn "in the center of it all"
where the rooms are so "comfortable and luxurious" that "even a
Rockefeller would feel at home" (he built the place in 1937); there's a
"beautiful new gym", golf, mint juleps and a "pleasing" (if "out of the
'50s") dining room; as for the service, "every staff member addresses
you by name."

Williamsburg Lodge ☺ | ▽ 22 | 23 | 22 | 24 | $300

310 S. England St. | 757-229-1000 | fax 757-565-8444 | 800-447-8679 |
www.colonialwilliamsburg.org | 323 rooms

"Centrally located" in the historic district and a "short stroll" to the
Colonial restoration, this retreat is a "great place to stay with kids" and
some of the "best value for money" in Williamsburg; its recently renovated rooms feature a "folk-art feel" that's like "going back to a more
peaceful, gracious time", made even better by the "charming, efficient
staff" and "delicious" dining both on-site and at its sister properties.

Washington

Seattle

TOPS IN AREA

26 Willows Lodge
25 Salish Lodge
24 Inn at Langley
   Grand Hyatt
23 Fairmont Olympic

	ROOMS	SERVICE	DINING	FACIL.	COST

Alexis Hotel ⓗ🐾🛏️👙Ⓢ | 21 | 22 | 20 | 18 | $299

1007 First Ave. | 206-624-4844 | fax 206-621-9009 | 866-356-8894 |
www.alexishotel.com | 121 rooms, 32 suites

Just "steps from Pioneer Square" and "Pike Place Market", this
"small", "secluded" Kimpton boutique offers "modern" rooms ("no
two are alike") with "a flair for drama" – though there's "never any
from the cordial staff" that "treats you like royalty"; the daily "wine
hour is a great chance to meet other guests", as is the "cozy" wood-
paneled bar featuring more than 50 single-malt scotches.

Andra, Hotel ⓗ👙 | ▽ 23 | 23 | 24 | 19 | $279

2000 Fourth Ave. | 206-448-8600 | fax 206-441-7140 |
877-448-8600 | www.hotelandra.com | 25 rooms, 90 suites,
4 studios

A chic, comfortable Scandinavian-style "haven" close to restaurants,
Nordstrom's flagship store and the Pike Place Market, this "pretty
cool", pet-friendly Downtown member of Small Luxury Hotels of the
World offers "excellent" room service from Tom Douglas' Lola restaurant
and "wonderful" rooms with a contemporary "hep cat" feel, flat-panel
TVs and "lovely" sheets; earning further kudos are the "pleasant" staff
and the on-site babysitting services.

Bellevue Club Hotel 👙👗Ⓢ🔍 | ▽ 24 | 22 | 21 | 25 | $275

11200 SE Sixth St. | Bellevue | 425-454-4424 | fax 425-688-3197 |
800-579-1110 | www.bellevueclubhotel.com | 64 rooms, 3 suites

It "just gets better and better" at this "best-in-Bellevue" boutique
member of Small Luxury Hotels of the World, distinguished by "unbeatable" "athletic facilities" including a new 15,000-sq.-ft. exercise
complex and an "indoor Olympic-size swimming pool"; other pluses
are a "fabulous" spa, unique rooms (plus three distinctive suites), a
"welcoming" staff and a "great" Pacific Rim restaurant.

Edgewater, The 👙👗 | 22 | 23 | 20 | 20 | $289

2411 Alaskan Way, Pier 67 | 206-728-7000 | fax 206-441-4119 |
800-624-0670 | www.edgewaterhotel.com | 211 rooms, 12 suites

It's all about "the views, the views, the views" at this "coolest little
spot in Seattle" that hangs over Elliott Bay and offers "beautiful" Puget
Sound panoramas ("get a waterside room"); service is "uncommonly
friendly" and the "small" quarters – with "fantastic fireplaces, fuzzy
bear footrests" and "wonderful tubs" – are "quite charming in their
Ralph Lauren/Paul Bunyan way"; even if foodies fret over the "limited
dining choices", others eat up the fact that "Led Zep and the Beatles
both stayed here."

Fairmont Olympic ✕ⓗ👙👗 | 23 | 24 | 23 | 23 | $419

411 University St. | 206-621-1700 | fax 206-623-2271 | 800-821-8106 |
www.fairmont.com | 234 rooms, 216 suites

"Still the queen of the city", this "fantastic" Italian Renaissance "classic" oozes "old-world charm" with "spectacular" public spaces, service that's "superb without being fawning" and a "beautiful" indoor
pool; couple that with "lovely" lodging featuring "the most comfortable beds this side of a five-star hotel" (some say rooms are "tired",
but an ongoing renovation aims to fix that) and the "always great"
Georgian Room restaurant, and this is the place to go.

	ROOMS	SERVICE	DINING	FACIL.	COST
[NEW] **Four Seasons** 👪 🐕 🔭 Ⓢ	-	-	-	-	$365

99 Union St. | 206-749-7000 | fax 206-749-7099 | 800-819-5053 | www.fourseasons.com | 147 rooms

Located within a five-minute stroll of the Seattle Art Museum and Pike Place Market, this new branch of the luxury hotel group features local artwork, views of Elliott Bay and Puget Sound and a rooftop with a fireplace and a pool boasting a lighted bottom that depicts the night sky; expect rooms with iPod docks, WiFi and plasma TVs, a Pacific Northwest restaurant with floor-to-ceiling windows and a 6,000-sq.-ft. spa with treatment areas that overlook the Sound.

	ROOMS	SERVICE	DINING	FACIL.	COST
Grand Hyatt 🔭	27	24	22	24	$350

721 Pine St. | 206-774-1234 | fax 206-774-6120 | 800-223-1234 | www.hyatt.com | 312 rooms, 113 suites

"Ask for a room facing Elliott Bay" at this "outstanding" Downtown high-rise where the "chic" quarters offer "stunning views" and "every modern detail you could possibly imagine", from "remote blinds" and iPod docks to "enormous bathrooms and tubs"; "while it's not cheap", the "pleasant and professional staff", "excellent location" (some say it's the "best in Seattle for shopping"), on-site spa and resident Ruth's Chris Steak House ease the pain.

	ROOMS	SERVICE	DINING	FACIL.	COST
[Z] **Inn at Langley, The** 🍴 Ⓗ 🐕 🔭 Ⓢ	25	21	27	23	$275

400 First St. | Langley | 360-221-3033 | fax 360-221-3033 | www.innatlangley.com | 22 rooms, 4 suites, 2 cottages

Whatever you do, "don't miss" the "intimate, fabulous" meals by chef/general manager Matt Costello at this "absolutely beautiful" "getaway spot" built on a bluff in the "charming" art community of Whidbey Island; expect "to-die-for" water views, "amazing massages at the on-site spa", a "friendly and helpful staff" and "ultramodern rooms" with "fantastic soaking tubs", outdoor balconies and wood-burning fireplaces.

	ROOMS	SERVICE	DINING	FACIL.	COST
Inn at the Market 🔭	23	23	19	19	$235

86 Pine St. | 206-443-3600 | fax 206-448-0631 | 800-446-4484 | www.innatthemarket.com | 56 rooms, 7 suites

So close to Pike Place Market you can "watch the fish fly", this "cool", "charming" inn has fans hooked on its "attentive staff", ivy-draped courtyard, "rooftop patio" with "million-dollar views" of Elliott Bay and the Olympic Mountains, and "upscale" "rooms that ooze with quaint B&B style"; still, even with the "terrific" Cafe Campagne on-site and that "fantastic location", there are those who say it's "nothing to write home about."

	ROOMS	SERVICE	DINING	FACIL.	COST
Marriott Waterfront 🍴 🔭	23	21	19	21	$299

2100 Alaskan Way | 206-443-5000 | fax 206-256-1100 | 800-455-8254 | www.marriott.com | 345 rooms, 13 suites

With an "ideal location" for strolling Pike Place Market ("just take the elevator up"), this waterfront chainster has the "best views" of Elliott Bay and the Olympic Mountains from "modern" rooms with CD players and iPod docking stations (half have balconies), even if it can be "pretty noisy" "hearing everyone on the street"; the "fun, retro pool", "extremely kind" staff and on-site Fish Club by Todd English are further pluses.

	ROOMS	SERVICE	DINING	FACIL.	COST

Mayflower Park Hotel ℗ — ∇ 21 | 26 | 24 | 19 | $269

405 Olive Way | 206-623-8700 | fax 206-382-6996 | 800-426-5100 |
www.mayflowerpark.com | 133 rooms, 28 suites

"There should be more places like this" "venerable" 1927 Downtown
hotel at Pike Place Market, where the "impeccably trained" staff is
"friendly" and "helpful"; the "charming", "historic" interior includes
20th-century antiques as well as rooms with Queen Anne–style furnishings, while the "terrific" bar and restaurant (Oliver's and Andaluca,
respectively) are "fun" places "to hang out."

Monaco, Hotel ⚶♨ — 22 | 22 | 19 | 18 | $349

1101 Fourth Ave. | 206-621-1770 | fax 206-621-7779 | 888-474-8397 |
www.monaco-seattle.com | 144 rooms, 45 suites

"Staying here makes me happy" sigh those sold on the "funky" Kimpton
style of this Downtown hotel, from the "pet-friendly" crimson-and-
yellow rooms full of "quirky charm" ("love the in-room goldfish") to
the "colorful", "airy" public spaces with "zany, mismatched" decor
and eye-catching murals; regulars further relish the "free wine in the
lobby each night" and a "can-do staff" that "treats you well, in a dem-
ocratic kind of way."

1000, Hotel ⚶♨ⓢ — ∇ 26 | 24 | 22 | 23 | $425

1000 First Ave. | 206-957-1000 | fax 206-357-9457 | 877-315-1088 |
www.hotel1000seattle.com | 101 rooms, 19 suites

"Shhh . . . don't tell anyone about this hidden gem" whisper enthusiasts of this "calming escape" with a central Downtown location that's
a "place to see and be seen"; "trendy without being weird", it boasts
"sleek rooms" with "high-tech amenities" ("waterfall bathtub",
plasma TVs) and solid customer service, so most say this "cool" spot
is "batting 1000."

Pan Pacific ⚶♨ⓢ — - | - | - | - | $425

2125 Terry Ave. | 206-264-8111 | fax 206-654-5049 | 877-324-4856 |
www.panpacific.com | 150 rooms, 10 suites

Pan Pacific's latest U.S. entry, this three-year-old in the South Lake
Union neighborhood offers Hirsch Bedner–designed rooms with "rich
fabrics", 32-inch plasma TVs and baths with European-size tubs and
shoji-screen-style walls to open up the space if desired; other highlights include an on-site Vida Wellness spa, WiFi and an "impressive"
staff that "greets" guests "by name" and includes personal stewards;
N.B. it's part of the 2200 Development, which features condominiums
and a Whole Foods Market.

Salish Lodge & Spa ✕♨ⓢ — 25 | 24 | 25 | 25 | $409

6501 Railroad Ave. SE | Snoqualmie | 425-888-2556 |
fax 425-888-2533 | 800-272-5474 | www.salishlodge.com |
85 rooms, 4 suites

"Rustic charm" meets the "high life" at this resort nestled in the
"Cascade Mountains" 45 minutes from Seattle where you can "snag a
room with a Snoqualmie Falls view" (once highlighted in the 1990 TV
show *Twin Peaks*), and relax in front of your own fireplace; the "superb
dining" includes "to-die-for" breakfasts, an "excellent" spa offers
"wonderful massages" and the "spectacular location" is "unbeatable";
just be prepared for "busloads of visitors" outside viewing the Falls.

	ROOMS	SERVICE	DINING	FACIL.	COST

Sheraton ⚲👥

| 20 | 19 | 15 | 19 | $329 |

1400 Sixth Ave. | 206-621-9000 | fax 206-621-8441 | 800-325-3535 | www.starwoodhotels.com | 1235 rooms, 23 suites

The completion of "agonizing" renovations and additions to this "conveniently located" Downtown chainster "finally make it a pleasant place to stay once again" say fans of the "fantastic", "spacious" rooms with "skyline views" in the new tower, the "best hotel pool" in town and an "unbeatable" location for theater, shopping and Pike Place Market; even if a few still find it "generic", it's a "well-managed", "reasonably" priced property.

Sorrento Hotel, The ✕⚲👥

| 23 | 22 | 20 | 22 | $349 |

900 Madison St. | 206-622-6400 | fax 206-343-6155 | 800-426-1265 | www.hotelsorrento.com | 34 rooms, 42 suites

"They don't build hotels like this" "grand" "landmark" "anymore" assert admirers of this 1909 Italian Mission–style "classic" of First Hill, where the "welcoming" mahogany-lined lobby with a fireplace and bar is "very old-school"; "traditional" rooms with French press coffee makers, Egyptian cotton linens and marble baths, "good" service" and the "wonderful" Hunt Club restaurant make it "well worth a weekend stay."

Watertown 👥

| - | - | - | - | $189 |

4242 Roosevelt Way NE | 206-826-4242 | fax 206-315-4242 | 866-944-4242 | www.watertownseattle.com | 80 studios, 20 suites

If you're "visiting Washington U.", this "hip" University District" boutique is "the place to stay" agree admirers who love the "gracious" service, "stylish" smoke-free rooms with Aveda bath amenities and the loaner bikes available to explore nearby parks and trails; those who "would go back in a heartbeat" also credit the "reasonable prices" and the "free breakfast buffet and afternoon snacks."

Westin 🛗⚲👥

| 23 | 20 | 17 | 20 | $399 |

1900 Fifth Ave. | 206-728-1000 | fax 206-728-2259 | 888-625-5144 | www.westin.com | 857 rooms, 34 suites

This "circular", "sprawling" Downtown chaninster "in the center of everything" ("convenient to shopping and not far from other attractions") is a "dependable" "standby for business and leisure", touting "large", "updated" rooms (be sure to get one on a "higher floor" with a "view of the city") outfitted with Heavenly beds, "top-notch restaurants" and a "nice gym"; still, the disgruntled dis "tired" rooms in "need of a makeover."

Westin Bellevue 🛗👥

| ▽ 26 | 22 | 16 | 23 | $359 |

600 Bellevue Way NE | Bellevue | 425-638-1000 | fax 425-638-1060 | 888-937-8461 | www.westin.com | 311 rooms, 26 suites

A "sleek" three-year-old business hotel "across from a major shopping mall" and 15 minutes from Downtown Seattle, this chainster offers "fantastic", "stylish" rooms that are "much better than a typical Westin" with 32-inch flat-screen TVs, complimentary daily newspapers, and signature Heavenly beds and Heavenly shower/baths; the fourth-floor Truce spa, an indoor heated lap pool and "great meeting facilities" cater to the corporate crowd, but the two on-site restaurants could be better.

ROOMS | SERVICE | DINING | FACIL. | COST

[Z] Willows Lodge 🍴♨🔭[S] 27 | 25 | 27 | 24 | $315

14580 NE 145th St. | Woodinville | 425-424-3900 | fax 425-424-2580 | 877-424-3930 | www.willowslodge.com | 80 rooms, 4 suites

With a "superb spa", "a prime location" in Washington wine country (30 minutes from Seattle) and two "excellent" restaurants (Barking Frog and the "ultrasuperior" Herbfarm), this modernist "Pacific Northwest lodge" is a "romantic", "secluded" "getaway"; "everything you need", including "modern", "romantic" rooms with fireplaces, luxe baths and "beds that help you melt away", along with a "wonderful staff", is present for a "perfect" weekend.

Woodmark Hotel on Lake Washington ♨🔭[S] ▽ 24 | 22 | 20 | 25 | $310

1200 Carillon Point | Kirkland | 425-822-3700 | fax 425-822-3699 | 800-822-3700 | www.thewoodmark.com | 79 rooms, 21 suites

With its absolutely "stunning" Lake Washington location and views of the Seattle skyline and the Olympic Mountains, it's no wonder why fans turn to this "wonderful" Kirkland hotel (10 minutes outside Seattle) for "business", "leisure" and special occasions such as "weddings"; among the in-room amenities are a soaking tub and flat-screen TVs, while attractions include a full-service spa, vinocentric restaurant and a complimentary tour of the lake aboard the hotel's 28-ft. vintage Chris Craft.

W Seattle ♨🔭 23 | 20 | 18 | 19 | $354

1112 Fourth Ave. | 206-264-6000 | fax 206-264-6100 | 888-625-4988 | www.whotels.com | 417 rooms, 9 suites

The "corner rooms" at this "swank spot" are "worth the $$$" for their "fantastic views" say those who love the "hip" decor, Bliss bath products and "great beds" at this "super location"; but those who feel deaf from the "bar's pounding techno music", blind in the "dimly lit halls" and chilled by the "too cool", "dressed in black" staff are "not having fun."

Spokane

Davenport Hotel & Tower [H]♨🔭[S] ▽ 28 | 25 | 23 | 26 | $299

10 S. Post St. | 509-455-8888 | fax 509-624-4455 | 800-899-1482 | www.thedavenporthotel.com | 563 rooms, 48 suites

"Don't even think about staying anywhere else in Spokane" say luxurists lured to this "recently remodeled" 1914 "crown jewel" with a "stunning" Spanish Renaissance lobby overflowing with turn-of-the-century gilding, flowers and stained glass; the "nicely appointed rooms" (with "lots of antiques and beautiful linens"), "impeccable service", on-site spa and "beautiful ballrooms" make this a "romantic" "return to the past" - and "just what the love doctor ordered!"

Tacoma

[NEW] Murano, Hotel ♨[S] - | - | - | - | $259

1320 Broadway Plaza | 253-572-3200 | fax 253-591-4105 | 888-862-3255 | www.hotelmuranotacoma.com | 299 rooms, 20 suites

The city that's home to a Museum of Glass now has a hotel named for the Venetian glass-blowing island and including lots of it, in this ambitious and edgy new hotel with an incredible art collection, courtesy of hotelier Gordon Sondland; each floor opens to work of a different glass artist, while sleek rooms boast flat-panel TVs, iPod docks, a pillow menu and baths lined with Carrera marble; 24-hour fitness and business centers, and a spa, are further draws, but it's the unique creations (i.e. a sewn glass corset by Susan Taylor Glasgow) that are the stars.

Winthrop

Sun Mountain Lodge ♀♻️♨️☺️🔍 | - | - | - | - | $205 |

604 Patterson Lake Rd. | 509-996-2211 | fax 509-996-3133 | 800-572-0493 | www.sunmountainlodge.com | 96 rooms, 16 cabins

This kind of "solitude is not available anywhere else" sigh sojourners who've visited this "lovely" lodge spread across 3,000 acres in the North Cascade mountains (four-and-a-half hours from Seattle); "no matter the season", you'll find an "extraordinary" mountain setting, "gorgeous" rooms (most have no TVs) and activities such as hiking, biking, horseback riding, ice-skating and cross-country skiing.

West Virginia

White Sulphur Springs

Ⓩ Greenbrier, The ♀✕⊕♨️⬆️☺️🔍 | 25 | 27 | 25 | 29 | $389 |

300 W. Main St. | 304-536-1110 | fax 304-536-7854 | 800-453-4858 | www.greenbrier.com | 581 rooms, 211 cottages

"Absolutely unique for its atmosphere" and "exemplary service", this "time warp" whose colorful Dorothy Draper decor "never goes out of style" is "almost heaven" to its fans who would "happily spend the rest of their days" strolling the gardens, teeing off at a course that's "worth the trip alone", practicing the "ancient art of falconry", floating in the infinity pool and "loving" the spa treatments; "you pay" for the "essence of luxury", but you "can't beat this grandaddy of them all."

Wisconsin

Chetek

Canoe Bay ✕♨️ | 28 | 27 | 25 | 28 | $350 |

Rte. 3, #28 | 715-924-4594 | fax 715-924-2078 | www.canoebay.com | 5 rooms, 1 suite, 16 cottages, 1 villa

"For "pure romantic bliss" "you won't be disappointed" at this Relais & Châteaux "grown-ups-only getaway" set among three private lakes on 280 wooded acres (two hours east of Minneapolis); the "dreamlike accommodations" with "first-rate creature comforts" (personal sauna and steam shower), "spectacular" service ("impeccable attention to detail") and "outstanding food" are "worth every penny."

Kohler

Ⓩ American Club, The ♀✕♨️⬆️☺️🔍 | 25 | 25 | 24 | 27 | $285 |

444 Highland Dr. | 920-457-8000 | fax 920-457-0299 | 800-344-2838 | www.destinationkohler.com | 211 rooms, 29 suites

A "class act in the middle of golf heaven", this Tudor-style "paradise for bathroom fanatics" ("big enough for a family of four" with Kohler installations and Ann Sacks' tiles) is a "world-class resort and spa" where "high-end" quarters and the "superb" Immigrant restaurant help to create an "ultimate" hotel experience; other pluses include advance tee times at the "incredible Blackwolf Run and Whistling Straits (the latter was voted No. 1 in our *America's Top Golf Courses* Survey) and complimentary access to an extensive health and racquet club.

Lake Geneva

Grand Geneva Resort & Spa 👫🔭⛳Ⓢ⛷🎾 ▽ 19 | 21 | 20 | 24 | $329

7036 Grand Geneva Way | 262-248-8811 | fax 262-249-4763 | 800-558-3417 | www.grandgeneva.com | 304 rooms, 51 suites

A "redone Playboy resort" with "gorgeous views", this "family-friendly" "getaway close to Chicago" (90 minutes northwest, and an hour southwest of Milwaukee) keeps the kids hopping with its "many amenities", including an indoor/outdoor water park, two pools and a snowboard park, plus 36 holes of golf; figure in the "nice spa" and "pleasant dining service" and some say it's "as good as it gets", even as others sniff that the "closet-sized rooms" "could use a little design overhaul."

Milwaukee

Pfister Hotel, The Ⓗ🐕🔭Ⓢ 22 | 24 | 23 | 23 | $309

424 E. Wisconsin Ave. | 414-273-8222 | fax 414-273-5025 | 800-558-8222 | www.thepfisterhotel.com | 225 rooms, 82 suites

The "grande dame of Milwaukee", this 1893 Downtown Victorian is an "elegant", "sophisticated" "unexpected pleasure"; the "lobby is gorgeous", the "charming", though "smallish", rooms are "beautiful" and the top-floor bar with views is "wonderful", so even if a few modernists deem it "tired", most find a "unique" "Midwestern classic."

Wyoming

Jackson Hole

[Z] **Amangani** 🔭Ⓢ 29 | 28 | 26 | 28 | $850

1535 NE Butte Rd. | Jackson | 307-734-7333 | fax 307-734-7332 | 877-734-7333 | www.amanresorts.com | 40 suites

"It doesn't get better than this" Amanresorts-owned "small luxury hotel" in a "drop-dead beautiful setting" that boasts 40 "oversized rooms designed to perfection" with "dramatic views of the Tetons"; regulars report "unparalleled service", a "swimming pool that climbs to the sky", a "lovely spa" and a "great", though "pricey", restaurant; in short, this "best choice" near Jackson Hole and Yellowstone is "in a league of its own."

[Z] **Four Seasons Resort Jackson Hole** 👫🍴☕🐕🔭Ⓢ⛷ 27 | 27 | 25 | 28 | $695

7680 Granite Loop | Teton Village | 307-732-5000 | fax 307-732-5001 | 800-295-5281 | www.fourseasons.com | 106 rooms, 18 suites, 27 condos

It's "beautiful inside and out" at this "ski-in/ski-out" "lodge of your dreams" "in the heart of the Tetons", where the "warm and welcoming" staff, "amazing" Westbank Grill, "excellent" spa and "hot cider and s'mores on demand" may have you thinking you've "died and gone to heaven"; off the slopes, snowbodies chill with "après skiing at its best" and in "wonderful" rooms "decorated in the truest Rocky Mountain flair", complete with walk-in closets and soaking tubs; P.S. this is a "great launching pad for Yellowstone", "only 90 minutes away."

Jackson Lake Lodge ⚅🏔️👥   ▽ | 19 | 19 | 19 | 21 | $199 |

US Hwy. 89 N. | Moran | 307-543-2811 | fax 307-543-3143 | 800-628-9988 | www.gtlc.com | 37 rooms, 348 cottages

Wake up to "moose outside the door" at this "rustic but attractive" seasonal lodge within Grand Teton National Park that's "away from the hustle and bustle of Downtown" Jackson Hole; yes, it's "more of a motel than a hotel" and the "food needs improvement", but "people come for the view, not the food"; P.S. there are "no TVs or even radios", but you can hike, fish, horseback ride or simply "watch the day break" from your deck.

Jenny Lake Lodge ✕⚇👥 | 22 | 25 | 24 | 23 | $550 |

Inner Loop Rd. | Moran | 307-733-4647 | fax 307-543-3358 | 800-628-9988 | www.gtlc.com | 37 cabins

"If this is roughing it, sign me up" say enthusiasts of this "charming and welcoming" "slice of heaven" in "spectacular" Grand Teton National Park, 13 miles north of the Jackson Hole Airport; rates for the "old-fashioned cabins" include "excellent" breakfasts and dinners ("locals go there just to eat, for a treat!"), but no phones or TVs – all the better to conserve energy for wildlife viewing, horseback riding and "walking into the valleys between the peaks."

Rusty Parrot Lodge 👥Ⓢ | 23 | 25 | 26 | 21 | $405 |

175 N. Jackson St. | Jackson | 307-733-2000 | fax 307-733-1422 | 800-458-2004 | www.rustyparrot.com | 30 rooms, 1 suite

"In a place one might not expect" (Downtown Jackson) lies this "elegant but not pretentious" Small Luxury Hotels member that satisfies siesta seekers with "pretty rooms", most harboring wood-burning fireplaces and homey touches ("love the teddy bears"); included in the rate are "perfect" Western-style breakfasts, and there's also a "great spa", "dancing at the cowboy bar" and an "excellent" staff that "couldn't be nicer."

Snake River Lodge & Spa 🚶Ⓢ🏊‍♂️   ▽ | 21 | 21 | 20 | 23 | $455 |

7710 Granite Loop Rd. | Teton Village | 307-732-6000 | fax 307-732-6009 | 866-975-7625 | www.snakeriverlodge.com | 93 rooms, 55 condos

A "fabulous location" in Teton Village that's "close to lots to do" keeps habitués hightailing it to this RockResorts lodging "with a real Western feel"; however, except for the "work-out facilities and spa, which are terrific", some hiss this "grand old dame is starting to show her age" (rooms are "fine but fairly standard") and the "dining leaves much to be desired."

Teton Mountain Lodge & Spa 🚶Ⓢ👥🎿 | - | - | - | - | $289 |

3385 Cody Ln. | Teton Village | 307-734-7111 | fax 307-734-6956 | 800-631-6271 | www.tetonlodge.com | 55 rooms, 62 suites, 28 studios

Rustic luxury is what this slopeside Jackson Hole ski resort is all about; the accommodations feature stone fireplaces, hardwood floors, luxury baths and custom kitchens (in some), while a new three-story, 12,000-sq.-ft. holistic spa offers private couples suites and a rooftop hot tub with panoramic views; thanks to trails for biking, hiking, dogsledding and snowmobiling, it's not just for downhill racers.

Yellowstone Nat'l Park

Old Faithful Inn ⊕

| 16 | 18 | 14 | 22 | $119 |

1 Grand Loop Rd. | Yellowstone National Park | 307-344-7901 | fax 307-344-7456 | 866-439-7375 | www.yellowstoneparknet.com | 329 rooms

"Forget everything else and go for the Yellowstone location and the history" of this "creaky" 1904 "national park treasure" that's akin to "camping out in a hotel" given the "rustic", "sparsely furnished rooms"; don't expect terrific accommodations or service at what some call "your grandpa's hotel" (both "could be nicer"), but it's the "best there is in the park" and just a "few steps from Old Faithful"; P.S. "bring a good book" because "after hiking" "there's nothing else to do."

INDEXES

Hotel Types

Indexes list the best in each category. Listings are arranged by state and are followed by nearest major city.

ALL-INCLUSIVE

ARIZONA
🆉 Canyon Ranch | *Tucson* — 24
Miraval Spa | *Tucson* — 24
Tanque Verde Ranch | *Tucson* — 20

CALIFORNIA
Alisal | *Santa Barbara* — 17
Cal-a-Vie | *San Diego* — -
Golden Door | *San Diego* — 24
Seven Gables Inn | *Carmel* — 24
Two Bunch | *Palm Springs* — 19

COLORADO
C Lazy U Ranch | *Denver* — 22
Home Ranch | *Clark* — -
Keyah Grande | *Pagosa Springs* — -

GEORGIA
Ldg./Little St. Simon | *GA Coast* — 23

HAWAII
Kona Village Resort | *Big Island* — 25

MASSACHUSETTS
🆉 Canyon Ranch | *Lenox* — 22

MICHIGAN
Grand Hotel | *Mackinac Is.* — 22

MONTANA
Triple Creek Ranch | *Darby* — 29

NEW HAMPSHIRE
Balsams | *Dixville Notch* — 19

NEW MEXICO
Taos Inn | *Taos* — 18

NEW YORK
Elk Lake Lodge | *Adirondacks* — -
🆉 Point | *Adirondacks* — 27

PENNSYLVANIA
Glendorn | *Bradford* — -
🆉 Lodge/Woodloch | *Hawley* — 23
Skytop Lodge | *Poconos* — 15

TENNESSEE
🆉 Blackberry Farm | *Walland* — 28

TEXAS
🆉 Lake Austin Spa | *Austin* — 25

UTAH
Sundance | *Salt Lake City* — 23

VERMONT
🆉 Twin Farms | *Woodstock* — 29

VIRGINIA
Tides Inn | *Irvington* — 22

WYOMING
Jenny Lake Ldg. | *Jackson Hole* — 22

BEACH RESORT

ALABAMA
Marriott | *Point Clear* — 21

CALIFORNIA
Bacara Resort | *Santa Barbara* — 26
Bernardus Lodge | *Carmel* — 26
Casa Del Mar | *LA* — 25
🆉 Casa Palmero | *Carmel* — 29
del Coronado | *San Diego* — 20
🆉 Four Seasons | *San Diego* — 27
Four Seasons | *Santa Barbara* — 26
🆉 NEW Grand/Mar | *San Diego* — 26
Half Moon/Lodge | *Half Moon Bay* — 23
Hilton La Jolla | *San Diego* — 20
Hyatt Resort | *OC Beaches* — 24
Lodge/Torrey Pines | *San Diego* — 25
Loews | *LA* — 20
Loews | *San Diego* — 21
Marriott | *OC Beaches* — 20
Marriott Coronado | *San Diego* — 23
🆉 Montage | *OC Beaches* — 27
Monterey Plaza | *Carmel* — 22
Ojai Valley Inn | *Santa Barbara* — 25
🆉 Post Ranch Inn | *Carmel* — 28
🆉 Ritz-Carlton | *OC Beaches* — 27
San Ysidro | *Santa Barbara* — 26
🆉 St. Regis | *OC Beaches* — 27
Surf/Sand | *OC Beaches* — 21
Westin | *Palm Springs* — 21

FLORIDA
🆉 Acqualina | *Miami* — 28
Amelia Is. Plant. | *NE Florida* — 22
Boca Raton | *Ft. Lauderdale* — 21
Breakers | *Palm Bch.* — 24
Casa Marina Resort | *Keys* — 21
Casa Ybel | *Ft. Myers* — 20

40,000 places to eat, drink, stay & play – free at ZAGAT.com

Cheeca Lodge	*Keys*	21
Colony Beach	*Sarasota*	18
Disney's Vero Beach	*Vero Bch.*	23
Don CeSar Bch.	*Tampa*	21
Doral Golf	*Miami*	19
Fairmont	*Miami*	26
Fisher Island	*Miami*	23
Fontainebleau	*Miami*	18
Ginn Hammock	*Palm Coast*	–
Hawk's Cay Resort	*Keys*	21
Hilton	*Ft. Lauderdale*	21
Hyatt	*Keys*	23
Hyatt	*Naples*	25
Jupiter Beach	*Palm Bch.*	20
Lago Mar Resort	*Ft. Lauderdale*	20
La Playa Beach/Resort	*Naples*	22
✑ Little Palm Island	*Keys*	27
Loews	*Miami*	21
Longboat Key Club	*Sarasota*	22
Marco Beach Resort	*Naples*	24
Marco Is. Marriott	*Naples*	22
Marriott	*Ft. Lauderdale*	21
Naples Grande	*Naples*	24
PGA National	*Palm Bch.*	17
Pier Hse. Resort	*Keys*	20
Ponte Vedra Inn	*NE Florida*	25
NEW Regent Bal Harbour	*Miami*	–
Renaissance	*Tampa*	24
✑ Ritz-Carlton	*Naples*	27
✑ Ritz-Carlton	*NE Florida*	26
Ritz-Carlton	*Palm Bch.*	26
Ritz-Carlton	*Sarasota*	26
Ritz-Carlton Key Bisc.	*Miami*	24
Ritz-Carlton S. Bch.	*Miami*	25
Sanibel Resort	*Ft. Myers*	21
South Seas Resort	*Ft. Myers*	21
Sunset Key/Cottages	*Keys*	26
Westin	*Ft. Lauderdale*	24

GEORGIA

✑ Cloister	*GA Coast*	27
Jekyll Is. Club	*GA Coast*	21
✑ Lodge/Sea Is.	*GA Coast*	28

HAWAII

Fairmont	*Big Island*	25
Fairmont	*Maui*	27
Four Seasons/Manele	*Lanai*	27
✑ Four Seasons Resort	*Big Island*	29
✑ Four Seasons Resort	*Maui*	28
Grand Hyatt	*Kauai*	24
Grand Wailea	*Maui*	24
Halekulani	*Oahu*	25

Hanalei Bay Resort	*Kauai*	20
Hapuna Bch. Prince	*Big Island*	23
Hilton Kauai	*Kauai*	21
Hilton Hawaiian Vill.	*Oahu*	20
Hilton Waikoloa Vill.	*Big Island*	21
Hyatt	*Maui*	22
JW Marriott	*Oahu*	26
Kahala	*Oahu*	25
Kapalua Villas	*Maui*	23
Kauai Marriott	*Kauai*	21
Kona Village Resort	*Big Island*	25
Maui Prince	*Maui*	19
Mauna Lani Resort	*Big Island*	24
Moana Surfrider	*Oahu*	21
✑ Ritz-Carlton	*Maui*	25
Sheraton	*Maui*	22
Turtle Bay Resort	*Oahu*	21
Westin	*Maui*	22

MAINE

NEW Hidden Pond	*S. Coast*	–
Inn by the Sea	*Portland*	21
Samoset	*Rockport*	19

MARYLAND

Hyatt	*Eastern Shore*	21

MASSACHUSETTS

Chatham Bars	*Cape Cod/Is.*	22
Ocean Edge	*Cape Cod/Is.*	21
Wequassett	*Cape Cod/Is.*	21

MICHIGAN

Grand Hotel	*Mackinac Is.*	22

NEW JERSEY

Atlantic City Hilton	*Atlantic City*	18
Harrah's Resort	*Atlantic City*	21

NEW YORK

Gurney's Inn	*Long Island*	17

OREGON

Salishan Spa	*Gleneden Bch.*	24

PUERTO RICO

El Conquistador	*Fajardo*	21
El San Juan	*San Juan*	20
Las Casitas Village	*Fajardo*	26
Rio Mar Beach	*San Juan*	22
Ritz-Carlton	*San Juan*	24

SOUTH CAROLINA

Marriott	*Hilton Head*	21
Myrtle/Marriott	*Myrtle Bch.*	24
Sea Pines Resort	*Hilton Head*	22
Westin	*Hilton Head*	21
Wild Dunes Resort	*Charleston*	21

U.S. VIRGIN ISLANDS

Buccaneer | *St. Croix*	23
Caneel Bay | *St. John*	23
Ritz-Carlton | *St. Thomas*	25
Westin | *St. John*	21

VERMONT

Basin Harbor | *Lake Champlain*	19

VIRGINIA

Tides Inn | *Irvington*	22

WISCONSIN

Grand Geneva | *Lake Geneva*	19

BED & BREAKFAST/ INN

ARIZONA

Arizona Inn | *Tucson*	23
Hacienda del Sol | *Tucson*	19
Hermosa Inn | *Phoenix/Scott.*	22
L'Auberge/Sedona | *Sedona*	23

CALIFORNIA

Albion River | *N. CA Coast*	24
Applewood | *Wine Co.*	19
☑ Auberge/Soleil | *Wine Co.*	28
Carneros Inn | *Wine Co.*	28
Deetjen's | *Carmel*	15
Fess Parker | *Santa Barbara*	21
Gaige House Inn | *Wine Co.*	28
Green Gables | *Carmel*	24
Harvest Inn | *Wine Co.*	23
Inn Above Tide | *SF*	26
Inn/Southbridge | *Wine Co.*	20
Inn/Spanish Gdn. | *Santa Barbara*	26
Inn/Rancho Santa Fe | *San Diego*	21
Kenwood Inn | *Wine Co.*	26
☑ L'Auberge Carmel | *Carmel*	25
Madrona Manor | *Wine Co.*	23
Maison Fleurie | *Wine Co.*	18
Malibu Beach Inn | *LA*	20
Milliken Creek Inn | *Wine Co.*	26
Mission Ranch | *Carmel*	21
Napa River Inn | *Wine Co.*	22
Petite Auberge | *SF*	20
Seven Gables Inn | *Carmel*	24
Simpson Hse. | *Santa Barbara*	25
Spindrift Inn | *Carmel*	23
St. Orres | *N. CA Coast*	–
Tickle Pink Inn | *Carmel*	24
Villagio Inn | *Wine Co.*	24
Vintage Inn | *Wine Co.*	23
Vintners Inn | *Wine Co.*	25

Whale Watch | *N. CA Coast*	24
White Swan Inn | *SF*	22

COLORADO

Cliff House/Pikes | *CO Springs*	–

CONNECTICUT

Boulders | *New Preston*	20
Homestead Inn | *Greenwich*	21
Inn/National Hall | *Westport*	27
Mayflower Inn | *Washington*	27
Saybrook Point | *Old Saybrook*	21

DELAWARE

Inn/Montchanin | *Wilmington*	26

DISTRICT OF COLUMBIA

Tabard Inn | *DC*	16

FLORIDA

Chalet Suzanne | *Tampa*	16
WaterColor Inn | *Panhandle*	27

GEORGIA

Ballastone | *Savannah*	26

LOUISIANA

Nottoway | *White Castle*	24

MAINE

Breakwater Inn | *S. Coast*	20
Captain Lord | *S. Coast*	27
Cliff House | *S. Coast*	20
Harraseeket Inn | *Freeport*	20
Inn by the Sea | *Portland*	21
☑ White Barn Inn | *S. Coast*	25

MARYLAND

Antrim 1844 | *Baltimore*	24
Inn/Perry Cabin | *Eastern Shore*	25

MASSACHUSETTS

Charlotte Inn | *Cape Cod/Is.*	23
Chatham Bars | *Cape Cod/Is.*	22
Jacob Hill Inn | *Boston*	28
Jared Coffin Hse. | *Cape Cod/Is.*	21
Wauwinet | *Cape Cod/Is.*	25
Wequassett | *Cape Cod/Is.*	21
White Elephant | *Cape Cod/Is.*	23

NEW JERSEY

Bernards | *Bernardsville*	20
Queen Victoria | *Cape May*	22

NEW MEXICO

Inn of the Anasazi | *Santa Fe*	24
Inn on the Alameda | *Santa Fe*	22
Taos Inn | *Taos*	18

NEW YORK

Beekman Arms | *Hudson Valley* — 18
Elk Lake Lodge | *Adirondacks* — ⌐
Friends Lake Inn | *Adirondacks* — 22
Inn at Irving Pl. | *NYC* — 24
Maidstone Arms | *Long Island* — 18
Mill House Inn | *Long Island* — 24
Mirror Lake Inn | *Adirondacks* — 23
Ram's Head Inn | *Long Island* — 16
Troutbeck Estate | *Amenia* — 18

NORTH CAROLINA

Fearrington Hse. | *Pittsboro* — 24
Greystone Inn | *Asheville* — 24
Inn on Biltmore | *Asheville* — 25
Richmond Hill | *Asheville* — 23

OREGON

Columbia Gorge | *Hood River* — 20
Stephanie Inn | *Cannon Bch.* — 27
Z Tu Tu' Tun Lodge | *Gold Bch.* — 26

PENNSYLVANIA

Hilton Inn | *Philadelphia* — 19

RHODE ISLAND

Castle Hill Inn | *Newport* — 23
Francis Malbone | *Newport* — 25
1661 Inn | *Block Is.* — ⌐

SOUTH CAROLINA

Inn/Middleton Pl. | *Charleston* — ⌐
Planters Inn | *Charleston* — 22
Wentworth Mansion | *Charleston* — 27

TEXAS

Inn/Dos Brisas | *Washington* — ⌐

UTAH

Goldener Hirsch Inn | *Park City* — 21

VERMONT

Green Mtn. Inn | *Stowe* — 22
Inn/Essex | *Lake Champlain* — 21
Inn/Sawmill | *S. VT* — 22
Inn/Shelburne | *Lake Champlain* — 22
Old Tavern/Grafton | *S. VT* — 21
Pitcher Inn | *Central Vermont* — 25

VIRGINIA

Clifton Inn | *Charlottesville* — 21
Goodstone Inn | *DC Metro* — ⌐
Z Inn/Little Wash. | *Washington* — 28
L'Auberge Provençale | *White Post* — 23
Williams. Colonial | *Williamsburg* — 23

WASHINGTON

Z Inn at Langley | *Seattle* — 25
Inn at the Market | *Seattle* — 23
Z Willows Lodge | *Seattle* — 27

WISCONSIN

Canoe Bay | *Chetek* — 28

WYOMING

Old Faithful Inn | *Yellowstone* — 16

BOUTIQUE

ARIZONA

Hacienda del Sol | *Tucson* — 19
Valley Ho | *Phoenix/Scott.* — 24

CALIFORNIA

Avalon | *LA* — 18
Z Bel-Air | *LA* — 27
Campton Pl. | *SF* — 24
Z Château du Sureau | *Yosemite* — 27
Chateau Marmont | *LA* — 21
Clift | *SF* — 20
Garden Court | *SF* — 24
Grafton on Sunset | *LA* — 19
Healdsburg | *Wine Co.* — 24
Hollywood Roosevelt | *LA* — 17
Huntington | *SF* — 21
Inn Above Tide | *SF* — 26
Inn Marin | *SF* — ⌐
Inn/Rancho Santa Fe | *San Diego* — 21
NEW Ivy | *San Diego* — 24
Kabuki | *SF* — 20
La Playa | *Carmel* — 18
L'Auberge Del Mar | *San Diego* — 23
La Valencia | *San Diego* — 22
Monaco | *SF* — 20
Mondrian | *LA* — 19
Mosaic | *LA* — 23
NEW Nick's Cove | *N. CA Coast* — 25
Orchard | *SF* — 22
NEW Palomar | *LA* — ⌐
Palomar | *SF* — 22
Petite Auberge | *SF* — 20
Serrano | *SF* — 18
Solamar | *San Diego* — 26
Standard | *LA* — 16
Standard Downtown | *LA* — 19
Stanford Ct. | *SF* — 21
Sunset Tower | *LA* — 21
Upham | *Santa Barbara* — 20
Viceroy | *LA* — 21
Viceroy | *Palm Springs* — 21
Vitale | *SF* — 25

White Swan Inn | *SF*	22
W San Francisco | *SF*	23
W Westwood | *LA*	22

COLORADO

Boulderado | *Denver*	19
Cliff House/Pikes | *CO Springs*	-
Curtis | *Denver*	-
Jerome | *Aspen*	22
Keyah Grande | *Pagosa Springs*	-
Loews | *Denver*	21
Monaco | *Denver*	22
St Julien | *Denver*	26
Teatro | *Denver*	24

CONNECTICUT

Homestead Inn | *Greenwich*	21

DISTRICT OF COLUMBIA

George | *DC*	21
Helix | *DC*	23
Madera | *DC*	20
Monaco | *DC*	20
Topaz | *DC*	21

FLORIDA

Brazilian Court | *Palm Bch.*	23
Casa Monica | *NE Florida*	23
Celebration | *Orlando*	21
Chesterfield | *Palm Bch.*	20
Delano | *Miami*	21
NEW Gansevoort South | *Miami*	26
Grove Isle | *Miami*	26
Hilton Bentley Bch. | *Miami*	21
Hotel, The | *Miami*	19
Marquesa | *Keys*	25
Mayfair | *Miami*	23
National | *Miami*	18
Raleigh | *Miami*	19
Setai | *Miami*	26
Shore Club | *Miami*	16
Tides | *Miami*	26
Townhouse | *Miami*	22
Victor | *Miami*	22

GEORGIA

Ldg./Little St. Simon | *GA Coast*	23
Mansion/Forsyth | *Savannah*	26
NEW Mansion/Peachtree | *Atlanta*	-
W Atlanta Perimeter | *Atlanta*	21

HAWAII

Sheraton | *Kauai*	20

ILLINOIS

Burnham | *Chicago*	25
Drake | *Chicago*	20
James | *Chicago*	24
Monaco | *Chicago*	21
Park Hyatt | *Chicago*	27
Sutton Place | *Chicago*	23
Whitehall | *Chicago*	20

IOWA

Vetro | *Iowa City*	-

LOUISIANA

Bourbon Orleans | *New Orleans*	18
Maison Dupuy | *New Orleans*	22
Soniat House | *New Orleans*	26
W French Quarter | *New Orleans*	23

MARYLAND

Inn/Perry Cabin | *Eastern Shore*	25

MASSACHUSETTS

☑ Blantyre | *Lenox*	26
Eliot | *Boston*	23
Fifteen Beacon | *Boston*	24
Lenox | *Boston*	19
Marlowe | *Boston*	23
Nine Zero | *Boston*	23
☑ Wheatleigh | *Lenox*	26

MICHIGAN

Townsend | *Detroit*	24

MINNESOTA

Chambers | *Mpls./St. Paul*	25
Grand Hotel | *Mpls./St. Paul*	24

NEBRASKA

NEW Omaha Magnolia | *Omaha*	-

NEVADA

Hard Rock | *Las Vegas*	20

NEW HAMPSHIRE

Manor/Golden Pond | *White Mtns.*	-

NEW JERSEY

NEW Chelsea | *Atlantic City*	-
Congress Hall | *Cape May*	19

NEW MEXICO

NEW Encantado | *Santa Fe*	-

NEW YORK

Alex | *NYC*	21
Algonquin | *NYC*	16
American | *Long Island*	17
Benjamin | *NYC*	21
Blue Moon | *NYC*	-
NEW Bowery | *NYC*	21
Bryant Park | *NYC*	22

Carlton	*NYC*	20
Castle/Hudson	*Westchester*	23
Chambers	*NYC*	21
Elysée	*NYC*	22
Gansevoort	*NYC*	20
NEW Gild Hall	*NYC*	-
Gramercy Park	*NYC*	22
Hotel/Rivington	*NYC*	23
Iroquois	*NYC*	21
Library	*NYC*	21
Z Lowell	*NYC*	25
Mansfield	*NYC*	14
Maritime	*NYC*	17
Mercer	*NYC*	23
Michelangelo	*NYC*	24
Muse	*NYC*	23
Night	*NYC*	16
Plaza Athénée	*NYC*	22
NEW Ravel	*NYC*	-
Royalton	*NYC*	20
Sherry-Netherland	*NYC*	24
Shoreham	*NYC*	21
NEW Six Columbus	*NYC*	-
60 Thompson	*NYC*	20
Soho Grand	*NYC*	19
Tribeca Grand	*NYC*	20
Wales	*NYC*	18
W New York	*NYC*	14

NORTH CAROLINA

Siena	*Durham*	24

OHIO

Blackwell	*Columbus*	23

OREGON

Benson	*Portland*	20
Columbia Gorge	*Hood River*	20
Heathman	*Portland*	20
Lucia	*Portland*	19
Monaco	*Portland*	22
RiverPlace	*Portland*	27

PENNSYLVANIA

Z Rittenhouse	*Philadelphia*	26
Sofitel	*Philadelphia*	24

PUERTO RICO

Bravo Beach	*Vieques*	-
El Convento	*San Juan*	21
Z Horned Dorset	*Rincon*	26
Water & Beach Club	*San Juan*	18

SOUTH CAROLINA

Mills House	*Charleston*	20
Planters Inn	*Charleston*	22

TENNESSEE

Madison	*Memphis*	22

TEXAS

Ashton	*DFW*	25
Derek	*Houston*	22
NEW Joule	*DFW*	-
Lancaster	*Houston*	18
NEW NYLO Plano	*DFW*	-
Palomar	*DFW*	25
Z Rosewood	*DFW*	26
Valencia Riverwalk	*San Antonio*	26
Zaza	*DFW*	26

UTAH

Monaco	*Salt Lake City*	21

VERMONT

Reluctant Panther	*S. VT*	27

VIRGINIA

Z Keswick Hall	*Charlottesville*	26
Morrison Hse.	*DC Metro*	23

WASHINGTON

Alexis	*Seattle*	21
Andra	*Seattle*	23
Bellevue Club	*Seattle*	24
Davenport	*Spokane*	28
Edgewater	*Seattle*	22
Inn at the Market	*Seattle*	23
Mayflower Park	*Seattle*	21
Monaco	*Seattle*	22
NEW Murano	*Tacoma*	-
1000	*Seattle*	26
Sorrento	*Seattle*	23
Watertown	*Seattle*	-

WYOMING

Rusty Parrot	*Jackson Hole*	23

BUSINESS-ORIENTED

CALIFORNIA

Hilton Checkers	*LA*	19
Marriott Marina	*San Diego*	19
Millennium Biltmore	*LA*	17
Omni	*LA*	20
Z Peninsula	*LA*	27
Renaissance	*LA*	22
Sofitel	*SF*	21
W Westwood	*LA*	22

DELAWARE

du Pont	*Wilmington*	24

DISTRICT OF COLUMBIA

Fairmont	*DC*	23
Z Four Seasons	*DC*	26

HOTEL TYPES

Hay-Adams	DC	24
JW Marriott	DC	21
Mandarin Oriental	DC	27
Park Hyatt	DC	24
Ritz-Carlton	DC	26
Z Ritz-Carlton Georgetown	DC	27

FLORIDA
| Conrad | Miami | 23 |
| JW Marriott | Miami | 22 |

GEORGIA
| Hilton | Atlanta | 19 |
| InterContinental | Atlanta | 26 |

ILLINOIS
Conrad	Chicago	26
Drake	Chicago	20
Embassy Suites	Chicago	21
Fairmont	Chicago	23
Z Four Seasons	Chicago	27
Hilton Suites	Chicago	22
Palmer Hse. Hilton	Chicago	19
Park Hyatt	Chicago	27
Z Peninsula	Chicago	29
Ritz-Carlton	Chicago	26

KANSAS
| Sheraton | Overland Park | 19 |

LOUISIANA
Hilton Riverside	New Orleans	19
JW Marriott	New Orleans	19
Le Pavillon	New Orleans	19
Loews	New Orleans	26
Monteleone	New Orleans	22
Omni	New Orleans	21
Ritz-Carlton	New Orleans	25
Royal Sonesta	New Orleans	20
Z Windsor Court	New Orleans	24

MARYLAND
NEW Gaylord Nat'l	Baltimore	-
NEW Hilton	Baltimore	-
Marriott	Baltimore	23

MASSACHUSETTS
NEW Le Méridien Cambridge	Boston	22
NEW Liberty	Boston	24
Westin Boston Water.	Boston	22

MINNESOTA
| Marquette | Mpls./St. Paul | 24 |

NEVADA
| Z Bellagio | Las Vegas | 26 |

Caesars	Las Vegas	22
Z Four Seasons	Las Vegas	27
MGM Grand	Las Vegas	19
Mirage	Las Vegas	19
Z Wynn	Las Vegas	28

NEW JERSEY
| Hilton | Short Hills | 22 |

NEW MEXICO
| Eldorado | Santa Fe | 22 |

NEW YORK
NEW Duane Street	NYC	-
Embassy Suites	NYC	22
Z Four Seasons	NYC	28
Kitano	NYC	22
Loews Regency	NYC	23
Millenium Hilton	NYC	21
NY Marriott Downtown	NYC	19
Ritz-Carlton Central Pk.	NYC	27
Waldorf=Astoria	NYC	21

OHIO
| Hilton Cincinnati | Cincinnati | 16 |

PENNSYLVANIA
| Park Hyatt | Philadelphia | 22 |

TEXAS
Driskill	Austin	23
Fairmont	DFW	22
Four Seasons	Houston	25
Hilton	Austin	20
Hilton Americas	Houston	21
Hilton Anatole	DFW	20
JW Marriott	Houston	20
Z Ritz-Carlton	DFW	28

UTAH
| Grand America | Salt Lake City | 27 |

WASHINGTON
Fairmont	Seattle	23
NEW Four Seasons	Seattle	-
Grand Hyatt	Seattle	27
Sheraton	Seattle	20

CONDOMINIUM

CALIFORNIA
| Silverado Resort | Wine Co. | 18 |

FLORIDA
Atlantic Resort	Ft. Lauderdale	26
Casa Ybel	Ft. Myers	20
Conrad	Miami	23

Fisher Island	*Miami*	23
Ginn Hammock	*Palm Coast*	-

HAWAII

Hanalei Bay Resort	*Kauai*	20
Kapalua Villas	*Maui*	23

IDAHO

Sun Valley Resort	*Sun Valley*	21

MASSACHUSETTS

Four Seasons	*Boston*	27

NEW YORK

Elk Lake Lodge	*Adirondacks*	-
Whiteface Lodge	*Adirondacks*	23

SOUTH CAROLINA

Sea Pines Resort	*Hilton Head*	22

WYOMING

☑ Four Seasons	*Jackson Hole*	27

CONVENTION

ALABAMA

Renaissance	*Birmingham*	25

ARIZONA

Hilton El Conquistador	*Tucson*	19
Hyatt	*Phoenix/Scott.*	21
Phoenician	*Phoenix/Scott.*	26
Ritz-Carlton	*Phoenix/Scott.*	22
Westin	*Tucson*	22

CALIFORNIA

Fairmont	*SF*	22
Hilton La Jolla	*San Diego*	20
Loews	*LA*	20
Loews	*San Diego*	21
MacArthur Pl.	*Wine Co.*	25
Manchester Gr. Hyatt	*San Diego*	22
Mark Hopkins	*SF*	22
Nikko	*SF*	22
Omni	*SF*	22
Resort/Squaw Creek	*Lake Tahoe*	22
Ritz-Carlton	*LA*	24
Stanford Ct.	*SF*	21
Westin St. Francis	*SF*	20

COLORADO

☑ Broadmoor	*CO Springs*	26
C Lazy U Ranch	*Denver*	22
Denver Marriott	*Denver*	19
Westin	*Denver*	21

CONNECTICUT

Foxwoods Resort	*Ledyard*	20

DELAWARE

du Pont	*Wilmington*	24

DISTRICT OF COLUMBIA

Fairmont	*DC*	23
Renaissance	*DC*	21
Willard InterCont.	*DC*	24

FLORIDA

Biltmore	*Miami*	23
Boca Raton	*Ft. Lauderdale*	21
Don CeSar Bch.	*Tampa*	21
Gaylord Palms	*Orlando*	22
Hyatt	*Orlando*	21
International Plaza	*Orlando*	-
Loews	*Miami*	21
Loews Portofino	*Orlando*	24
Loews Royal Pacific	*Orlando*	20
Marco Is. Marriott	*Naples*	22
Marriott	*Orlando*	20
Peabody	*Orlando*	21
☑ Ritz-Carlton	*Orlando*	27
Ritz-Carlton	*Sarasota*	26
Rosen Shingle	*Orlando*	23
Walt Disney Dolphin	*Orlando*	19
Walt Disney Swan	*Orlando*	21
Westin	*Ft. Lauderdale*	24

GEORGIA

Hyatt	*Atlanta*	20
InterContinental	*Atlanta*	26
Ritz-Carlton Buckhead	*Atlanta*	24

HAWAII

Grand Hyatt	*Kauai*	24
Hilton Hawaiian Vill.	*Oahu*	20
Hilton Waikoloa Vill.	*Big Island*	21
Hyatt	*Maui*	22
Hyatt	*Oahu*	20
Marriott	*Oahu*	21
☑ Ritz-Carlton	*Maui*	25
Sheraton	*Maui*	22
Sheraton	*Oahu*	19

ILLINOIS

Fairmont	*Chicago*	23
InterContinental	*Chicago*	22
Westin	*Chicago*	22

INDIANA

Westin	*Indianapolis*	20

IOWA

Vetro	*Iowa City*	-

KANSAS

Sheraton | *Overland Park* — 19

LOUISIANA

Hilton Riverside | *New Orleans* — 19
InterContinental | *New Orleans* — 23
Marriott | *New Orleans* — 18
Renaissance | *New Orleans* — -
Westin | *New Orleans* — 21
W New Orleans | *New Orleans* — 23
Wyndham | *New Orleans* — 23

MAINE

Samoset | *Rockport* — 19

MARYLAND

NEW Hilton | *Baltimore* — -
Hyatt | *Baltimore* — 22
Marriott | *Baltimore* — 23

MASSACHUSETTS

Boston Marriott | *Boston* — 20
Taj | *Boston* — 22
Westin Copley | *Boston* — 22

MICHIGAN

Westin | *Detroit* — 24

MISSOURI

Chase Park Plaza | *St. Louis* — 22
Renaissance | *St. Louis* — 23
Ritz-Carlton | *St. Louis* — 24

NEVADA

JW Marriott | *Las Vegas* — 27
Loews | *Las Vegas* — 22
MGM Grand | *Las Vegas* — 19
Paris Las Vegas | *Las Vegas* — 20
Venetian | *Las Vegas* — 27

NEW JERSEY

Caesars | *Atlantic City* — 18

NEW YORK

InterContinental | *NYC* — 20
🅩 Mandarin Oriental | *NYC* — 28
Marriott | *NYC* — 20
Waldorf=Astoria | *NYC* — 21

NORTH CAROLINA

Westin | *Charlotte* — 23

OHIO

Ritz-Carlton | *Cleveland* — 24

OREGON

Westin | *Portland* — 21

PENNSYLVANIA

Loews | *Philadelphia* — 23
Omni | *Pittsburgh* — 22
Westin | *Philadelphia* — 23

PUERTO RICO

Rio Mar Beach | *San Juan* — 22

RHODE ISLAND

Westin | *Providence* — 23

SOUTH CAROLINA

Myrtle/Marriott | *Myrtle Bch.* — 24
Sea Pines Resort | *Hilton Head* — 22
Westin | *Hilton Head* — 21

TENNESSEE

Gaylord Opryland | *Nashville* — 19

TEXAS

Hilton | *Austin* — 20
Hilton Americas | *Houston* — 21
Hilton Anatole | *DFW* — 20
JW Marriott | *Houston* — 20
Renaissance | *Austin* — 20

UTAH

Grand America | *Salt Lake City* — 27
Little America | *Salt Lake City* — 20
Snowbird | *Salt Lake City* — 17

VERMONT

Basin Harbor | *Lake Champlain* — 19

VIRGINIA

Homestead | *Hot Springs* — 21
Lansdowne | *DC Metro* — 20
Ritz-Carlton Pentagon | *DC Metro* — 25
Ritz-Carlton Tysons | *DC Metro* — 25

WASHINGTON

Sheraton | *Seattle* — 20
Westin | *Seattle* — 23
Westin Bellevue | *Seattle* — 26

COTTAGES/VILLAS

ARIZONA

🅩 Boulders | *Phoenix/Scott.* — 26
Hermosa Inn | *Phoenix/Scott.* — 22
L'Auberge/Sedona | *Sedona* — 23
Los Abrigados | *Sedona* — 22
Royal Palms | *Phoenix/Scott.* — 24

CALIFORNIA

Ahwahnee | *Yosemite* — 20
Cal-a-Vie | *San Diego* — -
Calistoga Ranch | *Wine Co.* — 26

Carneros Inn | *Wine Co.* 28
Casa Madrona | *SF* 23
🅉 Château du Sureau | *Yosemite* 27
Chateau Marmont | *LA* 21
Hyatt | *Palm Springs* 22
La Costa Resort | *San Diego* 22
La Playa | *Carmel* 18
La Valencia | *San Diego* 22
Le Parker Méridien | 22
  Palm Springs
MacArthur Pl. | *Wine Co.* 25
Mission Ranch | *Carmel* 21
🆕 Nick's Cove | *N. CA Coast* 25
🅉 Peninsula | *LA* 27
🅉 Post Ranch Inn | *Carmel* 28
Quail Lodge | *Carmel* 23
San Ysidro | *Santa Barbara* 26
Simpson Hse. | *Santa Barbara* 25
St. Orres | *N. CA Coast* -
Tickle Pink Inn | *Carmel* 24
Two Bunch | *Palm Springs* 19
Upham | *Santa Barbara* 20
Ventana Inn | *Carmel* 25
Viceroy | *Palm Springs* 21

CONNECTICUT
Spa/Norwich Inn | *Norwich* 20
Winvian | *New Preston* -

DELAWARE
Bellmoor | *Rehoboth Bch.* 25

FLORIDA
Amelia Is. Plant. | *NE Florida* 22
Cheeca Lodge | *Keys* 21
🅉 Disney's Bch. Club Villas | 27
  Orlando
🅉 Disney's BoardWalk Villas | 27
  Orlando
Disney's Old Key W. | *Orlando* 25
Disney's Saratoga | *Orlando* 27
Fisher Island | *Miami* 23
Hawk's Cay Resort | *Keys* 21
PGA National | *Palm Bch.* 17
South Seas Resort | *Ft. Myers* 21
Sunset Key/Cottages | *Keys* 26
Villas/Grand Cypress | *Orlando* 26
WaterColor Inn | *Panhandle* 27

GEORGIA
Château Élan | *Braselton* 23
🅉 Ritz-Carlton | *Lake Oconee* 26

HAWAII
Fairmont | *Maui* 27
🅉 Four Seasons Resort | *Big Island* 29

Hana-Maui | *Maui* 27
Kapalua Villas | *Maui* 23
Turtle Bay Resort | *Oahu* 21

LOUISIANA
Maison Dupuy | *New Orleans* 22
Soniat House | *New Orleans* 26

MAINE
🆕 Hidden Pond | *S. Coast* -
🅉 White Barn Inn | *S. Coast* 25

MASSACHUSETTS
🅉 Blantyre | *Lenox* 26
Ocean Edge | *Cape Cod/Is.* 21
White Elephant | *Cape Cod/Is.* 23

NEVADA
Hyatt | *Incline Vill.* 21
MGM Grand | *Las Vegas* 19

NEW HAMPSHIRE
Manor/Golden Pond | *White Mtns.* -

NEW YORK
Elk Lake Lodge | *Adirondacks* -
Gurney's Inn | *Long Island* 17
Maidstone Arms | *Long Island* 18
🅉 Mirbeau Inn | *Catskills* 27
Mohonk Mtn. Hse. | *Catskills* 18

NORTH CAROLINA
Pinehurst Resort | *Pinehurst* 20

PUERTO RICO
Bravo Beach | *Vieques* -
🅉 Horned Dorset | *Rincon* 26
Las Casitas Village | *Fajardo* 26

SOUTH CAROLINA
Inn/Palmetto | *Hilton Head* 29
Sea Pines Resort | *Hilton Head* 22
Wild Dunes Resort | *Charleston* 21
🅉 Woodlands | *Charleston* 26

TENNESSEE
🅉 Blackberry Farm | *Walland* 28

U.S. VIRGIN ISLANDS
Buccaneer | *St. Croix* 23
Caneel Bay | *St. John* 23
Westin | *St. John* 21

VERMONT
Basin Harbor | *Lake Champlain* 19
Inn/Sawmill | *S. VT* 22
Inn/Shelburne | *Lake Champlain* 22
Trapp | *Stowe* 19
🅉 Twin Farms | *Woodstock* 29

VIRGINIA
Clifton Inn | *Charlottesville* 21

WASHINGTON
🔲 Inn at Langley | *Seattle* 25

WEST VIRGINIA
🔲 Greenbrier | 25
  White Sulphur Springs

WISCONSIN
Canoe Bay | *Chetek* 28

WYOMING
Jackson Lake Ldg. | *Jackson Hole* 19

DESTINATION & RESORT SPA

ARIZONA
🔲 Canyon Ranch | *Tucson* 24
Miraval Spa | *Tucson* 24
Phoenician | *Phoenix/Scott.* 26
🔲 Sanctuary | *Phoenix/Scott.* 26

CALIFORNIA
Bacara Resort | *Santa Barbara* 26
Cal-a-Vie | *San Diego* -
Golden Door | *San Diego* 24
La Costa Resort | *San Diego* 22
L'Auberge Del Mar | *San Diego* 23
Milliken Creek Inn | *Wine Co.* 26
Miramonte | *Palm Springs* 23
🔲 Montage | *OC Beaches* 27
🔲 St. Regis | *OC Beaches* 27
Two Bunch | *Palm Springs* 19

COLORADO
Lodge/Cordillera | *Beaver Creek* 25

CONNECTICUT
Hyatt | *Greenwich* 18
Saybrook Point | *Old Saybrook* 21
Spa/Norwich Inn | *Norwich* 20

FLORIDA
Boca Raton | *Ft. Lauderdale* 21
Buena Vista Palace | *Orlando* 20
Jupiter Beach | *Palm Bch.* 20

HAWAII
🔲 Four Seasons Resort | *Big Island* 29
🔲 Four Seasons Resort | *Maui* 28
Grand Wailea | *Maui* 24

IDAHO
Coeur d'Alene | *Coeur d'Alene* 25

LOUISIANA
Iberville Suites | *New Orleans* 20

MASSACHUSETTS
🔲 Canyon Ranch | *Lenox* 22

NEW JERSEY
Seaview | *Atlantic City* 19

NEW MEXICO
El Monte Sagrado | *Taos* 25

NEW YORK
Gurney's Inn | *Long Island* 17
🔲 Mirbeau Inn | *Catskills* 27

PENNSYLVANIA
Nemacolin | *Farmington* 25

PUERTO RICO
Las Casitas Village | *Fajardo* 26

TEXAS
🔲 Lake Austin Spa | *Austin* 25

WEST VIRGINIA
🔲 Greenbrier | 25
  White Sulphur Springs

WYOMING
Snake River Ldg. | *Jackson Hole* 21

GOLF RESORT

ALABAMA
Marriott | *Point Clear* 21
Renaissance | *Birmingham* 25

ARIZONA
Arizona Biltmore | *Phoenix/Scott.* 23
Arizona Grand | *Phoenix/Scott.* 19
🔲 Boulders | *Phoenix/Scott.* 26
Fairmont | *Phoenix/Scott.* 25
Hilton | *Sedona* 23
Hilton El Conquistador | *Tucson* 19
Hyatt | *Phoenix/Scott.* 21
JW Marriott | *Tucson* 25
JW Marriott Camelback | 23
  Phoenix/Scott.
JW Marriott Desert | 24
  Phoenix/Scott.
Ldg./Ventana Canyon | *Tucson* 22
Loews | *Tucson* 24
Phoenician | *Phoenix/Scott.* 26
Pointe Hilton Squaw | 19
  Phoenix/Scott.
Pointe Hilton Tapatio | 19
  Phoenix/Scott.
Sheraton | *Phoenix/Scott.* 23

Westin | *Phoenix/Scott.*	24
Westin | *Tucson*	22
Wigwam Golf | *Phoenix/Scott.*	24

CALIFORNIA

Alisal | *Santa Barbara*	17
Bacara Resort | *Santa Barbara*	26
Barona Valley Ranch | *San Diego*	19
Cal-a-Vie | *San Diego*	–
Carmel Valley Ranch | *Carmel*	23
🄩 Casa Palmero | *Carmel*	29
Desert Springs | *Palm Springs*	21
Fairmont | *Wine Co.*	21
🄩 Four Seasons | *San Diego*	27
🄩 NEW Grand/Mar | *San Diego*	26
Hilton La Jolla | *San Diego*	20
Hyatt | *Palm Springs*	22
Inn/Spanish Bay | *Carmel*	26
La Costa Resort | *San Diego*	22
La Quinta | *Palm Springs*	22
🄩 Lodge/Pebble Bch. | *Carmel*	26
Lodge/Torrey Pines | *San Diego*	25
Ojai Valley Inn | *Santa Barbara*	25
Quail Lodge | *Carmel*	23
Rancho Bernardo | *San Diego*	21
Renaissance | *Palm Springs*	21
Resort/Squaw Creek | *Lake Tahoe*	22
Silverado Resort | *Wine Co.*	18
🄩 St. Regis | *OC Beaches*	27
Westin | *Palm Springs*	21

COLORADO

🄩 Broadmoor | *CO Springs*	26
Keystone Resort | *Keystone*	20
Lodge/Cordillera | *Beaver Creek*	25
Park Hyatt | *Beaver Creek*	23
Peaks Resort | *Telluride*	20
Sonnenalp | *Vail*	27

CONNECTICUT

Foxwoods Resort | *Ledyard*	20
NEW MGM Grand | *Ledyard*	–

FLORIDA

Amelia Is. Plant. | *NE Florida*	22
Boca Raton | *Ft. Lauderdale*	21
Breakers | *Palm Bch.*	24
Disney's Saratoga | *Orlando*	27
Doral Golf | *Miami*	19
Fairmont | *Miami*	26
Ginn Hammock | *Palm Coast*	–
Hyatt | *Naples*	25
Hyatt | *Orlando*	21
JW Marriott | *Orlando*	24
La Playa Beach/Resort | *Naples*	22

Longboat Key Club | *Sarasota*	22
Marco Is. Marriott | *Naples*	22
Marriott | *Orlando*	20
PGA National | *Palm Bch.*	17
Ponte Vedra Inn | *NE Florida*	25
🄩 Ritz-Carlton | *NE Florida*	26
🄩 Ritz-Carlton | *Orlando*	27
Ritz-Carlton | *Sarasota*	26
🄩 Ritz-Carlton Golf | *Naples*	26
Rosen Shingle | *Orlando*	23
Saddlebrook | *Tampa*	22
Villas/Grand Cypress | *Orlando*	26
Westin | *Ft. Lauderdale*	24

GEORGIA

Château Élan | *Braselton*	23
🄩 Cloister | *GA Coast*	27
🄩 Lodge/Sea Is. | *GA Coast*	28
🄩 Ritz-Carlton | *Lake Oconee*	26
Westin | *Savannah*	24

HAWAII

Fairmont | *Big Island*	25
🄩 Four Seasons/Koele | *Lanai*	27
Four Seasons/Manele | *Lanai*	27
🄩 Four Seasons Resort | *Big Island*	29
Hapuna Bch. Prince | *Big Island*	23
Hilton Waikoloa Vill. | *Big Island*	21
JW Marriott | *Oahu*	26
Kapalua Villas | *Maui*	23
Maui Prince | *Maui*	19
Mauna Lani Resort | *Big Island*	24
🄩 Ritz-Carlton | *Maui*	25
Turtle Bay Resort | *Oahu*	21
Westin | *Maui*	22

IDAHO

Coeur d'Alene | *Coeur d'Alene*	25
Sun Valley Resort | *Sun Valley*	21

ILLINOIS

Eagle Ridge Resort | *Galena*	19

INDIANA

NEW West Baden Springs | *Indianapolis*	–

MAINE

Samoset | *Rockport*	19

MARYLAND

Hyatt | *Eastern Shore*	21

MASSACHUSETTS

Cranwell Resort | *Lenox*	21
Ocean Edge | *Cape Cod/Is.*	21
Wequassett | *Cape Cod/Is.*	21

MICHIGAN
Grand Hotel | *Mackinac Is.* 22

NEVADA
Loews | *Las Vegas* 22
Ritz-Carlton | *Las Vegas* 27

NEW HAMPSHIRE
Balsams | *Dixville Notch* 19
Mount Wash. | *White Mtns.* 18

NEW JERSEY
Grand Cascades | *Hamburg* -
Seaview | *Atlantic City* 19

NEW MEXICO
Hyatt Tamaya | *Albuquerque* 23

NEW YORK
Otesaga | *Cooperstown* 21
Sagamore | *Adirondacks* 21

NORTH CAROLINA
Ballantyne | *Charlotte* 24
Grove Park Inn | *Asheville* 20
Pinehurst Resort | *Pinehurst* 20

OREGON
Salishan Spa | *Gleneden Bch.* 24
Sunriver | *Mt. Bachelor* 21

PENNSYLVANIA
Hershey | *Hershey* 22
Nemacolin | *Farmington* 25
Skytop Lodge | *Poconos* 15

PUERTO RICO
El Conquistador | *Fajardo* 21
Las Casitas Village | *Fajardo* 26
Rio Mar Beach | *San Juan* 22

SOUTH CAROLINA
Marriott | *Hilton Head* 21
Inn/Palmetto | *Hilton Head* 29
🄳 Sanctuary | *Kiawah Is.* 28
Sea Pines Resort | *Hilton Head* 22
Westin | *Hilton Head* 21
Wild Dunes Resort | *Charleston* 21

TENNESSEE
Gaylord Opryland | *Nashville* 19

TEXAS
Barton Creek | *Austin* 23
Four Seasons | *DFW* 25
Hyatt | *San Antonio* 23
Westin La Cantera | *San Antonio* 22

U.S. VIRGIN ISLANDS
Buccaneer | *St. Croix* 23

VERMONT
Basin Harbor | *Lake Champlain* 19
Equinox | *S. VT* 20
Stratton Mtn. Resort | *S. VT* 19
Woodstock Inn | *Woodstock* 22

VIRGINIA
Boar's Head | *Charlottesville* 19
Homestead | *Hot Springs* 21
Kingsmill Resort | *Williamsburg* 19
Lansdowne | *DC Metro* 20

WEST VIRGINIA
🄳 Greenbrier | 25
  White Sulphur Springs

WISCONSIN
🄳 American Club | *Kohler* 25
Grand Geneva | *Lake Geneva* 19

SKI RESORT

ALASKA
Alyeska Resort | *Anchorage* 21

CALIFORNIA
Resort/Squaw Creek | *Lake Tahoe* 22
Tenaya Lodge | *Yosemite* 19

COLORADO
Beaver Creek Ldg. | *Beaver Creek* 24
Home Ranch | *Clark* -
Keystone Resort | *Keystone* 20
Lodge/Cordillera | *Beaver Creek* 25
Lodge at Vail | *Vail* 23
Park Hyatt | *Beaver Creek* 23
Peaks Resort | *Telluride* 20
🄳 Ritz-Carlton | *Beaver Creek* 28
Sonnenalp | *Vail* 27
St. Regis | *Aspen* 26
Vail Cascade Resort | *Vail* 22

IDAHO
Sun Valley Resort | *Sun Valley* 21

ILLINOIS
Eagle Ridge Resort | *Galena* 19

MASSACHUSETTS
🄳 Canyon Ranch | *Lenox* 22
Cranwell Resort | *Lenox* 21

MONTANA
Resort/Paws Up | *Missoula* -
Triple Creek Ranch | *Darby* 29

NEW HAMPSHIRE
Balsams | *Dixville Notch*   19
Mount Wash. | *White Mtns.*   18

NEW YORK
Mohonk Mtn. Hse. | *Catskills*   18
Otesaga | *Cooperstown*   21
Sagamore | *Adirondacks*   21

OREGON
Sunriver | *Mt. Bachelor*   21

PENNSYLVANIA
Nemacolin | *Farmington*   25
Skytop Lodge | *Poconos*   15

UTAH
Goldener Hirsch Inn | *Park City*   21
Snowbird | *Salt Lake City*   17
Stein Eriksen Lodge | *Park City*   24
Sundance | *Salt Lake City*   23

VERMONT
Equinox | *S. VT*   20
Stratton Mtn. Resort | *S. VT*   19
Topnotch | *Stowe*   21
Trapp | *Stowe*   19
Woodstock Inn | *Woodstock*   22

VIRGINIA
Homestead | *Hot Springs*   21

WASHINGTON
Salish Lodge | *Seattle*   25
Sun Mtn. Lodge | *Winthrop*   -

WISCONSIN
Z American Club | *Kohler*   25
Grand Geneva | *Lake Geneva*   19

WYOMING
Z Four Seasons | *Jackson Hole*   27
Snake River Ldg. | *Jackson Hole*   21
Teton Mnt. Ldg. | *Jackson Hole*   -

HOTEL TYPES

Special Features

Indexes list the best in each category. Listings are arranged by state and are followed by nearest major city.

BUTLERS

ARIZONA
🅩 Boulders | *Phoenix/Scott.* 26
Fairmont | *Phoenix/Scott.* 25

CALIFORNIA
🅩 Château du Sureau | *Yosemite* 27
🅩 Four Seasons | *San Diego* 27
Hyatt | *Palm Springs* 22
NEW Ivy | *San Diego* 24
La Valencia | *San Diego* 22
🅩 St. Regis | *OC Beaches* 27
St. Regis | *SF* 27
Vitale | *SF* 25

COLORADO
Keyah Grande | *Pagosa Springs* -
Park Hyatt | *Beaver Creek* 23
St. Regis | *Aspen* 26

CONNECTICUT
Mohegan Sun | *Norwich* 23

DISTRICT OF COLUMBIA
Ritz-Carlton | *DC* 26
St. Regis | *DC* 23
Willard InterCont. | *DC* 24

FLORIDA
Boca Raton | *Ft. Lauderdale* 21
Brazilian Court | *Palm Bch.* 23
Conrad | *Miami* 23
Hawk's Cay Resort | *Keys* 21
NEW Regent Bal Harbour | *Miami* -
Ritz-Carlton | *Palm Bch.* 26
Ritz-Carlton S. Bch. | *Miami* 25
Setai | *Miami* 26
St. Regis | *Ft. Lauderdale* 27
Tides | *Miami* 26
Victor | *Miami* 22

GEORGIA
🅩 Cloister | *GA Coast* 27
🅩 Lodge/Sea Is. | *GA Coast* 28
Ritz-Carlton Buckhead | *Atlanta* 24

HAWAII
Grand Wailea | *Maui* 24
Hapuna Bch. Prince | *Big Island* 23
Mauna Lani Resort | *Big Island* 24
🅩 Ritz-Carlton | *Maui* 25

ILLINOIS
InterContinental | *Chicago* 22

LOUISIANA
Harrah's | *New Orleans* 23

MAINE
🅩 White Barn Inn | *S. Coast* 25

MARYLAND
Hyatt | *Eastern Shore* 21

MASSACHUSETTS
Taj | *Boston* 22
🅩 Wheatleigh | *Lenox* 26

MISSOURI
Ritz-Carlton | *St. Louis* 24

NEVADA
Ritz-Carlton | *Las Vegas* 27

NEW MEXICO
Eldorado | *Santa Fe* 22

NEW YORK
St. Regis | *NYC* 27
Waldorf=Astoria | *NYC* 21

OHIO
Ritz-Carlton | *Cleveland* 24

PENNSYLVANIA
Ritz-Carlton | *Philadelphia* 24

PUERTO RICO
El Convento | *San Juan* 21
Las Casitas Village | *Fajardo* 26
Ritz-Carlton | *San Juan* 24

TEXAS
St. Regis | *Houston* 25

VIRGINIA
Morrison Hse. | *DC Metro* 23
Ritz-Carlton Tysons | *DC Metro* 25

CASINOS

CALIFORNIA
Barona Valley Ranch | *San Diego* 19

CONNECTICUT

Foxwoods Resort | *Ledyard*   20
NEW MGM Grand | *Ledyard*   -
Mohegan Sun | *Norwich*   23

FLORIDA

Seminole Hard Rock | 20
  Ft. Lauderdale

INDIANA

NEW West Baden Springs | -
  Indianapolis

LOUISIANA

Harrah's | *New Orleans*   23

MICHIGAN

NEW MGM Grand | *Detroit*   26

NEVADA

Z Bellagio | *Las Vegas*   26
Caesars | *Las Vegas*   22
Green Valley Ranch | *Las Vegas*   24
Hard Rock | *Las Vegas*   20
Hyatt | *Incline Vill.*   21
JW Marriott | *Las Vegas*   27
Loews | *Las Vegas*   22
Mandalay Bay | *Las Vegas*   24
MGM Grand | *Las Vegas*   19
Mirage | *Las Vegas*   19
Orleans | *Las Vegas*   18
Z NEW Palazzo | *Las Vegas*   28
Palms Casino Resort | *Las Vegas*   20
Paris Las Vegas | *Las Vegas*   20
Planet Hollywood | *Las Vegas*   18
Red Rock | *Las Vegas*   27
Rio All-Suite | *Las Vegas*   20
Treasure Island | *Las Vegas*   -
Venetian | *Las Vegas*   27
Z Wynn | *Las Vegas*   28

NEW JERSEY

Atlantic City Hilton | *Atlantic City*   18
Borgata | *Atlantic City*   26
Caesars | *Atlantic City*   18
Harrah's Resort | *Atlantic City*   21
Tropicana | *Atlantic City*   16

PUERTO RICO

El Conquistador | *Fajardo*   21
El San Juan | *San Juan*   20
Las Casitas Village | *Fajardo*   26
Rio Mar Beach | *San Juan*   22
Ritz-Carlton | *San Juan*   24

CHILDREN NOT ADVISED

(Call to confirm policy)

ARIZONA

Z Canyon Ranch | *Tucson*   24
Miraval Spa | *Tucson*   24
Royal Palms | *Phoenix/Scott.*   24

CALIFORNIA

Z Auberge/Soleil | *Wine Co.*   28
Cal-a-Vie | *San Diego*   -
Deetjen's | *Carmel*   15
Gaige House Inn | *Wine Co.*   28
Golden Door | *San Diego*   24
Kenwood Inn | *Wine Co.*   26
Z L'Auberge Carmel | *Carmel*   25
Les Mars | *Wine Co.*   28
Madrona Manor | *Wine Co.*   23
Milliken Creek Inn | *Wine Co.*   26
Seven Gables Inn | *Carmel*   24
Two Bunch | *Palm Springs*   19
Ventana Inn | *Carmel*   25

CONNECTICUT

Boulders | *New Preston*   20
Homestead Inn | *Greenwich*   21
Mayflower Inn | *Washington*   27

FLORIDA

Z Little Palm Island | *Keys*   27
Marquesa | *Keys*   25
Standard | *Miami*   20

GEORGIA

Ballastone | *Savannah*   26
Z Lodge/Sea Is. | *GA Coast*   28
Ldg./Little St. Simon | *GA Coast*   23

LOUISIANA

Soniat House | *New Orleans*   26

MAINE

Captain Lord | *S. Coast*   27
Z White Barn Inn | *S. Coast*   25

MASSACHUSETTS

Z Blantyre | *Lenox*   26
Z Canyon Ranch | *Lenox*   22
Charlotte Inn | *Cape Cod/Is.*   23
Jacob Hill Inn | *Boston*   28
Wauwinet | *Cape Cod/Is.*   25
Z Wheatleigh | *Lenox*   26

MISSISSIPPI

Monmouth Plantation | *Natchez*   26

MONTANA

Triple Creek Ranch | *Darby*   29

SPECIAL FEATURES

NEW HAMPSHIRE
Manor/Golden Pond | *White Mtns.* ⌐|

NEW JERSEY
Virginia | *Cape May* 23|

NEW YORK
Friends Lake Inn | *Adirondacks* 22|
Inn at Irving Pl. | *NYC* 24|
🇿 Mirbeau Inn | *Catskills* 27|
🇿 Point | *Adirondacks* 27|

OREGON
Stephanie Inn | *Cannon Bch.* 27|

PENNSYLVANIA
🇿 Lodge/Woodloch | *Hawley* 23|

PUERTO RICO
Bravo Beach | *Vieques* -|
🇿 Horned Dorset | *Rincon* 26|

RHODE ISLAND
Francis Malbone | *Newport* 25|

TENNESSEE
🇿 Blackberry Farm | *Walland* 28|

TEXAS
🇿 Lake Austin Spa | *Austin* 25|

VERMONT
🇿 Twin Farms | *Woodstock* 29|

VIRGINIA
L'Auberge Provençale | *White Post* 23|

WASHINGTON
🇿 Inn at Langley | *Seattle* 25|

WISCONSIN
Canoe Bay | *Chetek* 28|

WYOMING
Rusty Parrot | *Jackson Hole* 23|

CITY VIEWS

ARIZONA
Ritz-Carlton | *Phoenix/Scott.* 22|

CALIFORNIA
Avalon | *LA* 18|
Campton Pl. | *SF* 24|
Clift | *SF* 20|
🇿 Four Seasons | *SF* 27|
Four Seasons Bev. Hills | *LA* 25|
Grafton on Sunset | *LA* 19|
Grand Hyatt | *SF* 20|
Hilton Checkers | *LA* 19|

Huntington | *SF* 21|
🆕 InterContinental | *SF* 25|
Kabuki | *SF* 20|
Le Méridien | *SF* 23|
Le Merigot | *LA* 23|
🆕 London W. Hollywood | *LA* -|
Mandarin Oriental | *SF* 27|
Mark Hopkins | *SF* 22|
Marriott Gaslamp | *San Diego* 23|
Marriott Marina | *San Diego* 19|
Millennium Biltmore | *LA* 17|
Mondrian | *LA* 19|
Nikko | *SF* 22|
Omni | *LA* 20|
Omni | *San Diego* 22|
Orchard | *SF* 22|
🆕 Palomar | *LA* -|
Palomar | *SF* 22|
🇿 Peninsula | *LA* 27|
Serrano | *SF* 18|
Solamar | *San Diego* 26|
Spindrift Inn | *Carmel* 23|
Standard | *LA* 16|
Standard Downtown | *LA* 19|
Stanford Ct. | *SF* 21|
St. Regis | *SF* 27|
Westgate | *San Diego* 23|
Westin Market St. | *SF* 21|
W San Diego | *San Diego* 21|

COLORADO
Curtis | *Denver* -|
Grand Hyatt | *Denver* 22|
Jerome | *Aspen* 22|
Monaco | *Denver* 22|
St Julien | *Denver* 26|
Teatro | *Denver* 24|
Westin | *Denver* 21|

DISTRICT OF COLUMBIA
🇿 Four Seasons | *DC* 26|
JW Marriott | *DC* 21|
Mandarin Oriental | *DC* 27|
Palomar | *DC* 23|
Park Hyatt | *DC* 24|
Ritz-Carlton | *DC* 26|
🇿 Ritz-Carlton Georgetown | *DC* 27|

FLORIDA
Casa Monica | *NE Florida* 23|
Conrad | *Miami* 23|
Delano | *Miami* 21|
Four Seasons | *Miami* 26|
🆕 Gansevoort South | *Miami* 26|
Hotel, The | *Miami* 19|

JW Marriott | *Miami*	22
Z Mandarin Oriental | *Miami*	27
Naples Grande | *Naples*	24
Ritz-Carlton Coconut | *Miami*	26

GEORGIA

Four Seasons | *Atlanta*	25
Hilton | *Atlanta*	19
InterContinental | *Atlanta*	26
JW Marriott | *Atlanta*	21
NEW Mansion/Peachtree | *Atlanta*	-
Omni | *Atlanta*	20
Ritz-Carlton | *Atlanta*	26
NEW W Atlanta Midtown | *Atlanta*	-
W Atlanta Perimeter | *Atlanta*	21
Westin | *Atlanta*	23

ILLINOIS

Burnham | *Chicago*	25
Conrad | *Chicago*	26
Drake | *Chicago*	20
Z Four Seasons | *Chicago*	27
InterContinental | *Chicago*	22
Monaco | *Chicago*	21
Omni | *Chicago*	24
Palmer Hse. Hilton | *Chicago*	19
Z Peninsula | *Chicago*	29
Ritz-Carlton | *Chicago*	26
Sofitel | *Chicago*	25
Sutton Place | *Chicago*	23
Swissôtel | *Chicago*	23
NEW Trump Int'l | *Chicago*	-
Westin | *Chicago*	22
Whitehall | *Chicago*	20

KENTUCKY

21c Museum | *Louisville*	27

LOUISIANA

Harrah's | *New Orleans*	23
Hilton Riverside | *New Orleans*	19
InterContinental | *New Orleans*	23
JW Marriott | *New Orleans*	19
Le Pavillon | *New Orleans*	19
Loews | *New Orleans*	26
Maison Dupuy | *New Orleans*	22
Marriott | *New Orleans*	18
Monteleone | *New Orleans*	22
Renaissance | *New Orleans*	-
Z Windsor Court | *New Orleans*	24

MARYLAND

NEW Gaylord Nat'l | *Baltimore*	-
NEW Hilton | *Baltimore*	-
Hyatt | *Baltimore*	22

MASSACHUSETTS

Boston Marriott | *Boston*	20
Charles | *Boston*	23
Commonwealth | *Boston*	24
Fifteen Beacon | *Boston*	24
Four Seasons | *Boston*	27
NEW Le Méridien Cambridge | *Boston*	22
Marlowe | *Boston*	23
Marriott Copley | *Boston*	20
Marriott Long Wharf | *Boston*	20
Millennium Bostonian | *Boston*	21
Nine Zero | *Boston*	23
Ritz-Carlton | *Boston*	25
Royal Sonesta | *Boston*	21
Taj | *Boston*	22
Westin Boston Water. | *Boston*	22
Westin Copley | *Boston*	22

MICHIGAN

NEW MGM Grand | *Detroit*	26
St. Regis | *Detroit*	-

MINNESOTA

Marquette | *Mpls./St. Paul*	24
NEW W Minneapolis | *Mpls./St. Paul*	-

MISSOURI

NEW Four Seasons | *St. Louis*	29
Renaissance | *St. Louis*	23

NEBRASKA

NEW Omaha Magnolia | *Omaha*	-

NEVADA

Z Bellagio | *Las Vegas*	26
Z Four Seasons | *Las Vegas*	27
Green Valley Ranch | *Las Vegas*	24
Hard Rock | *Las Vegas*	20
JW Marriott | *Las Vegas*	27
Mandalay Bay | *Las Vegas*	24
MGM Grand | *Las Vegas*	19
Mirage | *Las Vegas*	19
Z NEW Palazzo | *Las Vegas*	28
Palms Casino Resort | *Las Vegas*	20
Rio All-Suite | *Las Vegas*	20
Signature/MGM Grand | *Las Vegas*	27
Treasure Island | *Las Vegas*	-
Venetian | *Las Vegas*	27
Z Wynn | *Las Vegas*	28

NEW JERSEY

NEW Chelsea | *Atlantic City*	-

SPECIAL FEATURES

NEW MEXICO

La Fonda	*Santa Fe*	19

NEW YORK

Blue Moon	*NYC*	-
NEW Bowery	*NYC*	21
Bryant Park	*NYC*	22
Carlton	*NYC*	20
Carlyle	*NYC*	25
Chambers	*NYC*	21
NEW Duane Street	*NYC*	-
Elysée	*NYC*	22
Embassy Suites	*NYC*	22
NEW Empire	*NYC*	-
Z Four Seasons	*NYC*	28
Gansevoort	*NYC*	20
Gramercy Park	*NYC*	22
Hotel/Rivington	*NYC*	23
Inn at Irving Pl.	*NYC*	24
InterContinental	*NYC*	20
Iroquois	*NYC*	21
Jumeirah Essex Hse.	*NYC*	22
Kitano	*NYC*	22
Le Parker Méridien	*NYC*	21
London NYC	*NYC*	23
Z Lowell	*NYC*	25
Z Mandarin Oriental	*NYC*	28
Maritime	*NYC*	17
Mercer	*NYC*	23
Michelangelo	*NYC*	24
Millenium Hilton	*NYC*	21
Millennium UN	*NYC*	22
Muse	*NYC*	23
NY Marriott Brooklyn Br.	*NYC*	21
NY Marriott Downtown	*NYC*	19
New York Palace	*NYC*	25
Night	*NYC*	16
Peninsula	*NYC*	26
Plaza Athénée	*NYC*	22
NEW Ravel	*NYC*	-
Renaissance	*NYC*	22
Ritz-Carlton Battery Pk.	*NYC*	27
Ritz-Carlton Central Pk.	*NYC*	27
Royalton	*NYC*	20
Sherry-Netherland	*NYC*	24
Shoreham	*NYC*	21
NEW Six Columbus	*NYC*	-
Soho Grand	*NYC*	19
Tribeca Grand	*NYC*	20
Trump Int'l	*NYC*	23

NORTH CAROLINA

Richmond Hill	*Asheville*	23

OHIO

Blackwell	*Columbus*	23
Hilton Cincinnati	*Cincinnati*	16

OREGON

Benson	*Portland*	20
Heathman	*Portland*	20
Westin	*Portland*	21

PENNSYLVANIA

Z Four Seasons	*Philadelphia*	26
Hilton Inn	*Philadelphia*	19
Park Hyatt	*Philadelphia*	22
Z Rittenhouse	*Philadelphia*	26
Ritz-Carlton	*Philadelphia*	24
Sofitel	*Philadelphia*	24
Westin	*Philadelphia*	23

PUERTO RICO

El Convento	*San Juan*	21

RHODE ISLAND

Westin	*Providence*	23

SOUTH CAROLINA

Charleston Pl.	*Charleston*	25

TENNESSEE

Hermitage	*Nashville*	27
Loews Vanderbilt	*Nashville*	21

TEXAS

Adolphus	*DFW*	23
Derek	*Houston*	22
Four Seasons	*Austin*	25
Four Seasons	*Houston*	25
Hilton	*Austin*	20
Hilton Americas	*Houston*	21
Icon	*Houston*	24
InterContinental	*Houston*	21
NEW Joule	*DFW*	-
JW Marriott	*Houston*	20
La Mansión del Rio	*San Antonio*	21
Lancaster	*Houston*	18
Menger	*San Antonio*	17
Omni	*Houston*	20
Palomar	*DFW*	25
Stoneleigh	*DFW*	22
St. Regis	*Houston*	25
Valencia Riverwalk	*San Antonio*	26
Watermark	*San Antonio*	27
W Dallas-Victory	*DFW*	22
Westin Riverwalk	*San Antonio*	22
Zaza	*DFW*	26

UTAH

Grand America | *Salt Lake City* — 27
Little America | *Salt Lake City* — 20
Monaco | *Salt Lake City* — 21

VIRGINIA

Jefferson | *Richmond* — 24
Morrison Hse. | *DC Metro* — 23
Ritz-Carlton Tysons | *DC Metro* — 25

WASHINGTON

Alexis | *Seattle* — 21
Davenport | *Spokane* — 28
Edgewater | *Seattle* — 22
Fairmont | *Seattle* — 23
NEW Four Seasons | *Seattle* — -
Grand Hyatt | *Seattle* — 27
Monaco | *Seattle* — 22
1000 | *Seattle* — 26
Pan Pacific | *Seattle* — -
Sheraton | *Seattle* — 20
Watertown | *Seattle* — -
W Seattle | *Seattle* — 23

WISCONSIN

Pfister | *Milwaukee* — 22

DRAMATIC DESIGN

ARIZONA

Arizona Biltmore | *Phoenix/Scott.* — 23

CALIFORNIA

Ahwahnee | *Yosemite* — 20
Argonaut | *SF* — 23
Calistoga Ranch | *Wine Co.* — 26
Clift | *SF* — 20
Grafton on Sunset | *LA* — 19
Z NEW Grand/Mar | *San Diego* — 26
Healdsburg | *Wine Co.* — 24
NEW InterContinental | *SF* — 25
NEW Ivy | *San Diego* — 24
Kabuki | *SF* — 20
NEW London W. Hollywood | *LA* — -
Mondrian | *LA* — 19
Omni | *San Diego* — 22
Palomar | *SF* — 22
Z Post Ranch Inn | *Carmel* — 28
Raffles L'Ermitage | *LA* — 27
St. Orres | *N. CA Coast* — -
St. Regis | *SF* — 27
Viceroy | *LA* — 21
Viceroy | *Palm Springs* — 21

COLORADO

Z Broadmoor | *CO Springs* — 26

Curtis | *Denver* — -
St Julien | *Denver* — 26

CONNECTICUT

Homestead Inn | *Greenwich* — 21

DISTRICT OF COLUMBIA

Helix | *DC* — 23
Madera | *DC* — 20
Z Ritz-Carlton Georgetown | *DC* — 27
St. Regis | *DC* — 23

FLORIDA

Biltmore | *Miami* — 23
Conrad | *Miami* — 23
Delano | *Miami* — 21
Fontainebleau | *Miami* — 18
NEW Gansevoort South | *Miami* — 26
National | *Miami* — 18
NEW Regent Bal Harbour | *Miami* — -
Rosen Shingle | *Orlando* — 23
Shore Club | *Miami* — 16

GEORGIA

Mansion/Forsyth | *Savannah* — 26
NEW Mansion/Peachtree | *Atlanta* — -
Z Ritz-Carlton | *Lake Oconee* — 26

HAWAII

Z Four Seasons Resort | *Big Island* — 29
Hilton Waikoloa Vill. | *Big Island* — 21
Kona Village Resort | *Big Island* — 25

ILLINOIS

Burnham | *Chicago* — 25
Monaco | *Chicago* — 21
Park Hyatt | *Chicago* — 27
Sofitel | *Chicago* — 25
NEW Trump Int'l | *Chicago* — -

INDIANA

NEW West Baden Springs | *Indianapolis* — -

MASSACHUSETTS

Fifteen Beacon | *Boston* — 24
Marlowe | *Boston* — 23
Nine Zero | *Boston* — 23

MICHIGAN

NEW MGM Grand | *Detroit* — 26

MINNESOTA

Graves 601 | *Mpls./St. Paul* — 26

MISSOURI

NEW Four Seasons | *St. Louis* — 29

SPECIAL FEATURES

MONTANA
Resort/Paws Up | *Missoula* —

NEVADA
Z Bellagio | *Las Vegas* 26
Z NEW Palazzo | *Las Vegas* 28
Paris Las Vegas | *Las Vegas* 20
Red Rock | *Las Vegas* 27
Ritz-Carlton | *Las Vegas* 27
NEW Trump Int'l | *Las Vegas* 21
Venetian | *Las Vegas* 27
Z Wynn | *Las Vegas* 28

NEW MEXICO
Inn of the Anasazi | *Santa Fe* 24

NEW YORK
NEW Bowery | *NYC* 21
Carlton | *NYC* 20
Gramercy Park | *NYC* 22
Maritime | *NYC* 17
NEW Six Columbus | *NYC* —
Waldorf=Astoria | *NYC* 21
Whiteface Lodge | *Adirondacks* 23

OREGON
Lucia | *Portland* 19

PENNSYLVANIA
Loews | *Philadelphia* 23
Ritz-Carlton | *Philadelphia* 24

TENNESSEE
Lodge/Buckberry | *Gatlinburg* —

TEXAS
Cibolo Creek Ranch | *Marfa* —
Rosewood Crescent | *DFW* 25
Valencia Riverwalk | *San Antonio* 26
Zaza | *DFW* 26

UTAH
Goldener Hirsch Inn | *Park City* 21

WASHINGTON
1000 | *Seattle* 26

WISCONSIN
Canoe Bay | *Chetek* 28

WYOMING
Z Amangani | *Jackson Hole* 29
Z Four Seasons | *Jackson Hole* 27

FISHING

ALABAMA
Marriott | *Point Clear* 21

ALASKA
Alyeska Resort | *Anchorage* 21

ARIZONA
Fairmont | *Phoenix/Scott.* 25
L'Auberge/Sedona | *Sedona* 23
Tanque Verde Ranch | *Tucson* 20

CALIFORNIA
Ahwahnee | *Yosemite* 20
Alisal | *Santa Barbara* 17
Loews | *San Diego* 21
Malibu Beach Inn | *LA* 20
Manchester Gr. Hyatt | *San Diego* 22
Resort/Squaw Creek | *Lake Tahoe* 22
Ritz-Carlton | *Half Moon Bay* 27
Z Ritz-Carlton | *OC Beaches* 27
Ritz-Carlton | *LA* 24
Tamarack | *Mammoth Lakes* 15

COLORADO
Home Ranch | *Clark* —
Lodge/Cordillera | *Beaver Creek* 25
Lodge at Vail | *Vail* 23
Park Hyatt | *Beaver Creek* 23
Peaks Resort | *Telluride* 20
Pines Lodge | *Beaver Creek* 24
St. Regis | *Aspen* 26
Vail Cascade Resort | *Vail* 22

CONNECTICUT
Boulders | *New Preston* 20
Winvian | *New Preston* —

FLORIDA
Amelia Is. Plant. | *NE Florida* 22
Boca Raton | *Ft. Lauderdale* 21
Breakers | *Palm Bch.* 24
Casa Marina Resort | *Keys* 21
Cheeca Lodge | *Keys* 21
Colony Beach | *Sarasota* 18
Z Disney's Bch. Club Villas | *Orlando* 27
Z Disney's BoardWalk Villas | *Orlando* 27
Disney's Caribbean Bch. | *Orlando* 19
Disney's Contemporary | *Orlando* 20
Disney's Coronado | *Orlando* 19
Z Disney's Ft. Wilderness | *Orlando* 24
Disney's Grand Floridian | *Orlando* 25
Disney's Old Key W. | *Orlando* 25
Disney's Port Orleans/Fr. Q. | *Orlando* 21
Disney's Port Orleans/River | *Orlando* 22

Disney's Vero Beach | *Vero Bch.*	23
Disney's Yacht Club | *Orlando*	23
Don CeSar Bch. | *Tampa*	21
Fairmont | *Miami*	26
Fisher Island | *Miami*	23
Four Seasons Resort | *Palm Bch.*	24
Grove Isle | *Miami*	26
Hawk's Cay Resort | *Keys*	21
Hyatt | *Naples*	25
La Playa Beach/Resort | *Naples*	22
Z Little Palm Island | *Keys*	27
Longboat Key Club | *Sarasota*	22
Marco Beach Resort | *Naples*	24
Marriott | *Ft. Lauderdale*	21
Ponte Vedra Inn | *NE Florida*	25
Z Ritz-Carlton | *Orlando*	27
Ritz-Carlton | *Palm Bch.*	26
Ritz-Carlton Key Bisc. | *Miami*	24
Ritz-Carlton S. Bch. | *Miami*	25
Rosen Shingle | *Orlando*	23
Saddlebrook | *Tampa*	22
Sanibel Resort | *Ft. Myers*	21
Shore Club | *Miami*	16
South Seas Resort | *Ft. Myers*	21
Sunset Key/Cottages | *Keys*	26
Villas/Grand Cypress | *Orlando*	26
WaterColor Inn | *Panhandle*	27
Westin | *Ft. Lauderdale*	24

GEORGIA

Z Cloister | *GA Coast*	27
Ldg./Little St. Simon | *GA Coast*	23
Z Ritz-Carlton | *Lake Oconee*	26

HAWAII

Fairmont | *Big Island*	25
Fairmont | *Maui*	27
Four Seasons/Manele | *Lanai*	27
Z Four Seasons Resort | *Big Island*	29
Z Four Seasons Resort | *Maui*	28
Hapuna Bch. Prince | *Big Island*	23
Hyatt | *Maui*	22
Kapalua Villas | *Maui*	23
Kona Village Resort | *Big Island*	25
Mauna Lani Resort | *Big Island*	24
Sheraton | *Maui*	22
Westin | *Maui*	22

ILLINOIS

Eagle Ridge Resort | *Galena*	19

MARYLAND

Hyatt | *Eastern Shore*	21
Inn/Perry Cabin | *Eastern Shore*	25

MASSACHUSETTS

Chatham Bars | *Cape Cod/Is.*	22
Cranwell Resort | *Lenox*	21
Wauwinet | *Cape Cod/Is.*	25

MICHIGAN

Iroquois/Beach | *Mackinac Is.*	22

MISSISSIPPI

Monmouth Plantation | *Natchez*	26

MISSOURI

Chateau on Lake | *Branson*	23

MONTANA

Resort/Paws Up | *Missoula*	-
Triple Creek Ranch | *Darby*	29

NEVADA

Loews | *Las Vegas*	22
Ritz-Carlton | *Las Vegas*	27

NEW HAMPSHIRE

Balsams | *Dixville Notch*	19
Mount Wash. | *White Mtns.*	18

NEW MEXICO

Bishop's Lodge | *Santa Fe*	19

NEW YORK

Elk Lake Lodge | *Adirondacks*	-
Friends Lake Inn | *Adirondacks*	22
Gurney's Inn | *Long Island*	17
Mirror Lake Inn | *Adirondacks*	23
Mohonk Mtn. Hse. | *Catskills*	18
Otesaga | *Cooperstown*	21
Z Point | *Adirondacks*	27
Sagamore | *Adirondacks*	21
Whiteface Lodge | *Adirondacks*	23

NORTH CAROLINA

Greystone Inn | *Asheville*	24
Pinehurst Resort | *Pinehurst*	20

PENNSYLVANIA

Glendorn | *Bradford*	-
Nemacolin | *Farmington*	25
Skytop Lodge | *Poconos*	15

PUERTO RICO

El Conquistador | *Fajardo*	21
Z Horned Dorset | *Rincon*	26
Las Casitas Village | *Fajardo*	26

SOUTH CAROLINA

Charleston Pl. | *Charleston*	25
Inn/Palmetto | *Hilton Head*	29
Sea Pines Resort | *Hilton Head*	22

SPECIAL FEATURES

Westin | *Hilton Head* 21
Wild Dunes Resort | *Charleston* 21

TENNESSEE
🏠 Blackberry Farm | *Walland* 28
Lodge/Buckberry | *Gatlinburg* -

TEXAS
Cibolo Creek Ranch | *Marfa* -

U.S. VIRGIN ISLANDS
Caneel Bay | *St. John* 23
Ritz-Carlton | *St. Thomas* 25
Westin | *St. John* 21

UTAH
Goldener Hirsch Inn | *Park City* 21
Snowbird | *Salt Lake City* 17
Stein Eriksen Lodge | *Park City* 24
Sundance | *Salt Lake City* 23

VERMONT
Basin Harbor | *Lake Champlain* 19
Equinox | *S. VT* 20
Inn/Sawmill | *S. VT* 22
Stratton Mtn. Resort | *S. VT* 19
🏠 Twin Farms | *Woodstock* 29
Woodstock Inn | *Woodstock* 22

VIRGINIA
Boar's Head | *Charlottesville* 19
Homestead | *Hot Springs* 21
🏠 Keswick Hall | *Charlottesville* 26
Kingsmill Resort | *Williamsburg* 19
Tides Inn | *Irvington* 22

WASHINGTON
Edgewater | *Seattle* 22
Sun Mtn. Lodge | *Winthrop* -
Woodmark | *Seattle* 24

WEST VIRGINIA
🏠 Greenbrier | *White Sulphur Springs* 25

WISCONSIN
Canoe Bay | *Chetek* 28

WYOMING
🏠 Four Seasons | *Jackson Hole* 27
Teton Mnt. Ldg. | *Jackson Hole* -

HIKING/ WALKING TRAILS

ALABAMA
Marriott | *Point Clear* 21
Renaissance | *Birmingham* 25

ALASKA
Alyeska Resort | *Anchorage* 21

ARIZONA
Arizona Biltmore | *Phoenix/Scott.* 23
Arizona Grand | *Phoenix/Scott.* 19
Arizona Inn | *Tucson* 23
🏠 Boulders | *Phoenix/Scott.* 26
🏠 Canyon Ranch | *Tucson* 24
El Tovar | *Grand Canyon* 16
🏠 Enchantment | *Sedona* 26
Fairmont | *Phoenix/Scott.* 25
🏠 Four Seasons | *Phoenix/Scott.* 27
Hacienda del Sol | *Tucson* 19
Hilton El Conquistador | *Tucson* 19
Hyatt | *Phoenix/Scott.* 21
JW Marriott | *Tucson* 25
JW Marriott Camelback | *Phoenix/Scott.* 23
JW Marriott Desert | *Phoenix/Scott.* 24
L'Auberge/Sedona | *Sedona* 23
Ldg./Ventana Canyon | *Tucson* 22
Loews | *Tucson* 24
Miraval Spa | *Tucson* 24
Pointe Hilton Squaw | *Phoenix/Scott.* 19
Pointe Hilton Tapatio | *Phoenix/Scott.* 19
Renaissance | *Phoenix/Scott.* 21
🏠 Sanctuary | *Phoenix/Scott.* 26
Sheraton | *Phoenix/Scott.* 23
Tanque Verde Ranch | *Tucson* 20
Westin | *Phoenix/Scott.* 24
Westward Look | *Tucson* 20
Wigwam Golf | *Phoenix/Scott.* 24

CALIFORNIA
Ahwahnee | *Yosemite* 20
Albion River | *N. CA Coast* 24
Alisal | *Santa Barbara* 17
🏠 Auberge/Soleil | *Wine Co.* 28
Bacara Resort | *Santa Barbara* 26
Balboa Bay Club | *OC Beaches* 24
Barona Valley Ranch | *San Diego* 19
Cal-a-Vie | *San Diego* -
Calistoga Ranch | *Wine Co.* 26
Carmel Valley Ranch | *Carmel* 23
Carneros Inn | *Wine Co.* 28
🏠 Casa Palmero | *Carmel* 29
🏠 Château du Sureau | *Yosemite* 27
Deetjen's | *Carmel* 15
Fairmont | *Wine Co.* 21
🏠 Four Seasons | *San Diego* 27

Four Seasons Westlake	*LA*	25
Gaige House Inn	*Wine Co.*	28
Garden Court	*SF*	24
Golden Door	*San Diego*	24
Z NEW Grand/Mar	*San Diego*	26
Heritage House	*N. CA Coast*	25
Highlands Inn	*Carmel*	23
Hilton La Jolla	*San Diego*	20
Hyatt	*Palm Springs*	22
Inn Above Tide	*SF*	26
Inn/Spanish Bay	*Carmel*	26
Inn/Rancho Santa Fe	*San Diego*	21
La Quinta	*Palm Springs*	22
L'Auberge Del Mar	*San Diego*	23
La Valencia	*San Diego*	22
Lodge/Torrey Pines	*San Diego*	25
MacArthur Pl.	*Wine Co.*	25
Marriott Coronado	*San Diego*	23
Z Meadowood	*Wine Co.*	27
Miramonte	*Palm Springs*	23
Z Montage	*OC Beaches*	27
NEW Nick's Cove	*N. CA Coast*	25
Z Post Ranch Inn	*Carmel*	28
Quail Lodge	*Carmel*	23
Rancho Bernardo	*San Diego*	21
Z Rancho Valencia	*San Diego*	28
Renaissance	*Palm Springs*	21
Resort/Squaw Creek	*Lake Tahoe*	22
Ritz-Carlton	*Half Moon Bay*	27
Z Ritz-Carlton	*OC Beaches*	27
San Ysidro	*Santa Barbara*	26
Seven Gables Inn	*Carmel*	24
Silverado Resort	*Wine Co.*	18
Simpson Hse.	*Santa Barbara*	25
NEW Solage	*Wine Co.*	23
Z St. Regis	*OC Beaches*	27
Tamarack	*Mammoth Lakes*	15
Tenaya Lodge	*Yosemite*	19
Two Bunch	*Palm Springs*	19
Ventana Inn	*Carmel*	25
Viceroy	*Palm Springs*	21
Villagio Inn	*Wine Co.*	24
Vintage Inn	*Wine Co.*	23
Westin	*Palm Springs*	21
Whale Watch	*N. CA Coast*	24

COLORADO

Z Broadmoor	*CO Springs*	26
C Lazy U Ranch	*Denver*	22
Home Ranch	*Clark*	-
Keystone Resort	*Keystone*	20
Z Little Nell	*Aspen*	27
Lodge/Cordillera	*Beaver Creek*	25

Lodge at Vail	*Vail*	23
Park Hyatt	*Beaver Creek*	23
Peaks Resort	*Telluride*	20
Pines Lodge	*Beaver Creek*	24
Z Ritz-Carlton	*Beaver Creek*	28
Sonnenalp	*Vail*	27
St Julien	*Denver*	26
Teatro	*Denver*	24
Vail Cascade Resort	*Vail*	22

CONNECTICUT

Boulders	*New Preston*	20
Mayflower Inn	*Washington*	27
Winvian	*New Preston*	-

FLORIDA

Amelia Is. Plant.	*NE Florida*	22
Atlantic Resort	*Ft. Lauderdale*	26
Boca Raton	*Ft. Lauderdale*	21
Brazilian Court	*Palm Bch.*	23
Breakers	*Palm Bch.*	24
Colony Beach	*Sarasota*	18
Z Disney's Bch. Club Villas	*Orlando*	27
Z Disney's BoardWalk Villas	*Orlando*	27
Disney's Caribbean Bch.	*Orlando*	19
Disney's Contemporary	*Orlando*	20
Disney's Coronado	*Orlando*	19
Z Disney's Ft. Wilderness	*Orlando*	24
Disney's Old Key W.	*Orlando*	25
Disney's Port Orleans/Fr. Q.	*Orlando*	21
Disney's Port Orleans/River	*Orlando*	22
Doral Golf	*Miami*	19
Fisher Island	*Miami*	23
Ginn Hammock	*Palm Coast*	-
Grove Isle	*Miami*	26
Hawk's Cay Resort	*Keys*	21
Hyatt	*Orlando*	21
Jupiter Beach	*Palm Bch.*	20
JW Marriott	*Orlando*	24
Z Little Palm Island	*Keys*	27
Marriott	*Ft. Lauderdale*	21
Marriott	*Orlando*	20
PGA National	*Palm Bch.*	17
Z Ritz-Carlton	*Naples*	27
Z Ritz-Carlton	*NE Florida*	26
Z Ritz-Carlton	*Orlando*	27
Ritz-Carlton	*Palm Bch.*	26
Rosen Shingle	*Orlando*	23
Saddlebrook	*Tampa*	22

Sanibel Resort	*Ft. Myers*	21
Shore Club	*Miami*	16
Villas/Grand Cypress	*Orlando*	26
WaterColor Inn	*Panhandle*	27

GEORGIA

Château Élan	*Braselton*	23
Z Cloister	*GA Coast*	27
Jekyll Is. Club	*GA Coast*	21
Z Ritz-Carlton	*Lake Oconee*	26

HAWAII

Fairmont	*Big Island*	25
Fairmont	*Maui*	27
Four Seasons/Manele	*Lanai*	27
Z Four Seasons Resort	*Big Island*	29
Z Four Seasons Resort	*Maui*	28
Grand Hyatt	*Kauai*	24
Grand Wailea	*Maui*	24
Halekulani	*Oahu*	25
Hana-Maui	*Maui*	27
Hapuna Bch. Prince	*Big Island*	23
Hilton Kauai	*Kauai*	21
Hilton Waikoloa Vill.	*Big Island*	21
JW Marriott	*Oahu*	26
Kapalua Villas	*Maui*	23
Maui Prince	*Maui*	19
Mauna Lani Resort	*Big Island*	24
Z Ritz-Carlton	*Maui*	25

IDAHO

Sun Valley Resort	*Sun Valley*	21

ILLINOIS

Eagle Ridge Resort	*Galena*	19

MAINE

Bar Harbor Inn	*Bar Harbor*	21
NEW Hidden Pond	*S. Coast*	-
Inn by the Sea	*Portland*	21
Z White Barn Inn	*S. Coast*	25

MARYLAND

Hyatt	*Eastern Shore*	21
Inn/Perry Cabin	*Eastern Shore*	25

MASSACHUSETTS

Z Blantyre	*Lenox*	26
Z Canyon Ranch	*Lenox*	22
Cranwell Resort	*Lenox*	21
Jacob Hill Inn	*Boston*	28
Ocean Edge	*Cape Cod/Is.*	21
Wauwinet	*Cape Cod/Is.*	25
Wequassett	*Cape Cod/Is.*	21
White Elephant	*Cape Cod/Is.*	23

MICHIGAN

Dearborn Inn	*Detroit*	18
Grand Hotel	*Mackinac Is.*	22
Iroquois/Beach	*Mackinac Is.*	22

MISSISSIPPI

Monmouth Plantation	*Natchez*	26

MISSOURI

Chateau on Lake	*Branson*	23

MONTANA

Resort/Paws Up	*Missoula*	-
Triple Creek Ranch	*Darby*	29

NEVADA

Hyatt	*Incline Vill.*	21
Loews	*Las Vegas*	22
Ritz-Carlton	*Las Vegas*	27

NEW HAMPSHIRE

Balsams	*Dixville Notch*	19
Mount Wash.	*White Mtns.*	18
Wentworth by Sea	*Newcastle*	25

NEW JERSEY

Grand Cascades	*Hamburg*	-
Seaview	*Atlantic City*	19

NEW MEXICO

Bishop's Lodge	*Santa Fe*	19
El Monte Sagrado	*Taos*	25
Hyatt Tamaya	*Albuquerque*	23

NEW YORK

Castle/Hudson	*Westchester*	23
Elk Lake Lodge	*Adirondacks*	-
Friends Lake Inn	*Adirondacks*	22
Gurney's Inn	*Long Island*	17
Mohonk Mtn. Hse.	*Catskills*	18
Oheka Castle	*Long Island*	25
Otesaga	*Cooperstown*	21
Z Point	*Adirondacks*	27
Sagamore	*Adirondacks*	21
Troutbeck Estate	*Amenia*	18
Whiteface Lodge	*Adirondacks*	23

NORTH CAROLINA

Ballantyne	*Charlotte*	24
Fearrington Hse.	*Pittsboro*	24
Greystone Inn	*Asheville*	24
Inn on Biltmore	*Asheville*	25
Pinehurst Resort	*Pinehurst*	20
Richmond Hill	*Asheville*	23

OREGON

Salishan Spa	*Gleneden Bch.*	24
Sunriver	*Mt. Bachelor*	21

Z Timberline Ldg. | *Mt. Hood* 16

Z Tu Tu' Tun Lodge | *Gold Bch.* 26

PENNSYLVANIA

Glendorn | *Bradford* -

Hershey | *Hershey* 22

Z Lodge/Woodloch | *Hawley* 23

Nemacolin | *Farmington* 25

Skytop Lodge | *Poconos* 15

PUERTO RICO

Z Horned Dorset | *Rincon* 26

Las Casitas Village | *Fajardo* 26

Ritz-Carlton | *San Juan* 24

RHODE ISLAND

Castle Hill Inn | *Newport* 23

SOUTH CAROLINA

Marriott | *Hilton Head* 21

Inn/Middleton Pl. | *Charleston* -

Inn/Palmetto | *Hilton Head* 29

Myrtle/Marriott | *Myrtle Bch.* 24

Z Sanctuary | *Kiawah Is.* 28

Sea Pines Resort | *Hilton Head* 22

Wild Dunes Resort | *Charleston* 21

Z Woodlands | *Charleston* 26

TENNESSEE

Z Blackberry Farm | *Walland* 28

Lodge/Buckberry | *Gatlinburg* -

TEXAS

Barton Creek | *Austin* 23

Cibolo Creek Ranch | *Marfa* -

Derek | *Houston* 22

Four Seasons | *Austin* 25

Four Seasons | *DFW* 25

Houstonian | *Houston* 23

Hyatt | *San Antonio* 23

Inn/Dos Brisas | *Washington* -

Z Lake Austin Spa | *Austin* 25

Renaissance | *Austin* 20

Westin Riverwalk | *San Antonio* 22

U.S. VIRGIN ISLANDS

Caneel Bay | *St. John* 23

Ritz-Carlton | *St. Thomas* 25

UTAH

Goldener Hirsch Inn | *Park City* 21

Snowbird | *Salt Lake City* 17

Stein Eriksen Lodge | *Park City* 24

Sundance | *Salt Lake City* 23

VERMONT

Equinox | *S. VT* 20

Inn/Essex | *Lake Champlain* 21

Inn/Sawmill | *S. VT* 22

Inn/Shelburne | *Lake Champlain* 22

Old Tavern/Grafton | *S. VT* 21

Reluctant Panther | *S. VT* 27

Stratton Mtn. Resort | *S. VT* 19

Topnotch | *Stowe* 21

Trapp | *Stowe* 19

Z Twin Farms | *Woodstock* 29

Woodstock Inn | *Woodstock* 22

VIRGINIA

Boar's Head | *Charlottesville* 19

Clifton Inn | *Charlottesville* 21

Goodstone Inn | *DC Metro* -

Homestead | *Hot Springs* 21

Z Keswick Hall | *Charlottesville* 26

Kingsmill Resort | *Williamsburg* 19

Tides Inn | *Irvington* 22

Williams. Colonial | *Williamsburg* 23

Williams. Inn | *Williamsburg* 23

WASHINGTON

Salish Lodge | *Seattle* 25

Sun Mtn. Lodge | *Winthrop* -

Z Willows Lodge | *Seattle* 27

Woodmark | *Seattle* 24

WEST VIRGINIA

Z Greenbrier | *White Sulphur Springs* 25

WISCONSIN

Z American Club | *Kohler* 25

Canoe Bay | *Chetek* 28

Grand Geneva | *Lake Geneva* 19

WYOMING

Z Amangani | *Jackson Hole* 29

Z Four Seasons | *Jackson Hole* 27

Jackson Lake Ldg. | *Jackson Hole* 19

Jenny Lake Ldg. | *Jackson Hole* 22

Old Faithful Inn | *Yellowstone* 16

Snake River Ldg. | *Jackson Hole* 21

Teton Mnt. Ldg. | *Jackson Hole* -

ISLAND SETTINGS

CALIFORNIA

del Coronado | *San Diego* 20

Loews | *San Diego* 21

Marriott Coronado | *San Diego* 23

FLORIDA

Amelia Is. Plant. | *NE Florida* 22

Brazilian Court | *Palm Bch.* 23

Casa Ybel | *Ft. Myers* — 20
Cheeca Lodge | *Keys* — 21
Colony Beach | *Sarasota* — 18
Disney's Vero Beach | *Vero Bch.* — 23
Fisher Island | *Miami* — 23
Grove Isle | *Miami* — 26
Hawk's Cay Resort | *Keys* — 21
Hyatt | *Keys* — 23
🆉 Little Palm Island | *Keys* — 27
Longboat Key Club | *Sarasota* — 22
Marco Beach Resort | *Naples* — 24
Marco Is. Marriott | *Naples* — 22
Marquesa | *Keys* — 25
Pier Hse. Resort | *Keys* — 20
🆉 Ritz-Carlton | *NE Florida* — 26
Ritz-Carlton Key Bisc. | *Miami* — 24
South Seas Resort | *Ft. Myers* — 21
Sunset Key/Cottages | *Keys* — 26
WaterColor Inn | *Panhandle* — 27

GEORGIA

🆉 Cloister | *GA Coast* — 27
Jekyll Is. Club | *GA Coast* — 21
🆉 Lodge/Sea Is. | *GA Coast* — 28
Ldg./Little St. Simon | *GA Coast* — 23

HAWAII

Fairmont | *Big Island* — 25
Fairmont | *Maui* — 27
🆉 Four Seasons/Koele | *Lanai* — 27
Four Seasons/Manele | *Lanai* — 27
🆉 Four Seasons Resort | *Big Island* — 29
Grand Hyatt | *Kauai* — 24
Grand Wailea | *Maui* — 24
Halekulani | *Oahu* — 25
Hanalei Bay Resort | *Kauai* — 20
Hana-Maui | *Maui* — 27
Hapuna Bch. Prince | *Big Island* — 23
Hawaii Prince Waikiki | *Oahu* — 21
Hilton Waikoloa Vill. | *Big Island* — 21
Hyatt | *Maui* — 22
JW Marriott | *Oahu* — 26
Kahala | *Oahu* — 25
Kapalua Villas | *Maui* — 23
Kauai Marriott | *Kauai* — 21
Kona Village Resort | *Big Island* — 25
Marriott | *Oahu* — 21
Maui Prince | *Maui* — 19
Mauna Lani Resort | *Big Island* — 24
Moana Surfrider | *Oahu* — 21
🆉 Ritz-Carlton | *Maui* — 25
Sheraton | *Maui* — 22
Westin | *Maui* — 22

MASSACHUSETTS
Charlotte Inn | *Cape Cod/Is.* — 23
Jared Coffin Hse. | *Cape Cod/Is.* — 21
Wauwinet | *Cape Cod/Is.* — 25

MICHIGAN
Grand Hotel | *Mackinac Is.* — 22
Iroquois/Beach | *Mackinac Is.* — 22

NEW HAMPSHIRE
Wentworth by Sea | *Newcastle* — 25

NEW YORK
Ram's Head Inn | *Long Island* — 16

PUERTO RICO
Bravo Beach | *Vieques* — -
El Conquistador | *Fajardo* — 21
El Convento | *San Juan* — 21
El San Juan | *San Juan* — 20
🆉 Horned Dorset | *Rincon* — 26
Las Casitas Village | *Fajardo* — 26
Rio Mar Beach | *San Juan* — 22
Ritz-Carlton | *San Juan* — 24

RHODE ISLAND
1661 Inn | *Block Is.* — -

SOUTH CAROLINA
Sea Pines Resort | *Hilton Head* — 22
Wild Dunes Resort | *Charleston* — 21

U.S. VIRGIN ISLANDS
Buccaneer | *St. Croix* — 23
Caneel Bay | *St. John* — 23
Ritz-Carlton | *St. Thomas* — 25
Westin | *St. John* — 21

WASHINGTON
🆉 Inn at Langley | *Seattle* — 25

MOUNTAIN SETTINGS/VIEWS

ALASKA
Alyeska Resort | *Anchorage* — 21

ARIZONA
Arizona Grand | *Phoenix/Scott.* — 19
🆉 Canyon Ranch | *Tucson* — 24
🆉 Enchantment | *Sedona* — 26
Fairmont | *Phoenix/Scott.* — 25
🆉 Four Seasons | *Phoenix/Scott.* — 27
Hacienda del Sol | *Tucson* — 19
Hermosa Inn | *Phoenix/Scott.* — 22
Hilton | *Sedona* — 23
Hilton El Conquistador | *Tucson* — 19
Hyatt | *Phoenix/Scott.* — 21

JW Marriott | *Tucson*	25
JW Marriott Camelback | *Phoenix/Scott.*	23
JW Marriott Desert | *Phoenix/Scott.*	24
L'Auberge/Sedona | *Sedona*	23
Ldg./Ventana Canyon | *Tucson*	22
Loews | *Tucson*	24
Miraval Spa | *Tucson*	24
Phoenician | *Phoenix/Scott.*	26
Pointe Hilton Squaw | *Phoenix/Scott.*	19
Pointe Hilton Tapatio | *Phoenix/Scott.*	19
Renaissance | *Phoenix/Scott.*	21
Ritz-Carlton | *Phoenix/Scott.*	22
Royal Palms | *Phoenix/Scott.*	24
⛋ Sanctuary | *Phoenix/Scott.*	26
Tanque Verde Ranch | *Tucson*	20
Valley Ho | *Phoenix/Scott.*	24
Westin | *Tucson*	22
Westward Look | *Tucson*	20
Wigwam Golf | *Phoenix/Scott.*	24

CALIFORNIA

Ahwahnee | *Yosemite*	20
Alisal | *Santa Barbara*	17
Bacara Resort | *Santa Barbara*	26
Barona Valley Ranch | *San Diego*	19
Bernardus Lodge | *Carmel*	26
Calistoga Ranch | *Wine Co.*	26
Carmel Valley Ranch | *Carmel*	23
⛋ Château du Sureau | *Yosemite*	27
Desert Springs | *Palm Springs*	21
Fairmont | *Wine Co.*	21
Fairmont | *LA*	21
Fairmont | *SF*	22
Fess Parker | *Santa Barbara*	21
Four Seasons | *Santa Barbara*	26
Four Seasons Silicon | *SF*	26
Harvest Inn | *Wine Co.*	23
Healdsburg | *Wine Co.*	24
Hyatt | *Palm Springs*	22
La Quinta | *Palm Springs*	22
Miramonte | *Palm Springs*	23
Ojai Valley Inn | *Santa Barbara*	25
⛋ Post Ranch Inn | *Carmel*	28
Quail Lodge | *Carmel*	23
Renaissance | *LA*	22
Resort/Squaw Creek | *Lake Tahoe*	22
Ritz-Carlton | *Half Moon Bay*	27
San Ysidro | *Santa Barbara*	26
NEW Solage | *Wine Co.*	23

Sunset Tower | *LA*	21
Tamarack | *Mammoth Lakes*	15
Tenaya Lodge | *Yosemite*	19
Ventana Inn | *Carmel*	25
Viceroy | *Palm Springs*	21
Westin | *LA*	22

COLORADO

Beaver Creek Ldg. | *Beaver Creek*	24
Boulderado | *Denver*	19
⛋ Broadmoor | *CO Springs*	26
C Lazy U Ranch | *Denver*	22
Cliff House/Pikes | *CO Springs*	-
Curtis | *Denver*	-
Grand Hyatt | *Denver*	22
Home Ranch | *Clark*	-
Jerome | *Aspen*	22
JW Marriott | *Denver*	25
Keyah Grande | *Pagosa Springs*	-
Keystone Resort | *Keystone*	20
⛋ Little Nell | *Aspen*	27
Lodge/Cordillera | *Beaver Creek*	25
Lodge at Vail | *Vail*	23
Park Hyatt | *Beaver Creek*	23
Peaks Resort | *Telluride*	20
Pines Lodge | *Beaver Creek*	24
⛋ Ritz-Carlton | *Beaver Creek*	28
Sonnenalp | *Vail*	27
St Julien | *Denver*	26
St. Regis | *Aspen*	26
Teatro | *Denver*	24
Vail Cascade Resort | *Vail*	22
Westin | *Denver*	21

CONNECTICUT

Boulders | *New Preston*	20

GEORGIA

NEW Mansion/Peachtree | *Atlanta*	-

HAWAII

Ala Moana | *Oahu*	18
Fairmont | *Big Island*	25
⛋ Four Seasons/Koele | *Lanai*	27
Hanalei Bay Resort | *Kauai*	20
Hana-Maui | *Maui*	27
Hilton Waikoloa Vill. | *Big Island*	21
Hyatt | *Maui*	22
JW Marriott | *Oahu*	26
Sheraton | *Maui*	22

IDAHO

Knob Hill | *Ketchum*	-
Sun Valley Resort | *Sun Valley*	21

SPECIAL FEATURES

MASSACHUSETTS

ℤ Blantyre | *Lenox* — 26
ℤ Canyon Ranch | *Lenox* — 22
Cranwell Resort | *Lenox* — 21
ℤ Wheatleigh | *Lenox* — 26

MISSOURI

Chateau on Lake | *Branson* — 23

MONTANA

Resort/Paws Up | *Missoula* — _|
Triple Creek Ranch | *Darby* — 29

NEVADA

Green Valley Ranch | *Las Vegas* — 24
Hard Rock | *Las Vegas* — 20
Hyatt | *Incline Vill.* — 21
JW Marriott | *Las Vegas* — 27
Loews | *Las Vegas* — 22
Red Rock | *Las Vegas* — 27
Treasure Island | *Las Vegas* — _|

NEW HAMPSHIRE

Balsams | *Dixville Notch* — 19
Manor/Golden Pond | *White Mtns.* — _|
Mount Wash. | *White Mtns.* — 18

NEW JERSEY

Grand Cascades | *Hamburg* — _|

NEW MEXICO

Bishop's Lodge | *Santa Fe* — 19
Eldorado | *Santa Fe* — 22
El Monte Sagrado | *Taos* — 25
NEW Encantado | *Santa Fe* — _|
Hyatt Albuquerque | *Albuquerque* — 18
Hyatt Tamaya | *Albuquerque* — 23
Inn of the Anasazi | *Santa Fe* — 24

NEW YORK

Elk Lake Lodge | *Adirondacks* — _|
Mirror Lake Inn | *Adirondacks* — 23
Mohonk Mtn. Hse. | *Catskills* — 18
ℤ Point | *Adirondacks* — 27
Sagamore | *Adirondacks* — 21
Troutbeck Estate | *Amenia* — 18
Whiteface Lodge | *Adirondacks* — 23

NORTH CAROLINA

Grove Park Inn | *Asheville* — 20
Inn on Biltmore | *Asheville* — 25
Richmond Hill | *Asheville* — 23

OREGON

Columbia Gorge | *Hood River* — 20
Sunriver | *Mt. Bachelor* — 21
ℤ Timberline Ldg. | *Mt. Hood* — 16
ℤ Tu Tu' Tun Lodge | *Gold Bch.* — 26

PENNSYLVANIA

Glendorn | *Bradford* — _|
Nemacolin | *Farmington* — 25
Skytop Lodge | *Poconos* — 15

PUERTO RICO

El Conquistador | *Fajardo* — 21
Rio Mar Beach | *San Juan* — 22

TENNESSEE

ℤ Blackberry Farm | *Walland* — 28
Lodge/Buckberry | *Gatlinburg* — _|

TEXAS

Barton Creek | *Austin* — 23
Renaissance | *Austin* — 20

UTAH

Goldener Hirsch Inn | *Park City* — 21
Grand America | *Salt Lake City* — 27
Little America | *Salt Lake City* — 20
Monaco | *Salt Lake City* — 21
Snowbird | *Salt Lake City* — 17
Stein Eriksen Lodge | *Park City* — 24
Sundance | *Salt Lake City* — 23

VERMONT

Equinox | *S. VT* — 20
Green Mtn. Inn | *Stowe* — 22
Inn/Essex | *Lake Champlain* — 21
Inn/Sawmill | *S. VT* — 22
Inn/Shelburne | *Lake Champlain* — 22
Old Tavern/Grafton | *S. VT* — 21
Pitcher Inn | *Central Vermont* — 25
Reluctant Panther | *S. VT* — 27
Stratton Mtn. Resort | *S. VT* — 19
Topnotch | *Stowe* — 21
Trapp | *Stowe* — 19
ℤ Twin Farms | *Woodstock* — 29
Woodstock Inn | *Woodstock* — 22

VIRGINIA

Clifton Inn | *Charlottesville* — 21
Goodstone Inn | *DC Metro* — _|
Homestead | *Hot Springs* — 21
ℤ Inn/Little Wash. | *Washington* — 28
ℤ Keswick Hall | *Charlottesville* — 26
L'Auberge Provençale | *White Post* — 23

WASHINGTON

Edgewater | *Seattle* — 22
Grand Hyatt | *Seattle* — 27
Inn at the Market | *Seattle* — 23
Marriott | *Seattle* — 23
Salish Lodge | *Seattle* — 25
Sun Mtn. Lodge | *Winthrop* — _|

Watertown | *Seattle* —|
Woodmark | *Seattle* 24
W Seattle | *Seattle* 23

WEST VIRGINIA
☑ Greenbrier | *White Sulphur Springs* 25

WYOMING
☑ Amangani | *Jackson Hole* 29
☑ Four Seasons | *Jackson Hole* 27
Jackson Lake Ldg. | *Jackson Hole* 19
Jenny Lake Ldg. | *Jackson Hole* 22
Rusty Parrot | *Jackson Hole* 23
Snake River Ldg. | *Jackson Hole* 21
Teton Mnt. Ldg. | *Jackson Hole* —|

NOTEWORTHY NEWCOMERS

CALIFORNIA
☑ Grand/Mar | *San Diego* 26
Hard Rock | *San Diego* 20
InterContinental | *SF* 25
Ivy | *San Diego* 24
London W. Hollywood | *LA* —|
Nick's Cove | *N. CA Coast* 25
Palomar | *LA* —|
Solage | *Wine Co.* 23

CONNECTICUT
MGM Grand | *Ledyard* —|

DISTRICT OF COLUMBIA
Donovan House | *DC* —|
Liaison Capitol Hill | *DC* —|

FLORIDA
Gansevoort South | *Miami* 26
Regent Bal Harbour | *Miami* —|

GEORGIA
Mansion/Peachtree | *Atlanta* —|
W Atlanta Midtown | *Atlanta* —|

ILLINOIS
Blackstone | *Chicago* —|
Dana | *Chicago* —|
InterContinental | *Chicago* —|
Trump Int'l | *Chicago* —|

INDIANA
West Baden Springs | *Indianapolis* —|

MAINE
Hidden Pond | *S. Coast* —|

MARYLAND
Gaylord Nat'l | *Baltimore* —|
Hilton | *Baltimore* —|

MASSACHUSETTS
Indigo | *Boston* —|
Le Méridien Cambridge | *Boston* 22
Liberty | *Boston* 24
Renaissance | *Boston* —|

MICHIGAN
MGM Grand | *Detroit* 26

MINNESOTA
W Minneapolis | *Mpls./St. Paul* —|

MISSOURI
Four Seasons | *St. Louis* 29

NEBRASKA
Omaha Magnolia | *Omaha* —|

NEVADA
☑ Palazzo | *Las Vegas* 28
Trump Int'l | *Las Vegas* 21

NEW JERSEY
Chelsea | *Atlantic City* —|
Water Club | *Atlantic City* —|

NEW MEXICO
Encantado | *Santa Fe* —|

NEW YORK
Bowery | *NYC* 21
Duane Street | *NYC* —|
Empire | *NYC* —|
Gild Hall | *NYC* —|
Jane | *NYC* —|
Ravel | *NYC* —|
Ritz-Carlton | *Westchester* 27
Six Columbus | *NYC* —|

NORTH CAROLINA
Proximity Hotel | *Greensboro* 23

TENNESSEE
Indigo | *Nashville* —|

TEXAS
Joule | *DFW* —|
NYLO Plano | *DFW* —|

VIRGINIA
Palomar | *DC Metro* —|
Westin | *DC Metro* —|

WASHINGTON
Four Seasons | *Seattle* —|
Murano | *Tacoma* —|

NO TVS/PHONES

(In-room)

CALIFORNIA
Alisal | *Santa Barbara* | 17
Deetjen's | *Carmel* | 15
Seven Gables Inn | *Carmel* | 24
St. Orres | *N. CA Coast* | -
Whale Watch | *N. CA Coast* | 24

COLORADO
C Lazy U Ranch | *Denver* | 22
Home Ranch | *Clark* | -

FLORIDA
🄯 Little Palm Island | *Keys* | 27

GEORGIA
Ldg./Little St. Simon | *GA Coast* | 23

HAWAII
Kona Village Resort | *Big Island* | 25

MARYLAND
Antrim 1844 | *Baltimore* | 24

NEW YORK
Elk Lake Lodge | *Adirondacks* | -
🄯 Point | *Adirondacks* | 27

TEXAS
Cibolo Creek Ranch | *Marfa* | -

U.S. VIRGIN ISLANDS
Caneel Bay | *St. John* | 23

OFFBEAT/FUNKY

ARKANSAS
Peabody, The | *Little Rock* | 20

CALIFORNIA
Avalon | *LA* | 18
Carneros Inn | *Wine Co.* | 28
Casa Madrona | *SF* | 23
Chateau Marmont | *LA* | 21
NEW Ivy | *San Diego* | 24
Kabuki | *SF* | 20
Le Parker Méridien | *Palm Springs* | 22
NEW London W. Hollywood | *LA* | -
Mondrian | *LA* | 19
Serrano | *SF* | 18
Standard Downtown | *LA* | 19
Stanford Park | *SF* | 23
St. Orres | *N. CA Coast* | -

COLORADO
Curtis | *Denver* | -
Monaco | *Denver* | 22
Teatro | *Denver* | 24

CONNECTICUT
Homestead Inn | *Greenwich* | 21

DISTRICT OF COLUMBIA
George | *DC* | 21
Helix | *DC* | 23
Madera | *DC* | 20
Monaco | *DC* | 20

FLORIDA
Delano | *Miami* | 21
NEW Gansevoort South | *Miami* | 26
Hotel, The | *Miami* | 19
Mayfair | *Miami* | 23
Seminole Hard Rock | *Ft. Lauderdale* | 20
Victor | *Miami* | 22

GEORGIA
Mansion/Forsyth | *Savannah* | 26

HAWAII
Hana-Maui | *Maui* | 27
Kona Village Resort | *Big Island* | 25
Outrigger Waikiki | *Oahu* | 19

ILLINOIS
Monaco | *Chicago* | 21

LOUISIANA
Le Pavillon | *New Orleans* | 19

MASSACHUSETTS
NEW Le Méridien Cambridge | *Boston* | 22
Marlowe | *Boston* | 23
Nine Zero | *Boston* | 23

MINNESOTA
Graves 601 | *Mpls./St. Paul* | 26

NEVADA
Hard Rock | *Las Vegas* | 20
Planet Hollywood | *Las Vegas* | 18
Rio All-Suite | *Las Vegas* | 20

NEW YORK
Library | *NYC* | 21
Maritime | *NYC* | 17
Mercer | *NYC* | 23
Night | *NYC* | 16
Royalton | *NYC* | 20

OREGON
Lucia | *Portland* | 19

PUERTO RICO
Water & Beach Club | *San Juan* 18

TEXAS
Derek | *Houston* 22
Driskill | *Austin* 23
Magnolia | *DFW* 24
Menger | *San Antonio* 17

VERMONT
Pitcher Inn | *Central Vermont* 25
Trapp | *Stowe* 19

VIRGINIA
Goodstone Inn | *DC Metro* -

WASHINGTON
Monaco | *Seattle* 22

WYOMING
Old Faithful Inn | *Yellowstone* 16

POWER SCENES

ARIZONA
JW Marriott | *Tucson* 25

CALIFORNIA
🅩 Bel-Air | *LA* 27
🅩 Beverly Hills Hotel | *LA* 26
Beverly Wilshire | *LA* 25
🅩 Casa Palmero | *Carmel* 29
Chateau Marmont | *LA* 21
Clift | *SF* 20
Fairmont | *SF* 22
🅩 Four Seasons | *SF* 27
Four Seasons Bev. Hills | *LA* 25
🅩 NEW Grand/Mar | *San Diego* 26
Hilton Checkers | *LA* 19
InterContinental | *LA* 21
JW Marriott | *SF* 22
Mandarin Oriental | *SF* 27
Mondrian | *LA* 19
🅩 Peninsula | *LA* 27
Raffles L'Ermitage | *LA* 27
🅩 Ritz-Carlton | *SF* 26
St. Regis | *SF* 27
Westin | *LA* 22
W San Diego | *San Diego* 21

COLORADO
Brown Palace | *Denver* 20
Jerome | *Aspen* 22
🅩 Little Nell | *Aspen* 27
Lodge/Cordillera | *Beaver Creek* 25
St. Regis | *Aspen* 26
Teatro | *Denver* 24
Westin | *Denver* 21

DELAWARE
du Pont | *Wilmington* 24

DISTRICT OF COLUMBIA
🅩 Four Seasons | *DC* 26
Hay-Adams | *DC* 24
Madison/Loews | *DC* 19
Renaissance | *DC* 21
Ritz-Carlton | *DC* 26
🅩 Ritz-Carlton Georgetown | *DC* 27
St. Regis | *DC* 23
Willard InterCont. | *DC* 24

FLORIDA
Fontainebleau | *Miami* 18
National | *Miami* 18
🅩 Ritz-Carlton | *Naples* 27
Victor | *Miami* 22

GEORGIA
🅩 Cloister | *GA Coast* 27
Four Seasons | *Atlanta* 25
InterContinental | *Atlanta* 26
NEW Mansion/Peachtree | *Atlanta* -
Ritz-Carlton Buckhead | *Atlanta* 24
🅩 Ritz-Carlton | *Lake Oconee* 26

HAWAII
Halekulani | *Oahu* 25
JW Marriott | *Oahu* 26
Kahala | *Oahu* 25

ILLINOIS
🅩 Four Seasons | *Chicago* 27
Park Hyatt | *Chicago* 27
🅩 Peninsula | *Chicago* 29
Ritz-Carlton | *Chicago* 26
NEW Trump Int'l | *Chicago* -

INDIANA
Conrad | *Indianapolis* 27

LOUISIANA
Omni | *New Orleans* 21
Ritz-Carlton | *New Orleans* 25
🅩 Windsor Court | *New Orleans* 24
W New Orleans | *New Orleans* 23

MASSACHUSETTS
Boston Harbor | *Boston* 24
Fifteen Beacon | *Boston* 24
Four Seasons | *Boston* 27
Langham | *Boston* 21
Ritz-Carlton | *Boston* 25
Taj | *Boston* 22
Wauwinet | *Cape Cod/Is.* 25

SPECIAL FEATURES

MICHIGAN

NEW MGM Grand | *Detroit*	26
Townsend | *Detroit*	24

MINNESOTA

Graves 601 | *Mpls./St. Paul*	26

MISSOURI

NEW Four Seasons | *St. Louis*	29

NEVADA

Z Bellagio | *Las Vegas*	26
Z NEW Palazzo | *Las Vegas*	28
Palms Casino Resort | *Las Vegas*	20
NEW Trump Int'l | *Las Vegas*	21
Venetian | *Las Vegas*	27
Z Wynn | *Las Vegas*	28

NEW YORK

Carlyle | *NYC*	25
Z Four Seasons | *NYC*	28
Garden City | *Long Island*	23
Gramercy Park | *NYC*	22
Jumeirah Essex Hse. | *NYC*	22
Le Parker Méridien | *NYC*	21
Z Mandarin Oriental | *NYC*	28
Maritime | *NYC*	17
New York Palace | *NYC*	25
Peninsula | *NYC*	26
Z Point | *Adirondacks*	27
Ritz-Carlton Battery Pk. | *NYC*	27
Royalton | *NYC*	20
Trump Int'l | *NYC*	23
Waldorf=Astoria | *NYC*	21

OREGON

Benson | *Portland*	20
Heathman | *Portland*	20

PENNSYLVANIA

Park Hyatt | *Philadelphia*	22
Z Rittenhouse | *Philadelphia*	26
Ritz-Carlton | *Philadelphia*	24

TEXAS

Adolphus | *DFW*	23
Derek | *Houston*	22
Driskill | *Austin*	23
Four Seasons | *Houston*	25
Houstonian | *Houston*	23
Icon | *Houston*	24
Z Rosewood | *DFW*	26

VIRGINIA

Jefferson | *Richmond*	24

ROMANTIC

ARIZONA

L'Auberge/Sedona | *Sedona*	23
Royal Palms | *Phoenix/Scott.*	24
Z Sanctuary | *Phoenix/Scott.*	26
Valley Ho | *Phoenix/Scott.*	24

CALIFORNIA

Z Auberge/Soleil | *Wine Co.*	28
Z Bel-Air | *LA*	27
Bernardus Lodge | *Carmel*	26
Z Beverly Hills Hotel | *LA*	26
Bodega Bay | *N. CA Coast*	23
Calistoga Ranch | *Wine Co.*	26
Carmel Valley Ranch | *Carmel*	23
Casa Madrona | *SF*	23
Z Château du Sureau | *Yosemite*	27
Claremont Resort | *SF*	18
Four Seasons | *Santa Barbara*	26
Z NEW Grand/Mar | *San Diego*	26
Healdsburg | *Wine Co.*	24
Highlands Inn | *Carmel*	23
Inn Above Tide | *SF*	26
Inn/Spanish Bay | *Carmel*	26
Inn/Spanish Gdn. | *Santa Barbara*	26
Inn/Rancho Santa Fe | *San Diego*	21
Kenwood Inn | *Wine Co.*	26
La Costa Resort | *San Diego*	22
La Playa | *Carmel*	18
Z L'Auberge Carmel | *Carmel*	25
L'Auberge Del Mar | *San Diego*	23
La Valencia | *San Diego*	22
Maison Fleurie | *Wine Co.*	18
Z Meadowood | *Wine Co.*	27
Milliken Creek Inn | *Wine Co.*	26
Miramonte | *Palm Springs*	23
Orchard | *SF*	22
Quail Lodge | *Carmel*	23
Z Rancho Valencia | *San Diego*	28
San Ysidro | *Santa Barbara*	26
Seven Gables Inn | *Carmel*	24
Shutters | *LA*	25
Silverado Resort | *Wine Co.*	18
NEW Solage | *Wine Co.*	23
Solamar | *San Diego*	26
Tickle Pink Inn | *Carmel*	24
Ventana Inn | *Carmel*	25
Villagio Inn | *Wine Co.*	24
Vintners Inn | *Wine Co.*	25
Vitale | *SF*	25
Westin St. Francis | *SF*	20
Whale Watch | *N. CA Coast*	24
White Swan Inn | *SF*	22

COLORADO

Boulderado | *Denver* — 19
Keyah Grande | *Pagosa Springs* — -
Z Little Nell | *Aspen* — 27
Lodge/Cordillera | *Beaver Creek* — 25
Sonnenalp | *Vail* — 27

CONNECTICUT

Inn/National Hall | *Westport* — 27
Mayflower Inn | *Washington* — 27

DELAWARE

Bellmoor | *Rehoboth Bch.* — 25

FLORIDA

Buena Vista Palace | *Orlando* — 20
Casa Monica | *NE Florida* — 23
Disney's Bch. Club Resort | *Orlando* — 22
Z Disney's Bch. Club Villas | *Orlando* — 27
Disney's BoardWalk Inn | *Orlando* — 24
Z Disney's BoardWalk Villas | *Orlando* — 27
Disney's Contemporary | *Orlando* — 20
Disney's Wilderness | *Orlando* — 24
Ginn Hammock | *Palm Coast* — -
Grove Isle | *Miami* — 26
Z Little Palm Island | *Keys* — 27
Marquesa | *Keys* — 25
Mayfair | *Miami* — 23
Standard | *Miami* — 20
Walt Disney Dolphin | *Orlando* — 19
Walt Disney Swan | *Orlando* — 21

GEORGIA

Ballastone | *Savannah* — 26
Z Ritz-Carlton | *Lake Oconee* — 26

HAWAII

Fairmont | *Big Island* — 25
Z Four Seasons/Koele | *Lanai* — 27
Z Four Seasons Resort | *Big Island* — 29
Z Four Seasons Resort | *Maui* — 28
Hana-Maui | *Maui* — 27
Kona Village Resort | *Big Island* — 25
Moana Surfrider | *Oahu* — 21
Turtle Bay Resort | *Oahu* — 21

IDAHO

Knob Hill | *Ketchum* — -

ILLINOIS

Drake | *Chicago* — 20
Whitehall | *Chicago* — 20

INDIANA

NEW West Baden Springs | *Indianapolis* — -

LOUISIANA

Soniat House | *New Orleans* — 26

MAINE

Z White Barn Inn | *S. Coast* — 25

MARYLAND

Antrim 1844 | *Baltimore* — 24
Inn/Perry Cabin | *Eastern Shore* — 25

MASSACHUSETTS

Charlotte Inn | *Cape Cod/Is.* — 23
Jacob Hill Inn | *Boston* — 28
Marlowe | *Boston* — 23
Z Wheatleigh | *Lenox* — 26

MISSISSIPPI

Monmouth Plantation | *Natchez* — 26

NEVADA

Platinum | *Las Vegas* — -
Red Rock | *Las Vegas* — 27

NEW JERSEY

Queen Victoria | *Cape May* — 22

NEW YORK

Algonquin | *NYC* — 16
Carlyle | *NYC* — 25
Castle/Hudson | *Westchester* — 23
Inn at Irving Pl. | *NYC* — 24
Z Lowell | *NYC* — 25
Z Point | *Adirondacks* — 27

NORTH CAROLINA

Grove Park Inn | *Asheville* — 20

PENNSYLVANIA

Glendorn | *Bradford* — -

PUERTO RICO

Z Horned Dorset | *Rincon* — 26

SOUTH CAROLINA

Inn/Palmetto | *Hilton Head* — 29

TENNESSEE

Z Blackberry Farm | *Walland* — 28
Lodge/Buckberry | *Gatlinburg* — -

TEXAS

Galvez | *Galveston* — 18
La Mansión del Rio | *San Antonio* — 21

U.S. VIRGIN ISLANDS

Buccaneer | *St. Croix* — 23
Caneel Bay | *St. John* — 23

SPECIAL FEATURES

UTAH

Goldener Hirsch Inn | *Park City* · 21

VERMONT

Inn/Sawmill | *S. VT* · 22
Pitcher Inn | *Central Vermont* · 25
Z Twin Farms | *Woodstock* · 29

VIRGINIA

Boar's Head | *Charlottesville* · 19
Goodstone Inn | *DC Metro* · –
Z Inn/Little Wash. | *Washington* · 28
L'Auberge Provençale | *White Post* · 23
Morrison Hse. | *DC Metro* · 23

WASHINGTON

Z Inn at Langley | *Seattle* · 25
Sorrento | *Seattle* · 23

WISCONSIN

Canoe Bay | *Chetek* · 28

SAILING

ALABAMA

Marriott | *Point Clear* · 21

CALIFORNIA

Alisal | *Santa Barbara* · 17
del Coronado | *San Diego* · 20
Loews | *San Diego* · 21
Malibu Beach Inn | *LA* · 20
Manchester Gr. Hyatt | *San Diego* · 22
Marriott Marina | *San Diego* · 19
Ritz-Carlton | *Half Moon Bay* · 27
Z Ritz-Carlton | *OC Beaches* · 27
Ritz-Carlton | *LA* · 24

CONNECTICUT

Boulders | *New Preston* · 20

FLORIDA

Amelia Is. Plant. | *NE Florida* · 22
Atlantic Resort | *Ft. Lauderdale* · 26
Boca Raton | *Ft. Lauderdale* · 21
Cheeca Lodge | *Keys* · 21
Clearwater/Marriott | *Tampa* · 18
Colony Beach | *Sarasota* · 18
Z Disney's Bch. Club Villas | *Orlando* · 27
Disney's Caribbean Bch. | *Orlando* · 19
Disney's Contemporary | *Orlando* · 20
Disney's Grand Floridian | *Orlando* · 25
Disney's Old Key W. | *Orlando* · 25
Disney's Polynesian | *Orlando* · 22
Disney's Port Orleans/Fr. Q. | *Orlando* · 21

Disney's Port Orleans/River | *Orlando* · 22
Don CeSar Bch. | *Tampa* · 21
Fairmont | *Miami* · 26
Fisher Island | *Miami* · 23
Four Seasons Resort | *Palm Bch.* · 24
Grove Isle | *Miami* · 26
Hawk's Cay Resort | *Keys* · 21
Hyatt | *Keys* · 23
Hyatt | *Naples* · 25
Hyatt | *Orlando* · 21
La Playa Beach/Resort | *Naples* · 22
Z Little Palm Island | *Keys* · 27
Longboat Key Club | *Sarasota* · 22
Marco Beach Resort | *Naples* · 24
Marriott | *Ft. Lauderdale* · 21
Ponte Vedra Inn | *NE Florida* · 25
Z Ritz-Carlton | *Naples* · 27
Z Ritz-Carlton | *NE Florida* · 26
Ritz-Carlton | *Palm Bch.* · 26
Ritz-Carlton Key Bisc. | *Miami* · 24
Ritz-Carlton S. Bch. | *Miami* · 25
Sanibel Resort | *Ft. Myers* · 21
Shore Club | *Miami* · 16
Sunset Key/Cottages | *Keys* · 26
Villas/Grand Cypress | *Orlando* · 26
Walt Disney Swan | *Orlando* · 21
WaterColor Inn | *Panhandle* · 27
Westin | *Ft. Lauderdale* · 24

GEORGIA

Z Cloister | *GA Coast* · 27
Z Ritz-Carlton | *Lake Oconee* · 26

HAWAII

Fairmont | *Big Island* · 25
Fairmont | *Maui* · 27
Four Seasons/Manele | *Lanai* · 27
Z Four Seasons Resort | *Big Island* · 29
Z Four Seasons Resort | *Maui* · 28
Grand Wailea | *Maui* · 24
Hapuna Bch. Prince | *Big Island* · 23
Hilton Waikoloa Vill. | *Big Island* · 21
Hyatt | *Maui* · 22
JW Marriott | *Oahu* · 26
Kapalua Villas | *Maui* · 23
Kona Village Resort | *Big Island* · 25
Mauna Lani Resort | *Big Island* · 24
Sheraton | *Maui* · 22
Westin | *Maui* · 22

MAINE

Bar Harbor Inn | *Bar Harbor* · 21
Samoset | *Rockport* · 19
Z White Barn Inn | *S. Coast* · 25

MARYLAND
Hyatt | *Eastern Shore* 21
Inn/Perry Cabin | *Eastern Shore* 25

MASSACHUSETTS
Chatham Bars | *Cape Cod/Is.* 22
Cranwell Resort | *Lenox* 21
Wauwinet | *Cape Cod/Is.* 25
Wequassett | *Cape Cod/Is.* 21

MISSOURI
Chateau on Lake | *Branson* 23

NEVADA
Hyatt | *Incline Vill.* 21
Loews | *Las Vegas* 22

NEW YORK
Ram's Head Inn | *Long Island* 16
Sagamore | *Adirondacks* 21
Whiteface Lodge | *Adirondacks* 23

PUERTO RICO
⚡ Horned Dorset | *Rincon* 26
Las Casitas Village | *Fajardo* 26
Ritz-Carlton | *San Juan* 24

SOUTH CAROLINA
Charleston Pl. | *Charleston* 25
Inn/Palmetto | *Hilton Head* 29
Sea Pines Resort | *Hilton Head* 22
Westin | *Hilton Head* 21
Wild Dunes Resort | *Charleston* 21

U.S. VIRGIN ISLANDS
Caneel Bay | *St. John* 23
Ritz-Carlton | *St. Thomas* 25
Westin | *St. John* 21

UTAH
Goldener Hirsch Inn | *Park City* 21

VERMONT
Basin Harbor | *Lake Champlain* 19

VIRGINIA
Tides Inn | *Irvington* 22

WASHINGTON
Edgewater | *Seattle* 22
Sun Mtn. Lodge | *Winthrop* –
Woodmark | *Seattle* 24

SCUBA/SNORKELING

CALIFORNIA
La Valencia | *San Diego* 22
Malibu Beach Inn | *LA* 20

Manchester Gr. Hyatt | *San Diego* 22
⚡ Ritz-Carlton | *OC Beaches* 27
Whale Watch | *N. CA Coast* 24

FLORIDA
Boca Raton | *Ft. Lauderdale* 21
Breakers | *Palm Bch.* 24
Casa Marina Resort | *Keys* 21
Cheeca Lodge | *Keys* 21
Don CeSar Bch. | *Tampa* 21
Fairmont | *Miami* 26
Fisher Island | *Miami* 23
Four Seasons Resort | *Palm Bch.* 24
Grove Isle | *Miami* 26
Hawk's Cay Resort | *Keys* 21
Hyatt | *Keys* 23
La Playa Beach/Resort | *Naples* 22
⚡ Little Palm Island | *Keys* 27
Longboat Key Club | *Sarasota* 22
Marco Beach Resort | *Naples* 24
Marriott | *Ft. Lauderdale* 21
Ritz-Carlton | *Palm Bch.* 26
Ritz-Carlton Key Bisc. | *Miami* 24
Ritz-Carlton S. Bch. | *Miami* 25
Shore Club | *Miami* 16
South Seas Resort | *Ft. Myers* 21
Sunset Key/Cottages | *Keys* 26
WaterColor Inn | *Panhandle* 27
Westin | *Ft. Lauderdale* 24

GEORGIA
⚡ Cloister | *GA Coast* 27

HAWAII
Fairmont | *Big Island* 25
Fairmont | *Maui* 27
Four Seasons/Manele | *Lanai* 27
⚡ Four Seasons Resort | *Big Island* 29
⚡ Four Seasons Resort | *Maui* 28
Grand Hyatt | *Kauai* 24
Grand Wailea | *Maui* 24
Hanalei Bay Resort | *Kauai* 20
Hapuna Bch. Prince | *Big Island* 23
Hilton Waikoloa Vill. | *Big Island* 21
Hyatt | *Maui* 22
JW Marriott | *Oahu* 26
Kahala | *Oahu* 25
Kapalua Villas | *Maui* 23
Kona Village Resort | *Big Island* 25
Mauna Lani Resort | *Big Island* 24
Moana Surfrider | *Oahu* 21
⚡ Ritz-Carlton | *Maui* 25
Sheraton | *Maui* 22
Westin | *Maui* 22

SPECIAL FEATURES

MISSOURI

Chateau on Lake | *Branson* 23

PUERTO RICO

El Conquistador | *Fajardo* 21
🎲 Horned Dorset | *Rincon* 26
Las Casitas Village | *Fajardo* 26
Rio Mar Beach | *San Juan* 22

U.S. VIRGIN ISLANDS

Buccaneer | *St. Croix* 23
Caneel Bay | *St. John* 23
Ritz-Carlton | *St. Thomas* 25
Westin | *St. John* 21

UTAH

Goldener Hirsch Inn | *Park City* 21

SPA FACILITIES

ALABAMA

Marriott | *Point Clear* 21
Renaissance | *Birmingham* 25

ALASKA

Alyeska Resort | *Anchorage* 21

ARIZONA

Arizona Biltmore | *Phoenix/Scott.* 23
Arizona Grand | *Phoenix/Scott.* 19
🎲 Boulders | *Phoenix/Scott.* 26
🎲 Canyon Ranch | *Tucson* 24
🎲 Enchantment | *Sedona* 26
Fairmont | *Phoenix/Scott.* 25
🎲 Four Seasons | *Phoenix/Scott.* 27
Hacienda del Sol | *Tucson* 19
Hilton | *Sedona* 23
Hilton El Conquistador | *Tucson* 19
Hyatt | *Phoenix/Scott.* 21
JW Marriott | *Tucson* 25
JW Marriott Camelback | *Phoenix/Scott.* 23
JW Marriott Desert | *Phoenix/Scott.* 24
L'Auberge/Sedona | *Sedona* 23
Ldg./Ventana Canyon | *Tucson* 22
Loews | *Tucson* 24
Los Abrigados | *Sedona* 22
Miraval Spa | *Tucson* 24
Phoenician | *Phoenix/Scott.* 26
Pointe Hilton Squaw | *Phoenix/Scott.* 19
Pointe Hilton Tapatio | *Phoenix/Scott.* 19
Royal Palms | *Phoenix/Scott.* 24
🎲 Sanctuary | *Phoenix/Scott.* 26
Sheraton | *Phoenix/Scott.* 23

Valley Ho | *Phoenix/Scott.* 24
Westin | *Phoenix/Scott.* 24
Westin | *Tucson* 22
Westward Look | *Tucson* 20
Wigwam Golf | *Phoenix/Scott.* 24

CALIFORNIA

🎲 Auberge/Soleil | *Wine Co.* 28
Bacara Resort | *Santa Barbara* 26
Balboa Bay Club | *OC Beaches* 24
Barona Valley Ranch | *San Diego* 19
Bernardus Lodge | *Carmel* 26
🎲 Beverly Hills Hotel | *LA* 26
Beverly Hilton | *LA* 21
Beverly Wilshire | *LA* 25
Bodega Bay | *N. CA Coast* 23
Cal-a-Vie | *San Diego* –
Calistoga Ranch | *Wine Co.* 26
Carneros Inn | *Wine Co.* 28
Casa Del Mar | *LA* 25
Casa Madrona | *SF* 23
🎲 Casa Palmero | *Carmel* 29
🎲 Château du Sureau | *Yosemite* 27
Claremont Resort | *SF* 18
del Coronado | *San Diego* 20
Desert Springs | *Palm Springs* 21
Disney Grand Cal. | *LA* 22
Fairmont | *SF* 22
Fairmont | *Wine Co.* 21
Fairmont | *LA* 21
Fairmont | *SF* 22
🎲 Four Seasons | *San Diego* 27
🎲 Four Seasons | *SF* 27
Four Seasons | *Santa Barbara* 26
Four Seasons Bev. Hills | *LA* 25
Four Seasons Silicon | *SF* 26
Four Seasons Westlake | *LA* 25
Golden Door | *San Diego* 24
🎲 NEW Grand/Mar | *San Diego* 26
NEW Hard Rock | *San Diego* 20
Harvest Inn | *Wine Co.* 23
Healdsburg | *Wine Co.* 24
Hilton Checkers | *LA* 19
Huntington | *SF* 21
Hyatt Resort | *OC Beaches* 24
Hyatt | *Palm Springs* 22
Hyatt | *San Diego* 20
Inn/Spanish Bay | *Carmel* 26
Inn/Rancho Santa Fe | *San Diego* 21
NEW InterContinental | *SF* 25
InterContinental | *LA* 21
Island | *OC Beaches* 25
Kenwood Inn | *Wine Co.* 26

La Costa Resort | *San Diego*	22
Lafayette Park | *SF*	21
Langham Huntington | *LA*	24
La Playa | *Carmel*	18
La Quinta | *Palm Springs*	22
L'Auberge Del Mar | *San Diego*	23
Le Merigot | *LA*	23
Le Parker Méridien | *Palm Springs*	22
⧈ Lodge/Pebble Bch. | *Carmel*	26
Lodge/Torrey Pines | *San Diego*	25
Loews | *LA*	20
Loews | *San Diego*	21
MacArthur Pl. | *Wine Co.*	25
Manchester Gr. Hyatt | *San Diego*	22
Marriott | *OC Beaches*	20
Marriott | *SF*	19
Marriott Coronado | *San Diego*	23
⧈ Meadowood | *Wine Co.*	27
Milliken Creek Inn | *Wine Co.*	26
Miramonte | *Palm Springs*	23
Mission Inn | *Riverside*	19
Mondrian | *LA*	19
⧈ Montage | *OC Beaches*	27
Monterey Plaza | *Carmel*	22
Ojai Valley Inn | *Santa Barbara*	25
Omni | *LA*	20
Palace | *SF*	21
⧈ Peninsula | *LA*	27
⧈ Post Ranch Inn | *Carmel*	28
Quail Lodge | *Carmel*	23
Raffles L'Ermitage | *LA*	27
Rancho Bernardo | *San Diego*	21
⧈ Rancho Valencia | *San Diego*	28
Renaissance | *Palm Springs*	21
Renaissance | *LA*	22
Resort/Squaw Creek | *Lake Tahoe*	22
Ritz-Carlton | *Half Moon Bay*	27
⧈ Ritz-Carlton | *OC Beaches*	27
⧈ Ritz-Carlton | *SF*	26
Ritz-Carlton | *LA*	24
Shutters | *LA*	25
Silverado Resort | *Wine Co.*	18
Sofitel | *LA*	22
NEW Solage | *Wine Co.*	23
⧈ St. Regis | *OC Beaches*	27
St. Regis | *SF*	27
Sunset Tower | *LA*	21
Surf/Sand | *OC Beaches*	21
Tenaya Lodge | *Yosemite*	19
Two Bunch | *Palm Springs*	19
Ventana Inn | *Carmel*	25
Viceroy | *Palm Springs*	21

Villagio Inn | *Wine Co.*	24
Vitale | *SF*	25
Westgate | *San Diego*	23
Westin | *Palm Springs*	21
Westin St. Francis | *SF*	20
W San Diego | *San Diego*	21
W San Francisco | *SF*	23
W Westwood | *LA*	22

COLORADO

⧈ Broadmoor | *CO Springs*	26
Brown Palace | *Denver*	20
Hyatt | *Denver*	21
JW Marriott | *Denver*	25
Keyah Grande | *Pagosa Springs*	–
Keystone Resort | *Keystone*	20
Lodge/Cordillera | *Beaver Creek*	25
Monaco | *Denver*	22
Park Hyatt | *Beaver Creek*	23
Peaks Resort | *Telluride*	20
⧈ Ritz-Carlton | *Beaver Creek*	28
Sonnenalp | *Vail*	26
St Julien | *Denver*	26
St. Regis | *Aspen*	26
Vail Cascade Resort | *Vail*	22
Westin | *Denver*	21

CONNECTICUT

Foxwoods Resort | *Ledyard*	20
Hyatt | *Greenwich*	18
Mayflower Inn | *Washington*	27
NEW MGM Grand | *Ledyard*	–
Mohegan Sun | *Norwich*	23
Mystic Marriott | *Mystic*	20
Saybrook Point | *Old Saybrook*	21
Spa/Norwich Inn | *Norwich*	20

DELAWARE

Bellmoor | *Rehoboth Bch.*	25

DISTRICT OF COLUMBIA

Fairmont | *DC*	23
⧈ Four Seasons | *DC*	26
Madison/Loews | *DC*	19
Mandarin Oriental | *DC*	27
⧈ Ritz-Carlton Georgetown | *DC*	27
Willard InterCont. | *DC*	24

FLORIDA

⧈ Acqualina | *Miami*	28
Amelia Is. Plant. | *NE Florida*	22
Atlantic Resort | *Ft. Lauderdale*	26
Biltmore | *Miami*	23
Boca Raton | *Ft. Lauderdale*	21
Brazilian Court | *Palm Bch.*	23

Breakers | *Palm Bch.*	24
Buena Vista Palace | *Orlando*	20
Casa Marina Resort | *Keys*	21
Chalet Suzanne | *Tampa*	16
Cheeca Lodge | *Keys*	21
Clearwater/Marriott | *Tampa*	18
Colony Beach | *Sarasota*	18
Conrad | *Miami*	23
Delano | *Miami*	21
Disney's Animal King. | *Orlando*	24
Disney's Contemporary | *Orlando*	20
Disney's Coronado | *Orlando*	19
Disney's Grand Floridian | *Orlando*	25
Disney's Old Key W. | *Orlando*	25
Disney's Saratoga | *Orlando*	27
Don CeSar Bch. | *Tampa*	21
Doral Golf | *Miami*	19
Fairmont | *Miami*	26
Fisher Island | *Miami*	23
Fontainebleau | *Miami*	18
Four Seasons | *Miami*	26
Four Seasons Resort | *Palm Bch.*	24
NEW Gansevoort South | *Miami*	26
Gaylord Palms | *Orlando*	22
Ginn Hammock | *Palm Coast*	-
Grove Isle | *Miami*	26
Hawk's Cay Resort | *Keys*	21
Hilton | *Ft. Lauderdale*	21
Hyatt | *Keys*	23
Hyatt | *Naples*	25
International Plaza | *Orlando*	-
Jupiter Beach | *Palm Bch.*	20
JW Marriott | *Miami*	22
JW Marriott | *Orlando*	24
Lago Mar Resort | *Ft. Lauderdale*	20
La Playa Beach/Resort | *Naples*	22
ⓏLittle Palm Island | *Keys*	27
Loews | *Miami*	21
Loews Portofino | *Orlando*	24
Longboat Key Club | *Sarasota*	22
ⓏMandarin Oriental | *Miami*	27
Marco Beach Resort | *Naples*	24
Marco Is. Marriott | *Naples*	22
Marriott | *Ft. Lauderdale*	21
Marriott | *Orlando*	20
Mayfair | *Miami*	23
Naples Grande | *Naples*	24
Peabody | *Orlando*	21
PGA National | *Palm Bch.*	17
Pier Hse. Resort | *Keys*	20
Ponte Vedra Inn | *NE Florida*	25
NEW Regent Bal Harbour | *Miami*	-

Renaissance | *Orlando*	21
Renaissance | *Tampa*	24
Ⓩ Ritz-Carlton | *Naples*	27
Ⓩ Ritz-Carlton | *NE Florida*	26
Ⓩ Ritz-Carlton | *Orlando*	27
Ritz-Carlton | *Palm Bch.*	26
Ritz-Carlton | *Sarasota*	26
Ritz-Carlton Coconut | *Miami*	26
Ⓩ Ritz-Carlton Golf | *Naples*	26
Ritz-Carlton Key Bisc. | *Miami*	24
Ritz-Carlton S. Bch. | *Miami*	25
Rosen Shingle | *Orlando*	23
Saddlebrook | *Tampa*	22
Sanibel Resort | *Ft. Myers*	21
Seminole Hard Rock | *Ft. Lauderdale*	20
Setai | *Miami*	26
Shore Club | *Miami*	16
South Seas Resort | *Ft. Myers*	21
Standard | *Miami*	20
St. Regis | *Ft. Lauderdale*	27
Victor | *Miami*	22
Walt Disney Dolphin | *Orlando*	19
Walt Disney Swan | *Orlando*	21
WaterColor Inn | *Panhandle*	27
Westin | *Ft. Lauderdale*	24

GEORGIA

Château Élan | *Braselton*	23
Ⓩ Cloister | *GA Coast*	27
Four Seasons | *Atlanta*	25
InterContinental | *Atlanta*	26
Ⓩ Lodge/Sea Is. | *GA Coast*	28
Mansion/Forsyth | *Savannah*	26
NEW Mansion/Peachtree | *Atlanta*	-
Omni | *Atlanta*	20
Ⓩ Ritz-Carlton | *Lake Oconee*	26
NEW W Atlanta Midtown | *Atlanta*	-
Westin | *Savannah*	24

HAWAII

Fairmont | *Big Island*	25
Fairmont | *Maui*	27
Ⓩ Four Seasons/Koele | *Lanai*	27
Four Seasons/Manele | *Lanai*	27
Ⓩ Four Seasons Resort | *Big Island*	29
Ⓩ Four Seasons Resort | *Maui*	28
Grand Hyatt | *Kauai*	24
Grand Wailea | *Maui*	24
Halekulani | *Oahu*	25
Hana-Maui | *Maui*	27
Hapuna Bch. Prince | *Big Island*	23

Hawaii Prince Waikiki	*Oahu*	21
Hilton Kauai	*Kauai*	21
Hilton Hawaiian Vill.	*Oahu*	20
Hilton Waikoloa Vill.	*Big Island*	21
Hyatt	*Maui*	22
Hyatt	*Oahu*	20
JW Marriott	*Oahu*	26
Kaanapali Beach	*Maui*	17
Kahala	*Oahu*	25
Kauai Marriott	*Kauai*	21
Marriott	*Oahu*	21
Mauna Lani Resort	*Big Island*	24
Outrigger Reef	*Oahu*	16
Outrigger Waikiki	*Oahu*	19
🄩 Ritz-Carlton	*Maui*	25
Sheraton	*Kauai*	20
Sheraton	*Maui*	22
Turtle Bay Resort	*Oahu*	21
Westin	*Maui*	22

IDAHO

Coeur d'Alene	*Coeur d'Alene*	25
Sun Valley Resort	*Sun Valley*	21

ILLINOIS

NEW Dana	*Chicago*	-
Eagle Ridge Resort	*Galena*	19
Fairmont	*Chicago*	23
🄩 Four Seasons	*Chicago*	27
James	*Chicago*	24
Park Hyatt	*Chicago*	27
🄩 Peninsula	*Chicago*	29
Renaissance	*Chicago*	23
Ritz-Carlton	*Chicago*	26
NEW Trump Int'l	*Chicago*	-
Whitehall	*Chicago*	20
W Lakeshore	*Chicago*	20

INDIANA

Conrad	*Indianapolis*	27

KENTUCKY

21c Museum	*Louisville*	27

LOUISIANA

Iberville Suites	*New Orleans*	20
Loews	*New Orleans*	26
Monteleone	*New Orleans*	22
Ritz-Carlton	*New Orleans*	25

MAINE

Bar Harbor Inn	*Bar Harbor*	21
Breakwater Inn	*S. Coast*	20
Cliff House	*S. Coast*	20
Inn by the Sea	*Portland*	21
🄩 White Barn Inn	*S. Coast*	25

MARYLAND

NEW Gaylord Nat'l	*Baltimore*	-
Hyatt	*Eastern Shore*	21
Inn/Perry Cabin	*Eastern Shore*	25

MASSACHUSETTS

🄩 Blantyre	*Lenox*	26
Boston Harbor	*Boston*	24
🄩 Canyon Ranch	*Lenox*	22
Charles	*Boston*	23
Chatham Bars	*Cape Cod/Is.*	22
Cranwell Resort	*Lenox*	21
Four Seasons	*Boston*	27
InterContinental	*Boston*	25
Millennium Bostonian	*Boston*	21
Ocean Edge	*Cape Cod/Is.*	21
NEW Renaissance	*Boston*	-
Ritz-Carlton	*Boston*	25
Royal Sonesta	*Boston*	21
Wauwinet	*Cape Cod/Is.*	25
Westin Copley	*Boston*	22

MICHIGAN

Grand Hotel	*Mackinac Is.*	22
NEW MGM Grand	*Detroit*	26
St. Regis	*Detroit*	-

MINNESOTA

Grand Hotel	*Mpls./St. Paul*	24
Graves 601	*Mpls./St. Paul*	26

MISSOURI

Chase Park Plaza	*St. Louis*	22
Chateau on Lake	*Branson*	23
NEW Four Seasons	*St. Louis*	29

MONTANA

Resort/Paws Up	*Missoula*	-

NEVADA

🄩 Bellagio	*Las Vegas*	26
Caesars	*Las Vegas*	22
🄩 Four Seasons	*Las Vegas*	27
Green Valley Ranch	*Las Vegas*	24
Hard Rock	*Las Vegas*	20
Hyatt	*Incline Vill.*	21
JW Marriott	*Las Vegas*	27
Loews	*Las Vegas*	22
Mandalay Bay	*Las Vegas*	24
MGM Grand	*Las Vegas*	19
Mirage	*Las Vegas*	19
Orleans	*Las Vegas*	18
🄩 NEW Palazzo	*Las Vegas*	28
Palms Casino Resort	*Las Vegas*	20
Paris Las Vegas	*Las Vegas*	20
Planet Hollywood	*Las Vegas*	18

Platinum	*Las Vegas*	–
Red Rock	*Las Vegas*	27
Rio All-Suite	*Las Vegas*	20
Ritz-Carlton	*Las Vegas*	27
Signature/MGM Grand	*Las Vegas*	27
Treasure Island	*Las Vegas*	–
NEW Trump Int'l	*Las Vegas*	21
Venetian	*Las Vegas*	27
☒ Wynn	*Las Vegas*	28

NEW HAMPSHIRE

Balsams	*Dixville Notch*	19
Manor/Golden Pond	*White Mtns.*	–
Wentworth by Sea	*Newcastle*	25

NEW JERSEY

Atlantic City Hilton	*Atlantic City*	18
Borgata	*Atlantic City*	26
Caesars	*Atlantic City*	18
NEW Chelsea	*Atlantic City*	–
Congress Hall	*Cape May*	19
Grand Cascades	*Hamburg*	–
Harrah's Resort	*Atlantic City*	21
Hilton	*Short Hills*	22
Seaview	*Atlantic City*	19
Tropicana	*Atlantic City*	16
NEW Water Club	*Atlantic City*	–

NEW MEXICO

Bishop's Lodge	*Santa Fe*	19
Eldorado	*Santa Fe*	22
El Monte Sagrado	*Taos*	25
NEW Encantado	*Santa Fe*	–
Hyatt Tamaya	*Albuquerque*	23
La Fonda	*Santa Fe*	19
La Posada	*Santa Fe*	21

NEW YORK

Benjamin	*NYC*	21
Castle/Hudson	*Westchester*	23
NEW Empire	*NYC*	–
☒ Four Seasons	*NYC*	28
Gansevoort	*NYC*	20
Gramercy Park	*NYC*	22
Gurney's Inn	*Long Island*	17
Jumeirah Essex Hse.	*NYC*	22
Le Parker Méridien	*NYC*	21
☒ Mandarin Oriental	*NYC*	28
☒ Mirbeau Inn	*Catskills*	27
Mirror Lake Inn	*Adirondacks*	23
Mohonk Mtn. Hse.	*Catskills*	18
New York Palace	*NYC*	25
Plaza	*NYC*	25
NEW Ritz-Carlton	*Westchester*	27

Ritz-Carlton Battery Pk.	*NYC*	27
Ritz-Carlton Central Pk.	*NYC*	27
Sagamore	*Adirondacks*	21
St. Regis	*NYC*	27
Trump Int'l	*NYC*	23
Westin	*NYC*	23
Whiteface Lodge	*Adirondacks*	23
W New York	*NYC*	14
W Times Square	*NYC*	20

NORTH CAROLINA

Ballantyne	*Charlotte*	24
Greystone Inn	*Asheville*	24
Grove Park Inn	*Asheville*	20
Pinehurst Resort	*Pinehurst*	20
Richmond Hill	*Asheville*	23
Umstead	*Raleigh*	28

OHIO

Ritz-Carlton	*Cleveland*	24

OREGON

Columbia Gorge	*Hood River*	20
Monaco	*Portland*	22
Salishan Spa	*Gleneden Bch.*	24
Sunriver	*Mt. Bachelor*	21

PENNSYLVANIA

☒ Four Seasons	*Philadelphia*	26
Hershey	*Hershey*	22
☒ Lodge/Woodloch	*Hawley*	23
Loews	*Philadelphia*	23
Nemacolin	*Farmington*	25
Omni	*Philadelphia*	23
Omni	*Pittsburgh*	22
Park Hyatt	*Philadelphia*	22
☒ Rittenhouse	*Philadelphia*	26
Ritz-Carlton	*Philadelphia*	24
Skytop Lodge	*Poconos*	15

PUERTO RICO

Bravo Beach	*Vieques*	–
El Conquistador	*Fajardo*	21
El San Juan	*San Juan*	20
☒ Horned Dorset	*Rincon*	26
Las Casitas Village	*Fajardo*	26
Rio Mar Beach	*San Juan*	22
Ritz-Carlton	*San Juan*	24

RHODE ISLAND

Westin	*Providence*	23

SOUTH CAROLINA

Charleston Pl.	*Charleston*	25
Marriott	*Hilton Head*	21
Inn/Palmetto	*Hilton Head*	29

Myrtle/Marriott | *Myrtle Bch.* 24
☑ Sanctuary | *Kiawah Is.* 28
Sea Pines Resort | *Hilton Head* 22
Wentworth Mansion | *Charleston* 27
Westin | *Hilton Head* 21
Wild Dunes Resort | *Charleston* 21
☑ Woodlands | *Charleston* 26

TENNESSEE

☑ Blackberry Farm | *Walland* 28
Gaylord Opryland | *Nashville* 19
Hermitage | *Nashville* 27
Peabody | *Memphis* 19

TEXAS

Barton Creek | *Austin* 23
Four Seasons | *Austin* 25
Four Seasons | *DFW* 25
Four Seasons | *Houston* 25
Galvez | *Galveston* 18
Hilton | *Austin* 20
Hilton Americas | *Houston* 21
Hilton Anatole | *DFW* 20
Houstonian | *Houston* 23
Hyatt | *San Antonio* 23
Icon | *Houston* 24
InterContinental | *Houston* 21
☑ Lake Austin Spa | *Austin* 25
Menger | *San Antonio* 17
☑ Ritz-Carlton | *DFW* 28
Rosewood Crescent | *DFW* 25
Stoneleigh | *DFW* 22
St. Regis | *Houston* 25
Watermark | *San Antonio* 27
W Dallas-Victory | *DFW* 22
Westin La Cantera | *San Antonio* 22
Westin Riverwalk | *San Antonio* 22
Zaza | *DFW* 26

U.S. VIRGIN ISLANDS

Buccaneer | *St. Croix* 23
Caneel Bay | *St. John* 23
Ritz-Carlton | *St. Thomas* 25
Westin | *St. John* 21

UTAH

Grand America | *Salt Lake City* 27
Snowbird | *Salt Lake City* 17
Stein Eriksen Lodge | *Park City* 24
Sundance | *Salt Lake City* 23

VERMONT

Equinox | *S. VT* 20
Pitcher Inn | *Central Vermont* 25
Stratton Mtn. Resort | *S. VT* 19

Topnotch | *Stowe* 21
☑ Twin Farms | *Woodstock* 29
Woodstock Inn | *Woodstock* 22

VIRGINIA

Boar's Head | *Charlottesville* 19
Homestead | *Hot Springs* 21
☑ Keswick Hall | *Charlottesville* 26
Kingsmill Resort | *Williamsburg* 19
Lansdowne | *DC Metro* 20
Ritz-Carlton Tysons | *DC Metro* 25
Tides Inn | *Irvington* 22
Williams. Colonial | *Williamsburg* 23
Williams. Inn | *Williamsburg* 23
Williams. Lodge | *Williamsburg* 22

WASHINGTON

Alexis | *Seattle* 21
Bellevue Club | *Seattle* 24
Davenport | *Spokane* 28
NEW Four Seasons | *Seattle* -
☑ Inn at Langley | *Seattle* 25
NEW Murano | *Tacoma* -
1000 | *Seattle* 26
Pan Pacific | *Seattle* -
Salish Lodge | *Seattle* 25
Sun Mtn. Lodge | *Winthrop* -
☑ Willows Lodge | *Seattle* 27
Woodmark | *Seattle* 24

WEST VIRGINIA

☑ Greenbrier | 25
   White Sulphur Springs

WISCONSIN

☑ American Club | *Kohler* 25
Grand Geneva | *Lake Geneva* 19
Pfister | *Milwaukee* 22

WYOMING

☑ Amangani | *Jackson Hole* 29
☑ Four Seasons | *Jackson Hole* 27
Rusty Parrot | *Jackson Hole* 23
Snake River Ldg. | *Jackson Hole* 21

SPA FACILITIES: DIET/NUTRITION

ALABAMA

Marriott | *Point Clear* 21

ARIZONA

Arizona Grand | *Phoenix/Scott.* 19
☑ Boulders | *Phoenix/Scott.* 26
☑ Canyon Ranch | *Tucson* 24
☑ Enchantment | *Sedona* 26

⊠ Four Seasons	Phoenix/Scott.	27
Hilton El Conquistador	Tucson	19
JW Marriott Camelback	Phoenix/Scott.	23
Los Abrigados	Sedona	22
Miraval Spa	Tucson	24
Phoenician	Phoenix/Scott.	26
Royal Palms	Phoenix/Scott.	24
⊠ Sanctuary	Phoenix/Scott.	26
Westward Look	Tucson	20

CALIFORNIA

Bernardus Lodge	Carmel	26
Cal-a-Vie	San Diego	–
⊠ Casa Palmero	Carmel	29
Claremont Resort	SF	18
Desert Springs	Palm Springs	21
Fairmont	Wine Co.	21
⊠ Four Seasons	SF	27
Four Seasons	Santa Barbara	26
Golden Door	San Diego	24
Hilton Checkers	LA	19
Hyatt	Palm Springs	22
NEW InterContinental	SF	25
La Costa Resort	San Diego	22
Le Merigot	LA	23
Loews	LA	20
Loews	San Diego	21
Manchester Gr. Hyatt	San Diego	22
Marriott Coronado	San Diego	23
Miramonte	Palm Springs	23
Ojai Valley Inn	Santa Barbara	25
Quail Lodge	Carmel	23
Silverado Resort	Wine Co.	18
⊠ St. Regis	OC Beaches	27

COLORADO

⊠ Broadmoor	CO Springs	26
Park Hyatt	Beaver Creek	23
Peaks Resort	Telluride	20
St. Regis	Aspen	26
Vail Cascade Resort	Vail	22

CONNECTICUT

Mayflower Inn	Washington	27
Saybrook Point	Old Saybrook	21

DISTRICT OF COLUMBIA

Fairmont	DC	23

FLORIDA

Cheeca Lodge	Keys	21
Delano	Miami	21
Doral Golf	Miami	19
Fairmont	Miami	26
Fisher Island	Miami	23
Fontainebleau	Miami	18
Gaylord Palms	Orlando	22
Hyatt	Naples	25
Jupiter Beach	Palm Bch.	20
Longboat Key Club	Sarasota	22
Marco Is. Marriott	Naples	22
Marriott	Ft. Lauderdale	21
⊠ Ritz-Carlton	Orlando	27
Ritz-Carlton Key Bisc.	Miami	24
Shore Club	Miami	16

GEORGIA

Château Élan	Braselton	23
⊠ Cloister	GA Coast	27
NEW Mansion/Peachtree	Atlanta	–
⊠ Ritz-Carlton	Lake Oconee	26

HAWAII

⊠ Four Seasons Resort	Big Island	29
Grand Hyatt	Kauai	24
Grand Wailea	Maui	24
Hilton Hawaiian Vill.	Oahu	20
Hilton Waikoloa Vill.	Big Island	21
JW Marriott	Oahu	26
Mauna Lani Resort	Big Island	24
⊠ Ritz-Carlton	Maui	25
Westin	Maui	22

MARYLAND

Inn/Perry Cabin	Eastern Shore	25

MASSACHUSETTS

Boston Harbor	Boston	24
⊠ Canyon Ranch	Lenox	22
Cranwell Resort	Lenox	21

MINNESOTA

Grand Hotel	Mpls./St. Paul	24

MISSOURI

NEW Four Seasons	St. Louis	29

NEVADA

JW Marriott	Las Vegas	27
NEW Palazzo	Las Vegas	28
Ritz-Carlton	Las Vegas	27
Venetian	Las Vegas	27

NEW JERSEY

Hilton	Short Hills	22
Seaview	Atlantic City	19

NEW MEXICO

Bishop's Lodge	Santa Fe	19
El Monte Sagrado	Taos	25

NEW YORK
Gurney's Inn | *Long Island* 17
☒ Mirbeau Inn | *Catskills* 27

NORTH CAROLINA
Ballantyne | *Charlotte* 24

PENNSYLVANIA
Nemacolin | *Farmington* 25
Omni | *Philadelphia* 23

PUERTO RICO
El Conquistador | *Fajardo* 21
Las Casitas Village | *Fajardo* 26

SOUTH CAROLINA
☒ Sanctuary | *Kiawah Is.* 28

TEXAS
Barton Creek | *Austin* 23
Houstonian | *Houston* 23
Rosewood Crescent | *DFW* 25

UTAH
Stein Eriksen Lodge | *Park City* 24

VERMONT
Equinox | *S. VT* 20
Topnotch | *Stowe* 21

VIRGINIA
☒ Keswick Hall | *Charlottesville* 26

WASHINGTON
Bellevue Club | *Seattle* 24
Pan Pacific | *Seattle* -

WEST VIRGINIA
☒ Greenbrier | 25
White Sulphur Springs

WISCONSIN
☒ American Club | *Kohler* 25

WYOMING
☒ Four Seasons | *Jackson Hole* 27

SPA FACILITIES:
HYDROTHERAPY

ALABAMA
Marriott | *Point Clear* 21
Renaissance | *Birmingham* 25

ALASKA
Alyeska Resort | *Anchorage* 21

ARIZONA
Arizona Biltmore | *Phoenix/Scott.* 23
☒ Canyon Ranch | *Tucson* 24

☒ Enchantment | *Sedona* 26
Fairmont | *Phoenix/Scott.* 25
☒ Four Seasons | *Phoenix/Scott.* 27
Hilton | *Sedona* 23
Hilton El Conquistador | *Tucson* 19
Hyatt | *Phoenix/Scott.* 21
JW Marriott Desert | 24
Phoenix/Scott.
Los Abrigados | *Sedona* 22
Miraval Spa | *Tucson* 24
Royal Palms | *Phoenix/Scott.* 24
☒ Sanctuary | *Phoenix/Scott.* 26
Sheraton | *Phoenix/Scott.* 23
Westin | *Tucson* 22
Westward Look | *Tucson* 20
Wigwam Golf | *Phoenix/Scott.* 24

CALIFORNIA
Bacara Resort | *Santa Barbara* 26
Balboa Bay Club | *OC Beaches* 24
Bernardus Lodge | *Carmel* 26
☒ Beverly Hills Hotel | *LA* 26
Beverly Hilton | *LA* 21
Cal-a-Vie | *San Diego* -
Calistoga Ranch | *Wine Co.* 26
Carneros Inn | *Wine Co.* 28
Casa Madrona | *SF* 23
☒ Casa Palmero | *Carmel* 29
☒ Château du Sureau | *Yosemite* 27
Claremont Resort | *SF* 18
del Coronado | *San Diego* 20
Desert Springs | *Palm Springs* 21
Disney Grand Cal. | *LA* 22
Fairmont | *Wine Co.* 21
Fairmont | *SF* 22
☒ Four Seasons | *San Diego* 27
Four Seasons | *Santa Barbara* 26
Four Seasons Silicon | *SF* 26
Four Seasons Westlake | *LA* 25
Golden Door | *San Diego* 24
Hilton Checkers | *LA* 19
Hyatt Resort | *OC Beaches* 24
Hyatt | *Palm Springs* 22
Inn/Spanish Bay | *Carmel* 26
Kenwood Inn | *Wine Co.* 26
La Costa Resort | *San Diego* 22
La Quinta | *Palm Springs* 22
L'Auberge Del Mar | *San Diego* 23
Le Parker Méridien | 22
Palm Springs
☒ Lodge/Pebble Bch. | *Carmel* 26
Lodge/Torrey Pines | *San Diego* 25
Marriott Coronado | *San Diego* 23

Miramonte | *Palm Springs*	23		Fairmont | *Miami*	26
Mondrian | *LA*	19		Fisher Island | *Miami*	23
☑ Montage | *OC Beaches*	27		Fontainebleau | *Miami*	18
Monterey Plaza | *Carmel*	22		Four Seasons | *Miami*	26
Ojai Valley Inn | *Santa Barbara*	25		Gaylord Palms | *Orlando*	22
Quail Lodge | *Carmel*	23		Grove Isle | *Miami*	26
☑ Rancho Valencia | *San Diego*	28		Hyatt | *Keys*	23
Resort/Squaw Creek | *Lake Tahoe*	22		Hyatt | *Naples*	25
☑ Ritz-Carlton | *SF*	26		JW Marriott | *Orlando*	24
Silverado Resort | *Wine Co.*	18		La Playa Beach/Resort | *Naples*	22
NEW Solage | *Wine Co.*	23		Loews Portofino | *Orlando*	24
☑ St. Regis | *OC Beaches*	27		☑ Mandarin Oriental | *Miami*	27
Sunset Tower | *LA*	21		Marco Is. Marriott | *Naples*	22
Two Bunch | *Palm Springs*	19		Marriott | *Ft. Lauderdale*	21
Ventana Inn | *Carmel*	25		Mayfair | *Miami*	23
Villagio Inn | *Wine Co.*	24		PGA National | *Palm Bch.*	17
Vintage Inn | *Wine Co.*	23		**NEW** Regent Bal Harbour | *Miami*	–
Westin | *Palm Springs*	21		Renaissance | *Tampa*	24

COLORADO

			☑ Ritz-Carlton | *Naples*	27
☑ Broadmoor | *CO Springs*	26		☑ Ritz-Carlton | *Orlando*	27
Brown Palace | *Denver*	20		Ritz-Carlton | *Sarasota*	26
Lodge/Cordillera | *Beaver Creek*	25		Ritz-Carlton Key Bisc. | *Miami*	24
Monaco | *Denver*	22		Ritz-Carlton S. Bch. | *Miami*	25
Park Hyatt | *Beaver Creek*	23		Saddlebrook | *Tampa*	22
Peaks Resort | *Telluride*	20		Sanibel Resort | *Ft. Myers*	21
☑ Ritz-Carlton | *Beaver Creek*	28		Seminole Hard Rock | *Ft. Lauderdale*	20
St Julien | *Denver*	26		Shore Club | *Miami*	16
St. Regis | *Aspen*	26		Victor | *Miami*	22
			Walt Disney Swan | *Orlando*	21

CONNECTICUT

			Westin | *Ft. Lauderdale*	24
Foxwoods Resort | *Ledyard*	20			
Mohegan Sun | *Norwich*	23		**GEORGIA**	
Mystic Marriott | *Mystic*	20		Château Élan | *Braselton*	23
Spa/Norwich Inn | *Norwich*	20		☑ Cloister | *GA Coast*	27
			Four Seasons | *Atlanta*	25

DELAWARE

			NEW Mansion/Peachtree | *Atlanta*	–
Bellmoor | *Rehoboth Bch.*	25		☑ Ritz-Carlton | *Lake Oconee*	26

DISTRICT OF COLUMBIA

			Westin | *Savannah*	24
Fairmont | *DC*	23			
Mandarin Oriental | *DC*	27		**HAWAII**	
			Fairmont | *Maui*	27

FLORIDA

			☑ Four Seasons Resort | *Maui*	28
Amelia Is. Plant. | *NE Florida*	22		Grand Hyatt | *Kauai*	24
Biltmore | *Miami*	23		Grand Wailea | *Maui*	24
Boca Raton | *Ft. Lauderdale*	21		Halekulani | *Oahu*	25
Brazilian Court | *Palm Bch.*	23		Hana-Maui | *Maui*	27
Buena Vista Palace | *Orlando*	20		Hapuna Bch. Prince | *Big Island*	23
Cheeca Lodge | *Keys*	21		Hilton Hawaiian Vill. | *Oahu*	20
Colony Beach | *Sarasota*	18		Hilton Waikoloa Vill. | *Big Island*	21
Delano | *Miami*	21		Hyatt | *Maui*	22
Disney's Grand Floridian | *Orlando*	25		Hyatt | *Oahu*	20
Disney's Saratoga | *Orlando*	27		JW Marriott | *Oahu*	26
Doral Golf | *Miami*	19			

40,000 places to eat, drink, stay & play – free at ZAGAT.com

Kahala	*Oahu*	25	Mirage	*Las Vegas*	19
Mauna Lani Resort	*Big Island*	24	**Z NEW** Palazzo	*Las Vegas*	28
Z Ritz-Carlton	*Maui*	25	Palms Casino Resort	*Las Vegas*	20
Sheraton	*Maui*	22	Paris Las Vegas	*Las Vegas*	20
Turtle Bay Resort	*Oahu*	21	Rio All-Suite	*Las Vegas*	20
Westin	*Maui*	22	Ritz-Carlton	*Las Vegas*	27
			NEW Trump Int'l	*Las Vegas*	21
IDAHO			**Z** Wynn	*Las Vegas*	28
Coeur d'Alene	*Coeur d'Alene*	25		
Sun Valley Resort	*Sun Valley*	21	**NEW JERSEY**	
			Atlantic City Hilton	*Atlantic City*	18
ILLINOIS			Borgata	*Atlantic City*	26
Fairmont	*Chicago*	23	Caesars	*Atlantic City*	18
NEW Trump Int'l	*Chicago*	-	Harrah's Resort	*Atlantic City*	21
			Hilton	*Short Hills*	22
INDIANA			Seaview	*Atlantic City*	19
Conrad	*Indianapolis*	27		
			NEW MEXICO	
LOUISIANA			Bishop's Lodge	*Santa Fe*	19
Iberville Suites	*New Orleans*	20		
Monteleone	*New Orleans*	22	**NEW YORK**	
Ritz-Carlton	*New Orleans*	25	**Z** Four Seasons	*NYC*	28
			Gurney's Inn	*Long Island*	17
MAINE			Jumeirah Essex Hse.	*NYC*	22
Bar Harbor Inn	*Bar Harbor*	21	**Z** Mandarin Oriental	*NYC*	28
Cliff House	*S. Coast*	20	**Z** Mirbeau Inn	*Catskills*	27
Samoset	*Rockport*	19	Mohonk Mtn. Hse.	*Catskills*	18
			New York Palace	*NYC*	25
MARYLAND			Plaza	*NYC*	25
NEW Gaylord Nat'l	*Baltimore*	-	Sagamore	*Adirondacks*	21
Hyatt	*Eastern Shore*	21	Whiteface Lodge	*Adirondacks*	23
Inn/Perry Cabin	*Eastern Shore*	25	W New York	*NYC*	14
			W Times Square	*NYC*	20
MASSACHUSETTS				
Z Canyon Ranch	*Lenox*	22	**NORTH CAROLINA**	
Chatham Bars	*Cape Cod/Is.*	22	Ballantyne	*Charlotte*	24
Cranwell Resort	*Lenox*	21	Grove Park Inn	*Asheville*	20
InterContinental	*Boston*	25	Pinehurst Resort	*Pinehurst*	20
Millennium Bostonian	*Boston*	21		
Westin Copley	*Boston*	22	**OREGON**	
			Columbia Gorge	*Hood River*	20
MICHIGAN			Monaco	*Portland*	22
NEW MGM Grand	*Detroit*	26	Salishan Spa	*Gleneden Bch.*	24
			Sunriver	*Mt. Bachelor*	21
MINNESOTA				
Graves 601	*Mpls./St. Paul*	26	**PENNSYLVANIA**	
			Hershey	*Hershey*	22
MISSOURI			Nemacolin	*Farmington*	25
Chateau on Lake	*Branson*	23	Omni	*Philadelphia*	23
NEW Four Seasons	*St. Louis*	29		
			PUERTO RICO	
NEVADA			El Conquistador	*Fajardo*	21
Z Bellagio	*Las Vegas*	26	El San Juan	*San Juan*	20
Caesars	*Las Vegas*	22	**Z** Horned Dorset	*Rincon*	26
Green Valley Ranch	*Las Vegas*	24	Las Casitas Village	*Fajardo*	26
Hard Rock	*Las Vegas*	20	Rio Mar Beach	*San Juan*	22
Hyatt	*Incline Vill.*	21		
JW Marriott	*Las Vegas*	27		

SOUTH CAROLINA

Marriott | Hilton Head — 21
☑ Sanctuary | Kiawah Is. — 28

TENNESSEE

☑ Blackberry Farm | Walland — 28
Peabody | Memphis — 19

TEXAS

Barton Creek | Austin — 23
Four Seasons | Austin — 25
Four Seasons | DFW — 25
Hyatt | San Antonio — 23
☑ Lake Austin Spa | Austin — 25
☑ Ritz-Carlton | DFW — 28
Rosewood Crescent | DFW — 25
Stoneleigh | DFW — 22
Watermark | San Antonio — 27
W Dallas-Victory | DFW — 22
Westin Riverwalk | San Antonio — 22

U.S. VIRGIN ISLANDS

Buccaneer | St. Croix — 23
Ritz-Carlton | St. Thomas — 25

UTAH

Stein Eriksen Lodge | Park City — 24

VERMONT

Equinox | S. VT — 20
Stratton Mtn. Resort | S. VT — 19
☑ Twin Farms | Woodstock — 29

VIRGINIA

Boar's Head | Charlottesville — 19
Homestead | Hot Springs — 21
☑ Keswick Hall | Charlottesville — 26
Ritz-Carlton Tysons | DC Metro — 25
Tides Inn | Irvington — 22

WASHINGTON

Davenport | Spokane — 28
Pan Pacific | Seattle — -
Salish Lodge | Seattle — 25
Sun Mtn. Lodge | Winthrop — -
☑ Willows Lodge | Seattle — 27
Woodmark | Seattle — 24

WEST VIRGINIA

☑ Greenbrier | White Sulphur Springs — 25

WISCONSIN

☑ American Club | Kohler — 25
Grand Geneva | Lake Geneva — 19
Pfister | Milwaukee — 22

WYOMING

Snake River Ldg. | Jackson Hole — 21

SPA FACILITIES: MEDITATION

ALABAMA

Marriott | Point Clear — 21

ARIZONA

☑ Boulders | Phoenix/Scott. — 26
☑ Canyon Ranch | Tucson — 24
☑ Enchantment | Sedona — 26
☑ Four Seasons | Phoenix/Scott. — 27
Hacienda del Sol | Tucson — 19
JW Marriott Camelback | Phoenix/Scott. — 23
JW Marriott Desert | Phoenix/Scott. — 24
Loews | Tucson — 24
Miraval Spa | Tucson — 24
Phoenician | Phoenix/Scott. — 26
Royal Palms | Phoenix/Scott. — 24
☑ Sanctuary | Phoenix/Scott. — 26
Sheraton | Phoenix/Scott. — 23
Valley Ho | Phoenix/Scott. — 24

CALIFORNIA

Cal-a-Vie | San Diego — -
del Coronado | San Diego — 20
Desert Springs | Palm Springs — 21
Disney Grand Cal. | LA — 22
Fairmont | Wine Co. — 21
Golden Door | San Diego — 24
Hyatt | Palm Springs — 22
InterContinental | LA — 21
Langham Huntington | LA — 24
Le Merigot | LA — 23
Loews | LA — 20
Loews | San Diego — 21
☑ Meadowood | Wine Co. — 27
Miramonte | Palm Springs — 23
Ojai Valley Inn | Santa Barbara — 25
NEW Solage | Wine Co. — 23
☑ St. Regis | OC Beaches — 27
Sunset Tower | LA — 21

COLORADO

☑ Broadmoor | CO Springs — 26
Lodge/Cordillera | Beaver Creek — 25
Park Hyatt | Beaver Creek — 23
Peaks Resort | Telluride — 20

CONNECTICUT

Spa/Norwich Inn | Norwich — 20

FLORIDA

Amelia Is. Plant. | NE Florida — 22
Boca Raton | Ft. Lauderdale — 21

Brazilian Court | *Palm Bch.*	23
Cheeca Lodge | *Keys*	21
Delano | *Miami*	21
Don CeSar Bch. | *Tampa*	21
Doral Golf | *Miami*	19
Fairmont | *Miami*	26
Fisher Island | *Miami*	23
Fontainebleau | *Miami*	18
Four Seasons | *Miami*	26
Grove Isle | *Miami*	26
☑ Little Palm Island | *Keys*	27
Marco Beach Resort | *Naples*	24
Marco Is. Marriott | *Naples*	22
Marriott | *Ft. Lauderdale*	21
PGA National | *Palm Bch.*	17
Seminole Hard Rock | *Ft. Lauderdale*	20
Setai | *Miami*	26
Shore Club | *Miami*	16
Westin | *Ft. Lauderdale*	24

GEORGIA

☑ Cloister | *GA Coast*	27
Four Seasons | *Atlanta*	25
☑ Ritz-Carlton | *Lake Oconee*	26

HAWAII

Fairmont | *Big Island*	25
☑ Four Seasons Resort | *Big Island*	29
☑ Four Seasons Resort | *Maui*	28
Grand Hyatt | *Kauai*	24
Grand Wailea | *Maui*	24
Hapuna Bch. Prince | *Big Island*	23
Hilton Waikoloa Vill. | *Big Island*	21
Hyatt | *Maui*	22
JW Marriott | *Oahu*	26
Mauna Lani Resort | *Big Island*	24
☑ Ritz-Carlton | *Maui*	25

MARYLAND

Hyatt | *Eastern Shore*	21
Inn/Perry Cabin | *Eastern Shore*	25

MASSACHUSETTS

☑ Canyon Ranch | *Lenox*	22

NEVADA

Caesars | *Las Vegas*	22
Mandalay Bay | *Las Vegas*	24

NEW JERSEY

Harrah's Resort | *Atlantic City*	21
Hilton | *Short Hills*	22

NEW MEXICO

Bishop's Lodge | *Santa Fe*	19
El Monte Sagrado | *Taos*	25
La Posada | *Santa Fe*	21

NEW YORK

Gurney's Inn | *Long Island*	17
Mohonk Mtn. Hse. | *Catskills*	18

PENNSYLVANIA

Nemacolin | *Farmington*	25
☑ Rittenhouse | *Philadelphia*	26

PUERTO RICO

El Conquistador | *Fajardo*	21
☑ Horned Dorset | *Rincon*	26
Las Casitas Village | *Fajardo*	26
Ritz-Carlton | *San Juan*	24

SOUTH CAROLINA

☑ Sanctuary | *Kiawah Is.*	28

TEXAS

Barton Creek | *Austin*	23
Houstonian | *Houston*	23
☑ Lake Austin Spa | *Austin*	25
Watermark | *San Antonio*	27
Zaza | *DFW*	26

U.S. VIRGIN ISLANDS

Caneel Bay | *St. John*	23

UTAH

Snowbird | *Salt Lake City*	17

VERMONT

Topnotch | *Stowe*	21

WEST VIRGINIA

☑ Greenbrier | *White Sulphur Springs*	25

WISCONSIN

☑ American Club | *Kohler*	25
Grand Geneva | *Lake Geneva*	19

WYOMING

☑ Amangani | *Jackson Hole*	29

SPA FACILITIES: MINERAL SPRINGS

CALIFORNIA

Fairmont | *Wine Co.*	21
NEW Solage | *Wine Co.*	23
Two Bunch | *Palm Springs*	19

FLORIDA

Delano | *Miami*	21
Fontainebleau | *Miami*	18
Grove Isle | *Miami*	26

SPECIAL FEATURES

Marco Is. Marriott | *Naples* 22
Z Ritz-Carlton | *Naples* 27

INDIANA
NEW West Baden Springs | -
Indianapolis

NEVADA
Hard Rock | *Las Vegas* 20

NEW MEXICO
El Monte Sagrado | *Taos* 25

NEW YORK
Gurney's Inn | *Long Island* 17

NORTH CAROLINA
Grove Park Inn | *Asheville* 20

PENNSYLVANIA
Z Rittenhouse | *Philadelphia* 26

PUERTO RICO
Las Casitas Village | *Fajardo* 26

SOUTH CAROLINA
Z Sanctuary | *Kiawah Is.* 28

TEXAS
Barton Creek | *Austin* 23

VIRGINIA
Homestead | *Hot Springs* 21

WEST VIRGINIA
Z Greenbrier | 25
White Sulphur Springs

SPA FACILITIES:
WEIGHT LOSS

ARIZONA
Arizona Grand | *Phoenix/Scott.* 19
Z Boulders | *Phoenix/Scott.* 26
Z Canyon Ranch | *Tucson* 24
Z Enchantment | *Sedona* 26
Z Four Seasons | *Phoenix/Scott.* 27
JW Marriott Camelback | 23
Phoenix/Scott.
Miraval Spa | *Tucson* 24
Westin | *Phoenix/Scott.* 24

CALIFORNIA
Cal-a-Vie | *San Diego* -
Claremont Resort | *SF* 18
Fairmont | *Wine Co.* 21
Golden Door | *San Diego* 24
NEW InterContinental | *SF* 25
La Costa Resort | *San Diego* 22
Loews | *LA* 20

Loews | *San Diego* 21
Miramonte | *Palm Springs* 23
Ojai Valley Inn | *Santa Barbara* 25
Z St. Regis | *OC Beaches* 27

COLORADO
Z Broadmoor | *CO Springs* 26
Lodge/Cordillera | *Beaver Creek* 25
Park Hyatt | *Beaver Creek* 23
Peaks Resort | *Telluride* 20
St. Regis | *Aspen* 26

CONNECTICUT
Mayflower Inn | *Washington* 27

DISTRICT OF COLUMBIA
Fairmont | *DC* 23

FLORIDA
Cheeca Lodge | *Keys* 21
Delano | *Miami* 21
Don CeSar Bch. | *Tampa* 21
Doral Golf | *Miami* 19
Fairmont | *Miami* 26
Fisher Island | *Miami* 23
Fontainebleau | *Miami* 18
Hyatt | *Naples* 25
Marco Is. Marriott | *Naples* 22
Marriott | *Ft. Lauderdale* 21
Ritz-Carlton Key Bisc. | *Miami* 24
Seminole Hard Rock | 20
Ft. Lauderdale
Victor | *Miami* 22

GEORGIA
Z Ritz-Carlton | *Lake Oconee* 26

HAWAII
Z Four Seasons Resort | *Big Island* 29
Grand Hyatt | *Kauai* 24
Grand Wailea | *Maui* 24
Hapuna Bch. Prince | *Big Island* 23
Hilton Waikoloa Vill. | *Big Island* 21
JW Marriott | *Oahu* 26
Mauna Lani Resort | *Big Island* 24
Z Ritz-Carlton | *Maui* 25

MARYLAND
Inn/Perry Cabin | *Eastern Shore* 25

MASSACHUSETTS
Z Canyon Ranch | *Lenox* 22

NEVADA
JW Marriott | *Las Vegas* 27
Z NEW Palazzo | *Las Vegas* 28
Venetian | *Las Vegas* 27

NEW JERSEY
Hilton | *Short Hills* — 22

NEW MEXICO
Bishop's Lodge | *Santa Fe* — 19

NEW YORK
Le Parker Méridien | *NYC* — 21
Z Mirbeau Inn | *Catskills* — 27

NORTH CAROLINA
Westin | *Charlotte* — 23

PENNSYLVANIA
Nemacolin | *Farmington* — 25
Omni | *Philadelphia* — 23
Z Rittenhouse | *Philadelphia* — 26

PUERTO RICO
El Conquistador | *Fajardo* — 21
Las Casitas Village | *Fajardo* — 26
Ritz-Carlton | *San Juan* — 24

SOUTH CAROLINA
Z Sanctuary | *Kiawah Is.* — 28

TEXAS
Houstonian | *Houston* — 23

VERMONT
Stratton Mtn. Resort | *S. VT* — 19

VIRGINIA
Boar's Head | *Charlottesville* — 19
Z Keswick Hall | *Charlottesville* — 26

WEST VIRGINIA
Z Greenbrier | — 25
White Sulphur Springs

WISCONSIN
Grand Geneva | *Lake Geneva* — 19

SPA FACILITIES: YOGA

ALABAMA
Marriott | *Point Clear* — 21
Renaissance | *Birmingham* — 25

ARIZONA
Arizona Biltmore | *Phoenix/Scott.* — 23
Arizona Grand | *Phoenix/Scott.* — 19
Z Boulders | *Phoenix/Scott.* — 26
Z Canyon Ranch | *Tucson* — 24
Z Enchantment | *Sedona* — 26
Fairmont | *Phoenix/Scott.* — 25
Z Four Seasons | *Phoenix/Scott.* — 27
Hilton El Conquistador | *Tucson* — 19

Hyatt | *Phoenix/Scott.* — 21
JW Marriott Camelback | — 23
Phoenix/Scott.
JW Marriott Desert | — 24
Phoenix/Scott.
Ldg./Ventana Canyon | *Tucson* — 22
Loews | *Tucson* — 24
Los Abrigados | *Sedona* — 22
Miraval Spa | *Tucson* — 24
Phoenician | *Phoenix/Scott.* — 26
Pointe Hilton Squaw | — 19
Phoenix/Scott.
Royal Palms | *Phoenix/Scott.* — 24
Z Sanctuary | *Phoenix/Scott.* — 26
Sheraton | *Phoenix/Scott.* — 23
Valley Ho | *Phoenix/Scott.* — 24
Westin | *Phoenix/Scott.* — 24
Westin | *Tucson* — 22
Westward Look | *Tucson* — 20
Wigwam Golf | *Phoenix/Scott.* — 24

CALIFORNIA
Z Auberge/Soleil | *Wine Co.* — 28
Avalon | *LA* — 18
Bacara Resort | *Santa Barbara* — 26
Balboa Bay Club | *OC Beaches* — 24
Beverly Wilshire | *LA* — 25
Cal-a-Vie | *San Diego* — -
Calistoga Ranch | *Wine Co.* — 26
Carneros Inn | *Wine Co.* — 28
Z Casa Palmero | *Carmel* — 29
Z Château du Sureau | *Yosemite* — 27
Claremont Resort | *SF* — 18
del Coronado | *San Diego* — 20
Desert Springs | *Palm Springs* — 21
Fairmont | *SF* — 22
Fairmont | *Wine Co.* — 21
Z Four Seasons | *San Diego* — 27
Z Four Seasons | *SF* — 27
Four Seasons | *Santa Barbara* — 26
Four Seasons Silicon | *SF* — 26
Four Seasons Westlake | *LA* — 25
Golden Door | *San Diego* — 24
Z NEW Grand/Mar | *San Diego* — 26
Healdsburg | *Wine Co.* — 24
Huntington | *SF* — 21
Hyatt Resort | *OC Beaches* — 24
Hyatt | *Palm Springs* — 22
Inn/Southbridge | *Wine Co.* — 20
NEW InterContinental | *SF* — 25
InterContinental | *LA* — 21
Island | *OC Beaches* — 25
Langham Huntington | *LA* — 24

SPECIAL FEATURES

La Quinta	*Palm Springs*	22
Le Merigot	*LA*	23
Loews	*LA*	20
Loews	*San Diego*	21
Marriott Coronado	*San Diego*	23
Marriott Marina	*San Diego*	19
☒ Meadowood	*Wine Co.*	27
Miramonte	*Palm Springs*	23
☒ Montage	*OC Beaches*	27
Ojai Valley Inn	*Santa Barbara*	25
Palomar	*SF*	22
☒ Peninsula	*LA*	27
☒ Post Ranch Inn	*Carmel*	28
Quail Lodge	*Carmel*	23
☒ Rancho Valencia	*San Diego*	28
Resort/Squaw Creek	*Lake Tahoe*	22
Ritz-Carlton	*Half Moon Bay*	27
☒ Ritz-Carlton	*OC Beaches*	27
San Ysidro	*Santa Barbara*	26
Shutters	*LA*	25
NEW Solage	*Wine Co.*	23
Solamar	*San Diego*	26
☒ St. Regis	*OC Beaches*	27
Surf/Sand	*OC Beaches*	21
Two Bunch	*Palm Springs*	19
Ventana Inn	*Carmel*	25
Viceroy	*Palm Springs*	21
Villagio Inn	*Wine Co.*	24
Vintage Inn	*Wine Co.*	23
Vitale	*SF*	25
Westgate	*San Diego*	23
Westin	*Palm Springs*	21

COLORADO

☒ Broadmoor	*CO Springs*	26
Keystone Resort	*Keystone*	20
Lodge/Cordillera	*Beaver Creek*	25
Park Hyatt	*Beaver Creek*	23
Peaks Resort	*Telluride*	20
☒ Ritz-Carlton	*Beaver Creek*	28
Sonnenalp	*Vail*	27
St Julien	*Denver*	26
St. Regis	*Aspen*	26
Vail Cascade Resort	*Vail*	22

CONNECTICUT

Mayflower Inn	*Washington*	27
Saybrook Point	*Old Saybrook*	21
Spa/Norwich Inn	*Norwich*	20
Winvian	*New Preston*	-

DISTRICT OF COLUMBIA

Fairmont	*DC*	23
☒ Four Seasons	*DC*	26

George	*DC*	21
Mandarin Oriental	*DC*	27
Park Hyatt	*DC*	24
Topaz	*DC*	21

FLORIDA

☒ Acqualina	*Miami*	28
Biltmore	*Miami*	23
Boca Raton	*Ft. Lauderdale*	21
Breakers	*Palm Bch.*	24
Cheeca Lodge	*Keys*	21
Colony Beach	*Sarasota*	18
Delano	*Miami*	21
Don CeSar Bch.	*Tampa*	21
Doral Golf	*Miami*	19
Fairmont	*Miami*	26
Fisher Island	*Miami*	23
Fontainebleau	*Miami*	18
Four Seasons	*Miami*	26
Four Seasons Resort	*Palm Bch.*	24
Gaylord Palms	*Orlando*	22
Grove Isle	*Miami*	26
Hawk's Cay Resort	*Keys*	21
Hilton	*Ft. Lauderdale*	21
Hyatt	*Naples*	25
JW Marriott	*Orlando*	24
La Playa Beach/Resort	*Naples*	22
☒ Little Palm Island	*Keys*	27
Longboat Key Club	*Sarasota*	22
☒ Mandarin Oriental	*Miami*	27
Marco Beach Resort	*Naples*	24
Marco Is. Marriott	*Naples*	22
Marriott	*Ft. Lauderdale*	21
PGA National	*Palm Bch.*	17
Ponte Vedra Inn	*NE Florida*	25
Raleigh	*Miami*	19
Renaissance	*Tampa*	24
☒ Ritz-Carlton	*Naples*	27
☒ Ritz-Carlton	*NE Florida*	26
☒ Ritz-Carlton	*Orlando*	27
Ritz-Carlton	*Palm Bch.*	26
Ritz-Carlton	*Sarasota*	26
Ritz-Carlton Key Bisc.	*Miami*	24
Ritz-Carlton S. Bch.	*Miami*	25
Sanibel Resort	*Ft. Myers*	21
Setai	*Miami*	26
Shore Club	*Miami*	16
Standard	*Miami*	20
Westin	*Ft. Lauderdale*	24

GEORGIA

Château Élan	*Braselton*	23
☒ Cloister	*GA Coast*	27

Z Ritz-Carlton	*Lake Oconee*	26
Westin	*Savannah*	24

HAWAII

Fairmont	*Big Island*	25
Fairmont	*Maui*	27
Four Seasons/Manele	*Lanai*	27
Z Four Seasons Resort	*Big Island*	29
Z Four Seasons Resort	*Maui*	28
Grand Hyatt	*Kauai*	24
Grand Wailea	*Maui*	24
Hana-Maui	*Maui*	27
Hapuna Bch. Prince	*Big Island*	23
Hilton Waikoloa Vill.	*Big Island*	21
Hyatt	*Maui*	22
Hyatt	*Oahu*	20
JW Marriott	*Oahu*	26
Kahala	*Oahu*	25
Kauai Marriott	*Kauai*	21
Mauna Lani Resort	*Big Island*	24
Z Ritz-Carlton	*Maui*	25
Turtle Bay Resort	*Oahu*	21
Westin	*Maui*	22

IDAHO

Coeur d'Alene	*Coeur d'Alene*	25

ILLINOIS

Fairmont	*Chicago*	23
Monaco	*Chicago*	21
Z Peninsula	*Chicago*	29
Ritz-Carlton	*Chicago*	26

LOUISIANA

Harrah's	*New Orleans*	23
Loews	*New Orleans*	26
Westin	*New Orleans*	21

MAINE

Cliff House	*S. Coast*	20
Samoset	*Rockport*	19
Z White Barn Inn	*S. Coast*	25

MARYLAND

Hyatt	*Eastern Shore*	21
Inn/Perry Cabin	*Eastern Shore*	25
InterContinental	*Baltimore*	23

MASSACHUSETTS

Boston Harbor	*Boston*	24
Z Canyon Ranch	*Lenox*	22
Chatham Bars	*Cape Cod/Is.*	22
Cranwell Resort	*Lenox*	21
Marlowe	*Boston*	23
Ocean Edge	*Cape Cod/Is.*	21
Ritz-Carlton	*Boston*	25
Wauwinet	*Cape Cod/Is.*	25

MINNESOTA

Grand Hotel	*Mpls./St. Paul*	24

MISSOURI

Chase Park Plaza	*St. Louis*	22
Chateau on Lake	*Branson*	23

MONTA8.5NA

Triple Creek Ranch	*Darby*	29

NEVADA

Green Valley Ranch	*Las Vegas*	24
Hyatt	*Incline Vill.*	21
JW Marriott	*Las Vegas*	27
Loews	*Las Vegas*	22
Mandalay Bay	*Las Vegas*	24
Z NEW Palazzo	*Las Vegas*	28
Palms Casino Resort	*Las Vegas*	20
Ritz-Carlton	*Las Vegas*	27
Venetian	*Las Vegas*	27

NEW HAMPSHIRE

Mount Wash.	*White Mtns.*	18

NEW JERSEY

Congress Hall	*Cape May*	19
Harrah's Resort	*Atlantic City*	21
Hilton	*Short Hills*	22

NEW MEXICO

Bishop's Lodge	*Santa Fe*	19
El Monte Sagrado	*Taos*	25
Hyatt Tamaya	*Albuquerque*	23
La Posada	*Santa Fe*	21

NEW YORK

Gramercy Park	*NYC*	22
Gurney's Inn	*Long Island*	17
Le Parker Méridien	*NYC*	21
Z Mirbeau Inn	*Catskills*	27
Mirror Lake Inn	*Adirondacks*	23
Mohonk Mtn. Hse.	*Catskills*	18
Plaza	*NYC*	25
Z Point	*Adirondacks*	27
Sagamore	*Adirondacks*	21
St. Regis	*NYC*	27
Trump Int'l	*NYC*	23
Whiteface Lodge	*Adirondacks*	23

NORTH CAROLINA

Grove Park Inn	*Asheville*	20
Westin	*Charlotte*	23

OREGON

Monaco	*Portland*	22
Sunriver	*Mt. Bachelor*	21

SPECIAL FEATURES

PENNSYLVANIA
Hershey | *Hershey* — 22
Nemacolin | *Farmington* — 25
Park Hyatt | *Philadelphia* — 22
🗹 Rittenhouse | *Philadelphia* — 26
Ritz-Carlton | *Philadelphia* — 24
Skytop Lodge | *Poconos* — 15

PUERTO RICO
El Conquistador | *Fajardo* — 21
🗹 Horned Dorset | *Rincon* — 26
Las Casitas Village | *Fajardo* — 26
Ritz-Carlton | *San Juan* — 24

RHODE ISLAND
Westin | *Providence* — 23

SOUTH CAROLINA
Charleston Pl. | *Charleston* — 25
Myrtle/Marriott | *Myrtle Bch.* — 24
🗹 Sanctuary | *Kiawah Is.* — 28
Westin | *Hilton Head* — 21
Wild Dunes Resort | *Charleston* — 21

TENNESSEE
🗹 Blackberry Farm | *Walland* — 28

TEXAS
Barton Creek | *Austin* — 23
Four Seasons | *Austin* — 25
Four Seasons | *DFW* — 25
Hyatt | *San Antonio* — 23
🗹 Lake Austin Spa | *Austin* — 25
Watermark | *San Antonio* — 27
Zaza | *DFW* — 26

U.S. VIRGIN ISLANDS
Buccaneer | *St. Croix* — 23
Caneel Bay | *St. John* — 23
Ritz-Carlton | *St. Thomas* — 25
Westin | *St. John* — 21

UTAH
Snowbird | *Salt Lake City* — 17
Stein Eriksen Lodge | *Park City* — 24
Sundance | *Salt Lake City* — 23

VERMONT
Equinox | *S. VT* — 20
Stratton Mtn. Resort | *S. VT* — 19
Topnotch | *Stowe* — 21
Trapp | *Stowe* — 19
Woodstock Inn | *Woodstock* — 22

VIRGINIA
Boar's Head | *Charlottesville* — 19
🗹 Keswick Hall | *Charlottesville* — 26

Kingsmill Resort | *Williamsburg* — 19
Lansdowne | *DC Metro* — 20
Williams. Inn | *Williamsburg* — 23

WASHINGTON
Alexis | *Seattle* — 21
Bellevue Club | *Seattle* — 24

WEST VIRGINIA
🗹 Greenbrier | — 25
  White Sulphur Springs

WISCONSIN
🗹 American Club | *Kohler* — 25
Grand Geneva | *Lake Geneva* — 19

WYOMING
🗹 Amangani | *Jackson Hole* — 29
🗹 Four Seasons | *Jackson Hole* — 27
Snake River Ldg. | *Jackson Hole* — 21

SWIMMING POOLS, PRIVATE

ARIZONA
Arizona Inn | *Tucson* — 23
🗹 Enchantment | *Sedona* — 26
JW Marriott | *Tucson* — 25
JW Marriott Desert | — 24
  Phoenix/Scott.

CALIFORNIA
Balboa Bay Club | *OC Beaches* — 24
del Coronado | *San Diego* — 20
Four Seasons | *Santa Barbara* — 26
🗹 Rancho Valencia | *San Diego* — 28

HAWAII
Fairmont | *Maui* — 27
Mauna Lani Resort | *Big Island* — 24

IDAHO
Coeur d'Alene | *Coeur d'Alene* — 25

LOUISIANA
Nottoway | *White Castle* — 24

MASSACHUSETTS
Wequassett | *Cape Cod/Is.* — 21

PUERTO RICO
🗹 Horned Dorset | *Rincon* — 26

TEXAS
Hyatt | *San Antonio* — 23
Westin La Cantera | *San Antonio* — 22

UTAH
Snowbird | *Salt Lake City* — 17

VERMONT

Stratton Mtn. Resort | *S. VT* 19

VIRGINIA

Williams. Inn | *Williamsburg* 23

TRENDY PLACES

CALIFORNIA

🆉 Auberge/Soleil	*Wine Co.*	28
Avalon	*LA*	18
🆉 Bel-Air	*LA*	27
🆉 Beverly Hills Hotel	*LA*	26
Beverly Wilshire	*LA*	25
Casa Del Mar	*LA*	25
Chateau Marmont	*LA*	21
Clift	*SF*	20
🆉 Four Seasons	*SF*	27
Golden Door	*San Diego*	24
Healdsburg	*Wine Co.*	24
NEW Ivy	*San Diego*	24
NEW London W. Hollywood	*LA*	-
Mondrian	*LA*	19
NEW Palomar	*LA*	-
Palomar	*SF*	22
🆉 Peninsula	*LA*	27
🆉 Post Ranch Inn	*Carmel*	28
Raffles L'Ermitage	*LA*	27
Shutters	*LA*	25
Sofitel	*LA*	22
Solamar	*San Diego*	26
Standard Downtown	*LA*	19
St. Regis	*SF*	27
Sunset Tower	*LA*	21
Two Bunch	*Palm Springs*	19
Ventana Inn	*Carmel*	25
Viceroy	*Palm Springs*	21
Vitale	*SF*	25
Westin Market St.	*SF*	21
W San Diego	*San Diego*	21
W San Francisco	*SF*	23
W Westwood	*LA*	22

COLORADO

Curtis	*Denver*	-
Hyatt	*Denver*	21
Jerome	*Aspen*	22
🆉 Little Nell	*Aspen*	27
Lodge/Cordillera	*Beaver Creek*	25
Monaco	*Denver*	22
Park Hyatt	*Beaver Creek*	23
🆉 Ritz-Carlton	*Beaver Creek*	28
St Julien	*Denver*	26
St. Regis	*Aspen*	26
Teatro	*Denver*	24

CONNECTICUT

Homestead Inn	*Greenwich*	21
Inn/National Hall	*Westport*	27
Spa/Norwich Inn	*Norwich*	20

DISTRICT OF COLUMBIA

George	*DC*	21
Helix	*DC*	23
Monaco	*DC*	20

FLORIDA

Atlantic Resort	*Ft. Lauderdale*	26
Delano	*Miami*	21
Fontainebleau	*Miami*	18
NEW Gansevoort South	*Miami*	26
Hotel, The	*Miami*	19
Loews	*Miami*	21
🆉 Mandarin Oriental	*Miami*	27
National	*Miami*	18
NEW Regent Bal Harbour	*Miami*	-
Shore Club	*Miami*	16
Tides	*Miami*	26
Victor	*Miami*	22

GEORGIA

Indigo	*Atlanta*	18
InterContinental	*Atlanta*	26
Ritz-Carlton Buckhead	*Atlanta*	24

HAWAII

Halekulani	*Oahu*	25
Kahala	*Oahu*	25

ILLINOIS

Monaco	*Chicago*	21
Park Hyatt	*Chicago*	27
🆉 Peninsula	*Chicago*	29
Sutton Place	*Chicago*	23
NEW Trump Int'l	*Chicago*	-
W Lakeshore	*Chicago*	20

LOUISIANA

Renaissance	*New Orleans*	-
W French Quarter	*New Orleans*	23
🆉 Windsor Court	*New Orleans*	24
W New Orleans	*New Orleans*	23

MASSACHUSETTS

Fifteen Beacon	*Boston*	24
Nine Zero	*Boston*	23

MINNESOTA

Graves 601	*Mpls./St. Paul*	26

MISSOURI

NEW Four Seasons	*St. Louis*	29

NEVADA

Z Bellagio | *Las Vegas*	26
Hard Rock | *Las Vegas*	20
Z NEW Palazzo | *Las Vegas*	28
Palms Casino Resort | *Las Vegas*	20
Red Rock | *Las Vegas*	27
NEW Trump Int'l | *Las Vegas*	21
Z Wynn | *Las Vegas*	28

NEW JERSEY

Borgata | *Atlantic City*	26
NEW Chelsea | *Atlantic City*	-

NEW YORK

NEW Bowery | *NYC*	21
Chambers | *NYC*	21
Gansevoort | *NYC*	20
Gramercy Park | *NYC*	22
Hotel/Rivington | *NYC*	23
Z Mandarin Oriental | *NYC*	28
Maritime | *NYC*	17
Mercer | *NYC*	23
Muse | *NYC*	23
Night | *NYC*	16
Royalton | *NYC*	20
NEW Six Columbus | *NYC*	-
60 Thompson | *NYC*	20
Soho Grand | *NYC*	19
W Union Sq. | *NYC*	22

OREGON

Heathman | *Portland*	20
Lucia | *Portland*	19

PUERTO RICO

Las Casitas Village | *Fajardo*	26
Water & Beach Club | *San Juan*	18

TENNESSEE

NEW Indigo | *Nashville*	-

TEXAS

Derek | *Houston*	22
Icon | *Houston*	24
Palomar | *DFW*	25
W Dallas-Victory | *DFW*	22
Zaza | *DFW*	26

UTAH

Monaco | *Salt Lake City*	21

WASHINGTON

Monaco | *Seattle*	22
W Seattle | *Seattle*	23

WISCONSIN

Pfister | *Milwaukee*	22

WYOMING

Z Amangani | *Jackson Hole*	29
Z Four Seasons | *Jackson Hole*	27
Rusty Parrot | *Jackson Hole*	23

WATER VIEWS

ALABAMA

Marriott | *Point Clear*	21

ARIZONA

Hyatt | *Phoenix/Scott.*	21
L'Auberge/Sedona | *Sedona*	23

CALIFORNIA

Albion River | *N. CA Coast*	24
Bacara Resort | *Santa Barbara*	26
Bodega Bay | *N. CA Coast*	23
Calistoga Ranch | *Wine Co.*	26
Casa Del Mar | *LA*	25
Casa Madrona | *SF*	23
Z Château du Sureau | *Yosemite*	27
del Coronado | *San Diego*	20
Desert Springs | *Palm Springs*	21
Fairmont | *LA*	21
Z Four Seasons | *SF*	27
Four Seasons | *Santa Barbara*	26
Grand Hyatt | *SF*	20
Green Gables | *Carmel*	24
Highlands Inn | *Carmel*	23
Hilton La Jolla | *San Diego*	20
Huntington | *SF*	21
Hyatt Resort | *OC Beaches*	24
Inn Above Tide | *SF*	26
Inn/Southbridge | *Wine Co.*	20
Inn/Spanish Bay | *Carmel*	26
NEW InterContinental | *SF*	25
Island | *OC Beaches*	25
JW Marriott | *SF*	22
Langham Huntington | *LA*	24
La Playa | *Carmel*	18
Z L'Auberge Carmel | *Carmel*	25
L'Auberge Del Mar | *San Diego*	23
La Valencia | *San Diego*	22
Le Méridien | *SF*	23
Le Merigot | *LA*	23
Z Lodge/Pebble Bch. | *Carmel*	26
Lodge/Torrey Pines | *San Diego*	25
Loews | *LA*	20
Loews | *San Diego*	21
Malibu Beach Inn | *LA*	20
Manchester Gr. Hyatt | *San Diego*	22
Mandarin Oriental | *SF*	27
Mark Hopkins | *SF*	22

Marriott | *OC Beaches*	20
Marriott Coronado | *San Diego*	23
Marriott Gaslamp | *San Diego*	23
Marriott Marina | *San Diego*	19
Milliken Creek Inn | *Wine Co.*	26
Mission Ranch | *Carmel*	21
🅩 Montage | *OC Beaches*	27
Monterey Plaza | *Carmel*	22
Napa River Inn | *Wine Co.*	22
NEW Nick's Cove | *N. CA Coast*	25
Nikko | *SF*	22
Ritz-Carlton | *Half Moon Bay*	27
🅩 Ritz-Carlton | *OC Beaches*	27
Ritz-Carlton | *LA*	24
San Ysidro | *Santa Barbara*	26
Sofitel | *SF*	21
Spindrift Inn | *Carmel*	23
Stanford Ct. | *SF*	21
🅩 St. Regis | *OC Beaches*	27
St. Regis | *SF*	27
Surf/Sand | *OC Beaches*	21
Tamarack | *Mammoth Lakes*	15
Vitale | *SF*	25
Westgate | *San Diego*	23
Whale Watch | *N. CA Coast*	24

COLORADO

Beaver Creek Ldg. | *Beaver Creek*	24
🅩 Broadmoor | *CO Springs*	26
Vail Cascade Resort | *Vail*	22

CONNECTICUT

Boulders | *New Preston*	20
Inn/National Hall | *Westport*	27
Saybrook Point | *Old Saybrook*	21

DISTRICT OF COLUMBIA

Mandarin Oriental | *DC*	27
🅩 Ritz-Carlton Georgetown | *DC*	27

FLORIDA

🅩 Acqualina | *Miami*	28
Amelia Is. Plant. | *NE Florida*	22
Atlantic Resort | *Ft. Lauderdale*	26
Biltmore | *Miami*	23
Boca Raton | *Ft. Lauderdale*	21
Breakers | *Palm Bch.*	24
Buena Vista Palace | *Orlando*	20
Casa Marina Resort | *Keys*	21
Casa Monica | *NE Florida*	23
Casa Ybel | *Ft. Myers*	20
Celebration | *Orlando*	21
Chalet Suzanne | *Tampa*	16
Cheeca Lodge | *Keys*	21
Clearwater/Marriott | *Tampa*	18

Colony Beach | *Sarasota*	18
Conrad | *Miami*	23
Delano | *Miami*	21
🅩 Disney's Bch. Club Villas | *Orlando*	27
Disney's Contemporary | *Orlando*	20
Don CeSar Bch. | *Tampa*	21
Fisher Island | *Miami*	23
Fontainebleau | *Miami*	18
Four Seasons | *Miami*	26
Four Seasons Resort | *Palm Bch.*	24
NEW Gansevoort South | *Miami*	26
Ginn Hammock | *Palm Coast*	-
Grand Bohemian | *Orlando*	24
Grand Hyatt | *Tampa*	22
Grove Isle | *Miami*	26
Hawk's Cay Resort | *Keys*	21
Hilton | *Ft. Lauderdale*	21
Hilton Bentley Bch. | *Miami*	21
Hyatt | *Keys*	23
Jupiter Beach | *Palm Bch.*	20
JW Marriott | *Miami*	22
JW Marriott | *Orlando*	24
Lago Mar Resort | *Ft. Lauderdale*	20
La Playa Beach/Resort | *Naples*	22
🅩 Little Palm Island | *Keys*	27
Loews | *Miami*	21
Loews Portofino | *Orlando*	24
Loews Royal Pacific | *Orlando*	20
Longboat Key Club | *Sarasota*	22
🅩 Mandarin Oriental | *Miami*	27
Marco Beach Resort | *Naples*	24
Marco Is. Marriott | *Naples*	22
Marriott | *Ft. Lauderdale*	21
Marriott | *Orlando*	20
Naples Grande | *Naples*	24
PGA National | *Palm Bch.*	17
Pier Hse. Resort | *Keys*	20
Ponte Vedra Inn | *NE Florida*	25
Raleigh | *Miami*	19
NEW Regent Bal Harbour | *Miami*	-
🅩 Ritz-Carlton | *Naples*	27
🅩 Ritz-Carlton | *NE Florida*	26
🅩 Ritz-Carlton | *Orlando*	27
Ritz-Carlton | *Palm Bch.*	26
Ritz-Carlton | *Sarasota*	26
Ritz-Carlton Coconut | *Miami*	26
Ritz-Carlton Key Bisc. | *Miami*	24
Ritz-Carlton S. Bch. | *Miami*	25
Rosen Shingle | *Orlando*	23
Sanibel Resort | *Ft. Myers*	21
Setai | *Miami*	26
Shore Club | *Miami*	16

SPECIAL FEATURES

St. Regis	*Ft. Lauderdale*	27	Eagle Ridge Resort	*Galena*	19
Sunset Key/Cottages	*Keys*	26	Fairmont	*Chicago*	23
Tides	*Miami*	26	⚡ Four Seasons	*Chicago*	27
Victor	*Miami*	22	Hilton Suites	*Chicago*	22
Villas/Grand Cypress	*Orlando*	26	InterContinental	*Chicago*	22
Westin	*Ft. Lauderdale*	24	Monaco	*Chicago*	21
		Omni	*Chicago*	24

GEORGIA

⚡ Cloister	*GA Coast*	27
Jekyll Is. Club	*GA Coast*	21
⚡ Lodge/Sea Is.	*GA Coast*	28
⚡ Ritz-Carlton	*Lake Oconee*	26
Westin	*Savannah*	24

⚡ Peninsula	*Chicago*	29
Renaissance	*Chicago*	23
Ritz-Carlton	*Chicago*	26
Sofitel	*Chicago*	25
Sutton Place	*Chicago*	23
Swissôtel	*Chicago*	23
NEW Trump Int'l	*Chicago*	-
Westin	*Chicago*	22

HAWAII

Ala Moana	*Oahu*	18
Fairmont	*Big Island*	25
Fairmont	*Maui*	27
⚡ Four Seasons Resort	*Big Island*	29
Grand Hyatt	*Kauai*	24
Grand Wailea	*Maui*	24
Halekulani	*Oahu*	25
Hanalei Bay Resort	*Kauai*	20
Hana-Maui	*Maui*	27
Hapuna Bch. Prince	*Big Island*	23
Hawaii Prince Waikiki	*Oahu*	21
Hilton Kauai	*Kauai*	21
Hilton Hawaiian Vill.	*Oahu*	20
Hilton Waikoloa Vill.	*Big Island*	21
Hyatt	*Maui*	22
Hyatt	*Oahu*	20
JW Marriott	*Oahu*	26
Kaanapali Beach	*Maui*	17
Kahala	*Oahu*	25
Kapalua Villas	*Maui*	23
Kauai Marriott	*Kauai*	21
Marriott	*Oahu*	21
Maui Prince	*Maui*	19
Mauna Lani Resort	*Big Island*	24
Moana Surfrider	*Oahu*	21
Outrigger Reef	*Oahu*	16
Outrigger Waikiki	*Oahu*	19
⚡ Ritz-Carlton	*Maui*	25
Sheraton	*Kauai*	20
Sheraton	*Maui*	22
Sheraton	*Oahu*	19
Turtle Bay Resort	*Oahu*	21
Westin	*Maui*	22

IDAHO

Coeur d'Alene	*Coeur d'Alene*	25

ILLINOIS

Burnham	*Chicago*	25
Drake	*Chicago*	20

LOUISIANA

Harrah's	*New Orleans*	23
Hilton Riverside	*New Orleans*	19
JW Marriott	*New Orleans*	19
Loews	*New Orleans*	26
Marriott	*New Orleans*	18
Marriott Metairie	*New Orleans*	-
Monteleone	*New Orleans*	22
Nottoway	*White Castle*	24
Omni	*New Orleans*	21
Westin	*New Orleans*	21
⚡ Windsor Court	*New Orleans*	24
W New Orleans	*New Orleans*	23
Wyndham	*New Orleans*	23

MAINE

Bar Harbor Inn	*Bar Harbor*	21
Breakwater Inn	*S. Coast*	20
Inn by the Sea	*Portland*	21
⚡ White Barn Inn	*S. Coast*	25

MARYLAND

NEW Hilton	*Baltimore*	-
Hyatt	*Eastern Shore*	21
Inn/Perry Cabin	*Eastern Shore*	25
Marriott	*Baltimore*	23
Renaissance	*Baltimore*	21

MASSACHUSETTS

Boston Marriott	*Boston*	20
Charles	*Boston*	23
Chatham Bars	*Cape Cod/Is.*	22
Marlowe	*Boston*	23
Marriott Copley	*Boston*	20
Marriott Long Wharf	*Boston*	20
Ocean Edge	*Cape Cod/Is.*	21
Ritz-Carlton	*Boston*	25
Royal Sonesta	*Boston*	21

Wequassett | *Cape Cod/Is.*	21
Westin Boston Water. | *Boston*	22
Z Wheatleigh | *Lenox*	26
White Elephant | *Cape Cod/Is.*	23

MICHIGAN
Amway | *Grand Rapids*	23
Grand Hotel | *Mackinac Is.*	22
Iroquois/Beach | *Mackinac Is.*	22

MONTANA
Resort/Paws Up | *Missoula*	-
Triple Creek Ranch | *Darby*	29

NEVADA
Hyatt | *Incline Vill.*	21
Loews | *Las Vegas*	22
Ritz-Carlton | *Las Vegas*	27

NEW HAMPSHIRE
Manor/Golden Pond | *White Mtns.*	-
Wentworth by Sea | *Newcastle*	25

NEW JERSEY
Caesars | *Atlantic City*	18
NEW Chelsea | *Atlantic City*	-
Congress Hall | *Cape May*	19
Harrah's Resort | *Atlantic City*	21
Queen Victoria | *Cape May*	22
Seaview | *Atlantic City*	19
Tropicana | *Atlantic City*	16
Virginia | *Cape May*	23

NEW MEXICO
NEW Encantado | *Santa Fe*	-

NEW YORK
Castle/Hudson | *Westchester*	23
Danfords | *Long Island*	18
Embassy Suites | *NYC*	22
NEW Empire | *NYC*	-
Friends Lake Inn | *Adirondacks*	22
Gansevoort | *NYC*	20
Gurney's Inn | *Long Island*	17
Maidstone Arms | *Long Island*	18
Millennium UN | *NYC*	22
Mirror Lake Inn | *Adirondacks*	23
Mohonk Mtn. Hse. | *Catskills*	18
NY Marriott Downtown | *NYC*	19
Otesaga | *Cooperstown*	21
Ram's Head Inn | *Long Island*	16
Ritz-Carlton Battery Pk. | *NYC*	27
Westin | *NYC*	23

NORTH CAROLINA
Greystone Inn | *Asheville*	24
Pinehurst Resort | *Pinehurst*	20

OHIO
Hilton Cincinnati | *Cincinnati*	16
Ritz-Carlton | *Cleveland*	24

OREGON
Columbia Gorge | *Hood River*	20
RiverPlace | *Portland*	27
Stephanie Inn | *Cannon Bch.*	27
Z Timberline Ldg. | *Mt. Hood*	16
Z Tu Tu' Tun Lodge | *Gold Bch.*	26

PENNSYLVANIA
Z Four Seasons | *Philadelphia*	26
Z Lodge/Woodloch | *Hawley*	23
Skytop Lodge | *Poconos*	15

PUERTO RICO
Bravo Beach | *Vieques*	-
El Conquistador | *Fajardo*	21
El Convento | *San Juan*	21
El San Juan | *San Juan*	20
Z Horned Dorset | *Rincon*	26
Las Casitas Village | *Fajardo*	26
Rio Mar Beach | *San Juan*	22
Ritz-Carlton | *San Juan*	24

RHODE ISLAND
Castle Hill Inn | *Newport*	23
Francis Malbone | *Newport*	25
1661 Inn | *Block Is.*	-

SOUTH CAROLINA
Marriott | *Hilton Head*	21
Inn/Middleton Pl. | *Charleston*	-
Inn/Palmetto | *Hilton Head*	29
Mills House | *Charleston*	20
Myrtle/Marriott | *Myrtle Bch.*	24
Z Sanctuary | *Kiawah Is.*	28
Westin | *Hilton Head*	21
Wild Dunes Resort | *Charleston*	21

TENNESSEE
Madison | *Memphis*	22
Peabody | *Memphis*	19

TEXAS
Four Seasons | *Austin*	25
Galvez | *Galveston*	18
Hyatt | *San Antonio*	23
Inn/Dos Brisas | *Washington*	-
NEW Joule | *DFW*	-
Z Lake Austin Spa | *Austin*	25
La Mansión del Rio | *San Antonio*	21
Omni | *Houston*	20
Valencia Riverwalk | *San Antonio*	26
Watermark | *San Antonio*	27
Westin Riverwalk | *San Antonio*	22

SPECIAL FEATURES

U.S. VIRGIN ISLANDS

Buccaneer	*St. Croix*	23
Caneel Bay	*St. John*	23
Ritz-Carlton	*St. Thomas*	25
Westin	*St. John*	21

VERMONT

Inn/Sawmill	*S. VT*	22
Inn/Shelburne	*Lake Champlain*	22
Old Tavern/Grafton	*S. VT*	21
Topnotch	*Stowe*	21

VIRGINIA

Kingsmill Resort	*Williamsburg*	19
NEW Palomar	*DC Metro*	–
Tides Inn	*Irvington*	22

WASHINGTON

Alexis	*Seattle*	21
Edgewater	*Seattle*	22
Fairmont	*Seattle*	23
NEW Four Seasons	*Seattle*	–
Grand Hyatt	*Seattle*	27
Z Inn at Langley	*Seattle*	25
Inn at the Market	*Seattle*	23
Marriott	*Seattle*	23
1000	*Seattle*	26
Pan Pacific	*Seattle*	–
Salish Lodge	*Seattle*	25
Watertown	*Seattle*	–
Westin Bellevue	*Seattle*	26
Woodmark	*Seattle*	24
W Seattle	*Seattle*	23

WISCONSIN

Canoe Bay	*Chetek*	28
Pfister	*Milwaukee*	22

WYOMING

Z Amangani	*Jackson Hole*	29
Jackson Lake Ldg.	*Jackson Hole*	19

ALPHABETICAL PAGE INDEX

Listings followed by (C) are chains. Names are followed by nearest major city and state.

ALPHA INDEX

ALPHA INDEX

ALPHA INDEX

ALPHA INDEX

ALPHA INDEX

ALPHA INDEX